A Guide to Bird Finding in New Jersey

American Goldfinch, New Jersey's State Bird

DA Sibley 1985

A Guide to Bird Finding in New Jersey

Revised and Expanded Edition

William J. Boyle, Jr.

Drawings by David A. Sibley
and Shawneen Finnegan

Rutgers University Press
New Brunswick, New Jersey

Third paperback printing, 2008

Library of Congress Cataloging-in-Publication Data
Boyle, William J.
  A guide to bird finding in New Jersey / William J. Boyle, Jr. ; drawings by
  David A. Sibley and Shawneen Finnegan.—Rev. and expanded ed.
    p. cm.
  Includes bibliographical references and index.
  ISBN 0-8135-3084-9 (cloth : alk. paper) — ISBN 0-8135-3085-7
  (pbk. : alk paper)
    1. Bird watching—New Jersey—Guidebooks. 2. New Jersey—Guidebooks.
  I. Title.

QL684.N5 B68 2002
598'.07'23449—dc21   2001058672

British Cataloging-in-Publication information is available from the British Library.

Maps by William J. Boyle, Jr.

Manufactured in the United States of America

To Karen

Contents

Maps

Illustrations

Preface to the First Edition

The idea for this book developed from the *New Jersey Field Trip Guide* that I revised and rewrote for the Summit Nature Club in 1978. The original *Field Trip Guide*, published by the club in 1964, was a brief compilation of 22 birding spots around the state. It was assembled by Dick Lindner, the club's field trip chairman, and contained short descriptions of the locales with schematic maps and directions from Summit. In 1971, the *Field Trip Guide* was revised by Harold Crandall, with some additions and deletions to reflect the changing birding scene.

Because of the success of the *Field Trip Guide*, the 1971 edition was out of print by 1978. I undertook to revise and greatly expand the guide for a third edition (renamed the *New Jersey Field Trip Guide*), which covers 38 birding spots and is now in its fourth printing. The guide, however, provides only a limited amount of information on each birding spot and omits many good birding areas. In fact, the lack of a good bird-finding book covering the entire state of New Jersey led me think of writing such a book. I discussed the idea with the Executive Board of the Summit Nature Club in early 1983; the board was enthusiastic and agreed to help try to publish it.

When Rutgers University Press asked me in the spring of 1983 if I would be interested in writing a book about birdfinding in New Jersey, I had already formulated ideas about the structure of such a book. After the Press had reviewed my proposal and sample entries, the Summit Nature Club agreed that the Press would be a more appropriate vehicle for publishing the book, and graciously relieved me of any obligation to the club.

This book does not aim to be all-inclusive. Many good areas in New Jersey are not mentioned, but I think you will find that all of the best areas are included. The spots covered are entirely of my own choosing and necessarily reflect my own opinions about what constitutes a good birding spot. Except for a few of the sites mentioned as "Additional Birding Spots," I have birded in all the places covered in the book, visiting most of them many times.

Although the information given about each selection is largely based on my own experience, I have benefited greatly from the comments of my fellow birders who have read and commented on these entries. Most of the entries have been reviewed by one or more local experts more knowledgeable about the given area than I; the book was enormously improved by the generous assistance of these birders, whose names will be found in the Acknowledgments. However, I remain responsible for any errors of commission or omission. As I hope that the book will be sufficiently popular to warrant a revised edition in the future, I would appreciate readers bringing any errors to my attention through the publisher.

Certain matters of style are worth mentioning. I have chosen to capitalize the complete names of all bird and plant species; this is the practice adhered to in *American Birds, Birding, The Auk*, and most other birding journals. Furthermore, in lists of species with the same last name, as in Chipping, Field, Swamp, and Song Sparrow, I have chosen to capitalize the last name. Although books and journals are about evenly divided on this practice, I find the capitalized name easier to read.

Most of the distances in the directions are given in the form "*about* (so many) miles," because of inevitable differences in odometer readings among cars. Distance figures "from the exit ramp" of limited-access highways are measured from the end of the ramp. Wording of highway exit signs is enclosed in parentheses, e.g., "Follow I-287 north to Exit 18B (US 206 North, Bedminster, Netcong)." In most cases, road names and landmarks are given, and the maps should usually help you locate your position.

Preface to the Revised and Expanded Edition

The wish that I expressed in the preface to the first edition, "that the book will be sufficiently popular to warrant a revised edition in the future," has finally come to pass. After fifteen years and a half-dozen reprintings, the much-needed rewriting of the book has now taken place.

Several years ago, I contacted Rutgers University Press and inquired about its interest in producing a completely revised edition of the guide. The interest was there, and I actually made a couple of aborted attempts at the endeavor. I solicited comments and suggestions from birders, rewrote some of the sections, and redrew many of the maps using a computer graphics program. With the pressures of work and travel, however, I never really dug in and got the project underway, despite the constant inquiries from interested birders wanting to know "when are you going to update your book."

Finally, in autumn 2000, I again contacted Rutgers about inserting updates and corrections for a new printing of the first edition and inquired about interest in a completely revised second edition. The Press responded enthusiastically about its desire for a new edition, so I submitted a proposal. There followed many months of late nights and nonbirding weekends, much to the chagrin of my loving and neglected spouse. With a firm deadline and a determination to meet it, I have persevered and completed this new version of the guide.

As in the first edition, this book does not aim to be all-inclusive. Many good areas in New Jersey are not mentioned, but I think you will find that all of the best areas are included. I have tried to give some geographical balance to the regions, and in doing so had to omit some very good areas. The sections called "Additional Birding Spots in . . .," in the first edition have been eliminated, so that each site gets its own entry in the contents. The regions have been changed to conform more closely with county boundaries and those used by New Jersey Audubon Society, and within each region the entries are organized geographically by county. I have birded in almost all of the places covered in the book, and have visited most of them during the months spent on this revision. Finally, one stylistic change is the use of lower case in plurals of birds' names, as in Chipping and Song sparrows.

I hope that experienced birders, who have used the first edition and know many of the birding spots better than I do, will continue to find new sites of interest that compel a first visit, and maybe subsequent ones. Most of all, I hope that this newly revised edition will help to inspire a new generation of birders to explore the many places in New Jersey that offer a wealth of opportunity to the novice and veteran alike. Only by instilling in the youth of today an appreciation of nature and the intangible pleasures of seeing and admiring wild things can we hope to preserve the opportunity for future generations.

Acknowledgments for the First Edition

The writing of a book such as this, even for a state as small as New Jersey, involves the accumulation and presentation of much more information than one person can hope to know. During the 12 years that I have birded New Jersey intensively, I have learned much about many different parts of the state. Wherever I go, however, there are usually birders who are more knowledgeable about that particular area. I am fortunate to have been able to draw on the expertise of many fellow birders in writing this book, and I express my deep gratitude to all of them.

My special thanks go to my long-time friend and recent big-day companion Peter Bacinski, who made available all the material he had gathered for a similar, but unrealized, endeavor at writing a bird-finding guide to the state. Pete accumulated much of this information by soliciting accounts from New Jersey birders of their favorite local birding areas; these contributions are acknowledged below. Additional sources of information have been John and Justin Harding's *Birding the Delaware Valley*, the late James Akers' *All Year Birding in Southern New Jersey*, and numerous "Birdfinder's Guides" published by the New Jersey Audubon Society in *Records of New Jersey Birds*.

I am especially indebted to Tom Halliwell and Rich Kane, who read many of the individual entries and provided numerous helpful comments; and to Paul Buckley, who read the entire manuscript, field tested many of the entries, and made many valuable suggestions. Other birders who examined entries and added their knowledge are Peter Bacinski, Ray Blicharz, Joe Burgiel, Peter Dunne, Jerry Haag, Greg Hanisek, David Harrison, Brian Moscatello, Jim Meritt, Ted Proctor, Rick Radis, Bill Smith, Fred Tetlow and Wade Wander. The time and effort that each of them put into reviewing these selections are reflected in the thorough and thoughtful comments and suggestions that they provided. This book is much better because of their efforts, and I am sincerely grateful to each of them. Others who provided information, directly or indirectly, are the late Art Barber, Peggy Bayer, Philip Conroy, John Danzenbaker, Mike Hannisian, Charlie Leck, Len Little, John McNeil, John Moffet, Ken Prytherch, Richard Ryan, Joseph Schmeltz, John Serrao, Cathy

Smith, Len Soucy, Tom Southerland, Ken Tischner, Blanche Waddington, Floyd Wolfarth, Carl Woodward, Jr., and Steve Zipko.

Finally, I owe a special debt of gratitude to Gail Boyle, who read the first draft of every selection in the manuscript and provided innumerable suggestions for improving the clarity and consistency of the text.

Acknowledgments for the Revised and Expanded Edition

In reviewing the acknowledgments for the first edition, I can only reiterate my thanks and appreciation to the people who assisted in that initial endeavor. Even more than the first edition, however, the revised and expanded edition has benefited from the assistance of others. With the pressures of business and travel, I have not had the opportunities in the past decade or more to visit all of the places that are covered in this book with the frequency that I would like to have done. Nevertheless, I can say that I have been able to visit all but a few of the 128 birding sites described in the current edition.

Numerous birders, both close friends and generous people I know only by email, have contributed enormously to the completion of this revision. Without their help, this book would have been much longer in the making and would have suffered from innumerable errors of omission and commission that I could not have foreseen. Among the birders who have contributed information, suggestions, corrections, and advice are Margaret Atack, Marge Barrett, Charles Brine, Joe Burgiel, Hank Burk, Ward Dasey, Pete Dunne, Fred Pfeifer, Shawneen Finnegan, Peter Gannis, Kevin Karlson, Don Jones, Paul Lehman, Glenn Mahler, Brad Merritt, Mike Newlon, Evan Obercian, Bill Rawlyk, Tom Reed, Alan Schreck, Brian Vernachio, Jim Williams, and Jim Zamos.

A few friends have helped enormously in this revision, and I want to single them out for my sincere thanks. Paul Guris contributed most of the section on Dix WMA. Don Freiday provided the original write-ups for Voorhees State Park and Central Hunterdon County, in addition to all of the background information on Hoffman Park and Point Mountain Preserve. Fred Tetlow reviewed and revised High Point and Stokes Forest, and George Wenzelburger did the same for Assunpink and Allaire. David Harrison helped with Black River and Libby Herland with Wallkill WMA. Rick Radis showed me around Sparta Mountain and provided help for that entry, as well as Plainsboro Preserve. Tom and Margot Southerland provided updated information on Princeton, and Chip Krilowicz helped out in the greater Camden area, about which I knew next to nothing. Rich Kane was an invaluable resource on many areas, but especially Sherman-Hoffman, Kearny Marsh, and Conaskonk Point. August Sexauer reviewed my contribution on Hawkin Road, his special place, and Frank Winfelder sent me his write-up of Taylor Wildlife Refuge. Don Sutherland provided the background on Double Trouble State Park, and Fred Lesser helped with other Ocean County spots. Roger Johnson straightened out the Troy Meadows entry. Karla Risdon added suggestions for visiting Weis Ecology Center and Norvin Green State Forest, and Rick Weiman introduced me to High Mountain Park. Sandy Komito cleared up DeKorte Park. For several of the areas in Cumberland County, I drew upon the information provided in the *Birding Guide to Cumberland County, NJ*, which was researched and written for the county by Clay Sutton. Special thanks go to Ms. Christine Connelly for information about her Brightview Farm and permission to include it in this book.

Three individuals deserve special recognition for their contributions to the book, because without them it could not have been completed. They are Tom Bailey, Tom Halliwell, and Laurie Larson. Tom Bailey provided the original text for and revised many of the entries on central and southwestern New Jersey. Laurie reviewed and edited many of the entries for central and northwestern New Jersey, as well as the Annotated List, but her contributions represent an accumulation of ideas, suggestions, and comments dating back for more than a decade. In addition to reviewing many of the sections from northwest New Jersey, Tom Halliwell undertook to revise the Annotated List, based on his experience in co-authoring the *Birds of New Jersey* compendium. He and I spent many hours going over this list to arrive at a mutually agreeable summary.

Finally, I owe an enormous debt of gratitude to my long-suffering and immensely tolerant wife, Karen Thompson, who has endured the nine-month gestation period of the completion of this project. Her patience, understanding, encouragement, and thoughtful editing helped me through the long months of wondering if the effort was really worthwhile.

🦅

Birding New Jersey

Introduction

New Jersey is one of the smallest states, with only 7,836 square miles, and it has the greatest population density of any state. Nevertheless, the remarkable diversity of its birdlife surpasses that of many much larger states. The wealth of New Jersey's birdlife has been surveyed by Charles F. Leck (1984) in his book *The Status and Distribution of New Jersey's Birds* and more recently in *Birds of New Jersey*, published by New Jersey Audubon Society (1999). The latter book is based on the *Breeding Bird Atlas*, conducted 1993–1997, many years of Christmas Bird Count data, analysis of *Records of New Jersey Birds*, and reports submitted to the New Jersey Bird Records Committee.

Well over 400 species of birds have been recorded in New Jersey (about 420 species are well documented, and there are unsubstantiated reports of numerous others), and an active birder can hope to see more than 300 species in a year. A big-day team in May 1984 broke the previous record by finding 202 species in New Jersey in one day; this total was broken in 1987 with 205 species, and the record now tops 220. Only about a dozen states have big-day records of 200 or more species by teams following the rules of the American Birding Association. About 190 species nest in New Jersey in any given year; more than 200 species have nested here at least once.

The enormous variety of New Jersey's birdlife stems from a favorable geographical situation and a wide diversity of habitats. As a coastal state, New Jersey attracts an abundance of ducks, geese, shorebirds, gulls, terns, and other water-associated species. It lies on a major flyway for the migration of many of these birds, and serves as a nesting area or wintering ground for many others. In addition, the nearby offshore waters harbor a wide variety of pelagic birds. New Jersey's location on the mid-Atlantic coast results in an interesting mixture of northern and southern species. Many northern birds seen here are near the southern limit of their normal range in the East, such as Common and King eiders, Harlequin Duck, Barrow's Goldeneye,

Gyrfalcon, Iceland, and Glaucous gulls, Thick-billed Murre, Razorbill, Snowy Owl, Boreal Chickadee, Northern Shrike, Lapland Longspur, and Pine Grosbeak. Similarly, many southern species that are numerous or regular in New Jersey are rare or uncommon farther north along the East Coast; for example, Tricolored Heron, Yellow-crowned Night-Heron, White Ibis, Black Vulture, Mississippi Kite, American Avocet, Sandwich Tern, Carolina Chickadee, White-eyed Vireo, Yellow-throated, Prothonotary, and Kentucky warblers, Summer Tanager, Blue Grosbeak, Boat-tailed Grackle, and Orchard Oriole.

The convergence of north and south is reflected in the varied habitats found in New Jersey, from the salt marshes and hardwood swamps of the Delaware Bayshore to the hemlock glens and dry ridgetops of the Highlands and the Kittatinny Mountains. In between are the vast Pine Barrens of the coastal plain, with its cedar swamps and pine-oak woodlands, as well as the farm fields, lakes, rivers, swamps, and upland deciduous forest of the central and northern parts of the state. At Dividing Creek, Cumberland County, during the breeding season you'll find such typical southern birds as Chuck-will's-widow, Yellow-throated, Prothonotary, and Kentucky warblers, Summer Tanager, and Blue Grosbeak. Only 150 miles north in the Pequannock Watershed, the breeding birds include northern species such as Alder Flycatcher, Red-breasted Nuthatch, Winter Wren, Golden-crowned Kinglet, Blue-headed Vireo, Blackburnian Warbler, and occasionally Yellow-bellied Sapsucker, White-throated Sparrow, and Dark-eyed Junco.

Because of New Jersey's large population, its inclusion in two large metropolitan areas (New York City and Philadelphia), and the tourist attractions of its coastal beaches, much of the state has been urbanized, suburbanized, condominiumized, industrialized, or otherwise built upon. Even in the rural areas, the practices of agriculture are not usually beneficial to birdlife. Fortunately for the birder, a significant portion of the state has been preserved in the form of federal public lands; state, county, and local parks; state forests; Wildlife Management Areas (WMAs); private wildlife preserves; and other protected areas. The state parks and forests system includes almost 250,000 acres, while the WMAs administered by the New Jersey Division of Fish and Wildlife contain another 160,000 acres. The state has recently embarked on an ambitious program to preserve many thousands of acres over the next ten years. Thus, although much additional wildlife habitat is lost to development every year, many places remain for birders to pursue their hobby.

Birding by Season

As a coastal state with a diversity of inland habitats, New Jersey offers something for the birder at any season. Predictably, the coast has the greatest variety of birdlife most of the year, especially in the winter, but there are usually interesting species to be found elsewhere. The following suggestions are not meant to be comprehensive, but only to give ideas for places to visit in the various seasons. The locations mentioned are included in the regional maps, and directions are given in each individual chapter.

Many non-birders think of winter as a time when all the birds have gone south; to the birder in New Jersey, however, winter is a time to look for rarities and uncommon winter visitors. This is the time to visit Barnegat Light in search of Harlequin Duck, eiders, Purple Sandpiper, rare gulls, and possibly a Snowy Owl. The North Shore harbors many grebes, geese, ducks, gulls (including rarer ones like Black-headed, Little, Glaucous, Iceland, and Lesser Black-backed gulls), occasional alcids, and other water-associated species. Brigantine National Wildlife Refuge, too, has numbers of waterfowl plus numerous wintering raptors, including Rough-legged Hawk, Bald Eagle, and the occasional Golden Eagle. Cape May offers the greatest variety of birdlife at this season, because of the many wintering land birds and water birds.

In the north, Sandy Hook is a good spot for Red-necked Grebes, Snow Buntings, and winter rarities. Liberty State Park is favored by Short-eared Owl, Snowy Owl and, occasionally, Common Black-headed Gull. It has attracted both Red-necked and Eared grebes, as well as many ducks and gulls. The nearby Kearny Marsh and Hackensack Meadowlands still attract concentrations of gulls in winter, including rarities, but most of the garbage dumps that used to lure these scavengers are no longer active.

Winter is the time to check Ringwood State Park, Pequannock Watershed, Wawayanda State Park, High Point State Park, Stokes State Forest, Worthington State Forest, and Washington Crossing State Park for winter finches or other northern species. Alpha frequently has Short-eared Owl, Snow Bunting and Lapland Longspur. Princeton and the Stony Brook-Millstone Reserve are worth checking for owls, while nearby Rosedale Park usually has Eastern Bluebird. Trenton Marsh is a great spot for wintering Common Snipe, and the Delaware River downstream at Florence has become the state's prime winter gull-watching site, thanks to the massive dump across the river in Pennsylvania. In the southwestern part of the state, Fish House, Flood Gates, and Mannington Marsh are all excellent for wintering waterfowl, while the Delaware Bayshore of Salem and Cumberland counties (see Dividing Creek and Heislerville) has large numbers of wintering raptors.

With the arrival of spring, many of the wintering species depart and early migrants arrive. Late March brings the first Ospreys, Eastern Phoebes, swallows, and Pine Warblers. March is also a good time to look for Ross's Goose among the many Snow Geese in Salem County, as well as Brewer's or Yellow-headed blackbirds among the flocks of more common blackbirds. April is the month when many birders visit Pedricktown and Salem County in search of American Golden Plover, Ruff, and Upland Sandpiper. March and April are also good for migrant waterfowl at Assunpink WMA, Brigantine, Salem

County, Spruce Run State Recreation Area, and many other spots. By the end of April, most of the herons and egrets have returned to the coastal marshes, along with terns and early shorebirds. At Cape May, Sandy Hook, Palmyra, Garret Mountain, and Princeton, the songbird migration has begun in earnest, while at Parvin State Park and Belleplain State Forest, many of the local specialties such as Prothonotary Warbler and Louisiana Waterthrush are in full song.

May is the month when you want to be everywhere. The songbird and shorebird migrations reach their peak for a number of species during the first three weeks of the month. Birders flock to Princeton, Trenton Marsh, Bull's Island, and Garret Mountain to see warblers and other passerines, then head for the coast at Brigantine, Stone Harbor, and Cape May to look for shorebirds. By the end of the month, the variety has diminished, but it is the best time to visit the Delaware Bayshore at Reeds Beach, Moores Beach, Thompsons Beach, and East Point to see the spectacle of hundreds of thousands of Sanderlings, Semipalmated Sandpipers, Ruddy Turnstones, and Red Knots feeding on the eggs of horseshoe crabs.

By the beginning of June, the birding pace has slowed. This is the time to visit Belleplain State Forest, Parvin State Park, Glassboro Woods, Lebanon State Forest, and Dividing Creek in the southwest, and High Point State Park, Pequannock Watershed, Wawayanda State Park, and other places in the northwest in search of interesting breeding birds. June is also a good month for Mississippi Kite and other vagrants at Cape May and other coastal points. July is a slow month inland, because birdsong has diminished, but the higher parts of the northwest can provide enjoyable birding and hiking. Only the hardy brave the heat and insects of the Pine Barrens at this season! By midmonth, however, the fall shorebird migration is in full swing along the coast. Although the main shorebird migration lasts into October, the greatest numbers of birds are present in late July.

August brings the beginning of the fall songbird migration. This is a good time to visit Cape May, Sandy Hook, Palmyra, Princeton, and Rancocas for warblers and local specialties such as Yellow-bellied Flycatcher, Olive-sided Flycatcher, and Philadelphia Vireo, especially toward the end of the month. August is the best month along the south coast to see the massing flocks of Willets, American Oystercatchers and other shorebirds, and to search through the flocks of Common and Royal Terns for Sandwich and Roseate Terns.

September is the peak month for fall migration, and birders tend to concentrate on hot spots for migrants, including Brigantine, Island Beach State Park, and all the places mentioned in the preceding paragraph, especially Cape May. The hawk migration begins in earnest during September, as raptor enthusiasts head for Cape May, Montclair, Raccoon Ridge, and Sunrise Mountain. October brings the greatest variety to the hawk watches, and sees the last migrant songbirds pass through. These include sparrows (some much sought after, such as Lincoln's, Lark, Clay-colored, and the rare Henslow's sparrows), as well as Orange-crowned Warbler and other rarities. Along the coast, hundreds of loons, cormorants, and scoters pass by.

November is a good time to visit Island Beach and other spots along the coast for Red-throated Loon, Northern Gannet, Black-legged Kittiwake and migrant sea ducks. At the hawk watches, the season is winding down, but November is the best month for Golden Eagle, Northern Goshawk, Rough-legged Hawk, and Common Raven. Waterfowl gather at many coastal and inland locations, while most of the wintering songbirds have arrived. November is also a good month for rarities, so be sure to consult the Rare Bird Alerts (RBAs), listed in the following section. December is a good time to scout for rarities or late lingering species, in preparation for the Christmas Bird Counts that occupy most birders during the latter half of the month. With the new year, many birders retreat indoors, but winter can be an exciting season, as noted at the beginning of this section.

Rare Bird Alerts

New Jersey birders are fortunate in having access to multiple RBAs, which cover the state and adjacent areas of New York, Pennsylvania, and Delaware. These tape-recorded telephone messages run about five minutes and are changed at least once a week, usually on Wednesday or Thursday; they are often updated when a real rarity is discovered. The oldest of the RBAs is the New York RBA, sponsored by the National Audubon Society and the Linnaean Society of New York, phone (212) 979-3070. With the advent of the other RBAs, this alert now concentrates on Long Island and southern New York State. The Voice of New Jersey Audubon, sponsored by the New Jersey Audubon Society, covers bird sightings for the entire state, and is the most comprehensive for the New Jersey birder; phone (732) 872-2595. The Cape May Birding Hotline, run by the Cape May Bird Observatory, focuses mainly on Atlantic, Cape May, and Cumberland counties, phone (609) 898-2473. The Philadelphia Birdline, sponsored by the Delaware Valley Ornithological Club and the Philadelphia Academy of Natural Sciences, covers southern New Jersey, southeastern Pennsylvania, and most of Delaware, phone (215) 567-2473. Other useful regional tapes include Delaware, phone (302) 658-2737 (mostly the same as Philadelphia), Allentown, PA, phone (610) 252-3455, and Lower Hudson Valley, NY, phone (914) 666-6614. Although their emphasis is on rarities, all these alerts provide much useful information on more common breeding and migrant birds as well.

With the proliferation of access to the World Wide Web (the Internet), many birders get their rarity information on-line, where daily and even hourly news is available. The most popular source at this time is a list server

6 🐦 Birding New Jersey

called JerseyBirds, which is run from a computer at Princeton University. A list server works by taking e-mail messages and relaying them to all subscribers to the list. To subscribe to Jersey Birds, you send an e-mail to LIST-SERV@Princeton.edu with no subject and the single line in the body of the message: SUBSCRIBE JerseyBirds. Another excellent Web site is maintained by Jack Siler of Philadelphia at http://birdingonthe.net.

Birding Ethics

In an increasingly crowded and urbanized state, it is critical that birders be constantly aware of the need to respect the rights of property owners and of other birders and that they avoid jeopardizing the welfare of the birds. Most of the places discussed in this book, such as state parks and forests, national wildlife refuges, etc., are in public ownership. These public areas usually have rules and regulations governing hours of access and the types of activities allowed; certain sections are frequently off limits. The failure of individual birders to adhere to such rules has occasionally led to restrictions on the activities of all birders. A few of the areas covered are privately owned, with birders allowed access by the courtesy of the owners. When visiting them, be sure to leave things as you find them.

The most important aspect of birding ethics is attention to the welfare of the birds. Many species, especially those considered threatened and endangered, are easily disturbed on their nesting grounds; such disturbance can be harmful to such species' nesting success. Colonially nesting birds such as herons, egrets, gulls, and terns (including the state endangered Least Tern and Black Skimmer), are especially sensitive to the presence of humans (or their pets) around the colonies. Piping Plover, another endangered species in New Jersey, nests in very loose colonies along certain of the outer beaches. Although it may be difficult to avoid disturbing the plovers as you walk along the beach, don't linger in an area with an obviously agitated adult. Raptors are also especially sensitive to disturbance around the nest, and will occasionally abandon it, if pressured. If you know of or discover the nest of a hawk or an owl, avoid approaching it closely and be circumspect about revealing its presence to others. Nest locations for rare or endangered species, such as Northern Goshawk, Cooper's Hawk, Northern Harrier, Bald Eagle, and Short-eared Owl should be reported to the Nongame and Endangered Species Project of the New Jersey Division of Fish and Wildlife, but should otherwise be kept secret. Wintering owls also present a problem in birding ethics. Searching for and finding owls in winter can be challenging and fun, provided you use common sense. Don't break twigs or branches trying to obtain a better view; don't shake the tree or otherwise harass the owl and cause it to flush; don't go owling in large groups or make a lot of noise; and don't reveal the bird's location to people you don't know.

Finally, avoid overusing tape recorders. Tape recordings can be invaluable tools in locating and seeing many nocturnal or secretive species, such as rails, owls, and nightjars (Whip-poor-will and Chuck-will's-widow), plus certain wrens, warblers and sparrows. Playing these tapes too long, too loud or too frequently, however, may intimidate a bird on its nesting territory and cause it to desert. These actions also make it more difficult for other birders to find and locate the bird. The playing of tape recorders is now illegal in most federally owned and many state-owned parks and refuges. Playing a tape recording of Black Rail or any other endangered species in the state is expressly forbidden.

Playing a tape recording of a Screech-Owl will frequently attract all small songbirds in the area, eager to scold the intruding owl. Overuse of this technique is also undesirable for the birds and can be very annoying to other birders. Just as effective is learning to whistle an imitation of the owl. This is more satisfying because you are not relying on a mechanical device, and it is not as intrusive as the infernal machine. If you can't manage the owl whistle, vocalizations such as squeaking and "pishing" will often serve just as well.

How to Use This Book

The main body of the text describes birding areas in New Jersey. In order to help the reader locate sites within a particular part of the state, I have divided the state into six regions, which correspond closely to the regions used by New Jersey Audubon Society in *Records of New Jersey Birds*, a quarterly publication covering the state's birdlife. The only exception is that I have chosen to divide their Piedmont Region into Northeastern New Jersey and Central New Jersey. For the most part, these boundaries are along county lines, the exception being in the north, where Morris County and Passaic County are each divided between the Northwest and the Northeast. Map 1 shows the six regions and their boundaries. At the beginning of each regional section, you will find a map showing the locations of the various birding areas within that region with respect to some of the main roads; within the regional section, the areas are organized in geographical order, proceeding roughly from north to south. Because of the method of organization, each region does not cover a single, homogeneous habitat type; you will find some sites in the Northeast Region very similar to some in the Northwest Region, and some in the Southwest Region resembling others in the Central Region. However, I think you will find that each region as a whole has a distinctive character of its own.

Each of the detailed entries begins with a description of the birding area and some of its highlights, followed by directions on how to reach the site. At the end of the directions are the coordinates for the site from the *DeLorme New Jersey Atlas and Gazetteer*, which is available at most bookstores. You should also be able to find all the areas in this book using only my directions,

Map 1. The Birding Regions of New Jersey

with the help of a good roadmap for locating the various highways. In addition, county maps are indispensable for finding some of the smaller roads and out-of-the-way places. Both Hagstrom and Alfred B. Patton publish county maps for New Jersey, and between the two companies there is at least one map for every county. For more remote areas, United States Geological Survey (USGS) topographic maps are useful. These can be obtained from certain bookstores, and are even available on CD.

The main part of each entry, labeled "Birding," provides suggestions on how to bird a particular area and on some of the species that you might expect to find there. For some areas I have gone into considerable detail, whereas for others my description is fairly brief and refers you to sections on other, similar, areas for a listing of many of the species that you should look for. Many of the common and widespread species are normally not mentioned, but reference to the annotated checklist at the end of the book will tell you whether a particular bird is to be expected in the area or habitat you are birding.

Some of the smaller or lesser-known areas include only brief descriptions of the birding opportunities. Still other birding areas in the state are known to local birders, but not mentioned in this book. For the most part, they are similar to areas covered, but I'm sure that there are always new and worthwhile areas waiting to be discovered, so don't limit your horizons to the sites I have listed.

After the main body of the text, chapters on pelagic trips and on hawk watching suggest how and where to pursue these activities. These are followed by a bibliography of books and other publications useful to birders in New Jersey and a list of many of the nature and bird clubs in the state. An annotated checklist of New Jersey's birds that tells you briefly about the abundance and frequency of occurrence of each species, then suggests some places to look for it, is followed by the index. I have tried to make the index as comprehensive and useful as possible: Here you should find every reference to a species of interest or a location that you want to visit.

Some General Precautions

Carry a compass when visiting some of the more remote areas or when hiking the trails of any of the larger parks, forests, refuges, or WMAs. Many of the trails at places like Black River WMA, Scherman-Hoffman Sanctuaries, Higbee Beach (Cape May), and other spots are very wet in the morning after a heavy dew, so rubber boots or other waterproof footgear can make your outing more comfortable.

During the warmer months, insect pests can be a nuisance. Watch out for wood ticks, especially in shrubby, overgrown fields; they are most abundant in May and June, but can be found into the autumn. Any outing into a tick-infested area should be followed by a careful tick inspection. Even more troublesome are the abundant but tiny deer ticks. Many of these ticks carry Lyme disease, which is now widespread in New Jersey, so check for and remove ticks before they have a chance to burrow into your skin. Insect repellent supposedly helps to deter ticks; although they are a nuisance, they can be coped with and should not discourage you from exploring places where they occur.

Mosquitoes are present from spring through fall in the coastal marshes, and from about May to September in inland woodlands. Repellent works for them, except where they are especially abundant; in those places a headnet and long-sleeved clothing can provide some relief. Greenhead flies are exasperating pests at Brigantine National Wildlife Refuge (NWR) and other coastal marshes in July and August, while deer flies are persistent nuisances, especially in deciduous woodlands, during the summer months. A hat is a must when walking in deer fly country, as they insist on getting into your hair. Unfortunately, insect repellent seems to have little effect on the flies.

Common and Widespread Species

The species in the following lists are so frequently encountered that they are not normally mentioned in the text as occurring at a particular location. Permanent residents can be assumed to be present all year, whereas nesting or wintering species will be found during the appropriate seasons. Refer to the Annotated List for more information.

Deciduous Woodland

Red-bellied, Downy and Hairy woodpeckers, Northern Flicker, Eastern Wood-Pewee, Great Crested Flycatcher, Blue Jay, American Crow, Red-eyed Vireo, Black-capped (north) and Carolina (central and southern) chickadees, Tufted Titmouse, White-breasted Nuthatch, Blue-gray Gnatcatcher, Veery (north), Wood Thrush, American Robin, European Starling, Ovenbird, Scarlet Tanager, Common Grackle, Brown-headed Cowbird, and Baltimore Oriole.

Woodland Edge, Shrubby Fields, Suburbs, etc.

Many of the members of the preceding list, plus Mourning Dove, House Wren, Gray Catbird, Northern Mockingbird, Yellow Warbler, Common Yellowthroat, Indigo Bunting, Northern Cardinal, Eastern Towhee, Chipping Sparrow, Song Sparrow, White-throated Sparrow (winter), Dark-eyed Junco (winter), Red-winged Blackbird, House Finch, American Goldfinch, and House Sparrow.

Pine Barrens

Downy and Hairy woodpeckers, Northern Flicker, Eastern Wood-Pewee, Great Crested Flycatcher, Blue Jay, American Crow, Red-eyed Vireo, House Wren, Wood Thrush, American Robin, Gray Catbird, Brown Thrasher, Pine Warbler, Prairie Warbler, Ovenbird, Common Yellowthroat, Scarlet Tanager, Eastern Towhee, Song Sparrow, Common Grackle, Brown-headed Cowbird, and Baltimore Oriole.

Good Birding!

Ruffed Grouse

DA Sibley 1985

Northwest Region

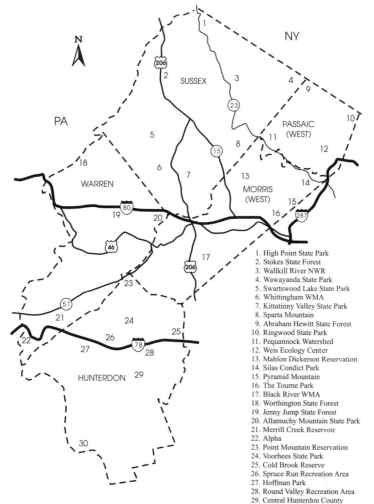

N

NY

PA

SUSSEX

PASSAIC
(WEST)

WARREN

MORRIS
(WEST)

HUNTERDON

1. High Point State Park
2. Stokes State Forest
3. Wallkill River NWR
4. Wawayanda State Park
5. Swartswood Lake State Park
6. Whittingham WMA
7. Kittatinny Valley State Park
8. Sparta Mountain
9. Abraham Hewitt State Forest
10. Ringwood State Park
11. Pequannock Watershed
12. Weis Ecology Center
13. Mahlon Dickerson Reservation
14. Silas Condict Park
15. Pyramid Mountain
16. The Tourne Park
17. Black River WMA
18. Worthington State Forest
19. Jenny Jump State Forest
20. Allamuchy Mountain State Park
21. Merrill Creek Reservoir
22. Alpha
23. Point Mountain Reservation
24. Voorhees State Park
25. Cold Brook Reserve
26. Spruce Run Recreation Area
27. Hoffman Park
28. Round Valley Recreation Area
29. Central Hunterdon County
30. Bull's Island (D & R Canal)

Map 2. Northwest Region

High Point State Park

High Point State Park occupies 13,400 acres of the Kittatinny Mountains in the extreme northwestern corner of the state. Bounded by Stokes State Forest on the south and by New York State on the north, it encompasses the highest elevation in New Jersey. Sitting atop High Point at 1,803 feet is a 220-foot tall obelisk that dominates the landscape for miles around.

Most of the land in the State Park was given in 1923 to the people of New Jersey by Col. Anthony Kuser, for whose ancestor the large Natural Area in the northern part of the park is named. This beautiful section of Sussex County contains several lakes, a few streams, numerous beaver swamps, two large bogs, and many hundreds of acres of ridges and valleys. The habitat and the birdlife is very similar to that in neighboring Stokes State Forest, so refer to that chapter for a list of the typical resident birds. High Point has some special places of its own, however, and these are covered in detail below. Noteworthy among the harder-to-find breeding birds are Common Raven, Hermit Thrush, Blue-headed Vireo, Nashville, Golden-winged and Blackburnian warblers, and occasionally Dark-eyed Junco.

At the headquarters, a Visitor Center features displays on the history and geology of the State Park; there are also restrooms. Ask for a copy of the park map, which shows the various trails and tells how they are marked.

Directions

The headquarters and information office at High Point State Park is on Rt. 23 at the crest of the Kittatinny Ridge. To reach this point:

From northeastern New Jersey, take I-80 west to Rt. 23 in Wayne, then follow Rt. 23 north for about 42 miles to the headquarters, which is on the left. [DeLorme 19, C-20]

From southern New Jersey, take the Garden State Parkway north to Exit 153 (Rt. 3, Clifton). Take Rt. 3 west for 1.5 miles until it merges with US 46, then follow Rt. 46 west for 4 miles to Rt. 23. Go north on Rt. 23 for about 42 miles to the headquarters.

From central New Jersey, the fastest of several routes is to take US 206 and I-287 to the junction with Rt. 23 in Butler; from there it is about 34 miles to the headquarters. Or, take US 206 north through Newton to Rts. 15 and 565. Continue straight ahead on Rt. 565 for 8 miles to Rt. 639, then straight on Rt. 639 for 1 mile to Rt. 23 in Sussex. The headquarters is about 8 miles north on Rt. 23.

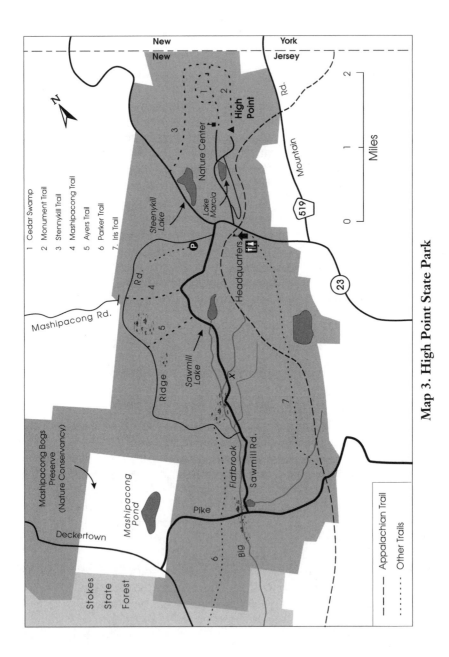

Map 3. High Point State Park

Legend:
1 Cedar Swamp
2 Monument Trail
3 Stennykill Trail
4 Mashipacong Trail
5 Ayers Trail
6 Parker Trail
7. Iris Trail

––– Appalachian Trail
······· Other Trails

New York
New Jersey

High Point

Nature Center

Lake Marcia

Stennykill Lake

Mountain Rd.

519

23

Miles
0 1 2

Headquarters

Mashipacong Rd.

Ridge Rd.

Sawmill Lake

Flatbrook

Sawmill Rd.

Pike

Big

Mashipacong Bogs Preserve (Nature Conservancy)

Mashipacong Pond

Deckertown

Stokes State Forest

N

Birding

This chapter will cover only a few of the birding spots, but you should explore some of the other trails if you have time.

Monument Trail

Across Rt. 23 from the headquarters is the entrance road to the northern part of High Point State Park. A fee is charged to enter this area in summer (it opens at 8 A.M.), but it is free at other seasons. Take this road for about 0.8 miles, past Lake Marcia on the right. At the far end of the lake, there is a sign for the nature center on the left; the drive to the center is about 200 yards. Another 0.2 miles along the main road, you will come to a fork at which the left fork leads to the cedar swamp (Kuser Natural Area). Follow the right fork for about 0.5 miles to the parking lot at High Point Monument.

During the summer, you can climb to the top of the monument, but the view from the parking lot is nearly as impressive. To the west beyond the Delaware River are the Pocono Mountains of Pennsylvania, to the north are the Shawangunk and Catskill Mountains of New York, and to the east lie the hills and valleys of the Highlands of New Jersey. Southwest along the Kittatinny Ridge, the Delaware Water Gap is visible almost 40 miles away, while Sunrise Mountain, a favorite hawk-watching spot, is about 10 miles distant.

Monument Trail leads northeast along the ridge for about 1 mile to the New York State Line; it starts at the far (northeast) end of the parking lot. The vegetation along the trail, dominated by Chestnut Oak, is typical of the dry ridgetops of the Kittatinnies. Birdlife is not abundant, but Hermit Thrush, Nashville Warbler (rare) and (occasionally) Dark-eyed Junco have been found nesting here, as well as the more common Prairie Warbler, Common Yellowthroat, and Eastern Towhee. The trail eventually reaches a gravel road that leads left to the cedar swamp. You can continue your hike to the swamp, which is covered in the next section, or retrace your steps to the parking lot.

Cedar Swamp

This, the centerpiece of the John Dryden Kuser Natural Area, is a legacy of the last ice age. It is a bog that has become densely overgrown with Atlantic White-Cedar and rhododendron, interspersed with Eastern Hemlock and Black Spruce. You might expect to encounter such a spot much further north, in the Adirondacks or the backwoods of Maine.

To reach the cedar swamp from the monument, drive back down the road about 0.5 miles, bear right at the fork, and continue about 0.3 miles to the Kuser Natural Area parking lot. The trail to the swamp is a continuation of the road, which is closed to traffic by a gate. After about 0.4 miles you will come to a fork. Go either way, since the trail makes a loop a little over 1 mile in length. A side trail from this loop goes north along the edge of the swamp and connects with the Monument Trail.

Northern Waterthrush is a common breeder in the cedar swamp, and Nashville Warblers sometimes nest here as well, although they are now quite rare. Compare this dense boggy habitat with the dry second-growth deciduous woods along Monument Trail where Nashville Warbler has also nested; this dual habitat preference is typical of Nashville. Black-throated Green, Blackburnian, Canada, and occasionally Magnolia warblers also nest in the cedar swamp. In winter, look for visiting Pine Siskin and Common Redpoll.

Sawmill Road

Drive back to the entrance at Rt. 23 and turn right. Go one-third of a mile and turn left onto Sawmill Rd. After 200 yards bear left at a fork and continue through a stretch of scrubby deciduous woods. The road then enters a more mature deciduous woods and passes Sawmill Lake and its campground. The tall trees around the Sawmill Lake dam are good for Cerulean Warbler in summer. New Jersey's first nest of Yellow-bellied Sapsucker was found on the campground loop road in 1998, and the birds returned in 1999 and 2000. About 2.5 miles from Rt. 23, just before the road crosses a small bridge, park your car on the shoulder. There is a large beaver swamp on the left. Cross the road and walk east a few hundred yards through a dark hemlock glen to a boggy area, known locally as Cat Swamp. Breeding birds of this glen and bog include Wood Duck, Hooded Merganser (rare), Ruffed Grouse, Acadian and Least flycatchers, Brown Creeper, Winter Wren, Blue-headed Vireo, Black-throated Green, Blackburnian, and Canada warblers, Northern and Louisiana waterthrushes, and Purple Finch.

After returning to your car, continue across the bridge along Sawmill Rd. After 0.8 miles, Ridge Rd. comes in on the right; in another 1.1 miles, Sawmill Rd. ends at the Deckertown Pike. There are two beaver swamps along this section of the road, one before and one after Ridge Rd. Here you might find migrant Olive-sided Flycatcher and nesting Great Blue Heron, Wood Duck, Eastern Kingbird, Tree Swallow, Brown Creeper, and Eastern Bluebird. You might be lucky enough to see a Barred Owl, roosting in a tree alongside the road, or a Black Bear, ambling along the roadside. Bears have become increasingly common in the park during the past ten years, and your chances of encountering one are fair. Many of them have become habituated to humans and show no fear; Do Not Feed Them!

Park on the left, before you get to heavily traveled Deckertown Pike. The large field and marsh on the right, known as Deckertown Swamp, was one of the most reliable places in New Jersey for nesting Alder Flycatcher for many years. Before beaver dams flooded the area, Alder and Willow flycatchers were here every year; with the higher water levels Alder has become less dependable. Willow Flycatcher is always here, however, along with Eastern Kingbird, Yellow and Chestnut-sided warblers, Common Yellowthroat and Swamp Sparrow. Orchard Oriole has nested nearby, and Golden-winged Warbler formerly nested in the scrubby growth on the south side of the road or to the north of the marsh. Watch for Red-shouldered Hawk and possibly Northern Goshawk.

Ridge Road

At this point, you can continue on into Stokes State Forest or turn around and explore more of High Point State Park. To reach Stokes, turn right onto Deckertown Pike, go 1.8 miles, then left on Crigger Rd. The junction with Grau Rd. is 1 mile ahead, and Steam Mill Campground another 0.4 miles beyond Grau Rd. To explore Ridge Rd., turn around on Sawmill Rd. and go 1.1 miles to the junction with Ridge Rd. and turn left.

Ridge Rd. makes a 5-mile loop through a variety of habitats before returning to Sawmill Rd., just 200 yards south of Rt. 23. There are several trail junctions along Ridge Rd. and one paved road, Mashipacong Rd., now blocked by a gate, on the left after about 3.5 miles. Just before you come to Ayers Trail (about 2.5 miles) there is a large marshy area on the right and a clearing where you can park. Within this is a bog with an impenetrable understory of shrubs, trees such as Tamarack and Black Spruce, and many other plants typical of more northerly climes. Birding from the edge, you may see or hear Northern Waterthrush, Nashville and Black-throated Blue warblers, Common Yellowthroat, and Swamp Sparrow.

Continue along Ridge Rd. until it rejoins Sawmill Rd., then turn left and go 0.1 miles to Rt. 23. A left turn will take you by Steenykill Lake, where birding around the boat ramp can be good, and down into the Delaware Valley at Port Jervis, NY. A right turn will head you back toward the rest of New Jersey.

🦆

Stokes State Forest

This beautiful section of the Kittatinny Mountains covers more than 15,000 acres of Sussex County in the northwest corner of the state. The forest ridges, valleys, streams, and ravines harbor a wide variety of resident and migrant birds. Elevation varies from about 460 feet just below Tillman Ravine to

1,653 feet at Sunrise Mountain. Stokes offers something for the birder at every season. In spring, it is an excellent place for migrants, whereas in summer you can find a diverse selection of breeding birds, including some species that, in New Jersey, nest only in the extreme northwestern part of the state. Late summer and fall bring migrant songbirds heading south, but it is mainly the hawk migration at Sunrise Mountain that draws birders at this season (see section on hawk watching). Late fall and winter are quiet at Stokes, but this is the time to search for winter finches in the birches and the hemlocks; it is also a good season to look for the increasingly abundant Wild Turkey.

During spring migration, you can expect to find here almost all the passerines that move through or nest in New Jersey. Some of the more interesting breeding birds are Sharp-shinned (rare) and Cooper's hawks, Northern Goshawk (uncommon), Red-shouldered Hawk, Ruffed Grouse, Wild Turkey, Barred Owl, Red-headed (rare) and Pileated woodpeckers, Acadian Flycatcher, Common Raven (rare, but increasing), Brown Creeper, Winter Wren, Golden-crowned Kinglet (rare), Eastern Bluebird, Hermit Thrush, Blue-headed Vireo, Golden-winged (uncommon), Nashville (uncommon), Black-throated Blue, Black-throated Green, Blackburnian, Cerulean, Worm-eating, Hooded, and Canada warblers, Northern and Louisiana waterthrushes, Dark-eyed Junco (rare) and Purple Finch (uncommon). Rarities that have been found in Stokes State Forest include Gyrfalcon, Band-tailed Pigeon, Black-backed Woodpecker, Boreal Chickadee, Townsend's Solitaire, and Varied Thrush.

Directions

From Exit 34 on I-80 (Rt. 15 North), follow Rt. 15 for 18 miles to its end at US 206. Continue straight ahead on Rt. 206 for about 7 miles to the Kittatinny Ridge through Culvers Gap, just past Culvers Lake on the right. The Appalachian Trail crosses the road just beyond the crest of the hill. Drive past the turnoff to Sunrise Mountain on the right, then past the turnoff to Kittatinny Lake on the left, to Coursen Road and the headquarters building on the right (0.6 miles beyond the Sunrise Mountain turnoff). Stop at the headquarters to obtain a map of the forest. [DeLorme 18, J-13]

From Hunterdon, Warren, or Somerset counties take US 206 north through Newton to the junction with Rt. 15, and proceed as described in the preceding paragraph.

Birding

There are many good birding areas within Stokes State Forest. The following list includes only a few of the better spots; additional exploration on your own might turn up equally good ones. A Sussex County map is useful for exploring the many back roads.

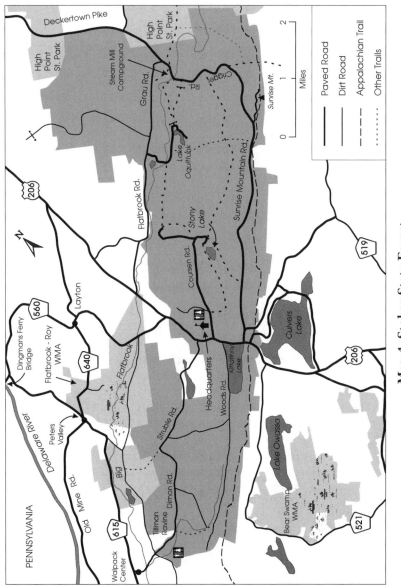

Map 4. Stokes State Forest

Kittle Field and Stony Lake

From the headquarters, continue north on Coursen Rd. From April through July, pause at a bridge a couple of hundred yards past the headquarters to listen for Louisiana Waterthrush. The birding is good along the road, which passes through mixed deciduous woods and Eastern Hemlock stands. After about 2 miles, you will come to a junction with Kittle Rd. on the left and the road to Stony Lake on the right. Turn left and immediately park on the left. The area around Kittle Field attracts migrants in the spring, and Blue-gray Gnatcatchers are always here. The hemlock grove around the picnic area has nesting Acadian Flycatcher and Black-throated Green Warbler.

From Kittle Field, continue northwest along the road for about one-half mile to a fork, where the main road goes right. This area is good for Blue-winged and Prairie warblers, and has long had Golden-winged Warbler, although this species may now be missing. At the end of the road is one end of Blue Mountain Trail, which leads to Lake Oquittunk, and has nesting Black-throated Green, Black-throated Blue, Blackburnian, Hooded, and Pine warblers.

Several good hiking trails begin at Stony Lake. The road to the lake is sometimes closed and there is a fee for parking in summer, but you can leave your car at Kittle Field and walk the one-quarter mile to the lake. Lackner Trail runs south along the west side of the lake, while Swenson Trail begins at the large parking lot at the end of the road into Stony Lake. Coursen Trail branches off on the right from Swenson Trail after about 100 yards. Pine Warbler nests in the spruce and pine groves a little further along Swenson Trail, as do Blackburnian and (sometimes) Black-throated Green warblers, and Blue-headed Vireo and Hermit Thrush.

Coursen Trail is especially good, as it runs south through mature deciduous woods, beaver swamp, and hemlock groves, and connects with Sunrise Mountain Rd. after about 1.2 miles (you can also park on Sunrise Mt. Road and hike the trail from the other direction). Black-throated Blue Warbler (now rare) is another of the specialties of this trail, as are Acadian Flycatcher, Blue-headed Vireo, and Hooded Warbler.

Some of the typical breeding birds of Stokes State Forest (in addition to those already noted), which can be found along Lackner, Coursen, and Swenson Trails, as well as elsewhere in the forest, are Green Heron, Wood Duck (beaver swamps), Broad-winged Hawk, American Woodcock, Black-billed and Yellow-billed cuckoos, Eastern Screech and Great Horned owls, Red-bellied Woodpecker, Eastern Phoebe (near water), Tree Swallow (beaver swamps), Cedar Waxwing, Yellow-throated Vireo, Blue-winged (scrubby second-growth), Yellow (wet, open areas), Chestnut-sided (in grown up clearcuts), and Black-and-white warblers, American Redstart, Rose-breasted Grosbeak, Eastern Towhee, Chipping Sparrow, plus all the more common species.

Sunrise Mountain

To reach Sunrise Mountain, return to US 206 via the headquarters and Coursen Rd. and turn left. Drive 0.6 miles to the signed turnoff for Sunrise Mountain at Upper North Shore Rd. (Rt. 636), and turn left. Go 0.2 miles and bear left onto Sunrise Mountain Rd.

Follow Sunrise Mountain Rd., which is a one-way road, for about 7 miles to the intersection with Crigger Rd. Along the way you will pass several trail junctions, where you can park and explore the woods. Bear right at the fork, 4.0 miles from Rt. 206, and continue another three-quarters of a mile to the Sunrise Mountain parking lot, where there are primitive toilets. Along the way, look and listen for Hooded, Black-throated Blue, and Worm-eating warblers. (See the chapter on hawk watching for more on Sunrise Mountain.)

Return to the intersection and turn right onto the one-way road. About 1.4 miles along this road, you can park on the shoulder and explore an old beaver swamp, now mostly overgrown, where Least Flycatcher and Hooded Merganser have nested. In another quarter-mile, park on the right opposite a Red Pine grove and follow the crude trail along another beaver swamp (known as Swenson Meadow). Least Flycatcher, Golden-winged Warbler (rare), and a variety of other songbirds nest here, and it is an excellent spot for migrants in late August–early September. Yellow-bellied and Olive-sided flycatchers and Philadelphia Vireo are all possibilities. Continuing on Crigger Rd. for another 0.8 miles will bring you to the bridge over the Big Flatbrook, just below Steam Mill Campground.

Steam Mill Campground

Continue over bridge for about 100 feet to a parking area on the left. A male Ruby-throated Hummingbird frequently displays around the parking area or down by the Big Flatbrook. Cerulean, and occasionally Hooded, warblers nest in these woods. Walk to the bridge across the Big Flatbrook. To your left is a beaver pond; a short trail leads away from the road on the far (east) side of the pond. Least Flycatcher nests along the trail, and the flooded areas at its end are good for nesting Eastern Kingbird and Eastern Bluebird and for migrant Olive-sided Flycatchers. Another, longer trail (Steam Mill Trail) leads west (downstream) along the Big Flatbrook into a dense grove of hemlocks. Barred Owl, Acadian Flycatcher, Blue-headed Vireo, Louisiana Waterthrush, and Black-throated Green and Blackburnian warblers nest along the first few hundred yards, and Hooded, Canada, and Black-throated Blue warblers are regular farther on, near where the trail intersects with an old road. Turn left on this road, which leads back to Crigger Rd. a few hundred yards from the Big Flatbrook (round trip about 1.5 miles). Alternatively, a right turn will take you through a hemlock grove to Lake Wapallane (look for Spotted Sandpiper) and the New Jersey School of Conservation.

Return to your car, and continue north on Crigger Rd. (you can't go back the way you came—it's one-way) past the entrance to Steam Mill Campground for about 0.3 miles to the intersection with Grau Rd., on the left. Continuing straight ahead will take you into High Point State Park, which is discussed elsewhere in this book. Instead turn left and follow Grau Rd. through an area where Worm-eating Warblers sing from the hillsides and you might hear Barred Owls hoot from deep in the woods. After about 1.7 miles, you will come to an old grove of Norway Spruce, on the left, just before the left turn for Lake Oquittunk and the New Jersey School of Conservation. This grove and the ones along the road past Lake Oquittunk Rd. have nesting Red-breasted Nuthatch (occasional), Golden-crowned Kinglets, Blue-headed Vireo, Hooded and Magnolia warblers, and sometimes both Broad-winged and Red-shouldered hawks.

Grau Road becomes Flatbrook Rd. at this point (no sign, however), so continue another 2.8 miles to US 206, staying left at the intersection with Hotalen Rd. after about 1.8 miles. Along the way, a brushy area on the right about 1 mile from the Lake Oquittunk turnoff and just before some old tennis courts, may have nesting Golden-winged Warbler. A left turn onto Rt. 206 will take you back to Coursen Rd. and the Headquarters in 1.7 miles, but to continue to the next section, turn right after 1.4 miles onto Struble Rd.

Tillman Ravine

Follow Struble Rd. for 4 miles (the main road becomes Dimon Rd., not marked, when Struble turns right as a dirt road) to Brink Rd. Turn right and go about 0.3 miles to the upper parking lot for Tillman Ravine on the left. A display board here describes some of the features of the ravine. There are primitive toilets here.

Tillman Ravine is a dark and beautiful place. Tillman Brook cascades downhill through a narrow gorge lined with hemlock, suffering heavily from the wooly adelgid infestation, and rhododendron. The trail from the parking lot leads first through a grove of Eastern White Pines, where Pine Warbler and Acadian Flycatcher nest, and then into the hemlocks. At the bottom of the ravine, another trail leads back to a second parking lot a few hundred yards downhill from the first. Some of the breeding birds here are Hermit Thrush, Blue-headed Vireo, Black-throated Green and Blackburnian warblers. Birds are not plentiful in the ravine, but it is worth a visit purely for its natural beauty.

Continue down Brink Rd. to the intersection with Mountain Rd. (not marked), turn left and drive a couple of miles to scenic Buttermilk Falls, watching for the now ubiquitous Wild Turkey.

Flatbrook–Roy Wildlife Management Area

Adjacent Flatbrook–Roy WMA has long been known as one of the better spots for Northern Shrike during those winters when this species comes south. Occasionally, winter finches, including Pine Grosbeak have been found here. From Coursen Rd. and US 206, go north on Rt. 206 for about one mile, then bear left onto Rt. 560 toward Layton. Go about 2.4 miles to the junction of Rt. 560 and Rt. 640 in Layton, and continue straight ahead on Rt. 640 where Rt. 560 turns right towards Dingmans Bridge.

In about 1.1 miles, you will enter the WMA, where there are fields and hedgerows on both sides. Scan the tops of the trees and hedgerows for the shrikes, which like to perch on the very top, especially when it is calm and sunny. In another 300 yards, an old road comes in on the left. If there are no barricades, this road can be driven for about 0.4 miles to its end at the Little Flatbrook. This stretch of the road is especially good for shrikes. In summer, nesting birds include Easter Bluebird, Blue-winged and Prairie warblers, Indigo Bunting, and Rose-breasted Grosbeak. Rt. 640 continues for another 0.7 miles to Peters Valley, passing through some additional good habitat along the way.

Culvers Lake

A trip to Stokes State Forest or Sunrise Mountain in late fall or early spring is not complete without a stop at Culvers Lake. This is best done on your way to the forest. From the junction of Rt. 15 and US 206, go north on Rt. 206 for about 4.6 miles to the junction with East Shore Rd. on the right, just past a Dairy Queen. Turn right and go about 1 mile to the Culvers Lake Association Clubhouse, on the left. This area is private, but birders are tolerated. It's best to park on the road and walk down the driveway of the clubhouse, which provides a good vantage point for scanning the lake. Most of the diving ducks have been seen here, including Common Merganser, Common Goldeneye, Long-tailed Duck and all three scoters; Red-necked Grebe is annual in early April.

A half-mile further, you will cross the Culvers Lake Causeway. Mute Swans and Ring-necked Ducks favor the shallower water on the right. Many Wood Ducks breed here, and Green Herons feed along the edges. On the left is a good view of the lake. In addition to the species just noted, Culvers Lake attracts loons, grebes, the occasional Bald Eagle, and many gulls, including Bonaparte's and Lesser Black-backed. Pomarine Jaeger and Red Phalarope have each been found once on the lake. If you continue around the lake for another 2 miles, you will rejoin US 206 just 200 yards from the turnoff for Sunrise Mountain.

Bear Swamp Wildlife Management Area

Nearby Bear Swamp WMA (2,054 acres), south of Lake Owassa, has nesting Broad-winged and Red-shouldered hawks, a good variety of waterfowl, including Wood Duck and Hooded Merganser, and many nesting passerines. To reach the WMA, take US 206 to the intersection with Rt. 521, 1 mile north of the intersection with East Shore Rd. and 1.2 miles south of Coursen Rd. Turn left onto Rt. 521 (signs for Lake Owassa), and drive about 2.5 miles to a parking area, on the left. A trail here leads into the woods.

From this point, continue another 2.5 miles on Rt. 521, which is called Kemah-Mecca Lake Rd. after it turns left. Here there is a larger parking lot, also on the left, with some crude trails that provide the best access to the swamp. Two other points of access to the WMA are on Rt. 533 (Kemah Lake Rd.) just north of Kemah Lake and on Rt. 655, one-half mile west of Rt. 533.

🦆

Wallkill River National Wildlife Refuge and Vicinity

The Wallkill River NWR, one of the newest additions to the refuge system, was established by Congress in 1990 to protect a 9-mile stretch of the Wallkill River primarily in Sussex County, with a small section in Orange County, New York. When acquisition is complete it will encompass more than 8,000 acres of diverse habitat that provide breeding grounds for a variety of songbirds and wading birds; woodlands and wetlands for migrant waterfowl, shorebirds, and songbirds; as well as some excellent wintering areas for raptors. More than 220 species have been recorded on the Refuge, and this list will grow as it sees more attention from birders.

The nearby grasslands and marshes of northern Wantage Township have an unusual assortment of breeding birds rarely found elsewhere in the state. With the ever increasing development pressure on the neighboring areas, one can only hope that some of this habitat will be preserved.

Directions

To reach the first birding stop in the Refuge, take Rt. 23 north from the intersection with I-287 for about 25 miles to Rt. 565 North (Glenwood Rd.), about 3 miles past the intersection with Rt. 94 in Hamburg. Turn right, and go about 200 yards to a parking area on the right for the Wood Duck Trail. [DeLorme 19, K-25]

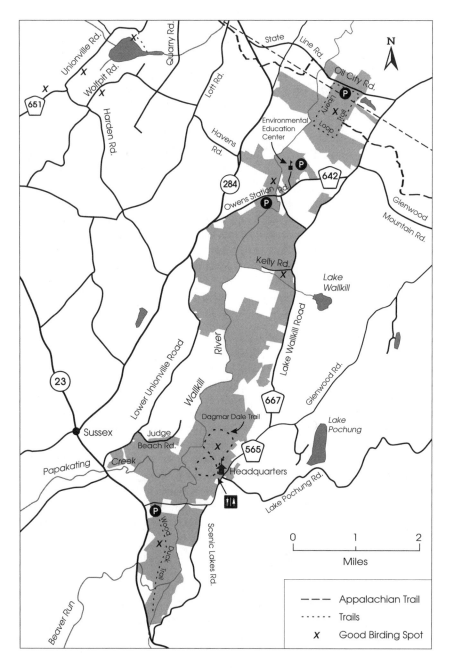

Map 5. Wallkill River NWR and Vicinity

Birding

The Wood Duck Trail runs along an old railroad bed for about 1.5 miles, passing through deciduous bottomland forest until it reaches the Wallkill River near Rt. 23. It is a good spot in spring and fall for migrant songbirds, but should be birded early before the noise from traffic on Rt. 23 becomes distracting. As the name suggests, Wood Ducks nest here and elsewhere along the river.

Return to your car along the same trail and continue on Rt. 565 for another 1.3 miles to the Refuge Headquarters, on the left, where you can obtain a bird list and map of the Refuge. There are public restrooms here open every day. The trail system is still in early stages of development, but the 3-mile long Dagmar Dale Nature Trail is planned, and will start at the headquarters and pass through grasslands and hardwood forests down to the Wallkill River.

Another good birding spot is Kelly Rd.; to reach Kelly Rd., continue on Rt. 565 for another mile, then bear left onto Lake Wallkill Rd. and drive about 2.4 miles, just past the turnoff for Lake Wallkill. Turn left onto Kelly Rd., and go a hundred yards or so until you are in the middle of the two fields on either side. This is the area where Sedge Wrens were discovered nesting in the late 1980s and both Alder and Willow Flycatcher have frequently occurred during the breeding season. Other common birds here include American Woodcock, House Wren, Common Yellowthroat, Song Sparrow, Indigo Bunting, and Baltimore Oriole.

From Kelly Rd., turn left onto Lake Wallkill Rd., and go about 0.7 miles to Bassetts Bridge Rd. (Rt. 665) and turn left. Drive about 0.6 miles to Owens Station Rd. and turn right. Go 0.25 miles to the entrance to the NWR Environmental Education Center, on the left. The driveway leads about 0.2 miles to the center, where there are restrooms and a short trail.

Return to Owens Station Rd. and turn right. When you come to the bridge over the Wallkill River (0.3 miles), stop, park, and scan the river for Solitary and Spotted sandpipers in migration and for Rough-winged Swallows from May through the summer. A Great Horned Owl usually nests somewhere within scope view of the bridge, so try to spot it. From the bridge, continue 1 mile to Rt. 284, watching for Bank Swallows in the sand pits along the way. Turn right onto Rt. 284 and go about 2.2 miles to Oil City Rd., on the right.

Turn right onto Oil City Rd., which becomes Lower Rd. when you cross the New York State line, and continue about 0.8 miles to State Line Rd. in New York. Turn right, and follow State Line Rd., which becomes Oil City Rd. when it crosses the Wallkill River, for about 0.8 miles to a parking lot, on the right. The 2.5-mile Liberty Loop Trail starts at the parking lot and makes a rectangular trek back into New Jersey before ending at the parking lot. This is a great place in winter for wintering raptors, including Rough-legged and

Red-tailed hawks, Short-eared Owl, and, occasionally Snowy Owl and Northern Shrike. The Short-eared Owls roost in the ditches during the day, but sometimes come out to hunt on cloudy days. The best time to see them is the last hour of daylight. The nearby sod farms and truck farms of Orange County, New York, often have American Golden-Plover, Upland Sandpiper, and Buff-breasted Sandpiper in fall migration.

The grasslands of upper Wantage Township and the Rockport (or Black Dirt) Marsh are distinct areas that are best in May and June. To reach them from the intersection of Rt. 23 and Rt. 565, continue northwest on Rt. 23 for another 5.6 miles to Unionville Rd. (Rt. 651), and turn right. Drive 1.3 miles to the intersection with Skytop Rd., on the left. Park here and check the pond on the left for Green Heron and other marsh birds, and the surrounding trees for Baltimore and Orchard orioles, Warbling Vireo, and other passerines.

The next 0.7 miles of Unionville Rd. pass through a farm with pastures on both sides. Bobolinks can usually be found from early May through June in the fields on the left. At the junction with Wolfpit Rd., stay left on Unionville Rd. At the top of the hill (0.1 miles), stop and listen for Vesper Sparrows, which nest in the fields here when they are left fallow. Continue about 0.2 miles, just past the farmhouse on the left, and pull off carefully on the right. Look and listen here for Grasshopper Sparrow up the hill to the left and for Eastern Meadowlark and (rarely) Sedge Wren in the wet grassy areas on the right.

Continue on Unionville Rd. for another 1.3 miles (about 1.6 miles from the junction with Wolfpit Rd.) past a large marsh on the left, and then a smaller one, also on the left, to a pullout on the right with enough room for about three cars. Park here and cross over the dirt berm on the right to join an old, abandoned road (shown as Black Dirt Rd. on some maps). This is private property, but the tenant welcomes birders, as long as they behave themselves.

A short distance down this trail, you will find a large open marsh on the right. This is known as both Rockport Marsh and Black Dirt Marsh (or Dirt Bag Marsh to the less respectful). Breeding birds here include Wood Duck, Mallard, Hooded Merganser, Green Heron, Great Blue Heron, American Bittern, Least Bittern, Pied-billed Grebe, Common Moorhen, Tree Swallow, Barn Swallow, Yellow Warbler, Northern Waterthrush, Common Yellowthroat, Swamp Sparrow, and many other species.

The next right turn off Unionville Rd. (1.1 miles) is Quarry Rd., which may have a variety of swallows, as well as Eastern Meadowlark. Follow Quarry Rd. south for about 1.5 miles to Wolfpit Rd., turn right, and go about 1.3 miles to the junction of Wolfpit and Harden Rd. Just before this intersection is a field where Vesper Sparrows sometimes nest. Turn right, staying on Wolfpit Rd. for another 0.4 miles to the junction with Unionville Rd. At this point, a left turn onto Unionville Rd. will lead you back to Rt. 23 in about 2 miles.

➤

Wawayanda State Park

Wawayanda State Park is the second largest state park in New Jersey, covering more than 10,500 acres in northeastern Sussex and northwestern Passaic Counties. Most of the park lies on the Wawayanda Plateau, a broad, relatively flat section of the New Jersey Highlands at an elevation of about 1,200 feet, situated between Bearfort Mountain on the southeast and Wawayanda Mountain on the west. To the south, the plateau continues into the Pequannock Watershed (covered in a separate chapter); to the north and west, the terrain drops off sharply to Vernon Valley and Wawayanda Creek.

The birdlife of Wawayanda State Park is similar to that of the neighboring Pequannock Watershed, though not quite as diverse. A wide variety of habitats and the moderately high elevation combine to give the area a long list of interesting nesting species. Birders seldom visit the park outside the breeding season, because most of the species are more readily found elsewhere. Ospreys visit the lake in spring and fall, but few waterfowl stop here in migration. The southeastern section of the park, including Bearfort Waters and Terrace Pond, is covered in the Pequannock Watershed chapter.

Among the more noteworthy species that nest in the park are Red-shouldered Hawk, Barred Owl, Pileated Woodpecker, Acadian Flycatcher, Brown Creeper, Winter Wren, Hermit Thrush, Blue-headed Vireo, Golden-winged, Black-throated Blue, Black-throated Green, Blackburnian, Cerulean, Worm-eating, Hooded, and Canada warblers, Northern and Louisiana waterthrushes, Dark-eyed Junco (rarely), and Purple Finch. These and many other species make Wawayanda a delightful place to spend a morning in late spring or in summer.

Directions

To reach the entrance to Wawayanda State Park, take Rt. 23 north from I-80 for about 17 miles to Rt. 513 (Union Valley Rd.). Go north on Rt. 513 for about 7.3 miles to a fork; bear left on Union Valley Rd. and go about 1.3 miles to another fork. Take the left fork, White Rd., for 0.3 miles to the Warwick Turnpike. Turn left onto the Warwick Turnpike and go about 4.4 miles to the park entrance, on the left. [DeLorme 20, J-9]

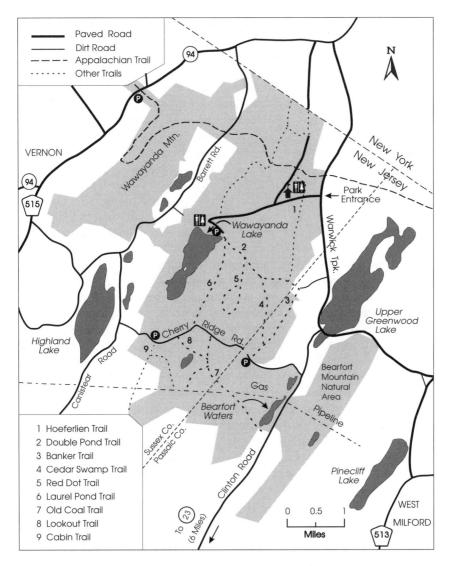

Legend

- ▬▬▬▬ Paved Road
- ───── Dirt Road
- ─ ─ ─ Appalachian Trail
- · · · · · Other Trails

N

94

VERNON

Wawayanda Mtn.

Barrett Rd.

94

515

New York
New Jersey

Park
Entrance

Wawayanda
Lake

Warwick Tpk.

2

6   5

1

4   3

Cherry Ridge Rd.

Upper
Greenwood
Lake

Highland
Lake

8

9

Canistear Road

7

Gas

Bearfort
Mountain
Natural
Area

Pipeline

1 Hoeferlien Trail
2 Double Pond Trail
3 Banker Trail
4 Cedar Swamp Trail
5 Red Dot Trail
6 Laurel Pond Trail
7 Old Coal Trail
8 Lookout Trail
9 Cabin Trail

Bearfort
Waters

Sussex Co.
Passaic Co.

Clinton Road

To 23
(6 Miles)

0   0.5   1

Miles

Pinecliff
Lake

WEST
MILFORD

513

Map 6. Wawayanda State Park

Birding

The entrance road reaches the park headquarters after about 0.3 miles; an entrance fee is charged in summer. The gate opens one-half hour before sunrise and closes one-half hour after sunset, although the collection booth is usually not manned before 8 A.M. If you arrive when the office is open, stop and get a trail map; one is also posted in the display case at the parking lot.

Birding at Wawayanda is on foot, using the numerous, but not always well marked, trails. These lead through a variety of interesting habitats that harbor many species of birds and some uncommon mammals. Black Bear, Bobcat, Beaver, and Porcupine occur within the park, but they are mainly nocturnal and you are unlikely to encounter them. Because of its unique plant and animal life, a large portion of the eastern section of the park has been designated a Natural Area under the New Jersey Natural Systems Act.

There are two parking areas from which to start your hike—the one at the headquarters and another, which provides better access to the trails, at the boat-rental concession. To reach it, follow the main park road to the parking lot at Wawayanda Lake, and continue through that parking area to the next one at the boat rental site. The trails are best covered with the aid of the trail map; several different routes for hikes are suggested.

Walk east from the parking lot for about 0.25 miles, past the dam and past an old iron furnace that was the focus of the small town of Double Pond that flourished here in the mid-1800s. Stay left at the dam on the dirt road that eventually becomes Laurel Trail. After about 250 yards, just across a wooden bridge, is a sign for Double Pond Trail on the left. Follow Double Pond Trail through the group campground and into a mature second-growth deciduous forest.

Some of the birds of the deciduous woods frequently encountered along this trail (and elsewhere in the park) during the nesting season are Broad-winged Hawk, Ruffed Grouse, Black-billed (uncommon) and Yellow-billed cuckoos, Eastern Screech and Great Horned owls, Pileated Woodpecker, Least Flycatcher, Eastern Kingbird, Brown Creeper, Cedar Waxwing, Chestnut-sided, Black-and-white, Hooded, and Canada warblers, American Redstart and Rose-breasted Grosbeak.

After about 0.4 miles, you will come to a wooden bridge across Wawayanda Creek and its open marshy edges. Here you will find Eastern Kingbird, Eastern Phoebe, Tree Swallow, Yellow Warbler, Louisiana Waterthrush, Common Yellowthroat, Song and Swamp sparrows, and Red-winged Blackbird. Continue past the junction with Red Dot Trail, through more deciduous woods and some hemlock groves to the junction with Cedar Swamp Trail on the right, about 1 mile from the beginning of Double Pond Trail. At this point you can go either way, but I suggest you try the Cedar Swamp Trail.

Cedar Swamp Trail leads to a swampy area where the dominant tree is the Atlantic White Cedar, the same species that grows in the cedar swamps of the New Jersey Pine Barrens. Northern and Louisiana waterthrushes are here; with luck you might find something unusual like a Nashville Warbler, a species that prefers this type of habitat further north but is an irregular nester in New Jersey. The trail emerges from the swamp into some rhododendron thickets and hemlock groves.

The hemlock woods have a few species not found in the deciduous forest, including Acadian Flycatcher (uncommon), Winter Wren (rare), Hermit Thrush (uncommon), Blue-headed Vireo, Black-throated Blue (rare), Black-throated Green (common), and Blackburnian warblers; and Dark-eyed Junco (very rare breeder). After about 1.1 miles on the Cedar Swamp Trail, you will come to a T intersection. At this point you can turn left and return via Banker Trail and Double Pond Trail, or turn right and return via Cherry Ridge Rd. and Laurel Pond Trail.

If you choose the left fork, go about 200 yards and take the left turn onto Banker Trail, which traverses a variety of habitats. It becomes hard to follow towards its north end, but keep to your left when you come to a small pond. After about 1.1 miles, the trail ends and a paved road begins. At this point you are no longer in the park. Go left onto a dirt road for about 0.2 miles, and then re-enter the park where the trail passes between two white posts. This is the eastern end of Double Pond Trail, which leads you back to the parking lot, a distance of about 1.8 miles.

If you turn right at the T intersection, go about 0.3 miles until the trail ends at Cherry Ridge Rd., a one-lane dirt road, and turn right. The first stretch passes through some open deciduous woods with a dense Mountain Laurel understory, where Hooded and Canada warblers are common. Further along are several hemlock glens where Acadian Flycatcher, Blue-headed Vireo, and Black-throated Blue Warbler may be found in summer.

After about a mile, on your left, you will pass the junction with Old Coal Rd., which leads through more deciduous woods and hemlock glens down to Bearfort Waters on Clinton Rd. Hooded and Canada warblers are common along the upper parts of Old Coal Rd. and Hermit Thrush is often in the hemlocks. About 0.3 miles along the Old Coal Rd., Lookout Trail leads to the right. This trail passes by Lake Lookout and rejoins Cherry Ridge Rd. in about 0.75 miles.

If you remain on Cherry Ridge Rd., after about 1.4 miles you'll reach the junction with Laurel Pond Trail on your right. (If you come to Lookout Trail on the left, you have missed Laurel Pond Trail. Go back one-third of a mile to the first trail on the left.) There is a marker at the beginning of Laurel Pond Trail, but vandals occasionally destroy the signs in this remote section of the park. From the junction of Cherry Ridge Rd. and Laurel Pond Trail, it is about 1.7 miles back to the parking lot.

Another interesting hike, covering about 6 miles, leads along Double Pond Trail, the William Hoeferlien Trail, a short section of the Appalachian Trail and Iron Mountain Rd. Use the trail map for this hike. You can start at either the day-use area or the headquarters parking lot. The habitat covered is similar to that on the hikes described above, except that there are more deciduous and less coniferous woods. The trails pass through some open areas where you will find Blue-winged and possibly Golden-winged warblers, Chipping Sparrow, and Indigo Bunting.

Cherry Ridge Rd., which was discussed briefly earlier, is one of the most interesting areas in the park. The road has been abandoned and you can no longer drive the length of it. The parts that are open are very rough and rocky, however, and may do severe damage to a low clearance vehicle. The best idea is to park in one of the parking areas at either end and walk the road.

To reach the east end of Cherry Ridge Rd. from the park entrance, turn right onto the Warwick Turnpike and go about 2.2 miles to Clinton Rd., on the right. Take Clinton Rd. south for about 0.8 miles to Cherry Ridge Rd., on the right. Follow Cherry Ridge uphill for about 1 mile to the entrance to Wawayanda State Park, marked by a sign, where you can park. Hooded Warbler is plentiful at this spot, which is about 0.2 miles from the junction with Banker Trail previously noted.

The west end of Cherry Ridge Rd. is much harder to find. From the park, it is most easily reached via the service gate on Wawayanda Rd., just west of the day-use area. This gate is open after 8 A.M., in summer only. From the service gate, follow Wawayanda Rd. for about 1.5 miles to the junction with Breakneck Rd. and Canistear Rd. Turn left onto Canistear and go about 1.2 miles to where the main road turns right and an unmarked road goes straight ahead down a hill. Take this unmarked road, which is Cherry Ridge Rd., past a lake on the right. Ignore the first right turn, but stay right at the next intersection and follow this road around a curve through a residential area until it takes off straight ahead into the woods. At this point you enter Wawayanda State Park; the distance from Canistear Rd. to the park is about 0.3 miles. Cherry Ridge Rd. can also be reached by driving north on Canistear Rd. from Route 23 for about 6.7 miles.

After you have entered the park the road gets rough, but there is a parking lot on the left in about one-quarter mile. Park here and continue on foot. In about 300 yards, Cabin Trail comes in on the right, while Cherry Ridge Rd. continues left. Follow Cabin Trail for about three-quarters of a mile to a gas pipeline right-of-way. Here, you can turn left and hike along the pipeline for about one-half mile to a beaver swamp, where Eastern Bluebirds nest. This swamp may be difficult to cross, but if you can, you'll come to a junction with Turkey Ridge Trail on the left after about 0.2 miles. Turkey Ridge Trail leads back to the Cabin Trail.

If you continue on Cabin Trail, across the pipeline, you will soon come to rhododendron and laurel thickets where Hooded and Canada Warblers abound and Black-throated Blue Warbler is an annual breeder. A trail on the left, after about 1.5 miles, leads down to a hemlock glen where Winter Wren, Hermit Thrush, Blue-headed Vireo, and Northern Waterthrush may be found.

The Appalachian Trail traverses the northern part of Wawayanda State Park. In the eastern section of the park, the trail follows a portion of Iron Mountain Rd. and passes within 0.4 miles of the park headquarters. The trail in the western section of the park crosses a relatively inaccessible area that is infrequently visited by birders. To reach the trail from the park, go out to the entrance, and follow Warwick Turnpike north into New York for 3 miles to its end at Route 94, New Milford Rd. Turn left onto Rt. 94 and go about 5.1 miles. Just before the junction with Maple Grange Rd. on the right is a parking area on the left. Park here and walk a short distance farther to the beginning of the Appalachian Trail, marked by white blazes.

The Appalachian Trail follows a gentle slope along the edge of some fields for about 0.4 miles, then starts a steep ascent of Wawayanda Mountain, climbing more than 700 feet in one-half mile. Along the way it passes through mature deciduous woods and a few hemlock groves, where you'll find a variety of birds. On top of the mountain the habitat is the open oak woodland with scattered Pitch Pines typical of the dry ridgetops of the Highlands and the Kittatinny Mountains. Here you will find Hermit Thrush, Veery, Worm-eating and Hooded warblers, Ovenbird, but little else.

A rock outcropping along the trail provides outstanding views of Vernon Valley below and the Kittatinny Mountains, with High Point Monument 13 miles to the northwest. It is also a good place to watch hawks in the fall, if you are up to the long climb. About one-half mile farther north along the talus of Wawayanda Mountain is the only stand of Red Pine in New Jersey believed to be native.

✈

Swartswood State Park and Vicinity

With over 700 acres of land and 600 acres of water, Swartswood State Park is a popular summer camping, picnicking, swimming, and boating area, but its two largest lakes are also excellent for waterfowl during migration and the colder months, when they are not frozen. Little Swartswood Lake is especially popular with diving ducks, while Swartswood Lake has attracted such rarities as Great Cormorant, Red-necked Grebe, and Eurasian Wigeon.

Nearby Paulins Kill Lake also offers good birding in the Paulinskill River WMA and the Paulinskill Valley Trail (the confusion about the spelling of the name is further compounded since *kill* means "river" or "stream").

Note: Although there is no hunting along the Paulinskill Valley Trail, the Paulinskill River WMA is open to hunters during hunting season (roughly October through December) every day but Sunday. Do not venture into the WMA during the hunting season, except on Sunday.

Directions

Take I-80 to Exit 25 (US 206), and drive north on US 206 for about 12 miles to the town of Newton. At the square in the center of Newton, US 206 makes a left turn at a traffic light, goes one block and makes a right turn, then, in only about 200 feet, comes to another traffic light at Mill Rd. Turn left onto Mill Rd. (Rt. 519), and go 0.4 miles to the light at Swartswood Rd. (Rt. 622), where there is a sign for Swartswood Lake State Park. Turn left onto Swartswood Rd. and follow it for about 4.4 miles to the intersection with Rt. 619 (East Shore Drive). Turn left, and go 0.6 miles to the entrance to the state park, on the right. [DeLorme 23, C-25]

Birding

Drive in the entrance road, past the park office (fee in summer; restrooms), and loop around to the left toward the large parking area and bathhouses (also restrooms). Park in the lot and walk down to the water to scan for waterfowl. In spring and fall, Common Loon, Pied-billed Grebe, Double-crested Cormorant, diving ducks, such as scaup, Common Goldeneye, Bufflehead, Common and Hooded mergansers, and Ruddy Duck, can often be seen swimming or diving on Swartswood Lake. This is often not the best vantage point, but provides a broad view of the lake and a chance to see where waterfowl may be concentrated. Red-throated Loon, Horned Grebe, Redhead, Canvasback, scoters, and Long-tailed Duck (Oldsquaw) occasionally drop in, the latter two usually when bad weather coincides with migration. Red-necked Grebe is noted in most years, typically in March through April. A spotting scope is very helpful at Swartswood.

Across the street from the park entrance is an extensive deciduous woodland with some Hemlock and Red Cedar. Duck Pond, Spring Lake, and a few other wet depressions are also located here. This area has not received much attention from birders, despite a fine network of trails.

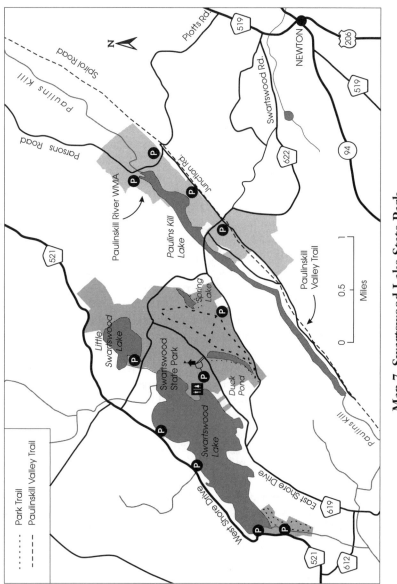

Map 7. Swartswood Lake State Park

Legend:
...... Park Trail
- - - Paulinskill Valley Trail

N

Spiral Road
Paulins Kill
Parsons Road
Plotts Rd.
519
Swartswood Rd.
NEWTON
206
519
94
622
Junction Rd.
Paulinskill River WMA
Paulins Kill Lake
Paulinskill Valley Trail
521
Little Swartswood Lake
Spring Lake
Swartswood State Park
Duck Pond
Swartswood Lake
West Shore Drive
East Shore Drive
619
521
612
Paulins Kill

0   0.5
Miles

To explore more of the lake and look for waterfowl, drive back to the park entrance and turn right. Drive about 2.5 miles to the intersection with Pond Brook Rd. (Rt. 612); along the way there are a couple of places where you can scan the lake, but access on this side is very limited. Turn right onto Pine Pond Rd. and go 0.8 miles to West Shore Rd. (Rt. 521), and turn right. Drive about 0.6 miles, then turn right into the parking lot at Keen's Grist Mill, which dates from the 1830s. The Mill Trail, a 1.2-mile loop, exits the parking lot and covers some steep terrain cloaked in Red Cedars. At its midpoint, the trail offers good views of the southern portion of the lake.

From the parking lot, turn right onto West Shore Rd., which follows the edge of the lake for over 2 miles. Parking areas or pullouts where you can scan for waterfowl are at 0.3 miles (a boat launch, from which you can walk a few hundred feet farther along the road to get excellent views of the south end), 1.4 miles, and 2.1 miles from the Grist Mill lot. Continue north to the intersection with Swartswood Rd. (Rt. 622), which is about 2.5 miles from the Grist Mill, and turn right. Drive 0.5 miles, then turn left into the short road to the parking lot at Little Swartswood Lake, where there is a boat launch and a portable toilet.

You can scan part of the lake from the boat launch, but the best vantage is to walk up the path to the picnic area and continue to the overlook at the edge of the lake. Although Little Swartswood is much smaller than Swartswood Lake, it is more secluded, and attracts a surprising variety of waterfowl. Pied-billed Grebe, Wood, Ring-necked, and Ruddy ducks, American Wigeon, Gadwall, and American Coot are regular, and many other species are seen occasionally. Bald Eagles have been noted here several times as well as at other places in the Swartswood area. Walk the trails counterclockwise along the shore in order to scan the swampy western cove of the lake, where birds sometimes retreat when disturbed. To complete this loop, turn left out of the entrance road onto Swartswood Rd., and go one-half mile back to the intersection with East Shore Rd.

For some woodland, hedgerow, and marsh birding at the Paulinskill River WMA or the Paulinskill Valley Trail, take Swartswood Rd. (Rt. 622) back toward Newton for 1.3 miles to the bridge over Paulins Kill Lake, then go another 0.3 miles to the intersection with Junction Rd., where there is a pulloff on the right side of Swartswood Rd. This is one access point for the Paulinskill Valley Trail, a trail that was once part of the right-of-way of the New York, Susquehanna, and Western Railroad, and now runs for 27 miles through parts of Warren and Sussex Counties. Look here for Louisiana Waterthrush by the stream flowing below the hill and for Alder Flycatcher, which has nested irregularly near the open wetland just below the pulloff.

Carefully drive across Swartswood Rd. onto Junction Rd., but pause in about 0.1 miles to check out the pond on the left, which often has Killdeer, Green, and Great Blue herons in the warmer seasons, and Green-winged Teal from fall to spring. Drive 0.9 miles (past the parking lot at 0.4 miles) and turn left under a railroad bridge onto Parsons Rd., then immediately right into the WMA parking lot. The Paulinskill River WMA includes the Paulinskill River, and a marsh at the head of Paulins Kill Lake, as well extensive fields, hedgerows, deciduous and Red Cedar woodlands. This area has not been birded extensively, but Eastern Kingbird, Blue-winged and Prairie warblers, Indigo Bunting, Eastern Towhee, and Field Sparrow should be found in summer, while Yellow-breasted Chat has nested in the hedgerows along Junction Rd.

From here you can either walk the 0.3 miles down Parsons Rd. to the marsh at the north end of Paulins Kill Lake or drive down, cross the bridge over the river, and park in the lot on the left. The marsh is an excellent place for Common Snipe, Solitary Sandpiper, and swallows in migration, and had its moment of glory in the summer of 1975 when both White Ibis and Purple Gallinule were present simultaneously. Unfortunately, the marsh has been overgrown with Purple Loosestrife and is less attractive to breeding birds than it once was. The marsh area and the shrubbery around the abandoned barns and house across the river are usually very good in migration for hawks, sparrows, bluebirds, wrens, and many common birds. It has also hosted several Northern Shrikes in winter.

To visit a very productive area of the Paulinskill Valley Trail, walk back under the railroad bridge to Junction Rd. Turn left and follow the road up and to the right. You'll soon see the marked trail where it crosses the road. A leisurely 1-mile walk to the left should produce Great Crested Flycatcher, Wood Thrush, Red-eyed and Yellow-throated vireos, Black-and-white and Worm-eating warblers, Ovenbird, Scarlet Tanager, and perhaps Pileated Woodpecker and Yellow-billed Cuckoo.

🖝

Whittingham Wildlife Management Area

Whittingham WMA, which contains more than 1,900 acres of fields, hedgerows, wooded limestone ridges and a large, spring-fed swamp that is the source of the Pequest River, is located near Newton, Sussex County. The Whittingham Tract is as well known for the abundance and variety of its ferns, including the bizarre Walking Fern, as it is for its birdlife. It not only supports an interesting diversity of breeding birds but also attracts many migrant songbirds in spring and fall.

Mammals inhabiting the swamp and surroundings include Mink, Beaver, River Otter, and Red Fox, but all are very shy and hard to see. Among the numerous amphibians are the rare Long-tailed and Four-toed salamanders. A 400-acre portion of the WMA has been set aside as a Natural Area.

Note: The Whittingham WMA is open to hunters during the hunting season (roughly October through December) every day but Sunday. Do not venture into the WMA during the hunting season, except on Sundays.

Directions

From I-80, Exit 25 (US 206 North, Newton), take Rt. 206 a little more than 6.0 miles to the only traffic light in Andover. Continue straight through this light for about 2.9 miles to the traffic light in Springdale. About 0.1 mile after the light, turn left onto Fredon-Springdale Rd. (Rt. 618). The only street sign is a small obscure one that reads "Fredon Road." In about one mile, there is a large WMA parking lot on the left. A more convenient parking place can be reached by continuing another 0.3 miles to an intersection, where you turn left (this is still the Fredon-Springdale Rd., although marked Spring Lake Trail in DeLorme). Go 0.4 miles to a small parking area on the left, where there is a gate across an old road. If the gate is open, turn left and drive down to a large parking lot; if the gate is closed, park near the main road and walk in. [DeLorme 23, F-27]

Birding

If you have parked outside the gate mentioned above, walk around it and down to the parking lot. At the far end of the lot, take the unpaved road to the right (if you take the one that goes straight, it will eventually lead you to the first parking lot). The road cuts across a large field (look for Field Sparrow, Indigo Bunting, and Blue-winged Warbler), crosses a hedgerow, then turns right as it meets a road coming from the left at a wooded limestone hill.

For several hundred yards, there are woods on the left and fields on the right. Next, the road enters the forest and, shortly thereafter, makes a sharp left turn. This is an excellent area for migrant landbirds and summer residents. In spring, check the trees at the small overgrown opening here for warblers, including Bay-breasted, Blackpoll, and Cerulean (which nests here). Some of the other, less common migrants to watch for are Swainson's and Gray-cheeked thrushes (mainly fall), Philadelphia Vireo (fall), both cuckoos (irregular breeders), and Mourning Warbler (spring).

A walk down the right side of the opening will lead to an old lime kiln. Just beyond is a pond surrounded by huge Silver Maples and Sycamores, where you may wish to explore for wildflowers and ferns, as well as for birds. Wood Duck, Pileated and Red-bellied woodpeckers, Great Crested

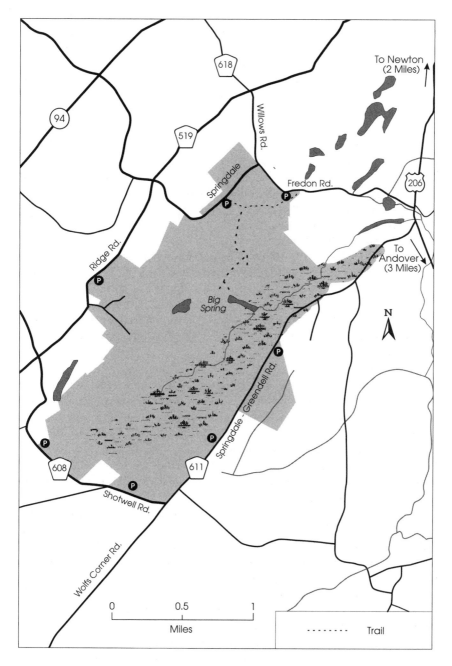

Map 8. Whittingham WMA

Flycatcher, Blue-gray Gnatcatcher, Yellow-throated Vireo, Cerulean Warbler, Scarlet Tanager, and Rose-breasted Grosbeak are among the species that nest near the pond. Eastern Phoebe nests under the same limestone ledges that may harbor Walking Fern or Maidenhair Spleenwort in their crevices. Acadian Flycatcher breeds at the far end of the pond and both Kentucky and Prothonotary warblers have nested in the past.

Return to the trail at the left bend and continue in the same direction. When the road forks, stay right and go up the hill. After a few hundred yards, you will emerge from the woods into a large, overgrown field. In or near the field nest Red-tailed and Broad-winged hawks, Wild Turkey, American Woodcock, Blue-winged Warbler, and Indigo Bunting. Follow the path to the right and, as you come down the hill, you should see water straight ahead. A path leads to the water where, with a little exploration, you can locate Big Spring as it emerges from the rocks at the base of a small cliff. This is the principal source of the Pequest River.

During May and late August to early September, check the dead snags around the spring for Olive-sided Flycatcher. Any flock of migrants should be checked for Yellow-bellied Flycatcher. The water at Big Spring never freezes and is an ideal place to find birds in winter. Several species of waterfowl, Belted Kingfisher, Yellow-bellied Sapsucker, Winter Wren, Eastern Bluebird, Yellow-rumped Warbler, or even an Eastern Phoebe could be the reward for a winter's hike.

The swamp and marsh extend about 0.25 miles to the northeast and one-half mile to the southwest from Big Spring, but there are no trails into or even around the edge of the area. It is easy to get lost, so exploration should be done cautiously and with the aid of a compass. Breeding birds have included Pied-billed Grebe (rare), Green Heron, Wood Duck, Virginia Rail, Sora, Common Moorhen, Willow Flycatcher, Canada Warbler, Northern Waterthrush, and other, more common, wetland species. Several mowed trails near Big Spring traverse some of the uplands portions of the northeastern part of the WMA.

To reach the other parts of the Whittingham tract, return to the junction of Fredon-Springdale Rd. and US 206, and turn right. Go 0.1 miles to the traffic light and turn right onto Springdale-Greendell Rd. (Rt. 611). There are two WMA parking lots on this road, the first on the left at 1.7 miles, and the second on the right at 2.3 miles. After the first mile, all of the land on the right (west) side of Rt. 611 is part of the WMA. You can explore the fields, woods, and swamps here, but the area is large and trails are few. Yellow-breasted Chat (irregular), Golden-winged Warbler (now rare), and Orchard Oriole have nested along the field-forest edge between the two parking lots. Eastern Meadowlark breeds in the fields south of the second lot.

Additional parking areas and WMA access can be reached by continuing on Rt. 611 for 0.6 miles from the second lot to Shotwell Rd. (Rt. 608). Turn right, then watch for parking lots on the right at 0.4 and 1.0 miles from Rt. 611. Continue on Shotwell Rd. for another mile, then turn right onto Ridge Rd. (Rt. 519) and go 0.7 miles to the last parking area.

☂

Kittatinny Valley State Park

One of the newer state parks, Kittatinny Valley includes more than 1700 acres in Andover Township, southeastern Sussex County. It is also the site of Aeroflex-Andover Airport, operated by the New Jersey Forest Fire Service, and includes the large Aeroflex Lake, as well as the smaller Gardner's Pond and Twin Lakes. In addition to the many trails within the park, the Sussex Branch Trail, a 21-mile path along an old railroad right-of-way, runs through the length of the park, from north to south.

Directions

Take I-80 to Exit 25 (US 206 North), and drive north on US 206 for a little more than 6 miles to the village of Andover. About 0.6 miles past the traffic light in Andover, turn right onto Limecrest Rd., Rt. 669. Go about 1 mile to the sign for the park entrance, turn left, then immediately right into the parking lot. [DeLorme 24, G-2]

Other parking areas are located on US 206 at the Sussex Branch Trail, 0.3 miles north of Limecrest Rd., and along Goodale Rd., which is 1 mile north of Limecrest Rd. on US 206.

Birding

The many trails through the park are worth exploring in spring, summer, or fall for migrant and resident songbirds, including most of the species expected at nearby Whittingham WMA. The lakes, particularly Whites Pond, can be excellent for waterfowl in migration.

Lake Aeroflex is a large, deep lake and is usually the last lake in the area to freeze, thus attracting diving ducks after the others have frozen. Between the airport and Limecrest Rd. is an extensive marsh/swamp that can produce Wood Duck, Green Heron, Warbling Vireo, Willow Flycatcher, and other marsh birds. Check the airport grass for Killdeer and bluebirds, and watch for Black Vultures among the Turkey Vultures overhead.

N

PSE&G

669

Lake
Aeroflex

Twin
Lakes

P

P

Goodale Road

P

Whites
Pond

Gardners
Pond

Lake
Lenape

517

206

P

Limecrest Rd.

Old Creamery Rd.

Andover - Sparta Rd.

517

0   0.25   0.5

Miles

ANDOVER

· · · · · · Park Trails

– – – – – Sussex Branch Trail

✈ Airport (Restricted)

Map 9. Kittatinny Valley State Park

One of the best spots, especially during migration, is a 1-mile section of the Sussex Branch Trail from the parking lot on US 206 to the trail's intersection with Goodale Rd. Warblers, thrushes, flycatchers, and vireos can often be seen well here. The best variety is often found in the area where water lies on both sides of the trail. Wilson's and Magnolia warblers are found during spring in the swampy depression on the left after passing the first field.

The tall trees on the rocky peninsula jutting left into Whites Pond may harbor Tennessee, Black-throated Green, Nashville, Blackburnian, and other warblers in May. In early September, try the short trail just before the marshy pond on the right for Philadelphia Vireo, Black-throated Blue Warbler, and many other migrants. Later in the month, check for Blue-headed Vireo. The marshy pond has nesting Virginia Rail, as well as Wood Duck, Least Flycatcher, Eastern Bluebird, and other common marsh birds, and is a good spot for Rusty Blackbird in late October.

In spring and fall, Whites Pond may have Belted Kingfisher, several swallow species, Pied-billed Grebe, Ring-necked Duck, Hooded and Common mergansers, Northern Pintail, American Wigeon, both teal, Black Duck, and Mallard. In late summer, when the water is low, check for Green Heron, Great Egret, Great Blue Heron, Killdeer, Solitary and Spotted sandpipers, yellowlegs, and other shorebirds. The section of trail beyond Whites Pond is densely forested and is particularly good for Pileated Woodpecker. Breeding birds here include Rose-breasted Grosbeak, Louisiana Waterthrush, Black-and-white Warbler, and Ovenbird.

For another good birding area in fall and early winter, park in the lot just south of Twin Lakes on Goodale Rd., 0.5 miles from US 206. The shrubby edges of the field between the lake and the road are excellent for migrant sparrows, including Fox, White-crowned, Lincoln's, and Savannah. The field on the left of the path to the boat launch usually has a large flock of American Pipits in late October and early November, and Northern Shrike has been seen here several times in early winter.

Continue another 0.5 miles along Goodale Rd. to the next parking area, on the right. Check the edges of the big field here for Wild Turkey and Eastern Bluebird, then cross the road and the Sussex Branch Trail to the gravel road that begins opposite the parking area. The trail leads to the north end of Twin Lakes, where Prairie Warbler has nested, then continues up a hill to an overgrown, abandoned stone barn. The area around the barn is good for migrants in spring and fall. Chestnut-sided Warbler and Indigo Bunting nest here. The cedars a bit farther along the trail have had Northern Saw-whet Owl in winter.

Other spots to try include the mixed deciduous/hemlock forest just south of this parking lot, where Black-throated Green Warblers nest and both crossbills have wintered, and the Sussex Branch Trail across the street and to the north of the parking lot.

☝

Sparta Mountain

The New Jersey Audubon Society's (NJAS) Sparta Mountain Sanctuary and the adjacent Sparta Mountain WMA provide additional birding opportunities in the Highlands in an area seldom visited by birders. The birdlife is similar to that of nearby Mahlon Dickerson Reservation and the Pequannock Watershed, but it includes some unique features of its own, such as the Edison Bog.

Directions

See Maps 12 and 13. From Northeastern New Jersey, take Rt. 23 west from its junction with I-287 (Exit 52B) for about 10 miles to the Oak Ridge Rd. exit. Bear right at the jughandle and cross over Rt. 23, going south on Oak Ridge Rd. Drive about 3 miles to the first traffic light and turn right onto Ridge Rd. Follow Ridge Rd. for 3 miles to Edison Rd., on the right, just past the sign for Paulist Fathers. Turn right onto Edison Rd., go about 150 yards, and park on the right by the fence. [DeLorme 24, E-13]

From the rest of New Jersey, take I-287 North to I-80 West, then go about 8 miles to Exit 34B (Rt. 15 North). Go 8.5 miles north to the Sparta Business District-Lake Mohawk exit. At the end of the ramp, make a right (this becomes Woodport Rd.) and continue 0.75 miles to a Texaco Station, on the right. Turn right onto East Mountain Rd., go 1 mile until it ends, and turn right onto Glen Rd. (County Rt. 620). Take Glen Rd. for about 3.5 miles, past a sign for Sparta Lake, and turn left onto Edison Rd. Go about 150 yards, and park on the right.

Birding

An NJAS kiosk at the edge of the woods has information about the sanctuary and a rough trail map. New trails have been prepared by the New York–New Jersey Trails Conference through the sanctuary and the adjacent Sparta Mountain WMA. Follow the trail to Rykers Lake, where there is fishing access, and stay right around the lake, following the NJAS signs. The trail is soon joined by the Highlands Trail, marked by teal blue blazes. After about one mile, the Highlands Trail turns north and the NJAS trail turns south to cross a stream. Shortly after the stream and just before the housing development, the trail divides. One part turns southeast to return to complete the loop around Rykers Lake. The second goes northwest into the WMA, where it eventually reaches the Edison parking area.

To reach the trailhead for the Edison area, continue west on Edison Rd. from the pullout for 1.6 miles to a short road and parking area on the right. Here there is a monument to Thomas A. Edison and the beginning of the trail to the old town of Edison. This trail continues to Edison Bog, but a more direct way is to continue on Edison Rd. for 0.2 miles to a pullout on the right. Park here and follow the trail left for a short distance to the beginning of a wide trail that is the remains of an old railroad bed.

Follow the railroad bed trail, which is popular with dirt bikers later in the day, for about a mile to a short side trail to an overlook that provides a good view of the bog. The New Jersey Audubon trail intersects at this point, and you can follow it either way as it circles the bog and rejoins the main trail, as shown on Map 13. Until the trails are better marked, a compass will be useful in finding your way.

The breeding birds of Sparta Mountain include about 18 species of warblers, including Golden-winged, Cerulean, and Black-throated Blue, and many other passerines, such as Hermit and Wood thrushes, Veery, Blue-headed, Red-eyed, and Yellow-throated vireos, Scarlet Tanager, and Rose-breasted Grosbeak. Wild Turkey and Ruffed Grouse are common and Common Raven probably nests.

Birding is often very good right along Edison Rd., which is lightly traveled early in the morning. A good spot for Golden-winged Warbler has been the power line cut reached by continuing west from the Edison Monument parking lot for another 0.7 miles. Park in the open area on the left and walk north along the power line to look for the warblers.

🦃

Abraham Hewitt State Forest

Although this scenic, undeveloped forest contains almost 2,000 acres of land on Bearfort Mountain in northwestern Passaic County, it is seldom visited by birders. Birdlife is similar to that in adjacent Pequannock Watershed areas, with such common breeding species as Ruffed Grouse, Pileated Woodpecker, Ovenbird, Hooded Warbler, and many others. An interesting 3.5-mile hike starts at the State Line Trail on Rt. 511, circles Surprise Lake and West Pond, then returns to the State Line Trail. A trail map is available at either Wawayanda State Park or Ringwood State Park.

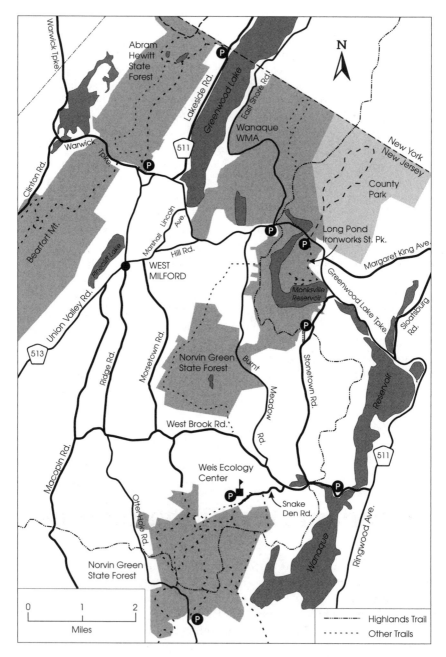

Map 10. Northern Passaic County

Directions

Take Rt. 23 west to Union Valley Rd. (Rt. 513), then follow Union Valley for 9 miles, through West Milford, to the junction with Rt. 511 at Greenwood Lake. Turn left onto Rt. 511 (Lakeside Rd.) and go 2.5 miles to just over the New York State line, where there is a place to park on the right. Walk back into New Jersey to a marina on the left, then cross the road. At the far side of the marina parking lot is a stream; walk along it until you see some blue-on-white markers on the trees indicating the beginning of the State Line Trail. [DeLorme 20, J-13]

Birding

See Map 10. The State Line Trail (blue blazes) makes a steep ascent of Bearfort Mountain, reaching a junction with the Ernest Walter Trail (yellow blazes) in about 0.4 miles. The Walter Trail makes a 2-mile loop around Surprise Lake and West Pond, joining the Appalachian Trail for a short section, then meeting the State Line Trail again after about 0.2 miles. The return on the State Line Trail is about 0.75 miles. In addition to those species noted above, look and listen for Great Crested Flycatcher, Hermit Thrush, Northern Waterthrush, and Eastern Towhee.

For the more ambitious hiker, take the Quail Trail (orange blazes), which branches off the Walter Trail on the southeast side of Surprise Lake, then return via the Bearfort Ridge Trail (white blazes) to rejoin the Walter Trail south of West Pond after about 4 miles.

▼

Ringwood State Park

This little-known state park, which borders on New York State, contains more than 2,600 acres in the Highlands of northern Passaic and Bergen counties. Most of the park is centered around two large estates, Ringwood Manor on the west and Skylands Manor on the east, which have mansions built in the nineteenth (Ringwood) or early twentieth (Skylands) centuries. A third section, Shepherd Lake, lies to the north. The park's wide variety of habitats includes shrubby fields, meadows, lakes, orchards, and gardens around the manor houses plus the extensive deciduous forest of the

Black-capped Chickadee

SHAWNEEN
FINNEGAN
2001

surrounding hillsides. There are numerous conifer plantings around both mansions and a large stand of Eastern Hemlocks on the southwest corner of Shepherd Lake.

Ringwood is an excellent spot for migrants in spring and fall and supports a diversity of breeding birds. The Bear Swamp Lake area (part of the Skylands Section) includes many of the characteristic breeding birds of the Ramapo Mountains, but it is remote, hard to get to, and seldom birded. The park is best known, however, as a good place to search for winter finches, especially Pine Grosbeaks, in invasion years, and for the Bohemian Waxwing that stayed for a month in February and March 1977.

Directions

Take I-287 to Exit 55 (Rt. 511, Wanaque). Go north on Rt. 511 (Ringwood Ave., which becomes Greenwood Lake Turnpike) for about 7.5 miles to the junction with Sloatsburg Rd. Turn right, following the signs for Ringwood Manor, onto Sloatsburg Rd. and drive about 2.5 miles to the entrance to the Ringwood Manor section of Ringwood State Park, on the left. Follow the entrance road for a few hundred yards to the parking lot. [DeLorme 21, M-17]

Birding

The hemlock and spruce plantings around the houses and parking lot at Ringwood Manor are good for northern finches during those winters in which these species come south (invasion years). Purple Finch and Evening Grosbeak are annual migrants in spring and fall, and are often present in the winter, as well. Pine Grosbeak, Red Crossbill (rare), White-winged Crossbill (rare), and Pine Siskin (most years) may all occur. In years when Pine Grosbeak is reported in northern New Jersey, there are almost always some here. A hiking trail follows the Ringwood River (really just a stream) north into New York. Another, longer trail departs from the west side of Sally's Pond (on the far side of the manor house from the parking lot), and explores some of the remote areas of the Ringwood Section to the north and west.

To reach the Skylands section of Ringwood State Park, follow the entrance road back to Sloatsburg Rd. and turn right. Go about 0.3 miles and turn left onto Morris Rd., following the sign for Skylands Manor. After about a mile, continue through the intersection with Shepherd Lake Rd. for about a hundred yards and turn left into a parking lot.

Just beyond the parking lot, a paved road (park vehicles only) bears left off the main road. Walk this side road, which leads past a couple of houses and other buildings. It is lined with evergreens and various other plantings and is a good spot in migration and in winter. The pavement ends after several hundred yards, just beyond a house on the left. Continue straight ahead

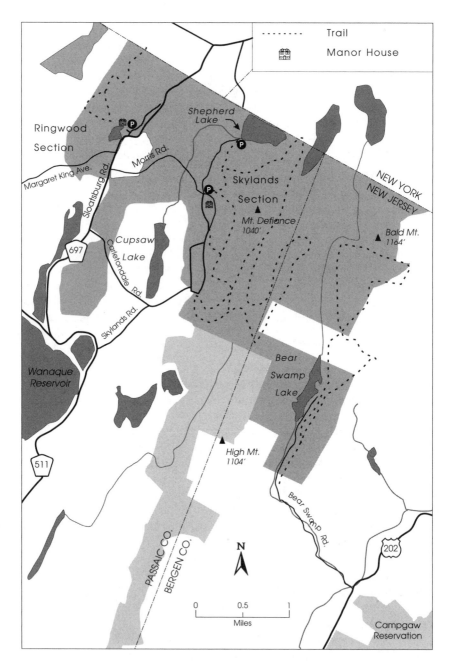

Trail ....
Manor House 🏛

Ringwood
Section

Shepherd
Lake

Morris Rd.

Margaret King Ave.

Sloatsburg Rd.

Skylands
Section

▲
Mt. Defiance
1040'

NEW YORK
NEW JERSEY

Bald Mt.
1164' ▲

Cupsaw
Lake

Carletondale Rd.

697

Skylands Rd.

Wanaque
Reservoir

Bear
Swamp
Lake

511

▲
High Mt.
1104'

Bear Swamp Rd.

202

PASSAIC CO.
BERGEN CO.

N
▲

0   0.5   1
Miles

Campgaw
Reservation

Map 11. Ringwood State Park

on a path through some shrubbery, until you come to a trail on the left. Here you will see some large spruces, which have had Pine Grosbeaks and White-winged Crossbills. Across the path from the spruces is an area of birches and other scrubby trees surrounding a small pond. Follow the trail that leads through the birches to check for Common Redpoll in winter and for warblers in migration. Beyond the birches is a grove of pines, where you might find Red-breasted Nuthatch in winter.

To the east of the road and trail just described is an extensive deciduous woods, with a couple of trails traversing it. Here you should find Pileated Woodpecker and other forest birds. To the west is a large open field lined with two rows of crab apples, where American Robins and Cedar Waxwings feed. Beyond the field are the main park road and the manor house, which is surrounded by numerous tree and shrub plantings that usually harbor a few birds, including Yellow-bellied Sapsucker, in winter.

South of the manor house, the main park road makes a mile-long loop (which you can walk or drive). Just after the road divides into the one-way loop, there is a hill on the left with numerous crab apples and wild roses. This is a favorite feeding area for robins and waxwings in winter, and it was here that a Bohemian Waxwing was found in February 1977.

Near the south end of the loop is the South (Cupsaw Lake) Entrance to Skylands; this gate is open only during the summer, when there is an admission charge to all sections of Ringwood State Park. About 200 yards past the South Entrance is an old road on the right that provides access to a maze of trails that traverse the southeastern half of the Skylands Section. You will need a trail map and a compass to explore these trails, but your efforts will be rewarded with some excellent birding. To the southeast of these trails, on the eastern slope of the Ramapo Mountains, is the Bear Swamp Lake Section of the State Park. To bird the Bear Swamp area, you should use a USGS topographic map and a compass, as there are no maintained trails that connect with the main body of Ringwood State Park.

To reach the Shepherd Lake Section of the state park from the first parking lot at Skylands Manor, turn right out of the parking lot onto the main road and go about 100 yards to Shepherd Lake Rd. Turn right and drive about one-half mile to the parking lot for Shepherd Lake. In migration, you may find a small number of diving ducks on the lake, including Ring-necked, Lesser Scaup, Common Goldeneye, Bufflehead, and Hooded and Common mergansers. A good birding trail follows the south shore of Shepherd Lake, through a grove of hemlocks, for more than one-half mile.

There are modern restrooms at Shepherd Lake, as there are at Ringwood Manor and at Skylands Manor. To return to Sloatsburg Rd. from the Shepherd Lake parking lot, you must retrace your route back to Morris Rd. at Skylands Manor, turn right and go 1 mile to the junction with Sloatsburg Rd.

✦

Pequannock Watershed

Newark's Pequannock Watershed has the greatest diversity of breeding birds in the state. It is a large and varied area, comprising more than 34,000 acres in Morris, Passaic, and Sussex counties, and lying entirely within the Highlands. The City of Newark owns the land, including five reservoirs that provide water to most of Newark and to several other municipalities. Except for the reservoirs and several ponds, the area is largely covered by second-growth woodland of varying degrees of maturity. A few overgrown fields remain along some of the major roads. Elevation ranges from 600 feet in the southeast, to just over 1,400 feet on some of the ridgetops.

As in other parts of the Highlands, the mixture of plateaus, ridges, and valleys supports a variety of vegetation and birdlife. Many of the birds nesting here, such as Winter Wren, Blue-headed Vireo, and Black-throated Blue and Blackburnian warblers, are typical of more northern climes, and are near the southern limit of their range east of the Appalachians. Conversely, a number of species of southern affinities, such as Acadian Flycatcher, Yellow-throated Vireo, Louisiana Waterthrush and Hooded Warbler, also are found here, the last being especially common.

Almost 120 species have been found nesting in the watershed since 1970, when the Urner Ornithological Club began conducting periodic breeding-bird surveys. Birding this area in the summer, you can always hope to find a species new to the state's list of breeding birds, as occurred in 1979 when a pair of Yellow-rumped Warblers was found nesting along Clinton Road. The watershed should not be neglected in winter, however, as the hemlock groves and spruce plantings are good for winter finches and other northern species during flight years.

Directions

You will need a hiking permit to park or wander off the main roads in the watershed. Although you can find many of the sought-after species by birding from the roadsides, you'll achieve a much greater appreciation of the birdlife of the area by hiking some of the many trails and roads open to permit holders. Hiking permits, which were $8 for nonresidents of Newark in 2002, can be obtained only by appearing in person at one of the offices of the Newark Watershed Conservation and Development Corporation. To reach the office

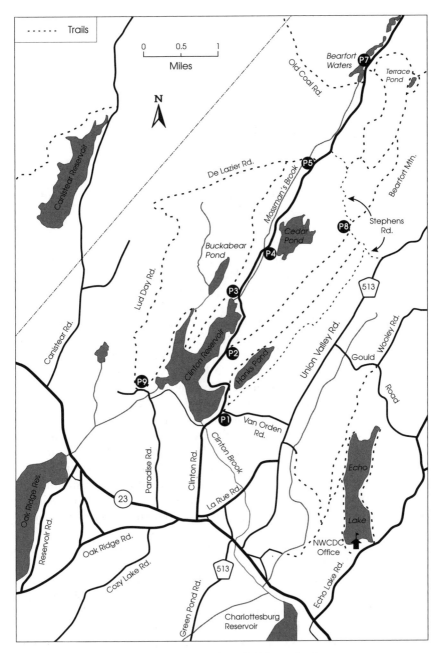

Map 12. Pequannock Watershed

in the watershed: From the intersection of Rts. 23 and 511 in Butler, go west on Rt. 23 for 5.4 miles to the Echo Lake Rd. exit. From the exit ramp, turn right onto Echo Lake Rd., and go 1 mile to the headquarters, on the left. With your permit (one for each person is required), you will be given a sticker for your car and a trail map for the watershed. The office is open weekdays from 8:00 A.M. to 4:00 P.M. and seasonally (roughly mid-March to Thanksgiving) on Saturdays from 8:00 A.M. to 1:00 P.M. Call them at (973) 697-2850 before going there to be sure. [DeLorme 25, E-22]

Birding

Return to Rt. 23 and continue straight ahead on a rough road that leads to an old house. The road to the left of the house (as you are facing it) leads to some of the areas around the Charlottesburg Dam. Here you may find several species that are uncommon elsewhere in the watershed. Among the birds that have been found here during the breeding season, although not necessarily nesting, are Black-crowned Night-Heron, Turkey Vulture, Red-tailed Hawk, Wild Turkey, Killdeer, Cliff Swallow, Northern Parula, Bobolink, and Eastern Meadowlark.

Go back to Rt. 23 and turn left (west); after 2.2 miles take the exit for Clinton Rd. Exit onto LaRue Rd., which intersects Clinton Rd. in about 100 feet. [DeLorme 25, D-19] Turn right and go 1.2 miles to Schoolhouse Rd. on the left, where a bridge crosses Clinton Brook. A small grove of old Norway Spruce here is a favored location of Pine Grosbeak and Pine Siskin in flight years. The dam for Clinton Reservoir is up the hill behind the grove, and the ruins of Clinton Furnace are just downstream from the bridge. Indigo Bunting and occasionally, Golden-winged Warbler nest below the dam, and Louisiana Waterthrush nests along the brook. Continuing along Clinton Rd., you will follow the edge of the reservoir for the next 2.5 miles (look for Common Loon in early spring), passing through a mixed hardwood forest dominated by oaks and also including ash, beech, Black Birch, hickories, and maples. In places where the trees are not too large, Mountain Laurel forms a dense understory.

Some of the birds to be looked for during the nesting season include Broad-winged Hawk, Yellow-billed and Black-billed cuckoos (numbers fluctuate), Pileated Woodpecker, Eastern Wood-Pewee, Great Crested Flycatcher and Veery (both abundant), Wood Thrush, Yellow-throated Vireo (scarce), Chestnut-sided and Black-and-white warblers, American Redstart, Worm-eating Warbler, Ovenbird (abundant), Hooded and Canada warblers (in Mountain Laurel), Scarlet Tanager, Rose-breasted Grosbeak, Rufous-sided Towhee, Chipping Sparrow, and Northern Oriole.

At 0.4 miles beyond the dam are Van Orden Rd. and a parking area marked P1. This is the starting point for two long trails, Hanks East and

Hanks West, that skirt Hanks Pond and follow the eastern side of Bearfort Mountain for 3 miles; shorter loops are possible using the trail map. Another 1.2 miles along Clinton Rd. is parking area P2, the origin of another long trail that goes to the Bearfort Fire Tower and intersects with several other trails. One mile further on is a bridge at the northern end of the reservoir and a right angle turn, where parking area P3 is located. Louisiana Waterthrush and Eastern Phoebe usually nest here, and Winter Wren has nested along the hillside just west of the road.

The next several miles of Clinton Rd. traverse some of the most interesting parts of the watershed, as the road parallels Mossman's Brook through hemlock glens, mature deciduous stands and younger oak-laurel habitat; the first 1.5 miles is especially productive. Be sure to stop at the hemlock grove 0.4 miles above P3, and at parking area P4, where Mossman's Brook passes under the road. Two trails leading off from either side of the road allow you to explore this habitat more thoroughly.

Species nesting here regularly are Red-shouldered Hawk, Great Horned and Barred owls, Ruby-throated Hummingbird, Least Flycatcher, Blue-headed Vireo (hemlocks), Blue-winged, Black-and-white, Black-throated Green (hemlocks), Blackburnian (mixed deciduous-hemlocks), and Chestnut-sided warblers (younger deciduous), Northern (wet areas near the brook) and Louisiana (along the brook) waterthrushes, Yellowthroat, Hooded, and Canada warblers (laurel), American Redstart, Rose-breasted Grosbeak, Chipping Sparrow, and Purple Finch (mainly deciduous). Winter Wren and Hermit Thrush are found in small numbers in the hemlock areas during most years. Other noteworthy species which nest in this area irregularly are Acadian Flycatcher, Red-breasted Nuthatch, Magnolia Warbler (rare), Yellow-rumped Warbler (rare), and Pine Siskin (after a big winter flight). During the winter of 1981-82, several Boreal Chickadees, hundreds of White-winged Crossbills and Pine Siskins, and a few Common Redpolls and Red Crossbills could be found along this stretch of road. Another big flight of crossbills occurred in late 1997.

Continue along Clinton Rd. to parking area P5, 1.3 miles beyond P4, stopping occasionally to listen for new species. Park on the left, where the road is widest, and walk down the abandoned road just ahead on your left, where an old iron gate is usually open. After about 100 yards, turn left onto another road; this is De Lazier Rd. on Map 12. White-throated Sparrows once nested in the open woods on your left. The road crosses Mossman's Brook, with a swampy area where Swamp Sparrow is common, then climbs through hemlocks and some mature deciduous stands for one-half mile. An open grassy area near the intersection of an old trail may have nesting Blue-winged and Cerulean warblers and Blue-headed Vireos. Other birds to be looked for along this road are Northern Goshawk, Red-shouldered Hawk, Brown Creeper, Hermit Thrush, Black-throated Blue, Black-throated Green,

Blackburnian, Hooded, and Canada warblers, and both waterthrushes. The loop trail that formerly connected to Clinton Rd. has been abandoned, so you must retrace your steps, or for the more adventurous, an interesting 10-mile hike covering a variety of terrain can be made via De Lazier Rd. and Lud Day Rd. to the southwest corner of Clinton Reservoir, returning via Clinton West and the Bearfort Waters-Clinton Trail.

One-half mile beyond P5 is the junction with Stephens Rd., on the right. Unfortunately, this area is an in-holding in the watershed and is slated for development. Stephens can be hiked all the way to the top of Bearfort Mountain, through areas that are good for Ruffed Grouse and Hermit Thrush, in addition to many species previously mentioned. The area to the south of the road includes Uttertown Bog, one of the few quaking bogs remaining in New Jersey and an area of outstanding botanical interest. Because of the environmental sensitivity of this area, it is closed except by special use permit. At the top of Bearfort Mountain is parking area P8, which can only be reached from Union Valley Rd. on the east. From here, the Fire Tower Trail goes south; after one-half mile you come to the fire tower and an exposed outcropping of rocks on the west side, which make a good hawk-watching location in the fall. From P8, another trail leads north into Wawayanda State Park, toward Terrace Pond.

From Stephens Rd., Clinton Rd. continues north into a small section of Wawayanda State Park that is isolated from the main body of the park. After 1.3 miles, you will reach a parking area on the left marked P7. Here a short trail leads to an elongated lake known as Bearfort Waters; this is a good spot for Red-shouldered Hawk, Least Flycatcher, Tree Swallow, and Eastern Bluebird. Across the road from the parking area, the Bearfort Waters-Clinton trail, marked with yellow blazes, goes south into the watershed. To reach the trail to Terrace Pond, walk north along Clinton Rd. for 0.4 miles to where a gas pipeline right-of-way provides a path up the side of Bearfort Mountain. About three-fourths of the way up, the trail to Terrace Pond, marked with blue blazes, takes off to the right. In about one-half mile, you will come to the pond, a delightful spot surrounded by cliffs and rhododendron thickets. Along the trail you may encounter Ruffed Grouse, Hermit Thrush, Veery, Ovenbird and Hooded Warbler, but birdlife is not abundant on the dry ridgetops of the Highlands. The trail circles the pond and connects with three other trails going off to the south, all of which eventually intersect Stephens Rd. These trails are not well marked, however, so they should be used with caution.

To visit some other areas in the watershed, return to the junction of Clinton Rd. and LaRue Rd., and turn left onto LaRue. Follow this for 0.7 miles and park on the roadside just before the bridge over Clinton Brook. The large grove of Norway Spruce on the west side of the road has nesting Golden-crowned Kinglet and Red-breasted Nuthatch; in winter there may be cross-bills or a Boreal Chickadee. To reach Stephens Rd., continue 0.7 miles to Union Valley Rd. Turn left and go 3.2 miles to Stephens Rd., on the left. This road climbs for 0.7 miles to P8 on the ridge of Bearfort Mountain; the road is very rough, so proceed with caution in an ordinary car. Dark-eyed Junco has nested along the upper parts of Stephens Rd.

Another interesting breeding bird area is the several spruce groves along Rt. 515. To reach them, return to the junction of Clinton Rd. and Rt. 23. Take Rt. 23 west for 4.3 miles to the exit for Rt. 515. There are three spruce groves and a marsh along this road, which are worth investigating. The first spruce grove is on the left, 2.3 miles north of Rt. 23. The second is reached by parking where an old road leads off to the right, 2.7 miles north of Rt. 23. Walk up this dirt road for about 0.3 miles to the grove on the left. The third grove is on the left, an additional 2.6 miles north on Rt. 515. All these groves should be checked for nesting Red-breasted Nuthatch and Golden-crowned Kinglet; in winter there may be northern finches. The marsh is 3.8 miles north of Rt. 23 on the right. Here you may find Golden-winged Warbler, American Kestrel, and Alder Flycatcher. These areas are best checked early in the morning, as they are right on Rt. 515 (except for the second spruce grove), and the traffic noise later in the day can make birding difficult.

Another spot that has had nesting Red-breasted Nuthatch and Golden-crowned Kinglet can be reached by returning to Rt. 23 and going east for 2.3 miles to the exit for Reservoir Rd. Follow this road for 1.1 miles to a spruce grove and listen for the two species. Another grove is a mile further on the right, just before Reservoir Rd. dead-ends at Oak Ridge Rd. To return to Rt. 23, make a U-turn and retrace your path, because a left turn onto Oak Ridge Rd. is not permitted.

A good spot for Blue-winged Warbler, Golden-winged Warbler and hybrids of these two species is a power line cut on Paradise Rd. Go east on Rt. 23 from Reservoir Rd. for about 1.2 miles to the jughandle left turn for Paradise Rd. Drive north on Paradise Rd. for about 1 mile to the power line cut and park. Walk west along the power line to search for the warblers. Red-shouldered Hawk also nests in this area.

Many other places can be explored in the watershed with the help of the trail map, but the areas covered here are the principal ones for the northern-nesting species that are hard to find elsewhere in the state.

Weis Ecology Center and Norvin Green State Forest

The Weis Ecology Center is a sanctuary of the NJAS, and includes a Nature Center and 150 acres of woodland. The sanctuary property is contiguous with the southern part of Norvin Green State Forest, which protects almost 8,000 acres of northern Passaic County. Together these preserves provide access to a variety of habitats typical of the Highlands of northern New Jersey.

Directions

See Map 10. Take I-287 to Exit 55 (Wanaque–Pompton Lakes, Rt. 511). Turn left onto Rt. 511 North, and go about 4 miles to Westbrook Rd., and turn left. Follow Westbrook Rd. for almost 2 miles, staying left when the road forks at 1.4 miles, to Snake Den Rd., on the left. Turn left and take Snake Den Rd. for 0.7 miles, staying left again when the road forks at 0.3 miles, to the entrance to Weis Ecology Center, on the right. Park by the stream or stay right to the parking area at the Nature Center. [DeLorme 25, C-27]

Birding

The Weis Center provides a convenient starting point for hiking the trails in the southern part of Norvin Green. Stop at the center to obtain a trail map. The numerous trails throughout the area (only major ones are shown on the map) are maintained by the New York–New Jersey Trails Conference, which publishes good trail maps of the entire area on water-resistant paper (for sale at the Weis Center).

Birdlife at Norvin Green is very similar to that in the nearby Pequannock Watershed, though not so diverse because it has less varied habitat. The newer Lake Sonoma section of the forest, accessible from Burnt Meadow Rd. or Stonetown Rd. has some excellent wetlands, but a much less developed trail system. The entire area receives inadequate attention from birders—a little exploration might turn up something unusual.

To explore some of the habitats at Weis-Norvin Green take the dirt road from the Visitor Center back toward Snake Den Rd. The spruce grove on the right becomes a Turkey and Black Vulture roost in late spring. As you continue along, the forsythia hedgerow on the left has both kinglets in early May and occasional Mourning Warbler later in the month. The canopy overhead is good for a variety of migrant warblers, including Nashville, Black-throated Green, Blackburnian, Bay-breasted, Magnolia, Blackpoll, and Canada.

At Snake Den Rd., stay left, and continue back out Snake Den for a short distance to the trailhead for the Wyanokie Circular (Red) and Mine (Yellow) trails. The trail passes along the edge of private property before entering the state forest. As you continue, Blue Mine Brook will be on your right, and you should watch and listen for Wild Turkey, Ruffed Grouse, Ovenbird and perhaps Barred Owl fledglings. After about 0.75 miles, there is a side trail to Blue Mine and the main trail crosses the brook.

When the trails diverge, stay left on the red marked Wyanokie Circular Trial for another half-mile or so to Wyanokie High Point, which offers a spectacular view of the Wanaque Reservoir and surrounding forests, and even New York City and the Catskills on a clear day. You can continue on the Wyanokie trail and make a 2 to 2.5 hour round trip back to the Visitor Center, or take the blue trail back to the old Snake Den Rd. for a shorter loop.

A shorter loop trail on the NJAS property, the W Trail follows Blue Mine Brook upstream, connecting with the Mine Trail and crossing the former site of the Winfield Farm. Along the way, you should encounter Louisiana Waterthrush, Worm-eating Warbler, Scarlet Tanager, and Rose-breasted Grosbeak. Other summer visitors and residents include Red-shouldered, Broad-winged, and Red-tailed hawks, Yellow-billed and Black-billed cuckoos, Whip-poorwill, Ruby-throated Hummingbird, Pileated Woodpecker, and sometimes Red-breasted Nuthatch.

The Wanaque Reservoir is a good spot for seeing Bald Eagles in winter. One viewpoint is on Westbrook Rd. From the Weis Center, return to Westbrook Rd. and turn right. Go about 1.2 miles, staying right at the fork to a sharp left curve, where there is a wide area to park on the left. Here you can scan part of the reservoir, including the cove directly east on the opposite side of the water that seems to be a favorite with the eagles. A spotting scope is indispensable. Another good spot is the Greenwood Lake Turnpike between Sloatsburg Rd. and the Monksville Dam. Continue on Westbrook Rd. back to Rt. 511 (Greenwood Lake Tpk.) and turn left. Go about 3.5 miles to Sloatsburg Rd., but continue straight ahead across the causeway. Park where you can, safely, in the next 2-mile stretch to scan for eagles.

✝

Mahlon Dickerson Reservation

This preserve is on a plateau in the New Jersey Highlands, near the northwestern corner of Morris County. Comprising almost 1300 acres, Mahlon Dickerson Reservation is the largest unit in the Morris County Park System.

Due to its moderately high elevation of 1,100 to 1,300 feet, and its combination of mature deciduous forest, hemlock groves, and bog, the park supports an interesting diversity of breeding birds. These include Ruffed Grouse, Wild Turkey, Hermit Thrush, Blue-headed Vireo, and a long list of warblers. The reservation is an out-of-the-way spot, and receives little attention from birders. It is very attractive, however, and is well worth a morning visit in May, June, or July.

Directions

Take I-80 West to Exit 34 (Rt. 15 North)—Exit 33 eastbound—just north of Dover. Go north on Rt. 15 for about 5 miles to Weldon Rd., following the signs for Milton. Follow Weldon Rd. northeast for about 4.5 miles, past the trailer site on the left and the campground on the right, to the entrance road to a family picnic area, on the left. Follow this road for about 100 yards to a parking area. [DeLorme 24, G-13]

Birding

At the parking area, there are primitive toilets and a directory showing the trails traversing Mahlon Dickerson Reservation. Weldon Rd. divides the park into two nearly equal sections, with the best birding in the northern half. The far northern border of the park, along the Sussex-Morris County line, crosses part of the Great Pine Swamp, an excellent birding area.

The reservation is mainly of interest because of the diverse selection of breeding birds. Hike some of the trails in the northern part of the park (with the help of a compass), and you should find many of the following species: Red-shouldered and Broad-winged hawks, Ruffed Grouse, Wild Turkey, American Woodcock, Black-billed and Yellow-billed cuckoos, Eastern Screech, Barred, and Great Horned owls, Pileated Woodpecker, Acadian Flycatcher, Brown Creeper, Winter Wren (rare), Hermit Thrush (uncommon), Blue-headed (hemlocks) and Yellow-throated vireos, Blue-winged, Chestnut-sided, Black-throated Green (hemlocks), Blackburnian, Black-and-white, Worm-eating, Hooded, and Canada warblers, American Redstart, Ovenbird, Northern and Louisiana waterthrushes, Rose-breasted Grosbeak, and Purple Finch, plus other, more common species. Worm-eating, Hooded, and Canada warblers usually sing from the woods around the parking lot.

An excellent morning's hike can be had by following the trail from the parking lot to the loop trail marked with white blazes. This trail passes through both coniferous and deciduous forest, past the highest point in Morris County, and skirts the edge of the Great Pine Swamp. Another good birding trail is the old Ogden Railroad Grade, accessible at the Saffin Pond

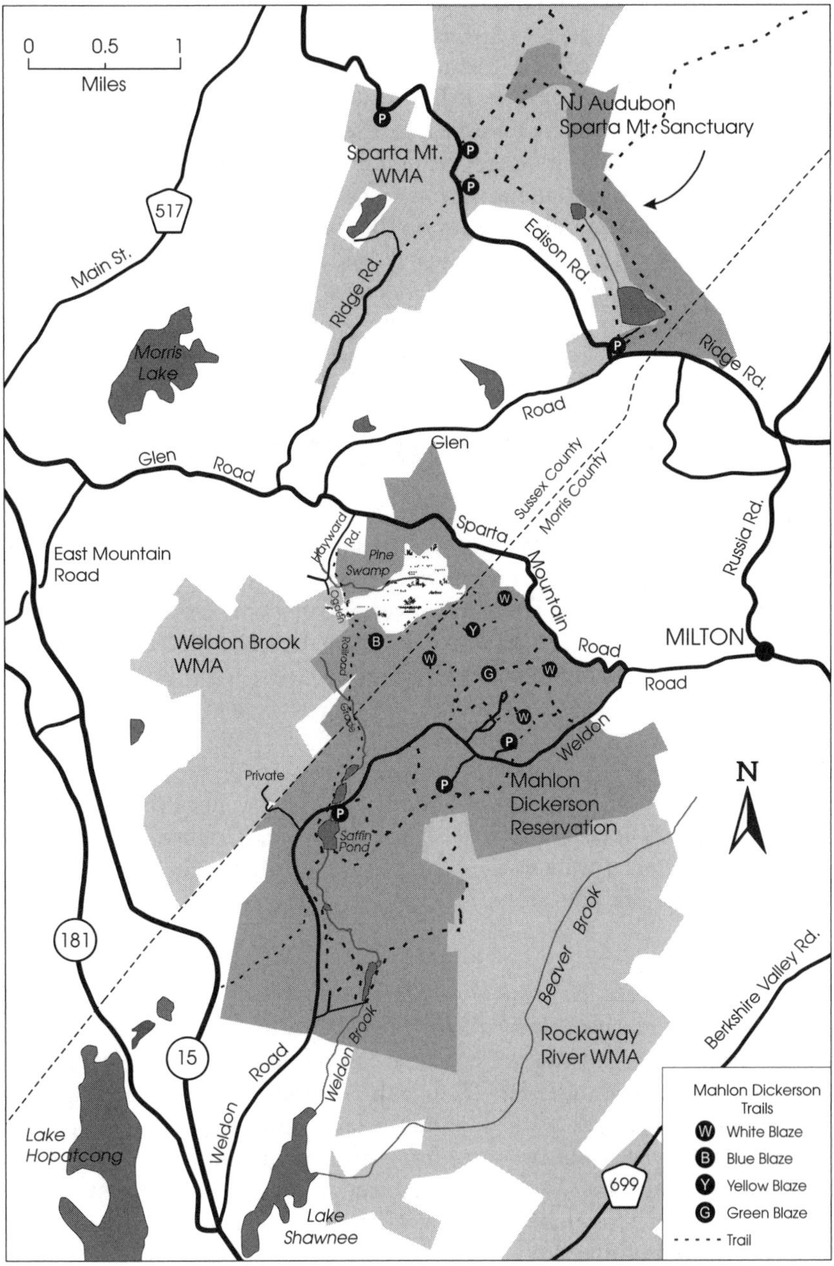

0
0.5
1
Miles
NJ Audubon
Sparta Mt. Sanctuary
Sparta Mt.
WMA
517
Main St.
Ridge Rd.
Edison Rd.
Ridge Rd.
Morris
Lake
Road
Glen
Glen
Road
Sussex County
Morris County
Hayward
Rd.
Sparta
Mountain
Road
Russia Rd.
East Mountain
Road
Pine
Swamp
Ogden
Railroad
Grass
Weldon Brook
WMA
MILTON
Road
Weldon
Mahlon
Dickerson
Reservation
Private
Saffin
Pond
N
181
Beaver Brook
Berkshire Valley Rd.
Rockaway
River WMA
15
Weldon Brook
Road
Weldon
Lake
Hopatcong
Lake
Shawnee
699
Mahlon Dickerson
Trails
White Blaze
Blue Blaze
Yellow Blaze
Green Blaze
Trail

Map 13. Mahlon Dickerson Reservation and Vicinity

parking lot. This is best done early in the morning, as the trail is very popular with mountain bikers.

Another point of access to the northern part of Mahlon Dickerson Reservation is along Sparta Mountain Rd. Drive out the entrance road to Weldon Rd. and turn left. Go about 1.1 miles, past some school buildings, to the first road on the left, which is Sparta Mountain Rd. Follow this winding road, which soon becomes dirt, for about 0.8 miles to where there is a trail (actually an abandoned road) on the left. Park on the side of Sparta Mountain Rd., and hike the trail, which after about a quarter mile, passes along the edge of the Great Pine Swamp (actually a rhododendron and Black Spruce bog).

▼

Silas Condict Park

A seven-acre lake, a few fields, and mature upland deciduous woods make up the small (265 acres) but attractive Silas Condict Park in the Highlands of northern Morris County. There are several hiking and cross-country skiing trails. Birdlife is similar to Mahlon Dickerson Reservation, but less diverse because of the park's much smaller size.

Directions

See Map 14. From the junction of State Rt. 23 and County Rt. 511 in Butler, go west on Rt. 23 for about 1 mile to Kinnelon Rd. (County Rt. 618). Turn left and drive about 1 mile to the park entrance, on the right—the first right turn after Ricker Rd. [DeLorme 25, G-24]

Birding

Drive in the entrance road for about 0.8 miles to the third and last parking lot. Two trails diverge from the north end of the lot, one (0.3 miles) leading north to an overlook above Rt. 23, and the second makes a loop around the highest point in the park (1,012 ft.) and the lake, returning to the first parking lot, about 300 yards from the third lot. This trail provides access to most of the habitats in the park. A more detailed trail map is available from the Morris County Park Commission or on their Web site at http://parks.morris.nj.us/asp/parks/info.asp.

▼

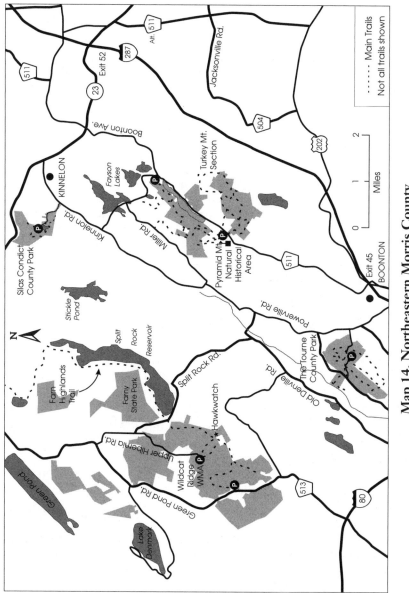

Map 14. Northeastern Morris County

- - - - - Main Trails
Not all trails shown

0	1	2

Miles

Green Pond

Lake Denmark

Green Pond Rd.

Upper Hibernia Rd.

Wildcat Ridge WMA

Hawkwatch

513

80

Split Rock Rd.

Old Denville Rd.

The Tourne County Park

Powerville Rd.

511

Exit 45
BOONTON

Pyramid Mtn. Natural Historical Area

511

Turkey Mt. Section

Fayson Lakes

Miller Rd.

Jacksonville Rd.

504

202

Boonton Ave.

23

Exit 52

287

Alt. 511

511

KINNELON

Kinnelon Rd.

Silas Condict County Park

Stickle Pond

Split Rock Reservoir

Farny State Park

Farny Highlands Trail

N

Pyramid Mountain

One of the newest acquisitions of the Morris County Park Commission, Pyramid Mountain Natural Historical Area, covering more than 1,000 acres, is preserved as a natural area. Five marked trails traverse the diverse fields, deciduous forests, rock outcroppings, and wetlands of the park. Pyramid Mountain is best known for a huge glacial erratic named Tripod Rock, which has been precariously balanced on three small boulders for the past 18,000 years.

Directions

From the south, take I-287 to Exit 45 (Wooton St., Boonton). Continue straight from the exit ramp on Park Ave. for 0.25 miles to Wooton St. and turn left. Coming from the north, turn left onto US 206 (Myrtle Ave.) at the end of the ramp and go 0.25 miles to Wooton St. and turn right. Drive 0.6 miles to the blinking red light at Rt. 511 (Boonton Ave.) and turn right. Go north on Rt. 511 for about 2.7 miles to the parking lot for the Visitor Center, on the left, opposite Mars Court. [DeLorme 25, K-23]

Alternatively, take Rt. 23 to its intersection with Rt. 511, 2 miles west of the junction of I-287 and Rt. 23. Go south on Rt. 511 for 4.4 miles to the parking lot, on the right.

Birding

The Visitor Center is open from 10:00 A.M. to 4:30 P.M. Friday to Sunday, but trail maps are available at the kiosk in the parking lot. An extensive and well-marked system of trails, some of which are shown on Map 14, covers both the Pyramid Mt. section west of Rt. 511 and the Turkey Mt. section east of Rt. 511. The Blue Trail, which provides access to the Pyramid Mt. section can be reached by following the signs at the parking lot.

From the parking lot, at about 600 feet above sea level, the Blue trail follows a powerline right-of-way, then rapidly ascends Pyramid Mt. to the crest at 934 feet elevation. Continuing for about one-half mile, past the junction with the Yellow trail, takes you past the short side trail to Lucy's Overlook, to the junction with the White trail. Stay right for about 200 feet along the White trail to Tripod Rock. Both the White and Blue trails pass through areas with numerous glacial erratics deposited here by the Wisconsin Glacier and provide magnificent views of the New York City skyline, 25 miles to the southeast.

Birdlife in the park is typical of the upland deciduous forests of northern New Jersey, although the drier ridgetops of Chestnut Oak and Mountain

Laurel have a limited variety. Some of the common residents include Wild Turkey and Pileated Woodpecker, in addition to the usual assortment of woodland species. Among the summer visitors are Great Blue Heron, Broad-winged Hawk, Eastern Wood-Pewee, Great Crested Flycatcher, Scarlet Tanager, and Rose-breasted Grosbeak. More than 100 species have been recorded in the park, and visitors during migration could probably add many more to the list.

A detailed trail map is also available on the Morris County Park Commission Web site at http://parks.morris.nj.us/asp/parks/info.asp.

🦆

The Tourne Park

Situated on the edge of the New Jersey Highlands, The Tourne is a 463-acre unit of the Morris County Park System that contains a variety of habitats, including upland deciduous forest and a fine stand of hemlocks. The park extends into Boonton, Denville, and Mountain Lakes, and has many hiking and nature trails, as well as family picnic sites.

Directions

See Map 14. Take I-287 to the Intervale Rd. exit in Parsippany, about 2 miles north of I-80. From the exit ramp turn left onto Intervale Rd., cross over the highway, and take the first right turn, Fanny Rd. Follow Fanny Rd., which soon merges with Powerville Rd., for about 1.2 miles to the park entrance on the left, at MacCaffrey Lane. [DeLorme 25, M-20]

A second entrance to the park is on the west side off Old Boonton Rd., about 1 mile north of Pocono Rd. The two entrance roads do not connect, but end at parking lots a few hundred feet apart.

Birding

Follow the MacCaffrey Lane entrance road for about one-half mile to its end at a parking lot next to a ball field, on the left. From Old Boonton Rd., it is also about one-half mile to the end at a small parking lot, on the right. From either area, walk east along the MacCaffrey Lane entrance road for a few hundred feet, to where the DeCamp Trail branches off on the left.

The DeCamp Trail makes a 1.2-mile loop with a modest elevation gain of about 350 feet to the highest point in the park (897 feet). Along the way it passes through mature deciduous woodland and a sadly endangered hemlock grove (infested with Wooly Adelgid) that harbor a good variety of breeding birds in late spring and summer. In winter the woods are quiet, with only the common residents and a few wintering sparrows. The many oaks and maples make the park attractive to migrant songbirds, especially in spring, but the area receives little attention at that time. Among the more interesting breeding birds are a variety of warblers, such as American Redstart, Black-and-white and Worm-eating warblers, Scarlet Tanager, and Rose-breasted Grosbeak.

☞

Black River Wildlife Management Area

Black River WMA in western Morris County near Chester, covers 3,000 acres of river bottom, freshwater marsh, swampy woodland, upland deciduous woods and fields. Nearly 200 species of birds have been found here in recent years, and an amazing variety (about 100 species) nest. Spring and summer are the best seasons at Black River, but it is worth visiting at any time of the year.

Although birders have long visited the Black River area occasionally, not until 1979 did David Harrison begin the thorough field studies that have revealed the full potential of this attractive spot. Among the more interesting breeding species are Least Bittern, Virginia Rail, Sora, Screech, Great Horned, and Barred owls, Alder Flycatcher, Marsh Wren, Chestnut-sided (common), Cerulean, Worm-eating, Kentucky, Hooded, and Canada warblers, Northern and Louisiana waterthrushes, Yellow-breasted Chat, Bobolink, and Grasshopper Sparrow.

Note: Black River is a very popular WMA, and is heavily used by hunters from October through December, except on Sundays, when no hunting is allowed. On other days during this season, confine your visits to the paved roads. There are portable toilets near the Firearms Training Area at the headquarters, except in winter.

Directions

There are several points of access to Black River WMA, and it boasts many good birding spots. The area most frequently visited by birders includes the bridge over the Black River at Pleasant Hill Rd. and the abandoned railroad bed that parallels the river, starting a short distance south of the bridge. To

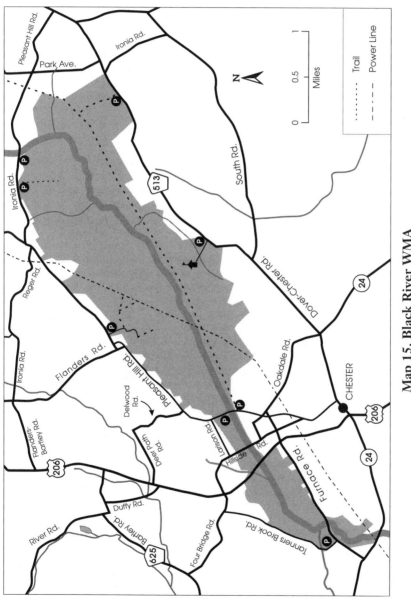

Map 15. Black River WMA

reach this point: From southern or central New Jersey take I-287 to Exit 22B (US 206 North, Bedminster and Netcong), about 1 mile north of I-78. Go 10 miles north on US 206 to the intersection with Rt. 24 in Chester, then continue straight ahead on Rt. 206 for 0.8 miles to the intersection with Furnace Rd. Turn right, go about 0.2 miles to the second stop sign, and turn left onto Pleasant Hill Rd. Follow this for 0.4 miles to a small parking area on the right. If this is full, continue on Pleasant Hill Rd. across the bridge over the Black River to a larger parking area, on the left. [DeLorme 30, E-5]

From northeastern or northwestern New Jersey, take I-80 to Exit 27 (US 206 South). Go south on Rt. 206 for about 7 miles to Furnace Rd., the first intersection after crossing the bridge over the inconspicuous Black River (0.3 miles). Turn left onto Furnace Rd. and proceed as described above.

Birding

From the Pleasant Hill Rd. parking area, where Least Flycatcher and Warbling Vireo usually nest, walk the road to the bridge across the Black River. This is a good spot for waterfowl (especially Ring-necked Duck and Hooded Merganser) and Spotted and Solitary sandpipers in migration, and in the breeding season for Least Bittern, rails, Willow Flycatcher, Tree and N. Rough-winged swallows, Barn Swallow (under the bridge), Marsh Wren, Yellow Warbler, Common Yellowthroat, Red-winged Blackbird, Swamp Sparrow (abundant), and Song Sparrow.

From the parking area on the south side of the bridge, you can walk east along the trail provided by an abandoned railroad bed. This trail runs for several miles, following the Black River on the left, to Ironia Rd. It is excellent during spring migration, when about 30 species of warblers and many other songbirds can be found, and is one of the best areas for breeding birds in the WMA. During June, more than 70 nesting species can be found along the first 2 miles of the trail.

Other nesting birds along this stretch of the river are Green Heron, Canada Goose, Wood Duck, Common Moorhen (scarce), both cuckoos (most years), Eastern Kingbird, Cedar Waxwing, Yellow-throated Vireo, Blue-winged, Chestnut-sided, Black-and-white, and Canada warblers, Ovenbird, Rose-breasted Grosbeak, and Field Sparrow. Eastern Screech, Great Horned and Barred owls all can be heard in this area at night, but seeing one or finding a nest is difficult. Less than one-half mile along the railroad bed, Ruby-throated Hummingbird has nested regularly in a swampy area on the right (south) side of the trail. Louisiana Waterthrush is usually here also. At least one pair of Alder Flycatchers nests each year in the swampy woods between one-half and three-quarters of a mile in from Pleasant Hill Rd., making this one of the most reliable spots for that species in New Jersey. Acadian Flycatcher is another occasional breeder here, making this one of the few places in the state where breeding Acadian, Alder, Willow, and Least flycatchers are known to occur together.

Worm-eating, Kentucky, and Hooded warblers nest on a hillside above the railroad bed. To reach this point, go about 1.25 miles in from Pleasant Hill Rd. to an underground cable right-of-way, marked by yellow or orange numbered markers on top of poles. Follow the right-of-way uphill for about 400 yards to a knoll on the left, where the warblers nest. (This spot can also be reached from the parking area at the headquarters, as discussed later.)

You can easily retrace your steps to your car and explore some other birding spots in the Black River WMA, including sites along Pleasant Hill Rd., Ironia Rd., Dover-Chester Rd. (two areas), and a small section west of US 206, which is accessible from Furnace Rd. Descriptions of these sites follow.

Pleasant Hill

To reach this area from the parking lot by the bridge, continue north on Pleasant Hill Rd. for about 1.7 miles, to a dirt road on the right marked by a Black River WMA sign. Turn into this road and then turn immediately left into a parking area. Walk along the dirt road for 0.3 miles to a large clearing that was formerly a parking area.

The grove of pines at the clearing has had Long-eared Owls in winter. Walk back up the entrance road for about 200 yards to an orange gate on the right that marks the beginning of one of the many mowed trails that crisscross this portion of the WMA. Using a compass, follow the trails in a generally eastward direction for a little less than one-half mile until you come to an underground cable right-of-way. Along the way, in the fields and hedgerows, you may encounter Red-tailed Hawk, Tree Swallow, Purple Martin, Eastern Bluebird, Brown Thrasher, White-eyed Vireo, Grasshopper and Field sparrows, Indigo Bunting, Bobolink, and Eastern Meadowlark.

Turn right at the cable right-of-way, which cuts a 30-foot-wide swath through some mature deciduous woodland, and head south toward the river. There is no path along the cable cut, so by late summer the Bracken Fern and Hay-scented Fern may be waist high. After about one-half mile, a steep hill leads down to the river. Species to be expected here are Willow Flycatcher, Brown Creeper, House Wren, Yellow-throated Vireo, Cerulean, Worm-eating, and Canada warblers, and many others already mentioned.

Another interesting area can be reached by turning left (northeast) instead of right at the cable cut. Follow the cut northeast for about 0.25 miles, until you come to a stream. Turn right and follow the stream for a half-mile down to the river. The going is not easy, but along the way you may find Alder Flycatcher, Brown Creeper, White-eyed Vireo, Cerulean Warbler, Yellow-breasted Chat, and other species.

Ironia Road

Return to Pleasant Hill Rd. and go right. Drive about 1.8 miles, bearing right after 1.3 miles onto Ironia Rd. (Pleasant Hill Rd. forks left), to a WMA parking lot on the right. Explore the woods, fields, and hedgerows, starting at the orange gate at the east end of the lot. In the fall, this area is good for migrants, including Philadelphia Vireo. Nesting species include Belted Kingfisher, Purple Martin, Brown Creeper, Brown Thrasher, White-eyed Vireo, Canada Warbler, Indigo Bunting, and Bobolink.

Continue on Ironia Rd. for one-half mile to a bridge across the Black River. On the right is Lillian Lake, which is really just a wide section of the river; it is good for migrant waterfowl in spring. Northern Waterthrush are usually found near the bridge. Beware of the No Parking signs here, and do not leave your car or you may get a parking ticket.

Ironia

The next birding stop in our tour of Black River WMA is reached by continuing east from the bridge on Ironia Rd. for about 0.9 miles to the stop sign at Park Ave. Turn right and go 0.8 miles to the junction with Rt. 513, the Dover-Chester Rd. Turn right and drive about 0.35 miles to a WMA parking lot on the right. Park near the far (east) end of the lot.

Go through the gate at the northeast corner of the lot and follow the mowed path. Bear left at the first two trail junctions until you start down a long tree-lined path that is obviously an old road. The road eventually narrows to a trail, and emerges, after about 0.4 miles, onto the cleared right-of-way for the power line previously mentioned. Continue on the trail as it descends toward the river and enters a superb stand of bottomland deciduous woods. Another 300 yards will bring you to the trail along an abandoned railroad bed. By turning left and walking along the railroad bed for about 1.5 miles, you will come to a stream at a rise in the path. Along the way, you may encounter Ruffed Grouse, Northern Waterthrush, Canada Warbler, and many of the species previously noted.

At the stream, the power line is very close to the railroad bed; about 50 yards before you reach the stream, you will pass a trail on the left. You can walk up the trail to the right-of-way, and return along the power line clearing. Some of the species that nest along the power line are Red-tailed Hawk, Black-billed Cuckoo, Chestnut-sided, Prairie, Cerulean, and Hooded warblers, Yellow-breasted Chat, Scarlet Tanager, Indigo Bunting, Eastern Towhee, and Field Sparrow.

Headquarters

The headquarters of Black River WMA is reached by continuing west along Rt. 513 for about 1.9 miles to a parking lot on the right. From the west end of the lot, take the trail to the dirt road that leads toward the headquarters. This area is excellent for sparrows in winter, and for Winter Wren in migration. It also has nesting Broad-winged Hawk, Ring-necked Pheasant, Eastern Phoebe, and Yellow-breasted Chat. Walk along the dirt road for about 300 yards, until you come to a three-way fork. Continue straight ahead on the middle fork toward a Firearms Training Area sign, and follow the trail for about 200 yards downhill to the power line cut. Turn left and follow the power line for about 0.3 miles to the underground cable cut. The hillside on your left—the same spot described in the initial section—has nesting Worm-eating, Kentucky, and Hooded warblers. By turning right at the cable cut and heading north down the hill, you will reach the abandoned railroad bed along the Black River.

To return to Rt. 206, continue west on Rt. 513 for about 1.7 miles to a five-way intersection at Rt. 24. Go straight ahead on Rt. 24 for about 1 mile to the intersection with Rt. 206.

⚐

Worthington State Forest

This 5,830-acre state forest in Warren County, which includes the New Jersey side of the famous Delaware Water Gap, contains some of the most scenic and rugged terrain in the state. Elevations range from about 300 feet along the Delaware River, to 1,549, and include the 1,527-foot Mt. Tammany, which overlooks the gap. Worthington State Forest takes in a variety of habitat, from the bottomlands along the river, through steep hillsides with climax deciduous forest and hemlock-shrouded ravines, to the dry ridgetops of the Kittatinny Mountains. Nestled in the forest is beautiful Sunfish Pond, a glacial lake lying at 1,382 feet in a broad valley between two ridges. Most of the land adjoining Worthington is in the Delaware Water Gap National Recreation Area, which may eventually comprise as much as 70,000 acres of land along the Delaware River in Pennsylvania and in Sussex and Warren Counties in New Jersey.

Birdlife in Worthington State Forest is as diverse as the terrain. Old Mine Rd. along the Delaware River is excellent for migrants in spring and fall; it supports an interesting variety of breeding birds and is a good area for winter finches during invasion years. Bald Eagles are regularly seen along the river in winter. Most of the state forest, including all of the higher elevations, is accessible only on foot; reaching it usually involving a strenuous hike of several miles. Consequently, the area receives insufficient attention from birders. Those who spend the time and effort to explore Worthington State Forest, however, will find many birds of interest.

Directions

Take I-80 west toward Pennsylvania and the Delaware Water Gap. Just after you pass through the gap, watch for a rest area sign on the right, and pull in. If you miss the rest area, take the next exit (the last one in New Jersey), and turn left from the exit ramp, following the signs for the National Recreation Area Information Center. Drive past the information center (or stop and get a map) to the next intersection. Turn left and follow the road under the highway to a stop sign. Then turn right for a short drive to the rest area. [DeLorme 22, I-7]

Birding

If you are prepared for a strenuous hike, this is a good place to start. There are two parking lots, with a trail leaving from each. Tammany Trail (marked by red blazes) starts at the first parking area and climbs almost 1,200 feet to the summit of Mt. Tammany in just 1 mile. It is a steep, rocky, moderately difficult trail and is not particularly birdy. You might find nesting Wild Turkey, Winter Wren, Hermit Thrush, or Dark-eyed Junco, however.

The trail that leaves from the second parking area (0.2 miles further along) is Dunnfield Hollow Trail, which follows the Appalachian Trail for about 0.75 miles. Dunnfield Creek is a clear, rock-strewn stream that still supports native Brook Trout. The creek begins high on the Kittatinny Ridge near Sunfish Pond, and falls more than 1,000 feet to the Delaware River in less than 4 miles. Dunnfield Hollow Trail branches from the Appalachian Trail on the right as an abandoned road (marked by blue blazes), that follows Dunnfield Creek for another 1.5 miles to an old sawmill. It then climbs a steep ravine and rejoins the Appalachian Trail after about 0.75 miles. Turn left (southwest) on the Appalachian Trail (marked by white blazes) to return to your car. If you are adventuresome, a right turn at the junction with the Appalachian Trail will take you on a 1.8-mile hike to Sunfish Pond.

About 0.4 miles up the Dunnfield Hollow Trail there is a fork, where the blue-blazed trail goes right and Dunnfield Hollow Trail bears left. The

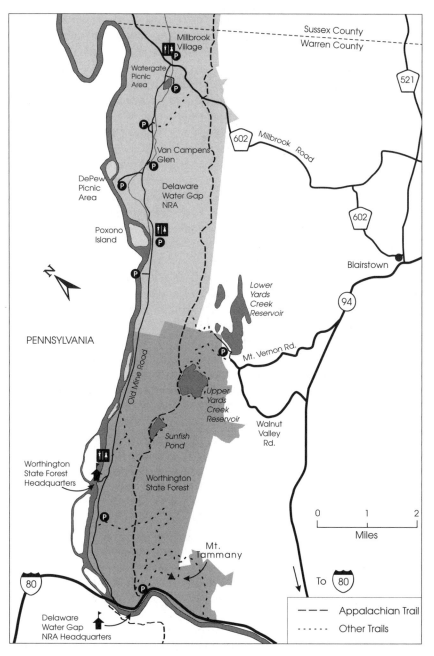

Map 16. Worthington State Forest

blue-blazed trail leads to the summit of Mt. Tammany, where it connects with Tammany Trail (which leads to the first parking area). You can thus hike a 3.5-loop via Tammany Trail and the blue-blazed trail, or a 5-mile loop via Dunnfield Hollow Trail to the sawmill and back on the Appalachian Trail.

The blue-blazed trail, Dunnfield Hollow Trail, and Appalachian Trail have many more birds than Tammany Trail, as they pass through a variety of habitats, including the dry ridgetop oak woods; dark hemlock glens; and mature deciduous woods of oak, maple, beech, and Yellow Birch. The understory consists of rhododendron or Mountain Laurel in some areas, and deciduous trees and shrubs such as Flowering Dogwood and Witch Hazel in others.

Typical breeding birds of Worthington State Forest include Wood Duck, Broad-winged Hawk, Ruffed Grouse, Wild Turkey, American Woodcock, Black-billed and Yellow-billed cuckoos, Eastern Screech, Great Horned, and Barred owls, Chimney Swift, Ruby-throated Hummingbird, Pileated Woodpecker, Acadian and Least flycatchers, Brown Creeper, Cedar Waxwing, Blue-headed (hemlocks) and Yellow-throated vireos, Chestnut-sided, Black-throated Green, Blackburnian, Cerulean, Black-and-white, Worm-eating, Hooded, and Canada warblers, American Redstart, Northern Waterthrush, Rose-breasted Grosbeak, and many other, more common, species. Some of the less common nesting species which should be searched for are Cooper's Hawk, Northern Goshawk, Red-shouldered Hawk, Whip-poor-will, Common Raven, Winter Wren, Eastern Bluebird, Hermit Thrush, Nashville Warbler, Northern Parula, White-throated Sparrow, and Purple Finch.

To explore more of the state forest, continue on I-80 for 0.7 miles from the Dunnfield Natural Area parking lot to Exit 1, the last exit in New Jersey; turn right from the exit ramp onto Old Mine Rd. Go north on Old Mine Rd. for about 1 mile to the Far View parking lot, on the right. A one-half mile stretch of Old Mine Rd. just north of I-80 is open only to one-way traffic, which is controlled by a traffic light.

From the Far View parking lot, the Beulahland Trail makes a steep ascent of the ridge. After about 1 mile (and 1,000 feet of elevation), it intersects the Appalachian Trail at the same point as the trail from Dunnfield Hollow. An interesting hike can be made by turning left on the Appalachian Trail and continuing about 1.8 miles to Sunfish Pond, a delightful spot to enjoy your lunch. This beautiful glacial lake was nearly turned into a pumped storage reservoir by an electric power company during the 1960s, but the resulting uproar caused the plans to be changed and the pond is now a protected natural area within the state forest.

The 1.5-mile hike around Sunfish Pond is interesting, but not very birdy. To complete your hike, return south along the Appalachian Trail for about one-half mile to Campsite No. 2, which you passed on your way north. Here the trail marked by blue blazes leads to the right. This trail, an abandoned road, leads downhill to Old Mine Rd. in about 1.4 miles (stay left when the

Common Merganser

SHANNEEN FINNEGAN 2001

road forks after about 1 mile). Turn left and walk the 1.9 miles back to your car along Old Mine Rd., which has little traffic and good birding.

From the Far View parking lot, drive north on Old Mine Rd., stopping occasionally to look and listen for birds. Any of the stops along Old Mine Rd. may have migrants in spring and fall, especially where the road passes close to the Delaware River. In fall, winter, or spring, walk down to the river to look for Common Goldeneye, Common Merganser, and Bald Eagle. Osprey is a regular migrant along the river in April and September to October. The hemlock groves and spruce plantings are worth checking for northern finches in winter.

Golden-crowned Kinglets have nested in the spruce grove about 1.2 miles north of the Far View Parking Lot. Hooded Warbler is a common breeding bird along this stretch of Old Mine Rd., and Northern Parula is regular. Yellow-breasted Chat can be found in some of the brushy fields along Old Mine Rd., and Prairie Warbler is regular in the fields near Van Campens Glen. Kentucky Warbler is usually present every year, but is rare and hard to find. Common Mergansers can be seen courting in the Delaware River from about Poxono Island north, and broods have been seen early in the summer.

The entrance to the State Forest Headquarters is on the left, about 1.3 miles north of the Far View parking area. Follow the entrance road about 200 yards down to the parking area, where there are toilets open year round. In winter, walk down to the river to scan for Bald Eagles and waterfowl.

If you have time, you may wish to continue north along Old Mine Rd., and explore other areas within the Delaware Water Gap National Recreation Area. The Poxono Island boat launch, about 4.7 miles north of the State Forest Headquarters, is especially good in winter for Bald Eagles. Another particularly attractive spot in spring and summer is Van Campens Glen, which is on the right about 1.8 miles north of the Poxono Island boat access. Two miles past Van Campens Glen is the restored village of Millbrook, where in summer, National Park Service personnel re-enact the daily chores common a hundred years ago. At Millbrook, the Blairstown-Millbrook Rd. (Rt. 602) turns south and crosses the Kittatinny Mountains at Millbrook Gap before descending into Blairstown. From Blairstown, you can follow Rt. 521 back to I-80.

▼

Jenny Jump State Forest

Jenny Jump State Forest and the adjacent areas along Shades of Death Rd. (now called Shades Rd.) in Warren County are known for their interesting diversity of breeding birds and for the excellent passage of migrant songbirds in May. The forest consists of several unconnected land parcels totaling more than 1,100 acres. The largest unit, and the only one readily accessible to the public, runs for about 2 miles along Jenny Jump Mountain near Hope. Shades Rd. follows the base of the mountain for several miles above the Pequest River Valley, and takes in a variety of habitats ranging from sod farms, swampy areas, and overgrown fields to dense, mature deciduous woods on steep hillsides.

Along Shades Rd. you can expect to find most of the flycatchers, swallows, thrushes, vireos, warblers, and sparrows that pass through northwestern New Jersey in May, including such hard-to-find species as Olive-sided Flycatcher, Yellow-bellied Flycatcher, Gray-cheeked Thrush (uncommon), and Golden-winged Warbler. Some of the interesting breeding birds at Jenny Jump and Shades Road have included Ruffed Grouse, Brown Creeper, Alder Flycatcher, Winter Wren, Hermit Thrush, Golden-winged, Northern Parula, Cerulean (common) and Worm-eating warblers (common).

Directions

From northeastern New Jersey, take I-80 west to Exit 12 (Rt. 521, Hope and Blairstown). From the exit ramp, turn left onto Rt. 521. Go about 1 mile, into Hope, and turn left onto Route 519. Drive about 1 mile, then turn right onto Shiloh Rd., where there is a sign for Jenny Jump State Forest. Follow this for almost 3 miles, bearing left at the first junction and right at the second, to the entrance to the state forest on the left. [DeLorme 23, M-19]

From central New Jersey, an alternative is to take Rt. 31 north to the intersection with Rt. 519 in Bridgeville, Warren County. Turn right and go 7 miles to Hope, then proceed as described in the preceding paragraph.

Birding

Enter Jenny Jump State Forest, drive about 200 yards, then turn left onto the oval drive that leads to the headquarters; stop at the office for a map of the forest. Continue up the hill on the entrance road to the parking lot for the Notch Picnic Area, where the trails begin. The Summit Trail begins at the north end of the parking lot, near the restrooms. Follow this trail for about 0.4 miles to a vista, at almost 1,100 feet elevation, that overlooks the scenic Pequest Valley to the east.

The Summit Trail continues for another 300 yards to a trail junction where you have three choices: (1) You can turn right onto the Spring Trail, which makes a steep descent to about 900 feet elevation, then loops around to the south and west and returns to the parking lot. (2) You can turn left and return to the parking lot via the Swamp Trail. (3) The final option, if you are

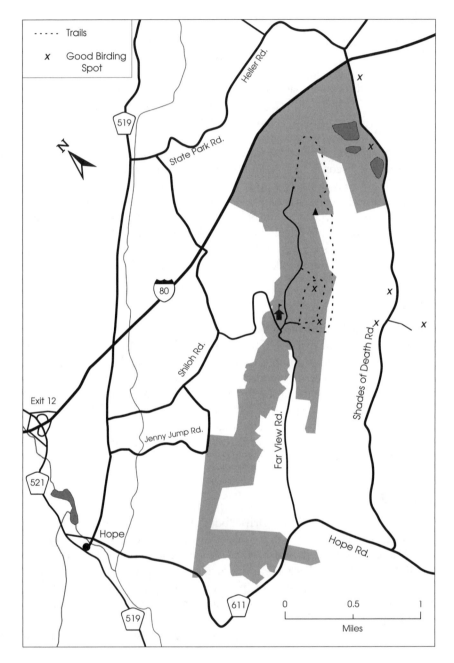

Trails
X   Good Birding
     Spot

Heller Rd.

519

State Park Rd.

80

Shiloh Rd.

Exit 12

521

Jenny Jump Rd.

Far View Rd.

Shades of Death Rd.

Hope

Hope Rd.

611

519

| 0 | 0.5 | 1 |

Miles

Map 17. Jenny Jump State Forest

prepared for a longer hike, is to continue straight ahead on the Summit Trail, which eventually reaches Group Campsite "B" at the extreme northern end of the forest after about 0.7 miles. You can then return to the parking lot by the old road that leads south from the group campsite, through the main camping area. Turn left onto the Swamp Trail near the south end of the camping area, and proceed another one-half mile back to your car.

Jenny Jump is seldom visited during migration, when Shades Rd. and other places are more productive, but an interesting variety of nesting birds can be found here from May through July. These include Turkey Vulture, Broad-winged and Red-tailed hawks, Ruffed Grouse, Wild Turkey, Black-billed and Yellow-billed cuckoos, Eastern Screech and Great Horned owls, Pileated Woodpecker (fairly common), Brown Creeper (in Hemlock glens), Winter Wren (rare on rocky slopes), Eastern Bluebird, Cedar Waxwing, Blue-winged, Chestnut-sided (common), Black-throated Green (in Hemlocks), Prairie, Cerulean (common in tall deciduous trees), Black-and-white, Worm-eating (common on wooded slopes), Hooded, and Canada warblers, American Redstart, Rose-breasted Grosbeak, Indigo Bunting, Chipping Sparrow, Field Sparrow, and many other summer and year-round residents.

To reach Shades Rd., return to the state forest entrance and turn left onto Far View Rd. Go about 1.6 miles to Rt. 611, then turn left. Drive 0.7 miles and turn onto the first paved road on the left, which is Shades Rd.

The Pequest Valley, on your right, is a large, flat expanse of truck farms and sod farms. The sod farms attract a variety of grassland shorebirds in August and September. About 0.7 miles along Shades Rd. is the headquarters of Liberty Sod Farms, on the right. The management usually permits birders to park at the headquarters and walk along the roads that criss-cross the sod areas; if you are interested, stop and inquire. You may also see Great Blue Herons from the large rookery (225+ nests) a few miles across the valley, American Kestrel, and a smattering of songbirds.

Shades Rd. soon enters a beautiful deciduous woods, with stands of mature Sugar Maple, Black Walnut, ashes, oaks, Slippery Elm, and many other species. You can park at either of two pullouts, one at 2.4 miles north of Rt. 611 and the second at 2.7 miles, and walk along the lightly traveled road. In May, the woods are alive with many migrant passerines, while in June and July you will find a diverse selection of breeding birds. Many of the species noted for Jenny Jump State Forest also nest along Shades Rd.; in addition there have been Northern Parula and Yellow-throated Vireo.

Shades Rd. can also be reached from Exit 19 (Allamuchy-Hackettstown) of I-80 at Rt. 517. Follow Rt. 517 south for about 5 miles into Hackettstown, then turn right (west) onto US 46. Continue for about 5 miles to Great Meadows, then turn right onto Rt. 611 at the sign for Hope. Shades Rd. is 1.7 miles ahead, on the right.

⌐

Allamuchy Mountain and Stephens State Parks

These two state parks (which are both administered from the Stephens State Park Office) cover more than 9,000 acres in Morris, Sussex, and Warren Counties. The area is mostly undeveloped, and consists of mature deciduous forest, fields, some conifer plantings, and a few native Eastern Hemlock groves. There are several lakes and ponds, as well as some streams that feed into the Musconetcong River, which runs through the southern portion of the area. Birding in migration can be excellent, especially along the Sussex Branch Trail and in the Deer Park section. The parks also support a wide diversity of breeding birds, with at least 17 species of nesting warblers.

The historic Morris Canal passed through the region, and remains of its corridor and associated structures can be seen in a few places, especially at Waterloo Village (fee), a restored nineteenth century canal village offering numerous programs and cultural activities, and along the Morris Canal Greenway Trail, which follows the old towpath below the village.

Directions

There are four main points of access. To reach the section of the Sussex Branch Trail near Jefferson Lake, take I-80 to Exit 25 (US 206 North, Newton). Go about 0.4 miles and take the first right off the long exit ramp (International Trade Center/Waterloo Village). When you come to the traffic light at Continental Drive (0.5 miles, by the Wyndam Hotel), turn right and go 1.1 miles to the T intersection with Waterloo Road. Drive directly across the intersection and park in the cinder parking lot (portable toilet). [DeLorme 24, L-2]

Birding

The scenic 2-mile stretch of the 21-mile long Sussex Branch Trail, between Waterloo Rd. and Cranberry Lake, passes through streamside and upland deciduous forest for most of this length, and is home to many interesting breeding birds. Among them are Broad-winged and Cooper's hawks, Wild Turkey, Yellow-billed Cuckoo, Screech, Great-horned and Barred owls, Pileated

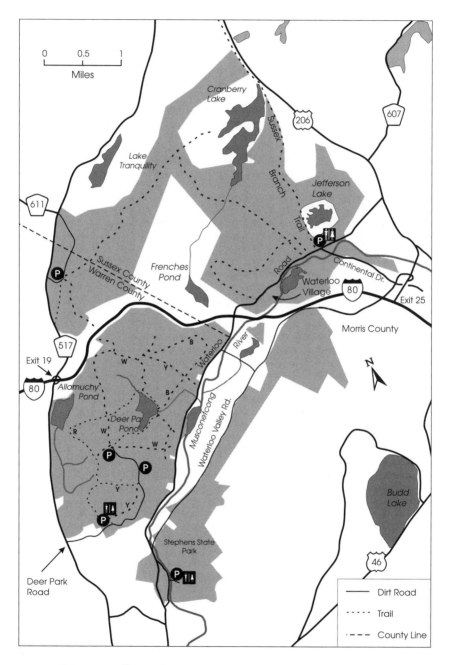

Map 18. Allamuchy Mountain and Stephens State Parks

Woodpecker, Yellow-throated and Warbling vireos, Cerulean (just north of Jefferson Lake), Black-and-white, and Worm-eating warblers, American Redstart (abundant), Ovenbird, and Louisiana Waterthrush (along the streams).

Jefferson Lake, one-half mile north of the parking lot, can have Belted Kingfisher, waterfowl, and all of the swallows in migration. The bushes and trees along the trail at the lake can be alive with migrant landbirds on a good day in May or late August to early September. About one-half mile north of the lake, a small waterfall on the right marks another good spot. The Highlands Trail (blue markers) crosses the stream just above the falls and leads into a mixed deciduous/Hemlock forest where Acadian Flycatcher, Solitary Vireo, Hermit Thrush, and Black-throated Green Warbler all breed.

Continuing along the Sussex Branch Trail for another 0.3 miles, you will find a large beaver pond/marsh on the right, which has had Olive-sided Flycatcher in migration, and usually hosts breeding Least Flycatcher.

There are several side trails setting off from the Sussex Branch Trail. Those leading west into the higher and more remote parts of Allamuchy Mountain State Park are well worth exploring for Ruffed Grouse and for Northern Waterthrush and Canada Warbler in boggy swamps. To do any serious exploring in this area, however, you should have a good topographic map and a compass.

Deer Park

To reach the Deer Park section, take I-80 to Exit 19 (Rt. 517, Allamuchy, Hackettstown). Turn left onto Rt. 517 South and go about 2.3 miles to Deer Park Rd., on the left, shortly after Mattar's Restaurant. Take this road for 0.7 miles to the main parking lot, by the outhouses. There is a display board showing some of the roads and trails that you can drive or walk. Trail maps are usually available here, as well. [DeLorme 23, N-25]

The dam by the small pond opposite the outhouses can be excellent for migrants. Tennessee and Wilson's warblers, among others, are regular in May, and the trees around the pond often hold an Olive-sided Flycatcher in late August. The large spruce trees by the road can be good for Cape May Warbler. A short walk back along the entrance road leads to a grove of evergreens worth checking for owls, thrushes, and kinglets.

From the main parking lot, the road continues 1 mile to parking lot 1, just past the only house that you will encounter. The road is unpaved and rough, but is passable in a normal car if you drive slowly. In winter, the road is often closed beyond this point. If it is open, you can drive another 0.6 miles to parking lot 2, where the road is always closed to vehicular traffic. You can walk the dirt road the remaining mile or so to Deer Park Pond, or hike some of the numerous color-coded trails; be alert for mountain bikers, however.

In May and June, the road between the main parking lot and lot 2 is excellent for migrant and breeding warblers. Bay-breasted is often seen in May in the tall trees near the stream crossing, while nesting warblers include Blue-winged, Yellow, Chestnut-sided, Prairie, Cerulean, Black-and-white, American Redstart, Worm-eating, Ovenbird, Louisiana Waterthrush, Kentucky, Common Yellowthroat, and Hooded. Kentucky Warbler is often found in the woods several hundred yards before you reach the house, but you should listen for it all along the route. Also listen for Prairie Warblers along the field edges at lot 1 and for Cerulean Warbler in the tall trees about 0.3 miles past that lot.

Hooded Warbler and Chestnut-sided Warbler can be found at scattered locations along this route, and both Mourning Warbler (May) and Connecticut Warbler (September) have been seen here, as well. Some other nesting species to seek are Ruby-throated Hummingbird, Eastern Bluebird, Veery, Rose-breasted Grosbeak, and Field Sparrow.

The stretch of road past parking lot 2 can yield Common Redpoll in invasion winters (in the birches) and the lake itself can have migrant waterfowl, such as Ring-necked Duck and Hooded Merganser. Across the path from the tall spruce trees at the far end of the lake are numerous small spruces that have held a N. Saw-whet Owl in several winters.

Northwest Section

Another part of the park north of I-80 can be reached by turning right onto Rt. 517 from the I-80 exit ramp at Exit 19. Drive north on Rt. 517 for about 1.3 miles, turn right onto a dirt road, and go 0.2 miles, watching the fields on either side for Wild Turkey. Just after the road makes a right angle turn to the left, you should park on the left. Just ahead is another dirt road going up to the right. Hike up this road for about 0.1 miles and, when the road bends left, bear right onto a trail that leads up toward the top of Allamuchy Mt. Be sure to take a compass so you don't get lost. Ruffed Grouse occur farther up the mountain, and there are a couple of small evergreen groves that occasionally host a N. Saw-whet Owl. This area of dense deciduous forest has not been well explored in the breeding season and may be rewarding for the adventurous birder-hiker. [DeLorme 23, K-26]

Stephens State Park

Stephens State Park can also provide some interesting birding. From the Sussex Branch Trail parking lot described above, turn right (west) onto Waterloo Rd., and drive 5.9 miles to an acute left turn (there is a poorly visible State Park sign). Take this road 0.4 miles to the bridge over the Musconetcong

River, on the right, and cross this bridge to the parking lot, where there are restrooms and a picnic area.

There are numerous pine groves in the park that are worth exploring. In summer, Pine Warbler breeds, and from fall to spring it is often possible to find Red-breasted Nuthatch, Yellow-bellied Sapsucker, Golden-crowned Kinglet, or a roosting owl. Red Crossbills have been seen here, as well. To locate most of the pines, walk back across the bridge and ascend the steep stairs to the campground area. Another large pine grove is located across Waterloo Rd. from the campground. [DeLorme 29, A-26]

✝

Merrill Creek Reservoir

Merrill Creek Reservoir is a pumped-storage hydroelectric project that was constructed by damming the creek atop Scotts Mountain in southwestern Warren County. Although the 650-acre reservoir inundated a beautiful and very productive spot for migrant songbirds, it provides a good haven for migrant waterfowl in spring and fall, and the surrounding 2,000 acres of protected forests and fields attract an interesting selection of migrant and breeding landbirds.

The best spot for waterfowl is the Overlook Parking Area, from which such unusual species as Pacific Loon, Greater White-fronted Goose, Barrow's Goldeneye, and Sabine's Gull have been seen. This is also the site of an annual fall hawk watch. In addition to a loop trail that circles the entire 5-mile shoreline of the reservoir, there are a number of shorter trails that are accessible from the Visitor Center.

Directions

To reach the Visitor Center, take I-78 West to Exit 4, Warren Glen/Stewartsville. Turn right, and go north on Stewartsville Rd., Rt. 637, for 1.8 miles to a blinker light. Turn right onto Rt. 638, Washington St., and continue about 2.4 miles to Rt. 57. Go across Rt. 57 diagonally onto Montana Rd. After 2 miles, bear left at a Y-intersection and go another 0.3 miles to Merrill Creek Rd. Turn left and follow the signs to the Visitor Center parking lot.

To reach the Overlook Area Parking lot, take I-78 West to Exit 3, US 22, the last exit in New Jersey. Go about 1.1 miles to the second traffic light and turn right onto Rt. 519 North. Drive about 2.8 miles on Rt. 519, crossing

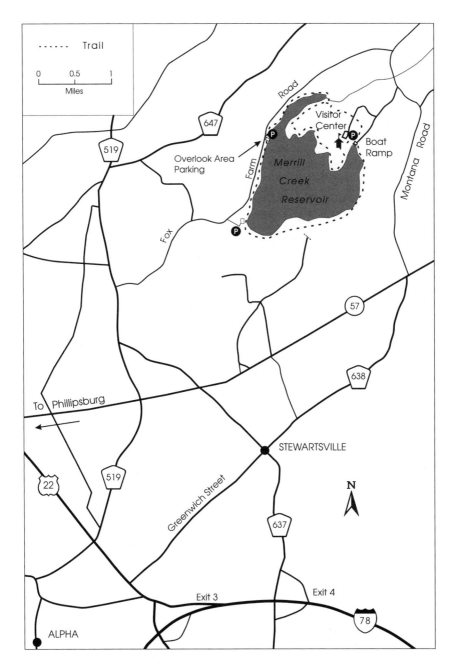

Map 19. Merrill Creek Reservoir

Rt. 57, and turn right onto Fox Farm Rd., where there is a small sign for Merrill Creek Res. Go about 2.6 miles, bearing right at the fork after one mile, to the entrance to the parking area, on the right.

Birding

At the Overlook Area Parking lot, the birding is straightforward—scan the reservoir and the skies for waterfowl and raptors, respectively. A spotting scope is indispensable for checking the water, as the birds may be widely dispersed and quite distant. Migrant ducks begin to arrive early in the fall, and include a good variety of diving ducks, plus a few dabblers. Scaup, Common Goldeneye, and Bufflehead are the most frequent visitors, but Barrow's Goldeneye has been seen a couple of times. Scoters and Long-tailed Ducks occasionally stop by in foul weather. Snow Geese and Brant are often seen migrating overhead, but seldom come in to the reservoir. Greater White-fronted Goose has been found in the company of the many migrant and resident Canada Geese. Both Common and Red-throated loons are regular visitors later in the season, and Pacific Loon has been recorded once. Bald Eagles are regular visitors in winter and are likely to nest in the near future.

From the Visitor Center, use the trail map available there to explore the woods and fields on the north side of the reservoir. The bird list for Merrill Creek includes more than 230 species, among them most of the regular migrant songbirds that pass through New Jersey, plus a good variety of species that stay to nest in the diverse habitat surrounding the reservoir. Although the area receives less attention during both spring and fall migration than some more popular areas, its position along a mountain ridge provides a favorable situation for songbird as well as raptor flights.

☞

Alpha (Oberly Road)

Oberly Road is a short farm road in extreme southwestern Warren County. Although it is only 1.5 miles long, in winter it is one of the best inland locations in the state for Snow Bunting and Lapland Longspur. During the summer, an interesting variety of grassland nesting species can be found here, including Eastern Meadowlark, Vesper, Savannah, and Grasshopper sparrows; and Bobolink. In migration a variety of ground-feeding birds passes through. Although this site was planned for a housing development, it was saved by the heroic efforts of the Pohatcong Grasslands Association, led by the late Dick Dunlap.

Directions

Take I-78 west to Exit 3 (Phillipsburg), the last exit in New Jersey. Make the jughandle turn at the traffic light, following the signs for Alternate Rt. 22 toward Alpha. Take Alt. Rt. 22 to the next light (about 0.8 miles) and turn left onto 519 south; follow this for 1.5 miles through Alpha. Continue past the Alpha Lumber Co., under I-78, then take the first right onto Rt. 635. Go about 1.3 miles and turn onto unmarked Oberly Rd., on the right. [DeLorme 34, A-4]

Birding

The entire 1.5-mile length of Oberly Rd. traverses land that has been preserved, but leased back to farmers, so do not stray from the road. The birds you will find here depend as much on the condition of the fields as on the season. For the first mile the road passes through cultivated fields, but one or more of these may lie fallow. In winter, the acres of corn stubble are attractive to Horned Lark and occasionally Eastern Meadowlark. Snow Bunting and Lapland Longspur (uncommon but regular) prefer the barest of fields. In winter, when the farmers spread manure, the birds tend to gather around the freshest deposits. After a fresh snow, the plow-scraped road shoulders also may be productive. The best way to find the birds is to drive slowly along Oberly Rd. (and also along Rt. 635), stopping to scan the fields at intervals. Snow Buntings never stay in one place for more than a few minutes, so you will see them fly up and land repeatedly.

Along this stretch of road, Water Pipit is occasional in early winter, Northern Harrier is common, and Rough-legged Hawk is present in most years. Short-eared Owl is often seen in winter; to look for owls, park in a spot with a wide view of the area about one-half hour before dark. The owls course over the fields as they hunt, pausing occasionally to perch on a post or on the ground.

After about 1 mile, the road passes between farm buildings. The last half-mile has sparrows at all seasons. The small fields here are bordered with shrubs and trees and provide better cover than the open fields on the south end of the road. In winter look for American Tree, Field, Savannah, Song, White-throated, and White-crowned (uncommon) sparrows and Dark-eyed Junco. Vesper Sparrow is rare in winter and Dickcissel has been found once.

During migration, all the species mentioned above (except Dickcissel) are regular. In addition, look for Chipping, Grasshopper, Fox, Lincoln's (mainly fall), and Swamp sparrows, and Bobolink. In fall, there may be migrating raptors overhead; they tend to follow the nearby ridges and the Delaware River, only 1 mile to the west.

In summer, several of the grassland species remain to nest, depending on the condition of the fields. Fallow fields are likely to have Grasshopper

Sparrow, Bobolink, and Eastern Meadowlark. Horned Lark and Vesper Sparrow like cornfields, while Savannah Sparrow seems to prefer large alfalfa fields. The latter two species are now very uncommon nesting birds in New Jersey.

At its north end, Oberly Rd. ends at Carpentersville Rd. Turn right, go 0.4 miles to a fork, then bear right onto Rt. 642. Follow this for about 0.9 miles into Alpha to the intersection with Rt. 519. To rejoin I-78 (Rt. 22), go left for 0.4 miles, then right onto Alt. Rt. 22, which merges with I-78 in about 1 mile.

For an alternate route through additional birding territory, turn left on Carpentersville Rd. and follow it through more fields and then along the Delaware River for about 2.5 miles. At the village of Carpentersville, turn left onto Rt. 635 and follow it back to Rt. 519 near the Alpha Lumber Co.

⌖

Point Mountain Section
(Musconetcong River Reservation)

One of the jewels of the Hunterdon County Park System, this 697-acre preserve at the northern tip of the county has more than 4 miles of trails through its diverse and sometimes steep terrain, from the scenic Musconetcong River to the top of the Musconetcong Ridge. Most of the park is heavily forested, but there are also old farm fields, streams, and a panoramic view from 935-foot Point Mountain, where hawks can be observed migrating in the fall. More than 160 species of birds have been recorded here, including numerous migrants both spring and fall, and almost 90 species of breeding birds. Many of the typical woodland nesting species can be found here, such as Ruffed Grouse, Wild Turkey, several woodpeckers, including Pileated, Red-eyed Vireo, Wood Thrush, Veery, Worm-eating, Cerulean, Chestnut-sided, Hooded, and Kentucky warblers, Northern Parula, American Redstart, Summer Tanager, and Rose-breasted Grosbeak. Common Merganser nests along the river.

Directions

Take I-78 to Rt. 31 North (Exits 16 & 17) and go north on Rt. 31 for 6.5 miles to the traffic light at Rt. 632 (Asbury-Anderson Rd.). Turn right and drive 4 miles to the intersection with Rt. 57. Turn right and go 0.2 miles to the first traffic light at Point Mountain Rd., and turn right. Drive one-half

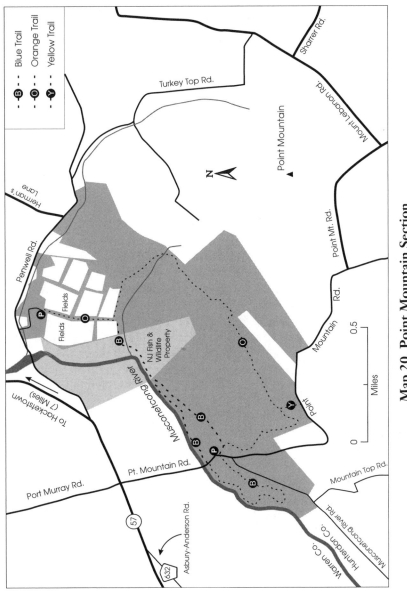

Map 20. Point Mountain Section

mile downhill, crossing the Musconetcong River, to a parking area on the left. [DeLorme 29, H-20]

From the northeast it is easier to take I-80 to US 46 (Exit 26), drive west on US 46 for 8 miles to Rt. 182 (Mountain Ave.) in Hackettstown. Turn left and go 1 mile to the light at Rt. 57 and turn right. Take Rt. 57 for almost 7 miles to the traffic light at Point Mountain Rd., and turn left.

Another parking area is off Penwell Rd., which intersects Rt. 57 0.3 miles east of Point Mountain Rd. Go one-half mile to the second driveway after crossing the river; the gravel road leads 200 yards to a parking area.

Birding

The downstream section of the Blue Trail makes a one-half mile loop along the river, passing through forest and a small patch of open field. The upstream section is a 1-mile loop, with giant sycamores along the river and a woodland of black birch, oak, maple, and tulip trees. Both trails start near the bridge over the Musconetcong River, where Ruby-throated Hummingbird, Great Crested and Acadian flycatchers, Warbling Vireo, Blue-gray Gnatcatcher, Cerulean Warbler, Northern Parula, American Redstart, Louisiana Waterthrush, and Baltimore Oriole may be found. Yellow-throated Warbler has been seen here and may someday nest. Several pairs of Common Mergansers nest along this stretch of the river, and can often be seen from the bridge or flying along the river; also watch for Wood Duck.

For a longer hike, the upstream part of the Blue Trail connects with the Orange Trail that connects the Penwell Rd. and Point Mountain parking areas. The round trip via the Orange Trail is 3 miles, but along the way you should encounter Louisiana Waterthrush and Acadian Flycatcher along the streams, and Kentucky, Hooded, and Worm-eating warblers on the upper slopes. For a short but strenuous hike to the Point Mountain overlook, drive uphill on Point Mountain Rd. from the parking lot for about 0.7 miles to a small pulloff on the left at the start of the trail. Follow the trail uphill to the overlook, where the Yellow Trail connects with the Orange Trail. The overlook is a good hawk watch in autumn, and you may see resident Broadwinged Hawks in summer, plus resident Red-tailed and Cooper's hawks, and Black and Turkey vultures.

From the Penwell Rd. parking area, the Orange Trail passes along several fields and hedgerows before entering the woods. Here you will find species such as soaring Black and Turkey vultures, Red-tailed Hawk, Chimney Swift, several species of swallows, Willow Flycatcher, Eastern Kingbird, Northern Mockingbird, Chestnut-sided, Prairie, and Blue-winged warblers, Field and Song sparrows, Indigo Bunting, and Orchard Oriole. The easiest way to get

to the Penwell Rd. parking area from Point Mountain Rd. is to return to
Rt. 57 and head east for 0.3 miles, as described above.

🦅

Voorhees State Park

Sitting atop a mountain ridge at the southern end of the New Jersey Highlands, this small (625 acres) but beautiful park served as a camp for the Civilian Conservation Corps during the Depression. Today, the extensive forest of
tall deciduous trees and planted conifers serves as a magnet for migrant songbirds and supports a nice mix of breeding birds. Because of its location, the
park is especially good in spring migration, when more than 20 species of
warblers can be found on a good day.

Voorhees is home to the New Jersey Astronomical Association, which offers regularly schedules programs open to the public. The 26-inch Newto-
nian reflector telescope is one of the largest privately owned telescopes in
New Jersey.

Directions

Take I-78 west to Exit 17 (Rt. 31 North, Clinton, and Washington). Go north
on Rt. 31 toward Washington for 2 miles to the traffic light at Rt. 513 North,
and turn right. Follow Rt. 513 through High Bridge for 2.9 miles, then turn
left onto Observatory Rd. (the High Acres entrance road. [DeLorme 29, L-21]

Birding

Drive in Observatory Rd. past a pine plantation (listen for Pine Warbler) for
0.2 miles to a small parking area on the left at a scenic overlook. Scan for
Broad-winged Hawk, which nests in the park, and for Black Vulture, Cooper's Hawk, and other raptors. A trail behind the signboard at the parking lot
leads into woods and up to the observatory entrance in 0.3 miles. By walking
up this trail and back down the road to your car, you may find breeding
Pileated and Red-bellied woodpeckers, Red-eyed and Yellow-throated vireos,
Blue-gray Gnatcatcher, Veery, Wood Thrush, Black-and-white, Worm-eating,
and Hooded warblers, American Redstart, Rose-breasted Grosbeak, Scarlet
Tanager, Baltimore Oriole, and other woodland species. This area can also be
excellent for Swainson's Thrush and migrant warblers in spring.

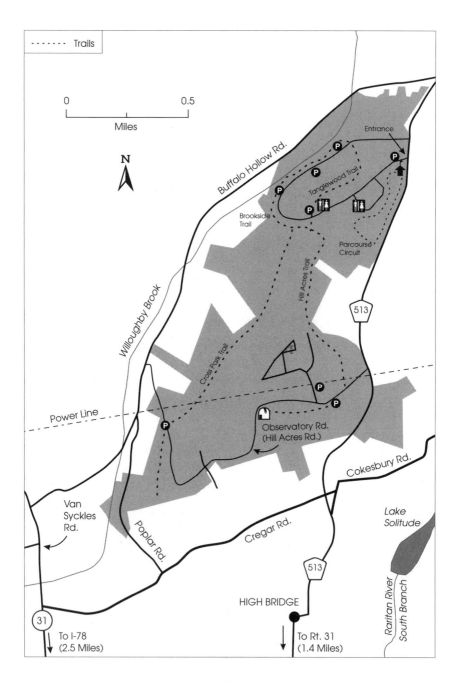

Map 21. Voorhees State Park

From the parking area, walk down the road about 100 yards to the Hill Acres Trail. The trail crosses a powerline cut after about 50 yards, then reenters the woods, where you may find Kentucky Warbler in the first hundred yards, if you are lucky. Return to the powerline and follow it uphill to the entrance road to the group campsite. Along the powerline and in the campground you will find nesting Chestnut-sided, Prairie, and Blue-winged warblers, Common Yellowthroat and Indigo Bunting, plus migrants in season. Yellow-billed Cuckoos are sometimes here, as well. Walk out the campground entrance road to Observatory Rd. and go left about 300 feet to your car.

Return to Rt. 513, turn left, and drive 0.9 miles to the main entrance to the State Park, on the left. The headquarters building, with hummingbird feeders, is on the left, just before the gate; listen for Hooded Warbler behind the office. Stop and pick up a trail map, then continue on the entrance road, which makes a 1.2-mile loop back to Rt. 513. The gate opens at 8:00 A.M., but you can park and walk in if you arrive earlier.

Bird along the entrance road to the main parking area (one-half mile), where there are restrooms. From here, the Brookside and Tanglewood Trails make a pleasant 1.2-mile loop through the deciduous woods of tulip trees, oaks, maples, and hickories, interspersed with occasional 70-year old conifer plantings. Some of the other birds that can be found here in spring and early summer are Ruffed Grouse, Wild Turkey, Great-crested Flycatcher, Cedar Waxwing, Louisiana Waterthrush (along Willoughby Brook), and Swamp Sparrow. Most of the migrant warblers pass through in May, including Mourning in late May to early June, and Olive-sided Flycatcher is a rare migrant, as well.

ᛏ

Cold Brook Reserve

This 308-acre preserve in eastern Hunterdon County consists mainly of farm fields and hedgerows. It is an outstanding spot in fall and early winter for migrant sparrows and other birds of this open habitat. Local birder Evan Obercian has run up some very impressive single-day totals of the sometimes elusive Vesper Sparrow, Lincoln's Sparrow, and White-crowned Sparrow. Other noteworthy species seen here include White-fronted Goose, Golden Eagle, Northern Shrike, Clay-colored Sparrow, and Dickcissel.

Directions

Take I-78 to Exit 24 (Rt. 523, Oldwick) and go north on Rt. 523. In 1 mile, Rt. 523 turns right, but continue straight ahead on Rt. 517, High St. Go one-half mile, through the center of Oldwick, to the entrance to Cold Brook Reserve, on the left. The entrance is easy to miss and is just 0.1 miles past the main intersection in Oldwick.

Birding

From the parking area, start up the dirt road marked for authorized vehicles only. A trail map for the area should be available, but the open aspect of the property makes it easy to explore. The main trail leads along a tree line at the edge of the fields. There are numerous hedgerows separating the fields and any of these can harbor migrant or wintering songbirds, plus a few permanent residents.

The numbers of sparrows can be staggering, with the common Song, Swamp, Field, Chipping, White-throated, and Savannah sparrows accompanied by the less common Vesper, Lincoln's, and White-crowned sparrows. As many as 20 to 30 Lincoln's Sparrows have been encountered on a tour of the fields in early October, and this is one of the best places in Hunterdon County to find Vesper Sparrow. Other species to be looked for here are Grasshopper, Clay-colored, and Nelson's Sharp-tailed sparrows, as well as the possible Lark Sparrow. Later in the season there will be American Tree Sparrow and Fox Sparrow, plus abundant Dark-eyed Juncos. A few warblers are found during migration, and Connecticut Warbler is a regular in fall.

Follow one of the trails that leads down to the stream that forms the northern boundary of the property. The stream flows into Cold Brook across Rt. 517. The bushes along the stream are another good spot for migrants in this attractive little park, which can be thoroughly covered in a couple of hours.

Cold Brook is a good location for Northern Shrike in late fall and winter, and, when the fields are plowed, attracts large flocks of American Pipit. Smaller flocks of Horned Lark are often present throughout the winter, with the occasional Lapland Longspur among them. The large flock of migrant and resident Canada Geese that frequents the fields often has a Snow Goose or even a White-fronted Goose among them in fall or winter. Another winter feature is the small roost of Northern Harriers that hunt over the fields and gather together for protection in the evening, when they can be seen flying into the roost.

Another good spot nearby is the section of Black River Rd. along the Lamington River. From the center of Oldwick, go east on Church St., which soon becomes Vliettown Rd., for 1.8 miles to the triangle intersection at Black River Rd. The fields along the road here and in the 1.5-mile stretch of Black River Rd. south (to the right) to Lamington Rd. have nesting Bobolink and Eastern Meadowlark, a few pairs of Savannah Sparrows and usually American Kestrel. The woods along the stretch of road near the river can be outstanding for migrant songbirds in spring, mid-April through May. Wood Duck and Louisiana Waterthrush nest along the river, as does Common Merganser on occasion. A small pond on the right side heading south can be good in migration for shorebirds, including both yellowlegs, Spotted Sandpiper, Solitary Sandpiper, and large numbers of Common Snipe (100+ seen).

🦆

Spruce Run Recreation Area

Spruce Run Recreation Area covers almost 2,000 acres of reservoir and shoreline near Clinton in northern Hunterdon County. It is one of the best inland locations in the state for observing migratory waterbirds, being rivaled only by Assunpink and Mannington Marsh. Together with adjacent Clinton WMA, which contains 1,115 acres, Spruce Run offers a diversity of habitat with a wide variety of birdlife.

Migratory waterfowl occur at Spruce Run from September to April, many species staying until they are frozen out in winter. The variety includes most of the species of ducks and geese that regularly occur in New Jersey, except for a few sea ducks. Loons and grebes are also present at these times. Late summer usually brings an influx of herons and egrets, as well as an excellent collection of migratory shorebirds if the water levels in the reservoir are low (as they often are).

Some of the species that have occurred here in recent years, including a few not often seen at inland sites in New Jersey, are Red-necked Grebe (almost annual), Tricolored Heron, Eurasian Wigeon, Long-tailed Duck, Black Scoter, Lesser Golden-Plover, Piping Plover, Whimbrel, Buff-breasted Sandpiper, Red Phalarope, Pomarine Jaeger, Lesser Black-backed Gull, Forster's Tern, Least Tern, Black Skimmer, and Northern Shrike.

Note: The Recreation Area is crowded with bathers and boaters in summer. The WMA is heavily used by hunters, especially from October through December (except on Sundays). Be sure to wear bright clothing, preferably blaze orange, if you enter the area on a hunting day.

Directions

Take I-78 west from its interchange with I-287 for 13 miles, to Exit 17 (Rt. 31 North, Clinton, and Washington). Go north on Rt. 31 toward Washington for about 3.3 miles to the traffic light at Van Syckles Rd., a well-marked left turn with signs for Spruce Run Recreation Area. Turn left and go about 200 yards to a parking area on the left. [DeLorme 29, M-19]

From the Trenton area, it is quicker to take Rt. 31 north all the way to Van Syckles Rd., a distance of about 37 miles from downtown Trenton.

From northwestern New Jersey, take US 206 to Netcong, Rt. 46 to Hackettstown (8 miles), Rt. 57 to Washington (10 miles), and Rt. 31 south to Van Syckles Rd. (about 7 miles).

Birding

The most productive areas for shorebirds, herons, and egrets are the places where Spruce Run and Mulhockaway Creek flow into the reservoir. The stream that you cross just after turning onto Van Syckles Rd. is Spruce Run; Mulhockaway Creek is discussed shortly. In late summer and fall (roughly mid-July through September), when the water level in the reservoir is low, a large expanse of grassy mud flats is exposed along the shore; these are extensive where Spruce Run flows into the reservoir.

From the first parking area on Van Syckles Rd., walk out onto the mud flats (knee boots are advisable). Here you may find an interesting variety of shorebirds—at least 27 species have been recorded at the reservoir, many of them at this spot. Black-bellied and Semipalmated plovers, Killdeer, Greater and Lesser yellowlegs, Spotted, Semipalmated, Western, Least, and Pectoral sandpipers, Dunlin, Short-billed Dowitcher, and Common Snipe are some of the more common, regularly occurring species. The goodies that bring birders to this spot are Lesser Golden-Plover and Baird's and Buff-breasted sandpipers, which occur annually. Other shorebirds that are found here with some frequency include Ruddy Turnstone (rare), Sanderling, Solitary, White-rumped, and Stilt sandpipers, and Long-billed Dowitcher. This northeastern corner of the reservoir is also a good spot for herons and egrets in late summer, although Mulhockaway Creek is better.

Continue west along Van Syckles Rd., watching for waterfowl offshore along the way. After about 1 mile, you will come to a road for the boat launch area on the left. Follow this road for about one-half mile to the launch site, at the end of a peninsula. This peninsula is an excellent place to observe waterfowl offshore and is a gathering place for gulls and terns. Caspian, Common, Forster's, Least (once) and Black terns all have appeared here, usually in late summer to early fall; Caspian Tern occurs annually, in spring and fall; and Pomarine Jaeger was found once. The launch area is excellent for Horned Lark

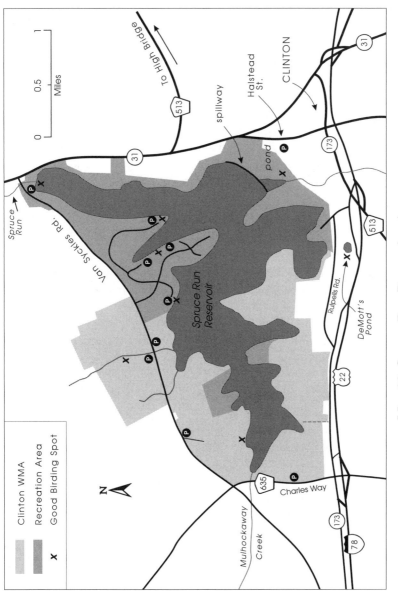

Map 22. Spruce Run Recreation Area

Clinton WMA

Recreation Area

x Good Birding Spot

N

0   0.5

Miles

To High Bridge

513

31

Spruce Run

Van Syckles Rd.

Spruce Run Reservoir

spillway

pond

Halstead St.

CLINTON

173

31

513

Rupells Rd.

DeMott's Pond

22

635

Charles Way

Mulhockaway Creek

173

78

and Snow Bunting in winter. The cove to the west, known as Boat Launch Cove, has been a favorite area for Eurasian Wigeon over the years.

Return to Van Syckles Rd. and go another 0.4 miles to the entrance to the Recreation Area, on the left. A fee is charged here in summer for this popular swimming area, and the gate does not usually open until 8 A.M. Just past the tollbooth, turn right and follow the road to a parking area that over-looks the western end of the reservoir. This is a good spot for finding migra-tory waterfowl, especially diving birds such as Common and Red-throated loons, Common, Hooded, and Red-breasted mergansers, and even the occa-sional Long-tailed Duck, White-winged Scoter, or Black Scoter.

When you return to the main entrance road, continue straight ahead, following the sign for family picnicking. Picnic area 3 provides a good view of the birds in Boat Launch Cove, including Eurasian Wigeon. In addition to the overlook and several picnic areas, the Recreation Area includes a large bathing beach, a boat rental area, and a campground (all except the camp-ground are open to the public). Although most of the natural vegetation has been destroyed and replaced with grass, there are a few fields and patches of woodland left; these can be good for songbirds, especially sparrows, in migra-tion. Northern Shrike wintered here one year.

Go back to Van Syckles Rd. and continue west for about one-half mile to where Black Brook flows into the reservoir. There is a parking area on the left before you reach the brook and a smaller one on the right after you cross the brook; you are now in the Clinton WMA. Park in the smaller area on the right, and walk up the dirt road that runs north along Black Brook. Yellow-breasted Chat is a common breeder in the multiflora rose tangles along this road, and the many other species here include Willow Flycatcher, Acadian Flycatcher (up the brook), White-eyed Vireo, and Chestnut-sided Warbler (abundant). This area can be great for migrants in both spring and fall; Olive-sided Flycatcher is regular in late summer–early autumn.

To find shorebirds and herons in the fall, continue on Van Syckles Rd. for 0.9 miles to an unmarked parking area on the left, just before the administra-tion building for the WMA. If you come to the sign for the Clinton WMA, you have gone too far. From the parking area, walk west along the road for about 200 yards, 50 feet past the WMA sign. Turn left just before a line of trees, and walk southeast toward the reservoir.

Follow the tire tracks and trails for about one-half mile. This will bring you to the reservoir near the north bank of Mulhockaway Creek, where a large expanse of mudflat is usually exposed in late summer. This is frequently the best spot for shorebirds, but the walking can be difficult—knee boots are definitely advisable. It is also the best area for wandering herons and egrets. All of New Jersey's herons and egrets, except Yellow-crowned Night-Heron, have occurred here; Tricolored Heron is rare, however. Do not attempt this walk on a Saturday or weekday during hunting season because it is unsafe.

Take Van Syckles Rd. back to Rt. 31 and turn right. After about 1.8 miles bear right onto Halstead St. (Rt. 513). Go another 0.4 miles to the Clinton Community Center on the right, and park in the lot. Walk across the ball field to a chain-link fence overlooking the outlet pond of Spruce Run Reservoir. This is often the best spot for waterfowl and has often had a flock of Redheads in the spring. Other diving ducks are fond of this spot as well, perhaps because it is not as deep as most of the reservoir. Puddle ducks come to roost but not to feed, and Eurasian Wigeon is a regular visitor.

Continue down Halstead, which soon becomes Lehigh St., for about 0.4 miles to the intersection with Rt. 173. Turn right and go 0.7 miles to the intersection where Rt. 513 goes straight and Rt. 173 turns right. Turn right and go 0.4 miles to a small pond on the right, DeMott's Pond. Despite its modest size, this Clinton city park is a good spot for Snow Goose, Wood Duck, Eurasian Wigeon, other ducks, and a small variety of gulls, mainly Ring-bills.

From DeMott's Pond, continue on Rt. 173, which merges briefly with I-78, for 2.4 miles to the traffic light at Charlestown Rd. (Rt. 635). Turn right and drive 0.4 miles to an unmarked WMA parking lot on the right. Park here and walk in the old road. The overgrown fields and hedgerows and second-growth woodlands have a variety of breeding birds, such as Yellow Warbler and Indigo Bunting, but are especially good for migrants in the fall. Lincoln's Sparrow is a regular visitor.

✦

Hoffman Park

This 354-acre preserve is one of the newest acquisitions of the park system and contains some excellent grassland habitat with nesting Eastern Bluebird, Grasshopper Sparrow, and Bobolink. There is a marked trail system and an information board at the parking lot.

Directions

Take I-78 to Exit 11 (Rt. 173, W. Portal, Pattenburg), make a loop following the signs for Pattenburg to cross over to the south side of I-78 and take the first left onto Baptist Church Rd. Go 1.2 miles to the entrance to the park, staying right at the fork after 0.2 miles, on the left. If the gate is not open (it opens at 9:00 A.M.) park on the side of the entrance road so as not to block the gate and walk in. Otherwise, drive in 0.2 miles to the parking area, where there is a portable toilet. [DeLorme 35, B-15]

Birding

The fields on both sides of the entrance road between the gate and the parking lot are good for the grasslands species, including Savannah Sparrow, Grasshopper Sparrow, Bobolink, and Eastern Meadowlark. Upland Sandpiper has not yet occurred here, but the fields certainly look appropriate and there is hope that this rarity may someday settle in.

In addition to the fields, the park includes 25 ponds, the largest of which is Manny's Pond, deciduous woodlands, where many common species nest, and some wet meadows in the eastern part of the park. The trees around the parking lot attract migrant songbirds in spring, as do the wet woods at the north end of Manny's Pond in both spring and fall. The hedgerows along the entrance road and Hairpin Lane have nesting Brown Thrasher and Willow Flycatcher.

The woods to the east of Manny's Pond have a good variety of the typical species of deciduous woodlands, including Pileated and Red-bellied woodpeckers, Veery, Wood Thrush, several warbler species, Scarlet Tanager, Rose-breasted Grosbeak, and others. The fields and edges are good for sparrows in October and November and for Northern Harrier, American Kestrel, and Savannah Sparrow in winter.

ᛣ

Round Valley Recreation Area

Round Valley Reservoir is the largest body of fresh water in the state. It is located within the Round Valley State Recreation Area, which covers over 3,600 acres in northeastern Hunterdon County and offers a variety of outdoor activities such as swimming, boating, hiking, and camping. There is an entry fee to the Recreation Area in summer. For birders, however, it is the other three seasons that are of interest.

The reservoir attracts diving birds, mainly loons, in spring and fall. Flocks of gulls begin to gather in late fall and remain through the winter. Rarities that have appeared here include Pacific Loon, Red-necked Grebe,

Red-necked Phalarope, and Lesser Black-backed Gull. A pair of Bald Eagles nest on a hillside on the northeastern corner of the reservoir.

Directions

Take I-78 west to Exit 20A (Lebanon), 10 miles west of I-287. Go about 0.3 miles to the traffic light at Rt. 22 and turn right. Follow Rt. 22 west for about 0.8 miles to the jughandle turn for Round Valley Recreation Area. Take this access road for about 0.8 miles to the junction with Rt. 629 (no street sign). Turn left onto this road, then immediately right into the parking area. [DeLorme 35, B 23-24]

Birding

Scan the cove at the boat launch area, where there is an unobstructed view of the reservoir. Round Valley is the prime inland location for Common Loon in New Jersey. Counts of 100 or more are not exceptional in October and November; smaller numbers are present in the spring. Some Red-throated Loons are usually mixed in with the Commons (as many as 40 have been seen), and a Pacific Loon was present for two weeks in November 1978. A few Horned Grebes stop off at the reservoir in spring and fall, and Red-necked Grebe, a rare annual visitor, has been recorded from October to March.

The number of gulls at Round Valley begins to build in late fall and may surpass 1,000. Herring Gull is the most common species, followed closely by Ring-billed Gull. Great Black-backed Gull is found in lesser numbers and Bonaparte's Gull (high count of 50), Iceland Gull, and Lesser Black-backed Gull have also been seen. Double-crested Cormorants drop into the reservoir occasionally, as do Tundra Swans and a variety of diving ducks, but overall, nearby Spruce Run Reservoir is much more attractive to most kinds of waterfowl.

Before leaving the boat launch cove, scan the shoreline of the reservoir for Snow Buntings, which appear often in winter. Turn left onto Rt. 629 and immediately left on the access road. Go about 0.8 miles to the Recreation Area entrance. Go in, take the first right turn (0.5 miles), and proceed for 0.3 miles to a parking lot overlooking a narrow section of the reservoir. The extensive groves of pines to your left may have northern finches or owls in winter. A hiking and riding trail begins here that follows the south and east sides of the reservoir for about 9 miles.

The small lagoon that has been diked off as a swimming area attracts a few diving ducks in winter, when it is not frozen. To reach this area, return to

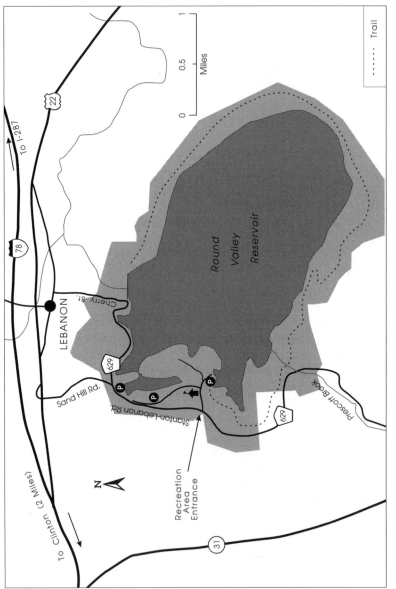

Map 23. Round Valley Recreation Area

the entrance road and continue straight ahead to one of the several parking areas on the right that overlook the bathing pond.

Restrooms at the Recreation Area are open year-round. A trip to Round Valley is easily combined with one to nearby Spruce Run Recreation Area.

⸸

Central Hunterdon County

The Hunterdon County Park System has assembled a collection of mostly small, but interesting preserves along the watershed of the South Branch of the Raritan River that offer diverse birding opportunities. A selection of birding sites suggested by Don Freiday, who contributed most of the material for this section, are covered here. Trail maps for these and other sections are available at the park headquarters at 1021 Highway 31, Lebanon.

Directions

From the north, take I-78 to Exit 17 (Rt. 31). Follow the directions for Rt. 31 South, Flemington, then drive south on Rt. for 5 miles to Stanton Station Rd. and make the jughandle U-turn to go north on Rt. 31. Proceed 0.4 miles to the Hunterdon County Park System Headquarters (closed Sundays). [DeLorme 35, E-23]

From the south, take Rt. 31 North from I-95 north of Trenton for about 17 miles to the traffic circle where US 202 and Rt. 31 divide. Continue north on Rt. 31 for 6 miles to the park headquarters on the right, 0.4 miles north of the traffic light at Stanton Station Rd.

Birding

The trails for the 73-acre Hunterdon County Arboretum start at the headquarters parking area. Once a commercial nursery, the collection of distinctive trees, shrubs, and both native and exotic plants can be alive with migrant songbirds in spring. If you hit it right, it's possible to run up a list of 20 or more species of wood warblers, plus many other species of passerines. If you don't hit it right, the arboretum can be dead. Fortunately, because of its small size, you will know right away how the birding is going to be.

From the south end of the parking area, walk east on the service road, which ends at a T. Look and listen in the spruce trees for migrants such as Cape May Warbler and for nesting Golden-crowned Kinglet and Red-breasted

Nuthatch. Walk left at the T, then right on a grass trail that leads to a wooden bridge over a small brook. Short trails lead in either direction along the stream. Check the tall oaks and larches for migrants, which seem to concentrate along the stream or near the pond and wetland area downstream of the bridge.

Assiscong Marsh Natural Area, at 24 acres the largest marsh in Hunterdon County, is located on the floodplain of Assiscong Creek, just upstream from its confluence with the south branch of the Raritan River. From the Arboretum, go north on Rt. 31 for 1.3 miles to the next jughandle U-turn at Payne Rd. Head south on Rt. 31 for about 3.8 miles to the traffic light at Bartles Corner Rd. (Rt. 612), and turn left. Drive 0.6 miles to the sharp left turn onto River Rd. at the intersection with Rt. 523. Go 0.2 miles to the parking area on the right.

A trail leads into the woods from the parking area, but the best birding is along River Rd., which is unpaved and lightly traveled. From autumn through spring, as long as the water is open, the marsh attracts a wide selection of waterfowl. Especially in migration, all of the puddle ducks can be found here, as well as a few divers, such as Ring-necked Duck and Hooded Merganser. When the water level is low, as it often is in spring or late summer, the marsh also attracts a variety of shorebirds, including Spotted Sandpiper, Solitary Sandpiper, both yellowlegs, Least Sandpiper, and Common Snipe.

Wood Ducks breed at the marsh, with up to 18 males seen at one time in early spring. Scan the back edges of the marsh for teal and the occasional American Bittern, which is seen annually but apparently does not breed. Sora and Virginia Rail are also heard sporadically in May. Great Blue Herons nest nearby and six species of swallows can sometimes be seen during migration.

To return to Rt. 31, turn right from the parking area onto River Rd. and go 0.9 miles, passing a horse training facility along the way, where you should watch for Eastern Bluebird, Killdeer, and blackbirds. At Rt. 31, turn right and go 1.6 miles to Stanton Station Rd. Make the jughandle left turn, go 0.3 miles to Lilac Dr. and turn right. Drive 0.4 miles to the entrance to Echo Hill Environmental Education Area, turn right and proceed 0.2 miles to the parking area.

Echo Hill is a 76-acre park dominated by stands of Norway Spruce, White and Red pines planted by the Civilian Conservation Corps in the 1930s. These conifers host nesting Cooper's Hawk, Great Horned Owl, Red-breasted Nuthatch, Golden-crowned Kinglet, and Pine Warbler. Check the spruces around the parking area, then walk up the service road at the north side of the lot, through the spruces, to a field with scattered eastern red cedars, where Prairie Warbler nests and migrants may be found.

In late fall or winter, check the conifers for Yellow-bellied Sapsucker, the cedar thickets for Hermit Thrush, Cedar Waxwing, and Yellow-rumped Warbler, and everywhere for owls (including N. Saw-whet Owl) and winter finches. Be sure to check the pond, on the southeast side below the buildings, where Green Heron, Great Blue Heron, Belted Kingfisher, and a surprising variety of ducks may be found.

Another little-known spot nearby that often has interesting birds is the Hamden Pumping Station, where the South Branch of the Raritan River is dammed. From Echo Hill, continue north on Lilac Dr. for 0.8 miles to a stop sign. Turn left, continuing on Lilac Dr., for another 1.8 miles to the stop sign at Wellington Dr. Go 1 mile and turn left onto Hamden Rd., which crosses the South Branch and bears left. At the intersection with Landsdowne Rd. (one-half mile), continue straight ahead a short distance and park on the shoulder on the left. Walk down Hamden Rd. to the barrier where it dead ends, cross the barrier, and check the impoundment for waterbirds.

Among the species seen at the pumping station are Pied-billed Grebe, Double-crested Cormorant, Great Cormorant (rare), Common and Hooded mergansers, Gadwall, American Wigeon, Green-winged and Blue-winged teal, Mallard, Black Duck, and Bufflehead. Check the shore for Killdeer, Spotted Sandpiper, and American Pipit (fall). Belted Kingfisher, Cliff Swallow and N. Rough-winged Swallow nest around the impoundment. To return to I-78, return to the intersection of Hamden Rd. and Wellington Dr. and turn left. Go 1.5 miles to West Main St. (Rt. 173, Old Route 22) in Clinton, turn left and go one-half mile to the junction with I-78, where you can go either east or west.

🦆

Bull's Island

Bull's Island is an 80-acre section of the Delaware and Raritan Canal State Park about 20 miles up the Delaware River from Trenton. The island was created by the digging of the canal during the nineteenth century. It is one of the most accessible examples of the riparian habitat along the Delaware and is best known among birders for the variety of interesting species that nest here, especially Acadian Flycatcher, Cliff Swallow, and several species of warbler: Yellow-throated, Northern Parula, Cerulean, and Louisiana Waterthrush. It is also an excellent place to observe the spring migration.

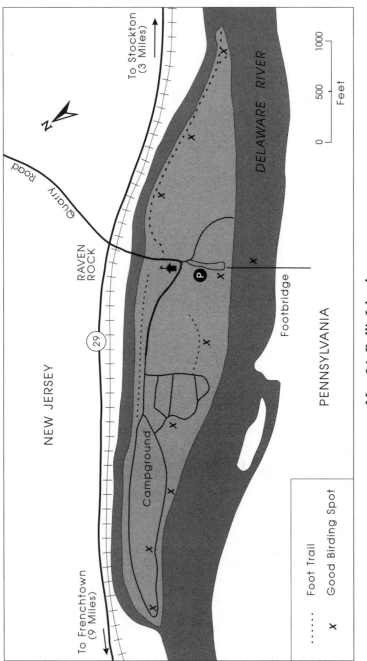

NEW JERSEY

To Frenchtown
(9 Miles)

29

RAVEN
ROCK

Quarry Road

To Stockton
(3 Miles)

N

Campground

DELAWARE RIVER

P

Footbridge

PENNSYLVANIA

0   500   1000

Feet

Foot Trail
x   Good Birding Spot

Map 24. Bull's Island

Directions

From the north, take I-287 or Rt. 22 to their intersections with US 202 in Somerville, then follow Rt. 202 south for 26 miles to the exit for NJ Rt. 29 north. Go north for about 6 miles to the entrance to Bull's Island, on the left. Cross the bridge over the canal and continue straight ahead to the parking area.

From the northern part of the New Jersey shore, take I-195 west to Trenton, then follow the signs for I-295. Go west on I-295 (becomes I-95) for 9 miles to the exit for Rt. 29 north. Stockton is 10 miles north on Rt. 29, and Bull's Island another 3 miles. From southern New Jersey or the Philadelphia area, go north on I-95 from Philadelphia, then take the Rt. 29 North exit just after crossing the Delaware. Proceed as described above.

Birding

The best time to visit Bull's Island is from late April through June. Mid-May is best for the spring migration, while the many nesting songbirds are especially conspicuous and easy to find in late May and early June. The park receives little attention during the fall migration, when the dense foliage makes birding difficult. Winter is the dullest season, with only a few resident songbirds and occasionally a roosting owl. The river may harbor some waterfowl, especially Canada Geese, Common Goldeneye, and Common Merganser, and there are usually good numbers of wintering raptors along Rt. 29 (mainly vultures and Red-tailed Hawks, but sometimes Bald Eagles).

The most interesting feature of Bull's Island is its small population of nesting Yellow-throated Warblers. The first males arrive during the last half of April and begin singing from the tops of the tall American Sycamores, which dominate the island. These birds are of the race *albilora* (formerly called Sycamore Warbler). This race is the typical breeding subspecies of the Mississippi Valley and is here near the extreme northeastern limit of its range. The nearest significant population of *albilora* is in West Virginia, so the Delaware Valley birds represent a disjunct colony. Sycamore Warblers are distinguished from the race *dominica*, which breeds in southern New Jersey, by having white instead of yellow lores (that part of the face between the eye and the bill), and by their slightly different song. They have been found nesting along the Delaware from Bull's Island north to about Flatbrookville.

The northern two-thirds of the island is now largely developed for picnicking and camping. A pleasant picnic area is located just beyond and to the right (north) of the parking area as you enter; Chipping Sparrow is a common nester in the evergreen plantings scattered around the nearby field, and Cerulean Warblers are often right around the parking lot. The paved road on the right, just past the headquarters, leads to the campground; to enter it, you must stop for a permit. For birders, though, the campground is mainly a place to walk through to observe some of the migrant and nesting species (please be courteous to the campers, who have paid for the privilege of staying there, and do not enter occupied campsites). Yellow-throated and Cerulean warblers, although found everywhere on the island in most years, are more common on the northern part with its many huge sycamores. Northern Rough-winged Swallow also can usually be found at the north end.

Between the campground and the picnic area is a low area, which is under water when the Delaware River floods. Thickly wooded, this spot is a favorite of migrant waterthrushes. In 1983, a pair of Northern Parulas was observed building a nest using some of the debris left hanging from trees—the first confirmed nesting attempt for New Jersey in many years. The species was once a common breeder throughout the state, but disappeared with the decline of the *Usnea* lichen (Old Man's Beard) that they prefer for building their nests. After adapting to new construction materials in the absence of its old favorite, it has once again become a regular summer resident.

The large oak and maple trees bordering the parking area usually have nesting Cerulean Warbler and Northern Oriole, and sometimes Orchard Oriole. At the far end of the parking lot, the footbridge leading across the Delaware River to Pennsylvania is a good place to look for waterfowl in winter, soaring raptors at any season, and swallows in spring. Barn and Cliff swallows nest under the bridge, while both N. Rough-winged and Tree swallows nest nearby and can be seen hawking insects over the river. Bank Swallow is usually present as well, but is not as common as the other swallows.

Another good birding area on Bull's Island is the southern one-third, most of which has been designated a Natural Area. To bird this area, walk back toward the entrance from the parking lot. Just opposite the headquarters, a poorly maintained trail leads down the bank to the canal, which it follows to the southern end of the island, passing among mature sycamores, Silver Maples, River Birches, and Box Elders. The path is lined with Jewelweed, Poison Ivy, and Stinging Nettle, so be careful what you touch. Jewelweed is supposed to soothe the stings of the nettle; if you should contact some nettle (you'll feel the burning right away), crush some Jewelweed leaves and rub them on the spot—maybe it will help. Another interesting feature of this walk along the canal is the large Ostrich Ferns, which are at their best along this stretch of the Delaware and which unfurl their fiddleheads in late spring.

Yellow-throated Warbler may be anywhere along this stretch of the island, but they are hard to spot as the males sing from the tops of the sycamores; a little squeaking or pishing may bring one down for a closer look. In May, listen for Acadian Flycatcher, another specialty of the park. Warbling Vireo and Cerulean Warbler nest on the southern part of the island, and Northern Parula may be here as well. Other species common in these woods are Wood Duck and Spotted Sandpiper (along the canal), Red-bellied Wood-pecker, Fish Crow, Carolina Wren, Veery, Blue-gray Gnatcatcher, Yellow-throated Vireo, and Louisiana Waterthrush.

After reaching the end of the trail, you will have to turn back, either re-tracing your steps along the towpath or following one of the makeshift trails closer to the river; any of these routes will lead you back to the parking lot. There are modern restrooms in the campground and usually portable toilets at the parking area.

Barred Owl

David Sibley 1985

Northeast Region

1. Ramapo Reservation
2. Campgaw Reservation
3. Ramapo Mountain State Forest
4. Allendale Celery Farm
5. Palisades Park Overlooks
6. Tenafly Nature Center
7. High Mountain
8. Garrett Mountain Reservation
9. Rifle Camp Park
10. Troy Meadows

11. Old Troy Park
12. Lake Parsippany
13. Jockey Hollow
14. Great Swamp NWR
15. Eagle Rock Reservation
16. South Mountain Reservation
17. Kearny Marsh
18. DeKorte Park
19. Liberty State Park
20. Watchung Reservation

Map 25. Northeast Region

Ramapo Valley Reservation

Located in the northwestern corner of Bergen County, this park contains more than 2,000 acres of bottomland and hillside along the Ramapo River and the slopes of the Ramapo Mountains. Many trails traverse the varied terrain, where the birdlife is similar to that in Ringwood State Park and in nearby Campgaw Reservation. A trail map is available at the headquarters or at the Bergen County Wildlife Center on Crescent Ave. in Wyckoff. The gate opens at 8:00 A.M.

Directions

See Map 26. Follow the directions for Campgaw Reservation, but instead of leaving Rt. 208 at Ewing Ave., continue another 2 miles to US 202 in Oakland. Turn right onto US 202 and drive about 5.0 miles to the park entrance, on the left. [DeLorme 26, C-7]

Birding

Most of the birding at Ramapo is along the trails that climb the gentle slopes of the Ramapo Mts. The park receives little attention from birders, so additional effort could quickly add to the knowledge of birdlife here.

🦆

Campgaw Reservation

The 1,351 acres of this Bergen County Park contain most of Campgaw Mountain, a 2-mile-long ridge in the northwestern part of the county. Ramapo Valley Rd. forms part of the northwestern boundary of the reservation. The Ramapo River runs along this road, separating Campgaw Mountain from the Ramapo Mountains. Elevations in the park range from about 300 feet along Ramapo Valley Rd. to 751 feet atop Campgaw Mountain. Most of the habitat consists of deciduous forest in various stages of succession, but there are a few patches of hemlocks. The borders of the ski area and the power line right-of-way provide some shrubby fields and edge habitat.

Like Eagle Rock Reservation, nearby Ramapo Valley Reservation, and other similar places in northeastern New Jersey, Campgaw Reservation is best during spring and fall migration.

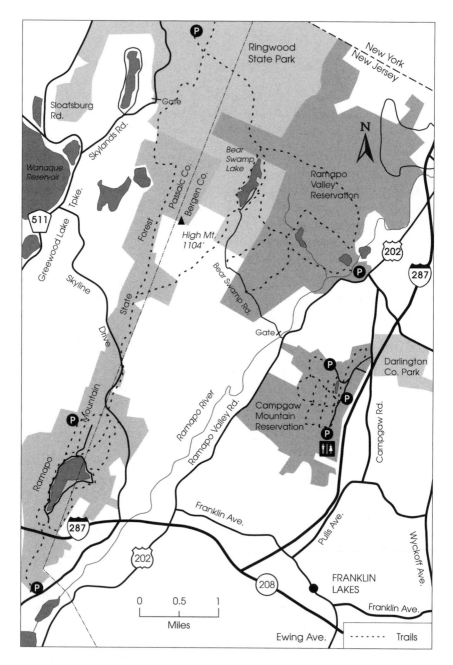

Map 26. Ramapo Valley and Campgaw Reservations

Directions

See Map 26. Take the Garden State Parkway to Exit 160 (Fair Lawn). From the exit ramp, turn left onto Paramus Rd., then go about one-half mile to the exit for Rts. 4 and 208 (Fair Lawn and Hawthorne); this will put you on Rt. 4. After about 0.3 miles, bear right onto Rt. 208 toward Oakland. Follow Rt. 208 for about 8 miles to the Ewing Ave. exit. Turn right onto Ewing Ave., go about 0.3 miles, and turn left onto Franklin Ave. Proceed about 0.8 miles and turn right onto Pulis Rd. Continue for 1.5 miles, turn left onto Campgaw Rd., and drive 1.7 miles to the Campgaw Reservation entrance road, on your left. Proceed for about one-half mile, staying left at the junction with the road to the ski area, until you come to a parking lot on the left for the Deer Picnic Area. There are some restrooms about 200 yards farther along the entrance road. [DeLorme 26, D-7]

Alternatively, take I-287 north to Exit 59 (Franklin Lakes, Rt. 208). Take the first exit onto Colonial Rd. north. Go to the first light (Franklin Ave.) and turn right. Turn left onto Pulis Rd. (about 0.2 miles) and proceed as described previously.

Birding

The trees and shrubs around the parking lot are good for migrant songbirds. Take the marked Hemlock Trail for several hundred yards; soon you will come to a small pond on the right and then to the marked junction with Indian Trail on the left. The area around this junction is one of the best birding spots in the park.

Walk up Indian Trail (yellow blazes), which climbs the ridge, roughly paralleling the ski slopes, in about one-half mile. At the top, you can turn left on Rocky Ridge Trail (blue blazes), or continue straight ahead a short distance to Old Cedar Trail (red blazes). Old Cedar Trail is the longer of the two, as it descends the ridge on the western slope, heads south for a while, then reclimbs the ridge to join Rocky Ridge Trail. From this junction, Rocky Ridge Trail continues south, then heads back down the eastern slope to rejoin the main park road just west of the campground. The total distance from Indian Trail to the main road is about 2.3 miles; it is another 0.4 miles back to the parking lot.

During May and August to September, you may expect to find most of the common migrant songbirds that pass through New Jersey. Connecticut Warbler has been recorded, and sought-after species such as Olive-sided and Yellow-bellied Flycatchers, Gray-cheeked Thrush, and Philadelphia Vireo probably occur in fall. Additional breeding birds to look for are Broad-winged Hawk, Belted Kingfisher, Yellow-throated Vireo, Brown Creeper, Veery, Wood Thrush, Yellow-throated Vireo, Blue-winged, Yellow, Chestnut-sided, and Black-and-white warblers, American Redstart, Ovenbird, Northern Waterthrush, Common Yellowthroat, Scarlet Tanager, Rose-breasted Grosbeak, Indigo Bunting, Baltimore Oriole, and American Goldfinch.

Nearby Ramapo Valley Reservation (also a Bergen County Park) and Ramapo Mountain State Forest offer further birding opportunities in this area.

🦆

Ramapo Mountain State Forest

This long, narrow state forest stretches more than 5.5 miles along the ridgetops of the Ramapo Mountains. Although it covers 2,336 acres, the forest averages only about one-half mile in width. It has many marked trails and includes the Ramapo Lake Natural Area. A trail map is available at Ringwood State Park. The birdlife here is similar to that in nearby Ringwood State Park, Campgaw Reservation, and Ramapo Valley Reservation, but less varied.

Directions

See Map 26. Follow the directions for the Skyline Drive Hawk Lookout in the Hawk-Watching section. There are two parking areas; the main one (well-marked by signs) is on the left, 0.3 miles after you turn off West Oakland Ave. onto Skyline Dr. A second, unmarked place to park is on the left, 1.1 miles past the first parking area. Connecting trails at both spots lead to Ramapo Lake. [DeLorme 26, E-3]

Birding

Because it consists of mainly ridgetop habitat, the birdlife of the state forest lacks the diversity to be found in some nearby preserves. Typical breeding species here include Red-eyed Vireo, Veery, Wood Thrush, Black-and-white, Blue-winged, Chestnut-sided, Hooded warblers, Ovenbird, American Redstart, Scarlet Tanager, and Eastern Towhee.

🦆

Allendale Celery Farm

The Allendale Celery Farm is a haven for wildlife amidst the residential and industrial developments of northwestern Bergen County. Although it was once an active celery farm, the site has lain fallow since 1951, and is now an 107-acre wildlife preserve owned by the Borough of Allendale. The centerpiece of this little park is a 48-acre marsh of Cattails and *Phragmites* that attracts a variety of migrant and nesting birds.

More than 230 species of birds have been observed at the Celery Farm since 1953, mainly by Stiles Thomas and members of the Fyke Nature Association. Among the interesting nesting species are Least Bittern, Wood Duck, Virginia Rail, Willow Flycatcher, Marsh Wren, and Ring-necked Pheasant. Although it is not known as a hotspot for rarities, the Celery Farm has attracted some noteworthy species over the years, including Glossy Ibis, Black Rail, Northern Goshawk, Golden Eagle, Sandhill Crane, Upland Sandpiper, Common Barn Owl, Common Raven, Sedge Wren, Northern Shrike, and Prothonotary, Yellow-throated, and Connecticut warblers.

Directions

Take the Garden State Parkway north to Exit 163 (Rt. 17). Follow Rt. 17 north for about 7.2 miles to the Allendale exit. Go west on E. Allendale Ave. for exactly 1 mile to Franklin Turnpike, turn right, and go about 0.2 miles to the small parking lot, on the right. [DeLorme 26, E-11]

Birding

Cross a small wooden bridge to reach the main trail, a 1-mile loop installed by the Fyke Nature Association. It follows the perimeter of the marsh that forms the southern half of the preserve. Two unmarked trails branch off on the north side of the marsh into wet deciduous woodland. A leisurely walk around the loop trail takes about two hours.

In April, look for migrant American Bittern and Common Snipe (both uncommon); this is also when the nesting Wood Ducks are setting up housekeeping. A variety of sparrows are present, mainly on the edges of the fields around the northern and western parts of the tract. These include Field, American Tree, Savannah, Song, Swamp, and White-throated sparrows and Dark-eyed Junco. Song and Swamp sparrows remain to nest in good numbers.

Other common nesting birds are Canada Goose, Mallard, Yellow Warbler, Common Yellowthroat, and Red-winged Blackbird. Tree Swallows nest in the tubes that have been put out for them, replacing the boxes often

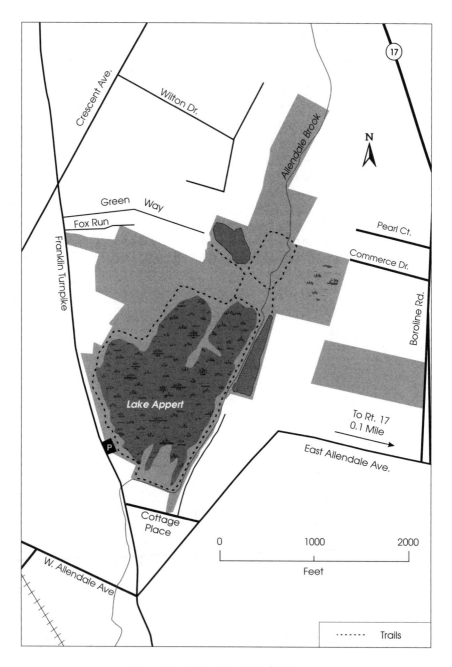

Map 27. Allendale Celery Farm

usurped by House Sparrows. Many of the common birds of lowland deciduous forest can be found in the wooded northern section.

Fall migration brings large flocks of ducks and Canada Geese into the marsh at dusk; this is the time for the greatest variety of waterfowl. It is also the best time to look for some of the less common migrants that show up regularly, including Olive-sided Flycatcher (September) and Lincoln's and White-crowned sparrows. Bobolinks are common in September and early October. Spectacular blackbird roosts have occurred here at times, as in the fall of 1981 when up to a million European Starlings, Common Grackles, and other blackbirds gathered in the evenings.

Winter is unexciting at the Celery Farm, especially after the water freezes. In milder years, Virginia Rails have overwintered occasionally, as have American Bitterns. There are always sparrows and some of the common permanent residents, but you won't run up a long list of species. Still, a rarity might show up at this welcome oasis on a cold winter day.

❧

Palisades Park Overlooks

Two overlooks along the Palisades Interstate Parkway are good spots during migration for loons, waterfowl, hawks, and songbirds. State Line Overlook is best in fall, the Alpine Overlook best in spring. The bigger birds tend to be high and difficult to spot, while the passerines move through the trees along the top of the Palisades or fly along the cliff top.

Directions

See Map 28. Take I-95 to the exit for Palisades Interstate Parkway at the west end of the George Washington Bridge. Drive north on the Parkway for about 5.5 miles to the Alpine Overlook, a well-marked exit on the right. State Line Overlook, another 3.5 miles north on the Parkway, is also well marked. [DeLorme 27, K-24]

Birding

In spring, the edges of the parking area at the Alpine Overlook can be full of migrant songbirds following the Palisades north. The best prospect is to find a good spot and let the birds come to you. In autumn, the State Line Overlook is an excellent hawk-watching spot. Many other migrants pass by, but as at most hawk watches, the best thing to do is wait and scan the skies repeatedly.

🦅

Tenafly Nature Center

The Tenafly Nature Center and Lost Brook Preserve is a small, private reserve in northeastern Bergen County, near the Palisades of the Hudson River, comprising nearly 50 wooded acres and a pond. It serves as a sanctuary for plants and animals, an educational facility, and a passive recreational area in the midst of suburbia. Despite the small size, its favorable location makes it an excellent spot to observe the migration in spring and fall, with almost 200 species recorded there.

The adjacent Green Brook Sanctuary is a private, densely wooded preserve atop the New Jersey Palisades in Alpine and Tenafly, Bergen County. This 165-acre sanctuary provides excellent birding and spectacular views of the Hudson River and nearby Manhattan. Owned by the Palisades Nature Association, Green Brook is open only to members, who pay tax-deductible annual dues. More than 230 species of birds have been recorded here, including most of the common species that regularly migrate through New Jersey. Rarities have included Swallow-tailed Kite, Golden Eagle, Boreal Chickadee, Orange-crowned Warbler, Henslow's Sparrow, Yellow-headed Blackbird, and all of the winter finches. Write the Palisades Nature Association at P. O. Box 155, Alpine, NJ 07620 for information about membership. [DeLorme 27, L-23]

Directions

Take I-95 towards the George Washington Bridge to the next-to-last exit in New Jersey, Exit 72 (Rt. 9W). Go north on Rt. 9W for about 4 miles (don't take the Interstate Palisades Parkway) to East Clinton Ave., and turn left. Drive 1.75 miles to Engle Ave., turn right, and go 0.7 miles to the T intersection at Hudson Ave. Turn right onto Hudson and go 0.7 miles to the entrance to the park, and park in the lot on the right, opposite the Nature Center. [DeLorme, 27, L-22]

Birding

Tenafly and Lost Brook are at their best during the spring and fall migrations, when you can expect to see a good diversity of songbirds on a good day. Twenty-two species of warblers are listed as common or uncommon in

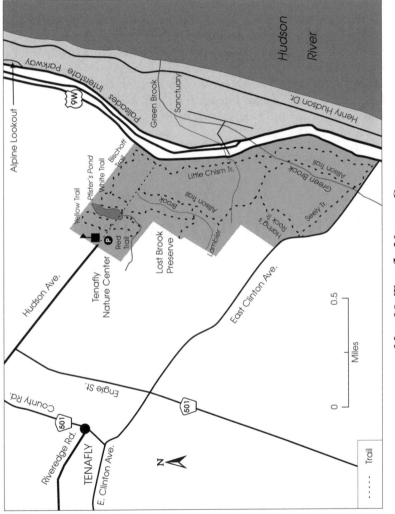

Alpine Lookout

Palisades Interstate Parkway

9W

Green Brook
Sanctuary

Henry Hudson Dr.

Hudson
River

Pfister's Pond
Bischoff
Trail
White Trail
Yellow Trail

Little Chism Tr.

Allison Trail
Green Brook

Brook
Allison Trail

Seely Tr.
Haring's
Rock Tr.

Red
Trail

Tenafly
Nature Center

Lost Brook
Preserve

Lambier

Hudson Ave.

East Clinton Ave.

Engle St.

Riveredge Rd.

County Rd.

501

TENAFLY

E. Clinton Ave.

501

N

0   0.5

Miles

Trail

Map 28. Tenafly Nature Center

spring, with another seven seen occasionally. All of the vireos occur, although Red-eyed is the only breeder and Philadelphia is rare in fall. Thrushes are regular and Wood Thrush and Veery both nest, but Gray-cheeked and (presumably) Bicknell's are rare. Among the many warblers, only Ovenbird and Common Yellowthroat stay to nest, but such attractive species as Scarlet Tanager, Rose-breasted Grosbeak, and Baltimore Oriole are annual breeders.

The main trail is a continuation of Hudson Ave., but there are several side trails that branch off in the first several hundred yards. The Yellow Trail and the White Trail both pass along the edges of Pfister's Pond, where you may find Wood Duck and Mallard, and perhaps a Green Heron. You can make a loop of the park via a couple of trails. Take the White Trail to Bischoff Trail, Little Chism Trail, branch off to Allison Trail, Seely Trail, Haring's Rock Trail, Allison Trail again, Purple Trail, and Red Trail for a complete tour. Depending on the traffic noise from Rt. 9W, you may want to avoid part of Little Chism Trail.

☛

High Mountain Park Preserve

This 1,104-acre preserve in Wayne Township and North Haledon, Passaic County, is one of the least-known birding spots in northeastern New Jersey. Jointly owned by the Nature Conservancy, Wayne Township, and the State of New Jersey, and created as a preserve in 1993, High Mountain is a natural oasis amid urban sprawl. It is situated in the small, outlier Preakness Range of the Watchung Mountains, where its rolling topography provides panoramic vistas, including a view of New York City, less than 20 miles away, from the summit of High Mountain. In addition to being a good spot for birds in migration, it harbors an unusual variety of plants, some quite rare in New Jersey.

Directions

From the intersection of I-80 and Rt. 23 North, go 1 mile north on Rt. 23 to Alps Rd. Turn right and go 2 miles to the traffic light at the intersection of Alps and Ratzer Rds. Turn right onto Ratzer Rd. and proceed 1 mile to Valley Rd. Turn left and go 0.7 miles to Hamburg Turnpike. Turn right and drive 1 mile to College Rd., on the left (same turn as for Wayne General Hospital). Turn left into College Rd., proceed 1 mile, and turn right into Parking Lot 6 of William Paterson University. Use the top tier. [DeLorme 26, K-6]

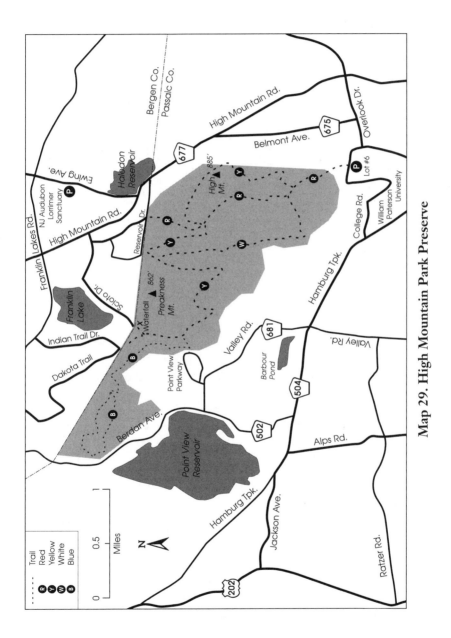

Map 29. High Mountain Park Preserve

From the west, take I-80 to Exit 53 and follow the signs for Rt. 46 East. From the merger with Rt. 46 East, continue about one-half mile to the exit for Riverview Dr. North (Rt. 640). Go 1.5 miles north to Valley Rd. and turn right. Continue on Valley Rd. for about 3.2 miles to Hamburg Tpk. and proceed as described in the preceding paragraph.

Birding

The preserve is one of the largest tracts of forested land in the Piedmont region of northern New Jersey, and contains a mixture of woodlands and wetlands, with nine different ecological communities. The trails in the park have been maintained by the New York-New Jersey Trail Conference since the 1940s, now in cooperation with Nature Conservancy volunteers. They are not difficult (the elevation gain to the top of High Mt. [885 ft.] is about 450 feet), but they are extremely rocky. Sturdy hiking boots are a must.

The best times to visit High Mountain for birds are in spring and fall migration, although the preserve has a good variety of nesting species in early summer. During May, many of the migrant songbirds found at nearby Garret Mountain can be seen here as well, although the numbers and variety are not as great. The birds are more difficult to see because High Mountain doesn't have the open, parklike environment of Garret. However, if you want to do some searching on your own, without crowds of birders, it offers a delightful, secluded haven for a morning's outing.

At the present time, the only public access is from the William Paterson University parking lot. Follow the Red Trail from the northwest corner of the parking lot for about one-half mile to the junction with the Yellow Trail, on the right. The Yellow Trail climbs to the top of High Mountain in another one-half mile, providing an outstanding view of New York City to the east, if the weather is clear. Yet another one-half mile or so will bring you back to a second junction of the Red and Yellow trails. At this point, you can turn left onto the Red Trail and return about 1.3 miles back to the parking lot, or stay on the Yellow Trail, which meanders through the preserve for a couple of miles to Buttermilk Falls, a small waterfall cascading down some columnar basalt. On your return, make the right onto the White Trail after about 1.5 miles, and continue to the Red Trail back to the parking lot. Note that not all of the trails are marked, so stick to the marked one, unless you know your way around.

Among the breeding birds of High Mountain, in addition to the more common species, are Yellow-billed Cuckoo (most years), Eastern Wood-Pewee, Great Crested Flycatcher, Veery, Wood Thrush, American Redstart, Louisiana Waterthrush, Black-and-white Warbler, Worm-eating Warbler (abundant), Scarlet Tanager, Rose-breasted Grosbeak, and Baltimore Oriole. In fall, the songbird migration is similar to Garret Mountain, but you'll probably have better luck elsewhere. The crest of High Mountain itself, however, is an excellent, if little-used, hawk watch at that season.

Haledon Reservoir and Lorrimer Sanctuary

Two other good birding spots nearby are the Haledon Reservoir and the NJAS Lorrimer Sanctuary, both off Ewing Avenue in Franklin Lakes. From Parking Lot 6, turn right and go about 0.2 miles to Overlook Dr. Turn left and drive 0.25 miles to Belmont Ave. and turn left. Proceed 1.3 miles to High Mountain Rd., bear left, and go 1 mile to Ewing Ave., and turn right. The north end of the reservoir, where you can park, is 0.3 miles farther. The entrance to Lorrimer Sanctuary is 0.4 miles ahead, on the left.

Walker Avenue

To reach Walker Ave., go north on Rt. 23 from the junction of I-80 and Rt. 23 for 1.4 miles to the exit for Newark-Pompton Pike. Cross over Rt. 23 and go 0.2 miles to Ryerson Ave., and turn left. Drive about 0.6 miles on Ryerson to Walker Ave., turn right, and go one short block, then turn left onto Ford St. and park on the right. The large body of water on the right, several acres in extent, was formed by dredging for fill for I-287, and has become a magnet for waterbirds of many species. Visit this spot any time from September through May to see a variety of ducks, herons, shorebirds, and other species. The site was once the location of one of the earliest transatlantic radio transmission towers.

➤

Garret Mountain Reservation

This Passaic County park sits atop the First Watchung Mountain just south of Paterson. The habitat is similar to that of Eagle Rock Reservation, but the songbird migration is outstanding in spring and fall. Garret Mountain has a pond that attracts waterfowl and an overlook that provides a spectacular view of northeastern New Jersey. Formerly a well-kept local secret, it has only recently become known to more birders as the best spot in New Jersey, and surely it is one of the best in the East, to observe the spring migration. Since being introduced to this spot by Kevin Karlson in the late 1980s, I have returned every spring to enjoy the marvels of Garret.

During the spring migration, one can expect to see most of the migrant warblers that pass through New Jersey, as well as many of the other passerines,

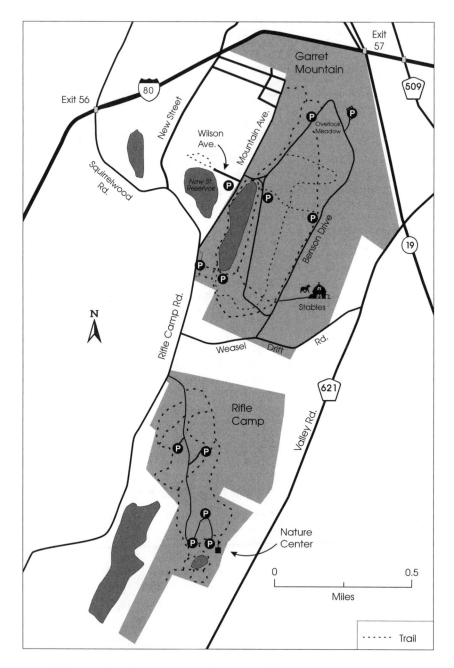

Map 30. Garret Mountain Reservation and Rifle Camp Park

from flycatchers through finches, that occur in the state. Even some of the more southerly species, such as Prothonotary Warbler and Yellow-throated Warbler show up occasionally. The species total rivals that of the Princeton of 30 years ago, although the numbers of birds will probably never be seen again, but at the beginning of the twenty-first century, Garret Mountain is the premier spot in the state for spring migrants.

Directions

Take I-80 to Exit 56A (Squirrelwood Rd., West Paterson). Drive south on Squirrelwood Rd. for 0.4 miles and bear right onto Rifle Camp Rd. Go about 0.2 miles and park on the left, just past the intersection with Mountain Ave. An alternative spot to park that fills up early is reached by turning left onto Mountain Ave., driving about 0.2 miles to a parking area on the left, just across the small bridge. [DeLorme 26, N-7]

Birding

Garret Mountain is at its best from the end of April through the third week in May, but continues to attract migrants into early June. It is much less frequently birded during the autumn migration, but can be a very productive area at that season, as well. The secret to Garret's productivity in spring appears to stem from its position atop and at the very end of the First Watchung Mountain. The Watchung ridges have long been known as excellent pathways for migrant passerines, but Garret has the added bonus of being the end of the line, so to speak, for a bird following the ridges. As a result, birds that arrive during the early morning hours tend to stay in the park for most of the day. While other migrant traps tend to diminish in activity by mid-morning, Garret can produce good birding into the afternoon.

Almost any area in the park can provide good birding during the spring migration, but certain areas tend to be better than others. The trails around Barbour's Pond, especially at the north end, the west side, and the south end, are often the best, but the woods at the end of Wilson Avenue and the higher part of the park along Benson Drive can be excellent, as well. The central part of the park, enclosed by Benson Drive, is sometimes referred to as the "Dead Zone" because of the lack of activity, but it is also the best area for seeing migrant thrushes, including Swainson's, Gray-cheeked, and (presumably) Bicknell's.

One strategy commonly employed by Frank Bobowski and Ken Sampras, the deans of Garret Mountain birders and daily fixtures in the park, is to bird the area at the north end of Barbour Pond first, followed by the woods along the western shore and beyond the south end, then gradually work uphill as the morning warms. Kevin usually does the reverse and starts at the south end of the pond. Depending on word-of-mouth as to what areas are hot, a detour to the end of Wilson Avenue or just south of Overlook Meadow may be in order. It is easy to spend an entire morning tracing and retracing the many paths at Garret, as you are likely to find something new each time around.

Because so many different migrants pass through Garret Mountain in spring, it is difficult to single out any particular species as being unique. You can expect a good assortment of flycatchers (including Olive-sided Flycatcher later in May), any of the swallows over Barbour Pond and New Street Reservoir, excellent numbers of thrushes in the dead zone (especially the third week of May), all of the vireos except Philadelphia (Warbling Vireo nests along the west shore of Barbour Pond), and most of the wood-warblers (Mourning Warbler is a specialty during the last ten days of May). Scarlet Tanager and Rose-breasted Grosbeak are common, as is Baltimore Oriole. Orchard Orioles are usually present and may stay to nest. Because of the lack of suitable habitat, sparrows are not particularly abundant.

After birding Garret Mountain, you may want to make a stop at nearby Rifle Camp Reservation, also a Passaic County Park, where there are restrooms and information at the Nature Center.

🦃

Rifle Camp Park

This Passaic County park sits atop the First Watchung Mountain just south of Paterson. The habitat is similar to that of nearby Garret Mountain Reservation, although the songbird migration, while excellent in spring and fall, is not as outstanding as at Garret. It is especially good for thrushes, including Swainson's, Gray-cheeked, and probably Bicknell's, and for Olive-sided Flycatcher. In fall, hawks are visible from the Rifle Camp Nature Center.

Directions

Take I-80 to Exit 56A (Squirrelwood Rd., West Paterson). Drive south on Squirrelwood Rd. for 0.4 miles and bear right onto Rifle Camp Rd. Continue another 0.9 miles to the entrance to Rifle Camp Park, on the left. The Nature Center, where there are restrooms, is at the last parking lot, about 1 mile from the entrance. [DeLorme 26, N-7]

Wood Thrush

Birding

The trail along the cliffline above the Nature Center provides a great view of lower Hudson Valley and New York City to the east and of migrant raptors following the ridge in autumn. You can continue on this trail, which is marked by parcourse exercise stations, to make a loop through much of the park. Along the way, you will pass through open areas, picnic grounds, and woods edges where you may encounter a wide variety of migrant songbirds in May and August to September. The thrushes, Wood Thrush and Veery, plus those already mentioned, are most often encountered in the quiet, open woodlands. You may be lucky enough to hear the migrants singing, which is the only reliable way to distinguish Gray-cheeked from Bicknell's.

From the Nature Center parking lot, drive back downhill 0.2 miles to a parking lot on the left. A trail from the south corner of the lot leads downhill to a small pond that is one of the most reliable places in the state for Olive-sided Flycatcher in spring, usually in late May. Northern Waterthrush is usually here, as well, plus Ovenbird, Common Yellowthroat, Great Crested Flycatcher, and migrants. The trail makes a loop back to the parking lot.

☞

Troy Meadows

Troy Meadows, near Parsippany in eastern Morris County, has long been famous as the premier freshwater marsh in the state. Like the Great Swamp, it is a remnant of glacial Lake Passaic that once covered more than 200 square miles of north central New Jersey. The marsh is an excellent place in spring and early summer to see and hear many of the freshwater marsh birds that are otherwise difficult to find. Also, the swampy woods and overgrown fields around the edges of Troy Meadows are good for migrants in spring and fall. In winter, a variety of sparrows and wintering raptors augment the limited number of permanent residents and lingering summer visitors.

Some of the nesting marsh birds that formerly drew birders to Troy Meadows are American Bittern (now very rare), Least Bittern (now rare), Wood Duck (common), King Rail (very rare), Virginia Rail, Sora (uncommon), Alder Flycatcher, Willow Flycatcher, and Marsh Wren. Among the migrants are Philadelphia Vireo (fall), Orange-crowned Warbler (rare), Lincoln's and White-crowned sparrows, and Rusty Blackbird. Northern Harrier, Rough-legged Hawk, and (occasionally) Short-eared Owl are prime attractions in winter. Rarities that have occurred at Troy Meadows include Bald

Eagle, Golden Eagle, Sandhill Crane (two records), Sedge Wren (formerly nested), Northern Shrike, and Yellow-headed Blackbird.

Because of the proximity of I-80 and I-280, which significantly reduced the size of Troy Meadows, it is now difficult to hear the early-morning calls of distant marsh birds due to the traffic from the highways. Nearby development and consequent siltation have reduced the value of the area to wildlife. Although it is seldom visited by birders anymore, it remains an interesting and worthwhile area to bird, and can still produce many of the expected marsh birds.

Directions

There are several points of access to Troy Meadows; to reach the best area: From Bergen or Passaic counties, take I-80 west to Exit 47 (US 46 West). Make a U-turn at the first opportunity, and head east on US 46. About 0.3 miles after you go under I-80, bear right onto Edwards Rd. Go 0.8 miles to the stop sign at New Rd., and turn right. Cross over I-280, and turn right onto a service road. Do *not* turn onto the entrance ramp to I-280, but carefully continue just beyond it to a parking area on the left at the end of the guard rails, *after* you turn right to parallel I-280. Here an old dirt road leads south into the woods. When parking and walking, watch out for broken glass and other litter. [DeLorme 31, C-25]

From the rest of northeastern or southern New Jersey or the Philadelphia area, take either the Garden State Parkway or the New Jersey Turnpike north to I-280. Go west on I-280 to Exit 1 (Edwards Rd.); turn left, cross over I-280, and proceed as described in the preceding paragraph.

From central New Jersey, take I-287 north to Exit 41A (I-80), then go east on I-80 for about 2 miles to Exit 47 (I-280). Take I-280 for 1 mile to the first exit (Exit 1). Turn right, go about 50 feet and take the first right turn. Park on the left at the end of the guard rail.

From northwestern New Jersey, take I-80 east to I-280 and proceed as just described.

Birding

The best area for marsh birds was formerly the boardwalk that runs for more than 2 miles along a power line that crosses the meadows from I-280 on the northwest to Willow Pl., off Ridgedale Ave. in East Hanover, on the southeast. Unfortunately, the boardwalk has mostly collapsed and is no longer safe to walk. With wading boots you can explore the edges of the marsh, but beware of the deep muck if you lose your footing.

Early morning is the best time to visit Troy Meadows, as this is when the marsh birds are most vocal. The hour before dawn is a good time to listen for

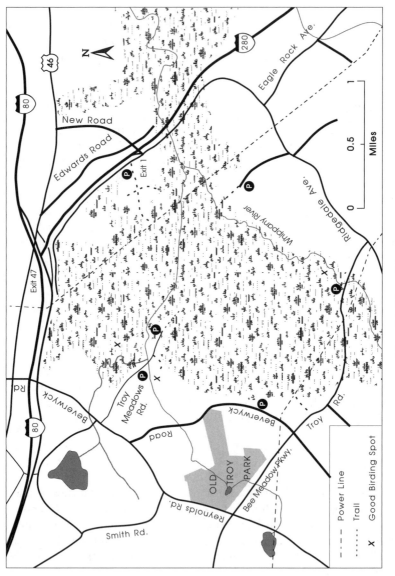

Map 31. Troy Meadows

Power Line – – – –
Trail ....
Good Birding Spot x

the *coo-coo-coo* of the Least Bittern and the "pumping" of American Bittern. Late April and May are best for these species, and for Virginia Rail and Sora. After dawn, patience may be rewarded with a glimpse of some of these species; a tape recording of the calls is also helpful in luring them into view, but use tapes sparingly so as not to disturb the birds unduly.

To reach the edge of the marsh, follow the dirt road from the parking area into the woods for a couple of hundred yards. Along the way, you will pass through wet deciduous woodland that is excellent for migrant songbirds, including a wide variety of warblers. When you come to a field, take the middle path across it toward some more woods, continuing a short distance through these to the edge of a large marsh. This whole area is becoming increasingly overgrown, so you may have to do a little exploring to find a path to the marsh.

In addition to the species already noted, birds resident in the marsh during the nesting season are Great Blue Heron (you can see their nests in the trees ahead), Green Heron (common), Mallard, Belted Kingfisher (nests nearby), Eastern Kingbird, Tree Swallow, Yellow Warbler, Common Yellowthroat, Swamp Sparrow, and Red-winged Blackbird (the last four abundant). Willow Flycatcher and Marsh Wren are very common in this section of the meadows; Alder Flycatcher is rare. Look for Wood Ducks around the many houses scattered through the marsh. One especially impressive feature of the marsh is the number of muskrat houses; they occupy every available patch of water as far as the eye can see.

Retracing your steps to your car, you can take side trails to the left or right to explore more of the wooded areas at this site. To your right at the open field is an old homestead with some large evergreens that occasionally harbor Long-eared Owls or a Great Horned Owl in winter. Red-tailed Hawks nest in the woods nearby, as do Great Horned Owl and Barred Owl. Eastern Screech-Owl can be found throughout the area. You may be fortunate enough to encounter a Red Fox; this attractive resident is common at Troy Meadows.

Troy Meadows Road

To reach the next stop at Troy Meadows, return to your car, drive back over I-280 on New Rd. for about 0.6 miles to the traffic light at US 46, and turn left. Go west on US 46 for about 2 miles to the traffic light at Beverwyck Rd. and turn left. Go about 0.8 miles and turn left onto Troy Meadows Rd. After about one-half mile you will come to a pipeline right-of-way; beyond this the pavement ends and the road enters a swampy woodland. You can continue another 0.3 miles to the end of the road, where there is a dirt parking area, or park on the right at the metal gate between the pipeline and the end of the road. If you follow the path behind the gate, it will soon join the pipeline in an area where Pileated Woodpeckers have nested in recent years.

Return to the road and walk the pipeline northeast (toward I-80) for a couple of hundred feet, then take the path on the right. In a short distance you will come to a metal ladder-type bridge across a stream. Search this area in winter for Red-headed Woodpecker and sparrows.

Bird along the road between the pipeline and the end of the road, then walk along the line of trees that heads southeast from the end of the road out into Troy Meadows. This tree line follows what was once a road that crossed the meadows. Here you will find many of the species that occur in the northern part of the marsh, but not as much variety. This is a good spot for Virginia Rail and Alder Flycatcher. Tree Swallows nest in the boxes put out for them.

Beverwyck Road

This spot on the southern edge of Troy Meadows can be reached by returning to Beverwyck Rd. and turning left. Drive south on Beverwyck for about 1.5 miles (Beverwyck makes a sharp left after about 250 yards), and turn left into a paved parking area. If you come to South Hall Ct., on the left, you have gone 100 feet too far.

At the east side of the driveway, a path will take you to a pipeline, another good spot for Alder Flycatcher. Turn right and walk south along the pipeline toward Troy Rd. The shrubby overgrown fields on both sides of the pipeline are good for Willow Flycatcher in summer and sparrows in the fall. Lincoln's Sparrow is regular in October, along with Chipping, Field, Savannah, Vesper, Fox, Song, Swamp, White-throated and White-crowned (uncommon) sparrows, and Dark-eyed Junco. Orange-crowned Warbler has been found in the weedy fields in fall, and both Henslow's Sparrow and Clay-colored Sparrow have occurred.

Return to your car and go left onto Beverwyck Rd., then make the left turn at the traffic light onto Troy Rd. Go about 1 mile to a parking area on the left, just before the bridge over the Whippany River. Follow the path north along the river for a few hundred feet to another good area for Alder Flycatcher. The birds normally do not nest in the same area every year, so you may have to search for them.

☝

Old Troy Park

This 100-acre county park in eastern Morris County is known for its excellent passerine migration, especially in fall. It gained fame during the 1970s as the home of a male Lawrence's Warbler; this bird (or its progeny) returned to the park in spring for a dozen years, last appearing in 1981. Thirty or more species of warbler are found here during August and September, along with most *Empidonax* flycatchers and many thrushes, vireos, and sparrows.

Among the sought-after species seen here are Yellow-bellied (regular in fall) and Acadian (summer) flycatchers, Gray-cheeked Thrush (mainly fall), Philadelphia Vireo (regular in fall), Kentucky, Connecticut (fall), and Mourning warblers, and Lincoln's Sparrow.

Directions

See Map 32. Take I-80 west to Exit 47 (Parsippany). Go about 1 mile to the traffic light at Beverwyck Rd. and turn left (from the west, take I-80 to Exit 46, Beverwyck Rd. and turn right). Take Beverwyck Rd. for 1 mile to a fork, and bear right onto Reynolds Rd. Follow this for 0.6 miles to the park entrance on the left. A display board at the parking lot shows a map of the park; there are many trails, but they are not marked. If the gate is closed, continue another 0.1 miles to another gate on the left, where there is room to park. [DeLorme 31, C-22]

From the south, take I-287 to Exit 39 (Rt. 10 East, Whippany). Take Rt. 10 for about 0.7 miles to the Parsippany exit, then turn left onto Parsippany Rd. (Rt. 511). Just after crossing over Rt. 10 (200 yards), take the right turn onto Reynolds Rd. The park entrance is about 1.4 miles ahead, on the right.

Birding

The trails can be covered in an hour of leisurely birding. Start at the far (east) side of the picnic area and follow the trail into the woods. When the trail forks, you can go either way, because you should return on the other. The left fork leads to some of the more mature deciduous woodland, which can be excellent for warblers and other songbirds in spring. Eventually, the trail leads downhill to the pond. The pond was once good for ducks and shorebirds, but was "improved" to remove most of the vegetation around and in it, and has seldom had much since. You might still see a Green Heron or Spotted Sandpiper along the edges.

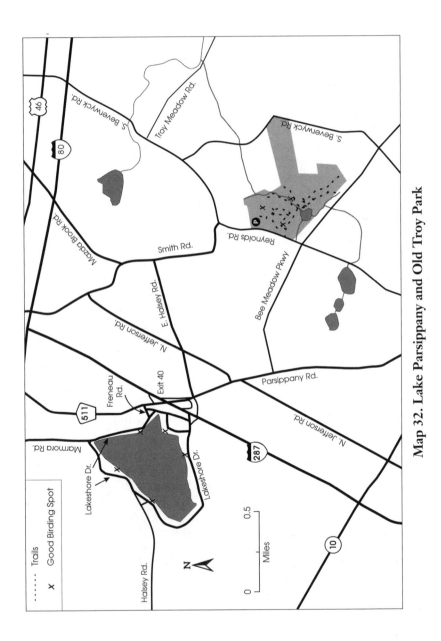

Map 32. Lake Parsippany and Old Troy Park

Continue on the trail past the pond and up the old road where there is the second gate mentioned above. Just before the gate, the trail turns right and goes through overgrown second-growth woodland until it rejoins the other fork near the picnic area.

🦆

Lake Parsippany

This small, artificial lake in eastern Morris County attracts a surprising diversity of waterfowl, primarily in late fall/early winter before the lake freezes, and in early spring after the ice has thawed. Averaging less than one-half mile across and nowhere very deep, Lake Parsippany is especially popular with diving ducks. When the water is frozen, gulls use the ice as a roosting area, and large numbers of them gather on the thawing ice in late February or March.

Directions

From the south take I-287 through Morristown. Take Exit 40 (Lake Parsippany) to the traffic light at Parsippany Rd. Turn left, cross over I-287, then take the first left turn onto Freneau Rd. (0.3 miles). Go immediately left onto Califon Rd. for 0.3 miles, then bear right at the T intersection onto Georgene Ct., which ends at Lake Shore Dr. after one short block. Continue straight ahead on Lake Shore Dr. This is the starting point for the loop drive. Lake Shore Dr. runs all the way around the lake; the complete loop is 2.3 miles.

From the north or east, take I-80 to I-287 in Parsippany, then take I-287 south for 1 mile to Exit 40B (Lake Shore Dr., Lake Parsippany). The exit puts you on Georgene Ct. at Califon Rd. Georgene Ct. ends at Lake Shore Dr. in one short block. Continue as described above. [DeLorme 31, C-21]

Birding

There are several good vantage points for scanning the lake; a spotting scope is helpful. The best place is just past the spillway, 0.2 miles from the starting point at Lake Shore Dr. There is a strip of grass and trees along the right and space to park between the Johnson Beach bathhouse and a boathouse belonging to the Lake Parsippany Property Owners Association. No Trespassing signs are posted, but at the seasons you will be there no one shows any concern for birders. From here continue around to the opposite shore, where the road is close to the lake from mile 1.0 to mile 1.6. Another good viewing spot is at Drewes Beach, 2.0 miles from the start.

During October the first migrant diving ducks appear. Ruddy Duck is common, with flocks of up to 500, and is joined in November by good numbers of Common Mergansers. Bufflehead, Lesser Scaup, Canvasback, and Ring-necked Duck are present in small numbers, while Redhead, Common Goldeneye, and Hooded and Red-breasted mergansers drop in occasionally. Other diving birds also appear: American Coot can be abundant, Common Loon and Horned and Pied-billed grebes are regular, and Red-necked Grebe has been found a few times. A variety of dabbling ducks stop in for brief visits, but only the resident Mallards remain.

After the lake freezes over in December, gulls gather to roost on the ice. In some years there are hundreds, in other years only a few dozen, but with the elimination of garbage dumps in the area, gull numbers have been greatly diminished. The less common gulls, Glaucous, Iceland, and Lesser Black-backed are seldom seen here anymore.

In the spring, as soon as there is open water, the diving birds start to re-appear. Most of the same birds present in fall also occur in spring. Common Mergansers are especially plentiful, and March to April is the best time to look for Red-necked Grebe (very rare). Spring 2001 produced some spectacular numbers of birds, with at least 19 species of waterfowl on the lake in mid-March, including an unprecedented 3,500 Ring-necked Ducks.

After completing the loop, you will be back at the intersection of Georgene Ct. and Lake Shore Dr. To return to I-287 southbound, turn left and follow Georgene Ct. two short blocks to the entrance ramp. To reach I-287 northbound, turn left onto Califon Rd., follow it back to Freneau Rd., then turn right onto Parsippany Rd. Cross over the Interstate and take the entrance ramp on the right marked I-287 North.

▼

Jockey Hollow

(Morristown National Historical Park)

The Jockey Hollow section of Morristown National Historical Park preserves more than 1,000 acres of land rich in history. It was here that General George Washington set up quarters for his Continental Army during the winters of 1777–78 and 1779–80. The Morristown area provided a source of food, water, and fuel wood, while the nearby Watchung Ridges enabled the lookouts to observe the activities of the British, 30 miles to the east in New York City. In addition to its historical attributes, the park is also an excellent place to observe spring migration and has a good variety of breeding birds.

Jockey Hollow today probably looks much the way it did 200 years ago when Washington's troops camped here, except that the forest is a gradually maturing second-growth woodland of maples, oak, hickories, and towering Tulip trees rather than the mature forest that existed then. The American Chestnut that dominated the forest in Colonial times is gone, a victim of the Chestnut blight; only short-lived sprouts remain as reminders of this magnificent tree.

A few fields around the old Wick farm and several parade grounds are the only open areas in the park. The rest is upland deciduous forest that harbors a good variety of migrant and breeding birds in spring and summer. Among the more noteworthy species are Winter Wren (March to April and October), Pileated Woodpecker, Brown Creeper (all year), Louisiana Waterthrush (April to July), Northern Waterthrush (May to September), Hooded Warbler (May to August) and Kentucky Warbler (May to July). Fall migration is more easily observed elsewhere; in winter, Jockey Hollow is as barren of birds as it is of leaves.

Directions

From the north, take I-287 south to Exit 33 (Harter Rd.). From the exit ramp go left onto Harter Rd. and follow it for about 0.9 miles to Mount Kemble Ave. (Rt. 202). Go left (south) for about 2.2 miles to the traffic light at Tempe Wick Rd. Turn right and go 1.4 miles to the sign at the park entrance road, on the right. Follow the entrance road for 0.3 miles to the Visitor Center parking area. The Visitor Center is open from 9:00 A.M. to 5:00 P.M. daily, except Thanksgiving, Christmas, and New Year's Day. Park roads are open every day of the year; the official opening time is 9:00 A.M., but in practice the gates are open by 7:30 A.M. or earlier, and close at sunset. [DeLorme 30, H-14]

From the south, take I-287 north to Exit 30B (Rt. 202, N. Maple Ave.). Watch for the brown signs with white lettering that direct you to the exit for Jockey Hollow—do *not* take Exit 30A (N. Maple Ave., Basking Ridge), which comes just before the Rt. 202 exit. Follow N. Maple for 0.2 miles to the traffic light at Rt. 202. Turn right onto Rt. 202 and go about 1.8 miles to the traffic light at Tempe Wick Rd. Turn left and proceed as described in the preceding paragraph.

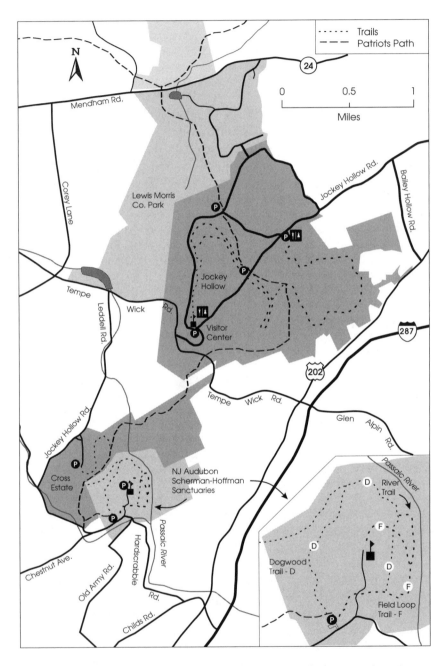

Map 33. Jockey Hollow (Morristown National Historical Park)

Birding

An extensive network of trails and fire roads covers the park (see the map). The most productive for birding are generally the Aqueduct Trail and the Wildflower Trail, both of which parallel a stream that has some swampy areas and that passes between wooded hillsides with a variety of birds. To reach the parking lot where these trails start, take Cemetery Rd. from the Visitor Center for 1.2 miles to the junction of Grand Parade Rd. Go right on Grand Parade for about 0.6 miles to Jockey Hollow Rd. Turn right and go about 0.4 miles to the parking lot, on the right.

The starting point for the Aqueduct Trail is at the far end of the parking lot. The trail gradually works its way uphill along the stream to a point just below Cemetery Rd., then turns back to finish near its starting point. Round trip is about 1.3 miles; the walking is easy, but the trail can be very muddy in spring.

The Wildflower Trail is located on the opposite (south) side of Jockey Hollow Rd. One end of it is near the entrance to the parking lot, the other is a couple of hundred feet beyond the parking lot, just past the bridge over the stream. Start at the bridge and check for Eastern Phoebes. The Wildflower Trail is somewhat more strenuous than the Aqueduct Trail, but is by no means difficult. There is a short loop (about one-half mile) and a long loop (about 1 mile). This trail, too, can be very muddy in spring. You must cross the stream on rocks in several places, which can be tricky if the water is high.

The two trails have similar birds. Late winter and early spring is a good time to look for woodpeckers, as they tend to be active and noisy. Red-bellied, Downy, Hairy, and Pileated woodpeckers and Northern Flicker are all fairly common; Yellow-bellied Sapsucker is an uncommon migrant. The park is especially known for its resident Pileated Woodpeckers. Listen for their loud, bugle-like call (slower than the similar call of the Flicker) or slow, resonant drumming.

By early April, the first Eastern Phoebes and Louisiana Waterthrushes will have arrived and your chances of finding a migrant Winter Wren are good. Broad-winged Hawk, a common breeder, usually turns up by the middle of the month. The bulk of the migrant and breeding songbirds do not begin to appear until the end of April, and the middle two weeks of May is the time of greatest activity.

The list of migrants includes many flycatchers (Yellow-bellied mainly in fall), all of the thrushes (Gray-cheeked and, presumably, Bicknell's), both kinglets, five vireos (Philadelphia in fall only), most of the warblers, and a variety of sparrows, blackbirds, and finches. Solitary Sandpiper, Spotted Sandpiper and Common Snipe have been found along the streams in spring and a variety of hawks can be expected overhead during the fall migration.

Many of the spring migrants remain to nest. The breeding birds, some of which are permanent residents, include Black-billed and Yellow-billed cuckoos, Least and Acadian flycatchers, Eastern Kingbird, Tree and Barn swallows, Brown Creeper, Carolina and House wrens, Eastern Bluebird, White-eyed, Yellow-throated, Warbling, and Red-eyed vireos, Blue-winged, Yellow, Chestnut-sided, Black-and-White, Worm-eating, Kentucky, Hooded (rare), and Canada warblers, American Redstart, Northern and Louisiana Waterthrushes, Rose-breasted Grosbeak, Indigo Bunting, Chipping, Field, and Song sparrows. Most of the other familiar species of deciduous woodlands are here as well.

Winter is the bleakest season at Jockey Hollow, as in all New Jersey deciduous forests. A few wintering hawks may be present, including any of the accipiters. Northern Saw-whet Owls have been found roosting in the Red Cedars near the Wildflower Trail. Field, Fox (rare), Song, White-throated, and American Tree sparrows and Dark-eyed Juncos inhabit the woods and field edges at this season, and are occasionally joined by winter finches.

To return to the Visitor Center from the parking lot for the Aqueduct and Wildflower Trails, continue on Jockey Hollow Rd. for about 0.7 miles. There are two other entrances to the park (see map); one of these is through Lewis Morris County Park, a 750-acre unit of the Morris County Park system. The habitat here is similar to Jockey Hollow, but the park also has numerous picnic areas and playing fields. The other entrance is from Western Ave., which runs south from Morristown to the northeastern boundary of the park, where it becomes Jockey Hollow Rd.

The nearby Cross Estate section of the park regularly has nesting Kentucky Warbler. Return to the entrance on Tempe Wick Rd. and turn right. Go 0.75 miles to Jockey Hollow Rd., and turn left. The entrance to the park is about 1.2 miles on the left. Follow the entrance road to the parking lot and walk the trail to the left, listening for the *churree-churree-churree* of the warbler.

🦆
Great Swamp National Wildlife Refuge

Great Swamp NWR is an 8,000-acre refuge consisting primarily of hardwood swamp, marsh, and some open water; in addition it has areas of upland deciduous woods, overgrown fields, and pastures maintained by periodic mowing. The swamp escaped becoming the New York metropolitan area's fourth major airport only through the efforts of concerned citizens; today it is a haven for wildlife in the midst of southern Morris County's ever-expanding suburbia.

The refuge is divided into a wilderness area and a management area. The wilderness area was established by an Act of Congress in 1968, and comprises the eastern two-thirds of the swamp. It has a number of maintained trails, but is otherwise left untouched. The management area, the western one-third of the swamp, has several large ponds, where water levels are controlled to provide optimal habitat for the resident and migrant waterfowl, and numerous fields that are mowed periodically to provide feeding and nesting habitat for a wide variety of wildlife. You can drive along Pleasant Plains Rd., which bisects the area, and you can walk the trails and visit the observation blinds at the Wildlife Observation Center off Long Hill-New Vernon Rd.

More than 200 species of birds occur on the refuge, plus a wide variety of mammals, reptiles, amphibians, and fish. About 90 species of birds nest here. The mammals most likely to be encountered are the abundant White-tailed Deer and Muskrat, plus Gray Squirrel, Chipmunk, Raccoon, and Eastern Cottontail. Opossum, Long-tailed Weasel, Striped Skunk, and Red Fox are all common, but highly nocturnal. River Otter are seen on occasion. Among the more interesting reptiles and amphibians are the state-endangered Bog Turtle and Blue-spotted Salamander.

Directions

All directions for locations within Great Swamp NWR start at the Wildlife Observation Center (WOC) on Long Hill-New Vernon Rd. in Harding Township, Morris County. The WOC can be reached as follows: From the east, take Rt. 24 west to the Morris Ave. exit in Summit; this puts you on River Rd. Follow River Rd. south for 1.1 miles, cross the bridge over the Passaic River into Chatham, and take the first left, also called River Rd. After a traffic light at 1.3 miles, continue straight ahead on River Rd. for one-half mile and bear right at the fork when the road curves to the left; you are still on River Rd. Continue for 1.4 miles and turn right onto Fairmount Ave. Take the second left turn (0.2 miles) and follow Meyersville Rd. 2.5 miles to the circle in Meyersville. Turn right onto New Vernon Rd. and go 1.9 miles to the WOC entrance, on the left, marked by a small stone gate. On the way, you will cross White Bridge Rd. and the name of the road you are on will change (there are no markers, however) from New Vernon Rd. to Long Hill Rd. when you cross from Long Hill Township into Harding Township by the refuge sign. [DeLorme 31, K-17]

From the north, take I-287 south to Exit 33 (Harter Rd.), and stay to the right as you come around the cloverleaf onto Harter Rd. Go 0.3 miles and

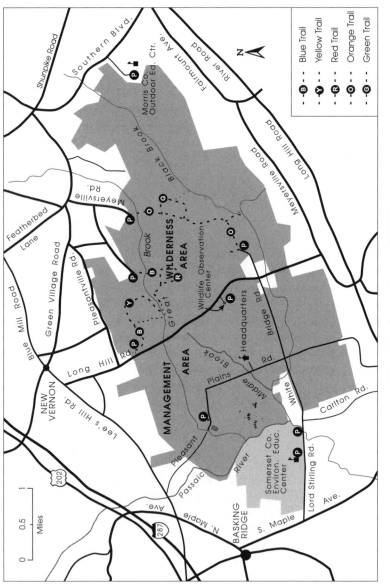

-🅑- -	Blue Trail
-🅨- -	Yellow Trail
-🅡- -	Red Trail
-🅞- -	Orange Trail
-🅖- -	Green Trail

Map 34. Great Swamp NWR

turn right onto James St. Proceed 1.1 miles, turn right on Blue Mill Rd., and drive 0.8 miles, staying left at the fork and proceeding through the traffic light, where the road name changes to Lee's Hill Rd. Go 0.4 miles and turn left onto Long Hill Rd. opposite the Harding Township School. The WOC entrance is 2.2 miles ahead, on the right.

From the south, take I-287 north to Exit 30A (N. Maple Ave., Basking Ridge). Follow N. Maple for one-half mile to the first traffic light. Turn left onto Madisonville Rd., and go 2.7 miles (the name changes to Lee's Hill Rd. when you cross a small dam). Turn right onto Long Hill Rd. (opposite the Harding Township School) and proceed 2.2 miles to the WOC entrance, on the right.

Birding

The Great Swamp can be interesting at any season, but the most productive times to visit are during spring migration in April and May and the nesting season, which is primarily May through July. The nesting season is a time of great activity in the swamp, with almost ninety species of birds found nesting in 1983, and about one hundred species known or suspected to have nested within the past 20 years. The abundance and variety of the breeding birds make the swamp an exciting place to visit at this season. In the fall, there are many migrant passerines and waterfowl, but the dense vegetation makes them hard to see. In winter, raptors and sparrows abound.

The area is called a swamp for good reason, and many of the trails will be wet or muddy. Waterproof footgear, although not an absolute necessity, can make your outing more comfortable. The abundant deerflies can make many of the woodland trails unbearable from late June to mid-August. A hat is a must and a headnet can provide welcome relief from these persistent insects.

Wildlife Observation Center

The WOC has a large parking lot, self-service information center, restrooms, and trails to two observation blinds, which are good for viewing some of the birdlife, especially in the spring and also in winter if the bird feeders are filled. Take the right trail past the restrooms to the boardwalk that leads to one blind. In spring and summer, watch for Virginia Rails and Common Yellowthroat around the boardwalk; Swamp Sparrow is here at any season. The blind may permit close looks at Great Blue Heron, Green Heron, Wood Duck, Green-winged and Blue-winged Teal, Mallard, or perhaps something unusual.

Returning to the parking lot area, take the left trail that leads to the other blind. This is a longer trail (about 0.3 miles), and leads through wet woodland that has many of the common birds of the swamp. The blind looks out over some small ponds and fields. Wood Ducks can be closely observed here, especially in the spring, and Great Blue Herons from the nearby heronries are frequently seen feeding. The Great Swamp is the best place in the state and one of the best in the country for observing Wood Duck. More than 500 pairs usually nest on the refuge and can be easily found in the spring on the many ponds or sitting on top of the hundreds of nest boxes provided for them. Great Blue Herons have also established several colonies in the swamp.

Rarities show up here on occasion—Bald Eagle, Northern and Loggerhead shrikes, and Yellow-headed Blackbird have all been seen from the blind. If the bird feeder near the blind is kept filled in winter, it offers the chance to see some of the local birds at close range. Red-bellied Woodpecker, Blue Jay, Black-capped Chickadee, Tufted Titmouse, White-breasted Nuthatch, Red-winged Blackbird, and Northern Cardinal are all regular visitors to the feeder, as are Tree, White-throated, Swamp, and Song sparrows.

Long Hill Road Trail Access

The Long Hill Rd. parking area provides access to several trails in the Wilderness Area. From the WOC entrance road, turn left onto Long Hill Rd. and go 1.2 miles to the small parking area on the right at the pipeline clearing. The Blue Trail meanders through the swamp for 2.4 miles to the parking area at Woodland Rd., but you can make a shorter 1.8-mile loop by returning on the Yellow Trail. Along the trail you should encounter many of the typical birds of the swamp. Listen for woodpeckers—five species may be nesting in the woods: Red-bellied, Downy, Hairy, and Pileated woodpeckers, plus Northern Flicker. All but Pileated are common.

Just before the junction with the Yellow Trail, the Blue Trail comes to Great Brook, continues through some mature woods, then follows the brook for a while. This is a good area in spring migration for flycatchers (including Olive-sided), thrushes, vireos, and warblers. In August and September watch for Yellow-bellied Flycatcher and Philadelphia Vireo.

If you continue on the Blue Trail, you veer south away from the brook for several hundred yards, then come to a brushy field where the trail forks. The right fork is the Red Trail, which makes a one-half mile loop through wet woodlands with fairly mature stands of oak and maple, and through some scrubby areas dominated by Gray Birch, before eventually rejoining the Blue Trail.

Some of the birds that nest along the Red Trail are Wood Duck, American Woodcock, Yellow-billed Cuckoo, Eastern Screech and Barred owls, Least Flycatcher, Eastern Kingbird, White-eyed Vireo, Tree Swallow, Brown Creeper, Carolina Wren, Eastern Bluebird, Northern Mockingbird, Brown Thrasher, Blue-winged and Black-and-White warblers, American Redstart, Scarlet Tanager, Rose-breasted Grosbeak, Chipping, Field, and Song sparrows, plus all the common species of deciduous woods and shrubby fields listed.

Woodland Road

From the Long Hill parking area, go right on Long Hill Rd. for 0.2 miles to Pleasantville Rd. Turn right, go 1.7 miles to the first right turn, which is Miller Rd. Proceed on Miller for 1.0 miles to the T at Woodland Rd. Turn right and go one-half mile to the parking area at the end. The east end of the Blue Trail begins here, and you can make a 1-mile loop via the Red Trail, already described.

About 100 yards down the trail, you will come to a bridge across Great Brook. To your left is a large expanse of marsh. If the water is low, this may hold a small variety of shorebirds in the spring, including Greater and Lesser yellowlegs, Solitary, Spotted, and Least sandpipers, and occasionally a Semipalmated or Pectoral Sandpiper, Dunlin, or Short-billed Dowitcher. The Blue Trail passes through a grove of large old American Beech trees where Scarlet Tanagers and Veeries abound; otherwise the birds are mainly the same as those noted for the Red Trail.

Meyersville Road

The old Meyersville Rd., marked as the Orange Trail, can be reached from either end. To reach the north end, follow the directions for Woodland Rd., but turn left at the T intersection of Miller Rd. with Woodland Rd. and go one-half mile to Meyersville Rd. Turn right and continue 0.7 miles to the parking area. To reach the south end from the WOC, go right on Long Hill Rd. for 0.8 miles to White Bridge Rd. Turn left and proceed 0.6 miles to the parking area.

Meyersville Rd. passes through a variety of habitats, including Red Maple swamp, drier deciduous woods, overgrown fields, marsh, and even an old orchard and some Norway Spruce plantings. The road itself is only about 1.5 miles, but there are two side trail loops (shown on trail map) and a couple of dead-end spurs that increase the total trail length to about 3 miles. Because of the diversity of habitat, most of the breeding birds of the Great Swamp can be found here.

Starting from the southern end, you will be near a Great Blue Heron rookery and may see the birds flying to and from feeding areas. Near the beginning of the trail, there is usually a Least Flycatcher in the wet woods on the right. Eight species of flycatcher were found nesting along this road in 1983, including all four of the state's breeding species of *Empidonax* flycatchers. A short distance ahead a loop trail branches off to the left through a field and near some ponds surrounded by willows. Both Alder and Willow

White-throated Sparrow

SHAWNEEN FINNEGAN 2001

flycatchers have been found nesting here, although the Alder has not occurred recently. Willow Flycatcher is common and widespread throughout
the swamp, but the only other spot where Alder Flycatcher has nested is in
the management area off Pleasant Plains Rd. Acadian Flycatcher was found
nesting in 1983 for the first time in many years; the pair was in a wooded area
containing some large maples near the north end of Meyersville Rd. The
other flycatchers nesting here are Eastern Wood-Pewee, Eastern Phoebe,
Great Crested Flycatcher, and Eastern Kingbird.

Meyersville Rd. is a good place for hawks (Red-tailed, Red-shouldered,
and American Kestrel) and owls (Screech, Great Horned, and Barred), and
formerly had nesting Ruffed Grouse, although they seem to have disappeared
from the refuge. The marsh on the east side of the road opposite the orchard,
about one-half mile from the northern end, has Least Bittern and Virginia
Rail. King Rail occurs in migration and could stay to nest. Near the northern
end of the road, a footbridge crosses Loantaka Brook; the marsh here has occasional bitterns and several Marsh Wrens.

Pleasant Plains Road

A drive along Pleasant Plains Rd. through the management area can be very
productive for hawks in the winter and for Eastern Bluebird at any other season. Red-tailed Hawk is common along the road from November to March
(also nests here); other species to be looked for are Red-shouldered Hawk,
Rough-legged Hawk (rare), Northern Harrier, and American Kestrel. Turkey
Vultures from the nearby Bernardsville roost are conspicuous during most
winters, and are often joined by a few Black Vultures. Red-headed Woodpeckers often winter in the refuge, mainly in the management area near the
closed bridge at Primrose Brook.

To reach Pleasant Plains Rd. from the WOC, turn right onto Long Hill
Rd. and go 0.9 miles to the intersection with White Bridge Rd. Turn right
and go 1.1 miles to the next intersection, which is Pleasant Plains Rd. Go
right again, and in 0.3 miles you will come to a gate at the refuge boundary.
The gate is open from 8:00 A.M. (often earlier) to dusk. The gate at the far
end, at the bridge over Primrose Brook, a distance of 1.5 miles, is perma-
nently closed. Except for the short distance from the main gate to the long
driveway on the right, which leads to the refuge headquarters, the road is
unpaved and can get quite muddy at times. The office is open from 8:00
A.M. to 4:30 P.M., weekdays, and has bird checklists, trail maps, and other
information.

As you drive along Pleasant Plains Rd., watch the wires and trees for
Eastern Bluebirds. The refuge maintains a very successful nest-box program
and now has several dozen pairs of bluebirds nesting in both boxes and natural cavities. The birds are conspicuous most of the year, especially in the late

summer after the young have fledged, though the numbers in winter are somewhat reduced. Other species in the fields, woods, and man-made ponds along the road are Canada Goose, Wood Duck, American Woodcock, Great Horned Owl (in old Red-tailed Hawk nests), Tree Swallow (in boxes), Eastern Meadowlark (rarely), plus many of the more common species. In early May, hordes of swallows of all six species swarm over the fields in search of insects. All but Cliff Swallow are seen throughout the summer, although Bank and N. Rough-winged swallows do not nest within the refuge boundaries.

Adjacent to the driveway to the headquarters is a shallow pond that is sometimes full of water, sometimes dry. This new addition (1999) can be very productive for shorebirds in spring and fall and for waterfowl later in the year. It regularly has up to 50 Common Snipe in late fall–early winter, and has attracted such rarities as Eurasian Green-winged Teal and Ruff. It is especially popular with Green-winged Teal, Northern Pintail, Northern Shoveler, and American Wigeon.

Watch the fields along Pleasant Plains for Red Fox early in the morning, especially in the spring when the kits are about and have yet to learn to fear man. About two hundred yards before the closed bridge there is a parking area and overlook on the right. The large nests in the dead trees to the north are used by Great Blue Herons and, if you visit from April to July, you will see them standing at the nests or flying to and from them on feeding forays. This spot is also a good vantage point to scan the trees to the left for Red-headed Woodpecker, which often winters here, and has had Northern Shrike on several occasions. Just before reaching the north gate, there is a man-made pond on the left that is favored by Pied-billed Grebe, Ring-necked Duck and Hooded Merganser, and occasionally other divers, such as Ruddy Duck and Lesser Scaup. At the bridge, check for Warbling Vireo and Orchard Oriole.

South Mountain Reservation

South Mountain Reservation encompasses 2,047 acres in the southwestern part of Essex County. A little over 3 miles long from north to south, it extends from the crest of the First Watchung Mountain on the east to that of the Second Watchung on the west. The west branch of the Rahway River runs the entire length of the preserve. Most of the reservation is covered with mature deciduous woods, and small areas of thickets, fields, and conifer plantings. Because of its location along the mountain ridges, South Mountain is a good spot for migrant songbirds in spring and fall. The reservation supports most of the breeding birds expected for this primarily deciduous woodland habitat; in winter, the park is quiet and birds are scarce.

More that 200 species have been recorded in the park, including some rare or uncommon species. Many of the records of waterfowl, shorebirds, gulls, and terns are from the Orange Reservoir, located next to the zoo. The reservoir is very difficult to bird, since most of it is surrounded by a high fence that restricts the view; there are a few good vantage points for scanning the water, however. The remainder of the reservation has many places to park, picnic areas, and 20 miles each of bridle and hiking trails.

Directions

A good place to park and explore some of the trails and streams in South Mountain is the Tulip Springs picnic area.

From the south or east, take the New Jersey Turnpike or the Garden State Parkway to I-280. Go west on I-280 to Exit 10 (Northfield Ave., Orange, S. Orange, and Montclair). At the exit ramp traffic light, turn left onto Northfield Ave. and go about 2.4 miles until you pass the South Mountain Skating Arena and Turtle Back Zoo on the left. Exit right just after you pass the left turn for the zoo entrance, turn left onto Pleasant Valley Way, and proceed to the traffic light. Continue straight through the traffic light, where the road name changes to Cherry Lane. Drive about 0.9 miles, then turn left onto a park road that leads about 100 yards to the parking lot and picnic area at Tulip Springs (bear right when the road forks just after you turn off Cherry Lane). [DeLorme 31, H-1]

From the west, take I-280 east to Exit 8A (Prospect Avenue). Go south on Prospect Ave. for 1.5 miles to Northfield Rd. and turn right. The Cherry Lane intersection is about 1.4 miles ahead; proceed as described above.

Birding

The Tulip Springs and Hemlock Falls areas are excellent for migrant warblers and other songbirds in the spring. From Tulip Springs there are two ways to reach the Hemlock Falls area. You can walk along the river from the picnic area at Tulip Springs, which will lead you under South Orange Ave., and turn left onto a bridle trail about 200 yards past the underpass. Or, you can bird your way from the picnic area through the pine woods uphill along a trail marked by a yellow dot and cross South Orange Ave. on the equestrian bridge. The yellow dot trail begins just south of the parking area at Tulip Springs, on the opposite side of the road. All these areas are best explored with the help of a trail map, which is available from the Essex County

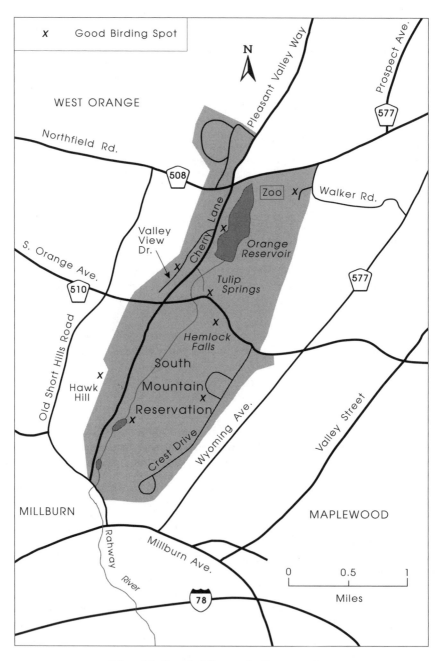

Map 35. South Mountain Reservation

Department of Parks, Recreation, and Cultural Affairs, 115 Clifton Avenue, Newark, NJ 07104.

One of the best areas in the reservation during the breeding season is the slope to the west of Crest Dr., south of South Orange Ave. There are several points of access to the numerous trails that traverse the hillside and lead down to the ponds along the Rahway River. To get to Crest Dr. from the Tulip Spring picnic area, return to Cherry Lane and turn left. Drive up the hill for about 1 mile, then turn right onto Crest Dr. In 0.25 miles, you come to a loop road that circles Summit Field; there are several parking areas along this loop. Alternatively, you can continue on Crest Dr. for 1.5 miles to the circle at the end of the road, where there is parking.

Other good birding spots include the rhododendron thickets along Valley View Dr. (turn off Cherry Lane at the Oakdale sign, about one-half mile north of Tulip Springs) and the Hawk Hill area in the southwestern part of the park. The migrant and breeding birds at South Mountain are much the same as those at nearby Eagle Rock Reservation; refer to the next section for a list of some of the species you should expect to find.

✝

Eagle Rock Reservation

This 408-acre preserve of the Essex County Park Commission sits atop the First Watchung Mountain in West Orange (with small sections extending into Verona and Montclair) at an average elevation of about 600 feet. Because of its position along this basalt ridge, Eagle Rock Reservation is an excellent spot for migrant passerines in spring and, especially, in fall. The lack of habitat variety limits the diversity of nesters, but the list of breeding birds contains some interesting species, such as Acadian Flycatcher (occasional), Northern Waterthrush, Worm-eating, Hooded, and Kentucky warblers (all three irregular), and Canada Warblers.

Directions

From northeastern or southern New Jersey, take the Garden State Parkway or the New Jersey Turnpike to their intersections with I-280. Go west on I-280 to Exit 8B, Prospect Ave. (Rt. 577), in West Orange, about 3.6 miles west of the Parkway. Drive north on Prospect Ave. for 0.4 miles to the second traffic light at Eagle Rock Ave., and turn right. Go 0.3 miles, and turn left at the entrance to Eagle Rock Reservation. [DeLorme 32, E-4]

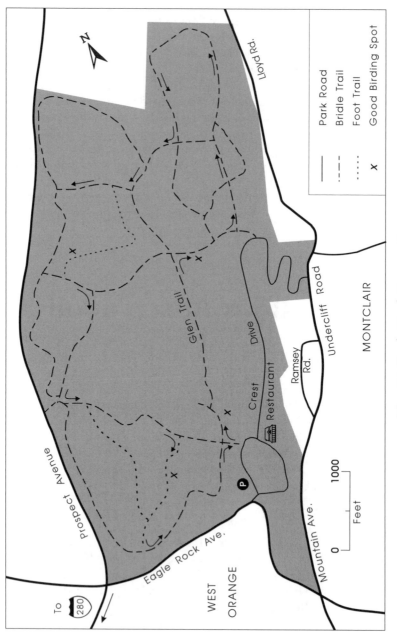

Map 36. Eagle Rock Reservation

From the west, take I-80 east to the junction with I-280, then follow I-280 for about 8 miles to Exit 8B and proceed as described in the preceding paragraph.

Birding

Follow the entrance road for about 0.4 miles, part of the way around a large oval drive, and park on the left opposite a small brick building, where another road (Crest Dr.) turns off to the right. Along the way you will pass a stone wall where you can look out to the east for a spectacular view of the New York skyline. Just past the stone wall is an elegant and expensive restaurant.

Eagle Rock Reservation has about 7 miles of bridle trails and another 3.5 miles of foot trails, which together cover every part of the park. The bridle trails are wider, better maintained, and easier to follow than the foot trails, and cover most of the same ground. There is very little equestrian traffic, especially early in the morning. The trails are easy to follow with the help of a compass and a fairly good trail map that is available from the Essex County Park Department. Avoid trails near Prospect Ave.

The vegetation is a mixture of woods and thickets typical of the hills of the Piedmont Plateau in northern New Jersey. It reflects second-growth woodland in every stage of development, with mixed oaks, black birch, aspen, and various shrubs along the dry ridgetops, and a richer forest of oaks, maples, birches, beech, tulip-tree, sweet gum, ash, dogwood, sassafras, sycamore, and many other trees and shrubs in the cooler and wetter basins and ravines. Many of the migrant and breeding birds at Eagle Rock are found in the thickets along the streams and ravines. The route suggested on Map 36 covers all these habitats.

Walk along the oval entrance road to a gravel path on the right, which leads past an old stone privy. Stay right on the gravel trail at the next intersection; this is marked as the Glen Trail on the map, but there are no posted signs. Glen Trail is one of the best birding areas in the park. Follow this trail along a stream for about 200 yards and then bear right where the trail leads left to a maintenance building.

The suggested route can be covered in a couple of hours. Some of the breeding birds you might hope to find are Black-billed and Yellow-billed cuckoos, Eastern Screech and Great Horned owls, Pileated Woodpecker, Blue-winged, Black-and-white, Worm-eating, Kentucky, Hooded, and Canada warblers (all rare to uncommon), American Redstart (rare), Northern Waterthrush, Rose-breasted Grosbeak, Indigo Bunting, and other more common species.

In migration, look for Osprey, Sharp-shinned, Red-shouldered, and Red-tailed hawks, American Kestrel, Ruby-throated Hummingbird, Yellow-bellied Sapsucker, Olive-sided, Yellow-bellied, and Least flycatchers, Eastern

Phoebe, various swallows, Red-breasted Nuthatch, Winter Wren (April and October best), kinglets, all of the thrushes, Cedar Waxwing, vireos (including Philadelphia in September), warblers, Fox, and Swamp sparrows. Winter visitors include Golden-crowned Kinglet, American Tree and White-throated sparrows, Dark-eyed Junco, and occasional winter finches such as Pine Siskin and Common Redpoll.

Eagle Rock Reservation is open from 6:00 A.M. to 10:00 P.M. To obtain a copy of the trail map, phone or write the Essex County Dept. of Parks, Recreation, and Cultural Affairs, 115 Clifton Ave., Newark, NJ 07104 (201-482-6400).

❧

Kearny Marsh

Kearny Marsh, which includes one of the better freshwater marshes in New Jersey, is located near the southern end of the Hackensack Meadowlands, in heavily urban Hudson County. The western part was created accidentally in the early 1970s, when the pumps draining an area surrounded by railroad and roadbed embankments failed to keep pace with greatly increased drainage into the site. Today, this marsh covers 342 acres, and is bordered on one edge by a 63-acre abandoned landfill overgrown with weeds, shrubs, and small trees. The eastern part is a semitidal area bounded by the New Jersey Turnpike and Amtrak Railroad Tracks, and is now much better for birds than the western part.

Kearny Marsh has become an outstanding breeding ground for a number of different waterbirds, some of which, such as Pied-billed Grebe and Ruddy Duck, rarely nest elsewhere in the state. It also provides a roost for large numbers of herons and egrets in late summer, has a good-to-excellent shorebird migration in May and July to August, and harbors a variety of unusual species in winter, including a Black-crowned Night-Heron roost. The marsh is an interesting place to visit at any season, but especially in summer.

Among the birds that have nested or are thought to have nested at Kearny Marsh during the past 20 years, the following are especially noteworthy: Pied-billed Grebe (common), Least Bittern (common), Black-crowned Night-Heron, Yellow-crowned Night-Heron (uncommon), Gadwall, Green-winged Teal, Ruddy Duck, Common Moorhen (abundant), American Coot (now rare, formerly abundant), and Blue Grosbeak. Some of the rarer or unusual species that have been found here during that time are White Ibis,

Black-necked Stilt, Ruff, Wilson's, Red-necked, and Red phalaropes, Iceland, Lesser Black-backed, and Glaucous gulls, Large-billed and Gull-billed terns, and Yellow-headed Blackbird.

Directions

From the north and south, take the New Jersey Turnpike north to Exit 15W (I-280, Newark, the Oranges). Coming north, be sure to stay left when the turnpike forks just north of Exit 14. After the tollbooth, stay to the right, following the signs for Harrison Ave. Go west on Harrison Ave. for about 0.7 miles to the traffic light at Schuyler Ave. Turn right onto Schuyler and drive north for about 1.2 miles to a traffic light and a sign on the right at the entrance to Gunnel Oval, a Kearny city park. Turn right into Gunnel Oval, drive around to the northeast corner of the park near the tennis courts, and park. [DeLorme 32, H-10]

From the west, take I-280 east to the Harrison Ave. exit in Harrison. Go left on Harrison Ave. for about 0.8 miles to the traffic light at Schuyler Ave. Turn left onto Schuyler and proceed as described in the preceding paragraph.

Birding

Birding at Kearny Marsh West is done from the shoreline of the impoundment. Some birders climb the railroad embankment that forms the north boundary and walk east along the tracks. This is **NOT** recommended, as the tracks are heavily used and one is trespassing to walk on them. From the tennis courts, walk east for a short distance to an abandoned railroad bed near the western edge of the marsh. If a low water level coincides with shorebird migration, this can be an outstanding spot.

The shorebird area can be scoped from the edge of the marsh, although the lack of height can make it difficult. This northwest corner is where the rare shorebirds noted above have been seen, however. Other species that appear here regularly in migration are Black-bellied and Semipalmated plovers, Killdeer, Greater and Lesser yellowlegs, Solitary, Spotted, Semipalmated, Least, White-rumped (rare), and Pectoral sandpipers, Short-billed Dowitcher, and Common Snipe.

It is difficult to see the entire expanse of marsh, which is largely overgrown with *Phragmites*, except for one large pond, a network of canals, and a few smaller areas of open water.

In and around the large pond, you can see the nesting species in summer. In addition to the species noted above, other nesting waterbirds are Green Heron, Canada Goose, Mallard, American Black Duck, and Gadwall. Some species that have occurred during the breeding season and may have nested are Snowy Egret, Little Blue Heron, Wood Duck, Northern Shoveler, and Sora. There are no trees or boxes for the Wood Ducks, but they might attempt to nest in the side of muskrat houses, of which there are dozens.

Kearny Marsh is especially valuable as a freshwater marsh because of the large numbers of several unusual breeding birds, most of which now nest in Kearny Marsh East. The area is one of the few breeding sites of Pied-billed Grebes in New Jersey (single pairs nest at a half-dozen other places). Similarly, the few pairs of Ruddy Duck represent virtually the entire nesting population for the state. The number of Least Bitterns is difficult to estimate because of the species' secretive nature; however, there probably are one or two dozen pairs between Kearny and the Sawmill WMA. Common Moorhen is abundant but the numbers of American Coot (formerly 400+ pairs) are down to fewer than 20 pairs, mostly in Kearny East. Late afternoon and evening in spring and summer is a good time to visit the marsh, since many of the birds are active and conspicuous at that time.

To reach Kearny Marsh East, drive back out to Schuyler Ave. and turn right. Go 1 mile to the traffic light at Belleville Pike and turn right. Continue approximately 2 miles to the Janitex plant, on the left, just before the Amtrak railroad tracks. Between the Janitex driveway and the Amtrak tracks is a second road, now paved, that runs along the tracks to the Hackensack River. Take this road to the gated fence and park outside the gate, on the right.

Walk through the gate and along the paved road, with the river on your right and impoundments on the left. Most of the species that used to nest in Kearny West now nest in Kearny East, including Pied-billed Grebe, Common Moorhen, American Coot, and Least Bittern. Ruddy Duck nests in the Kingsland impoundment at nearby DeKorte Park.

In late summer, the marsh becomes a roost for large numbers of herons and egrets from elsewhere, including Great Blue Heron, Great Egret, Tricolored Heron, and as many as 500 Snowy Egrets.

Relatively few landbirds nest at the marsh and most of these are on the landfill. The marsh is host to Marsh Wren, Yellow Warbler, Common Yellowthroat, Swamp Sparrow, and Red-winged Blackbird. The landfill accommodates Indigo Bunting, American Goldfinch, and Northern Mockingbird. Birds regularly found in migration on the landfill are Bobolink (May and July to October), a variety of warblers in the copses (May and September), and a good mix of sparrows, including White-crowned and Fox sparrows, in fall and winter.

Numerous species of gulls and terns appear at Kearny Marsh during migration and in winter. In May or late summer, Caspian, Common, Forster's, and Black terns appear. Large-billed Tern (the second North American record) and Gull-billed Tern have each been seen once. In winter, a few Iceland,

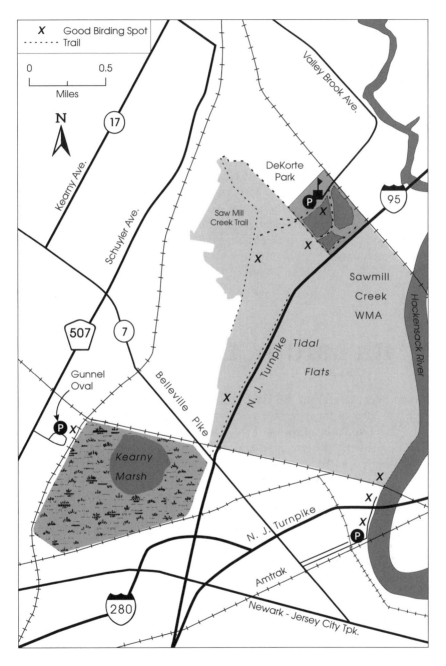

Map 37. Kearny Marsh and DeKorte Park

Lesser Black-backed, and Glaucous gulls are found amidst the large flocks of gulls on the pond.

When it is not completely frozen, the marsh usually holds some of the breeding birds that try to overwinter, such as Pied-billed Grebe, Black-crowned Night-Heron, American Coot, and Common Moorhen. Kearny East usually has some open water due to the flow of the Hackensack River. Yellow-headed Blackbird has been found a few times in winter as well as in spring and summer. Northern Harrier and Rough-legged Hawk are frequently seen here in winter.

The Sawmill Creek WMA, which lies along both sides of the New Jersey Turnpike north of the Belleville Pike, is excellent for shorebirds and waterfowl in migration, especially in May and in July to October. To reach it, walk north along the river from the gate at Kearny East to the railroad tracks that cross the river. The Sawmill marsh can be observed from the north side of the railroad embankment. Low tide is best (tides here are about three hours later than at Sandy Hook).

☝

Richard W. DeKorte Park

When birders talk about the Hackensack Meadowlands, they are usually referring to parts of the extensive Hackensack River marshes that are included in the DeKorte Park, a project of the Hackensack Meadowlands Commission (HMC). Formerly the site of several garbage dumps, the area attracts a variety of water-associated birds to the ponds and tidal mudflats. Among the unusual species that have appeared here in the past 30 years are White Ibis, Fulvous Whistling-Duck, American Golden Plover (annual), Hudsonian (annual) and Marbled godwits, Baird's (annual), Curlew, and Buff-breasted sandpipers, Ruff, Wilson's and Red-necked phalaropes, Franklin's Black-headed, Thayer's, Iceland, Lesser Black-backed and Glaucous gulls, Blue Grosbeak (formerly an annual nester), Dickcissel (nested in 1974), and Yellow-headed Blackbird.

Directions

To reach DeKorte Park from everywhere but northwestern New Jersey, take the New Jersey Turnpike to Exit 16W (Secaucus and Rutherford). Take Rt. 3 west for about 1.5 miles, then take the exit for Rt. 17 South. Follow the ramp back over Rt. 3 to a traffic light at Polito Ave., where there is a sign for DeKorte Park. Turn left, and go about 0.6 miles to the end of Polito at Valley Brook Rd., turn left, and continue about 1.7 miles to the end at the parking lot for DeKorte Park and the HMC; drive past the building and park near the southeast corner of the lot.

Alternatively, you can take the Garden State Parkway to Exit 153 (Rt. 3), then go east on Rt. 3 for about 5 miles to the second exit for Rt. 17 South (Lyndhurst); there is a sign for DeKorte Park and the HMC. Proceed straight ahead at the traffic light onto Polito Ave. Go about 0.6 miles to the end of Polito at Valley Brook Rd., turn left, and continue about 1.7 miles to the end. [DeLorme 32, F-12]

From northwestern New Jersey, take I-80 east to US 46 in Wayne, and then exit onto Rt. 3 in Clifton. Follow Rt. 3 for about 6.5 miles to the Rt. 17 South exit in Lyndhurst and proceed as above.

Birding

The best birding areas in the 2,000-acre DeKorte Park are now an impounded pool known as the shorebird pool (99 acres), a large tidal flat (581 acres), and a former garbage dump (90 acres). Some of these land uses will change substantially in the next few years; however, the impoundment and tidal flat are in a marshland preservation zone and will continue to attract shorebirds and gulls.

Late summer and fall is the shorebird season at the Meadowlands. The modern new headquarters of the HMC and its adjacent Environmental Center are on the shore of the large, shallow impoundment known to birders as the shorebird pool. It is a good spot for migrant waterfowl in spring, shorebirds in the fall (July through October), and gulls in winter. To bird it thoroughly, you must walk around the perimeter, a little more than 1.5 miles.

The water level in the shorebird pool is regulated by floodgates. If a low level is maintained in August and September, the pool provides good feeding and resting areas for migrant shorebirds. At high tide, the nearby tidal flats along the Hackensack River are submerged, and many birds seek refuge in the impoundment. Some species use the impoundment at all tides. In recent years, the water level has been kept high to reduce the threat of botulism and to keep the water deep enough to encourage ducks and wading birds to please the visitors to the HMC's catering business. Unfortunately, this means that the shorebirding is much less productive. However, you can still find most of the common species and, occasionally, phalaropes. Breeding birds include Pied-billed Grebe, Common Moorhen, Gadwall, Ruddy Duck, and Blue-winged Teal. Snowy and Common egrets, Black-crowned Night-Heron, and Glossy Ibis are regular visitors in late summer and early fall.

To bird the shorebird pool, walk south from the parking lot a short distance to a dike that runs east-west, then turn left. This is called the Transco Trail. As you walk east toward the New Jersey Turnpike, which you can see about one-half mile ahead, the pool will be on your left and the large tidal flat on your right. Large numbers of shorebirds, mainly Lesser Yellowlegs, Least and Semipalmated sandpipers, and Short-billed Dowitchers gather on the flats to feed when the tide is out. Just before you reach the Turnpike, the dike ends at a junction with a dike running north-south. Here you can turn left to continue the walk around the shorebird pool or turn right and walk along the edge of the tidal flat for about 0.3 miles. The viewing conditions in the morning are usually better on this side of the flat, especially later in the season. The tidal flats to the south on both sides of the Turnpike are part of the Sawmill Creek WMA; they can be reached on foot from the Belleville Pike (see the preceding Kearny Marsh section).

A new trail, the Sawmill Creek Trail, opened in 2001, traverses the Sawmill Creek WMA mud flats from the west end of the Transco Trail southeast for about 1.1 miles to a former landfill in Kearny. This will eventually extend to the Belleville Pike. The trail is also accessible from the Lyndhurst Nature Preserve, which is directly across the Transco Trail from the parking lot. Sawmill Creek Trail could be very productive, because it allows access to some new shorebird areas that could not previously be reached.

Winter is the season for gulls at the Meadowlands, although the numbers are greatly reduced from the days when the dumps were active. You can usually still find a Lesser Black-backed Gull or two among the roosting Herring, Great Black-backed and Ring-billed gulls, and an occasional Iceland or Glaucous Gull. Other winter visitors to the Hackensack Meadowlands are Red-tailed Hawk, Rough-legged Hawk, which can be quite common in flight years, and American Kestrel. A few ducks and shorebirds linger around the pools if the water isn't frozen, and numerous sparrows feed on the landfill on cold winter days.

➤

Liberty State Park

This 736-acre state park lies in the shadow of the Statue of Liberty, along the banks of the Hudson River in Jersey City. In addition to offering an impressive view of Miss Liberty and the Manhattan skyline, it is a good birding spot from late fall through spring. Red-necked Grebe, Great Cormorant, Eurasian Wigeon, Lesser Golden-Plover, Little, Black-headed, Iceland, and Glaucous gulls, Snowy Owl, and Boreal Chickadee are some of the more interesting birds that have been found here.

Most of Liberty State Park, which extends over abandoned and dilapidated railroad yards, is still undeveloped. The park is also home to the Liberty Science Center, which is a great place to take the kids when the birding is slow.

Directions

Take the New Jersey Turnpike Extension east from Exit 14 of the Turnpike for about 5 miles to Exit 14B (Jersey City). Stay left at the tollbooth, and turn left onto Bayview Ave., following the signs for Liberty State Park. After about 300 yards, keep to the right at a small traffic circle, where the road becomes Morris Pesin Dr. Continue about 0.3 miles farther, then turn into the first parking lot on the right. [DeLorme 33, L-15]

Birding

Scan the cove between the parking area and the jetty to the south for grebes, ducks, and gulls. Red-necked Grebes are occasionally seen here in winter. Scope the jetty, which is several hundred yards distant, for white-winged gulls. Also, look for Snowy Owl, which occur fairly regularly during invasion years. Double-crested Cormorants (year-round) and Great Cormorants (winter) also use the jetty as a resting place. Dunlin, Black-bellied Plover, and occasionally Purple Sandpiper frequent the jetty at high tide in the winter.

Continue east along the entrance drive for about 0.4 miles to the parking lot at the park office. Ring-billed Gulls gather to roost on the parking lot in winter, and should be checked for something rare. Walk south to the edge of the water, and scan for water birds—many species of grebes, loons, and waterfowl show up in the waters off the State Park during migration, and some of them stay for the winter. Among the more common ones are Brant, Canada Goose, Green-winged Teal, American Black Duck, Mallard, Gadwall, American Wigeon (plus the occasional Eurasian Wigeon), Canvasback, Greater and Lesser scaup, Common Goldeneye, Bufflehead, Red-breasted Merganser, and Ruddy Duck. Even Redhead, Long-tailed Duck, and all three scoters are found here regularly.

Follow the edge of the water east to the overlook along the river, the south end of the Liberty Walk, and scan for ducks and gulls; this is a good place to see Little Gull, especially in late spring. Continue around the edge until you reach a marsh along the north side of the entrance road. This is good for many of the puddle ducks and for Clapper Rail, and is also the best place to see Northern Harrier and Short-eared Owl in winter. For the

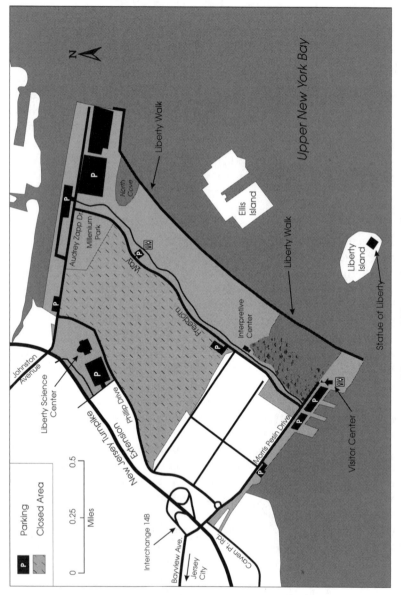

Map 38. Liberty State Park

ambitious, the 2-mile Liberty Walk to the Ferry Terminal provides good views of the harbor.

Walk west along the road overlooking the marsh for about 200 yards beyond the headquarters, to the beginning of the interpretive trail, which leads to the Interpretive Center. The many pine and shrub plantings along the trail, the marsh along the eastern edge, and the small freshwater pond at the north end of the trail offer a haven for migrant birds—a small oasis of food and shelter along the heavily urbanized waterfront of the Hudson River. Many sparrows and other songbirds can be found here from September through November, with lesser numbers during the winter. Lincoln's and White-crowned sparrows have proven to be regular migrants here, and a Boreal Chickadee discovered in late November 1983 stayed through the following March. The pines have harbored Long-eared Owls in winter, but they have become so sparsely vegetated that they don't offer much cover anymore.

Return to your car, then drive north along Liberty Way toward the Ferry Terminal. Check the grassy areas on the right for Snowy Owl in winter. At the T intersection, turn right. The parking areas along Audrey Zapp Dr. provide access to the boat basin on the north and the bayfront on the east.

⸙

Watchung Reservation

Largest of Union County's parks, the Watchung Reservation encompasses almost 2,000 acres between the ridges of the First and Second Watchung Mountains. The reservation is an excellent spot to observe the songbird migration in spring and fall, and supports an interesting diversity of breeding birds. Nesting species include American Woodcock, Red-bellied and Pileated woodpeckers, Chestnut-sided Warbler, Louisiana Waterthrush, and many other common birds of fields and deciduous woodlands. Prothonotary Warbler, Worm-eating Warbler (slopes along Glenside Ave.), and Kentucky Warbler (near the Deserted Village) have all been found nesting, but do not occur every year.

Directions

To reach the Trailside Nature and Science Center, where trail maps of the reservation are available, take US 22 to New Providence Rd. in Mountainside. Turn north onto New Providence Rd. and go about 1 mile (the name of

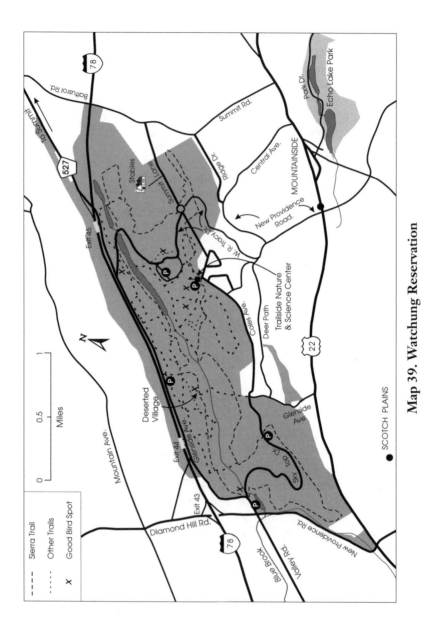

Map 39. Watchung Reservation

the road changes to Ackerman Ave. after about 0.7 miles) to the end at Coles Ave. Turn right and drive about 0.2 miles to the parking lot for the Nature Center, on the left. [DeLorme 31, M-24]

To reach the Deserted Village, take W. R. Tracy Dr. through the reservation to Glenside Ave. Turn left and go about 0.9 miles to unmarked Cataract Hollow Rd. on the left, just past Glenside Rd. on the right. Turn into Cataract Hollow Rd. and then immediately right into the parking area.

Birding

There are many trails throughout the park that can be explored with the trail map, a larger copy of which is available at the Nature Center. The Deserted Village area is especially good in spring for warblers and other migrants. From the parking lot, walk down Cataract Hollow Rd. for about 0.3 miles to the village area. Continue straight ahead on the Sierra Trail, then loop back via one of the other trails. The area along the Blue Brook usually has nesting Louisiana Waterthrush and Eastern Phoebe, among others. For a longer hike, you can take the Sierra Trail all the way to Little Seeley's Pond at the western edge of the park. Here you may find migrant shorebirds, as well as songbirds, and nesting Belted Kingfisher, Baltimore Oriole, and Eastern Bluebird.

The orange and yellow trails that start near the Nature Center can be good for both migrant and nesting species. Pileated Woodpecker usually nests along the orange trail, and the nursery area adjacent to the Nature Center has lots of food and good cover for nesting species. The field at the Scout Camping Area is a good spot in autumn for migrant sparrows, and Great Horned Owls often roost in the conifers in "The Loop." Both Great Horned and Barred owls are also often found in the pine woods near the Sky Top Picnic Area. Watchung Reservation is a real oasis in the midst of suburbia.

Bobolink

D. A. Sibley 1985

Central Region

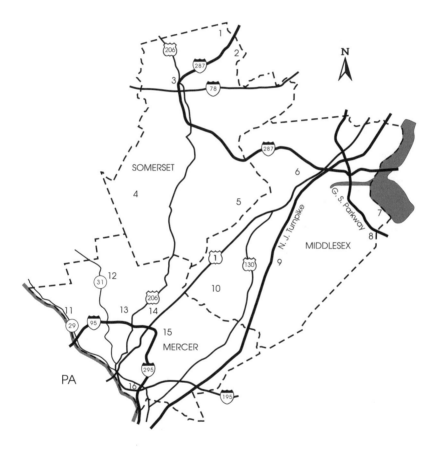

1. Scherman-Hoffman Sanctuaries
2. Lord Stirling
3. Robert J. Stahl Natural Area
4. Six Mile Run & D&R Canal
5. Sourland Mountains Preserve
6. Johnson Park
7. South Amboy
8. Cheesequake State Park
9. Jamesburg Park
10. Plainsboro Preserve
11. Washington Crossing State Park
12. Stony Brook-Millstone Reserve
13. Rosedale-Mercer Co. Park NW
14. Princeton
15. Mercer County Park
16. Trenton-Hamilton Marsh

Map 40. Central Region

Scherman-Hoffman Sanctuaries

These twin sanctuaries of the New Jersey Audubon Society include 263 acres of upland deciduous forest, fields, and flood-plain in the northeastern corner of Somerset County. The diversity of habitat provided by these nature preserves attracts a wide variety of both migrant and nesting birds; over 175 species have been recorded, of which about 60 nest in a typical year. Among the more interesting breeding species are Great Horned Owl, Pileated Woodpecker, Acadian Flycatcher, Brown Creeper, Eastern Bluebird, Worm-eating and Kentucky warblers, and Louisiana Waterthrush.

Spring migration at Scherman-Hoffman can be outstanding, with at least 25 species of warblers occurring in May, including the elusive Mourning Warbler. Other noteworthy spring migrants include Olive-sided Flycatcher (regular in late May to early June), Winter Wren (April to May and October to November), and Yellow-bellied Flycatcher (May).

Fall migration is also excellent at the sanctuaries, but the dense vegetation makes the birds harder to see than in spring. The first waves of warblers appear in mid-August, while September and October can produce spectacular flights of kinglets, thrushes, vireos, Yellow-rumped Warblers and blackbirds of several species. Among the more sought-after migrants are Olive-sided Flycatcher (August), Yellow-bellied Flycatcher (mainly September) and Connecticut Warbler (rare, in September).

Other interesting species that have occurred in recent years include winter finches, such as Common Redpoll, Pine Siskin, Red Crossbill, White-winged Crossbill and Pine Grosbeak (the latter two rare).

Directions

See Map 33. From the north, take I-287 south to Exit 30B (Bernardsville). From the exit ramp go a short distance to a traffic light at Rt. 202, then proceed straight ahead through the light onto Childs Rd. Go 0.2 miles, and bear right onto Hardscrabble Rd. After about 0.8 miles you will cross a bridge; the second driveway (uphill) on the right after the bridge is the entrance to the Hoffman Sanctuary. [DeLorme 30, I-13]

From the south, take I-287 north to Exit 30B (Rt. 202, N. Maple Ave.)—do *not* take Exit 30A (N. Maple Ave., Basking Ridge), which comes just before the Rt. 202 exit. Follow N. Maple Ave. for 0.2 miles to the traffic light at Rt. 202 and continue straight ahead as just described.

The Hoffman Sanctuary houses the office, bookstore, educational facilities, and restrooms. The offices are open from 9:00 A.M. to 5:00 P.M., Tuesday through Saturday, and noon to 5:00 P.M. on Sunday. Trail maps are available here. To reach the main parking lot for the trails, continue on Hardscrabble Rd. about 100 yards past the Hoffman driveway to the Scherman parking lot on the right. The trails are open every day until 5:00 P.M.

Birding

There are several marked trails, each of which offers some different habitat.

From the parking lot, take the trail toward the Hoffman Fields. In spring, the woods along the way ring with the marvelous songs of Wood Thrushes and Veeries; other woodland species are here as well: Eastern Wood-Pewee, Great Crested Flycatcher, Red-eyed Vireo, Scarlet Tanager, Northern Oriole, and many others. Just after crossing the driveway to the Hoffman Nature Center, the trail branches; the right path goes through the fields and the left path is part of the Dogwood Trail.

This area is good for Orchard Oriole in May, nesting Eastern Bluebird from March through June (present most of the year), Yellow-throated Vireo, Blue-winged Warbler and a variety of other migrant and breeding species. Some of the common nesting birds around the borders of the fields are House Wren, Gray Catbird, Northern Mockingbird, Brown Thrasher, Yellow Warbler, Common Yellowthroat, Northern Cardinal, Indigo Bunting, Eastern Towhee, Chipping, Field, and Song sparrows, Red-winged Blackbird, House Finch, and American Goldfinch.

At the junction of the Field Loop and the Dogwood Trail, continue along the Dogwood Trail, which gradually climbs the ridge above the sanctuary buildings. The top of the ridge is at an elevation of 600 feet, almost 300 feet above the Passaic River, which borders the Hoffman Fields. Along the way you will pass through deciduous woodland dominated by White and Red oaks, Red Maple, American Beech, and Tuliptrees, the latter occurring as tall, straight giants that tower over the forest.

There are many other varieties of trees and shrubs along the Dogwood Trail, some of which provide food and shelter to Pileated, Downy, Hairy, and Red-bellied woodpeckers. The Pileated Woodpeckers are most easily seen in March and April, when the pairs are busy courting and building their nests. Other species of birds to be found along the Dogwood Trail are Wild Turkey, Great Horned Owl (mainly in winter), Worm-eating Warbler, Kentucky Warbler (may nest), and Hooded Warbler (occasionally nests). In recent years, both Kentucky and Hooded warblers have nested just beyond the border of the sanctuary in the Cross Estate section of Morristown National Historical Park, accessible from Jockey Hollow Rd. or, on foot, via the Dogwood Trail.

Most of the familiar species of the upland deciduous forest can be found along the Dogwood Trail, including Broad-winged Hawk, Yellow-billed Cuckoo (numbers fluctuate), Black-and-white Warbler, American Redstart, and Rose-breasted Grosbeak. The trail eventually returns to the parking lot by way of Museum Trail, or you can take a detour on the Old Field Loop Trail that has many of the species already mentioned. If you take the Museum Trail, listen for the dry, rattling song of the Worm-eating Warbler, which usually sings from the hillside above the parking lot. This species, an annual breeder at the sanctuaries, usually arrives during the first week of May and departs by mid-August.

Another trail that can be interesting in spring is the River Trail that runs from Hardscrabble Rd. along the Passaic River, then upslope to a junction with the Dogwood Trail. This trail should not be attempted without wading boots. It has Wood Duck and Louisiana Waterthrush in spring, plus a good variety of nesting and migrant thrushes, vireos, and warblers. Recently, Acadian Flycatcher has begun nesting along the river.

In fall, any of the trails can be good for migrant passerines. The areas along the streams are prime spots for some of the less common transients such as Yellow-bellied and Olive-sided flycatchers, Winter Wren (October to November), Philadelphia Vireo and Connecticut Warbler (rare, in September). Winter brings a variety of sparrows to the feeders at the Hoffman Sanctuary and, in flight years, flocks of Pine Siskins, Purple Finches, and Common Redpolls.

⌖

Lord Stirling Park

This 900-acre park, which adjoins the Great Swamp NWR, has nearly 9 miles of hiking trails, including more than 1.5 miles of boardwalk. Bordering the Passaic River, the park contains a variety of both marshy and woodland habitats that support birdlife similar to that of the NWR. Approximately half the park is reserved for equestrian trails, where no pedestrians are allowed, and the remaining half is devoted to the conservation and nature programs of the Somerset County Environmental Education Center.

Almost 200 species of birds have occurred at the park, of which about 75 nest. Breeding species include Wood Duck, Great Horned and Barred owls, Red-bellied Woodpecker, Willow and Least flycatchers, Brown Creeper, Eastern Bluebird, and White-eyed, Yellow-throated, Red-eyed, and Warbling vireos. Spring and fall migrations bring a variety of waterfowl, hawks, a few

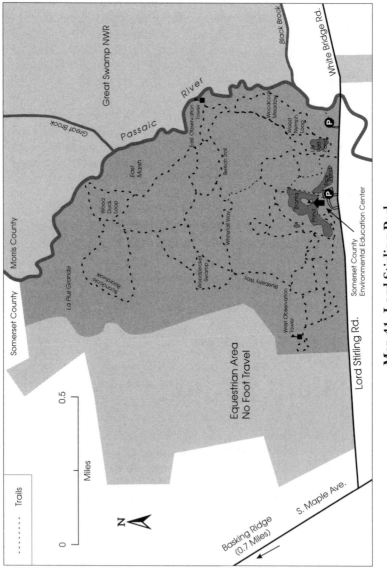

Map 41. Lord Stirling Park

Trails

Miles

0   0.5

N

Somerset County

Morris County

Great Swamp NWR

Great Brook

Passaic River

East Marsh

Wood Duck Loop

La Plus Grande

Boardwalk

Woodpecker Swamp

Whitetail Way

Beech Trail

East Observation Tower

Woodcock Meadow

Wood Nymph Song

Blueberry Way

West Observation Tower

Pratt's Pond

Branta Pond

Black Brook

White Bridge Rd.

P

P

Somerset County
Environmental Education Center

Lord Stirling Rd.

Equestrian Area
No Foot Travel

S. Maple Ave.

Basking Ridge
(0.7 Miles)

shorebirds, and many passerines. Winter is a quiet time, with only a few raptors and sparrows to augment the population of permanent residents. Rarities seen here have included Golden Eagle, Peregrine Falcon, Boreal Chickadee, and Northern Shrike.

Directions

Take I-287 to Exit 30A (N. Maple Ave., Basking Ridge). Follow N. Maple Ave. for about 1.7 miles to a fork, where you bear left onto S. Maple Ave. Continue another 1.0 miles to Lord Stirling Rd. and turn left. The Center is 1 mile ahead on the left. [DeLorme 31, L-15]

Birding

The Environmental Education Center is open 9:00 A.M. to 5:00 P.M. every day of the week, except major holidays. The trails are open from dawn to dusk, every day of the year.

In spite of the boardwalks and numerous bridges, you may encounter muddy conditions along some of the trails; rubber boots are recommended. The route suggested below is just one of many that you can take using the trail map, which is available at the Center, as are restrooms.

From the Environmental Education Center, which has Barn Swallow nesting under the eaves, walk out the red and yellow trail along Branta Pond on the left, where Canada Goose and Tree Swallow nest. Listen here for Orchard Oriole, which sometimes nests. Turn right where the red and yellow trails diverge, following the yellow. Stay right at the next two junctions, as you cross a field where Eastern Kingbird, Northern Mockingbird, Brown Thrasher, Eastern Bluebird, Blue-winged Warbler, Common Yellowthroat, Eastern Meadowlark, American Goldfinch, Field and Song sparrows nest.

When you pass Lily Pad Pond, you may flush Green Heron or Wood Duck. Continue past the observation blind, and leave the yellow trail at the next junction on the right. This trail, Wood Nymph Loop, follows along the edge of woods near the Passaic River and is an excellent spot for migrant songbirds in spring. Breeding birds here include Red-bellied Woodpecker, Eastern Phoebe, Tree and Barn swallows, Yellow-throated and Warbling vireos, Yellow Warbler, and Rose-breasted Grosbeak.

Turn right at the next trail junction, then right again on a trail that leads you 200 yards further to the East Observation Tower. Here you may see Mallard, Wood Duck, Eastern Kingbird, Yellow Warbler, Song and Swamp sparrows. Continue along the trail from the observation tower, taking a right turn at each new trail junction.

This route will take you along the edge of a field, where Ruby-throated Hummingbird, House Wren, White-eyed Vireo, Common Yellowthroat,

Northern Cardinal, Eastern Towhee, and Field Sparrow are breeders. Then you will enter a swampy Red Maple woodland. Barred Owl is a common resident in such habitat in the Great Swamp basin; it will probably take you many visits to see one, but you have a fair chance of hearing one giving its *who cooks for you, who cooks for you allll* call, especially in April and May. Barred Owls have a wide repertoire of other hoots and screams, which they often give even in the middle of the day, so be alert to the noises of the swamp.

You will soon come to a boardwalk across the East Marsh area; stay right at the next fork and follow the boardwalk down to the river. In June, you might find a female Wood Duck with her brood; in August, the banks are aflame with the scarlet of Cardinal Flower. Continue along the boardwalk for another 250 yards, then turn right at the next junction on the Boondocks Boardwalk. After a couple of hundred yards you will emerge into a large, open area where cattails are interspersed with Swamp Rose, Buttonbush, and willows. Great Blue and Green herons come to feed here, and nesting species include Virginia Rail, Sora, Willow Flycatcher, Eastern Kingbird, Marsh Wren, Gray Catbird, Cedar Waxwing, Yellow Warbler, Common Yellow-throat, Red-winged Blackbird, Swamp and Song sparrows.

The trail soon enters a forest of Pin Oak and Red Maple. Here and in the slightly drier stands of oaks, hickories, and birches farther along the red trail, you will encounter many of the common woodland species of the Great Swamp. Among the breeding birds are Yellow-billed and Black-billed cuckoos, Brown Creeper, Yellow-throated Vireo, Black-and-white Warbler, American Redstart, Rose-breasted Grosbeak, and many other, more common species.

The trail completes a long loop, then comes to another boardwalk junction; turn right, then right again at the next junction. From this point it is about 300 yards to the red trail. Take either fork and follow the red trail through a variety of woods and fields for about 1 mile back to the Environmental Center. The entire tour covers a little over 3 miles; it can be birded in 2 to 3 hours, depending on your pace.

In May, you will encounter many migrants in the woods, especially thrushes, vireos, and warblers. The park bird list includes 28 species of warblers, most of which occur as common spring migrants. Many of these same species return as fall migrants in August and September. They are followed in October by a variety of sparrows that includes Savannah, Vesper, Tree, White-crowned, White-throated, Fox, and Lincoln's sparrows, plus Dark-eyed Junco.

A small number of waterfowl and raptors pass through during the fall migration, as do a smattering of shorebirds. October and November bring Rusty Blackbird and Purple Finch. Winter birds usually include only the permanent residents, plus a few hawks and sparrows.

This well-maintained park has a varied and interesting birdlife, but it is not adequately covered by birders. Wandering Bald Eagles have shown up here increasingly during spring and summer in recent years, and diligent searching might turn up other rarities.

Warren Green Acres

This is another nearby site in Somerset County that is great for migrant sparrows and other birds of fields or wet woods in fall. From the Environmental Center, return to S. Maple Ave. and turn left. Drive one-half mile to Cross Rd., turn right and go to the stop sign at S. Finley Ave. Turn left, go 0.2 miles to the traffic light, and turn left onto Stonehouse Rd. Follow this road, which becomes Valley Rd. after 1.4 miles, for 1.9 miles to a traffic light, where Valley Rd. turns left. Continue straight ahead on King George Rd., across I-78, for 1.6 miles to Mountain Ave., the first left after the Interstate. Turn left onto Mountain Ave., and go about 1.1 miles to the unmarked entrance on the left, just beyond a bridge. Drive in about 200 yards to the circular parking area. The trails start at the gate at the northwest side of the parking area.

In addition to the migrant sparrows, other species seen here include Sandhill Crane and Sedge Wren, the latter of which has nested. Eastern Bluebird is here most of the year, as are Red-tailed Hawks and a variety of woodpeckers. The wet areas at the north of the park near the Passaic River are attractive to Great Blue Heron year-round, Green Heron in spring and summer, and Great Egret in late summer, and to a small variety of waterfowl, especially Black Duck, Mallard, and Wood Duck. Nesting warblers are not numerous, but you should find Blue-winged, Black-and-white, and Yellow warblers, and Common Yellowthroat. American Woodcock nests here, and the males can be seen performing their courtship flight from March to June.

The overgrown fields are especially attractive to sparrows in migration. Less-common migrants like White-crowned and Lincoln's sparrows are easily found here in early October. Migrant raptors, mainly Sharp-shinned and Cooper's hawks, take advantage of the abundant food supply.

The trail that leads in from the parking area soon branches, and you can take the right fork to make a complete circuit of the reserve. If you continue straight ahead, you will eventually come to some wet areas, where Sedge Wren has been found and herons and egrets search for food. The footing can be a bit muddy if there have been recent rains. There is no trail map available at present, but the area is not that large and you can't get lost. It is bounded on the north by the Passaic River, about one-half mile from Mountain Ave.

Robert J. Stahl Natural Area

This 170-acre Bedminster Township park offers some excellent grassland and riparian habitat. Grasshopper, Vesper, and Savannah sparrows, Bobolink, and Eastern Meadowlark have all nested in the open fields, although Grasshopper and Vesper not in recent years. Willow Flycatcher and Orchard Oriole (more common here than Baltimore Oriole) are easy to find in the hedgerows. In the woodlands and along the North Branch of the Raritan River, you can find Yellow-throated, White-eyed, Warbling, and Red-eyed vireos, a variety of warblers, Scarlet Tanager, and Rose-breasted Grosbeak, among others.

Directions

From the north, take I-287 south to Exit 18 (US 202/206 North). Stay in the curb lane a hundred yards and take the jughandle left turn at the first traffic light. Drive straight ahead across US 202/206 onto River Rd. You can park immediately on the right at the lot for the playing fields, but a better bet is to continue 0.3 miles to an old farm driveway on the right, where you can park if you don't block the entrance. There is room for two cars in a small lot on the left. [DeLorme 30, N-8]

From the south, take Exit 18B (US 202/206 North) and go about 0.25 miles to the jughandle turn.

Birding

Bedminster Township cooperated with the United States Fish and Wildlife Service, the New Jersey Department of Fish and Game, and the Soil Conservation Service in a series of habitat restoration projects at this site. Two acres of wetlands and two acres of wildflowers were restored in the early 1990s, and additional projects are underway. A signboard by the gate has a map of the area. As you walk up the driveway, the wetlands restoration area is on both sides, a large pond on the left and a smaller one on the right. The taller trees and hedgerows ahead are good for Willow Flycatcher and Orchard Oriole in late spring and summer.

The ponds can be good in spring or fall for migrant shorebirds, including Common Snipe, both yellowlegs, Spotted, Solitary, Least, and Semipalmated sandpipers. Killdeer and American Woodcock nest on the site, as does Green Heron. Great Blue Herons from a nearby rookery frequent the ponds.

Continuing up the road, be alert for Vesper and Savannah sparrows in migration and in summer. American Kestrel sometimes nests in the box along the driveway entrance, and Great Horned Owl, Red-tailed Hawk, and Cooper's Hawk have all nested along the back edge of the fields. As the road winds past the old farmstead, there are mowed trails along the hedgerows and fields. This area is good for Willow Flycatcher, Eastern Kingbird, Tree Swallow, Eastern Bluebird, Common Yellowthroat, and orioles. In the open fields you may find Grasshopper, Vesper, Savannah, Field, and Song sparrows, Eastern Meadowlark, and Bobolink.

The woods on the south side of River Rd. are the most productive for migrants and some of the breeding birds. A series of overgrown trails lead through the woods following the river. Northern Rough-winged and Barn swallows nest under the bridges, with Bank Swallow occasionally present. Nesting birds include Cedar Waxwing, Brown Thrasher, Wood Thrush, Chipping Sparrow, Eastern Towhee, Rose-breasted Grosbeak, and Baltimore Oriole. In winter, you can expect the usual migrant sparrows plus a few raptors. The continuing habitat restoration may change the picture for the better in the future.

✦

Six Mile Run and Delaware & Raritan Canal State Park

The Six Mile Run Reservoir Site in southeastern Somerset County is no longer planned for a reservoir at the present time, but the 3,000 acres of land acquired by the state in preparing for it are partially open to the public as a new state park. The fields and riparian woodlands provide habitat for a variety of migrant and nesting species. Because the area has not yet received much attention from birders, the birding possibilities are not well known. The Headquarters for the Delaware and Raritan Canal State Park is located on the same property, which provides access to the adjacent canal pathway. D&R Canal, which runs from Milford on the Delaware to the Raritan River in New Brunswick, is a 70-mile long linear park. There are numerous points of access to the park, which offers good riparian birding, especially in migration.

Directions

From northeastern New Jersey, take US 1 south through New Brunswick to Cozzens Lane, 2 miles past the junction with US 130, and turn right. Go 1 mile to Rt. 27, Lincoln Highway, and go right a short 250 yards to Skillmans Lane and turn left. Take Skillmans for 2.4 miles to S. Middlebush Rd., turn

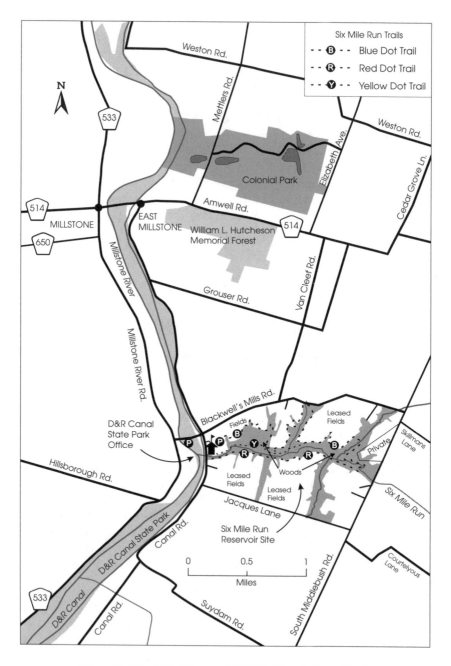

Map 42. Six Mile Run and D&R Canal State Park

right, go 100 yards and turn left onto Blackwells Mills Rd. Go 1.8 miles to the stop sign at Canal Rd., turn left and immediately left again into the parking lot, where there are portable toilets. [DeLorme 36, K-12]

From the south, take US 1 (accessible from I-295, or the New Jersey Turnpike, Exit 8, to US 130, Rt. 522 to Monmouth Junction and New Rd. to US 1) north to Cozzens Lane, 5 miles north of New Rd., and proceed as was already described.

From the west, take US 206 to Rt. 514, Amwell Rd., and go east on Rt. 514 for 3 miles to Rt. 533 in Millstone. Turn right and drive 2 miles to Blackwell Mills Rd., turn left, go 0.25 miles across the Millstone River and the D&R Canal to Canal Rd. Turn right, then immediately left into the parking lot.

Birding

Six Mile Run

There are now three well-marked trails at Six Mile Run, which can be hiked individually or combined to make short or long loops. The Blue Dot Trail starts just east of the parking lot and follows field edges and wooded areas on the north side of Six Mile Run for about 4 miles. The first field beyond the parking lot is good for Grasshopper Sparrow and Blue Grosbeak. The trail eventually crosses Six Mile Run and ends near South Middlebush Rd., where it connects with the Red Dot Trail. Along the way, there are two junctions with the Yellow Dot Trail that form 1-mile or 2.5-mile loops.

The Yellow Dot Trail starts behind the Headquarters building and follows the flood plain of Six Mile Run. It stays entirely within the woods and is very scenic, but it can also be very muddy and difficult to negotiate without hiking boots, especially at the western end. To reach the start of the Red Dot Trail, walk south along Canal Road past the bridge over Six Mile Run to the trail head. This trail runs for about 3 miles along the south side of the woods that follow the stream bed and connects with the Blue Dot Trail to make a 7-mile loop.

Both the Blue Dot and Red Dot trails pass along farm fields that are leased to local farmers, so do not stray from the trails. Because of the mixture of fields and woodlands, the three trails provide a nice variety of habitat for nesting Red-tailed Hawk, Wild Turkey, White-eyed Vireo, Wood Thrush, Eastern Bluebird, Blue-gray Gnatcatcher, Carolina Chickadee, Carolina Wren, Yellow and Black-and-white warblers, American Redstart, Common Yellowthroat, Scarlet Tanager, Rose-breasted Grosbeak, Indigo Bunting, Blue Grosbeak, Grasshopper, Field, and Song sparrows, Eastern Meadowlark, Baltimore and Orchard orioles, and American Goldfinch.

Six Mile Run may be good for songbirds in migration and a scattering of wintering species, but the site is too new for a good history to have been compiled. Hopefully, this entry will encourage more birders to visit.

Delaware & Raritan Canal State Park

The entire length of the park can be good for birding in migration and in early summer, with as many as 160 species recorded within the park, almost 90 of which have been recorded nesting. From Bakers Basin, just north of Trenton, to Millstone, a distance of about 20 miles, the historic towpath of the canal offers an excellent path for walking and some of the best birding in the park. There are numerous parking areas that allow one to bird selected parts of this stretch of the canal.

The Bakers Basin area is one of the best spots along the canal for migrants in spring. Although there is no official parking, you can usually find space along the road by the canal. Bakers Basin Rd. intersects US 1 at a traffic light 0.8 miles south of the junction of US 1 and I-95/295. Otherwise, there is parking one-half mile north at US 1. The Alexander Rd. parking area is mentioned in the Princeton entry. Another good spot is the Millstone Aqueduct parking area on Mapleton Rd., the first left turn north of Harrison St. on US 1; go one-half mile to the parking area, on the left, that provides a good view of Carnegie Lake.

Follow Mapleton Rd. another 2 miles to Rt. 27 in Kingston and continue straight ahead onto Church St., which merges with Kingston-Rocky Hill Rd. After about 1.6 miles you reach the traffic light at the intersection with Rt. 518. Continue straight ahead on Canal Rd. for about 3 miles to the Griggstown Causeway and turn left to another parking area. The D&R Canal State Park Headquarters is another 3.5 miles north along Canal Rd. In addition to the parking at the headquarters, there is another parking lot on Blackwell Mills Rd. The fields along Suydam Rd. and Canal Rd. between Suydam and Butler Rd. have had nesting Northern Bobwhite, Grasshopper Sparrow, Bobolink, Eastern Meadowlark, and Orchard Oriole in recent years.

🦆

Sourland Mountains Preserve

This 2,500-acre preserve in Hillsborough and Montgomery Townships, Somerset County, occupies a portion of the northeast point of the Sourland Region, a portion of the Piedmont which stretches southwest through southern Hunterdon and northern Mercer counties to the Delaware River. Most of the area that is currently accessible consists of upland deciduous woodland, mainly Tulip trees, oaks, maples, ashes, and hickories, with a few open fields and pipeline breaks. The name Sourland is supposedly derived from *sorrel-land*, which describes the sorrel (reddish-brown) soils encountered by the original German farmers.

Because of the elevated location along the eastern flyway, the Sourlands are excellent for migrant songbirds in spring and also good in fall. They support a good variety of nesting species, including a mix of both southern and northern species. Among the breeding birds are Wild Turkey, Pileated Woodpecker, Red-eyed and Yellow-throated vireos, Wood Thrush, Veery, Carolina Wren, Worm-eating, Blue-winged, Black-and-white, Yellow, Hooded, and Kentucky warblers, Ovenbird, American Redstart, Scarlet Tanager, Rose-breasted Grosbeak, Indigo Bunting, and Baltimore Oriole.

Directions

From the north, take US 206 south from the Somerville Circle for 6 miles to Amwell Rd. (Rt. 514). Turn right onto Amwell Rd. and drive about 2.9 miles to East Mountain Rd., and turn left. Go 2.0 miles to the entrance to the preserve on the right, and follow the entrance road to the parking area, where there are portable toilets and an information kiosk, at which trail maps are usually available. [DeLorme 36, K-5]

From the south, take US 206 north from I-95 through Princeton for 13 miles to Dutchtown-Harlingen Rd., and turn left. Go 1.5 miles to the Tintersection at Belle Mead-Blawenburg Rd., and turn right. Drive north for 1.25 miles, turn left onto East Mountain Rd. and go 1 mile to the entrance to the preserve, on the left.

Birding

Three well-marked trails depart from the parking area, the half-mile Pond-side trail (marked with a circle), the 1.4-mile Maple Flats Trail (marked with a triangle), and the more difficult 4-mile Ridge Trail (marked with a rectangle). All of the trails traverse somewhat rocky slopes, so good footwear is essential. From the trailhead, the trails lead immediately into the woods, where you may encounter migrants in spring and fall, as well as some of the breeding birds noted above. All of the trails eventually cross the Texas Eastern gas pipeline cut, where some of the birds of edge and open areas can be encountered. Blue-winged and Yellow warblers, Common Yellowthroat, Song and Field sparrows, and Indigo Bunting are common.

Both Black-capped Chickadee and Carolina Chickadee were found here during the breeding bird atlas, and a nearby banding station regularly nets birds intermediate between the two in size and plumage. Birders who want to

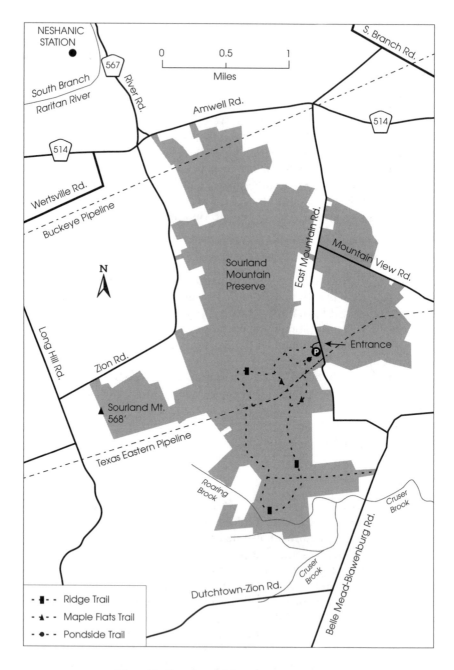

NESHANIC
STATION

567

South Branch
Raritan River

River Rd.

514

Wertsville Rd.

Buckeye Pipeline

S. Branch Rd.

Amwell Rd.

514

East Mountain Rd.

Mountain View Rd.

N

Sourland
Mountain
Preserve

Long Hill Rd.

Zion Rd.

P

Entrance

Sourland Mt.
568'

Texas Eastern Pipeline

Roaring
Brook

Cruser
Brook

Cruser
Brook

Belle Mead-Blawenburg Rd.

Dutchtown-Zion Rd.

Cruser
Brook

- ■ - Ridge Trail
- ▲ - Maple Flats Trail
- ● - Pondside Trail

Map 43. Sourland Mountains Preserve

study this problem will find excellent opportunities here. The two species adopt each other's songs and sing intermediate versions as well. Among the other species recorded nesting here during the atlas were Black Vulture and Winter Wren.

At the end of the trails, a small pond has Rough-winged, Barn, and Tree swallows in spring and summer, and may attract a Green Heron. Volunteers are planting shrubs and small trees around the edges of the pond, so even more species may be found here in the future. Somerset County, in cooperation with the state and the Delaware & Raritan Greenway, is pursuing a vigorous and active campaign to acquire additional parklands in the Sourlands. Hopefully, even more of these areas will become available to the public in the future.

🦃

Johnson Park

Lesser Black-backed Gull was the star attraction at Johnson Park, which is in the floodplain of the Raritan River in Highland Park and Piscataway. With the species' increasing abundance, it no longer creates much excitement. However, there are many other birds in this 600-acre Middlesex County park. In winter, Iceland Gull is regular, Glaucous Gull is rare but regular, and, during migration, a variety of shorebirds and songbirds stop off. More than 150 species, including about 55 that nest, have been recorded in the park, including a Lark Bunting, one of the few state records.

Directions

From northeastern New Jersey, southwestern New Jersey or the Philadelphia area, take the New Jersey Turnpike to Exit 9 (New Brunswick). Stay right at the tollbooth, and turn onto Rt. 18 west. Go about 2.9 miles and exit onto Rt. 27 north to Highland Park, then stay in the left lane as you cross the bridge over the Raritan River. Turn left at the end of the bridge onto River Rd., proceed 0.6 miles (passing under a railroad trestle) to the first traffic light, and turn left into Johnson Park. [DeLorme 37, I-20]

From coastal New Jersey, take the Garden State Parkway north to Exit 127 (I-287). Go west on I-287 for about 2.6 miles to the New Jersey Turnpike, then south on the Turnpike for 4.8 miles to Exit 9. Proceed as directed in the preceding paragraph.

From northwestern New Jersey, take I-287 south to the exit for Rt. 18 to Highland Park. Go about 3.5 miles on Rt. 18, then continue straight ahead on River Rd. when Rt. 18 turns right to cross the Raritan at the traffic light and new bridge. The next right turn is an entrance into the park, but to reach the same entrance given above, continue another mile to the next traffic light and turn right.

Birding

From October through March, numerous gulls gather to roost at Johnson Park along the Raritan River. The gulls are especially fond of an island in the river, opposite the zoo, which provides a good resting spot at low tide. During high tide, the gulls must either float on the water or join the flocks in the parking lots or playing fields. High tide occurs here about two or three hours later than at Sandy Hook.

As you drive into the park from the traffic light at River Rd., check the field on the right for gulls, especially in rainy weather. A little farther on you can see the river on the left; watch for concentrations of birds on the water. Sometimes in spring, when the current is strong, the birds play a game reminiscent of leapfrog on a moving sidewalk, in which they fly up the river, float downstream to the railroad bridge, then fly back upstream again to the front of the line.

About one-half mile from the entrance, you will see the zoo on the right and a pond on the left. The pond usually has many Canada Geese and Ring-billed Gulls; maybe a California Gull will show up here someday. Park on the right at the far (west) end of the pond, and walk around the end of the pond to the river, where you will see the island if the tide is low. This island and the ball fields that you passed earlier are the best places to see Lesser Black-backed Gull. The ball fields are especially good during, or just after, heavy rains.

The majority of the gulls at Johnson Park are Herring, Ring-billed, and Great Black-backed gulls, but in fall and spring you may find up to several hundred Laughing Gulls. In winter Iceland Gull is a regular visitor, with up to three birds at a time (usually in first winter dress), and Glaucous Gull has occurred several times.

Johnson Park has a moderately good fall shorebird migration for an inland location. Of regular occurrence are Killdeer, Greater and Lesser yellowlegs, Semipalmated Sandpiper (the most common species here), and Spotted, Western, Least, and Pectoral sandpipers. There are many records for American Golden Plover, while Common and Forster's terns are occasional late-summer visitors to the river.

The main area for songbirds lies to the west of Landing Lane, which is the first street west of the Rt. 18 bridge. To reach the birding spots, continue west along the park road from the zoo, and stay left at the next intersection. The road will pass under the Rt. 18 bridge, then come to a stop sign at Landing Lane. Continue straight ahead across Landing Lane, and park in one of the lots for the picnic groves. The best birding is between here and the west end of the park near the administration building, a distance of about 1 mile.

ⵣ

South Amboy

In the late 1960s and 1970s Little Gull and Black-headed Gull drew birders to the tidal mudflats at the southeast end of South Amboy on Raritan Bay. Shorebirding also proved to be good here, and there are numerous records for Curlew Sandpiper in addition to a long list of other shorebirds. Gulls and terns, including Black Tern, roost on the flats at low tide. Most of the overgrown landfill that bordered the shoreline has now been turned into an expensive housing development and a grass-covered park. Whether the remaining area will continue to produce species such as Horned Lark and Snow Bunting remains to be seen. The new park does provide good access to the bayshore for spring and fall shorebird migration and for wintering waterfowl.

Directions

From the north, take the Garden State Parkway south to Exit 123 (US 9 South), then take the first exit off Rt. 9 toward South Amboy, the Bordentown-Amboy Turnpike. Follow this road, which becomes Bordentown Ave. for about 1.4 miles to Broadway in South Amboy. Turn left, go two short blocks to John St., turn right, and go two blocks to the end. Turn right onto Rosewell St., and follow this road, which becomes John O'Leary Blvd., for about 0.4 miles to the entrance to Bayshore Park at Kenan Way. Proceed 0.3 miles to the far end of the parking area. [DeLorme 38, K-2]

From the south, take the Parkway north to the service area at Exit 123. Enter the service area and drive to the commuter parking area at the north end. Follow the commuter access road out the north end of the parking area to the Bordentown-Amboy Turnpike, and proceed as described in the preceding paragraph.

From the Philadelphia area, take the New Jersey Turnpike north to Exit 10 (Edison), then follow Rt. 440 east for about 2 miles to the Garden State Parkway south. Go 4 miles south on the Parkway to Exit 123.

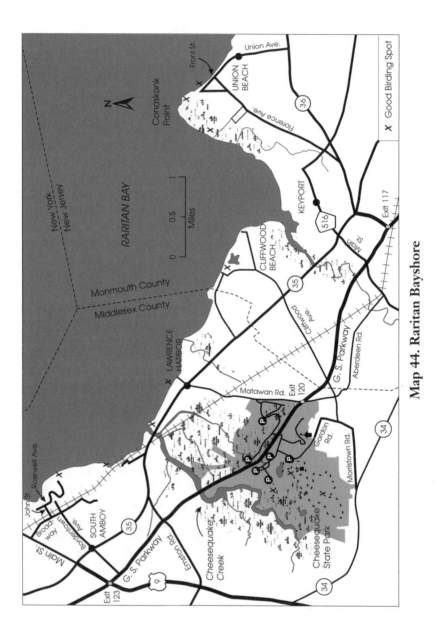

Map 44. Raritan Bayshore

Birding

The best birding spot is the mudflat around the mouth of a small stream almost one-half mile southeast of the parking lot at the park. Walk out to the bay, then head southeast along the shore, scanning ahead for shorebirds. Although the gulls and terns tend to concentrate around the stream, shorebirds may be found anywhere along the way, if some stones or mudflats are exposed. The best times for the shorebirds, gulls, and terns are the three hours before (better) and after low tide. (Low tide at South Amboy occurs approximately one-half hour later than the published tides for Sandy Hook). The shorebirds to be expected here are generally the same as those mentioned for Conaskonk Point.

When you reach a point where the shoreline bends sharply to the right, you are approaching the stream where the gulls and terns gather. If there are any around, you should spot them sitting on the mudflats offshore. Little Gull and Black-headed Gull have been found here at all seasons, but the best time for them is May, when they mingle with migrant flocks of Bonaparte's Gull which feed in Raritan Bay and pause to rest on the South Amboy mudflats when the tide is out. Numbers of Little Gull have declined steadily since the early 1970s, and they are no longer found here every year.

May is also a good time to find Black Tern at South Amboy, although the species is an uncommon spring migrant anywhere in New Jersey. Late July and August are better for Black Tern and for any other wandering terns. Shorebirding is also good in late summer, but birders find other places more attractive and productive.

In winter, rafts of scaup and other diving ducks float offshore, and gulls are abundant. Check the beach and the playing fields for flocks of Horned Lark and Snow Bunting; there might be a Lapland Longspur in with them.

The stream mouth where the gulls gather also can be reached from Rt. 35. To reach this spot, take Bordentown Ave. back to Rt. 35 and head south on Rt. 35. After about 2 miles, you will cross the bridge over Cheesequake Creek. Exit here and make the U-turn to head north on Rt. 35. Cross the bridge and take the first right turn, Morgan Ave. Go about 0.25 miles, ignoring the Dead End sign, and turn right onto North St., which turns left to become Cliff Ave. The road ends in another 0.25 miles at a large circle, which will probably have additional houses in the future. For now, park along the road, cautiously cross the railroad tracks (this is a heavily used commuter line), and follow the obvious path down to the shore. The stream mouth is several hundred yards to your left, northwest.

Cheesequake State Park

The Raritan Bay area in eastern Middlesex County is the site of this 1,000-acre state park. Cheesequake encompasses a range of habitats, including dry Pitch Pine woods, mature upland deciduous forest, freshwater marsh, salt marsh, and an Atlantic White Cedar swamp. A variety of birds visit the park, mainly during spring and fall migrations. Both Black-capped and Carolina Chickadees can be found here because the park lies within the narrow zone of overlap of these two species.

Directions

Take the Garden State Parkway to Exit 120 (Lawrence Harbor). Turn right onto Matawan Rd. and go about 0.2 miles (0.4 miles if coming from the south) and turn right onto Morristown Rd. at the sign for Cheesequake State Park. Go 0.3 miles to the traffic light at Gordon Rd., and turn right. The entrance to the State Park is 0.7 miles ahead. Continue past the tollbooth (a fee is charged in summer) about 200 yards to the first parking area for the trails and the interpretive center. [DeLorme 38, M-3]

Birding

The park receives very little attention from birders during the migration seasons, but the proximity to the coast should ensure a good variety of passerines and the marshes provide good habitat for waders, waterfowl, rails, and nesting Ospreys. A walk along one of the trails that start at the parking area for the Interpretive Center should produce an assortment of the common breeding birds of this transition zone between northern and southern vegetation types. The bird list of almost 200 species and a trail map can be obtained at either the park office or the Interpretive Center. Despite the proximity to the Garden State Parkway, the hiking trails are sheltered from the highway noise by the extensive forest.

▼

Jamesburg Park

A large (3,000+ acres) outlier of Pine Barrens habitat in southern Middlesex County, Jamesburg Park, a Middlesex County Park, in Helmetta contains many of the typical species of the Barrens. This is probably the northernmost spot in the state where Whip-poor-will is a common breeding bird; other nesting species include Common Nighthawk (probable), Purple Martin, Pine Warbler and Summer Tanager (in 1983). Common Loon, Great Blue Heron, and Osprey occur regularly in migration. The woods are accessible from Helmetta Blvd., Port St., and Washington Ave. Many sand roads lead off these paved roads into the woods. The sand roads can be walked, but not driven (access is blocked).

Directions

From Exit 8A of the New Jersey Turnpike, go east on Rt. 32 (Forsgate Dr.) for about 1.6 miles to the intersection with Half Acre Rd. Turn left and drive about 0.7 miles to Gatzmer Ave. Turn left, go one block, then turn right onto Lincoln Ave. Follow Lincoln, which soon becomes Helmetta Rd. and then Spotswood-Cranbury Rd., for about 2 miles to Maple St. in Helmetta. Turn left and drive about 0.1 miles to Helmetta Pond, on the left. [DeLorme 43, C-21]

Birding

Helmetta Pond has both open water and shrubby marshlands, which have the usual contingent of Warbling Vireo, various swallows, Yellow Warbler, Common Yellowthroat, Red-winged Blackbird, and Northern Oriole around the edges. Although not a well-known spot, the marshy edges must harbor such species as Virginia Rail, Common Moorhen, and perhaps Sora.

To explore the pine woods, continue another 0.3 miles to Helmetta Blvd. and turn left. Drive 0.3 miles to a dirt road, on the left, that leads into the woods. Port St. is another 0.4 miles ahead. To reach Washington Ave., turn left on Port and drive about one-half mile to the left; turn onto Washington. Port and Washington have little traffic, so you can park and bird along the road. Although there are many inholdings within the park, you can find a few spots along Washington Ave. and Port St. where you can park and explore the woods. Unfortunately, there is no map and no plans to make one.

☜

Plainsboro Preserve

The Plainsboro Preserve is a joint project of NJAS and the Township of Plainsboro, Mercer County. The newest NJAS Sanctuary building will open in mid-2002. The preserve encompasses 631 acres, including 50-acre McKormack Lake. Most of the site is transitional scrub, but there is mature beech forest, a sphagnum bog, and many very rare plants. Over 150 species of birds have been recorded during its brief history, and it is especially good for sparrows in the fall.

Directions

From north or south, take US 1 to the Scudders Mills Rd. exit in Plainsboro Turnpike., just east of Princeton. Exit onto Scudders Mills Rd. and follow it 2 miles to the traffic light at the intersection with Dey Rd. Make a left onto Dey Rd. and go about 1.6 miles to Scotts Corner Rd. Turn left onto Scotts Corner Rd. and follow it for about one-half mile, past Community Park on your left. The Preserve entrance is on your left almost directly across from a red brick water pumping station. [DeLorme 42, E-13]

Birding

There are about 5 miles of trails, but no good trail maps, as yet. One should become available in late 2002. From the parking area, walk past the gate on the dirt road that serves as the main trail along the south side of the lake. A variety of waterfowl can be found on the lake in spring and fall, and the ubiquitous Canada Geese are always present. The woods along the lake and the adjacent fields are good for migrant and wintering passerines, especially sparrows, goldfinches, buntings, and blackbirds.

Nesting birds at Plainsboro include Cooper's Hawk, Yellow-billed and Black-billed cuckoos, and Blue Grosbeak. Other common species can be found around the lake and in the taller deciduous woodlands along Shallow Brook. For this area, take the trail to the left (see map) after about 0.25 miles. There are two loops that pass through woods and fields, then eventually return to the starting point.

The main trail (road) continues near the lake, past the outlet of the lake at Devil's Brook, where you may find a Green Heron. Along the way, from late spring through summer, you will find numerous Yellow Warblers, Common Yellowthroats, Indigo Buntings, Chipping, Song, and Field sparrows. At a junction in the road there is an old abandoned building that will probably be torn down in the future. Here the path turns right and leads out a narrow peninsula in the lake. Additional trails will be available by the time this book appears, so this newly available preserve deserves exploration.

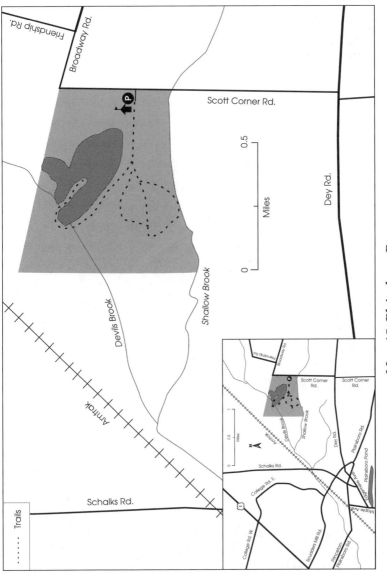

Map 45. Plainsboro Preserve

Trails
⋯⋯

Friendship Rd.

Broadway Rd.

Scott Corner Rd.

Dey Rd.

Devils Brook

Shallow Brook

Amtrak

Schalks Rd.

0   0.5
Miles

Broadway Rd.
Friendship Rd.
Scott Corner Rd.
Scott Corner Rd.
Devils Brook
Shallow Brook
Dey Rd.
Plainsboro Rd.
Plainsboro Pond
Maple Ave.
Plainsboro Rd.
Princeton
Scudders Mill Rd.
College Rd. E.
College Rd. W.
Schalks Rd.
0   0.5
Miles

Cedar Waxwing

Washington Crossing State Park

Situated on the east bank of the Delaware River, 8 miles north of Trenton, this 807-acre park preserves the site of a famous event in American history. On Christmas night, 1776, George Washington and his Continental Army crossed the river from Pennsylvania and marched toward Trenton, where they defeated the Hessians in a daring surprise attack—an event considered by many historians as the turning point of the Revolutionary War. Continental Lane, which runs the entire length of the park (about 1 mile), is the road over which Washington's soldiers marched. In addition to being an important historical site, Washington Crossing State Park is also a good birding area.

The park includes manicured lawns and gardens, fields, evergreen groves, and upland deciduous woods that attract a diversity of birds. Although it is not known as a place to see rare or unusual birds, it provides a good selection of the species that occur in the central Delaware Valley.

Directions

From northern New Jersey, take US 1 or US 206 south to I-295, north of Trenton. Turn right onto I-295 and proceed to Exit 3 (Scotch Rd.). From the exit ramp, turn right onto Scotch Rd. Drive 1.3 miles to Rt. 546 (Washington Crossing-Pennington Rd.), and turn left. Go 1.9 miles to the intersection with Rt. 579, and continue straight ahead on Rt. 546 for one-half mile to the park entrance, on the right.

From the northern part of the New Jersey shore, take I-195 west to its terminus at I-295, then follow I-295 north around Trenton and proceed as was already described.

From southern New Jersey take I-295 north around Trenton and proceed as described above.

Birding

Drive down the park entrance road for about 0.2 miles to Continental Lane and turn left. Go about 0.3 miles to the parking area on the left for the Visitor Center. After stopping in the Center, walk along Continental Lane for 0.3 miles to an overlook; continue across a pedestrian bridge that takes you over Rt. 29 to Washington's landing site on the banks of the Delaware. The numerous conifer plantings along Continental Lane have had Red and White-winged crossbills in winter; Common Redpoll has also been found in this

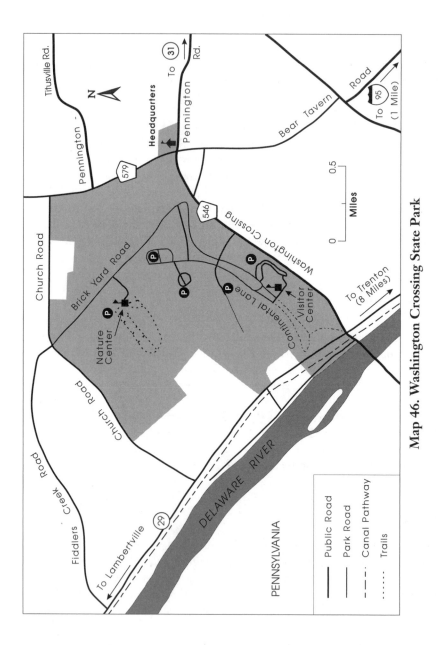

Map 46. Washington Crossing State Park

Titusville Rd.

Pennington -

Church Road

Church Road

Fiddlers Creek Road

To Lambertville

To 31

Headquarters

Pennington Rd.

579

546

Washington Crossing

Brick Yard Road

Nature Center

P

P

P

Continental Lane

P

P

Visitor Center

To Trenton (8 Miles)

Bear Tavern Road

To 95 (1 Mile)

0   0.5

Miles

DELAWARE RIVER

PENNSYLVANIA

N

Public Road

Park Road

Canal Pathway

Trails

area. Red-breasted Nuthatch, Brown Creeper, and Golden-crowned Kinglet can almost always be found here during the colder months.

Some of the best birding in Washington Crossing State Park is in the Natural Area, which encompasses about one-quarter of the park. To reach the Nature Center, where the trails through the Natural Area begin, drive north on Continental Lane from the Visitor Center parking lot for about 0.6 miles, to where the road loops around to return to the entrance. Turn right onto Brick Yard Rd. at the Nature Center sign, drive one-half mile, and turn left into the Nature Center driveway; the parking lot is about 300 yards ahead. Although the official opening time is 10:00 A.M., the road into the nature center is open by 8:00 A.M., and you are welcome to use the trails. If you arrive after the Center opens, you can stop in and obtain a trail map.

A network of trail loops traverses the natural area. If you don't have the trail map, you can make a general circuit of the trails by following the yellow trail (stay right at the first junction) to the white trail, the green trail, the blue trail, and then the red trail, which leads back to the Nature Center. These trails pass through a variety of mature and scrubby second-growth deciduous woodland.

The natural area may be an excellent spot for migrant songbirds in spring, but most birders choose to go to Princeton for spring migration, so relatively little is known about Washington Crossing. In summer, the breeding birds include most of the expected species for this habitat, including American Woodcock, Yellow-billed Cuckoo, Eastern Screech-Owl and Great Horned Owl, Red-bellied Woodpecker, Fish Crow (along the river), Carolina Chickadee, Carolina Wren, Brown Thrasher, Yellow-throated Vireo, Warbling Vireo (along the river), Blue-winged, Yellow, Black-and-white, and Prairie warblers (the last in cedars near the open-air theater), American Redstart, and Rose-breasted Grosbeak. The field at the corner of Rt. 579 and Church Rd. usually has a few nesting Bobolink and Eastern Meadowlarks. Cliff Swallows have nested irregularly under the bridge over the Delaware River.

The fall migration of songbirds also is inadequately covered at Washington Crossing. In late fall, ducks, geese, and gulls can be found along the Delaware River. To reach the parking lot that overlooks the river, return to the park entrance and go right onto Rt. 546. Drive 0.8 miles to the traffic light at Rt. 29, then continue straight ahead for a short distance to a parking lot on the right. From the banks of the river you can scan the water in both directions. Canada Goose, Mallard, Common Goldeneye, and Common Merganser are the most common waterfowl, but there is one record of Barrow's Goldeneye.

Southern Sourlands Preserves

A variety of properties in the southern part of the Sourland Mountains, spanning the boundary of Mercer and Hunterdon counties, have been preserved by the state, Hunterdon County, and the Delaware & Raritan Greenway. Most of these areas are characterized by upland deciduous woodlands that are excellent in migration and harbor a good selection of nesting birds in summer. The areas described here are the Northern Stony Brook Preserve (McBurney Woods), Sourland Mountain Preserve, Cedar Ridge Preserve, Sommer Park, and the Lindbergh Estate (Highfields). The D&R Greenway is actively pursuing other acquisitions in the area, however, so additional lands will soon be open to the public.

Directions

To reach the Northern Stony Brook Preserve, from the junction of US 206 and County Rt. 518 in Rocky Hill, Somerset County, go west of Rt. 518 for 6.5 miles to Greenwood Ave. (Hopewell-Wertsville Rd.) in the Borough of Hopewell. Turn right and drive 3.2 miles to Mountain Rd., on the left (the road name changes to Rileyville Rd. along the way). Turn left and go about 0.6 miles to the parking area, on the left. [DeLorme 35, N-26]

Birding

The Northern Stony Brook Preserve (McBurney Woods) comprises more than 300 acres (and growing) atop the Sourland Mountains in Hunterdon and Mercer counties. The main (Yellow) trail starts at the parking area and makes a 1.3-mile loop that can be lengthened by taking one of the side trails (Orange and Blue markings). These pass mainly through mature deciduous woodlands, then a few open areas and some younger woodlands. Additional parts of the preserve can be birded along Stony Brook Rd. and Mountain Church Rd., on the west and south, respectively (see map).

McBurney Woods can be an excellent spot for migrants in spring, with more than 20 species of warblers seen on some days. In addition, the preserve has a good assortment of nesting birds, including Wild Turkey, Ruffed Grouse, Pileated Woodpecker, Eastern Phoebe, Red-eyed Vireo, Wood Thrush, Veery, Black-and-white, Blue-winged, Kentucky, and Hooded warblers, Ovenbird, American Redstart, Louisiana Waterthrush, Rose-breasted Grosbeak, Scarlet Tanager, and Baltimore Oriole. American Woodcock and Cooper's Hawk are thought to nest there, as well.

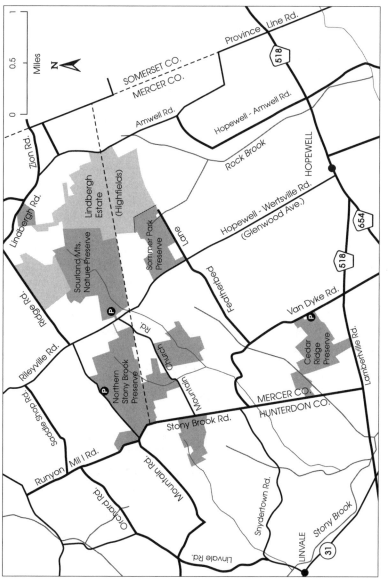

Map 47. Southern Sourland Mountains

SOMERSET CO.
MERCER CO.

Province Line Rd.

518

Amwell Rd.

Hopewell - Amwell Rd.

Rock Brook

Zion Rd.

Lindbergh Rd.

Lindbergh Estate
(Highfields)

Sourland Mts. Nature Preserve

Sommer Park Preserve

Hopewell - Wertsville Rd.
(Glenwood Ave.)

HOPEWELL

654

Ridge Rd.

Rileyville Rd.

Northern Stony Brook Preserve

Church Rd.

Featherbed Lane

518

Van Dyke Rd.

Cedar Ridge Preserve

Lambertville Rd.

Saddle Shop Rd.

Mountain Rd.

Stony Brook Rd.

MERCER CO.
HUNTERDON CO.

Runyon Mill Rd.

Orchard Rd.

Mountain Rd.

Snydertown Rd.

Stony Brook

Linvale Rd.

LINVALE

31

Miles

N

0   0.5   1

From the parking lot, turn right onto Mountain Rd. and return to the intersection with Rileyville Rd. Turn right, go one-half mile, then turn left into the entrance drive for the Sourland Mountains Nature Preserve, a 273-acre Hunterdon County park. The birding on the well-marked trails is similar to that in McBurney Woods, although not quite as good for migrants.

Turn left from the entrance road and go about 1 mile on Rileyville Rd. to Featherbed Lane, and turn left. Park along the road and look for a trail going north into the woods. The abandoned fields and second-growth and mature deciduous woodlands are now part of the Sommer Park Preserve of the D&R Greenway and have been the site of a bird-banding project of Hannah Sothers for more than 20 years. Featherbed Lane ends after one-half mile, and most of the land along the north side is part of the preserve, except for a few houses.

The east end of both the Sourland Mountains Nature Preserve and the Sommer Park Preserve adjoin Highfields, the former estate of Charles and Ann Morrow Lindbergh. It now houses a unit of the New Jersey State Corrections Department for troubled adolescents, but there are numerous trails and the land is open to the public. The best way to access these trails is from the adjoining two preserves.

Cedar Ridge Preserve is another growing property of the D&R Greenway at 80+ acres. From the intersection of Rileyville Rd. and Featherbed Lane, go west 1 mile on Featherbed to its end at Van Dyke Rd., and turn left. Go about 0.7 miles and park on the side of the road just before a small bridge. Follow the trail a short distance to a sign board, where the Cedar Ridge Trail is depicted. The 1.5-mile long trail will take you through a variety of habitats, along fields, and through deciduous woodland.

✝

Stony Brook-Millstone Watersheds Reserve

This 480-acre reserve near Pennington, Mercer County (owned by the Stony Brook-Millstone Watersheds Association), is one of the few places in New Jersey where Henslow's Sparrow has nested or attempted to nest in the last 30 years. The former grassland habitat has changed in the past 20 years, however, and species such as Savannah Sparrow, Grasshopper Sparrow, and Bobolink no longer nest there. Among the species that nest here now are Eastern Bluebird, Yellow-breasted Chat, Blue-winged and Yellow warblers, plus a good variety of the common field and woodland species typical of the central part of the state. Northern Saw-whet Owl is a regular winter visitor to the cedar woods, and Long-eared Owls are present some years.

Directions

There are two entrances to the reserve, one on Wargo Road and the other on Titus Mill Road. From the junction of US 1 and I-295 north of Trenton, follow I-295 (becomes I-95) west for 5 miles to Rt. 31. Go north on Rt. 31 for about 4.2 miles and turn right onto Titus Mill Rd.; continue about 1.4 miles to the driveway on the left that leads to the headquarters and parking lot. For the Wargo Rd. entrance, continue past the headquarters driveway for 0.3 miles to Wargo Rd. and turn left. Go about one-half mile to a gate on the left, just where the road takes a sharp right turn. There is limited parking on either side of the road before the turn. Walk through the gate to enter the reserve.

Birding

The reserve offers a mixture of weedy fields, cultivated fields (leased to nearby farmers), second-growth deciduous woods along the Stony Brook, scrubby Red Cedar woods, pine plantings, and a small pond with adjacent marshy area. Several marked trails pass through these diverse habitats. Here you will find most of the customary field and woodland birds of central New Jersey.

To bird the reserve in spring or summer, enter via the service road at the Wargo Rd. gate. This road curves around to the left, passing through vestiges of an old orchard and past the beginning of the Circle Trail on the left. Both Black-billed and Yellow-billed cuckoos are likely to be here, and, sometimes, an Orchard Oriole. Vesper Sparrows used to nest in the field bordering the Circle Trail and may still occur on occasion.

Continue on the service road, past another service road on the left (called Red Rd. after the red shale that colors the soil here), then past two old silos on the right (about 300 yards from the entrance). Next, you'll go by the starting point of the Stony Brook Trail on the left, some buildings on the right, and come to the pond. Canada Goose, Mallard, Tree Swallow (in boxes), and Swamp Sparrow nest around the edges of the pond and King Rail has occurred in the marshy areas.

Return to the starting point of the Stony Brook Trail. This trail runs west through some overgrown fields for almost a mile, then enters the woods and leads to Stony Brook; it turns south for 0.25 miles, then returns toward Wargo Rd. through the cedar woods and edges of the fields. Some of the fields were bulldozed in the mid-1990s to clear the shrubs and saplings, but

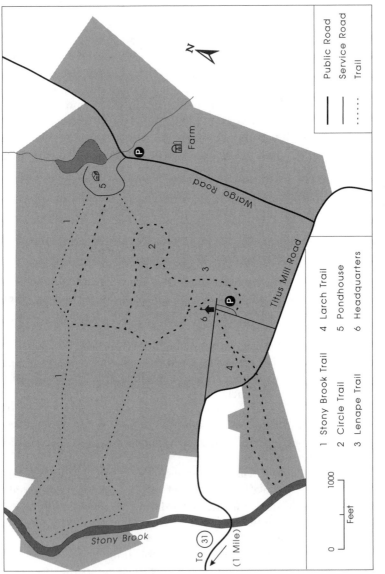

Map 48. Stony Brook-Millstone Watersheds Reserve

Public Road		
Service Road		
Trail		

1 Stony Brook Trail   4 Larch Trail
2 Circle Trail   5 Pondhouse
3 Lenape Trail   6 Headquarters

Farm

Wargo Road

Titus Mill Road

Stony Brook

To (31)
(1 Mile)

0   1000
Feet

N

the grasslands and the associated birds have not returned. Many other species of birds nest in the woods surrounding the fields, including Wood Duck, Red-tailed Hawk, four species of woodpecker, and a long list of songbirds. Turkey Vulture, Belted Kingfisher, N. Rough-winged Swallow, and Bank Swallow, which are not known to nest on the reserve, are frequent visitors. In March, the area is excellent for a woodcock watch—American Woodcocks nest in the woods around the fields and perform their spring courtship flight at dusk over the adjacent fields.

Fall migration brings a modest hawk flight, various warblers, an array of sparrows (including Vesper), and an occasional rarity such as Northern Phalarope and Western Kingbird. In winter, the reserve is quiet. A few bluebirds usually remain, and in the fields a variety of sparrows can be found, especially American Tree, Field, Song, Swamp, and White-throated sparrow, and Dark-eyed Junco. White-crowned Sparrow is an occasional visitor and Harris's Sparrow has occurred once. The reserve is one of the most reliable spots for Northern Shrike in invasion years.

Every winter, one or two N. Saw-whet Owls seek shelter in the cedars at the southwestern end of the fields. They are usually not very far in, but there are so many cedars and the foliage is so dense that you can look for hours without finding an owl.

🦆

Mercer County Park Northwest and Rosedale Park

These Mercer County Park Commission's adjacent units of almost 1,300 acres include an old park and a new one. Rosedale Park, with 475 acres, has long been a county park, and was formerly the most reliable place in New Jersey to see Loggerhead Shrike. Unfortunately, with the continued decline of the species, it is seldom reported anywhere in New Jersey anymore. Rosedale continues to be an excellent birding spot, however. Eastern Bluebird is a specialty of the park, along with a variety of raptors in winter, including an occasional Northern Goshawk. In 1995, the county acquired an 800-acre tract from AT&T, known as the Pole Farm because of the many telephone poles used as part of an overseas transmission service. It has both woods and fields, with several trails, and has had nesting Grasshopper and Savannah sparrows, Bobolink, Eastern Meadowlark, Yellow-breasted Chat, and Blue Grosbeak.

Directions

From most of New Jersey, take US 1, the New Jersey Turnpike or I-195 to I-295. Proceed north or west on I-295 to Exit 7 (Lawrenceville, US 206). Go north on US 206 for a short 0.3 miles to Lawrenceville Rd. (Rt. 546), and turn left. Continue on Lawrenceville Rd. for 1.8 miles, then bear right onto Federal City Rd. Take Federal City for about 1.1 miles to Blackwell Rd., and turn right. Go 0.2 miles to a parking area, on the left. [DeLorme 42, F-1]

Alternatively, take I-295 an additional 1.5 miles to Exit 5 (Federal City Rd.), and go 1.2 miles to the intersection with Lawrenceville Rd.

Birding

From the parking area, you have access to both parks. The Pole Farm is directly across the street. To bird Rosedale, walk the worn path through the woods directly away from the road from the parking lot. A short walk through the woods brings you to an open area where you can see fields with scattered cedars and small woodlots. There are no well-marked trails at Rosedale, but the best birding is generally in the fields and hedgerows east of the lake. Continue in a northeasterly direction for several hundred yards until you come to the overgrown fields. The areas on the north and east sides of the fields, where there are numerous cedars, are usually the best. In addition to the numerous Eastern Bluebirds, common breeders include Indigo Bunting, Yellow Warbler, and Field Sparrow.

For the Pole Farm tract, you can cross Blackwell Rd. to reach the trails or drive to the entrance to the tract. From the intersection of Federal City Rd. with Blackwell Rd., go east on Blackwell for 1 mile to the T intersection at Cold Soil Rd. Turn right and go south on Cold Soil Rd. for 1.1 miles to the intersection with Keefe Rd. The entrance to the park is on the right. [DeLorme 42, G-2]

The trails cover both the woods and the field edges of the park, where the species just noted can be found, along with many other, more common ones. Some of the fields are leased to farmers for cultivation, so stay on the trails and don't walk on the fields.

Winter birds in the two sections of the park include numerous raptors and many sparrows, including White-crowned and Tree. In winter 2000–2001, a large roost of Northern Harrier was located in the fields west of the old barn on Keefe Rd. Northern Shrike, N. Saw-whet Owl, and Long-eared Owl have been found and, as previously noted, the fields of Rosedale Park frequently had wintering Loggerhead Shrike in the 1970s and early 1980s. If the species ever recovers in numbers, they may someday return.

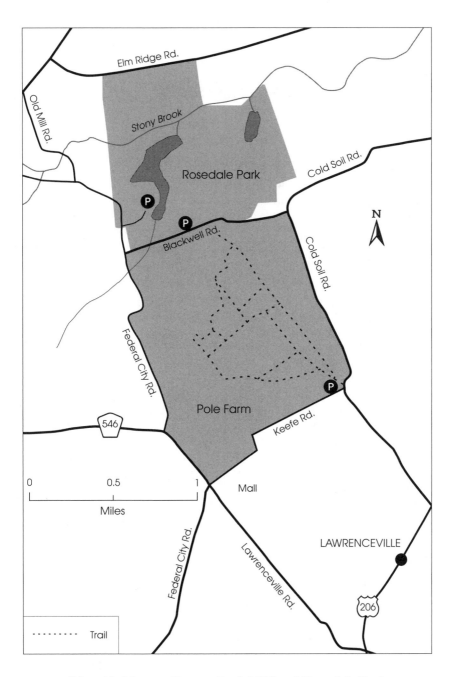

Map 49. Mercer County Park NW and Rosedale Park

ⲧ

Princeton
(Institute Woods and Rogers Refuge)

When birders talk about "Princeton," they are usually referring to the Charles H. Rogers Refuge, which is owned by Princeton Township, and the adjacent Institute Woods, which belong to the Institute for Advanced Studies. Covering almost 550 acres, these areas constitute one of the better spots in New Jersey for observing the spring migration of warblers and other songbirds. For poorly understood reasons—perhaps because of the overall decline in subtropical migrants combined with the encroaching suburbia—Princeton today is a mere shadow of its past. Still, on a good day in May, you can see more than 20 species of warblers here—a few people have even had 30 in times past. The Rogers Refuge includes a freshwater marsh that attracts many water birds.

The two areas support an interesting diversity of breeding birds and are also good for migrants during fall migration. Some species that nest on or near the ground, such as Eastern Towhee and Veery, however, have virtually disappeared because of the destruction of the understory and ground cover by deer. In winter, the woods are quiet. You can count on the common resident and wintering species, maybe a few owls, and, occasionally, winter finches.

About 200 species have been recorded in these combined areas over the past 50 years. Among the regular breeding birds are Wood Duck, Virginia Rail, Sora, Eastern Screech and Great Horned owls, Pileated Woodpecker, Warbling Vireo, Kentucky Warbler (now rare), and Orchard Oriole. Mourning Warbler is an annual visitor in late May and early June, as are Yellow-bellied Flycatcher, Philadelphia Vireo, and Connecticut Warbler in fall.

Directions

The most popular of several parking places at Princeton is along West Dr. near the entrance to the Rogers Refuge. To reach this spot:

From northeastern New Jersey, take US 1 south toward Princeton to the traffic overpass at Alexander St. Turn right onto Alexander St. (shown as Alexander Rd. on some maps), and go about 0.7 miles to West Dr., the first left turn after you cross two bridges—one over the Delaware and Raritan Canal and the other over Stony Brook. Drive about 0.3 miles to where the road

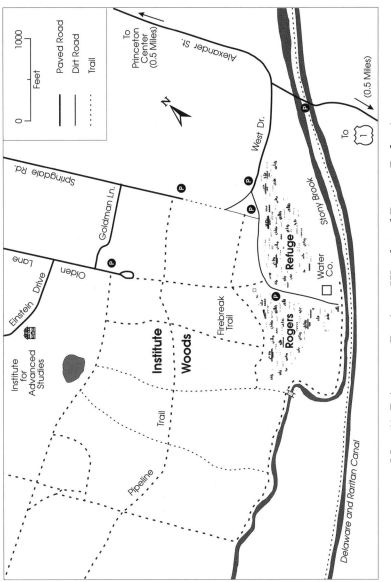

Map 50. Princeton (Institute Woods and Rogers Refuge)

Institute for Advanced Studies

Einstein Drive

Olden Lane

Goldman Ln.

Springdale Rd.

Institute Woods

Rogers Refuge

Firebreak Trail

Trail

Pipeline

Delaware and Raritan Canal

Stony Brook

Water Co.

West Dr.

Alexander St.

To Princeton Center (0.5 Miles)

To 1 (0.5 Miles)

Feet

0   1000

Paved Road
Dirt Road
Trail

N

forks and becomes dirt. Park along the side of the road here; the left fork leads to the Rogers Refuge.

From northwestern New Jersey, take US 206 south to the intersection with Rt. 27 (Nassau St.) in Princeton. Turn left onto Nassau St., then almost immediately right onto Mercer St. Drive about 0.2 miles to Alexander St. and turn left. Go about 1 mile to West Dr. and turn right. Proceed as described in the preceding paragraph.

From the New Jersey shore, take I-195 west to Trenton, then follow the signs for I-295. Take I-295 to the exit for US 1 north. Go north for 4 miles to the ramp exit for Alexander St. westbound, and continue as already described.

From southern New Jersey or the Philadelphia area, take I-95 or I-295 north around Trenton to the exit for US 1 North. Go north for 4 miles to the jughandle exit for Alexander St. westbound and continue as already described.

Birding

Everybody has a preferred way of birding Princeton, so the best thing to do is to familiarize yourself with some of the main roads and paths, then develop your own plan for covering the Rogers Refuge and the Institute Woods. The network of paths can be bewildering to the newcomer and there are no good maps available. The accompanying map is accurate as far as the major features are concerned; the positions of some of the trails may be a little off, but you should be able to find your way around. The following paragraphs suggest a way of covering most of the paths; it will take you about two hours to complete the walk—longer if the birding is good.

It is best to arrive early, however, because the birds songs and calls, which determine the way most species are discerned and located, decline dramatically after about nine o'clock. Being able to identify species by their song is a valuable skill here.

From West Dr., walk along the road that leads to the Charles H. Rogers Refuge and the Elizabethtown Water Company. The section of road from West Dr. to the marsh, about one-quarter mile, is often the best spot at Princeton for migrant songbirds in spring. The first three weeks in May are best, but there are early birds in late April and latecomers such as Olive-sided Flycatcher and Mourning Warbler later in May.

At the bend in the road where the marsh begins, there is a trail on the right that leads to a brick pump house. Kentucky Warbler nests in this spot in some years, and Yellow-throated Vireo sings from the tops of the tall trees overhead. Continuing along the dirt road, you will come to the marsh, which is where the rails nest. Tree Swallows are abundant after early April; they nest in the many boxes provided for them. Other common breeding birds around the marsh are Eastern Kingbird, House Wren, Blue-gray Gnatcatcher, Yellow

Warbler, Common Yellowthroat, Song and Swamp sparrows, Red-winged Blackbird, Northern Oriole, and American Goldfinch. Willow Flycatcher was formerly a reliable breeding bird at the north end of the marsh, but has become much less so in recent years. Continue along the dirt road toward the water company. Here, you will find some large willow trees along the road that usually have nesting Warbling Vireo and Orchard Oriole. When you come to Stony Brook, stop and listen for Prothonotary Warbler, which once nested in this area. Turn right and follow Stony Brook Trail along the stream. This is an excellent area in migration for thrushes, vireos, and warblers. After several hundred yards, you will come to an intersection with a trail that crosses Stony Brook on a suspension bridge to your left, where Acadian Flycatcher nests. Make a brief detour on this trail, by turning right and walking a short distance to a stream and marshy area on the right; it is an excellent area for migrant Solitary Sandpipers in the spring.

Return to the trail along Stony Brook, turn right, and bird along the brook. After another hundred yards or so, you will come to the junction of another trail on the right. This trail intersects the pipeline trail, which is the major trail running northeast-southwest through Institute Woods. Turn left onto the pipeline trail, and you will soon come to a spot where a stream passes under the trail and the path bends right. In addition to being a good area for migrant songbirds, this is also a traditional nesting spot for Kentucky Warbler. As you continue along this trail, you will come to a magnificent stand of American Beech on the right. The trees are very old, and this area may have never been logged. Turn right at the next trail junction, go about 50 yards, and cross through some woods to another trail on the right.

The next trail junction will be at the edge of the Princeton Battlefield State Park. Turn right and follow the trail that leads along the edge of some fields and shrubby woods to the next trail junction on the right; this is again the birch grove trail. Follow the trail for a few hundred yards to some pine plantings on the left, where you should check for owls in winter.

Just past the pine grove, the birch grove trail intersects the pipeline trail. Turn left and bird your way through the mixed deciduous woods for several hundred yards. After passing a couple of junctions with smaller trails, you will come to a wide, clear trail known as the firebreak trail. Turn right onto this trail, which passes between a mature deciduous stand on the right and some old pine plantings on the left.

The firebreak trail is one of the best birding trails at Princeton. As you walk along it, you will soon come to the edge of the marsh at Rogers Refuge, where the firebreak turns left and parallels the edge of the marsh. You will eventually cross a small stream and come to an intersection with another path. A left turn on this path will lead to some dense conifer plantings where Great Horned Owl can sometimes be found. A right turn on this path will lead to a gate where the trail continues out to the dirt road in Rogers Refuge.

If, instead of turning onto the side path, you continue straight ahead on the firebreak, you will pass by some dense tangles on the right that are a favorite spot for Mourning Warbler in late May and early June. After crossing a small stream, you will come to another gate that has been left unlocked in recent years. Continuing through the gate, you will emerge onto a dirt road and parking area which joins the entrance road to Rogers Refuge almost immediately to your right. If you parked along West Dr., your car will be a few hundred feet up the entrance road, to your left. Alternatively, you can turn left after the gate and bird along the dirt road (which soon intersects West Dr.) as far as the swim club.

Among the species that breed on Rogers Refuge or in the Institute Woods (in addition to those already mentioned) are Green Heron, Canada Goose, Mallard, Black Duck, American Woodcock, Chimney Swift, Belted Kingfisher, Red-bellied Woodpecker, Eastern Phoebe, Northern Rough-winged Swallow, Fish Crow, Carolina Chickadee, Brown Creeper (rare), Carolina Wren, Cedar Waxwing, Black-and-white Warbler, American Redstart, Rose-breasted Grosbeak, Indigo Bunting.

An interesting nearby spot is Turning Basin Park. The entrance is located on Alexander Rd. between the D&R Canal and the Stony Brook or about 0.1 miles south of the entrance to West Drive, the road into the Charles H. Rogers Refuge. A long path offers wooded views from the other side of the refuge, and since part of the path is somewhat elevated, you can often obtain nice vistas and be closer to the upper canopy. A nesting Willow Flycatcher can sometimes be found. Portable toilets are available here.

☞

Mercer County Park

This large park in central Mercer County attracts birders because of the interesting variety of breeding birds and the occasional appearance of rare or unusual species. Mercer County Park includes more than 2,500 acres of fields, deciduous woodlands, and streams in West Windsor Township, about 7 miles northeast of Trenton. The centerpiece of the park is 300-acre Lake Mercer, a prime birding spot. Although a portion of the park is devoted to recreational facilities, a large part will not be developed and will continue to be good for birding. The many fields and woodland edges are excellent in migration for sparrows. These areas also have had nesting Yellow-breasted Chat and Blue Grosbeak.

Directions

From northern New Jersey, take the New Jersey Turnpike south to Exit 8 (Hightstown, Rt. 33). Follow Rt. 33 West into Hightstown. From the junction with Rt. 571 in Hightstown, continue on Rt. 33 for 1.8 miles until the road merges with US 130. Go 0.9 miles farther from this junction and exit right at the sign for Windsor. Drive another 0.9 miles to the center of Windsor, and turn right onto Church St. (Rt. 641). Church St. soon becomes Windsor Rd., and after 2.2 miles it intersects Rts. 535 (Old Trenton Rd.) and 526 in Edinburg. Turn left onto Rt. 535 and go one-half mile to the park entrance, on the right. [DeLorme 42, J-8]

From coastal New Jersey, take the Garden State Parkway to I-195, then go west on I-195 for about 25 miles to Exit 5 (US 130 North)—the first exit after the New Jersey Turnpike. Drive north on Rt. 130 for 0.9 miles, then turn left onto Rt. 526. In about 0.3 miles, where Rt. 526 joins Rt. 33 at an angle, immediately turn right, staying on Rt. 526. Go 3 miles to the intersection with Rt. 535, Old Trenton Road. Turn left onto Rt. 535 and continue one-quarter mile to the park entrance, on the right.

From southwestern New Jersey or the Philadelphia area, take the New Jersey Turnpike north to Exit 7A (I-195). Go west on I-195 for 2 miles to Exit 5 (US 130), and proceed north on US 130 as described in the preceding paragraph.

Mercer County Park can also be approached from the west via US 1. Exit onto Quakerbridge Rd. (Rt. 533), and go southeast for about 2.2 miles to Hughes Dr. Turn left and drive about 0.7 miles to the west entrance to the park, on the left.

Birding

The main road across the park is a wide boulevard about 2 miles long. Drive in about 1 mile from either Rt. 535 on the east or Hughes Dr. on the west, to the road that leads to the parking lot for the boathouse on the north side of the road. Park in the lot, which is where a Scissor-tailed Flycatcher spent two weeks in the fall of 1984, and walk down to Lake Mercer. The paved walkway that extends into the lake provides an excellent vantage point for scanning the water and shore in all directions.

In late summer and early fall, small numbers of herons and egrets appear at the lake to feed, some of them lingering for months. Great Egret and Great Blue Heron are the two most common species, but Little Blue Heron

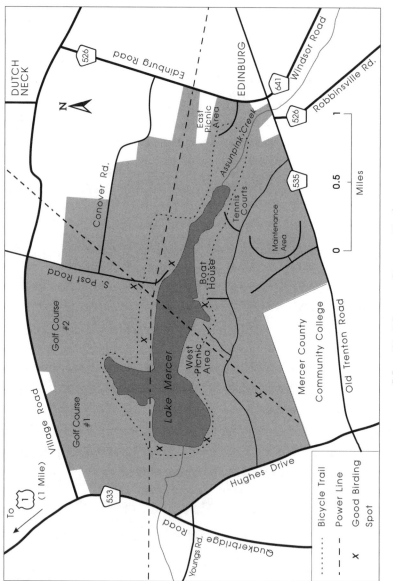

Map 51. Mercer County Park

and Snowy Egret are also regular visitors. A variety of shorebirds can be found at Lake Mercer from July through October along the edges.

Gulls and (occasionally) terns often roost on Lake Mercer. Ring-billed Gull is the common species, but other regulars are Herring Gull in the colder months and Laughing Gull in the warmer months. Bonaparte's Gull has occurred, both Least and Forster's terns have been found on the lake in late summer and fall, and Caspian Tern is to be expected. Lake Mercer also is a good spot for migrant waterfowl in March through April and October through November.

During the hunting season, many ducks from nearby Lake Assunpink flee to Mercer County Park. Some of the regular visitors are Tundra Swan, Canada Goose, Wood Duck, Green-winged and Blue-winged teal, Mallard, Northern Pintail, Ring-necked Duck, Hooded Merganser, and Ruddy Duck. The lake is regularly home to one of the largest concentrations of Common Mergansers in the state, thousands being present in spring just after the ice begins to thaw. In addition to the waterfowl, Pied-billed Grebe and Double-crested Cormorants are regular migrants in spring and fall and the latter may nest in the flooded woodlands at the east end of the lake.

To visit another part of the park, drive out the west entrance to Hughes Dr. and turn right. Go about 0.7 miles to Quakerbridge Rd., turn right, and continue about 0.75 miles farther to Village Rd., then turn right. Go about 1.7 miles on Village Rd. to the intersection with Post Rd., and turn right onto S. Post Rd. Follow S. Post Rd. for about 1 mile to its end at a dirt parking area on the north shore of Lake Mercer.

The woods and fields here are good for nesting and migrant birds; the power line rights-of-way also provide good paths for exploring this part of the park. Walking west under the power lines you will soon come to a depression that can be a bit wet and very weedy. This is an excellent spot for migrant sparrows, including White-crowned and Lincoln's sparrows. Blue Grosbeaks nest along the right-of-way. In addition to those species already mentioned, Northern Bobwhite, Brown Thrasher, Yellow-breasted Chat, and Eastern Meadowlark are among the approximately 60 species that nest in the park.

The final point of access to the park is the east picnic area. To reach it from the parking lot on the north shore, go north on S. Post Rd. for about one-half mile to Conover Rd. on the right. Turn right and proceed to Edinburg Rd., Rt. 526. Turn right and drive about 0.6 miles to the entrance to the picnic area, on the right. Great Horned Owl, Yellow-billed Cuckoo, and Eastern Phoebe have been found nesting here, and there is access to a nice riparian woods at the footbridge over Assunpink Creek. If you continue past the entrance to the picnic area for another 0.2 miles, you will come to the junction of Rts. 526, 535, and 641 in Edinburg.

☛

Hamilton-Trenton Marsh

(John A. Roebling Memorial Park)

John A. Roebling Memorial Park (Hamilton-Trenton Marsh, as it is known to birders) is an excellent place to observe spring migration in late April and early May and is well known for its variety of nesting marsh birds. The park, a unit of the Mercer County Park System, is located in Hamilton Township on the southeast side of Trenton. It is the most accessible part of a large system of wetlands that extends for about 3 miles along the Delaware River between Trenton and Bordentown and up to 1 mile inland. Some of the local specialties are Pied-billed Grebe, Least Bittern, American Bittern (now very rare), King Rail (rare), Virginia Rail, Sora, Common Moorhen, and Marsh Wren.

The park comprises about 300 acres of marshes, ponds, streams, second-growth bottomland deciduous woods, and thickets of viburnum and other shrubs. More than 210 species of birds have been recorded here, mainly by Ray Blicharz and members of the Trenton Naturalists Club. Many birders come here in late April, because the birds arrive here about one week earlier than in the northern part of the state. The D&R Greenway has done an outstanding job of rehabilitating the park and providing both additional trails and oversight.

Directions

From the north, take the New Jersey Turnpike south to Exit 7A (I-195) and follow I-195 west for 5 miles to Exit 2 (Rt. 206, S. Broad St.). Turn left at the exit, then go 0.1 mile to the traffic light and turn right onto S. Broad St. Follow this west (through the White Horse Circle where it becomes Rt. 206) for 2.3 miles to Sewell Ave. on the left. (Sewell Ave. is in the 1800 block, one block east of the conspicuous green steeple of Holy Angels Church.) Turn left onto Sewell and follow it through three intersections (stop signs) to its end (0.2 miles), where a dirt road bears off to the left and down a hill. Follow the dirt road down the hill and park at the beginning of the causeway that separates Spring Lake on the left from a marshy pond on the right. [DeLorme 42, N-3]

Alternatively, take either Rt. 31 or Rt. 206 south into Trenton, where these routes intersect; then follow Rt. 206 south. From the point where Rt. 206 crosses over US 1, Sewell Ave. is about 2.0 miles, on the right.

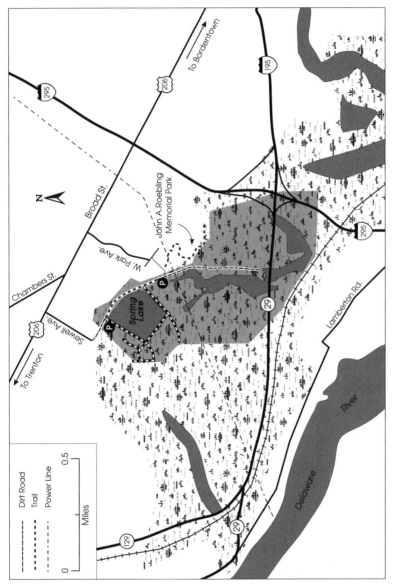

Map 52. Hamilton-Trenton Marsh

From the Philadelphia area, take US 1 north across the toll bridge into Trenton, then take the first exit; bear right, following the signs for Rt. 29. After about 0.2 miles, turn left onto the John Fitch Parkway (Rt. 29), which soon becomes Lamberton St. (This area was under construction in 2001 and the directions may have changed). Turn left onto Lalor St. (about 1 mile total from exit ramp), following the signs for Rt. 206 South. Go 1.1 miles to S. Broad St. and turn right. Sewell Ave. is 0.2 miles ahead on the right.

From southern New Jersey, take the New Jersey Turnpike north to Exit 7 (Bordentown). Turn north onto Rt. 206 and go about 5 miles to the White Horse Circle. Sewell Ave. is another 1.6 miles ahead on the left.

Birding

Spring Lake is good for migrant waterfowl (especially Ring-necked Duck in March through April and October through November) and for nesting Pied-billed Grebe. The marshy area to the right has nesting Common Moorhen. Willow Flycatcher, Yellow Warbler, and Carolina Wren are common around the borders of the marsh. As you walk along the edge of the marsh, watch for Least Bittern, Green Heron, and Spotted Sandpiper (all nesters), Black-crowned Night Heron, and Common Snipe, all of which are common migrants in late April to early May.

At the far end of the causeway (about 400 yards), a path leads off to the left along the lake and a footbridge leads straight ahead across a creek. Cross the footbridge and follow the path into the woods; it is excellent for migrant songbirds in spring and fall, but the first stretch is very muddy.

Rusty Blackbirds are abundant in the wet woodland in late April, and with luck you might flush an American Woodcock. Early migrants such as Sharp-shinned and Broad-winged hawks, Yellow-bellied Sapsucker, Eastern Kingbird, Golden-crowned and Ruby-crowned kinglets, Blue-gray Gnatcatcher, Hermit Thrush, White-eyed and Blue-headed vireos, Yellow, Palm, Yellow-rumped, and Black-and-white warblers, Louisiana and Northern waterthrushes, and Purple Finch are regular here and easy to see before the leaves come out. In May, you can expect cuckoos, Ruby-throated Hummingbird, flycatchers, and a long list of migrant thrushes, vireos, warblers, and other songbirds.

The path through the woods is unmarked, but the area is not extensive and you're not likely to get lost. Eventually, you will have to return to the footbridge. When you do, turn right and take the path along the lake. All of the eastern swallows are usually present by the end of April, and can be seen hawking insects over the ponds. Migrant Ospreys find the fishing good, and sit in one of the tall dead trees to enjoy their catch.

After about 100 yards, the trail forks. Bear right toward the power transmission lines. This trail follows the border of an extensive marsh where many species nest, including Least Bittern, Wood Duck, King Rail (rare), Virginia Rail, Sora, American Coot, Eastern Kingbird, Tree Swallow, Marsh Wren, Yellow Warbler, Common Yellowthroat, and Swamp Sparrow.

Return to your parking area and walk along the dirt road. Just past Spring Lake, there is a storm sewer outlet where the marshes begin; this is an excellent spot in winter for Common Snipe, Rusty Blackbird, and even an occasional yellowlegs. About 0.7 miles from the causeway, you will come to a picnic area. In addition to being a pleasant spot to enjoy your lunch, the woods around the picnic grounds are excellent for migrant warblers in spring and fall and for Yellow-bellied Flycatcher and Philadelphia Vireo in fall. A new Nature Trail, accessible from the power line cut just east of the Park Ave. entrance road (see map) runs through the woods behind the picnic table, but the noise from nearby I-295 can make the birding difficult.

The D&R Greenway has developed a new trail starting at the scenic overlook on I-295, about 2 miles south of the junction with I-195, and it also has provided canoe launches along Crosswicks Creek. Birding by canoe provides a great way to get into parts of the marsh inaccessible by foot.

D A Sibley 1985

North Coast Region

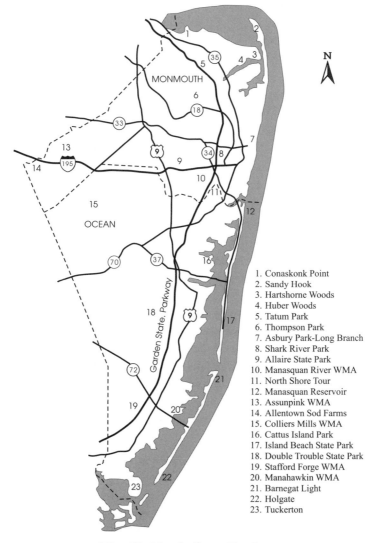

N

1. Conaskonk Point
2. Sandy Hook
3. Hartshorne Woods
4. Huber Woods
5. Tatum Park
6. Thompson Park
7. Asbury Park-Long Branch
8. Shark River Park
9. Allaire State Park
10. Manasquan River WMA
11. North Shore Tour
12. Manasquan Reservoir
13. Assunpink WMA
14. Allentown Sod Farms
15. Colliers Mills WMA
16. Cattus Island Park
17. Island Beach State Park
18. Double Trouble State Park
19. Stafford Forge WMA
20. Manahawkin WMA
21. Barnegat Light
22. Holgate
23. Tuckerton

Map 53. North Coast Region

Conaskonk Point

This area of salt marsh and beach at Union Beach on Raritan Bay, between Sandy Hook and South Amboy, is good for migrant terns and shorebirds from late spring through early fall. It provides a good vantage point for watching southbound loons and waterfowl in the fall. Winter finds rafts of scaup and other diving ducks offshore, a few raptors over the salt marsh, and Horned Lark and Snow Bunting on the beach. Gulls, including an occasional rarity, are present at all seasons. Conaskonk makes a good spot to spend an hour or two as part of a trip to Sandy Hook or South Amboy.

Some of the noteworthy species recorded at Conaskonk in recent decades are Hudsonian and Marbled godwits, Baird's and Curlew sandpipers, and Little and Black-headed gulls, and Snowy Owl. Caspian, Royal, and Black terns all occur in late summer. There are few species of breeding birds, but one of them is the sometimes elusive Saltmarsh Sharp-tailed Sparrow, which is abundant here. Others include American Oystercatcher and Boat-tailed Grackle.

Directions

Take the Garden State Parkway to Exit 117 (Keyport and Hazlet), and take Rt. 36 east (follow signs for Sandy Hook, Gateway National Recreation Area). Go about 2.6 miles from the tollbooth to the jughandle turn for Union Ave. north toward Union Beach. After about 0.8 miles, Union Ave. bears slightly left and becomes Front St.; continue another 0.3 miles to the intersection with Florence Ave. and park on the right overlooking the water. [DeLorme 38, L-8]

Birding

The parking areas along the waterfront in Union Beach provide a good view of the waters of Raritan Bay and the fishing weirs offshore. From spring through fall, but especially in late summer, terns can be seen sitting on the beach or flying back and forth fishing in the surf. Common and Least terns are the dominant species, since both breed nearby, but Caspian, Royal, and Black terns are annual visitors.

Gulls are most common in the winter, when Iceland, Glaucous, and Lesser Black-backed should be looked for, but Little Gull and Black-headed Gull occur among migrant flocks of Bonaparte's Gulls in spring or late fall. Double-crested Cormorants can be seen sitting on the fishing weirs at all seasons, and are joined by a few Great Cormorants in winter. Ospreys, both migrants and nesting birds from nearby Sandy Hook, also pause to rest on the weirs.

After scanning the bay, continue on Front St. another 0.25 miles to its end and park in the dirt parking area. Walk north along the beach, scanning the sod banks and mudflats for shorebirds, mainly Black-bellied and Semipalmated plovers, Semipalmated and Least sandpipers, and Short-billed Dowitcher. In a few hundred yards, you will come to a creek; in former times, you could cross the creek with knee boots at low tide, but the channel is now too deep. Some of the nesting species along the route from the parking lot to the creek are Willow Flycatcher, Fish Crow, Marsh Wren, Yellow Warbler, Common Yellowthroat, Song Sparrow, and Boat-tailed Grackle.

The best access to the shoreline west of the point and to the point itself is from Edmunds Ave. Turn right out of the parking lot onto Dock St. and go 0.4 miles back to Florence Ave. Turn right again, drive 0.25 miles to Edmunds Ave., the fourth street on the right, and turn right. Take Edmunds 0.25 miles to its end at a gate with No Parking and No Trespassing signs. Turn left onto Chingarora Ave., and park on the right off the pavement. A muddy dirt road leads around the gate for a few yards and rejoins the dirt extension of Edmunds Ave. The No Trespassing signs are intended to keep out vehicles, not pedestrians.

Walk the dirt road toward the beach, a distance of about 500 yards. Along the way you pass through an overgrown area with small trees and more Willow Flycatchers, Yellow Warblers, and Song Sparrows, then through an extensive salt marsh, where Clapper Rail, Willet, Marsh Wren, Saltmarsh Sharp-tailed Sparrow, and Seaside Sparrow nest. Northern Harriers hunt over the marsh in fall and winter, Rough-legged Hawk is sometimes present in winter, and both Merlin and Peregrine have been seen in migration. A variety of sparrows can be found in the weedy areas in winter, and Horned Lark and Snow Bunting are frequently on the beach.

At the beach, turn right toward Conaskonk Point, which is about one-half mile northeast. The sandbar at the point is a favorite resting place for gulls, terns, Black Skimmers, and shorebirds. Here and along the way you may find American Oystercatcher (nests in the salt marsh), Greater and Lesser yellowlegs, Ruddy Turnstone, Red Knot, Sanderling, White-rumped and Stilt sandpipers, and Dunlin, in addition to the species already noted.

Sandy Hook
(Gateway National Recreation Area)

Sandy Hook is not only an exciting place to discover birds, it is also unique from a geographical and historical perspective. The 5-mile long peninsula of Sandy Hook juts northward toward the center of Lower New York Bay, where its commanding position at the gateway to New York harbor has determined its history for 300 years. Since the late 1600s, Sandy Hook has been the site of forts, lighthouses, and later a Coast Guard Station. Today, as a 1,600-acre unit of Gateway National Recreation Area, it is an interesting historical spot and an extremely popular summer bathing beach. One benefit of the many years of military occupation is that, unlike most of the barrier islands in New Jersey, much of Sandy Hook has escaped development and retains an impressive array of habitats including holly forest, deciduous woods, beach, mudflats, and dunes.

As a coastal peninsula along a major flyway, "The Hook" is an outstanding place to find migrant birds in spring and fall. There is an excellent hawk migration in March and April, followed by waves of songbirds in May. In fall, the songbird migration holds strong from early August to the end of October, with an ever-changing kaleidoscope of species. Sandy Hook supports an interesting diversity of breeding birds during summer, although it is not regularly birded at that season because of the beach crowds. In winter, it is a good place to look for seabirds and waterfowl, the rarer gulls, winter finches, Snow Buntings, and longspurs.

The more sought-after species that occur regularly at Sandy Hook include Red-necked Grebe, Great Cormorant, Iceland, Glaucous, and Lesser Black-backed gulls, Yellow-bellied Flycatcher, Gray-cheeked Thrush, Philadelphia Vireo, Orange-crowned, Connecticut, and Mourning warblers, Lincoln's Sparrow, and Lapland Longspur. Rarities found here in recent years are Eared Grebe, Pacific Loon, Barrow's Goldeneye, Swallow-tailed Kite, Groove-billed Ani, Gray and Western kingbirds, Scissor-tailed Flycatcher, Townsend's Warbler, LeConte's, Clay-colored, and Lark sparrows, and Chestnut-collared Longspur. The variety of both expected and unexpected species makes Sandy Hook an exciting place to bird at any season. The recent arrival of New Jersey Audubon Society's Sandy Hook Bird Observatory on Hartshorne Dr. will provide a constant presence and source of information for birders.

Directions

Take the Garden State Parkway to Exit 117 (Keyport, Rt. 36). Go east on Rt. 36 for 13 miles, then follow the signs for the exit on the right just after you cross the bridge over the Navesink River. The exit road leads under the bridge and then to the entrance to Gateway National Recreation Area, Sandy Hook Unit, in about 0.3 miles. There is an entrance fee in summer. [DeLorme 45, B-20]

Birding

The first parking lot on the right, Lot B, is 0.2 miles past the entrance. From late fall to early spring, search here for loons, grebes, scoters and other sea ducks, and gulls; this has been one of the best spots on the coast for Red-necked Grebe. Lot C, one-half mile north of Lot B, is another good place to check the ocean off the breakwater; Little Gull has been seen here in winter.

From Lot C, continue north another one-half mile to the Visitor Center parking lot on the right. Walk across the busy road to the boardwalk that leads out to the edge of Spermaceti Cove. Great Cormorants often roost on the mudflats around the cove in winter, and Brant and Greater Scaup are usually abundant, the latter sometimes numbering over 10,000. Other winter ducks here are Black Duck, Bufflehead, Common Goldeneye, and Red-breasted Merganser.

The best place to observe goldeneyes and search for Barrow's Goldeneye is from the maintenance road opposite the road to parking Lot F (South Beach). From the Visitor Center lot, drive north about one-half mile and park in the lot in the middle of the road opposite a maintenance area. Walk north about 0.25 miles to the maintenance road on the left, which is closed by a gate. Go around the gate and walk the 0.25 miles to the water and scan for the goldeneyes.

Return to your car and continue north about 0.25 miles to the right turn for Lot F (South Beach); after about 0.4 miles, you will reach the parking lot. After parking, walk back along the road for about 200 yards, and turn right on a path that leads north into the woods. This is excellent for spring and fall migrant songbirds, including some of the less common species, such as Yellow-bellied Flycatcher, Gray-cheeked Thrush, Philadelphia Vireo, Connecticut Warbler (mainly September), and Mourning Warbler (late May to early June). Look and listen for chickadees; the resident species at Sandy Hook is the Black-capped Chickadee, while the resident species on the nearby mainland at Highlands is the Carolina Chickadee. The trail continues for a little over one-half mile, and eventually meets the paved road to North Beach. Near its northern end are some groves of planted pines that attract migrants and crossbills in winter during invasion years.

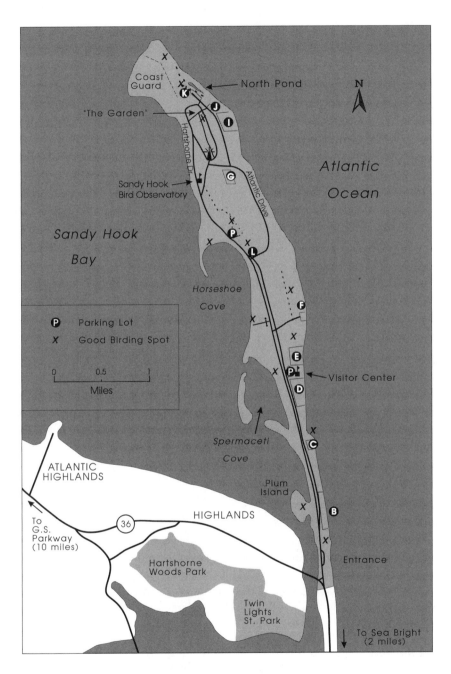

Coast Guard

North Pond

N

"The Garden"

Hartshorne Dr.

Sandy Hook Bird Observatory

Atlantic Drive

Atlantic Ocean

Sandy Hook Bay

K

J

I

G

P

L

F

Horseshoe Cove

P Parking Lot

X Good Birding Spot

0   0.5
Miles

E

P

D

Visitor Center

X

C

Spermaceti Cove

Plum Island

X

B

ATLANTIC HIGHLANDS

To G.S. Parkway (10 miles)

36

HIGHLANDS

Hartshorne Woods Park

Twin Lights St. Park

Entrance

To Sea Bright (2 miles)

Map 54. Sandy Hook

Return to parking Lot F and walk south along the beach for a short distance to a trail that leads inland toward a large area surrounded by a chain-link fence. This is the maintenance area, which is also accessible from parking Lot E near the Visitors Center. The fence along the maintenance area, especially the eastern side, is excellent for migrant sparrows in October. In addition to all the common species, White-crowned and Lincoln's sparrows are regular, and Lark Sparrow and Clay-colored Sparrow usually appear each year.

Drive back to the main road from Lot F and turn right. In about 0.7 miles, you will come to a junction with a right turn for North Beach. Continue straight ahead another 0.3 miles, past Lot L, and turn into the parking area for the group camping area, where there is a portable toilet. Cross the street and walk toward the beach to scan Horseshoe Cove. Winter birds here include Horned Grebe, Great Cormorant, Bufflehead, Common Goldeneye, and Red-breasted Merganser. When a Barrow's Goldeneye is present, it can sometimes be seen from here. The marsh on the north side of the path is good for rails and herons, and often has a nesting Osprey.

Return to the parking lot and take the trail on the left, just before the first parking spot. This leads through some woods that can be great for migrants, especially in the fall. After a couple of hundred yards, the path emerges into an open area with a concrete roadway and an old rusty metal building. This area is good for Winter Wren and sparrows in spring and fall. Follow the path that leads around the left side of the building into a holly woods, with a dense tangle of cat briar and other undergrowth. This is an excellent spot in migration for many songbirds, including skulkers such as Winter Wren, Gray-cheeked Thrush, Connecticut Warbler, and Mourning Warbler.

After a short distance, you will emerge into a clearing with a yellow brick building on the left. Just ahead on the right, another partly overgrown trail goes about 50 yards into the dense woods; this is another place to check for migrants. At this point, you can either retrace your steps back to the parking lot or continue down the road north of the yellow building. The next couple of hundred yards to the junction with the main road can also be outstanding for migrants. You can return to your car along the main road, or retrace your route through the woods.

From the parking lot, turn right. Drive north along the main road to the fork by the Nike missile. To visit the Sandy Hook Bird Observatory, take the left fork to the first building on the right, which is the Observatory. Otherwise, take the right fork and continue past the marine science laboratories and the next right turn, then bear right at the lighthouse. Stay right at the next junction until you come to a stop sign, just past an old battery fortress, a total distance of about 1.3 miles from the Horseshoe Cove parking lot. Park on the left and explore the area, shown as The Garden on the map. When the garden was cultivated, it used to be a great spot for migrant warblers and sparrows in the fall. Although it is no longer used, the area and the surrounding trees can still be good for migrants in spring and fall.

From the garden, take the road between the two houses, then the first right a short distance to parking Lot K. Drive all the way to the north end of Lot K and park. Follow the path north along the fence. Just inside the gate, there is another small gate on the right. Go through this and follow the trail through the poison ivy tangles to the Locust Grove, another good spot for migrants in spring and fall.

As you continue past the locust grove, you will come out on the top of the dunes overlooking North Pond, with the ocean and the entrance to New York Harbor in front of you. North Pond itself may have coots and a variety of ducks, Pied-billed Grebe, Belted Kingfisher, and rails. Numerous rarities have been found in this area, including Purple Gallinule, Groove-billed Ani, and Gray Kingbird. The dunes here are also good for migrant raptors, especially in spring, when Sandy Hook Bird Observatory maintains a migration watch from a platform just to your left. In fall, hundreds of migrant Blue Jays wander up and down the Hook, uncertain about where to go.

The trail continues to the left, past the observation platform, and intersects the Fisherman's Trail. A right turn here will lead you several hundred yards out to the beach, where Piping Plovers, and Least and Common terns nest. This is also a good spot for migrant shorebirds in fall and for Snow Buntings (with the occasional Lapland Longspur) in winter. A left turn at the Fisherman's Trail leads you a few yards back to the main path. Here, you can go right for about 50 yards along the fence by the government housing, then return on the path to the parking lot.

The beach is also accessible from Lot J, where a shorter hike takes you to the water's edge and an area popular with gulls and Snow Buntings. Turn left and go about 1 mile to the T intersection opposite Lot G. Turn right and drive past Lot G to the parking lot on the left, just before the stop sign. The area on the left between Lot G and the parking lot can be excellent for migrant sparrows, especially in October, when LeConte's Sparrow has been seen several times.

Some of the common breeding birds at Sandy Hook, in addition to those mentioned above, are Green Heron, Clapper Rail, Killdeer, American Woodcock, Herring Gull, Whip-poor-will, Eastern Kingbird, Black-capped Chickadee, Brown Thrasher, White-eyed Vireo, American Redstart, Common Yellowthroat, and Boat-tailed Grackle.

Hartshorne Woods

This Monmouth County park contains several hundred acres of upland deciduous forest on the highlands above Sandy Hook. The park has migrant songbirds in spring and fall and supports a small variety of breeding birds.

Directions

Take the Garden State Parkway to Exit 117 (Keyport, Rt. 36). Go east on Rt. 36 for 10 miles to Atlantic Highlands. Continue on Rt. 36 about 0.8 miles past the traffic light in Atlantic Highlands, then bear right at a traffic light onto Valley Road East., where Rt. 36 bears left. Go about 0.6 miles, then turn left onto Navesink Ave. A parking area for the park is about one-half mile ahead on the right. [DeLorme 45, A-18]

Birding

A trail guide is posted at the parking area and a trail map is usually available there, as well. Following the numerous trails, many of which are paved, you can explore the entire park in an hour or so. The mature deciduous woodland of oaks, sycamores, and Tulip trees can have a good variety of migrant warblers in early May, attracted to the insects to be found on the flowers and catkins of the trees. Other migrants to watch and listen for include flycatchers, thrushes, Scarlet Tanager, and Rose-breasted Grosbeak. The more protracted fall migration brings the same species, but birders generally focus their attention on nearby Sandy Hook.

❦

Huber Woods

This 255-acre park is one of the jewels of the Monmouth County Park System. Six miles of trails and an environmental center provide ample opportunity for nature study and bird watching, as well as an equestrian area.

Directions

Following the directions for Sandy Hook, take Rt. 36 east to Atlantic Highlands and turn right onto Grand Ave. Go south on Grand Ave., which

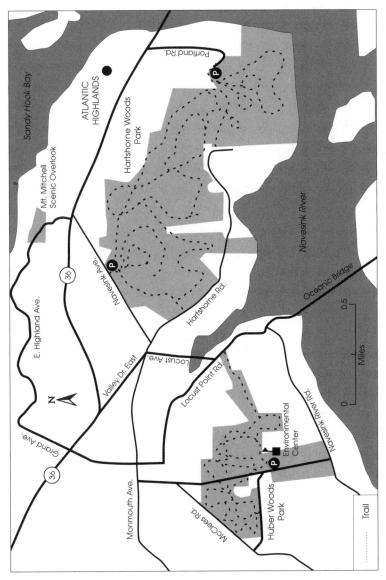

Map 55. Hartshorne Woods and Huber Woods

Sandy Hook Bay

Mt. Mitchell
Scenic Overlook

ATLANTIC
HIGHLANDS

Portland Rd.

Hartshorne Woods
Park

Navesink River

E. Highland Ave.

36

Navesink Ave.

Hartshorne Rd.

Oceanic Bridge

Valley Dr. East

Locust Ave.

0.5

Miles

Grand Ave.

36

Locust Point Rd.

Navesink River Rd.

Environmental
Center

0

Monmouth Ave.

McClees Rd.

Huber Woods
Park

N

Trail

becomes Navesink Ave., for one-half mile to Monmouth Ave. Turn right and drive 0.15 miles to Brown's Dock Rd, and turn left. Drive south on Brown's Dock Rd., staying left at the fork, for about 1 mile to the parking lot, on the left. [DeLorme 45, B-16]

Birding

The bird feeders at the Environmental Center are worth checking for Pine Siskin and other finches in winter, as well as the usual wintering songbirds. The trailhead for the various trails is just north of the parking lot. Here, the short Nature Loop takes you through some woods with a dense understory of mountain laurel, where you may find a variety of migrant birds in spring and fall.

The longer Many Log Run, Valley View, and Claypit Run trails allow you to explore the entirety of the park, most of which is covered by mature deciduous woods of tulip trees, maples, oaks, and hickories. Here you will find the typical woodland species, such as woodpeckers, Blue Jays, Carolina Chickadees, Tufted Titmice, and White-breasted Nuthatches, plus a variety of migratory breeding birds, such as Eastern Wood-Pewee, Red-eyed Vireo, Wood Thrush, American Redstart, Scarlet Tanager, and others.

☂

Tatum Park

This 368-acre unit of the Monmouth County Park System contains an interesting mix of deciduous woods, thickets, and tangles in a hilly section of Middletown. It is excellent for songbirds in migration and provides sufficient food and cover to harbor good numbers of birds in winter.

Directions

Take the Garden State Parkway to Exit 114 (Holmdel). From the exit ramp, turn left if coming from the north, right if coming from the south, onto Red Hill Rd. Go about 0.3 miles to the first intersection, where Red Hill Rd. bears slightly right. Continue on Red Hill Rd. for about 1.5 miles to the park's Red Hill Activity Center entrance, on the left. [DeLorme 44, B-11]

Birding

The park has five marked trails varying in length from the easy half-mile Holly Grove Trail that loops through a grove of mature holly trees to the moderate 2.3-mile Tatum Ramble Trail that explores a variety of fields and forest. The Holly Grove, Dogwood Hollow, and Indian Springs Trails can be accessed from the Red Hill parking area. For the two other trails, turn left onto Red Hill Rd. and go 0.4 miles to Holland Rd., the first intersection. Turn left and drive about one-half mile to the entrance to the Holland Activity Center on the left. The Tatum Ramble Trail and the Meadow Run Trail, a 1-mile loop off the Tatum Ramble Trail can be reached from this parking area.

Tatum Park is especially good for songbirds in migration in both spring and fall. It also has an assortment of breeding birds because of the diversity of habitat. Among these are Hairy, Downy, and Red-bellied woodpeckers, Eastern Wood-Pewee, Red-eyed Vireo, Carolina Chickadee, Tufted Titmouse, White-breasted Nuthatch, Wood Thrush, Ovenbird, American Redstart, Scarlet Tanager, and Baltimore Oriole. In winter, expect mainly the resident species, plus a few sparrows around the field edges.

✝

Thompson Park

This 665-acre park in Monmouth County has had an unusual number of rarities over the years. The fields, hedgerows, freshwater lake and riparian woodlands provide a diversity of habitat that ensures a good variety of both migrant, breeding, and wintering species. The park management plan is still somewhat in flux, with numerous recreational playing fields, but also with many of the fields in the western part of the park being leased for commercial farming. Among the unusual species recorded here in the past twenty years are Northern Shrike, Clay-colored Sparrow, and Lark Sparrow.

Directions

Take the Garden State Parkway to Exit 109 (Red Bank, Tinton Falls), and turn right, if coming from the north, left coming from the south, onto Newman Springs Rd. Go 2.3 miles (2.6, if you came from the south), past the main entrance to Thompson Park, and turn left on an unmarked dirt road, directly across from the Christian Brothers Academy. [DeLorme 44, F-10]

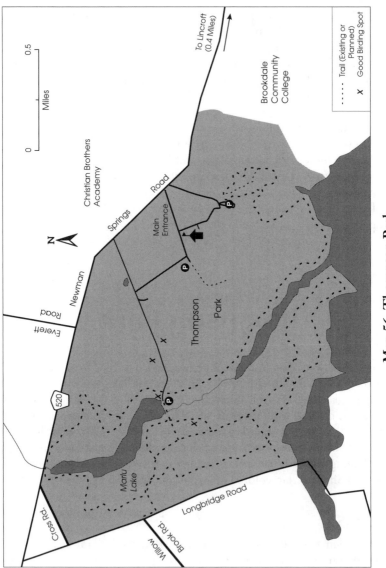

Map 56. Thompson Park

Legend:
- Trail (Existing or Planned)
- X Good Birding Spot

Christian Brothers Academy

Brookdale Community College

To Lincroft (0.4 Miles)

Springs Road

Main Entrance

Thompson Park

Newman

Everett Road

520

Marlu Lake

Cross Rd.

Willow Brook Rd.

Longbridge Road

N

Miles
0   0.5

Birding

Stop and check the small pond on the right a few hundred yards in from the highway for swallows, then continue past the park building to the farm fields. The area from here to Marlu Lake is a mixture of farm fields and hedgerows, with some trees. Most of the fields are leased for farming, so you won't find much during the growing season. In late fall and winter, however, the fields and hedgerows can be full of sparrows and other birds of this habitat. Northern Shrike has wintered several times, and the long list of sparrows includes Lincoln's (can be quite common in October), White-crowned, Vesper, Grasshopper, and Clay-colored (annual).

The lake can be good for a variety of dabbling and diving ducks from fall through spring, including Wood Duck, Ring-necked Duck, and Hooded Merganser. Beyond the lake there is another collection of hedgerows and fields, most of which are not farmed, but mowed annually. There is also a dense stand of deciduous woods along the stream from the outlet of the lake to the Swimming River Reservoir. There are several dirt roads through this area, and paths are kept open along the edges of the fields by mowing. Nesting species include Willow and Great Crested flycatchers, Cedar Waxwing, Brown Thrasher, Yellow Warbler, Common Yellowthroat, Scarlet Tanager, Field and Song sparrows, Indigo Bunting, Rose-breasted Grosbeak, Baltimore and Orchard orioles, and American Goldfinch. Numerous trails are planned or already laid out, and you can walk the dirt roads as well. The main trail leads south and makes a loop along the Swimming River Reservoir.

There are restroom facilities at the park headquarters, the second right turn if you head back toward the parkway on Newman Springs Rd., and a trail map will be available there in the near future.

✝

Asbury Park to Long Branch

The North Shore north of Belmar is not nearly as productive for birding as it is south of Belmar but has a few good spots of its own. This shorter tour can be followed as a sequel to the North Shore Tour, or undertaken by itself or in conjunction with a trip to Sandy Hook. Although the directions are from south to north, you should be able to follow the reverse, as well.

Directions

From the north or south, take the Garden State Parkway to Exit 102 (Asbury Park). Go east on Asbury Ave. for 1.7 miles to the junction with Rt. 66, then

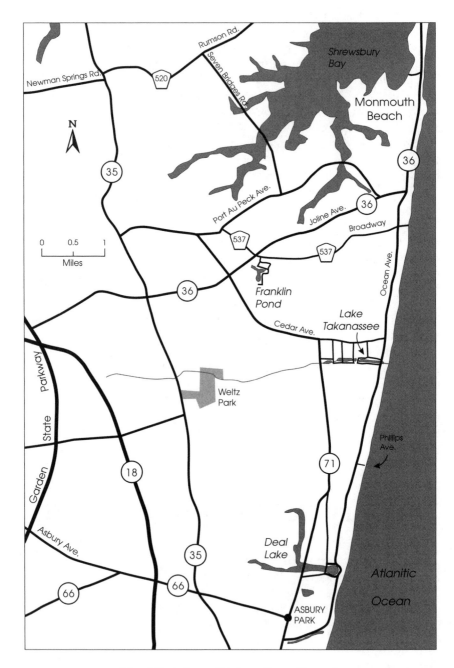

Map 57. Asbury Park to Long Branch

continue on Rt. 66 for 2.6 miles to the junction with Rt. 77, Main St., in Asbury Park. Turn left, and drive about 0.6 miles to Deal Lake, where Rt. 77 bends right to follow the lakeshore. [DeLorme 45, L-18]

From the south, take the Garden State Parkway to Exit 100 and follow the sign for Rt. 66 east toward Asbury Park. Go east on Rt. 66 for 2.2 miles to the junction with Asbury Ave. Continue as described in the previous paragraph.

Birding

In winter when the water is frozen, Deal Lake attracts large numbers of gulls that come to loaf and roost on the ice. In addition to the usual Ring-billed, Herring, and Great Black-backed, there is a good possibility of finding Lesser Black-backed Gull, and perhaps Iceland and Glaucous gulls. In some years, there are a few Bonaparte's Gulls as well, so check them for Little or Black-headed gulls, rare possibilities.

Continue along Deal Lake Rd. 0.7 miles to the east end of the lake (don't turn left when Rt. 71 crosses the lake), to a parking area, where you can scan the ocean. There is seldom much here, but the jetties in Asbury Park used to have the occasional eider. As the road turns back west along the north shore, take the second right, Ocean Ave. (if you come to Rt. 71, you've gone one block too far). Drive north about 1.6 miles to Phillips Ave., on the right. A short drive will take you to the beach, where a pier leads over the water. The beach to the north of the pier and the surrounding waters can have a variety of gulls and waterfowl.

Drive north another 1.6 miles to South Lake Drive, and turn left along the south shore of Lake Takanassee. This small and unimposing lake is remarkably good for waterfowl and gulls. It has traditionally been the preferred pond along the north shore for Bonaparte's Gull, and there are many records of Black-headed Gull, although there have been few in the past decade. Among the ducks to be expected here are Canvasback and Hooded Merganser.

After driving along the south shore (0.3 miles), the road loops back along the north shore. Don't complete the loop, but take the first left, Green Ave., 0.25 miles to Cedar Ave., and turn left. Go 0.2 miles and take the second left, Hoey Ave., about 0.25 miles and park beside the road. The tiny pond on the left (east) side of the road is favored by Hooded Merganser, Ring-necked Duck, and many other species. The much larger pond on the right has the same species, plus numerous American Coots and Ruddy Ducks. There is often a flock of American Wigeon here, and Eurasian Wigeon has been seen many times.

Turn right onto Overlook Ave. and continue across Woodgate Ave. to the T at Van Court Ave. Turn right and take the first left, Elinore Ave., along the north side of the last of the ponds. This pond, too, has been a good spot for Eurasian Wigeon, but is usually overrun with Canada Geese. At Rt. 71, turn right and drive 0.3 miles north to Norwood Ave., and turn right. Norwood soon become Cedar Ave., which you should take all the way to Ocean Ave. (1 mile). Turn left on Ocean Ave. (which becomes Ocean Blvd.) and go about 0.4 miles to Howland Ave., on the right.

This road makes a short loop along the bluff overlooking the beach and jetties. Over the years, this area has often had Harlequin Duck. When the road returns to Ocean Blvd., turn right and go one-half mile to Bath Ave. Go one block to Ocean Ave. and turn left. The jetties along Ocean are worth scanning for Purple Sandpipers and Sanderlings. Follow Ocean Ave. for about a mile, then turn left to rejoin Ocean Blvd. When you come to the junction with Rt. 36 in 200 yards, you can turn left to head back to the Garden State Parkway (about 7 miles), or continue north to Sandy Hook (about 6 miles).

☞

Shark River Park

Owned by the Monmouth County Park Commission, this park encompasses 725 acres of recreational facilities, woods, fields, and riparian habitat along the Shark River. The main entrance to the park is off Schoolhouse Rd., but there is also parking access along Gully Rd.

Directions

See Map 58. Take the Garden State Parkway to Exit 100 (Rt. 33). Go east on Rt. 33 for 0.4 miles, then turn right onto Schoolhouse Rd. The park entrance is about one-half mile on the left. Gully Rd. is about 0.4 miles east of Schoolhouse Rd. on Rt. 33. [DeLorme 44, M-13]

Birding

The recreational facilities and one short trail are on the west side of Schoolhouse Rd., while the majority of the land area of the park and most of the trails are on the east side of Schoolhouse Rd., south of Shark River. The rugged 0.75-miles Rivers Edge Trail provides access to the riparian habitat along the river, while the 3-mile Hidden Creek Trail traverses all the different habitats of the park and can be accessed from either Schoolhouse Rd. or Gully Rd.

Like other similar woodland areas near the coast, Shark River Park can be very good for migrant songbirds in spring and, especially, in fall. Birdlife is similar to that in nearby Allaire State Park, although not quite as diverse.

✝

Allaire State Park

This 3,035-acre park in southern Monmouth County contains an interesting mixture of oak-pine woodland, upland deciduous forest, and bottomland deciduous woodland along the Manasquan River. It is the site of a restored village that preserves a glimpse into the life of a mid-nineteenth century iron mining and smelting village. It is an excellent spot in spring for migrant warblers and other songbirds, and supports a diverse population of breeding birds. Fall migration is also good, but the area attracts fewer birders at that season, when the nearby coastal locations are more productive. Noteworthy breeding birds at Allaire are Acadian Flycatcher, Prothonotary, Kentucky, and Hooded warblers, and Northern Waterthrush. Yellow-throated Warbler has nested at least once.

Directions

From northern or southern New Jersey, take the Garden State Parkway to Exit 98 (I-195). Follow the sign for I-195, then go west on I-195 for almost 3 miles to Exit 31B (Rt. 547). Follow the exit ramp onto Rt. 547, then turn right almost immediately onto Allaire Rd. (Rt. 524). Go about 1.2 miles to the main park entrance, on the right. Follow the entrance road for several hundred yards to the large parking area at Allaire Village (past the parking area for the Nature Center). The gate is open from 8:00 A.M. to sunset. [DeLorme 50, B-11]

From west-central New Jersey, take I-195 east to Exit 31B (Rt. 547) and proceed as just described.

Birding

From the parking area at Allaire Village, walk west (to your right as you drive into the parking lot) along the path. This trail is the former towpath of a canal that dates from the foundry days of 150 years ago. The woods are excellent for migrant songbirds in the spring; here, you can expect to find most

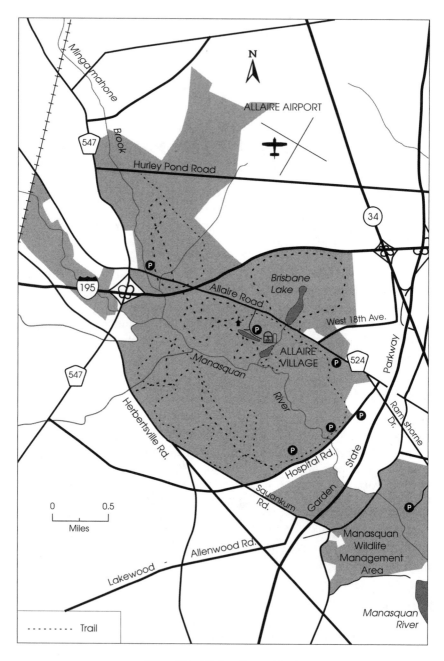

Map 58. Allaire State Park

species of flycatchers, kinglets, thrushes, vireos, warblers, tanagers, grosbeaks, and orioles that pass through New Jersey at that season.

After about 0.25 miles, you will pass a pond on the right that attracts migrant flycatchers. On the far side of the pond is the Nature Center. Continue along the towpath trail for another one-half mile until you approach the underpass at I-195, and turn onto a trail leading left. This trail makes a long loop through the mature deciduous woodland down to the Manasquan River, then eventually rejoins the towpath trail near the Nature Center.

Another productive trail is the nature trail that begins near the sawmill site, just below the fishing pond at Allaire Village. To reach this spot from the parking lot, walk east along the tow path past the Visitor Center, then turn right onto the path that parallels the fishing pond. You will soon come to an intersection of several paths, where the nature trail entrance is marked by a sign. This trail makes a circuit along the floodplain of the Manasquan River, where giant old American Sycamores and Silver Maples tower overhead. This is where Yellow-throated Warbler has nested.

Another good birding area at Allaire is the path around the pond at the family camping area. Drive back to Allaire Rd. and turn left. Go about 0.9 miles to a parking lot on the right, just beyond the entrance to the family camping area. The trail leads along the Mingamahone Brook, and is the best spot in the park for Prothonotary Warbler. Brisbane Lake has Ring-necked Ducks in early spring. It is located on Allaire Rd. about 0.4 miles east of the main park entrance.

A good spot for water birds is the pond belonging to the New Jersey Water Authority and the surrounding area. To reach this area from the main entrance, drive east on Allaire Rd. for about 1.3 miles to Hospital Rd., then turn right. Go about 0.25 miles to a small turn-out on the left, where you can park. Cross the road and walk the path past the Water Authority facility until you can see a fenced-in pond on the left. The pond has restricted access, but you can view it from the path. Numerous waterfowl occur here in winter, including Wood Duck, Gadwall, American Wigeon, Black Duck, Mallard, Northern Shoveler, Green-winged Teal (Eurasian Green-winged Teal has been seen), Ring-necked Duck, Hooded Merganser, and Ruddy Duck. A Sandhill Crane spent three days here in 1991 and Christmas Bird Counts have yielded American Woodcock, Common Snipe, Palm and Orange-crowned warblers, and Eastern Meadowlark. Breeding birds around the pond include Willow Flycatcher, Warbling Vireo, Eastern Bluebird, and Blue Grosbeak.

Approximately one-third of Allaire State Park lies south of the Manasquan River. This part of the park lies within the Pine Barrens, and contains all of the usual birds of that region. It is traversed by a hiking and horseback trail about 4 miles long (round trip), and is also crossed by an unimproved dirt road that is closed to traffic, but serves as an alternate trail. To reach this area from Allaire Rd., go south on Hospital Rd. for about 1.2 miles to a parking area on the right, where you can take the hiking/horseback trail.

To walk the dirt road, continue on foot 0.25 miles from the parking lot on Hospital Rd. to the road on the right. The dirt road is about 2 miles long and ends at Herbertsville Rd.; about 1.7 miles along it, a side road on the right leads north to the Manasquan River. To return to I-195 from the Hospital Rd. parking area, continue south for about one-half mile to Squankum Rd., go about 0.8 miles to Herbertsville Rd. (Rt. 549) and turn right again. Next, drive about 1.2 miles to Rt. 547 and turn right. I-195 is 0.3 miles ahead.

Breeding birds at Allaire, in addition to those already mentioned, include Wood Duck, Broad-winged Hawk, Eastern Screech, Great Horned, and Barred owls, Whip-poor-will, Red-bellied Woodpecker, Eastern Phoebe, Eastern Kingbird, Purple Martin, Carolina Wren, White-eyed and Yellow-throated vireos, Blue-winged, Yellow, Pine, Prairie, and Black-and-white warblers, American Redstart, Louisiana Waterthrush, Rose-breasted Grosbeak, and Indigo Bunting.

There are restrooms in the basement of the General Store near the main parking lot, and there is a snack bar at the adjacent Visitor Center. An entrance fee is charged at the main parking lot in summer.

☞

Manasquan River Wildlife Management Area

Located just east of the Garden State Parkway along the Monmouth-Ocean County Line, this 726-acre WMA includes both fields and deciduous woodland, as well as some riparian habitat along the Manasquan River. This spot receives little attention from birders, so it is difficult to assess its full potential, but it has many of the same species as nearby Allaire State Park. The location of the area is shown on Map 58.

Directions

Take the Garden State Parkway to Exit 98 (Rt. 34, Point Pleasant). Turn right onto Allenwood Rd. immediately after passing under the Parkway. Go 0.75 miles to the T intersection at Atlantic Ave. Spur Rt. 524), and turn left. Go 0.4 miles on Atlantic Ave., then continue straight ahead on Ramshorn Dr. when Atlantic Ave. turns left. Drive another 0.4 miles to the entrance road to the WMA, on the right. [DeLorme 50, C-13]

Birding

Drive in the entrance road for about 0.3 miles to the parking area, then explore the fields and hedgerows for migrants. The woods along the river are especially good for passerines. The portion of Manasquan WMA west of the river can be reached by driving back to Atlantic Ave., and turning left onto the Lakewood-Allenwood Rd. Go 0.2 miles, then turn left, still on Lakewood-Allenwood Rd., which crosses the river in about one-half mile. Two dirt roads (not open to vehicles) lead east into the WMA in the next half-mile. Park along the road and walk in.

✝

North Shore Tour

The New Jersey coast from Point Pleasant Beach to Long Branch is known to birders as the North Shore. It includes numerous freshwater ponds, estuaries, inlets, and oceanfront in Monmouth and northern Ocean counties. From October through March this area is excellent for loons, grebes, Northern Gannet, Great Cormorant, geese, ducks (dabblers, divers, and sea ducks), Purple Sandpiper, gulls, and occasionally, alcids.

Rarities that have been recorded along the North Shore in the past few decades include Eared and Western Grebes, Tufted Duck, Barrow's Goldeneye, Sooty Tern, Black-tailed Gull, Sabine's Gull, Dovekie, Common and Thick-billed murres, Black Guillemot, and Razorbill. Other noteworthy species that occur annually in varying numbers are Red-necked Grebe, Brown Pelican, Eurasian Wigeon, Common and King eiders, Harlequin Duck, Little, Common Black-headed, Iceland, Lesser Black-backed, and Glaucous gulls, and Black-legged Kittiwake.

Outlined in the sections that follow is a suggested tour that covers the area of interest. To bird the entire route takes at least half a day (longer if you do a sea watch at Manasquan Inlet), but you can omit parts of it to fit your schedule. In general, the area north of Shark River Inlet is less productive than that to the south. Regardless of where you come from, it is easiest to cover the coast from south to north, so the trip begins in Point Pleasant. A spotting scope is essential.

Directions

From the north, take the Garden State Parkway south to Exit 98 (Rt. 34). Follow Rt. 34 south for about 4 miles until it merges with Rt. 35. Continue

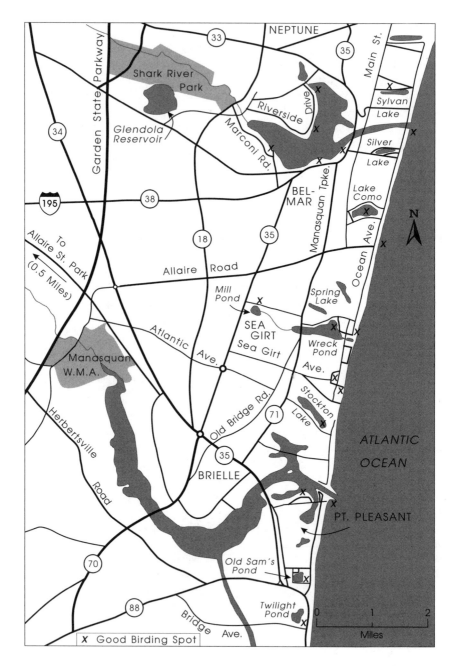

NEPTUNE

Shark River Park

Glendola Reservoir

Garden State Parkway

Riverside Drive

Marconi Rd.

Main St.

Sylvan Lake

Silver Lake

Lake Como

BEL-MAR

Manasquan Tpke.

N

Ocean Ave.

To Allaire St. Park (0.5 Miles)

Allaire Road

Mill Pond

Spring Lake

SEA GIRT
Sea Girt Ave.

Wreck Pond

Atlantic Ave.

Manasquan W.M.A.

Herbertsville Road

Old Bridge Rd.

Stockton Lake

71

ATLANTIC OCEAN

35

BRIELLE

PT. PLEASANT

Old Sam's Pond

Twilight Pond

Bridge Ave.

0   1   2
Miles

X Good Birding Spot

Map 59. North Shore

south on Rt. 35 for about 3.7 miles through the center of Point Pleasant Beach and into Bay Head. After you pass a McDonald's restaurant, you will come to the traffic light at Ocean Ave. Continue another 0.2 miles to Twilight Rd. and turn right. Go one block to Lake Ave. and turn left. Twilight Pond is on the right.

From the west, take I-195 east to its terminus at Rt. 34. Follow Rt. 34 south toward Point Pleasant, proceeding as just described.

From the south, take the Garden State Parkway north to Exit 88 (Rt. 70), then follow Rt. 70 north for about 2.3 miles to the junction with Rt. 88, on the right. Take Rt. 88 east for about 4.6 miles to Rt. 35. Bear right onto Rt. 35 south over the railroad tracks to the traffic light at Ocean Ave. Twilight Rd. is 0.2 miles ahead.

Birding

In addition to the usual domestic ducks, this pond is surprisingly attractive to diving ducks, especially Bufflehead, scaup, Canvasback, and Hooded Merganser. Common Goldeneye is occasional and Tufted Duck has turned up twice, about 30 years apart. Part of the pond that cannot be seen from Lake Ave. can be viewed by continuing 0.3 miles to Bridge Ave., turning right, then taking the first right on Club Dr.

Take Bridge Ave. east to the traffic light at Rt. 35 and turn left. Go one-half mile back to the light at Ocean Ave. and bear right onto Ocean. Drive 0.25 miles to Elizabeth Ave. and turn left. Lake of the Lilies (Old Sam's Pond to birders) is just ahead on the right. Despite its modest size, Old Sam's Pond was formerly one of the best of the shore ponds for seeing some of the diving ducks at close range. A large flock of Canvasbacks wintered here, along with smaller numbers of Redhead, Greater and Lesser scaup, Ruddy Duck and Pied-billed Grebe. Dabbling ducks that frequented the pond were American Black Duck, Mallard, Northern Pintail, Northern Shoveler, Gadwall, and American Wigeon. There are usually plenty of American Coot, although they are even more abundant on some of the ponds further north. Ecological changes of uncertain origin drastically diminished the popularity of this lake during the early 1990s, and one can only hope that it will regain its former appeal.

When the water is partly frozen in winter, gulls of several species come to sit on the ice and bathe in the water. In addition to the big three (Ring-billed, Herring, and Great Black-backed), Bonaparte's Gull is regular and Black-headed, Iceland, Lesser Black-backed, and Glaucous gulls occur almost every year.

After driving around the perimeter of Old Sam's, turn right onto Washington Ave. and go two blocks back to Ocean Ave. Turn left at Ocean and go about 1.1 miles to Broadway; you will pass Little Silver Lake on the left, which may have Bufflehead, wigeon, and scaup, among others. Turn right at Broadway and park on either side of the short, dead-end street. Walk out to the beach, then north to the dike that forms the south side of Manasquan Inlet, and continue to the end of the jetty.

In late fall, migrating loons and scoters can be seen heading south off the end of the jetties that protect the inlet. East or southeasterly winds at that season can bring large numbers of gannets close to shore, particularly in foggy or rainy weather. Parasitic Jaeger is occasionally seen from shore under these conditions in October; Black-legged Kittiwake is regular in November and December, and Purple Sandpiper can be found on the jetty throughout the winter. With a lot of luck you might find a Dovekie, Razorbill, or Thick-billed Murre in the inlet. Even Black Guillemot and Common Murre, two of the rarest alcids in New Jersey, have occurred once or twice.

The inlet is popular with gulls, especially Bonaparte's, from fall through spring. It has been one of the most reliable places for Black-headed Gull (although this species has declined considerably in recent years), and a good spot to look for Little, Iceland, and Glaucous as well. A Black-tailed Gull (an Asian species) was seen here several times in 1999.

Return to Ocean Ave. and turn right to the inlet. The road along the seawall (Inlet Dr.) winds around, past the Shrimp Box restaurant where Black-headed Gull is sometimes present, and rejoins Broadway. Turn right, cross the bridge, and turn right onto Channel Dr. Check the water wherever you can get to it between the restaurants and boat docks for gulls, including Lesser Black-backed and Black-headed. When Channel rejoins Broadway, go right, then make the right turn onto Rt. 35.

Cross the Manasquan River, which has lots of wintering Brant and scaup, and exit right onto Rt. 71 (about 1 mile from Broadway). Follow Rt. 71 north for about 1.6 miles to the traffic light at Sea Girt Ave. Turn right onto Sea Girt, cross the railroad tracks, and bear right (still Sea Girt Ave.) alongside the state police training center and National Guard parade grounds. Scan the parade grounds for the occasional flocks of Horned Lark and Snow Bunting (rarely accompanied by Lapland Longspur), in addition to the omnipresent Brant, Canada Geese, and gulls.

After about a mile, take the last left, First Ave. Go about 0.3 miles to Trenton Blvd., turn right, go to the end and scan the ocean and jetties. Next, turn around and take the first right, a dirt lane through an American Holly forest. After about 200 yards, there is a place to park on the left. This small city park has been a good place for Great Horned, Barred, and Long-eared owls in winter, as well as American Woodcock, Hermit Thrush, American Robin, and Cedar Waxwing.

Continue through the holly forest to the paved road, where you rejoin First Ave. Turn right at the third street, New York Blvd., and continue one block to Ocean Ave. Turn left and park on the right; scan the ocean for seabirds and the jetties for Purple Sandpiper. Drive north for about 200 yards to the dead end, then left onto Beacon Blvd. Go one block back to First Ave., turn right, cross over the bridge, then take the first left on Brown Ave. Go one block to 2nd Ave., and park along the road overlooking Wreck Pond.

After scanning the pond, continue along 2nd Ave. and make a left onto Ocean Rd. to skirt the pond. Turn left onto Shore Rd. and continue to the back of the second pond at Rt. 71, stopping to scan for ducks, geese, and gulls. At Rt. 71, turn around and retrace your route back to Ocean Rd., then turn left onto Union Ave. at the east end of the pond. Go two blocks to Ocean Ave.

Turn left (north) onto Ocean Ave. For the next 1.5 miles, the ocean is too far from the road for birding. If you have time, stop at a couple of places and walk out to the boardwalk to scan the water. Just before Lake Como the road approaches the beach, and you can scan the jetties for gulls and the ocean for seabirds. Turn left immediately before the brick arches and follow the road clockwise around Lake Como. In addition to a variety of the usual dabbling and diving ducks, the lake regularly has Eurasian Wigeon and Hooded Merganser, and is the American Coot capital of the North Shore.

After returning to Ocean Ave., continue north for about 1.3 miles to Shark River Inlet. Park on the right, just before the drawbridge and check the inlet and the jetties. Harlequin Ducks hang out here on occasion, and the inlet has been known to harbor an alcid or two. Black-legged Kittiwakes sometimes follow the fishing boats back to the inlet; scan the flocks of gulls with a scope as the birds approach the jetties, because the kittiwakes usually turn back before the boats enter the inlet.

Make a U-turn and head south to Fifth Ave. Turn right, then bear left along the shore of Silver Lake, which has had goodies such as Eurasian Wigeon and Lesser Black-backed Gull. (Red-crested Pochard and Mandarin Duck have been here as well, but they are escapees and can't be counted). Turn right at Eighth Ave. and follow it through Belmar for about one-half mile to Rt. 35. Turn left onto Rt. 35 and go 0.1 miles to the entrance to the Belmar Marina, on the right. The brick building (Belmar Marina Headquarters) on the right houses the Harbormaster Restaurant and has restrooms that are open all winter.

Continue just past the marina building and turn left to a parking area overlooking the marina. This is an excellent spot to scan the Shark River Estuary, the best place for wintering waterfowl along the north coast. Large numbers of grebes, geese, ducks, and gulls—as well as a few rarities—can be found here throughout the winter. Species to be expected around Shark River in winter are Pied-billed and Horned grebes, Great Blue Heron, Brant (abundant), Green-winged Teal, American Black Duck, Mallard, Northern Pintail, Northern Shoveler, Gadwall, Eurasian Wigeon, American Wigeon (abundant), Canvasback, Redhead, Ring-necked Duck, Greater and Lesser scaup, Common Goldeneye, Bufflehead, Hooded, Common, and Red-breasted mergansers, and Ruddy Duck. Wintering shorebirds include Black-bellied Plover, Sanderling, Dunlin, and sometimes both yellowlegs.

After scanning the estuary from this spot, continue along the marina to the west end, where there is a boat launch area. Watch the boat-mooring areas along the way for diving ducks and the occasional Red-necked Grebe. Check the estuary from the boat launch area, then go back out to Rt. 35 and turn right. Continue on to the traffic light at Belmar Blvd. (0.5 miles) and turn right. Just ahead on the right is a small bridge. Stop before the bridge and check out the ducks for the drake Eurasian Wigeon that likes to hang out here. Go another 0.5 miles and take the second right, Marconi Rd. When Marconi turns left after about 0.2 miles continue straight ahead on North Marconi Rd. down to the water. This is the best place to search for dabbling ducks and is the prime spot for Eurasian Wigeon. Hooded and Common mergansers also prefer this upper end of the estuary.

Shark River can also be birded from the north side. To reach it, go back up the hill to Marconi Rd. and turn right. Go right at the first stop sign (you're still on Marconi Rd.), and follow Marconi for about 1 mile to the next crossroads at Brighton Ave. (just beyond the Marconi Pump Station building on the right). Turn right, cross the bridge over Shark River, and take the first paved road on the right, S. Riverside Dr. Stay right when the road forks almost immediately, then continue straight ahead at the second crossroads (about 0.4 miles), down the hill to the water. Riverside Dr. follows the waterfront for about 1.4 miles, and offers numerous places to stop and scan.

When you reach the stop sign at Lakewood Rd. you have a big decision. If you have had enough for one day and are going south or west, a left turn will take you back to Rt. 18 south, then Rt. 38 and the Garden State Parkway. If you are going north, a right turn will take you to Sylvania Ave. (about 0.4 miles), which leads west to Rt. 33 and the Parkway.

✝

Manasquan Reservoir

A new birding spot opened in 1990, this 1,200-acre recreation area includes the 740-acre reservoir. Recreation facilities are managed by the Monmouth County Park Commission, and currently provide access at two points, the main parking area and boat ramp on Windeler Rd., where there is a large Nature Center, and a small parking lot on Georgia Tavern Rd., both open from 8:00 A.M. to dusk. A 5-mile-long perimeter trail circles the reservoir.

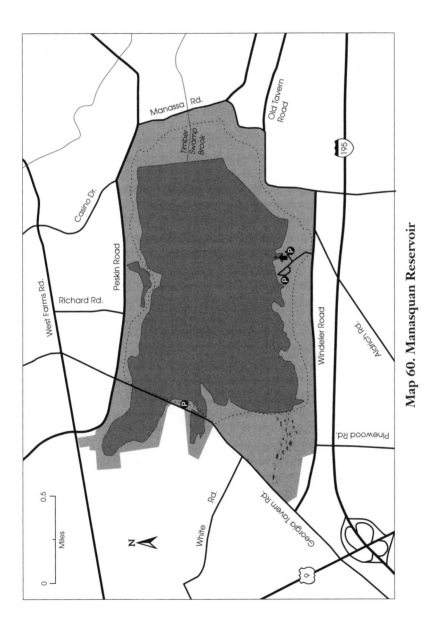

Map 60. Manasquan Reservoir

Directions

From the north or the coast, take the Garden State Parkway to Exit 98 (I-195). Go west on I-195 for about 7 miles to Exit 28B (Rt. 9 North). Turn immediately right at the traffic light onto Georgia Tavern Rd., go 0.3 miles and turn right onto Windeler Rd.; drive about 1.6 miles to the recreation area entrance, on the left. The second parking area is on Georgia Tavern Rd., about 1 mile beyond the turnoff for Windeler Rd. [DeLorme 50, A-5,6]

From the west, take the New Jersey Turnpike to Exit 7 (I-195), follow I-195 east for about to 21 miles to Exit 28B and proceed as described in the preceding paragraph.

Birding

The main birding attraction is waterfowl, which are best scanned from the viewing areas at the Nature Center or the causeway east of the parking area on Georgia Tavern Rd. Diving ducks, especially Common Merganser, frequent the new reservoir, as do Double-crested Cormorants, which probably nest here. Ospreys are common in migration and may soon choose to nest here, and Bald Eagles are seen occasionally in winter. Migrant songbirds can be found around the edges of the reservoir in spring and fall, but relatively few nest.

☛

Assunpink Wildlife Management Area

The Assunpink WMA comprises more than 5,400 acres of lakes, fields, hedgerows, and deciduous woodlands situated near the geographic center of New Jersey. Most of the tract is located in extreme western Monmouth County, but part is in Mercer County. Assunpink is an excellent inland place to observe migrant waterfowl, and it is also fairly good for shorebirds. Its diversity of habitats attracts a good selection of breeding birds.

Some of the species that occur regularly at Assunpink are Ring-necked Duck (up to 450), Common Merganser (up to 1,300), Kentucky and Hooded warblers, Yellow-breasted Chat, Blue Grosbeak, and Orchard Oriole. Rarities that have occurred here include Greater White-fronted Goose, Mississippi Kite, Sandhill Crane, Hudsonian Godwit, Western Kingbird, Ash-throated Flycatcher, Loggerhead Shrike, Henslow's Sparrow, and Brewer's Blackbird.

Note: As a WMA, Assunpink is heavily used by hunters from October through February (except on Sundays, when no hunting is allowed). On other days at this season, confine your visit to the parking lot at Lake Assunpink or the roads through the tract, and always wear some bright clothing.

Directions

To reach the parking lot at Lake Assunpink: From the north, take the New Jersey Turnpike south to Exit 8 (Hightstown), and follow Rt. 33 into town. Go left at the junction with Rt. 539, proceed one short block through the traffic light at Stockton St., then bear left at the fork where Rts. 539 and 33 diverge. Continue south on Rt. 539 south for about 4.8 miles to Herbert Rd. Turn left onto Herbert Rd., go about 2.0 miles to Imlaystown Rd., turn left, and proceed 1.2 miles to the parking lot at Lake Assunpink. [DeLorme 43, M16-17]

From the southwest, take the New Jersey Turnpike north to Exit 7A (I-195). Go east on I-195 for 2 miles to Exit 8 (Rt. 539). Take Rt. 539 north for about 2.1 miles to the junction with Herbert Rd. Turn right and proceed as described above. From the Trenton area, take I-195 east to Rt. 539.

From the east, take I-195 west from the Garden State Parkway Exit 98 for about 22 miles to Exit 11 (Imlaystown Rd.-Hightstown Rd.). Go north on Imlaystown Rd. for 2.6 miles to the parking lot at Lake Assunpink.

Birding

Lake Assunpink is the main attraction for birders. A wide variety of migrating ducks, geese, and other waterbirds stop here, especially in spring. The peak waterfowl seasons are February through April and October through December. A few species breed around the periphery of the lake.

Red-throated Loon is a rare visitor, mainly November to March, but Common Loon is regular in small numbers both in fall and in spring; a few are usually seen in May, and occasionally one lingers into mid-summer. Pied-billed Grebe is present year-round, though it is most common in November and March to April. Horned Grebe is a common migrant in spring and fall, while Red-necked Grebe is rare, but regular, usually appearing in March or April. Double-crested Cormorants are present most of the year, and may nest, and Great Cormorant has occurred several times.

Great Blue Heron is a year-round resident at Assunpink (most common in late summer), and Green Heron is a common summer resident. Many of the other herons and egrets can also be found here, especially in late summer when these species are prone to wander. American Bittern, Great and Snowy egrets, Little Blue Heron, Black-crowned and Yellow-crowned (rare) night-herons, and Glossy Ibis are all regular visitors to the shore of Lake Assunpink.

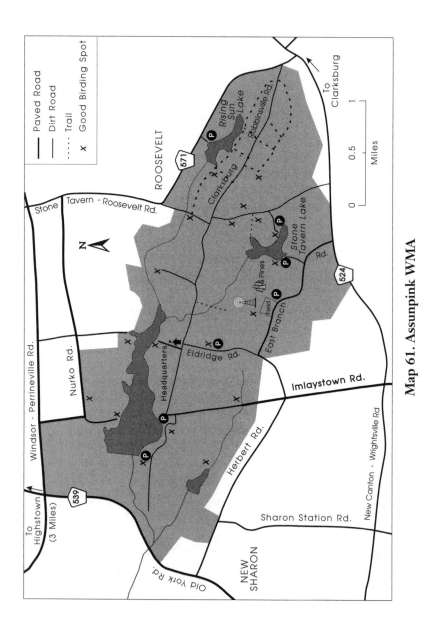

Map 61. Assunpink WMA

Legend:
— Paved Road
— Dirt Road
····· Trail
x Good Birding Spot

ROOSEVELT

Stone Tavern - Roosevelt Rd.

Rising Sun Lake

Robbinsville Rd.

To Clarksburg

Clarksburg

571

N

Stone Tavern Lake

Pines

524

Field

East Branch

Rd.

Nurko Rd.

Windsor - Perrineville Rd.

Headquarters

Eldridge Rd.

Imlaystown Rd.

To Highstown (3 Miles)

539

Herbert Rd.

Old York Rd.

NEW SHARON

Sharon Station Rd.

New Canton - Wrightsville Rd.

0   0.5   1

Miles

The best place for most of these birds is the marshy east end of the lake, which is difficult to reach (see Map 61).

The waterfowl migration starts as soon as the lakes are open, usually by mid-February. It peaks in March and continues strong through April; by mid-May, only the local breeders remain. In September, the first migrant teal and wigeon appear, but the biggest numbers and variety of species occur in October and November. Hunting pressure chases most of the birds off Lake Assunpink in the fall. Some remain until the lake freezes over, and a few stay for the winter in ice-free years, which included most of the 1990s. Species that occur regularly or occasionally are Mute Swan, Tundra Swan (uncommon), Snow Goose, Wood Duck (nests), Green-winged Teal, American Black Duck (nests), Mallard (nests), Northern Pintail, Blue-winged Teal, Northern Shoveler, Gadwall (uncommon), American Wigeon, Canvasback, Redhead, Ring-necked Duck, Greater Scaup, Lesser Scaup, Oldsquaw (rare), all three scoters (rare), Common Goldeneye (uncommon), Bufflehead, Hooded Merganser, Common Merganser (common), Red-breasted Merganser (uncommon), and Ruddy Duck.

A smattering of shorebirds stop off along the lakeshore; any area that has some mud may attract a few. The species seen here include Black-bellied and Semipalmated plovers, Killdeer, Greater and Lesser yellowlegs, Solitary and Spotted (nests) sandpipers, Sanderling (rare), Semipalmated, Western, Least, White-rumped (rare), and Pectoral (common in spring) sandpipers, Dunlin, Stilt Sandpiper (rare), Long-billed Dowitcher (rare), Common Snipe, American Woodcock (nests), and Wilson's and Red-necked phalaropes (both rare).

Small numbers of gulls and terns show up at Lake Assunpink in spring and again in late summer and fall. Ring-billed and Herring gulls are the regulars, but Laughing Gull occurs in small numbers and Bonaparte's Gull is occasional; Black-headed Gull has occurred twice and Iceland Gull once. Common, Forster's, Caspian, and Black terns appear annually in late summer and fall, but they are generally scarce; there are also records for Least and Gull-billed terns.

In May, June, and July, it is the breeding land birds that bring birders to Assunpink. The nesting species include Cooper's Hawk, American Kestrel (now rare), Wild Turkey, Northern Bobwhite (uncommon), Belted Kingfisher, Willow Flycatcher, White-eyed and Warbling vireos, Purple Martin, Carolina Chickadee, Blue-winged, Chestnut-sided (rare), Pine (rare), Prairie, Worm-eating, Kentucky, and Hooded warblers, American Redstart, Yellow-breasted Chat, Blue Grosbeak, Rose-breasted Grosbeak, and Orchard Oriole.

Blue Grosbeak frequently inhabits the hedgerow on the east border of the Lake Assunpink parking lot. To see some of the other breeding species, leave the parking lot and proceed back down Imlaystown Rd. Go about 200

Red-bellied Woodpecker

yards, then turn right onto another dirt road. Just after the road bends right are some large trees where Orchard Oriole and Warbling Vireo usually nest. After about 0.5 miles, the road climbs a little rise to a parking area shaded by two large old Sugar Maples and a Red Mulberry; Orchard Oriole is here, too.

Return to Imlaystown Rd., turn left toward Lake Assunpink, then right at the intersection onto Clarksburg-Robbinsville Rd. (no sign). The WMA headquarters is about 0.7 miles on the left; stop in for a map of the area if your visit is on a weekday. Along the way, listen for Willow Flycatcher, Yellow-breasted Chat, and Blue Grosbeak. Just before the headquarters is a dirt road that leads 0.3 miles to the shore of Lake Assunpink. As you drive down this road, you'll see a grass parking area and bleachers on the left, which are used by a model airplane club. If no one is there, pull in and park. In fall migration, check the fields and hedgerows here for sparrows, Bobolink, and Eastern Meadowlark. A Northern Shrike wintered here one year, and American Bittern and Sora have been seen along the lake edge. This is also a good vantage point to scan for ducks, herons, and hawks.

Go back to the main road; directly opposite the headquarters turn right onto Eldridge Rd. (no sign) and go about 0.25 miles to a parking area on the left. Listen here for Blue Grosbeak in the hedgerow and Grasshopper Sparrow in the grassy fields. Henslow's Sparrow has been seen in the wet fields on the right, just before the parking lot.

Drive back toward the headquarters, turn right, and go about 0.2 miles to a bridge across a marshy stream. Willow Flycatcher, Virginia Rail, and several other species breed here. Eastern Screech-Owls usually inhabit the Wood Duck boxes. About 200 yards farther on is a trail on the right, where you might find Blue Grosbeak, Indigo Bunting, Orchard Oriole, and plenty of Poison Sumac. About 1.5 miles past the headquarters, turn left on Stone Tavern-Roosevelt Rd., and drive about 0.3 miles to where Assunpink Creek crosses the road. Acadian Flycatcher and Prothonotary Warbler have been seen here in summer.

Drive back to Clarksburg-Robbinsville Rd. and turn left. Go about 100 yards, to the continuation of Stone Tavern-Roosevelt Rd., on the right, but continue straight ahead. The road becomes dirt and is sometimes in poor condition, although it is almost always driveable. Continue another 0.6 miles, passing several fields, until the road enters woods on both sides. Park in the first parking area on the right, just after entering the woods. Walk the trail uphill in summer to look for Yellow-billed Cuckoo, Eastern Screech-Owl, Great Crested Flycatcher, Veery, Black-and-white, Chestnut-sided, Kentucky, Hooded, and Worm-eating warblers, Ovenbird, American Redstart, Rose-breasted Grosbeak, and Scarlet Tanager. Wild Turkey and Pileated Woodpecker also occur here.

Return to your car and reverse your route for about 0.3 miles. Park on the left opposite a trail on the right (north) side. Follow this trail and turn left just before you enter a clearing. There are usual a couple of pairs of Kentucky Warblers along this stretch. Drive back to the intersection with Stone Tavern-Roosevelt Rd., and turn left. Pause here to check for Prairie and Blue-winged warblers, Yellow-breasted Chat, and Indigo Bunting. The road soon enters deciduous woodland that has nesting Kentucky and Hooded warblers. After about 0.4 miles, you will emerge from the woods at the top of a hill overlooking Stone Tavern Lake, which is largely hidden from view by trees and bushes. The entire perimeter of the lake is good for birds, and usually has Orchard Oriole and Blue Grosbeak in a few places; Western Kingbird has been seen here in winter. There are two spots where you can drive down to the lake, an excellent spot for Ring-necked Duck. The first is 0.3 miles ahead on the right, at the bottom of the hill.

Another good spot can be reached by parking on the north side of East Branch Rd., near the sharp bend. Walk north and then west along the edge of a field to an air navigation structure. This recently cleared area is good for sparrows, American Kestrel, and Northern Harrier in autumn, and for soaring raptors and vultures (both Turkey and Black). Three rows of planted pine trees at the northeast corner of the field are good for owls (both Long-eared and N. Saw-whet have been found here), and for Cedar Waxwing and Hermit Thrush in winter.

There are numerous other places in the Assunpink WMA that can be explored. In fall and winter, Nurko Rd. on the north side of Lake Assunpink (see Map 61) is excellent for sparrows, including Lincoln's (October) and White-crowned sparrows. Lark, Clay-colored, and Chipping sparrows have all been found in winter. The tree rows along the north side of the lake are also good for fall migrants; such sought-after species as Yellow-bellied Flycatcher, Mourning Warbler, and Connecticut Warbler occur regularly.

Assunpink is an excellent place to observe raptors during the fall migration and in winter. Turkey Vulture, Northern Harrier, Red-tailed Hawk, and American Kestrel are the commonest species, but Osprey and Sharp-shinned Hawk are common in migration; Coopers Hawk and Merlin are uncommon but regular. Broad-winged and Red-shouldered hawks nest on the area, and there are usually several reports of Bald Eagle every year. The wintering flocks of Horned Larks that sometimes visit the meadows near the south entrance to Assunpink sometimes include Lapland Longspur and Snow Bunting.

Allentown Sod Farms

Very little remains of the central New Jersey sod farms that once attracted flocks of migrant shorebirds to the area around Hightstown and Assunpink. The few remaining areas are near the town of Allentown in southwestern Monmouth County. The shorebirds that like to forage on sod farms, mainly Killdeer, American Golden Plover (September to October), Upland Sandpiper (mainly August), Baird's Sandpiper (September), and Buff-breasted Sandpiper (mainly September), can still be found here in some years.

Directions

Take I-195 to Exit 8 (Rt. 539, Allentown), which is 2 miles east of the New Jersey Turnpike and 28 miles west of the Garden State Parkway. Go south a few hundred yards on Rt. 539 to the sod farm, on the left.

Birding

There are two places for viewing the sod farm. The first is the stretch of Rt. 539 between the I-195 exit and the end of the sod farm. For the second, which is usually better, continue into the town of Allentown for about 0.8 miles from I-195 and turn left onto Rt. 526, Allentown-Red Valley Rd. Go about 0.6 miles to the firehouse on the left, where you can get a good view of much of the sod farm. Birding the Allentown sod farm is a matter of luck— are there any birds on the sod farm and, if so, can you see them? Because of a dip in the middle of the field, the birds are sometimes not in view even when present.

✝

Colliers Mills Wildlife Management Area

Colliers Mills WMA covers more than 12,000 acres of northwestern Ocean County, near the northern edge of the New Jersey Pine Barrens. Most of the upland areas are covered with the typical Pitch Pine and Scrub Oak vegetation of the Barrens, while the wetter areas support Atlantic White Cedar. There are a few areas with mixed deciduous woods and some hardwood swamps. Several impoundments provide habitat for migrant waterfowl.

The birds of Colliers Mills are those of the Pine Barrens, and are described in detail in the sections on Lebanon State Forest and Whitesbog. Noteworthy breeding birds include Red-headed Woodpecker, Eastern Bluebird, Northern Waterthrush, Grasshopper Sparrow, Blue Grosbeak, and Orchard Oriole. The area is not heavily birded during the breeding season, which is when you might find something really unusual. This would be a good place to do exploring during June and July, instead of visiting the better known spots.

Note: As a WMA, Colliers Mills is heavily used by hunters, mainly from October through December. If you visit during hunting season, stay on the roads and wear bright clothing or confine your trips to Sundays.

Directions

From northern New Jersey, take the New Jersey Turnpike south to Exit 7 (I-195). Go east on I-195 for about 2 miles to Exit 8 (Rt. 539). Follow Rt. 539 south through Allentown (watch for a sharp left turn) for about 10 miles to Colliers Mills Rd., which is about 1.4 miles south of the intersection of Rt. 539 and New Egypt-Cassville (Rt. 528). Turn left onto Colliers Mills Rd. (there is a WMA sign) and go 0.9 miles to the entrance to the WMA, which is straight ahead on the dirt road. [DeLorme 49, G-20]

From southwestern New Jersey or the Philadelphia area, take Rt. 70 east to the intersection with Rt. 539 near Whiting. Turn left (north) on Rt. 539 and go about 8.5 miles to Colliers Mills Rd.

From southern New Jersey, take Rt. 539 north from the Garden State Parkway for about 32 miles to Colliers Mills Rd.

Birding

Orchard Oriole usually nests in the trees around the bridge at the south end of Colliers Mills Lake, which is where you enter the WMA. Take the first left turn, just past the bridge, and drive along the lakeshore about 0.3 miles to a small parking area on the left. Walk to the north side of the parking area, to where a dirt road has been blocked by a pile of sand. Walk along the blocked road to search for birds of the Pine Barrens. Along your drive in, and along this walk, you will notice fields off to the right. The staff at Colliers Mills maintains a very active and productive bluebird trail, and some of the boxes are located in these fields.

You will soon come to a power line cut, where you can turn right and explore more of the area. When you come to a dirt road after about one-half mile, you can either turn around and retrace your steps, or turn right and walk through more of this pine-oak habitat. In about 0.7 miles, you will come to a junction with another dirt road, where you should turn right. Called

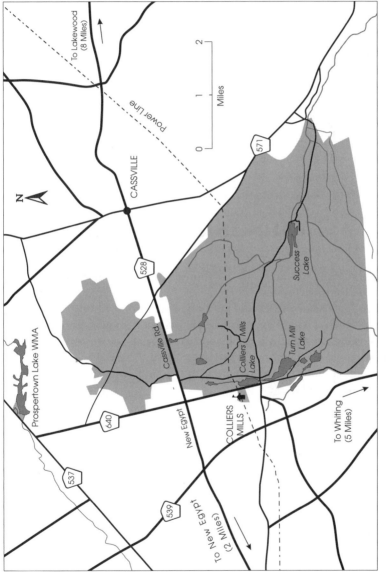

To Lakewood
(8 Miles)

Power Line

CASSVILLE

N

528

Cassville Rd.

Prospertown Lake WMA

640

537

New Egypt

COLLIERS
MILLS

539

To New Egypt
(2 Miles)

To Whiting
(5 Miles)

Colliers Mills
Lake

Turn Mill
Lake

Success
Lake

571

0   1   2

Miles

Map 62. Colliers Mills WMA

Success Rd. on some maps, this is the same entrance road that led you into the WMA. From here it is about a mile to the spot where you turned left after crossing the bridge. The road passes through a large cutover area, where you might find Red-headed Woodpecker.

Return to your car and drive back 0.3 miles to the entrance road (Success Rd.). A left turn leads you across the WMA from west to east to Rt. 571, a distance of about 5.3 miles. There are many interesting looking stops along the way. Most of the birds you will encounter on Success Rd. are the common species of the Pine Barrens, especially Brown Thrasher, Gray Catbird, Prairie Warbler, Pine Warbler, and Rufous-sided Towhee. After about 2.5 miles, you will reach Success Lake on the right, where you might find Green Heron, Wood Duck and other waterfowl, Osprey, Belted Kingfisher, and various swallows in migration.

🦆

Cattus Island Park

Cattus Island Park is located on the shores of Barnegat Bay, about 3 miles northeast of Toms River. Its 497 acres, managed by the Ocean County Parks and Recreation Department, contain a good selection of both Pine Barrens habitat and coastal salt marsh. Although it is not known for any rare or unusual species, the park is a good spot to see birds native to the bays and neighboring uplands of coastal New Jersey. Since these coastal areas are rapidly diminishing due to development, Cattus Island offers a birding environment not easily found in New Jersey.

Directions

Take the Garden State Parkway to Exit 82 (Rt. 37 East). Follow Rt. 37 east toward Seaside Heights for about 4.5 miles to Spur Rt. 549 (Fischer Blvd). Turn left, via a jughandle turn, onto Rt. 549 and go north about 2.1 miles to Cattus Island Blvd. Turn right and drive about 100 yards to the park entrance, on the left. Follow the entrance road for almost a mile to the parking area at the Cooper Environmental Center. [DeLorme 50, M-11]

Birding

Go into the nature center, which has restrooms, and obtain a copy of the trail map and a bird checklist. There are two main areas to the park, with two or

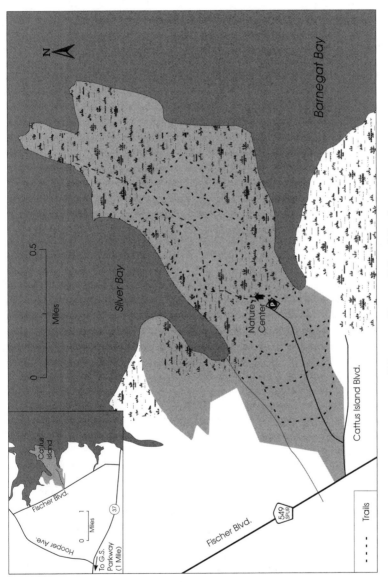

Silver Bay

Barnegat Bay

N

0.5

0

Miles

Nature
Center

P

Cattus Island Blvd.

Fischer Blvd.

549
SPUR

····· Trails

Cattus
Island

Fischer Blvd.

Hooper Ave.

37

To G.S.
Parkway
(1 Mile)

0   1

Miles

Map 63. Cattus Island Park

three trails in each area. The western area consists mainly of Pine Barrens woodland, with a short section of swamp and salt marsh along a boardwalk that starts on the south side of the Nature Center. The boardwalk connects with the red trail, which leads in turn to the blue trail and the yellow trail; all three trails wander through typical Pine Barrens habitats.

The eastern section of the park is perhaps more interesting, especially a maintenance road, which runs from the north side of the Nature Center across a salt marsh to an island, then over the island and across more salt marsh to another, smaller, island. Here the road ends on a point of land that separates Silver Bay on the west from Barnegat Bay on the east. The orange trail makes a circuit of the larger island, including a field where a mansion formerly stood.

Breeding birds in the western part of Cattus Island Park include Northern Bobwhite, Whip-poor-will, White-eyed Vireo, Carolina Wren, Brown Thrasher, Blue-winged, Yellow, Pine, Prairie, and Black-and-white warblers, and other typical Pine Barrens species.

The two islands and the salt marsh in the eastern part of the park offer a greater diversity of habitat than the western part of the park. Additional breeding birds here include Clapper Rail, Marsh Wren, and Saltmarsh Sharp-tailed, Seaside, and Swamp sparrows, and House Finch. In summer, various herons and egrets frequent the salt marsh, while offshore in migration and in winter there are many ducks and geese, especially diving ducks. A few species of shorebirds visit the tidal edges, mainly in fall. Numerous raptors pass through the park in migration, especially Northern Harrier and American Kestrel; Merlin and Peregrine Falcon are regular in the fall. Winter is a quiet time at Cattus Island, except for the waterfowl in Barnegat Bay. A stop at this attractive little park is easily combined with a visit to Island Beach State Park.

🦆

Island Beach State Park

Island Beach State Park contains one of the few unspoiled stretches of barrier island on the New Jersey coast. The park is almost 10 miles long, but is only a few hundred yards wide over most of its length. It retains the native vegetation of Dune Grass, Beach Plum, Bayberry, and American Holly, and a large portion of the park is protected as a botanical preserve.

Forming as it does part of our outer coastal strip, Island Beach is an excellent place to see both migrant landbirds and seabirds, especially in fall. Sea watching can be very productive in October and November, when such species as Northern Gannet, Parasitic Jaeger, and Black-legged Kittiwake regularly occur, along with thousands of loons, cormorants, geese, and ducks. Land birding can be frustrating because of the severely restricted access to most of the park, but such rarities as Orange-crowned Warbler, Clay-colored Sparrow, and Lark Sparrow are seen every year. Operation Recovery, a fall bird-banding project conducted at Island Beach for more than 40 years, has resulted in the capture of many rarities, some of which have never been observed elsewhere in New Jersey.

In winter, Island Beach has wintering loons, Great Cormorant, sea ducks, gulls, Snow Bunting, Lapland Longspur (rare), and occasionally a Snowy Owl. In addition to the birds mentioned above, rare or unusual species that have occurred here in recent years (other than netted birds) include Cory's Shearwater (rare from shore), Brown Pelican, Harlequin Duck (annual), Little Gull, and Smith's Longspur. Other vagrants have included Long-tailed Jaeger, Ivory Gull, and Bridled Tern.

Directions

Take the Garden State Parkway to Exit 82 (Rt. 37, Toms River). Go east on Rt. 37 for about 6.8 miles, crossing the bridge over Barnegat Bay, and exit right at the sign for Island Beach State Park, Seaside Park. After about 0.7 miles and several curves, you will be headed south on N. Central Ave. Continue south for another 2 miles to the state park entrance. An entrance fee is charged year round (higher in summer). [DeLorme 58, C-14]

Birding

Drive south along the park road, watching the roadside in fall for sparrows and the trees for perched Merlins and Peregrine Falcons. About 3.5 miles south of the tollbooth you will come to the first bathhouse, which offers indoor restrooms from spring through fall and outdoor portable toilets in winter. Walk along the left side of the building toward the beach, where there is a wooden platform at the edge of the dunes; the slight elevation of this platform makes it an excellent lookout for scanning the sea.

The best times for a sea watch are October and November, although winter and early spring can also be good. In fall, a good migration day can produce hundreds of Red-throated and Common loons, Double-crested Cormorant (mainly September to October), scaup, and scoters. Occasionally, mixed in with the other ducks, you will see a Common Eider, King Eider, or Harlequin Duck. Laughing Gull and Common Tern are abundant migrants at this season. If the winds are from the east, you may see dozens of Northern Gannets migrating or fishing offshore. Usually they stay at least a quarter-mile off, but sometimes they come closer. In November and December, you may see Black-legged Kittiwake as well. Other pelagic species that get blown close to shore on easterly winds are Parasitic Jaeger (September to October) and Cory's Shearwater (rare). In winter, there is a possibility of an alcid.

One of the best places at Island Beach for fall migrant sparrows has been the area around the new headquarters between the two bathhouses. From the first bathhouse, drive or walk to the south side of the parking lot, checking the edges of the lot for songbirds. Yellow-rumped Warblers are abundant, Orange-crowned Warbler is rare but regular, and many different kinds of sparrows can be expected in October and November. The headquarters area is just beyond the south end of the parking lot. Clay-colored and Lark sparrows have been seen here, Lincoln's and White-crowned sparrows are regular, and a Smith's Longspur spent a few days here in 1995.

Return to your car, and continue driving south along the park road, still watching the road edges for feeding sparrows. About 4.8 miles from the bathhouse, you will come to the end of the road at the last parking area. If you feel up to an invigorating hike, you can reach the south end of the park by walking along the beach for about 1.5 miles. Along the way, scan the ocean for seabirds and the dunes for Snow Bunting and for Snowy Owl, which has occurred here in some winters.

At the south end of the peninsula, a long jetty guards the north side of Barnegat Inlet. If the tide and weather permit, it is worth hiking out this jetty as far as you can. From late fall to early spring, you may find Harlequin Duck or eiders along the edges of the rocks (but they are usually on the Barnegat Light side of the inlet). Purple Sandpiper is common from late fall to May and other shorebirds, such as Sanderling, Dunlin, and Ruddy Turnstone, are often present as well.

Also, from late fall to early spring, a walk inland from the jetty along the inlet may produce Horned Lark, Snow Bunting, and occasionally, Lapland Longspur feeding in the grassy areas at the edges of the dunes. Large flocks of gulls sometimes gather at the southern end of Island Beach, so be sure to look for Iceland, Glaucous, and Lesser Black-backed gulls. At certain times, many hundreds of Bonaparte's Gulls gather to feed in the channel of Barnegat Inlet. At such times, you have a fair chance of seeing a Little Gull or a Black-headed Gull among them, but the gatherings are very erratic and unpredictable.

Double Trouble State Park and Vicinity

Double Trouble includes more than 5,000 acres of cedar swamp and pine barrens in eastern Ocean County. During late summer and fall, many Wood Ducks roost in the reservoir at the western end of the park. Among the more unusual breeding birds for this part of the state are Sharp-shinned Hawk, Acadian Flycatcher, Veery, Black-throated Green and Hooded warblers, Indigo Bunting, and Baltimore Oriole. Double Trouble Village preserves a former cranberry farm and packing plant, while Cedar Creek runs through the length of the park to provide fresh water for the bogs, swamps and the wildlife they support. Nearby Webbs Mill Bog has an interesting array of extraordinary plants, including Curly Grass Fern, and several sundews.

Directions

From the north, take the Garden State Parkway south to Exit 80 (US 9, Rt. 530). Stay left at the exit ramp and turn left onto Double Trouble Rd. (sign To Rt. 619). Go about 4 miles to a stop sign at Pinewald-Keswick Rd. (Rt. 618), then continue straight ahead to the park entrance, where there is a small parking lot. [DeLorme 58, D-5]

From the south, take the Garden State Parkway north to Exit 74 (Lacey Rd.). Drive east on Lacey Rd. for about 0.8 miles, then turn left onto Manchester Boulevard, go 0.6 miles to Western Blvd. and turn left again. Take Western Blvd. about 2 miles north to the stop sign at Rt. 618 (Veterans Blvd.), turn left and proceed about 1.8 miles to the entrance to the state park, on the left.

Birding

Take the trail on the west side of the parking lot (your right as you entered) along the north side of Mill Pond Bog. During the nesting season you should encounter many of the common species of the Pine Barrens, such as House Wren, Cedar Waxwing, Carolina Chickadee, Gray Catbird, Brown Thrasher, Pine Warbler, Eastern Towhee, Chipping and Field sparrows. In winter or migration, you may find kinglets, Brown Creeper, and Yellow-rumped Warblers.

After about 0.25 miles, the trail reaches Mill Pond Reservoir, where Belted Kingfishers sometimes nest and Tree Swallows and Purple Martins are present all summer. Watch overhead for the occasional Black Vulture among the ubiquitous Turkey Vultures, plus Red-tailed and, occasionally,

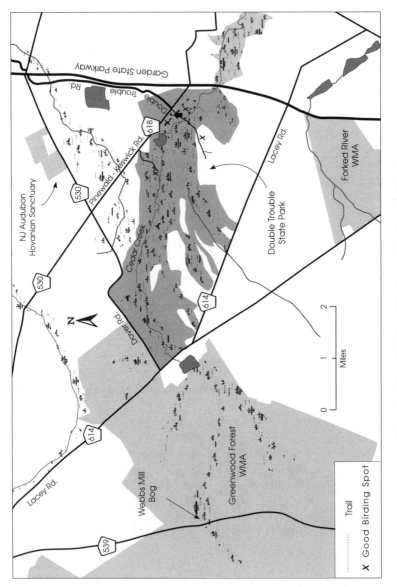

Map 64. Double Trouble State Park and Vicinity

Red-shouldered hawks. The reservoir is the best area in the park for water-fowl, with Mallard and Wood Duck in summer, Ring-necked Duck, Lesser Scaup, and Black Duck at other seasons. Great Blue Herons are present most of the year, while Green Heron is resident during the warmer months. If you continue on the trail across the floodgate, with the reservoir on your right, you'll come to a white cedar swamp where Black-throated Green and Black-and-white warblers nest. Beyond this point, the trail is usually flooded.

Returning to the parking area, walk south through the village. The last building along the trail is the old sawmill, and behind the sawmill is a maple swamp that has had nesting Acadian Flycatcher, Carolina Wren, Wood Thrush, White-eyed Vireo, and Hooded Warbler. Continuing on the trail, Mill Pond Bog will be on your right. It is rapidly becoming overgrown, but may have Common Yellowthroat and Song Sparrow. You will soon come to the bridge across Cedar Creek. Barn Swallows nest under the bridge, and a short trail on the right just past the bridge borders a cedar swamp with nesting Black-throated Green and Black-and-White warblers, and Ovenbird. The Maple Swamp on the left has nesting Veery.

If you continue south along the main trail (Deep Hollow Rd.), you will come to a power line right-of-way in about 200 yards. The clearing here provides nesting habitat for Common Nighthawk, Eastern Kingbird, Eastern Bluebird, and Prairie Warbler.

Returning to the bridge over Cedar Creek, follow the path downstream along the creek along the south edge of the maple swamp. Eventually the creek opens up into a small reservoir, where you can find Eastern Kingbird, Common Yellowthroat, Yellow Warbler, Song and Swamp sparrows, Red-winged Blackbird and Common Grackle.

To visit another interesting spot in the park, turn left on Pinewald-Keswick Rd. from the parking lot and drive about 1 mile to a dirt road on the left, just past the power line. Follow this dirt road, taking the first right fork into the woods, for about 0.7 miles to a canoe access point for Cedar Creek. Along the way, you will pass through some wet woods that look like they should harbor Prothonotary Warbler and other species during the breeding season.

Return to Pinewald-Keswick Rd., and turn left. Go 1.6 miles to County Rt. 530, turn right, and drive 1 mile to the sign for the New Jersey Audubon Hirair and Anna Hovnanian Sanctuary, on the left. There are currently no marked trails at the sanctuary, but you can drive the dirt roads or park along Rt. 530 and walk. The birding is typical of the Pine Barrens.

To reach Webbs Mill Bog and the surrounding Greenwood Forest WMA, return to the traffic light at the intersection of Rt. 530 and Pinewald-Keswick Rd. Turn right onto Rt. 530 and go 8 miles to the intersection with Rt. 539 in Whiting. Turn left onto Rt. 539 and drive about 5 miles to the sign and small parking area for Webbs Mill Bog, on the left. You can explore the bog using the boardwalks, but do not stray from them, as the bog is a very fragile place and the plants here are rare in New Jersey.

❦

Stafford Forge Wildlife Management Area

Stafford Forge WMA covers more than 17,000 acres of ponds and pine barrens in southern Ocean County, just west of the Garden State Parkway. Four contiguous ponds, which were created by a series of dams along Westecunk Creek, are the main attraction to both birds and birders. The southernmost pond, which is the largest and shallowest, was formerly attractive to Tundra Swan and Ring-necked Duck in migration. When the water level is low enough to expose the grassy areas around the shore in August and September, you may find Lesser Golden-Plover, Baird's and Buff-breasted sandpipers, along with numerous other shorebirds.

Note: Stafford Forge is a popular hunting area from October through December; visits at that season should be confined to the paved road or should be made on Sunday.

Directions

Take the Garden State Parkway to Exit 58 (Tuckerton and Warren Grove). From the exit ramp, turn right onto Rt. 539. Go 0.3 miles and turn right onto Rt. 606 (Forge Rd.). In about 1.3 miles, you will come to the large, southernmost pond on the left; carefully pull off on the shoulder and park. [DeLorme 65, 27-C,D] Coming east, you can also take Rts. 70 and 72 to Rt. 539, turn right, and go south for about 10 miles to Forge Rd., which is the last left turn before you come to the Parkway.

Birding

The large pond is the farthest downstream of the four ponds. It is frequented by waterfowl from fall through early spring, as long as the water is open, and formerly attracted flocks of 25 to 50 Tundra Swans. For some reason the spot is no longer attractive to the swans, but changes in water level and vegetation could change that again. The grassy edges of the pond have attracted modest numbers of shorebirds in some years; the best area is usually the southwestern shore of the pond (to your left as you face the pond) near the road. In addition to the rarities mentioned above, you might find Solitary, Spotted, or Pectoral sandpipers, or Common Snipe, among other shorebirds.

To reach the other ponds, continue along Forge Rd. to the far end of the first pond and turn left at the entrance to the WMA. Follow the entrance road between two fields, where Ring-necked Pheasant and Northern Bobwhite often call from the hedgerows, and turn left on another dirt road. Go about 0.6 miles on this road, then turn left onto a dirt road; in a few hundred yards you will come to the dike road that separates the second and third ponds. Continue along the dike, scanning the water for geese and ducks and the edges of the ponds for shorebirds. Wood Duck and Canada Goose are common visitors in the fall.

At the far end of the dike, you can turn either right or left on dirt roads. A right turn will lead you past a parking area to the dike that divides the third and fourth ponds. The fourth pond still has standing dead trees where Tree Swallow and Purple Martin nest in abundance. Turning right at the end of the dike between the third and fourth ponds will lead you back to the parking area noted above.

If you turn left after crossing the dike between the second and third ponds, the dirt road will take you along the shore of the second pond then lead away to the right into the woods. About 0.4 miles after turning left you will intersect another dirt road. Turn left, and after 0.4 miles you will come to Forge Rd., just west of your starting point by the first pond.

Most of Stafford Forge is covered with typical Pine Barrens vegetation, and harbors birds characteristic of this habitat. Approximately half the WMA lies west of Rt. 539, along both sides of Governor's Branch. This portion and its associated cedar swamp receives virtually no attention from birders. You might find something different there.

🦆

Manahawkin Wildlife Management Area

The Manahawkin WMA is a 1,064-acre tract of diverse habitat, including Pitch Pine and deciduous woodlands, fields, salt marsh, and several freshwater impoundments. It is best known for some unusual breeding species and for a number of rarities. The area was virtually unknown until the early 1970s, when the first rarity appeared; with increased attention many more were found, and the interesting nesting species of the area were discovered.

In subsequent years, the freshwater impoundments, which furnished most of the exciting records, have become overgrown with vegetation and have produced little of interest. As a result, the area is less frequently visited today than it was in the 1970s, and any occasional rarity that passes through here may escape unnoticed. Manahawkin is still a regular stop on winter trips, however, as it is one of the better spots in the state for wintering Northern Harrier, Rough-legged Hawk, and Short-eared Owl.

Note: the area is managed for hunting, so visits during the hunting season (roughly October through December) should be made on Sundays. On weekdays or Saturdays, do not wander off Stafford Ave.

Directions

From the intersection of Rt. 72 and the Garden State Parkway at Exit 63 (Manahawkin), take Rt. 72 east for about 1.5 miles to Rt. 9. Go north on Rt. 9 for 0.1 miles to a traffic light at Bay Ave., then take the next right onto Stafford Ave. In about 0.3 miles you will come to the blinking red light at Parker St. Continue straight ahead for 0.6 miles to Hilliard Blvd; just before reaching Hilliard you enter the boundary of the Manahawkin WMA. [DeLorme 59, B-18]

Birding

The woods along Stafford Ave. between Parker St. and Hilliard Ave. have nesting Hooded Warbler from mid-May through the summer. Stop along the road and listen for their song; singing males can frequently be coaxed into view by pishing or by an E. Screech-Owl call. Additional species present include the usual assortment of Carolina Chickadee, Gray Catbird, Eastern Towhee, and others.

Continue on Stafford Ave. After the stop sign at Hilliard, the road passes through more woodland for about 1 mile, and there are several paths that lead off to the right. These paths are worth exploring for migrants and for nesting species, such as Red-bellied Woodpecker, Acadian Flycatcher, Hooded Warbler, and other species typical of the coastal plain-deciduous woodlands. Just before the woods give way to salt marsh, there is a wet area with dead trees on the right. This spot has had nesting Prothonotary Warbler and Acadian Flycatcher and is a good place for migrant Olive-sided Flycatcher in late May and early June.

Whip-poor-will is abundant along this stretch of road and is joined by smaller numbers of Chuck-will's-widow. The best way to find these species is to park along the road at dusk or before dawn and wait until they start singing. Sometimes they come out and sit on the dirt road or perch on a branch of a nearby tree. In the poor light in which these birds are usually seen, field marks are inadequate for distinguishing the two species. Size is the best

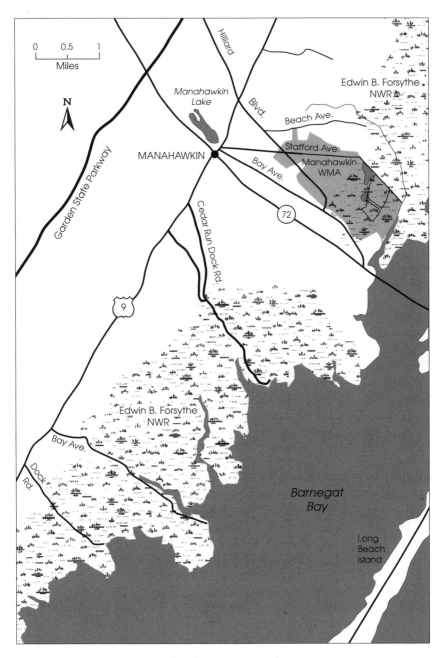

Map 65. Manahawkin WMA

distinction—Whip-poor-will is about the same size as an American Robin (though of different proportions), while Chuck-will's-widow is almost as big as a Rock Dove. Their songs differ mainly in the cadence, the strongest accent being on the *first* syllable for the Chuck-will's-widow and on the *last* syllable for the Whip-poor-will.

Just past a bend, the road emerges from the woods into an area of salt marsh on the left (part of Barnegat NWR) and an impoundment on the right (pond A on the map). Scan the pond for herons, waterfowl, and (if the water is low) shorebirds. One-half mile after you leave the woods, a dike on the right separates pond A from pond B. The five impoundments were originally constructed to study mosquitoes in shallow salt-water ponds. Now, they are mainly fresh and overgrown, but still attract some waterfowl. In summer, the dike harbors innumerable Yellow Warblers and Common Yellowthroats, as well as Song and Swamp sparrows, while pond B has nesting Least Bittern, Blue-winged Teal, and Mute Swans. At times, both of these ponds and the ones farther on have harbored such rarities as White Ibis, Cinnamon Teal, Black-necked Stilt, and Ruff, as well as more frequent desirables such as Wilson's Phalarope and Buff-breasted Sandpiper.

If the rest of Stafford Ave. is passable (after a heavy rain it sometimes isn't) continue on for another one-half mile to the end of the road at an old wooden bridge. The salt marsh on either side of the road and across the bridge has nesting Clapper Rail, Seaside Sparrow, and Saltmarsh Sharp-tailed Sparrow. In some years there have also been breeding Black Rail, both here and in the salt marsh north of Stafford Ave., opposite pond A. During the mid-1970s there were many reports of Black Rail at Manahawkin, since then, however, Black Rail reports have been sporadic.

To search for Black Rail, choose a warm, still, moonless night in late May or June. After 10:00 P.M., listen at various points along the road for the unique *kick-ee-doo* or *kee-kee-kerr* call of the male. Although the Black Rail is no bigger than a Song Sparrow, its call is very loud and carries a long way. If you should be so fortunate as to hear one, you might try to venture out into the salt marsh in the direction of the call, but beware of the many deep channels and mosquito ditches. Your best chance for approaching a rail will occur if you should hear one that is beyond the wooden bridge at the end of the road, for here the ditches can be crossed or circumvented. You will have to be very lucky to hear a Black Rail, let alone see one. It is illegal to play tape recordings of the Black Rail's call in order to attract it because the species is endangered in New Jersey.

In winter, the ponds are frozen and the woods are almost deserted. The salt marsh, however, is an excellent place for wintering Northern Harrier, Rough-legged Hawk, and Short-eared Owl, which can be observed from many points along Stafford Ave. Harriers and Rough-legs are about all day, but the owls usually appear only at dusk (although they occasionally are seen on gray overcast days).

A short drive south of Manahawkin, three other places are good in winter for Northern Harrier, Rough-legged Hawk, and, especially, Short-eared Owl. (1) Take Stafford Ave. back to its end at Rt. 9. Turn left and go south for about 1 mile to Cedar Run Dock Rd. Turn left and follow this road for 3.0 miles to the end; the last 2 miles go through salt marsh, where the hawks and owls may be seen. (2) Return to Rt. 9, turn left, and go about 4.0 miles to Bay Ave. in Parkertown. Turn left and follow Bay for about 2.5 miles to the end; the last mile or so is salt marsh. (3) Go back to Rt. 9, turn left, and go about 0.6 miles to Dock Rd. Turn left and follow Dock Rd. about 2 miles to the end. Obviously, if you are looking for Short-eared Owl at dusk, you won't be able to try all these spots. Any one of them should produce owls in season, but Dock Rd. has been the most reliable in recent years. To return to the Garden State Parkway, go north on Rt. 9 for about 5.5 miles to Rt. 72, then take Rt. 72 west for 1.4 miles to the Parkway.

🦆

Barnegat Light

The town of Barnegat Light is at the north end of Long Beach Island and is separated from Island Beach State Park by Barnegat Inlet, which connects the ocean and Barnegat Bay. Although the area is completely developed, there are several excellent birding spots. Because the area is bordered by water on three sides, the birds seen here are mainly those associated with water; large numbers of migrant landbirds do pass through in the fall, however. This is one of the best places in New Jersey to look for Northern Gannet, Common and King Eiders, Harlequin Duck, and Black-legged Kittiwake. You can also see here many of the other birds that migrate or winter along the coast, especially loons, geese, and ducks. Barnegat Light is worth visiting any time from October to April, with winter providing the most interesting—if also the coldest— birding.

Directions

From the intersection of Rt. 72 with the Garden State Parkway at Exit 63 (Manahawkin), go east on Rt. 72 for 7 miles, crossing the bridge to Long Beach Island. At the third (and last) traffic light after crossing the bridge turn left onto Long Beach Blvd. Follow this road north for about 8 miles and you

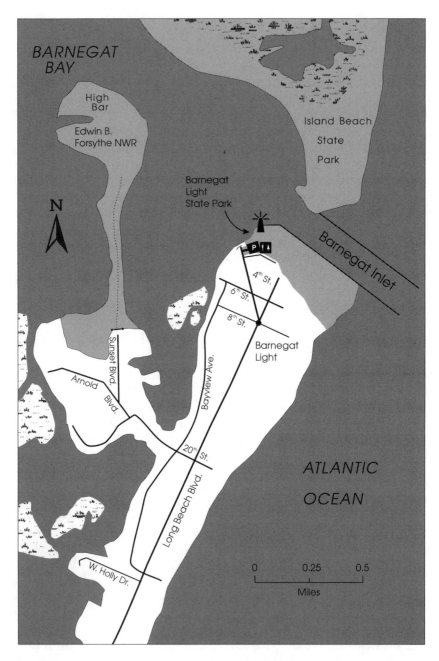

BARNEGAT
BAY

High
Bar

Edwin B.
Forsythe NWR

Island Beach

State

Park

Barnegat
Light
State Park

N

Barnegat Inlet

P

4ᵗʰ St.

6ᵗʰ St.

8ᵗʰ St.

Sunset Blvd.

Barnegat
Light

Arnold
Blvd.

Bayview Ave.

20ᵗʰ St.

ATLANTIC

OCEAN

Long Beach Blvd.

W. Holly Dr.

0   0.25   0.5

Miles

Map 66. Barnegat Light

will see the lighthouse. You are now in the town of Barnegat Light, the road name has changed to Central Ave., and you can follow the signs at the cross streets as they decrease from 30th Street. At 8th Street bear left onto Broadway and continue toward the end of the road. Just before the end, turn right into the parking lot for Barnegat Light State Park, where a fee is charged in summer. [DeLorme 58, L-12]

Birding

From the parking lot, walk out the path past the bathhouses and bear left to the base of the lighthouse. Here is the start of the jetty constructed in the early 1990s to replace an older one. This jetty stretches for about 1 mile, paralleling the one on the Island Beach side of the inlet. The first couple of hundred yards has a concrete walkway, which provides a vantage point for scanning the inlet and the Island Beach side of the inlet. A Snowy Owl occasionally winters at the inlet, so scan the north jetty and the beach cottages on Island Beach with a spotting scope. In winter, flocks of Bonaparte's Gulls frequently feed in the channel.

One of the highlights of birding Barnegat Light in the winter is the small flock of Harlequin Ducks that is present here. Numbering up to about 20, they often sit on the rocks along the edge of the jetty and can be observed at very close range. Although they can be found anywhere along the jetty, they frequently are in the first section with the paved walkway.

The ocean at the end of the jetty is the most reliable place in the state for King and Common eiders, but they are not present every year. You will have to walk all the way to the end of the jetty to see them. The quickest and safest way to get to the end is to climb down the rocks at the end of the paved walkway and go the rest of the way on the sand. As you go, watch in the dunes for Snow Bunting, Horned Lark, the occasional Lapland Longspur, and "Ipswich" Sparrow, a large, pale variety of Savannah Sparrow. The eiders are usually found about 100 yards to the south of the jetty feeding along the remnants of the old 8th Street jetty. If you can't find one here, you may want to climb up on the jetty and walk out to the end to scan, watching along the way for Purple Sandpipers, frequent visitors from November through March.

The inlet and the area around the end of the jetty are a favorite wintering site for Long-tailed Duck and Red-breasted Merganser. Sometimes there are rafts of Greater Scaup, all three scoters, Bufflehead, and a few Common Goldeneyes. A small flock of Brant usually frequents the near end of the jetty. In late fall, especially during November, large numbers of Red-throated and Common loons can be seen migrating just offshore. Northern Gannet is regular here at this season and, if the winds are from the east or southeast, you may see several hundred. These same winds occasionally bring Black-legged Kittiwake close to shore at this point.

Fall and early winter bring long skeins of scoters migrating south. Depending on the winds, they may fly from 100 yards to 1 mile or more offshore; easterly winds bring them closest. This season also brings migrant gulls from the north. Bonaparte's Gull appear some time in November to December, frequently by the hundreds; among them there is almost always a Little or a Common Black-headed Gull. With the arrival of the larger gulls in December, it is time to look for Glaucous, Iceland, and Lesser Black-backed gulls, which are seen around Barnegat Inlet annually.

Returning to the parking lot, check the bushes in fall for migrant passerines. Western Kingbird is seen here occasionally in fall or early winter. In winter, modern restrooms are open in the small building at the southwest corner of the parking lot; at other seasons use the restrooms in the bathhouses near the lighthouse.

Just outside the park, at the end of Broadway, a small parking area overlooks the bay side of the inlet. Here you can scan the sandbar islands for gulls and shorebirds; Gyrfalcon occasionally has been seen here, but you will be very lucky to see one. Large numbers of Brant, Red-breasted Merganser, and Long-tailed Duck are usually present in winter. Listen for the "owl-omelette" courtship call of the male Long-tailed Duck, which can be heard almost as frequently here as on the Arctic tundra where the species nests.

From the end of Broadway you can see a long spit of land that extends west into Barnegat Bay. This mile-long sandbar is known locally as High Bar or the dike, and is now part of the Barnegat Unit of Forsythe NWR. The outermost part of the bar, which was created by dredge spoil from Barnegat Inlet, has existed long enough for shrubs and small trees to grow, and supports a heronry in summer. The area is accessible on foot and is worth checking in winter for Snowy Owl and the ever-elusive Gyrfalcon.

To reach High Bar, go south on Broadway for two short blocks, turn right on 6th Street, then left onto Bayview Ave. As you drive south on Bayview, watch the boat channels for gulls and ducks; a female Harlequin Duck once wintered with the Mallards along here. The water tower to your left is a favorite perch for Snowy Owls when they are around, and a flock of Boat-tailed Grackles usually winters here. Turn right at 20th St., right again on Arnold Blvd. (the first street you come to), then immediately right on Sunset Blvd. Follow Sunset for about one-half mile to its end, then park on the street, being careful not to block the driveways of the houses. Cross through the fence and walk north to the end.

ᵀ

Holgate

Holgate Peninsula (the south end of Long Beach Island) is one of the few remaining relatively unspoiled stretches of barrier island left in New Jersey. It is roughly 2.5 miles long and constantly changing, with ocean beach, tidal mudflats on the bay side, salt marsh, and low dunes. The area above mean high tide is now a unit of Forsythe NWR, and is closed from April 1 to about August 31 to protect bird nesting colonies. Holgate supports some of the largest nesting colonies of Piping Plover, Common Tern, Least Tern, and Black Skimmer in the state. At other times, it is good for a variety of gulls, terns, and shorebirds in migration, and for wintering raptors, such as Rough-legged Hawk, Short-eared Owl, and the occasional Snowy Owl.

Directions

From the intersection of Rt. 72 with the Garden State Parkway at Exit 63 (Manahawkin), go east on Rt. 72 for 7 miles, crossing the bridge to Long Beach Island. At the third (and last) traffic light after crossing the bridge, turn right onto Bay Ave., which is also called Long Beach Blvd., depending on which municipality you are in. Follow this road south for 9 miles (and a couple of dozen traffic lights) to its end. There is a parking lot at the end, which is free except in summer. [DeLorme 59, L-17]

Birding

From late July through September, flocks of terns and shorebirds gather on the bay side at sandbars and mudflats. By late September the flocks have thinned somewhat, but there are still some migrant shorebirds, mainly juveniles, and this is a good time to look for godwits and other rarities.

The main birding areas at Holgate are near the south end of the peninsula, a walk of more than 2 miles from the parking lot. If you walk along the beach in late fall, watch for migrant waterfowl, loons, and Northern Gannets. After about 2 miles you will see a small cove on the bayside, with mudflats and a sandbar island that is completely covered at high tide. Cross over to the bayside here.

If possible, visits should be timed to coincide with the tides—the best birding conditions are usually found about halfway between low and high tides, preferably on the rising tide, although the several hours after high tide can be good also. At these times, terns and shorebirds gather on the mudflats or the sandbar island to feed or rest. (At low tide the birds are widely dispersed over the exposed mud, while at high tide the island is submerged, the mudflats limited, and the birds tend to fly off to other places). The walk down the beach is much easier on the hard-packed sand left by a falling tide than on the loose sand above the high water mark, so the best walking conditions do not always coincide with the best birding. Tides at Beach Haven Inlet occur at approximately the same time as at Cape May and Sandy Hook.

Summer resident Willets and American Oystercatchers gather in flocks of 50 to 100 after the breeding season. Dowitchers and Red Knots are abundant, and there are lesser numbers of Black-bellied Plovers, Sanderlings, and Semipalmated Sandpipers. Semipalmated Plovers are common migrants, and the local Piping Plovers feed on the mudflats as well as the ocean beaches, although they leave soon after the nesting season. Wilson's Phalarope and Hudsonian and Marbled godwits are annual visitors in small numbers.

From late fall through the winter, Holgate is a rather barren place. Offshore there are rafts of scaup, scoters, and Oldsquaw, plus a few loons, but one good reason for a visit is the possibility of finding a Snowy Owl. Almost every winter one of these vagrants from the north is seen here, and occasionally one stays for several weeks. Other winter visitors to be looked for are the Ipswich race of the Savannah Sparrow, Lapland Longspur, Snow Bunting, and Short-eared Owl. On the bayside, you can find a number of wintering waterbirds, including Bufflehead, Brant, Common Goldeneye, Horned Grebe, and possibly American Bittern.

⟩

Tuckerton Marshes

The Tuckerton Marshes, or simply Tuckerton as the area is known among birders, is an extensive area of salt marsh just south of the town of Tuckerton in Ocean County. Most of the area is within the 5,000-acre Great Bay WMA administered by the New Jersey Division of Fish and Wildlife. It is accessible by means of Great Bay Blvd., also known as Seven Bridges Rd. (there are only five), which traverses the marsh for 5 miles to its end at Little Egg Inlet. Tuckerton is known primarily as a shorebirding spot, but is also good for raptors, and the bushes along the road can harbor hordes of migrant songbirds after the passage of a fall cold front. American Oystercatcher is the specialty of the house and can be found here from early spring through fall. Interesting rarities, such as White-faced Ibis, Sandhill Crane, Curlew Sandpiper, and Black-throated Gray Warbler, are always a possibility during migration.

Directions

From the north, take the Garden State Parkway south to Exit 58 (Tuckerton). Follow Rt. 539 south for 3 miles to the traffic light at Rt. 9. Turn right and go about 0.2 miles to a fork (opposite a large lake) where Rt. 9 continues straight ahead and Great Bay Blvd. bears off to the left. Take the left fork onto Great Bay Blvd.; after about 1.6 miles you will emerge onto the salt marsh. [DeLorme 65, I-26]

From the south, take the Garden State Parkway north to Exit 50 (Rt. 9, New Gretna). Follow Rt. 9 through New Gretna for about 7 miles to Tuckerton. Just past a self-service car wash, turn right onto Gale Rd. Follow this road for about 1 mile until it dead-ends at Great Bay Blvd. Turn right and go 1 mile to where the road emerges from the salt marsh.

Birding

Great Bay Blvd. continues for 5 miles across the salt marsh, crossing 5 bridges along the way. Just before the first bridge (2.5 miles from Rt. 9) there is a parking area on the left side of the road. The marsh here is a favorite stopping-off place for Whimbrels, especially in the spring. In some years, they have been accompanied by an individual of one of the Eurasian races, formerly considered a separate species. These differ from our Whimbrel in having a conspicuous white wedge on the lower back, like a dowitcher. The last week of April through the second week in May is the best time to search through the flocks of Whimbrels, which may number more than 100.

As you cross the first bridge, you will see a sandy beach on either side of the road. If there are not too many cars and people around, these areas may have American Oystercatcher, Black-bellied Plover, or even Lesser Golden-Plover, and possibly Hudsonian Godwit in August and September. From late April through the summer and fall, Forster's Terns fish in the channel behind the boat dock to your right. Study them carefully, refer to your field guides, and compare them to the terns you will see at the end of the road, which are usually Common Terns.

The stretch of road between the first and second bridges (about 0.8 miles) is not very productive, but you should begin to see herons and egrets if your visit occurs between late April and early October. All of New Jersey's nesting herons and egrets are found at Tuckerton. Green-backed Heron is fairly common, Snowy and Great egrets are abundant and conspicuous, Great Blue Heron only slightly less so. This is an excellent place to observe Tricolored Heron at close range, as this species seems to prefer the open marshes here to the closed ponds at Brigantine NWR that are popular with the other species. Little Blue Heron is fairly common at Tuckerton, but may be more easily seen at Brigantine (as is Cattle Egret, which prefers to feed in drier

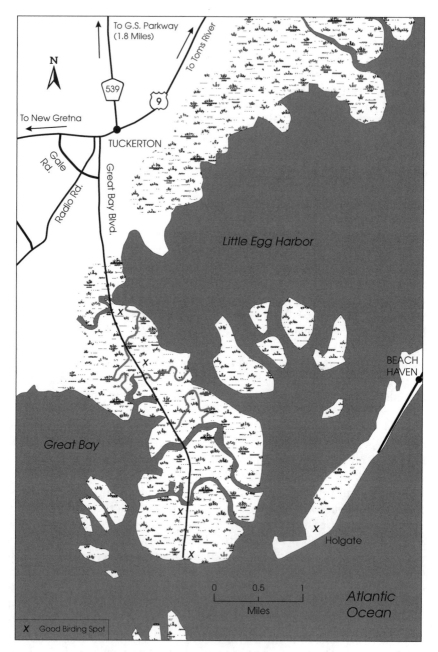

Map 67. Tuckerton Marshes

areas). Black-crowned Night-Heron is usually present, but is less active during the day and, therefore, somewhat less conspicuous than the others. Yellow-crowned Night-Heron, although present in small colonies just a few miles away, is seldom seen here. Glossy Ibis is abundant, and it is always worth checking them for a possible White-faced or White ibis, both of which have occurred here.

The section of road between the second and third bridges (about 0.5 miles) is usually more interesting, particularly when the tide is high enough to force the shorebirds away from the mudflats and onto the small shallow ponds that dot the salt marsh near the road. Beyond the third and fourth bridges (1.3 miles) there is even more of this type of habitat, which provides the best birding until you reach the end of the road.

Spring shorebirding is mostly confined to the month of May, but the fall migration here, as elsewhere, begins in early July and runs into October. During July and August, however, early-morning birding is recommended to avoid the automobile traffic. Most of the regularly occurring coastal shorebirds can be expected here. Black-bellied and Semipalmated plovers, American Oystercatcher, Greater and Lesser yellowlegs, Willet (abundant), Whimbrel, Hudsonian Godwit (uncommon in fall), Ruddy Turnstone, Red Knot, Sanderling, Semipalmated, Western (mainly fall), Least, White-rumped, Pectoral, and Stilt (fall) sandpipers, Purple Sandpiper (on the sod banks at the end of the road in winter and spring), Dunlin, Short-billed and Long-billed (mainly fall) dowitchers, Common Snipe, and Wilson's Phalarope (uncommon in fall). Rarer species that occasionally occur are Lesser Golden-Plover, Piping Plover (at the end of the road), Marbled Godwit, Curlew Sandpiper (formerly, at the end of the road), Ruff, and Red-necked Phalarope.

Between the third and fourth bridges, watch for the Osprey nest on the left (north) side; it has been occupied for many years. The road between the fourth and fifth bridges (about 1 mile) is less productive and is in poor condition. A flock of Boat-tailed Grackles frequently hangs out around the end of the road just before the fifth (and last) bridge.

When you cross the fifth bridge, you will see a long line of telephone poles going off to the right toward a former seafood processing plant on a distant island. Look for an Osprey nest atop one of the poles. The last stretch of road (0.8 miles) is lined with small shrubs, mainly bayberry. Under the right conditions, this vegetation can harbor hundreds of migrant passerines in September and October. Passage of a cold front during the day, followed by clearing skies and strong northwest winds overnight—the same conditions that bring massive flights to Cape May—forces many of the night-migrating songbirds well out to sea or out over the coastal marshes. At dawn they struggle landward, where the bushes along Great Bay Blvd. provide welcome shelter and a chance to recover from their long flight. The marshes along both sides of the road have nesting Sharp-tailed and Seaside sparrows, a few of which are present year-round. Clapper Rail is a common breeder, and the ponds along the roadside provide good feeding areas for herons, egrets, and shorebirds.

At the end of the road, extensive sodbanks are exposed at low tide, which occurs at about the same time as at Sandy Hook and 20 minutes later than at Barnegat Light. These are favorite feeding grounds for shorebirds, especially Black-bellied Plover (year-round), American Oystercatchers (spring through fall), Red Knot (spring, fall, occasionally in winter), and Dunlin (all winter). A wide variety of shorebirds can be found here from July through October; during the 1960s this was a favorite stopping place for Curlew Sandpipers, but none has been reported here in recent years.

Oystercatchers nest in the marsh about 0.25 miles north of the road's end, and they gather here and at nearby Holgate in large concentrations in late summer. Although Piping Plovers no longer nest here, one species that continues to nest is the Common Tern. Interestingly, this species and the oystercatcher have adapted here (and at many other sites in New Jersey) to nesting in the salt marsh, rather than in the grassy dune areas where they formerly nested, but were subject to frequent disturbance by people. A walk along the shore through the salt marsh to the north can be interesting and may turn up a few extra species of shorebirds, but waterproof boots are advised.

In winter, Tuckerton has little to offer. A few diving ducks gather in the channels and inlets, along with hoards of Brant; there are usually Black-bellied Plover and Dunlin, and sometimes Purple Sandpipers forage on the sod banks at the end of the road. Rough-legged Hawk and Northern Harrier are here, and perhaps Short-eared Owl.

Most birders try to combine a trip to Tuckerton with one to nearby Brigantine NWR, which has restrooms.

Kentucky Warbler

Southwest Region

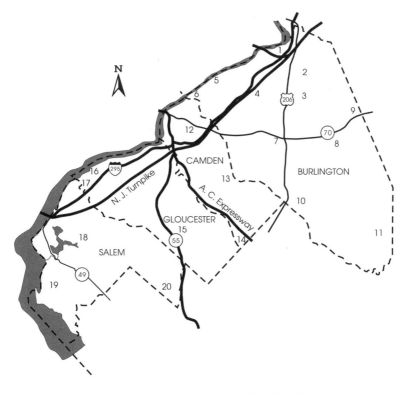

1. Florence
2. Brightview Farm
3. Pemberton Area
4. Rancocas State Park
5. Taylor Wildlife Refuge
6. Palmyra Cove Nature Park
7. Bear Swamp-Red Lion Preserve
8. Lebanon State Forest
9. Whitesbog
10. Wharton State Forest

11. Bass River State Forest
12. Pennypacker Park
13. Berlin Park
14. Winslow WMA
15. Floodgates
16. Pedricktown Marshes
17. Glassboro WMA
18. Northern Salem County
19. Southern Salem County
20. Parvin State Park

Map 68. Southwest Region

Florence

From the time of its "discovery" by Brian Sullivan in January 1997, the town of Florence, Burlington County, has been the hotspot for wintering gulls in New Jersey. Situated along the Delaware River opposite a monumental sanitary landfill at Tullytown, Pennsylvania, Florence provides excellent views of the birds soaring over the dump, or floating down the river. The more sought-after species, such as Glaucous, Iceland, and Lesser Black-backed gulls, are often commonplace, while the site has also produced numerous records of Thayer's Gull, as well as some yet-unaccepted reports of California, Mew, and Yellow-legged gulls.

Directions

The straightforward way to reach Florence from most of New Jersey is to take the New Jersey Turnpike to Pennsylvania Extension, Exit 6. Follow the Extension to the first exit, the last one in New Jersey, at US 130. At the end of the ramp, turn right onto US 130, and go 0.3 miles to the traffic light at Delaware Ave./Florence-Columbus Rd. Go through the light to make the jughandle left turn onto Delaware Ave., then continue about 2 miles on Delaware, which becomes Front St., to a small park and boat launch, Clark T. Carey Memorial Park, on the right, opposite Broad St. Alternatively, one can take I-295 to Exit 52, Florence-Columbus, and go west on Florence-Columbus Rd. for 1.9 miles to the traffic light at US 130. [DeLorme 47, D-26]

From the Trenton or Camden areas, take US 130 to the intersection with Delaware Ave., which is about 5 miles south of Bordentown and 5 miles north of the Burlington-Bristol bridge.

Birding

Gull-watching at Florence consists primarily of scanning the enormous flocks that sit on the water and gradually float downstream, then pick up and fly upstream to repeat the process. When the tide is low, several areas of mudflats are exposed on the Pennsylvania side of the river, and the birds can often be scoped at leisure, although they are a bit far away. Yet another pastime is to try to pick out rarities among the swarms of gulls wheeling over the landfill, although this is seldom very satisfying. Altogether, an estimated 30–40 thousand gulls visit the dump at the peak winter gathering.

There are two good vantage points for watching the gulls along the Delaware, the first being the park with the boat launch. To reach the second, continue west along Front St. for 0.5 miles to the H. Kenneth Wilkie River's Edge Park, on the right. Park in the parking lot and walk to the river, where there is a paved walkway that provides a good vantage point for birding. A spotting scope is an indispensable tool at Florence.

The gulls are present from late fall into the spring, and it is sometimes easier to spot the rarities when there aren't so many to sort through. Numbers of Lesser Black-backed Gulls seen here are amazing for a bird that is not yet known to nest in North America. Daily counts in excess of 30 are not uncommon, and there was a state high tally of 113 on Dec. 2, 1998. State record counts of Iceland (30+) and Glaucous (10+) gulls were noted there in early 1997, and both can be expected on any winter visit. A few Thayer's Gulls are being seen every winter, although these are by no means regular. Likewise, the difficulty in obtaining good photographs or videos has so far delayed the acceptance of such species as California Gull and Yellow-legged Gull.

In addition to the gulls, there are often other birds to keep things interesting. Bald Eagles are regular visitors, and sometimes perch in the trees on the Pennsylvania side. The Double-crested Cormorants that are common along the river are occasionally joined by a Great Cormorant or two. Among the various waterfowl that can be seen flying by or swimming in the river, Common Merganser is the most frequent of the diving ducks.

Gull-watching at Florence is usually a chilling and sometimes frustrating experience, and is strictly a week-day or Saturday morning venture. With few exceptions, the gulls are active only when the dump is active. The dump closes at about 1:00 P.M. on Saturday and is not open on Sunday.

The Wawa on Broad St. at 5th St. has coffee and hot chocolate, and there are public restrooms in the municipal building, 0.4 miles south of Front St. on Broad St., on the right.

⯆

Brightview Farm

This scenic 270-acre horse farm in western Burlington County, surrounded by encroaching housing developments, is one of the best places in New Jersey to see nesting Savannah Sparrow, Grasshopper Sparrow, Meadowlark, and Bobolink, and has hosted nesting Dickcissel on several occasions. Dickcissel is a rare and sporadic breeding bird in the state, confirmed nesting at only three different sites (not all in the same year) during the breeding bird atlas.

The success of these grassland species at Brightview Farm is entirely the result of delayed mowing by the generous landowner.

Directions

Take the New Jersey Turnpike to Exit 7, US 206. Go right (south) on US 206 for just 0.6 miles from the end of the exit ramp and turn left onto State Rt. 68. Take Rt. 68 for about 3.9 miles, then turn left and immediately right onto County Rt. 545 East (Bordentown Rd.) for about 1 mile to the entrance to Brightview Farm, on the left. [DeLorme 48, H-8]

Alternatively, take I-295 to Exit 52, Florence-Columbus. Go east on Florence-Columbus Rd., which is joined by Rt. 543 after 0.6 miles, for about 7 miles, continuing straight ahead onto Mt. Pleasant Rd. when Rt. 543 turns left. When Mt. Pleasant Rd. deadends at Rt. 545, turn right and go 0.2 miles to the entrance to Brightview Farm, on the left.

From southeastern New Jersey take US 206 north to the intersection with Rt. 537, Monmouth Rd., then turn right onto Rt. 537. Go about 6.3 miles to the intersection with Rt. 545, turn left onto Rt. 545, and 0.3 miles to the entrance to the farm, on the right.

Birding

Drive straight ahead past the buildings for about one-half mile, with fields on the left and woods on the right, until you come to an area with fields on both sides of the road. Here, the owner has installed a box on the fence holding a sightings log. Often, the target species are visible right from this location. Birders are allowed to walk the other roads and trails, but it's best to keep out of pastures with horses. From the corner where the log book is posted, walk along the road about 300 yards to a feeding stable on the left. Turn left here and walk the wide, grassy path between the pastures. Eastern Bluebird and Tree Swallow nest in the boxes along the path. At the end of the path is a wet area with woods beyond, where you may see Yellow Warbler, Common Yellowthroat, and Baltimore and Orchard orioles.

Remember that birding at Brightview is a gift and a privilege. Don't do anything to jeopardize the welfare of the birds or the largesse of the landowner who permits continued access to the farm by birders. By all means record your sightings in the log, including numbers, not just species.

Pemberton Area

(Dot and Brooks Evert Memorial Trail, Magnolia Road Swamp, North Branch Preserve, Pemberton Lake Wildlife Management Area)

These four sites, located just east and south of Pemberton, in western Burlington County, include a mixed woodland of swamp and upland species on the boundary between the Pinelands and the coastal plain, a wooded swamp, a wet, river-bottom deciduous woodland, and a shallow lake that was formerly a cranberry bog. The first three are especially good in spring and early summer for migrant and breeding passerines, while the lake attracts migrant and wintering waterfowl in the cooler months.

Directions

From the intersection of US 206, Rt. 38, and Rt. 530, 3 miles southeast of Mt. Holly, [DeLorme 48, M-3], take Rt. 530 (South Pemberton Rd.) east for 2.7 miles to the traffic light at Hanover St. (Rt. 616). Continue straight ahead on Rt. 530, but bear immediately right onto Magnolia Rd. (Rt. 644). Go about 4.5 miles to the intersection with Ong's Hat-Buddtown Rd. (Rt. 642), on the right, at the Magnolia Tavern. Turn right onto Ong's Hat Rd, and drive 1.4 miles to a small parking lot on the right and a sign for the Dot and Brooks Evert Memorial Trail. [DeLorme 56, B-7; note that the location marked in the DeLorme Atlas is in error.]

Birding

The nature trail makes a 1.5-mile loop, with a side leg, through this 170-acre preserve owned by the New Jersey Conservation Foundation. Its mature flood-plain forest along a stream with the curious name of Stop-the-Jade Run, contains a wet Red Maple swamp, where Prothonotary and Kentucky warblers can be found in spring and summer, and a somewhat drier Pitch Pine-Mountain Laurel section with Worm-eating, Pine, and Prairie warblers, White-eyed and Red-eyed vireos, Scarlet Tanagers, and many others; Hooded Warblers are found throughout. The diversity of flora and fauna along the Evert Memorial trail is a result of the position of the forest along an ecotone that separates the Pine Barrens of the younger, sandy Outer Coastal Plain from the deciduous forests of the older, richer soils of the Inner Coastal Plain. An informative trail guide is available in a sign-in box at the entrance

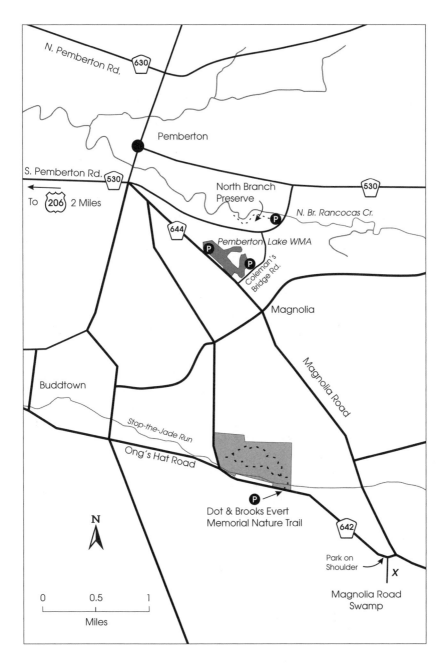

Map 69. Pemberton Area

and provides a narrative account of the different ecological features of the preserve.

To continue, drive back toward the intersection of Ong's Hat Rd. and Magnolia Rd., and park on the right shoulder, just before Ong's Hat Rd. bends left and ends at Magnolia Rd. An old dirt road leads into the woods from the south side of Ong's Hat Rd., but it is usually covered with water in places and wading boots are a must. This area is known as Magnolia Rd. Swamp, but only a small portion of the swamp is accessible from the road. Nevertheless, most of the interesting species can be easily found close to the trail. A couple of pairs of Prothonotary Warblers nest here and are usually very obliging. This is also one of the most southerly spots in the state for nesting Northern Waterthrush, with a pair usually on the left as you walk in. Hooded and Pine warblers are easily found here, as well as Louisiana Waterthrush. Other breeding species include Broad-winged Hawk, Yellow-billed Cuckoo, Acadian Flycatcher, Blue-gray Gnatcatcher, White-eyed Vireo, and Black-and-white Warbler.

Turn left onto Magnolia Rd. toward Pemberton, and go about 3 miles to Pemberton Lake WMA, on the right. This small, shallow, 82-acre lake was once a cranberry bog, but now attracts a variety of dabbling ducks, geese, and even Tundra Swans during the colder months. There is a small parking area at the sign for the WMA where you can stop and scan the lake. Another point of access is along Coleman's Bridge Rd., the last right turn before the lake.

The last stop is the North Branch Preserve. Continue toward Pemberton and the junction of Rt. 530 and Magnolia Rd., and turn right onto Rt. 530 (Pemberton Parkway), just before the traffic light. Go about 1.7 miles and turn left just before the bridge over Rancocas Creek into a short, paved road to a small parking area. A trail on the west side of the parking area leads into the deciduous bottomland forest, where Broad-winged and Cooper's hawks nest. This spot is good for migrant songbirds in spring and has an interesting assortment of nesting birds. Like most such spots, it's quiet in winter, except for the usual resident chickadees and titmice, plus a modest selection of wintering sparrows.

❦

Rancocas State Park

Rancocas State Park in western Burlington County encompasses almost 1,100 acres of mixed oaks and Virginia Pine woods, overgrown fields, lowland deciduous forest, freshwater streams, and marshes along the two branches of

Rancocas Creek—the only Pine Barrens stream that drains westward. Since 1977, the New Jersey Audubon Society has operated the Rancocas Nature Center at an old farmhouse in the northeast corner of the park.

Because of its location near the Delaware River, Rancocas harbors many migrant songbirds in spring. The breeding species are diverse, but not unusual. The fall migration is not as good as the spring, but the colder months can be very productive, with sparrows, occasional northern finches, and other wintering species.

Directions

Take the New Jersey Turnpike to Exit 5 (Mt. Holly and Burlington). From the exit ramp, go right (east) on Rt. 541, Mt. Holly-Burlington Rd. Go about 1.5 miles to the second traffic light, and turn right onto the Mt. Holly Bypass, following the sign to Rt. 38 (still Rt. 541). Drive 0.7 miles to the next traffic light, and turn right onto Rancocas Rd. The entrance to the Rancocas Nature Center is 1 mile ahead on the left.

Alternatively, you can take I-295 to Exit 45A (Rancocas Rd.). Go east for 1.7 miles to the entrance to the Nature Center, on the right. [DeLorme 47, K-25]

Birding

The nature trail and other trails accessible in the northern part of the park cover a good selection of the habitats available at Rancocas. The nature trail begins at the southeast corner of the parking lot and forms a loop of about 0.6 miles; a side trail about one-third of the way along (going clockwise) adds another 0.4 miles to the walk. The side trail leads to the marshes along the North Branch of Rancocas Creek, where you will find abundant Wild Rice, Arrow Arum, and other marsh plants.

In spring, Wood Duck, Green-winged Teal, Gadwall, Northern Pintail, Ring-necked Duck, and other species of waterfowl visit Rancocas Creek. Other migrants along the streams include Great Blue Heron, Osprey, Greater and Lesser yellowlegs, and Common Snipe. Although Rancocas is a little east of the main Delaware Valley flyway, it gets a good spillover of spring migrant songbirds, with as many as 24 species of warblers from late April through May, including Yellow-throated Warbler and Prothonotary warblers, Louisiana Waterthrush, and Yellow-breasted Chat.

Breeding birds at Rancocas include Green Heron, Wood Duck, Mallard, Red-tailed Hawk, Northern Bobwhite, American Woodcock, Yellow-billed Cuckoo, Eastern Screech and Great Horned owls, Chimney Swift, Belted Kingfisher, Red-bellied Woodpecker, Wood Thrush, Brown Thrasher,

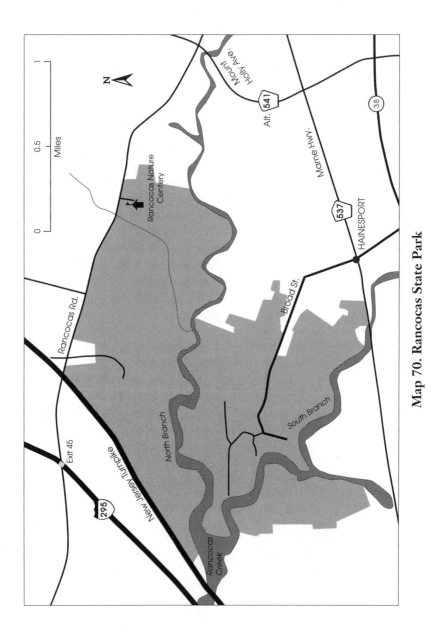

Map 70. Rancocas State Park

Yellow and Black-and-white warblers, Blue Grosbeak (since about 1980), Indigo Bunting, and Swamp Sparrow.

Fall migration is unspectacular, but it does bring many Bobolinks to the Wild Rice marshes along the creek, a good selection of warblers (especially Cape May and Yellow-rumped) from mid-September to mid-October, and a variety of sparrows to the fields and feeders later in the season. From November to March, you may find Northern Harrier and Sharp-shinned, Cooper's, and Red-tailed hawks hunting in the woods and marshes. Other species to look for at that season are Red-breasted Nuthatch, Eastern Bluebird, Hermit Thrush and (in flight years) Red and White-winged crossbills, Common Redpoll, and Pine Siskin.

The southern portion of the park can be reached by turning right (east) onto Rancocas Rd. and going 1.1 miles to Rt. 541 (the Mt. Holly Bypass). Turn right, and go 0.8 miles to Rt. 537 (Marne Highway). Drive about 1.1 miles, then turn right on Rancocas Ave., the first right turn after Broad St. After about 0.6 miles, Rancocas Ave. becomes dirt and enters the state park. Passable dirt roads continue almost to the confluence of the North and South branches of Rancocas Creek (about 1.2 miles), but caution is urged when the roads are wet and muddy. Park along the roads and explore the woods and the marshes along the creek.

❧

Taylor Wildlife Preserve

This small, privately owned preserve along the Delaware River in Cinnaminson, Burlington County, is the only remaining farm on the river between Trenton and Camden. Despite its small size, the diversity of habitat and its strategic position along the river, make it a magnet for migrant songbirds. Almost 250 species have been seen here in the past 20 years and, although it is primarily a spot to visit in spring or fall, the refuge has a good variety of breeding birds and some unusual wintering birds, as well. The New Jersey Natural Lands Trust holds a conservation easement on 89 of the 130 acres of the farm to preserve its beauty for coming generations.

Directions

To reach the refuge, take the New Jersey Turnpike to Exit 4 (Rt. 73) or I-295 to Exit 36 (Rt. 73), and drive north on Rt. 73 for about 5 miles to the exit for

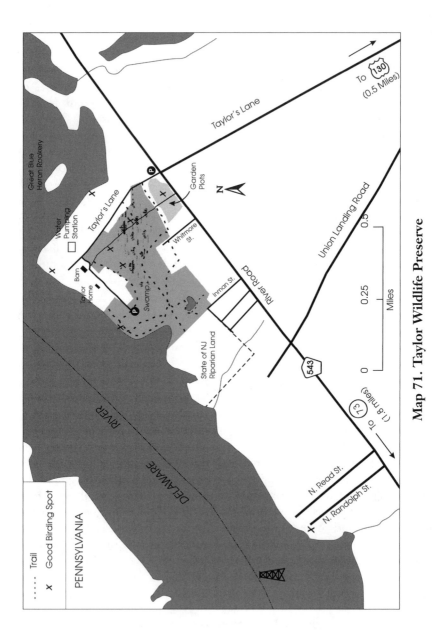

Map 71. Taylor Wildlife Preserve

US 130 North. Go north on US 130 for about 3 miles to the jughandle left turn onto Taylor's Lane. Go 1.4 miles on Taylor's Lane to River Rd., and continue straight ahead into the preserve. After about 0.4 miles, the road turns left and continues another 0.3 miles to a parking area. In wet weather or snowy weather, it may be prudent to park near the entrance to the preserve at River Rd. [DeLorme 47, J-15]

Birding

Because of the small size of the preserve, you can walk all of the trails at a leisurely birding pace in a couple of hours or less, including the trails on the adjacent 20-acre plot owned by the state of New Jersey. Spring and, especially, fall are best. Many migrant songbirds pass through here in spring, as at the nearby Palmyra Cove Nature Park, while September and October bring such sought-after species as Yellow-bellied Flycatcher, Philadelphia Vireo, Connecticut Warbler, and Lincoln's Sparrow. Many other rarities, including Western Kingbird, Northern Shrike, Lark Sparrow, Clay-colored Sparrow, and even Painted Bunting have occurred.

The main feature of the site is the beautiful marsh and swampy woodlands, a unique rarity in such a developed area. A dirt road that parallels Taylor's Lane serve as an excellent trail through the marsh for listening to the morning chorus of marsh birds and frogs in the spring. Among the breeding birds at Taylor Refuge are Least Bittern, Great Blue Heron, Green Heron, Wood Duck, Virginia Rail, Cooper's Hawk, Willow Flycatcher, Tree Swallow, Warbling and White-eyed vireos, Swamp Sparrow, and Orchard Oriole. Least Bittern and Virginia Rail have occurred in summer, and Cooper's Hawk, Red-shouldered Hawk, Black-billed and Yellow-billed cuckoos have all nested on occasion.

Another good area in fall is the collection of garden plots along River Rd., adjoining the Refuge (see map). After the growing season, these plots are very good for sparrows and the occasional Orange-crowned or Connecticut Warbler.

Winter birding along the river will produce Common Goldeneye and Common Merganser. The Randolph St. access to the Delaware River, 1.25 miles south of Taylor's Lane, is excellent for Great Cormorant, which often roost on the nearby navigation tower in winter, and this spot has even produced Barrow's Goldeneye.

Palmyra Cove Nature Park

Situated at the base of the Tacony-Palmyra Bridge, the Palmyra Cove Nature Park is an unlikely spot for one of the best migrant traps in New Jersey, but that it is. Created from former marshlands by the deposit of tons of dredge spoil from the Delaware River since World War II, the park is a magnet for a wide variety of migratory birds, and it has attracted an amazing selection of rarities in the past decade. In addition to being one of the best places in the state for Yellow-bellied Flycatcher, Philadelphia Vireo, Mourning and Connecticut warblers, and Lincoln's Sparrow, the 260+ species recorded here include White Pelican, Mississippi Kite, Franklin's Gull, Common Black-headed Gull, Snowy Owl, Ash-throated Flycatcher, Painted Bunting, Le-Conte's and Clay-colored sparrows, and Yellow-headed Blackbird.

Directions

To reach Palmyra from southern or northeastern New Jersey, take the New Jersey Turnpike to Exit 4, Rt. 73, or I-295 to Exit 36, Rt. 73. Go north on Rt. 73 toward the Tacony-Palmyra Bridge for about 5 miles to Souder St., the last traffic light, just before the bridge. Turn right and go about 300 yards, crossing Market St., to Temple Blvd. Turn left and go a short distance to the entrance to the Bridge Authority parking lot on the right, just past a sign that warns "Last turn before bridge." Turn into the lot and drive past the buildings, then down a dirt road toward the river and under the bridge. You will see a parking lot ahead on the right. [DeLorme 46, K-12]

Future plans call for relocating the entrance to the park to the traffic light at Souder St., where the entrance to the Flea Market is at present.

Birding

The 350-acre Palmyra Cove Nature Park is being developed jointly by the Burlington County Bridge Commission and the Burlington County Board of Chosen Freeholders. Plans call for an environmental education center, interpretive trails, and a boardwalk. While these plans have been slow to reach fruition, the public access to the park has made it an attractive birding area.

Palmyra was "discovered" by Tom Bailey in the early 1980s, and has gradually become a prime birding attraction in the greater Philadelphia-Camden area. The trail names shown on the map are those used by Tom and his associates, and they are not necessarily the names that will be used by the park management. Although the dominant feature of the site is the Big Pit,

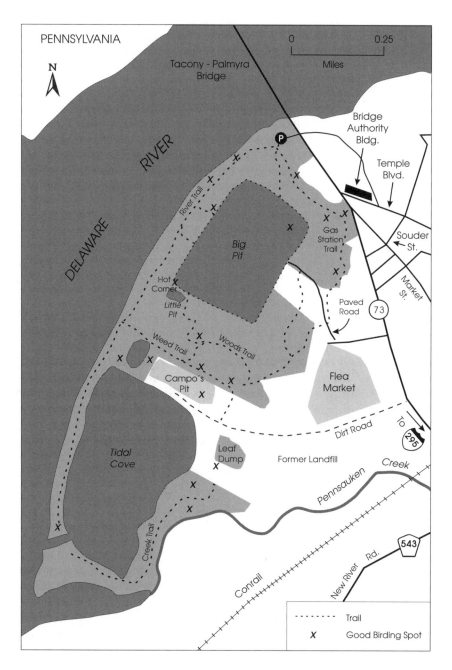

PENNSYLVANIA

N

Tacony - Palmyra
Bridge

0   0.25
Miles

Bridge
Authority
Bldg.

Temple
Blvd.

RIVER

DELAWARE

River Trail

Big
Pit

Gas
Station
Trail

Souder
St.

Hot
Corner

Little
Pit

Paved
Road

73

Market St.

Weed Trail

Woods Trail

Campo's
Pit

Flea
Market

Tidal
Cove

Leaf
Dump

Former Landfill

Dirt Road

To
295

Pennsauken   Creek

Creek Trail

Conrail

New River   Rd.

543

- - - - - - -   Trail

X   Good Birding Spot

Map 72. Palmyra Cove Nature Park

a large rectangular hole dug as a repository for future dredge spoils, the surrounding woodlands of second growth and more mature deciduous woodlands attract an outstanding variety of migrant songbirds in spring and, especially, in the fall. All of the common migrant songbirds can be found here in migration, and many shorebirds are attracted to the Big Pit in fall, when there is water in it.

The relatively short list of breeding birds does contain one stellar rarity, N. Saw-whet Owl. Other breeders are Pied-billed Grebe, Least Bittern, Peregrine Falcon (on the bridge), Willow Flycatcher, Marsh Wren, Warbling Vireo, Yellow Warbler, and Baltimore and Orchard orioles. While winter birding is generally pretty slow, spring and fall find the park full of birders seeking the common and not-so-common migrants.

All of the trails in the park can be traversed in a few hours, but Tom's recommended route is to follow the River Trail as it parallels the Delaware River. The woods along the trail are excellent for migrants early in the morning. After about 500 yards, follow the main trail as it bends to the left, away from the river, and ends at the Big Pit. In the fall, turn right on the dirt road that surrounds the Big Pit and walk a short distance until you reach the area between the Big Pit and the Little Pit. This area is known as the Hot Corner. Early in the morning, the rays of the sun warm this area first, and both birds and birders concentrate here.

By just standing at the Hot Corner, one can see or hear an amazing variety of species. Some found here in recent years include Whip-poor-will, Red-headed Woodpecker, Philadelphia Vireo, Golden-winged, Mourning, and Connecticut warblers, and Clay-colored Sparrow. After the first hour or two, the birds disperse and form feeding flocks.

In general, the area along the river is better in fall; in spring, the woods to the south and east of the Big Pit are usually productive. An especially good trail to check at both seasons is the Gas Station Trail. Many other trails wander around and through the woods, most of them shown on the map, and anyone can be productive when conditions are right. Don't neglect the Big Pit itself. Although sand was pumped into the northwest corner in 2000, it is still attractive to birds. Some of the species seen in the pit are Pied-billed Grebe (nests), American and Least bitterns, Glossy Ibis, Virginia Rail (nests), Sora, Common Moorhen, Stilt and Baird's sandpipers, Black Tern, Barn Owl, LeConte's Sparrow, and Dickcissel. Lincoln's Sparrow can be almost common in fall.

Another productive area is Campo's Pit, which is an active sand and gravel mining area. This is private property (Burlington County is negotiating to buy the land as open space), but the landowner has always allowed birders free access. Sparrows are abundant here in fall, especially along the Weed Trail on the north side. The wet area in the middle has produced

American Bittern, Sora, and Nelson's Sharp-tailed Sparrow. The pond usually has a nesting pair of Pied-billed Grebes and a few ducks in migration. Check the wood edges for migrant songbirds.

The Leaf Dumping Area is another good spot, mainly in the fall. This is also private property, so don't enter the area if workers are there. The area to the east of the Leaf Dump is a former landfill and has few birds, but the Creek Trail south of the Leaf Dump can be good for migrant warblers in the spring.

The large tidal cove on the southwestern edge of the park can be viewed from the River Trail. Future plans call for a boardwalk in the marsh here and a footbridge over the inlet, which would connect the River Trail with the Creek Trail. Least Bittern and Marsh Wren breed in the cove, which also attracts shorebirds and waterfowl in migration. Such unusual species as Tricolored Heron; Willet; and Franklin's, Common Black-headed, Iceland, and Glaucous gulls have been recorded here. In winter, large numbers of American Black Ducks can be found, along with Green-winged Teal and Northern Pintail.

The Delaware River is not particularly productive for birds at this spot. In winter, Bufflehead and Common Merganser are usually present in small numbers, sometimes accompanied by a few Common Goldeneye. Great Cormorant is regular, however, from November to March. In late summer, watch for Caspian and Forster's terns, then for Bonaparte's Gulls in October through November.

✝

Hawkin Road
(Bear Swamp-Red Lion Preserve)

Burlington County's Bear Swamp (almost every county in New Jersey has one), better known to birders by the name of the road that traverses it, may well be the Prothonotary Warbler capital of the state. It is also an outstanding spot to view the spring migration of songbirds attracted to the tall deciduous trees of this unique woodland; many of these species stay to nest. Although there are scattered residences along the length of Hawkin Rd., a total of 840 acres, almost one-third, of the roughly 3,000-acre swamp has been protected as the Bear Swamp-Red Lion preserve, a property of the New Jersey Natural Lands Trust.

Directions

The Bear Swamp portion of Hawkin Rd. (Hawkins Rd. on some maps) runs for 4 miles between Skeet Rd., just southeast of Medford and US 206, just south of Red Lion; most of the birding is along the western 2 miles. Take I-295 to Exit 34 (Rt. 70, Marlton Pike) for about 11 miles though Marlton and Medford to Skeet Rd., and turn right. Skeet Rd. is about 2.1 miles past the intersection with Rt. 541 in Medford. Go 0.6 miles to the intersection with Hawkin Rd. and turn left. [DeLorme 55, D-27] Alternatively, take the New Jersey Turnpike to Exit 4 (Rt. 73), go south on Rt. 73 for 3 miles to the intersection with Rt. 70, and turn left. Skeet Rd. is about 7.5 miles east.

To reach the east end of Hawkin Rd., take Rt. 70 or US 206 to the junction of these two roads at the Red Lion Circle. Go south on US 206 for 1.9 miles to the traffic light at Hawkin Rd., and turn right. The pavement ends after about 1 mile and resumes after another 2.1 miles, just 0.6 miles from the intersection with Skeet Rd.

Birding

For spring migration, the best bet is to park along the road and bird from the road. From the intersection of Hawkin Rd. and Skeet Rd., take Hawkin Rd. about 0.7 miles to the bridge over Little Creek. Park here, and walk the road in both directions to look and listen for migrants. Most of the regular migrant songbirds can be found here on a good day. The first two weeks in May are the best.

The swamp is also a delightful place in late spring-early summer for its variety of nesting birds. Mosquitoes are abundant, however, so be prepared. Among the breeding birds at Bear Swamp are Yellow-billed Cuckoo, White-eyed Vireo, Blue-gray Gnatcatcher, Blue-winged, Pine, Prairie, Black-and-white, Worm-eating, Kentucky, and Hooded warblers, Ovenbird, Louisiana Waterthrush, Common Yellowthroat, and Scarlet Tanager. Prothonotary Warbler is a specialty at Bear Swamp. August Sexauer of nearby Southampton has for some years maintained a nest box trail in the swamp for our only cavity-nesting warbler and has had outstanding success. Fifteen nest boxes are maintained and have typically been used by 7–10 pairs of warblers. In 1999, they fledged an impressive 35 young.

From the bridge over Little Creek, you can often see and hear Prothonotary Warbler, as well as Kentucky and Hooded warblers, Ovenbird, and Louisiana Waterthrush. To explore more of the swamp, take the trail that starts on the north side of the road, just east of the bridge. After about 100 yards, another trail branches off on the left. You can follow this trail, which is usually very muddy and requires knee boots, for several hundred yards until the creek stops further progress.

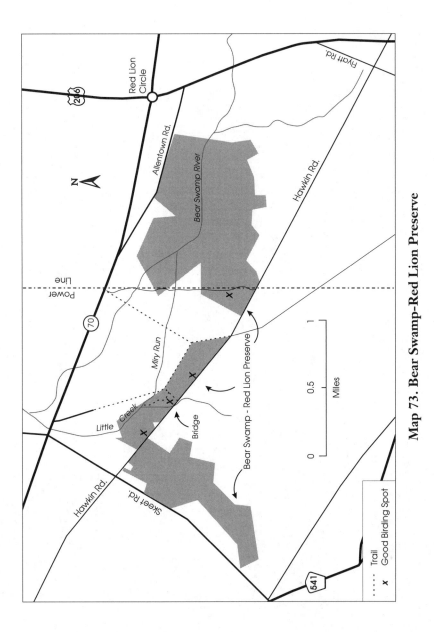

Map 73. Bear Swamp-Red Lion Preserve

Prothonotary Warbler

Return to the main trail and turn left. After another 100 yards or so, you will come to an old woods road (shown on some maps as Picketts Mill Rd.), which marks the current boundary of the preserve. You can bird to the left for several hundred yards of similar habitat. If you want a good hike through some of the other parts of the swamp, you can follow the road to the right (southeast) for about 1 mile to a power line. Along the way, you pass through drier, Pine Barrens-type habitat, plus additional swamp.

At the power line, you will come to a dirt maintenance road that runs under the lines. Turn right and you will come to Hawkin Rd. in about one-half mile. Here, on your right, you will see a sign marking the beginning of the Bear Swamp-Red Lion Preserve. The bridge over Little Creek is 1.2 miles to the right (northwest).

☂

Lebanon State Forest

Lebanon State Forest covers almost 30,000 acres in the heart of the New Jersey Pine Barrens in Burlington and Ocean counties. Like most of the pinelands, Lebanon receives relatively little attention from birders because of the uniformity of habitat and lack of diversity of birdlife. However, a number of unusual species were found nesting in the state forest during the early 1980s, mainly due to diligent field work by Wade and Sharon Wander and Ted Proctor. Their findings suggest that other surprises might await the inquisitive birder who is willing to explore some out-of-the-way places.

Unusual species that nest in Lebanon State Forest are Common Nighthawk, Red-headed Woodpecker, Brown Creeper, Eastern Bluebird, Black-throated Green Warbler, and Summer Tanager. Other birds that have been found nearby and should be sought here in summer are Hermit Thrush, Northern Waterthrush, and Canada Warbler.

Directions

Our tour of Lebanon State Forest begins at the traffic circle where Rts. 70 and 72 intersect, known as the Four Mile Circle. To reach this point:

From the intersection of US 206 and Rt. 70 (the Red Lion traffic circle) in Burlington County, take Rt. 70 east for about 8 miles to the Four Mile Circle. [DeLorme 56, D-11]

From the New Jersey shore, take either Rt. 70 southwest from Exit 88 of the Garden State Parkway for 27 miles or take Rt. 72 northwest from Exit 63 of the Parkway for 22 miles.

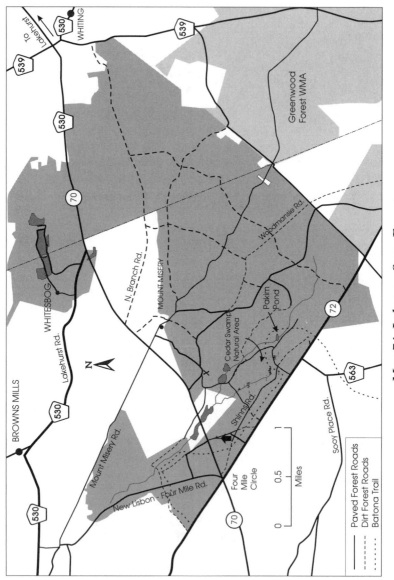

Map 74. Lebanon State Forest

Birding

Most of the roads in Lebanon State Forest are unpaved and are unmarked. At the headquarters (see below) you can get a map that shows the main roads, but it is better to use USGS topographic maps of the area (Lebanon State Forest is covered on the Browns Mills, Whiting, Chatsworth, and Woodmansie quadrangles). These are usually on sale at the forest headquarters.

From the Four Mile Circle, go east on Rt. 70 for about 100 yards to a dirt road (Shinn's Rd.) on the right. Turn onto it and almost immediately you will come to a junction where another dirt road goes left, paralleling Rt. 70; a second dirt road goes right toward Rt. 72, and Shinn's Rd. continues straight ahead, paralleling Rt. 72. Follow Shinn's Rd.

Parts of the oak-pine woods along the road have been selectively cut. This has provided habitat that is attractive to Summer Tanager and, at least formerly, Red-headed Woodpecker. The first 0.8 miles are especially good; stop periodically and listen for the raucous call of the woodpecker and the Robin-like song or "tucky-tuck" call of the tanager. Eastern Bluebirds also find the open woodlands desirable, and can often be found along Shinn's Rd. Other birds to be found along Shinn's Rd. include Broad-winged Hawk, Yellow-billed Cuckoo, Blue-winged, Pine, Prairie, and Black-and-white warblers, Indigo Bunting, Chipping Sparrow, and other typical Pine Barrens species. Although the woodpeckers seem to have abandoned this area, look for them in any of the more open woodland that you encounter throughout the forest.

About 1 mile in from Rt. 70, Shinn's Rd. intersects a paved road and continues as a paved road. The new headquarters building, which has restrooms, maps, and information, is just beyond the intersection, on the left. Continue about 0.6 miles to another intersection with a dirt road and turn left. In about 0.6 miles you will cross the bridge over Shinn's Branch, a typical Pine Barrens stream bordered by a dense cedar swamp.

About 200 yards beyond the bridge a sand road on the right parallels the edge of the swamp for almost a mile. Park along the dirt road and explore the sand road. You will have to wander off the road into the woods on the right to get close to the swamp. If you do, you may encounter Brown Creeper, Black-throated Green Warbler, and possibly Northern Waterthrush or Canada Warbler, in addition to many of the species previously mentioned.

Lebanon State Forest has many more cedar swamps that you can explore with the help of topographic maps. These include McDonald's Branch, about 1.5 miles east of Shinn's Branch; the North, Middle, and South Branches of Mount Misery Brook, which converge at Mount Misery, about 3.5 miles northeast of the forest headquarters; and Goose Pond, about 1 mile north of Pasadena, which lies along the abandoned Central Railroad of New Jersey. Long-eared Owl and Acadian Flycatcher have been found at Goose Pond in summer, and Sharp-shinned Hawk and N. Saw-whet Owl are possibilities. Hooded and Prothonotary warblers should also be looked for.

Several places in Lebanon State Forest have cranberry bogs with their associated reservoirs that provide habitat similar to Whitesbog, which is covered in a separate section. The most accessible of these is Reeves Bogs (at the X-symbol on the map northwest of Cedar Swamp); to reach this area, go north from the bridge across Shinn's Branch for 0.3 miles and turn left on another dirt road. Go 0.6 miles to a T intersection and turn right onto Woodmansie Rd. The bogs begin on the right in about 200 yards.

In addition to those species already noted, some of the other regular breeding birds of the Pine Barrens include Green Heron, Red-tailed Hawk (uncommon), Wild Turkey, American Woodcock, Black-billed Cuckoo, Ruby-throated Hummingbird, Willow Flycatcher, Eastern Phoebe, Purple Martin, Tree, N. Rough-winged, and Barn swallows, Fish Crow, Carolina Wren, Northern Mockingbird, White-eyed Vireo, Yellow Warbler, American Redstart, and Swamp Sparrow. Most of these species are less widely distributed in the barrens than those previously cited as typical of the area.

The Batona Hiking Trail, a well-marked foot trail, traverses 49 miles of varied habitats and landforms of the Pine Barrens. It begins at Ong's Hat on the western edge of Lebanon State Forest and covers 9.4 miles within the forest, passing near the headquarters building. The trail then turns south toward Wharton State Forest, reaching almost to Batsto before it heads east to its end at Bass River State Forest. Camping is permitted at several spots along the way; a trail map and camping permit can be obtained at the Lebanon State Forest headquarters.

If you camp in the state forest or stay in the area until dark, you may hear some of the nocturnal birds of the Pine Barrens. The most conspicuous voices of the night are those of Eastern Screech-Owl, Barred Owl, Common Nighthawk, and Whip-poor-will, which nest in the forest. The nighthawk is a rare breeder elsewhere in the state, but is locally common in the barrens. N. Saw-whet Owl has also been found in the Pine Barrens during the nesting season, and is probably more common than birders realize. Do a little exploring and see if you can find one.

🦃

Whitesbog

Whitesbog is a unique birding area in the New Jersey Pine Barrens that offers a variety of habitat. It is better known historically as the place where the first successful blueberry crops were cultivated. Now it comprises more than

3,000 acres of both abandoned and cultivated cranberry bogs, blueberry fields, reservoirs, swamps, ponds, streams, cedar bogs, fields in many stages of succession, and oak and Pitch Pine forest. The area, in northeastern Burlington County, is a part of the Lebanon State Forest and is operated as the Conservation and Environmental Studies Center.

More than 200 species of birds have been observed around Whitesbog, but it is mainly the waterfowl that attracts birders to the site. Nowhere else in New Jersey can you observe Tundra Swans at such close range. The most remarkable feature of the area is the flocks of Gull-billed Terns that have appeared here during August. Although this tern is considered to be an exclusively coastal species, Whitesbog is more than 20 miles from the nearest salt water.

Directions

From the junction of State Rt. 70 and County Rt. 530 on the Burlington-Ocean County Line, go west on Rt. 530 toward Browns Mills for 1.2 miles, then turn right at the sign for the Conservation and Environmental Studies Center. Follow this road for about 0.4 miles to the town of Whitesbog. [DeLorme 49, N-16]

Birding

The map shows a 3-mile tour, suggested by Len Little, that covers most of the interesting birding areas. By parking in appropriate places and hiking into the surrounding woods and fields, you can thoroughly investigate Whitesbog. Use caution in driving the narrow sandy roads through the bogs, especially during wet weather, because you can easily become mired.

Upon reaching the buildings at Whitesbog, turn right and follow the dirt road for about 0.5 miles until you come to a reservoir on the left. The bogs and reservoirs are the best places for birding, and harbor the many species of waterfowl and shorebirds that occur here. Tundra Swans can be found in late winter or early spring, as soon as the water is open. Their numbers may approach 400 in March and they can be studied at incredibly close range, especially if you stay in your car. The swans prefer the flooded cranberry bogs in the center of the suggested tour route. Among the other waterfowl that occur in large numbers on these ponds are Canada Goose, Wood Duck, Green-winged Teal, American Black Duck, Mallard, Northern Pintail, Blue-winged Teal, and Ring-necked Duck (up to 50). Hooded Merganser is regular in spring, and a variety of other ducks occur in limited numbers.

The spring migration of landbirds is not particularly noteworthy at Whitesbog, but the diversity of nesting species is greater than at most places in the Pine Barrens. Nesters include Pied-billed Grebe (rare as a breeder anywhere in the state), Green Heron, American Bittern (rare), Ruffed Grouse, King Rail (rare), Virginia Rail, Killdeer, Spotted Sandpiper, American Woodcock, Yellow-billed Cuckoo, Whip-poor-will, Common Nighthawk, and Chimney Swift. The list of nesting songbirds includes all of the characteristic species of the Pine Barrens, including Eastern Screech-Owl and Great Horned Owl, which are year-round residents.

In late summer when the reservoirs are partly drained, small numbers of shorebirds stop in on their way to the coast. At least twenty species have been observed, the most common being Greater and Lesser yellowlegs, and Semi-palmated, Least, and Pectoral sandpipers. American Avocet, Buff-breasted Sandpiper, and Baird's Sandpiper have all occurred.

Since 1980, flocks of Gull-billed Terns have been appearing at Whites-bog in late summer. The first birds arrive in July and peak numbers occur in mid-August; most depart by the beginning of September. In New Jersey, this species is normally confined to the salt marshes in the southern part of the state, where it nests in small numbers. The birds that come to Whitesbog take advantage of the low water levels in the bogs and reservoirs to feed on the abundant frogs, tadpoles, and insects. A flock of 70 Gull-billed Terns counted here on August 10, 1981, was the largest concentration ever recorded in the state.

Fall brings a few migrating raptors and many of the same species of waterfowl that occur in spring, although in smaller numbers. Both Golden Eagle and Bald Eagle have occurred during the winter, but otherwise only a few of the common resident species are present.

After completing the loop around the cranberry bogs, return to Rt. 530. There are no public restroom facilities at Whitesbog, but there are some at the Lebanon State Forest Headquarters off Rt. 72, just east of Rt. 70.

➤

Wharton State Forest

More than 100,000 acres of unspoiled wilderness invite the adventurous birder to explore this little known area of New Jersey. Wharton State Forest, in the heart of the Pine Barrens, lies mostly in southern Burlington County, with smaller sections in adjacent Atlantic and Camden Counties. It is a canoeist's paradise, with numerous rivers and streams that flow gently through cedar swamps, pine, and deciduous woods toward the Atlantic Ocean. US 206 crosses the western part of the tract at Atsion and there are a few other roads around the perimeter, but none in the interior. In fact, no other area in New

Jersey is further from a paved road than the central part of the Wharton Tract, as it was formerly known. There are numerous sand roads, however, that connect the former iron foundry towns of Atsion and Batsto with the ruins of Hampton Furnace, Quaker Bridge, Washington Forge, and many other places.

The Pine Barrens is better known for its interesting plants, reptiles, and amphibians (including the endangered Pine Barrens Tree Frog) than for its birds. The birdlife of Wharton State Forest is similar to that of Lebanon State Forest (covered in its own chapter). Some of the more unusual breeding birds to look and listen for are N. Saw-whet Owl (rare in summer), Common Nighthawk, Whip-poor-will, Brown Creeper, Eastern Bluebird, Hermit Thrush, Black-throated Green, Prothonotary, Hooded, and Canada warblers, and Summer Tanager. There is still much to be learned about the birdlife of the Pine Barrens, as was shown in 1981, when Ted Proctor discovered a previously unknown nesting population of Hermit Thrushes in Wharton State Forest.

Directions

From northern New Jersey, take the New Jersey Turnpike south to Exit 7 (Bordentown). Stay left through the tollbooth and merge onto US 206 South. Follow this for 37 miles to US 30 in Hammonton, then turn left. Go east on US 30 for about 1.4 miles to the intersection with Rt. 542 and turn left. In about 7 miles, you will come to Batsto Village Historical Site, which is also the state forest headquarters. [DeLorme 64, E-8]

From the north coast, take the Garden State Parkway south to Exit 52 (New Gretna). From the exit ramp, turn left onto Rt. 654, go 1 mile, and turn right onto US 9. Follow US 9 through New Gretna for about 1.5 miles to Rt. 542. Turn right onto Rt. 542 and go about 13 miles to Batsto.

From the south coast, take the Garden State Parkway north to Exit 50, New Gretna. Go about a mile north on US 9 to the junction with Rt. 542. Turn left onto Rt. 542 and proceed as previously described.

From the Philadelphia area, take the Atlantic City Expressway south to Exit 28 (Hammonton). Follow Rt. 54 toward Hammonton for about 2 miles to Rt. 542 and turn right. Batsto is about 9 miles.

Birding

Wharton State Forest is best explored with the help of USGS topographic maps. These can usually be purchased at either Lebanon State Forest headquarters (see Map 49) or Wharton State Forest headquarters in Batsto, where a less detailed map of the forest is also available. Most of Wharton lies within the Atsion, Chatsworth, Green Bank, Hammonton, Indian Mills, Jenkins, and Medford Lakes quadrangles.

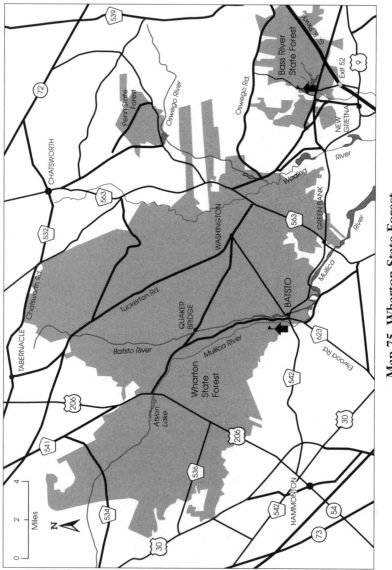

Map 75. Wharton State Forest

The nature trail at Batsto covers about 2 miles of Pine Barrens upland, where you will encounter a good sampling of the common birds. Most of the more interesting birds of the area are found along streams, in hardwood swamps, or around cedar swamps; such areas are best explored by canoe or by driving some of the sand roads with the help of topo maps. Many of the sand roads can be driven in an ordinary car, but do so with caution as you do not want to get stuck miles from the nearest telephone. It is best to ask the forest rangers about the condition of the roads.

Bird species associated with Pine Barrens cedar swamps (especially Red Maple-White Cedar swamps) are N. Saw-whet Owl (rare), Brown Creeper, Black-and-white, Prothonotary, Black-throated Green, and Canada warblers, and Louisiana (uncommon) and Northern (rare) waterthrushes. The drier, open oak-pine forests are where you may find Common Nighthawk, Whip-poor-will, Eastern Bluebird, Hermit Thrush, and Summer Tanager. Hermit Thrushes have been found near Quaker Bridge and about 2 miles northwest of Washington Forge. Prior to 1981, this species was not known to nest in New Jersey south of the highlands of the northwestern part of the state, although it is a regular breeder in similar pine-oak habitat on Long Island.

The Batona Hiking Trail, mentioned in the Lebanon State Forest chapter, also traverses 25 miles of varied habitat in Wharton State Forest, stretching from Evans Bridge to Batsto to Quaker Bridge to Apple Pie Hill. By exploring this and other areas of the state forest, you might locate some unusual species, like Red Crossbill and White-winged Crossbill, both of which nested farther north in the Pine Barrens in the 1930s. Or, you might happen upon the elusive Swainson's Warbler, which has never been proved nesting in New Jersey, though there are frequent rumors of its nesting in the swamps of the Barrens.

✝

Bass River State Forest

An attractive and popular campground on Lake Absegami is one of the main features of this 25,000-acre state forest. Conveniently located off the Garden State Parkway, the forest is near the popular birding spots of Brigantine NWR and Tuckerton. Here you will find typical Pine Barrens habitats, including many cedar swamps along the Bass River and the numerous small streams that traverse the area. Birdlife is similar to that in Lebanon State Forest, Stafford Forge, and Wharton State Forest, covered in separate sections.

Directions

From the north, take the Garden State Parkway to Exit 52 (New Gretna). Turn right (north) onto Rt. 654, go about 1 mile to the junction with Stage Rd., and follow the directions to the state forest campground. From the south, take the Garden State Parkway to Exit 50 (New Gretna, US 9). Follow US 9 into New Gretna for a little over a mile, then turn left onto Rt. 679 toward Chatsworth. Bear right after about 1.5 miles, turning off Rt. 679, which bears left, onto W. Branch Allen Rd. In another half-mile, you will come to a junction with Stage Rd.; turn right and follow the signs to the State Forest campground. [DeLorme 65, F-21]

Birding

In addition to the trails around Lake Absegami and the campground, there are numerous dirt roads that traverse the forest and provide access to a variety of habitats. French Coal Rd. and Dan Bridge Rd. both begin at Stage Rd., just 0.25 miles west of the junction of Stage Rd. with Rt. 654. French Coal Rd. parallels the West Branch of the Bass River, passing through good cedar swamp habitat, while Dan Bridge follows the East Branch of Bass River. One end of the Batona Trail, a 49-mile trek through the Pine Barrens of Bass River, Wharton, and Lebanon State Forest, is accessed at the Ranger Station.

✢

Pennypacker Park

Pennypacker/Greenwald Memorial Park occupies an 80-acre strip along the Cooper River in Haddonfield and Cherry Hill, Camden County. The Cherry Hill portion of this Camden County Park is mostly manicured lawns, but the Haddonfield section has some natural growth. Spring and fall migration are the most interesting times here, when a walk along the river can produce an excellent variety of songbirds, attracted to this oasis in a sea of urban sprawl.

Directions

From the intersection of State Rts. 70 and 41 in Cherry Hill, take Rt. 41 (Kings Highway) south for 0.9 miles, then turn right onto Park Blvd. Park in one of the designated areas on the left side of the road. [DeLorme 55, C-13]

Birding

An easy 1-mile walk follows the Cooper River from Kings Highway north and west as far as the park system headquarters. In addition to being a good spot for migrant songbirds, the park is the site where the first complete dinosaur skeleton was unearthed in 1858.

Berlin Park

This small, 140-acre, city park in Berlin, Camden County, contains an excellent stand of mature deciduous forest and is good for songbirds in migration. Basically a local birding spot, it has seldom been visited by birders from outside the area, but is worth a stop if you are in the area.

Directions

From Exit 4 of the New Jersey Turnpike, go south on Rt. 73 for about 10 miles to a traffic circle. Follow the sign to Rt. 30 access (Milford Rd.). Stay on this road 0.3 miles to the traffic light at Rt. 30, then continue across Rt. 30 (the road name changes to Berlin-Cross Keys Rd.) for 0.25 miles to Park Dr. Make a left turn onto Park Dr. and continue one-half mile to the park entrance. [DeLorme 55, J-18]

Birding

Berlin Park is best for migrant songbirds from late April through the first half of May, when the mixed woodland attracts vireos, warblers, Scarlet Tanager, Rose-breasted Grosbeak, and orioles to the emergent flowers and vegetation and the insects that feed on them. The stream-side riparian habitat along the headwaters of the Great Egg Harbor River provides some of the best birding.

Winslow Wildlife Management Area

Winslow, one of the least known WMAs, encompasses more than 6,000 acres along the Great Egg Harbor River in Camden and Gloucester counties. Access is rather limited and the woods along the river are almost impenetrable, but the habitat here is very interesting. The wooded swamps harbor numerous Prothonotary and Hooded warblers, and they look like prime habitat for Swainson's Warbler, which has not yet succeeded in nesting in New Jersey. This area certainly deserves further exploration during the breeding season.

Directions

Take the Atlantic City Expressway to Exit 33. At the end of the exit road, continue straight ahead across West Winslow-Williamstown Rd. onto Blue Anchor Fireline Rd. [DeLorme 63, D-21]

Birding

The birding in Winslow is basically from the numerous dirt roads that crisscross the area. All these roads can be sandy or muddy in places, so caution is advised. The open Pine Barrens habitat has the usual contingent of species, including nesting Yellow-billed Cuckoo, Eastern Wood-Pewee, Great Crested Flycatcher, Red-eyed and White-eyed vireos, Carolina and House wrens, Wood Thrush, Brown Thrasher, Pine, Prairie, Blue-winged, and Black-and-white warblers, Scarlet Tanager, Eastern Towhee, and Baltimore Oriole. Along streams and wet areas, look for Acadian Flycatcher, Yellow-throated Warbler, Prothonotary and Hooded warblers, Louisiana Waterthrush.

Many other species undoubtedly occur. Whip-poor-will is probably present in the nesting season, as well as Common Nighthawk. Red-headed Woodpecker and Summer Tanager occur in similar habitat elsewhere, and Yellow-throated Warbler is to be expected. Black-throated Green Warbler might breed in some of the dense cedar swamps. Do some exploring and add to the list.

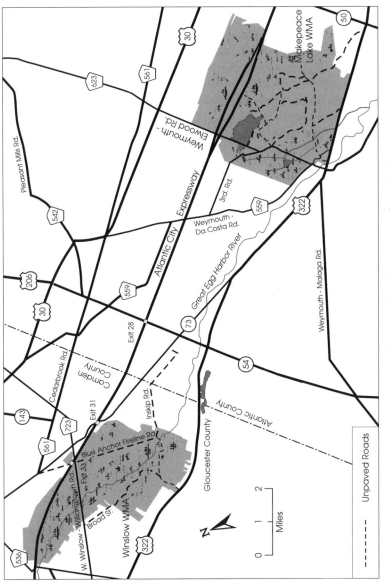

Map 76. Winslow and Makepeace Lake WMAs

Makepeace Lake WMA

Weymouth – Elwood Rd.

Pleasant Mills Rd.

Atlantic City Expressway

Weymouth - Da Costa Rd.

3rd. Rd.

Weymouth - Malaga Rd.

Great Egg Harbor River

Cedarbrook Rd.

Camden County

Exit 28

Inskip Rd.

Blue Anchor Fireline Rd.

Exit 31

Exit 33

W. Winslow - Williamstown Rd.

Broad St.

Winslow WMA

Gloucester County

Atlantic County

Miles

0   1   2

Unpaved Roads

N

Flood Gates

This spot, just north of the Commodore Barry Bridge in Gloucester County, often has the largest concentrations of wintering Ruddy Ducks in the state, but the numbers found along the Delaware River are much reduced from former times. Gulls, cormorants, and hawks are found here in winter and in migration, and in fall a variety of shorebirds occur on the mudflats at low tide. Great Cormorant is regular here in winter. In addition to the Ruddies, various other species of waterfowl winter along the river.

Directions

From Exit 2 of the New Jersey Turnpike, go west on US 322 for 4 miles to I-295. Drive north on I-295 for about 2 miles to the exit for Repaupo Rd. Take Repaupo Rd. west for about 0.6 miles to Rt. 44, where it becomes Flood Gates Rd. Continue straight ahead on Flood Gates Rd. for about 1.5 miles to the end, and park. [DeLorme 53, H-23]

Birding

Scan the water from the dikes; cormorants like to sit on the rock jetty to the north. Bald Eagles have recently begun nesting at sites along the river, and may occasionally be seen from Flood Gates. A spotting scope is helpful for identifying the waterfowl on the river.

🦆

Glassboro Wildlife Management Area

Glassboro WMA (or Glassboro Woods, as the area is known to birders) is a 2,337-acre tract located on the southeastern edge of Glassboro in central Gloucester County. It is an excellent place to observe the spring migration of songbirds and has an interesting variety of nesting species. Hooded Warbler is an abundant breeder, and Kentucky Warbler is perhaps more easily found here than anywhere else in New Jersey. Prothonotary Warbler, Worm-eating Warbler, and Louisiana Waterthrush are also among the 13 species of warblers that nest in the woods. Warbler flights also can be good in fall, when Connecticut Warbler has occurred.

Note: Glassboro Woods is managed for hunting. During the hunting season (September through December), visits should be made only on Sundays. The roads through the woods may be in bad shape in the early spring; portions of the roads have been washed away at times and there are no warning signs. By late spring, the roads are usually repaired.

Directions

Although there are four entrances to the WMA, the most accessible is the western entrance off Rt. 47 at Carpenter Ave., a good dirt road that bisects the tract. To reach this entrance:

From northern New Jersey, take the New Jersey Turnpike south to Exit 3 (Camden). Stay left after going through the tollbooth and merge onto Rt. 168 South (Black Horse Pike). Go about 0.9 miles to Rt. 41 and turn right. Follow Rt. 41 south for 5 miles to Rt. 47, then continue straight ahead on Rt. 47. After 5.8 miles you will pass the turnoff for US 322 West. From here it is about 1.2 miles to Stanger Ave. on the left, one of the entrances to the woods. If you continue past Stanger 0.5 miles, you will come to a dirt road on the left with a red gas pipeline marker on the corner. This is Carpenter Ave.; the Gloucester County Road Department is just beyond it on the right. [DeLorme 62, C-9]

Alternatively, take I-295 to Exit 26 (Rt. 42, the North-South Freeway), follow Rt. 42 for about 1.7 miles, and exit onto Rt. 55 South. Go about 10 miles to Exit 56 (US 322) and take US 322 East for 3 miles to the junction with Rt. 47. Turn right onto Rt. 47 and drive 1.7 miles to Carpenter Ave.

From coastal New Jersey, take the Atlantic City Expressway north to Exit 38 (Sicklerville). Turn left onto Sicklerville Rd. (Spur Rt. 536), and go about 2 miles to US 322. Turn right onto US 322 West and go 7 miles to the intersection with Rt. 47 in Glassboro. Carpenter Ave. is 1.7 miles south (left) on Rt. 47.

Birding

Most of Glassboro Woods is heavily wooded with areas of lowland deciduous swamp and oak-pine forest. A number of open patches and hedgerows are maintained for wildlife. The terrain is very flat, and the several streams that run through the tract create extensive wet areas where the swamp vegetation flourishes. Red Maple, Sweet Gum, Black Gum (Tupelo), Gray Birch, and Sassafras (the latter two around the drier edges) are the dominant trees, mixed with a few Atlantic White Cedars. The understory is a dense and impenetrable tangle of Sweet Pepperbush, Mountain Laurel, blueberries, azaleas, and other shrubs. The drier areas support a more open forest consisting

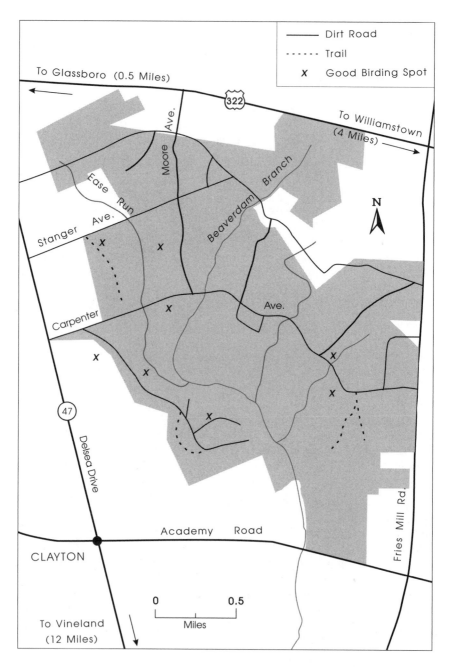

	Dirt Road
-----	Trail
X	Good Birding Spot

To Glassboro (0.5 Miles)

322

To Williamstown
(4 Miles)

Moore Ave.

Ease Run

Beaverdam Branch

Stanger Ave.

N

Carpenter

Ave.

47

Delsea Drive

Academy Road

Fries Mill Rd.

CLAYTON

0   0.5

Miles

To Vineland
(12 Miles)

Map 77. Glassboro WMA

of either mature oaks and hickories with a Scrub Oak-Mountain Laurel understory or a mixed oak-Pitch Pine woods.

The woods are at their best during spring migration. Although the flights are not as heavy and diverse as those in some of the better known areas farther north, they do produce a wide variety of warblers and other migrants. In addition, the woods have the virtue of being a quiet and little-used spot where one can bird in relative solitude. About 70 species of birds nest here, and May and early June are good times to search for them. Later in the summer, the bugs are so abundant that birding is difficult. The woods do not receive much attention in the fall, particularly after the hunting season begins, but the warbler flights in late August and September can be good.

There are several passable dirt roads through parts of the WMA, and numerous trails branch off from the roads. Carpenter Ave. bisects the area from Rt. 47 on the west to Fries Mill Rd. on the east, a distance of about 2.6 miles. The road goes through all of the available habitat types, so it makes a good place to start your birding; the western part is especially productive.

About 0.25 miles in from Rt. 47, a road branches off from Carpenter Ave. to the right. You can take this road south for about 1 mile until it dead-ends at a turnaround. On the left, the road parallels a stream through a swampy woodland; on the right are somewhat drier woods with a few clearings. At the end of the road is an open area of oaks and pines. Most of the characteristic species of the tract can be found along this road, including Northern Bobwhite, Yellow-billed Cuckoo, Red-bellied Woodpecker, Great Crested and Acadian flycatchers, Eastern Wood-Pewee, White-eyed Vireo, Carolina Wren, Blue-gray Gnatcatcher, Wood Thrush, Brown Thrasher, Blue-winged, Yellow, Pine, Prairie, Black-and-white, Kentucky, and Hooded warblers, American Redstart, Louisiana Waterthrush, Yellow-breasted Chat (open areas), and Scarlet Tanager.

Other noteworthy species that breed on the tract are Broad-winged Hawk, Eastern Screech, Great Horned, and (probably) Barred owls, Whip-poor-will, Ruby-throated Hummingbird, Cedar Waxwing, Yellow-throated Vireo, Prothonotary (along streams) and Worm-eating (irregular) warblers. A little additional field work in late May or early June might add Willow Flycatcher, Yellow-throated Warbler (has occurred in spring), Summer Tanager, Blue Grosbeak, or other species, to the list of breeding birds.

Return to Carpenter Ave. and turn right. About 0.6 miles farther on is the junction with Moore Ave. on the left. Kentucky Warbler nests in the woods around the field on the south side of this intersection. Moore Ave. goes north for about 1.3 miles to US 322. Along the way it passes through some oak woodlands where Hooded Warbler is abundant. About 0.6 miles up Moore Ave. is the junction with Stanger Ave., which leads west out to Rt. 47. Stanger crosses a stream called Little Ease Run where Prothonotary Warbler has nested for years.

Continuing east on Carpenter Ave. from Moore Ave., you will cross another stream, Beaverdam Branch, then pass through alternating sections of dry oak-pine woods and wet deciduous swamp until you reach the eastern end of the tract at Fries Mill Rd. Along the way there are numerous side trails that can be explored. The trails are mainly old roads that are no longer suitable for driving, however, they make for easy walking, although you may encounter some wet spots.

♈

Pedricktown Marsh

Pedricktown is famous for the (formerly) annual spring gathering of Ruffs in the marshes of Oldman's Creek, just north of town. Many other shorebirds stop off here in April, including Lesser Golden-Plover, Common Snipe, Pectoral Sandpiper, and both yellowlegs, but they yield center stage to the star attraction.

Directions

To reach the causeway across the marsh at Pedricktown: From northern New Jersey, take the New Jersey Turnpike south to Exit 2 (Swedesboro). After passing through the tollbooth, turn left onto US 322 West. Go 4 miles to I-295, and take I-295 southbound. Go about 1.6 miles to Exit 10 (Center Square Rd.) and turn right (west) onto Center Square Rd. (An alternative route is to take the Turnpike south to either Exit 7 or Exit 4 and cross over to I-295, then continue south to Exit 10 on I-295). Drive 1 mile to the first crossroads and turn left; this is Pedricktown Rd., although the street sign may be missing. After about 1 mile, the road becomes a causeway across the extensive marshes of Oldman's Creek. [DeLorme 53, L-19]

From the Philadelphia area, you can take either I-76 or I-676 to I-295, then go south to Exit 10 and proceed as above. Or, take I-95 south to the US 322 exit in Chester, then follow Rt. 322 across the Barry Bridge to US 130. Turn right onto 130, go about 1 mile, and turn left onto High Hill Rd., just past the marshes of Raccoon Creek. Pedricktown Rd. is about 1.3 miles ahead on the right; the marshes of Oldman's Creek are about 1.6 miles south on Pedricktown Rd.

From coastal New Jersey, take the Atlantic City Expressway to I-295, then go south for about 15 miles to Exit 10 at Center Square Rd.

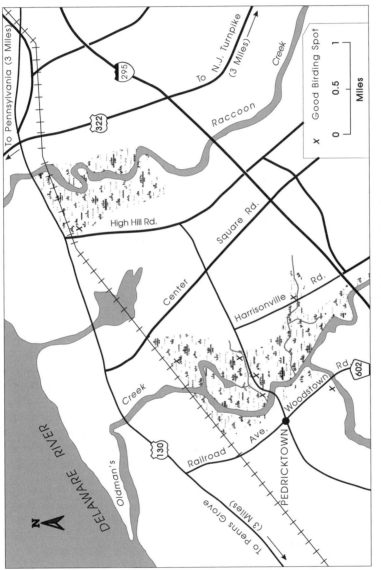

Map 78. Pedricktown Marsh

Birding

Pedricktown Rd. is a causeway across the marsh for about 0.6 miles to the bridge at Oldman's Creek, but the marshes extend for a couple of miles east and west of the road. At the monthly spring tides (at full and new moon), the road is under water. During the 1970s and 1980s, the first Ruffs, still in winter plumage, would arrive as early as the middle of March, although in some years none were found before April. By the time the last ones departed at the end of April, they would be in full breeding dress, each male different from the others, with the magnificent, colorful ruffs that give them their name. As many as a dozen individuals would pass through in some seasons, including several females (Reeves), attractive birds but not as spectacular as the males. The maximum number of males present at any one time was usually three or four.

In recent years, the Ruffs have become much less reliable. One can speculate that the large numbers from earlier years represented a single flock (Ruffs are known to migrate in small flocks) that was blown off course and ended up passing through Pedricktown. As the flock gradually aged and died off, there were few or no new recruits to maintain the tradition. Eventually, there was only the occasional stray that dropped into the marshes at Oldman's Creek.

The best times to find Ruffs and other shorebirds is usually one to three hours before high tide (best) or one to three hours after high tide. (High tide at Pedricktown occurs about five hours later than at Sandy Hook or Cape May, and about one-half hour earlier than at Philadelphia.) At low tide, the exposed mud flats are so extensive that picking out the birds is nearly hopeless. A spotting scope is indispensable. Finding a Ruff requires careful and frequent scanning of the mud flats. The rising tide forces the birds out of the more remote areas of this large system of marshes and (frequently) into the gradually dwindling spots closer to the Pedricktown causeway.

Migrant Tundra Swans stop off at Pedricktown in February and early March and sometimes linger into April; flocks of 200 to 300 are common. A variety of other spring migrant waterfowl can be seen, especially Green-winged Teal, which like to walk around on the mud and feed on the marsh vegetation, and Northern Pintail, which can occur in spectacular numbers (up to 50,000 in 1990). King Rail nests in the marshes and is occasionally seen swimming in one of the channels or scurrying across an open expanse of mud. The most common breeding bird, however, is the Common Moorhen, which vies with Muskrat for the title of most abundant animal on the Pedricktown marsh.

The first shorebirds, mainly Greater Yellowlegs, usually arrive in mid-March. By the end of the month, other species have begun to arrive, especially Lesser Yellowlegs, Common Snipe, and Pectoral Sandpiper. As many as

Pectoral Sandpiper

400 Pectorals have been seen in mid-April, making Pedricktown the best place in the state to observe this species. A few Lesser Golden-Plover (up to 15) appear in early April, and some of them stay to the end of the month. By the time they depart, one or two may have acquired most of the spectacular breeding plumage that we seldom see in New Jersey in the spring. Other species of shorebirds that occur regularly during April are Black-bellied and Semipalmated plovers, Killdeer, Spotted and Least sandpipers, Dunlin, and Short-billed Dowitcher.

Although shorebirds are the main attraction, Pedricktown has other things to see as well. Migrant hawks, mainly Northern Harriers, Broad-winged and Red-tailed hawks, and American Kestrels pass through in April. A pair of Peregrine Falcons has recently taken up residence under the nearby Commodore Barry Bridge and the pair is sometimes seen harassing the ducks and shorebirds over the marsh. In some years, a pair of Great Horned Owls nests in trees in the marsh.

Migrant swallows are a familiar sight over the marsh in April, when all of the eastern species can be expected (although Cliff Swallow is uncommon). By mid-April other early migrants start to appear, and they and the local residents tune up their spring songs. The marsh and nearby woods resound with the familiar songs of Eastern Phoebe, White-eyed Vireo, Carolina Chickadee, Carolina and House wrens, Gray Catbird, Northern Mockingbird, Brown Thrasher, Yellow Warbler, Common Yellowthroat, Eastern Towhee, Chipping, Song, and Swamp sparrows, Red-winged Blackbird, and House Finch.

After birding the marsh at Pedricktown, continue south across the bridge into town. Turn right at the first intersection (Railroad Ave.), and drive about 1.3 miles to US 130. The field diagonally across 130 to the left is frequently flooded in spring, and is an excellent spot for Common Snipe.

Another good shorebirding spot that receives relatively little attention is the marsh at Raccoon Creek. To reach it, go back to US 130 and turn right. Go north on 130 for about 1.6 miles to the second right turn, at High Hill Rd. Go about 100 yards on High Hill and park at the railroad tracks. The Raccoon Creek marsh extends for more than one-half mile to your left (northeast). By walking along the tracks (watch out for trains—the tracks are used occasionally), you'll have a good view of the marsh.

Another spot to check for shorebirds is where Harrisonville Rd. crosses part of the marshes of Oldman's Creek. From the north end of the Pedricktown Rd. causeway, go north for 0.3 miles to the first right turn, Harrisonville Rd. Go 0.7 miles and park on the right, just before the bridge.

WARNING: Do not park on the Pedricktown Rd. causeway; you may get a ticket and will annoy the local residents, whose good will is important to the welfare of the marshes.

Northern Salem County Tour

Salem County, an area long neglected by most of the state's birders, received increasing attention during the past 20 years because of the Ruffs at Pedricktown, Upland Sandpipers near Sharptown, American Golden-Plovers at Pedricktown and Mannington Marsh, and the growing population of Black Vultures when the species was still a rarity in New Jersey. Birders from the more populous regions discovered what the locals had known for many years: There are many good birds and birding areas in Salem County. The locations described here provide a sampling of the better spots, but there are many others to be investigated. Parvin State Park, a beautiful 1,125-acre preserve in southeastern Salem County, and Pedricktown are covered separately.

Directions

Take the New Jersey Turnpike to Exit 2 (US 322, Swedesboro). Go west on US 322 for 0.8 miles to Rt. 551 (Kings Highway). Follow Rt. 551 south for 5 miles through Swedesboro, where it becomes Auburn Rd., and continue to Auburn. Bear left in town, then take the first left turn, cross the New Jersey Turnpike, and turn immediately right onto Auburn-Sharptown Rd. Drive 1.8 miles south to Featherbed Lane and turn left. [DeLorme 61, C-21]

Birding

Just over one-half mile along Featherbed Lane, you will come to the crest of a hill that overlooks beautiful pastures on both sides of the road. The fields stretch for another one-half mile to Swedesboro Rd. (Rt. 620). Among the birds nesting in these fields are Savannah and Grasshopper sparrows, Bobolink, and Eastern Meadowlark. Upland Sandpipers formerly nested, and can still be seen occasionally during the last part of April.

Huge flocks of Snow Geese and Canada Geese feed on the pastures in spring, and the pond on the south side of the road attracts Ring-billed Gulls, Killdeer, and occasionally Ring-necked Ducks. In recent years, there have usually been one or two Ross' Geese among the Snows. Large flocks of Turkey Vultures usually can be seen soaring off to the east and south, and numerous Black Vultures are frequently among them. A Scissor-tailed Flycatcher was seen along Featherbed Lane in June 1982.

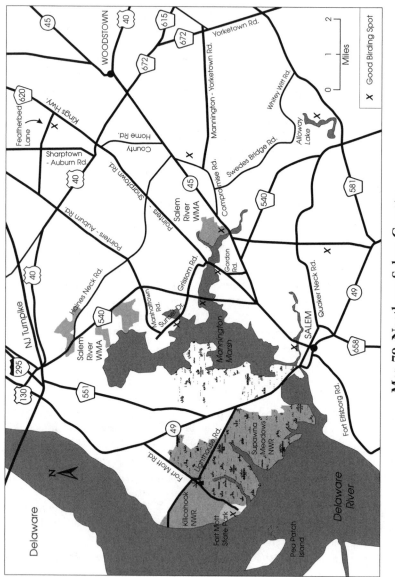

Map 79. Northern Salem County

Continue on Featherbed Lane to the stop sign at Swedesboro Rd., and turn right. Go a few hundred yards to a cattle feed lot on the right, where Brewer's Blackbird has been seen a few times in spring. Continue south for 1.5 miles to the intersection with US 40, and turn left. Follow Rt. 40 east for about 1.6 miles (watching for Black Vultures along the way) to the traffic light at Rt. 45. Turn right and go about 2.2 miles to the left turn onto Compromise Rd. (the second left after the Vo-Tech School). Compromise Rd. makes a 2.3-mile loop, eventually rejoining Rt. 45.

When Compromise Rd. rejoins Rt. 45, turn left onto Rt. 45 and go 0.4 miles and park on the right, just before the bridge across Mannington Creek at the upper reaches of Mannington Marsh. In addition to being a good area for Black Vulture and Bald Eagle, Mannington Marsh is an excellent spot for migrant waterfowl in spring and fall. Because it is tidal, there are a few good spots for shorebirds, as well. Herons and egrets from the nearby Pea Patch Island, Delaware, heronry (only about 8 miles away) fly over to feed in the extensive marshes. Great Blue and Little Blue herons, Great and Snowy egrets, Cattle Egret (in the fields), Black-crowned Night-Heron, and Glossy Ibis are common; Tricolored Heron is also seen. The area on the west side of the road is part of the Salem River WMA, and a trail leads through the reeds to a viewing platform.

The section of the marsh west of Rt. 45 to Swedesboro Rd., about 1 mile, is good for grebes and migrant waterfowl. Some birds, especially Canada Geese, winter at Mannington, but the greatest variety of species occurs in March and April. Pied-billed and Horned grebes are common in spring. Large flocks of Tundra Swans (several hundred) stop off on their way north, and there are usually a few Snow Geese among the Canadas. Green-winged Teal, Northern Pintail, Northern Shoveler, Gadwall, and American Wigeon are the common migrant dabbling ducks, while Ring-necked Duck, Common Merganser, and Ruddy Duck are the common divers. Eurasian Wigeon is an almost annual visitor in spring. The same species occur in the fall (October to November), but (except for the Canadas) usually in smaller flocks. The bridge on Rt. 45 is still the best viewing spot, but beware of the heavy traffic.

Continue south on Rt. 45 for another 1.2 miles, then turn right onto Gordon Rd.; follow this for 0.6 miles to its end, and turn right onto Swedesboro Rd. (Rt. 620). Go one-half mile and park on the shoulder of the causeway across Mannington Creek. Here you have a view east toward Rt. 45, and west, across a big expanse of water, toward Rt. 540. This is the best vantage point for observing migrant ducks, which seem to prefer the areas within one-half mile of Swedesboro Rd.

At the far end of the causeway, turn left onto Griscom Rd. and go 1.1 miles to Rt. 540 (Pointers-Auburn Rd.). Turn left on Rt. 540; in about 0.4 miles you will reach a long causeway that crosses Mannington Marsh. The best shorebirding area is on the right toward the northern end of the causeway.

Because there is no place to park along this heavily traveled road, the safest practice is to drive to the south end of the causeway, another 0.4 miles, where there is ample parking room, and walk back.

Shorebirding at Mannington Marsh is only possible when the tide is low; for several hours before and after high tide (which occurs about one hour earlier than at Philadelphia and four hours later than at Sandy Hook), the mud flats are underwater and the birds are elsewhere. The best month for migrants is April, before the marsh vegetation has grown too thick. If the flats are exposed, walk north along the causeway about three-quarters of the way across, and scan for American Golden-Plover on the mud where there is emerging vegetation. Check for Ruff, too—at least one is seen here every spring. As you walk back toward your car, check for roosting gulls farther out on the bare mudflats. Scan the gulls (mainly Ring-billed and Laughing) for Forster's and Caspian terns. This is probably the best spot in New Jersey for finding Caspian Tern in the spring.

Continue south on Rt. 540 to Rt. 45 (1.2 miles), bear right onto Rt. 45 and follow it into Salem to the intersection with Rt. 49 (2 miles). To reach Fort Mott, turn right and go west on Rt. 49 for about 2.8 miles, then bear left on Lighthouse Rd. Continue 2.4 miles to Fort Mott Rd., and turn left toward the park; the entrance is 1 mile ahead on the right. This 104-acre park preserves historic Fort Mott, built near the mouth of the Delaware River to guard the approach to Philadelphia from the sea. The fort looks across the river to Pea Patch Island and New Castle County, Delaware. An historical land grant establishes the boundary of Delaware as the low tide line on the New Jersey side for a 24-mile stretch of the river starting at the Pennsylvania state line. If you wade into the water at Fort Mott, you are in Delaware.

Pea Patch Island is about 1 mile away from the fort, and the herons and egrets that nest there can usually be seen perched in the trees or flying around. Black and Turkey vultures frequently roost in the trees and can sometimes be seen soaring over the island.

❧

Southern Salem County Tour

In addition to the more frequently visited northern parts of Salem County, there are also numerous good birding areas in the southern portion of the county. These include wintering and spring gathering areas for sparrows and blackbirds, plus the more remote expanses of Mad Horse Creek WMA and the Delaware Bay at the Salem Nuclear Power Plant.

Directions

Take the New Jersey Turnpike to Exit 1 (US 40, US 130, NJ 49). Follow the sign for Rt. 49 toward Salem, then follow Rt. 49 for 9 miles into Salem. When Rt. 49 crosses the bridge over the Salem River, it makes a right turn for one block, then a left turn. Instead of turning left, continue straight ahead onto S. Front St. Go 0.25 miles to the T at Grieves Parkway and turn left. Drive 0.2 miles and turn right onto Oak St., which merges with Chestnut St., then becomes Ft. Elfsborg Rd. (Rt. 625). In 1.5 miles from Grieves Parkway you will come to the intersection with Featherbed Lane, on the left. [De-Lorme 60, J-13]

Birding

Featherbed Lane runs south for 1.2 miles to its end at Amwellbury Rd. From late winter to early spring, but especially in March, large flocks of blackbirds forage in the fields in this part of Salem County, and Featherbed Lane is a good spot to search for them. Among the thousands of Common Grackles, Red-winged Blackbirds, and Brown-headed Cowbirds, there are usually a few Yellow-headed Blackbirds. Despite the striking coloration, they can be incredibly difficult to spot among the masses of blackbirds.

Continue along Ft. Elfsborg Rd. past Featherbed Lane for another 1.4 miles to the left turn at Rt. 624, Hancocks Bridge-Ft. Elfsborg Rd. In about 0.25 miles, you will come to Apple Blossom Farm, where White-crowned Sparrow is a regular winter visitor and Brewer's Blackbirds have occurred in some years. As you drive along Rt. 624 for another 1.4 miles, watch the fields for pipits, sparrows, and raptors. Great Horned Owls often nest in the trees along this road and can be seen in late winter to early spring sitting on their nests.

Stay right at the intersection with Amwellbury Rd. (Rt. 627), but continue straight ahead onto Money Island Rd. when Rt. 624 turns left. You can follow Money Island for about 1.2 miles to its end, but the best birding is usually in the first half-mile, especially around the junction with Acton Farm Rd. Dickcissel has been found here in some winters, and a good variety of sparrows, including White-crowned, can be expected.

Rejoin Rt. 624 via 0.9 mile-long Acton Farm Rd., then continue 1.2 miles to the intersection with Hancocks Bridge Rd. (Rt. 658), and turn right. Go 1.5 miles to the traffic light at Alloway's Creek Neck Rd. and turn right. Follow this road for 5.5 miles to the Salem Nuclear Generating Station. Along the way you'll pass numerous fields, some of which are often flooded in spring and attract migrant ducks and shorebirds.

The last 2 miles of the road are private, but they are open to the public for about 1.5 miles. The public is no longer allowed near the power plant.

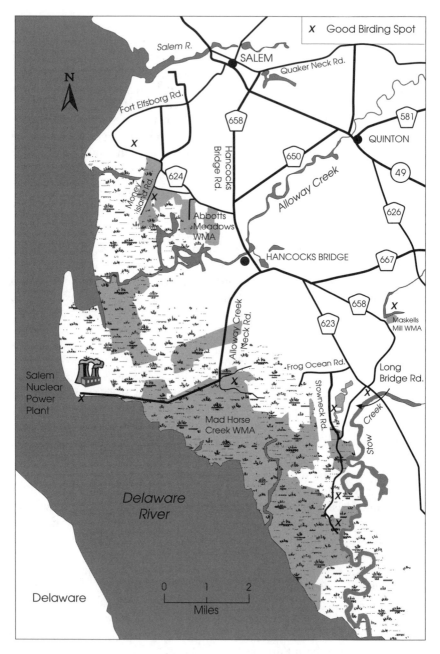

Map 80. Southern Salem County

The road runs through tidal marshes near the shore of Delaware Bay. Herons, egrets, and dabbling ducks can be seen in the marshes, and Canvasback and scaup gather offshore in the spring. Large numbers of waterfowl use the marshes in the fall. Ospreys that nest on the electrical transmission towers near the road are an annual attraction.

The marshes to the south and east of the private section of the road are part of the 5,826-acre Mad Horse Creek WMA, a popular fall waterfowl hunting area. At the sharp bend in the road near the east end of the private section of the road, two dirt roads lead off into some wooded spots in the WMA. You can park off the paved road and explore these dirt roads for local resident birds and for early migrants in spring.

To visit another interesting part of the WMA, return to Hancock's Bridge and continue straight ahead on Alloway's Creek Neck Rd. Bear right at the fork (0.3 miles beyond the junction with the Salem-Hancock's Bridge Rd.), and continue another 0.7 miles to Rt. 623, the Harmersville-Canton Rd. Turn right, go 3 miles to Canton, then park on the right, just before the bridge over Stow Creek. A short path leads to an observation platform, where you can see the Bald Eagle nest situated in a large Sycamore on the opposite side of Stow Creek.

Turn back toward Canton and take the first left, Long Bridge Rd. Follow Long Bridge for about a mile to the intersection with Stow Neck Rd. and turn left. This road wanders through the marsh for 2 miles until it ends at Pine Island, where there is a boat launch and parking area. Pine Island is a forested "island" of Pitch Pine, Loblolly Pine, oaks, and American Holly surrounded by marshes. It has many of the resident birds typical of the mainland and attracts small numbers of migrant songbirds in spring. It looks like the kind of place that might attract a pioneer Brown-headed Nuthatch, if one ever strayed over from Delaware. So far, nothing unusual has been found, but Boat-tailed Grackle has recently moved into this area—the farthest extension of its range up the Delaware Bayshore. Good numbers of Northern Harrier and Rough-legged Hawk can be seen along Stow Neck Rd. in winter.

Another good birding spot nearby is Maskells Mill Pond near Canton, a state WMA containing a 33-acre pond. Return to the junction of Long Bridge Rd. and Rt. 623 and turn right. Go about 100 yards to Rt. 658, Maskells Mill Rd., and turn left. Follow Rt. 658 for about 1.8 miles to the parking area for the WMA on the right.

☂

Parvin State Park

Parvin is a beautiful, 1,125-acre state park in southeastern Salem County. It is a good birding spot in migration, especially in the spring, and has a number of interesting breeding birds. For more than 30 years, Parvin has been noted for its nesting Prothonotary Warblers, which are especially common in the swampy areas along Muddy Run. Some of the other common breeding birds are Yellow-billed Cuckoo, Red-bellied Woodpecker, Acadian Flycatcher, Wood Thrush, Black-and-white, Kentucky, and Hooded warblers, Louisiana Waterthrush, and Scarlet Tanager. Barred Owl and Summer Tanager (uncommon) also nest here.

Directions

Follow the directions for Glassboro WMA, take Rt. 55 South from the North-South Freeway (Rt. 42), but do not exit at US 322. Instead, continue another 15 miles to Exit 35 (Rt. 674, Garden Rd.). Go west on Garden Rd. for 2.1 miles to Rt. 645 (State Park-Willow Grove Rd.) and turn left. Drive 2 miles on Rt. 645 to the junction with Rt. 540 (Centerton-Norma Rd.). Turn right and go about 1.2 miles to a gate on the left and a paved road that leads a short distance to a parking area; this spot is shown as Second Landing on the park map. If you arrive before 8 A.M., the gate probably will be locked. In that case, park along the entrance road, but do not block the gate. [DeLorme 62, L-6]

Birding

Parvin is heavily wooded, except for two lakes, Parvin and Thundergust, that cover 107 acres in the eastern part of the park. Parvin Lake is by far the larger of the two, and was created as a millpond around the turn of the century by damming Muddy Run, a tributary of the Maurice River. The land around the two lakes includes a bathing beach, two campgrounds, some cabins, and a picnic site.

The western part of the park, which has been designated a Natural Area, is more interesting for birds. Here the habitats range from a mixed hardwood-cedar swamp with dense vegetation, through a transition area of oaks, American Holly, Mountain Laurel, and Sassafras, to a very open oak-pine woods. Several trails and an unused paved road meander through this section of the park, offering visitors a sample of all the habitats.

From late April to early June is the best time to visit Parvin. Many migrants as well as the local breeding birds are present early in this period; later on, you will find only the breeding birds. By mid-June, the foliage is dense,

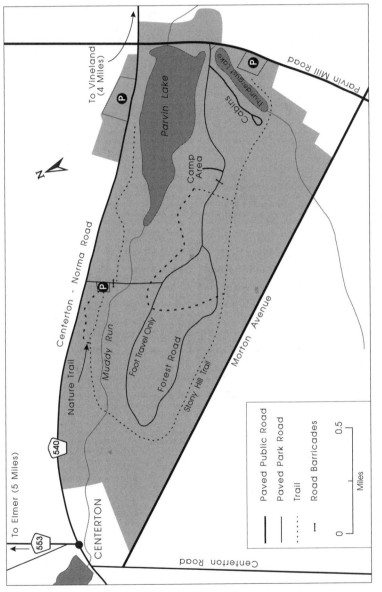

Map 81. Parvin State Park

To Vineland
(4 Miles)

Parvin Lake

Thundergust Lake

Cabins

Camp
Area

N

Centerton - Norma Road

Nature Trail

Muddy Run

Foot Travel Only

Forest Road

Stony Hill Trail

Morton Avenue

540

To Elmer (5 Miles)

553

CENTERTON

Centerton Road

Parvin Mill Road

Paved Public Road
Paved Park Road
Trail
Road Barricades

0   0.5

Miles

especially in the swampy areas, and the bugs are plentiful. The fall migration in late August and September is also productive, although the thick foliage makes birding difficult.

At the parking area there are picnic tables and some primitive toilets. A trail (the Nature Trail shown on the park map) leads down a few steps from the parking area and forks; take the left fork. You will immediately find yourself in the swamp that extends along both sides of Muddy Run for the length of the park. It is dominated by large Red Maple, Atlantic White Cedar and Black Gum trees, with a dense understory of Sweet Pepperbush, Leatherleaf, Mountain Laurel, and other shrubs. Although there are a few boardwalks, the going may get rather wet underfoot, especially in early spring.

In April and early May, a variety of migrant songbirds pause on their journey north to find food and shelter in the shrubs and trees along the trail. Some of the regular nesting birds of the swamp are Yellow-billed Cuckoo, Barred Owl, Red-bellied Woodpecker, Eastern Wood-Pewee, Acadian Fly-catcher, White-eyed, Yellow-throated (uncommon), and Red-eyed vireos, Blue-gray Gnatcatcher, Wood Thrush, Yellow, Black-and-white, Prothonotary, and Kentucky warblers, and Louisiana Waterthrush.

After about 0.25 miles, you'll reach a trail junction. To the right, the Nature Trail returns to the parking area. The left trail parallels Muddy Run for about 0.6 miles, then crosses the stream via a wooden bridge, where Prothonotary Warbler sings in spring. About 200 yards farther, on the left, is another fork. If you are short of time, the left trail will lead you quickly to Forest Rd., a paved road, where you should turn left; continue 0.6 miles until you reach two stone markers for a trail on the left. Take this trail to a paved path, turn left, and you'll be headed back to Second Landing.

If you are not pressed for time, continue straight ahead on the trail that is marked Stony Hill Trail on the park map. The trail emerges abruptly from the swamp, passes through a transition zone and enters an open mixed oak-Pitch Pine woodland. Breeding birds that you may encounter here (in addition to many of the species mentioned above) are Broad-winged Hawk, Northern Bobwhite, Eastern Screech-Owl, Whip-poor-will, White-breasted Nuthatch, Carolina Wren, Brown Thrasher, Cedar Waxwing, Blue-winged, Pine, Prairie, and Hooded warblers, Ovenbird (abundant), Summer Tanager (uncommon), and Scarlet Tanager.

About a mile beyond the fork mentioned above, you will come to another junction with a trail on the left. Follow the left fork, and you soon will cross Forest Rd. and enter an open oak woods, then an oak-holly woods. After about 0.3 miles you will cross Forest Rd. again. Continue another 100 yards and turn left on the paved path which leads to the parking area at Second Landing. You can hike the long loop—starting from the parking area and including parts of the Nature Trail and the Stony Hill Trail—and return to the parking area in two to three hours, depending upon the amount of time you spend birding.

The park map shows several other trails which you may enjoy exploring if you have the time. Although Parvin State Park may not have quite the abundance and diversity of birdlife enjoyed in some parts of the state, you will find few places in New Jersey that are more attractive.

DA Sibley 1985

Black Skimmers

South Coast
Region

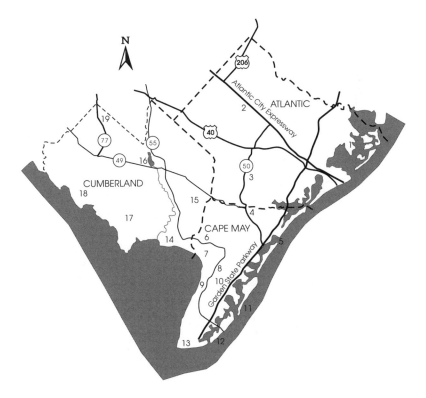

1. Brigantine NWR
2. Makepeace Lake WMA
3. Atlantic County Park
4. Tuckahoe WMA
5. Corson's & Townsend's Inlets
6. Belleplain State Forest
7. Jakes Landing Road
8. Beaver Swamp WMA
9. Cape May Bayshore
10. Cape May County Park

11. Stone Harbor
12. Ocean Dr. to Wildwood Crest
13. Cape May
14. Heislerville-Thompsons Beach
15. Peaslee WMA
16. Union Lake WMA
17. Dividing Creek
18. Dix WMA
19. Johnson Sod Farm

Map 82. South Coast Region

Brigantine (Forsythe) National Wildlife Refuge

Brigantine NWR, or "Brig" as it is affectionately known to birders, is famous throughout the United States as one of the two best birding spots in New Jersey, with Cape May being the other prime area. Near Atlantic City in northeastern Atlantic County, Brig embraces more than 20,000 acres of coastal salt marsh, islands, open bays and channels, bordered by fields, upland brush and woodlands. Two large fresh-brackish impoundments created by diking off about 1,600 acres of salt marsh are the main attraction for birds and, therefore, for birders. Although the refuge was established in 1939 primarily to aid in the protection and management of waterfowl along the Atlantic Flyway, especially Brant and Black Duck, it has become a haven for birds of many species from grebes to songbirds. Early in the 1980s the name was changed to Brigantine Division, Edwin B. Forsythe National Wildlife Refuge System, but to birders it will always be Brigantine.

Brigantine is an outstanding place to observe the migration of shorebirds in spring, summer, and fall, and to see migrant and wintering ducks, geese, and swans from October through April. In winter, raptors (including Bald and Golden eagles) are an added attraction, while the warmer seasons bring a variety of breeding herons and egrets, rails, gulls, and terns. The woods and fields attract a surprising variety of migrant songbirds in spring and fall, and a modest number of species nest in the mixed oak-pine forest that is typical of the coastal plain at the edges of the Pine Barrens.

Because of its proximity to the coast and its combination of saltwater, freshwater, and upland habitats, Brigantine attracts a wide variety of birds, including many rarities. The refuge checklist includes 270 species that occur regularly, but more than 300 species have been reported. Some of the more sought-after species that occur annually are Eurasian Wigeon, American Golden Plover, American Avocet, Hudsonian and Marbled godwits, Baird's and Curlew sandpipers, Ruff, Wilson's and Red-necked phalaropes, and Yellow-headed Blackbird. The rarities that have occurred from one to several times during the past 30 years include Eared Grebe, American White Pelican, White and White-faced Ibis, Fulvous Whistling-Duck, Black-bellied Whistling-Duck, Greater White-fronted and Ross' geese, Gyrfalcon, Purple Gallinule, Sandhill Crane, Wilson's Plover, Black-necked Stilt, Curlew Sandpiper, Spotted Redshank, Red-necked Stint, Little Stint, Black-tailed and Bar-tailed godwits, Red Phalarope, Lesser Black-backed Gull, Snowy Owl, Western Kingbird, Fork-tailed Flycatcher, Sedge Wren, Northern Wheatear,

Mountain Bluebird, Northern Shrike, and Clay-colored and Lark sparrows. Goodies such as these can occur at any season, so there is always a chance of finding something unusual at Brig.

Directions

From northern New Jersey, take the Garden State Parkway south to Exit 48 (US 9 South). Drive south on Rt. 9 for 6 miles to Great Creek Rd. in Oceanville, where there is a small sign pointing left to the refuge. Turn left, and, passing a sign that marks the entrance to the refuge, continue to a bridge that spans Doughty Creek, which forms ponds on both sides. Park at the edge of the road by the bridge. [DeLorme 71, A-19]

From the Philadelphia area or southwestern New Jersey, take the Atlantic City Expressway southeast to Exit 7 (Garden State Parkway North). Drive north on the Parkway for 3 miles to the service area at Mile 41. Drive into the service area and proceed to the far (north) end, following the signs for Jim Leeds Rd. The exit road to Jim Leeds Rd. is a commuter access road between the service-area exit for northbound traffic and the entrance for southbound traffic. From this short access road, turn right onto Jim Leeds Rd. Go 0.4 miles and bear left at the fork onto Great Creek Rd. (Jim Leeds Rd. continues straight ahead). Continue on Great Creek Rd. for 3.1 miles to Rt. 9; cross Rt. 9 and proceed to the bridge mentioned above.

From southern New Jersey, take the Garden State Parkway north to the service area at Mile 41, and proceed as just described.

Birding

Least Bittern and King Rail have nested along the marshy edges of Doughty Creek, but you will be lucky to see either one. Wood Duck, Blue-winged Teal, Virginia Rail, and Sora are resident during the breeding season, while Pied-billed Grebe and American Coot are likely visitors at other times, if the water is not frozen.

Continue along the paved entrance road for 0.3 miles, as it turns first right and then left, until you come to the parking lot, on the left. Here, there are modern restrooms and an information booth; the headquarters is across the road on the right. Stop in the information booth to obtain a checklist and to examine the book of recent bird sightings; the location of rarities can be determined with a grid map in the booth. The list of bird sightings, sometimes referred to as "the book of lies" by those who fail to find reported rarities, is an important means of communication among the birders who visit Brigantine. If you should find something unusual, by all means record it in the book, so that others can search for and enjoy your discovery.

The Jim Akers Trail behind the restrooms is worth exploring for migrant thrushes, vireos, and warblers in spring and fall; although Brigantine is not

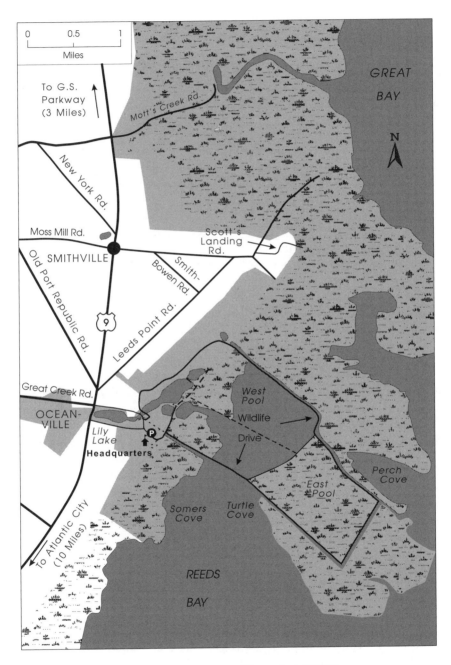

Map 83. Brigantine (Forsythe) NWR

considered a prime spot for migrant songbirds, an excellent variety of passerines can be found here in May and in August to September. In summer, you will find only the limited number of breeding species that reside in this Pine Barrens fringe habitat, while in winter the local population will be increased by migrant sparrows. Tree Swallows and Purple Martins use the boxes in the field near the parking lot; Loggerhead Shrike and Western Kingbird have been found here in fall.

Most of Brigantine is accessible only by boat, but an 8-mile auto tour route is the principal attraction for birders. The tour route circles dikes that contain the two large impoundments, the West Pool and the East Pool. During the 1990s, the West Pool was divided into two parts with the introduction of a new east-west dike. This is intended to provide better control of water levels. A high or rising tide is the best time to be on the dikes at Brig, so plan your trip accordingly. (Tides at Brig occur approximately one hour later than at Sandy Hook and Cape May.)

The tour starts at the parking lot; after about 200 yards, a small parking area on the right marks the beginning of the Leeds Eco-trail. A pamphlet is available at the information booth that describes this trail, which loops through a variety of habitats. The trail may provide a glimpse of Clapper Rail or Long-tailed Weasel, but it is best known for the Sedge Wrens that are sometimes found there in late fall and early winter. Mosquitoes can also be abundant during the warmer months, and Green-head and Deer flies are exasperating pests in July and August if there is no wind.

About 200 yards beyond the parking lot for the Leeds Eco-trail, the main tour route turns right onto the south dike, but the road you are on goes straight ahead. Continue straight ahead on this road, which passes a pond on the left and soon ends at the West Tower, which overlooks the Gull Pond and an adjacent area of shallow ponds and marsh. There you can expect Little Blue Heron; ducks in migration (especially Hooded Merganser); occasional shorebirds in migration (Common Snipe is regular); and gulls in fall, winter, and spring. In winter, the tower provides an excellent point for scanning the marshes to the east and the tree lines to the north and west for visiting Bald and Golden eagles.

Retrace your path to the main tour route, and turn left onto the south dike. At low tide, the channel on your right is an exposed mudflat where hundreds of peep (mainly Semipalmated Sandpipers) and yellowlegs feed in May and again from July through September. The marshes beyond the channel attract Glossy Ibis, Great Egret, and Snowy Egret, plus hordes of gulls (mostly Laughing Gulls in summer, Herring Gulls in winter). The channel on the left is part of the West Pool and is not tidal; other than a few Canada Geese, a Great Blue Heron, and some Common Moorhen, you are not likely to see much in it. The large expanse of *Phragmites* beyond the channel obscures any view of the water beyond.

After about 0.3 miles, you will come to the first mandatory birding stop, an open area in the *Phragmites* on the left about 100 yards across. If the water is not too high, this can be a very good spot for shorebirds in migration, especially in the fall. It is popular with Greater and Lesser yellowlegs, Stilt Sandpiper, Short-billed and Long-billed dowitchers, and (if the water level is low enough to expose some grassy areas) Pectoral and Least sandpipers. On the far side of the pool, an opening in the reeds provides a glimpse of a protected part of the West Pool, where many ducks gather in spring and fall. In November to December, you may see hundreds of Hooded Mergansers and some Common Mergansers, along with thousands of American Black Ducks, Mallards, Northern Pintail, Gadwall, Green-winged Teal, Northern Shoveler, and American Wigeon.

About 0.3 miles further along the dike is a water-control structure, used to regulate the water level in the south half of the West Pool. The West Pool covers about 900 acres, most of which is an open expanse of water, varying in depth from a few inches to a few feet. The water is fairly fresh, as it is supplied by rainfall and by Doughty Creek, which enters the pool near the West Tower. At low tide, the outlet from the pool is a favorite feeding area for Ruddy Turnstone and sandpipers, which can often be observed at close range. The channel that leads south to Somers Cove is a feeding area for ducks, herons, and egrets (especially Great Blue Heron), while the muddy flat across the channel from the water-control outlet is a roosting spot for shorebirds and Least and Forster's terns.

As you continue east along the dike, the *Phragmites* on the left gradually give way to the open water of the West Pool; here you can obtain an unobstructed view across to the north dike, about 1 mile away. Tens of thousands of ducks, geese, and swans use this pool as a resting and feeding area in migration. One or two Eurasian Wigeon are seen annually, mixed in with American Wigeon, and the Eurasian race of the Green-winged Teal has been found on occasion.

Large flocks of Canada and Snow geese visit the refuge in October to November and February to March, and most of them can usually be found on the West Pool or feeding in the marshes outside the dikes. One or two Greater White-fronted Geese have occurred with the Canadas several times during the past 15 years. A Ross' Goose that appeared with a flock of Snow Geese in January 1971 was the first New Jersey record. Since 1982 Ross' Goose has been an annual visitor to Brig. Tundra Swan is another migrant that prefers the north half of the West Pool; November and February are the best times to look for this elegant species (as many as 1,000 have been seen), but a few are present in mid-winter if the water is not frozen, and some linger into March. The introduced Mute Swan is now a common permanent resident in both the West Pool and the East Pool; its numbers are augmented by migrants in winter.

About 1 mile from the start of the south dike, you will come to the South Observation Tower. From this tower you may view the West Pool to the north and Turtle Cove and the surrounding marshes to the south. Climb the tower and scope the West Pool for waterfowl, gulls, terns, and shorebirds. American White Pelican was an annual visitor to Brigantine during the early 1980s, but has been less frequent in recent years. To the northeast you will see a tower with a box on top of it. This is the home of the resident pair of Peregrine Falcons.

Scan south from the observation tower across Turtle Cove. Double-crested Cormorants can be seen at any season sitting on poles far out in the bay. In fall, winter, and spring, the cove is a good spot for Horned Grebe and various diving ducks, such as Canvasback, scaup, Common Goldeneye, Bufflehead, and Red-breasted Merganser. Eared Grebe has been reported from this spot a couple of times. Large flocks of Brant, one of the species for which the refuge was created, winter on the bay to the south and feed on the marshes along the south dike. The Brant population has fluctuated widely in this century owing to such factors as loss of their principal winter food (eelgrass) and severe weather conditions in the high arctic. Approximately three-quarters of the western Atlantic Brant population winter in New Jersey, many of them in the bays and inlets around Brigantine.

On the right is the shore of Turtle Cove, where hordes of Ruddy Turnstones, Sanderlings, and Semipalmated Sandpipers gather to feed on horseshoe crab eggs in late May. This is one of several spots along the tour route where Northern Wheatear has occurred in fall.

The cross dike marks the beginning of the East Pool, which presents an entirely different aspect from the West Pool. Unlike the latter, the 700-acre East Pool has much more land than water; it is also more saline, being fed only by rainwater and by salt water from a water-control gate near the north end of the east dike. The many islands, with abundant *Phragmites* and shrubs, provide nesting habitat for Canada Geese and a variety of ducks, including Green-winged Teal (a rare breeder), American Black Duck, Mallard, Blue-winged Teal, Northern Shoveler, Gadwall, and Ruddy Duck (a rare breeder). This area also is a favorite feeding ground for herons and egrets from the nearby colonies. From April to October, look for American Bittern (rare), Great Blue Heron (also in winter), Great, Snowy, and Cattle (now uncommon) egrets, Little Blue and Tricolored herons, Black-crowned and Yellow-crowned (uncommon) night-herons, and Glossy Ibis. White Ibis (always immatures) has occurred numerous times, and several of the New Jersey records of White-faced Ibis are from the East Pool. Among the other breeding species are Forster's Tern (abundant), Gull-billed Tern, Marsh Wren, Yellow Warbler, Common Yellowthroat, Swamp and Song sparrows, and Red-winged Blackbird (watch for vagrant Yellow-headed Blackbirds among the flocks of Red-wings in late summer). Black Skimmers from nearby nesting colonies roost on the islands in the pool, and Boat-tailed Grackles and Fish Crows (abundant) feed along its edges. The marshes outside the dikes are full of nesting Clapper Rail, Saltmarsh Sharp-tailed Sparrow, and Seaside Sparrow.

Except for a couple of spots around the West Pool, the East Pool has been the place where shorebirds have congregated in recent years. Although the numbers and variety of shorebirds can be staggering, they tend to remain rather far from the dike, so a spotting scope is essential. Among the regularly occurring species are Black-bellied and Semipalmated plovers, American Golden Plover (rare), American Oystercatcher, American Avocet (uncommon in late summer to fall), Greater and Lesser yellowlegs, Willet (common breeder), Spotted Sandpiper, Upland Sandpiper (rare in late summer), Whimbrel (mainly in the grassy marshes outside the dikes), Hudsonian and Marbled godwits (both uncommon), Ruddy Turnstone, Red Knot, Semipalmated Sandpiper (abundant), Western Sandpiper (mainly in fall), Least Sandpiper, White-rumped Sandpiper, Baird's Sandpiper (rare, fall only), Pectoral Sandpiper, Dunlin, Curlew Sandpiper (rare), Stilt Sandpiper (fall), Buff-breasted Sandpiper (rare, fall), Ruff (rare), Short-billed Dowitcher, Long-billed Dowitcher (mainly in fall), Wilson's Phalarope, and Red-necked Phalarope (uncommon).

About 1.5 miles from the South Tower, you will come to the southeast corner of the East Pool, where the road turns left. Several hundred yards to the east of this corner is a mud flat known as the Godwit Flats. A Black-tailed Godwit and a Bar-tailed Godwit, both extreme rarities, were present at Brigantine during the summer of 1971, and were frequently seen on the Godwit Flats. Although the flats are readily accessible only by boat, some observers waded the channels and trudged across salt marsh to glimpse these birds. Marbled Godwits and Hudsonian Godwits were also present during that summer, and a few lucky birders were able to see all four of the world's species of godwit in one day, an achievement that may never have been equaled anywhere else.

As you drive north along the east dike, stop frequently to check out the ducks and shorebirds. Least Terns that nest on the nearby barrier islands frequently fish in the impoundment along with the many resident Forster's Terns. The terns fishing in the channel on the outside of the dike are usually Common Terns from the colonies in the salt marshes to the east. Snowy Owls have been seen on occasion in winter sitting on the dikes around the east pool.

After 0.7 miles, you will come to the northeast corner of the East Pool, where you turn left onto the north dike. The bay to your north is known as Perch Cove, a good spot for migrant and wintering Brant, bay ducks, and mergansers. There are many good spots for ducks and shorebirds along the north dike, so stop wherever you find concentrations of birds. In about 1.1 miles, the north end of the cross dike comes in from the left, and the road makes a dogleg right.

As you head west along the north dike, there are few places where you can get a glimpse of the water through the *Phragmites* on the left. To your right is a vast expanse of salt marsh, where Ospreys perch on poles in summer and Rough-legged Hawks hunt in winter; Northern Harriers are common all over the refuge at most times of the year. After about 1 mile, you will see the first of several small islands in the west pool, where Double-crested Cormorants, gulls, and terns roost. These islands are especially favored by Gull-billed and Caspian terns in late summer.

You will soon come to the end of the north dike, where you should be sure to scan the tree line to the north for roosting Bald Eagle in winter. These magnificent birds also like to sit on the ice or on islands in the West Pool, where they frequently find dead birds on which to feed.

The field on your left has had nesting Eastern Meadowlark and Grasshopper Sparrow (not recently). In late fall it is a favorite feeding ground for Canada Geese and Snow Geese, and Northern Shrike has occurred in winter along its eastern edge. At the southeast end of the field is an old hacking tower that was used in the mid-1970s for the first Peregrine Falcons introduced at Brigantine. In recent years, it has been the home of a pair of Barn Owls, which can sometimes be seen roosting in a corner of the box. The road turns left at the western edge of the field, the spot where New Jersey's first Mountain Bluebird spent part of an afternoon in November 1982.

After passing by another field, where Canada Geese feed, the tour road enters the woods. Here you will find the expected permanent residents and summer visitors for this oak-pitch pine type habitat, including American Woodcock. Both Chuck-will's-widow and Whip-poor-will nest in these woods; however, since you are not supposed to be in the refuge after dark, you might plan on searching for these species along nearby Leeds Point Road and Scott's Landing Road.

The tour road ends 1.6 miles from the end of the west dike, just after you cross another bridge over Doughty Creek, where the dirt road joins Great Creek Rd. You can park on the left just before the stop sign and explore some of the trails that lead along the creek and through the woods. To return to the parking lot at the headquarters, turn left and drive about 0.2 miles; if you have seen anything of interest, record it in the book at the information booth. To rejoin US 9, turn right and go 0.6 miles back to the traffic light.

Leeds Point and Scott's Landing Roads

These roads are excellent in summer for Chuck-will's-widow and Whip-poor-will, and in winter for eagles and other raptors. From the intersection of

Great Creek Rd. and US 9, go north on Rt. 9 for 0.1 miles, and bear right onto Leeds Point Rd. Follow this for about 2 miles to a stop sign and turn right. The second road on the right, after about 0.2 miles, is Scott's Landing Rd., a half-mile long road that leads down to the edge of the salt marsh. The woods along this road are home to the two nightjars from late April through the summer. At the landing, you can scan the tree line and marshes for raptors.

From the stop sign mentioned above, Leeds Point Rd. ends in about 1.5 miles at the village of Oyster Creek, where there is a favorite local restaurant. The first one-half mile or so passes through woods where the nightjars are common. The road then enters a large open expanse of salt marsh, where Bald Eagle and Golden Eagle are regular winter visitors, along with Rough-legged Hawk and numerous Northern Harriers.

It is easy to spend four to six hours at Brig if the birding is good. Particularly in shorebird season, a second trip around the dikes may yield a very different array of species.

✝

Makepeace Lake Wildlife Management Area

This large, but seldom-visited WMA sits astride the Atlantic City Expressway about 20 miles northwest of the city. The dominant feature of the 7,458-acre refuge is the large (300-acre), shallow Makepeace Lake, a popular fishing spot for Forster's Terns. Much of the upland habitat is typical Pine Barrens, but a substantial part is covered by impenetrable swamps and streams that feed into the Great Egg Harbor River near the southern border of the reserve. It has attracted some attention in recent years because of nesting King Rails, but otherwise it is sadly neglected by birders.

Directions

See Map 76. From the north, take the Atlantic City Expressway to Exit 28 (Rt. 54). Go 1 mile to Rt. 73, and turn left. Rt. 73 merges with US 322 in 2.3 miles, then continue on US 322 for 4.5 miles to Weymouth-Elwood Rd. (Rt. 559), and make the jughandle left turn. Continue straight ahead on Weymouth-Elwood Rd. when Rt. 559 turns left after one-half mile. After about 2.8 miles from US 322, you will come to Makepeace Lake on the right, where there is a small parking area, on the right. [DeLorme 64, K-1]

Birding

King Rails have been found at Makepeace Lake for a number of years in the marshy area on the west side of the road, opposite the parking area. As with all rails, hearing is easier than seeing. Although they will respond to a tape recording, use discretion in employing this tactic, as the birds have probably heard too many tapes. Virginia Rail is also present, so listen carefully.

The lake attracts a variety of waterfowl in migration and in winter when it is not frozen. Because it is so shallow, it tends to freeze quickly. Depending on the water level, lake edges can attract numerous shorebirds in migration, typically the regular inland migrants like Killdeer, Spotted, Solitary, Pectoral, Semipalmated, and Least sandpipers, Common Snipe, both yellowlegs, and Short-billed Dowitcher. Spotted Sandpiper nests along the lake, and Killdeer probably does, as well. Loafing Double-crested Cormorants can be seen here at any season, but they don't nest.

The birdlife in the woods and swamps is similar to nearby Winslow WMA and is described in that entry. As at Winslow, birding is mainly from the network of sandy, sometimes muddy dirt roads that crisscross the area. Some of the dense, impenetrable swamps along streams look very interesting, and a thorough study of the birdlife of the WMA might prove enlightening.

🦃

Atlantic County Park

Atlantic County Park at Estelle Manor is essentially unknown to most birders. Its 1,714 acres with 28 miles of marked trails include a diverse selection of habitats along South River and Stephens Creek, where the two streams flow into the Great Egg Harbor River about 4 miles south of Mays Landing. The park was once home to glass works, and also hosted a munitions factory during World War I, then became a game farm; the land was acquired by Atlantic County in 1974. It includes Pine Barrens uplands, ponds, cedar swamps, hardwood swamps, fields, streams, freshwater marshlands, and about 250 acres of developed recreational parkland.

As at Tuckahoe WMA, just a few miles south, the diversity of habitats at Atlantic County Park attracts a wide variety of migrants, Pine Barrens residents, and coastal birds. Among the breeding birds are Wood Duck, Marsh Wren, Acadian Flycatcher, and Yellow-throated and Prothonotary warblers. Ospreys and Great Blue Herons from nearby colonies fish along the streams in summer. The swamps are places where something interesting might be found nesting. Explore them and find out.

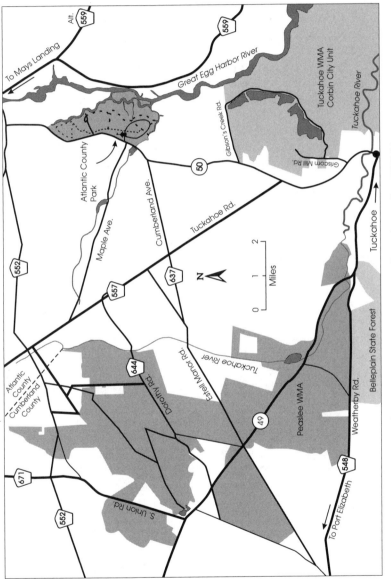

Map 84. Atlantic County Park and Peaslee WMA

Directions

From the north, take the New Jersey Turnpike south to Exit 3 (Runnymede, Rt. 168). Follow Rt. 168 south for 3 miles to Rt. 42, then go south on Rt. 42 (which becomes the Atlantic City Expressway) for 33 miles to Exit 17 (Rt. 50). Take Rt. 50 south for 6 miles to Mays Landing, where Rt. 50 joins US 40 for one-half mile. When Rts. 40 and 50 diverge, turn left onto Rt. 50, toward Cape May, and continue 3.7 miles to the Atlantic County Park entrance, on the left. If you arrive before the gate is opened (by 7:30 A.M.), turn left into the dirt road just beyond the entrance, and park in the space provided.

From the Philadelphia area, take the Atlantic City Expressway as described above.

From the New Jersey shore, take the Garden State Parkway to Exit 37 (Atlantic City Expressway). Go north for 5 miles to Exit 12 (US 40), then take Rt. 40 for 6 miles into Mays Landing and the junction with Rt. 50. Proceed as described above. From Cape May, the entrance to the park is about 7.5 miles north of the Tuckahoe River bridge on Rt. 50.

Birding

Drive in the entrance road for 0.1 miles to the modern new Nature Center. The center has restrooms, maps, and information. A 1.5-mile Nature Trail begins at the center and covers many of the habitats available at Atlantic County Park; you can hike the trail in a leisurely one-and-a-half hours. The many miles of trails provide access to all parts of the park.

A one-way 2.2-mile paved road also departs from the Nature Center, looping through the southern portion of the park. There are many places to stop along the way and explore the adjacent woods and trails. One especially good area to visit is the trail to the observation deck at Stephens Creek; this is part of the nature trail, but can also be reached by driving 0.8 miles along the loop road, where you can park on the right. Along this trail in summer, one can find Great Blue Heron, Osprey, Belted Kingfisher, Acadian Flycatcher, Blue-gray Gnatcatcher, Yellow-throated Warbler, American Redstart, and many other species. Another good point of access to Stephens Creek is the floating dock at the large picnic area, about 0.3 miles farther along the loop.

The best way to explore the more secluded northern portion of the park, about three-quarters of the park acreage, is to park at the Nature Center and hike the many trails that crisscross the area, some of them boardwalked to provide handicapped access. Most of these trails are abandoned railroad beds that date from the days of the munitions manufacture. Also remaining from the game farm days are the numbered markers on many of the trees. The trail map available at the Nature Center shows the locations of many of these numbers, and makes it easy to find your way around.

Other birds that nest at Atlantic County Park or visit the area in summer include Green Heron, American Black Duck, Turkey Vulture, Broad-winged and Red-tailed hawks, American Woodcock, Laughing Gull, Yellow-billed Cuckoo, Great Horned Owl, Whip-poor-will, Chimney Swift, Red-bellied Woodpecker, Eastern Phoebe, Eastern Wood-pewee, Eastern Kingbird, Great Crested Flycatcher, Purple Martin, Tree Swallow, Wood Thrush, Eastern Bluebird (in nest boxes), White-eyed Vireo, Blue-winged, Yellow, Pine, and Prairie warblers, Louisiana Waterthrush (in the northern part), and Scarlet Tanager.

☞

Tuckahoe (McNamara) Wildlife Management Area

The Lester G. McNamara WMA (formerly known as Tuckahoe-Corbin City WMA and still "Tuckahoe" to birders) encompasses almost 12,500 acres of salt marsh; fresh water rivers, marshes, and impoundments; and Pine Barrens woodland in Atlantic and Cape May counties. This diversity of habitat attracts a wide variety of birds. In addition to the typical birds of the Pine Barrens, you will find herons, egrets, ducks, geese, swans, shorebirds, gulls, terns, and wintering raptors, including Bald and Golden Eagles.

Among the more noteworthy breeding birds at Tuckahoe are Northern Harrier, Black Rail, Acadian Flycatcher, Yellow-throated, Prothonotary, and Hooded warblers. Rare or unusual species that have occurred include Wood Stork, Fulvous Whistling-Duck, Purple Gallinule, Ruff, Curlew and Buff-breasted sandpipers, and Pileated Woodpecker (rare in the Pine Barrens). Because it is not as productive or as famous as such nearby hot spots as Brigantine and Cape May, and because it is a little off the beaten path, Tuckahoe is not heavily birded. The long list of interesting species that summer, winter, or just visit here, suggests that additional attention from birders would be amply rewarded.

Note: As a WMA, Tuckahoe is heavily used by hunters from October through December (except on Sundays, when no hunting is allowed). You can still drive the roads at that season, but it is best to stay in your car.

Directions

Take the Garden State Parkway to Exit 25 (Ocean City and Marmora). From the exit ramp, turn west (right if coming from the north, left if coming from

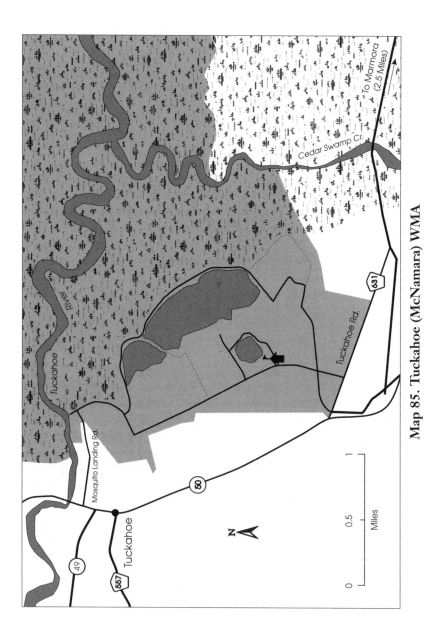

Map 85. Tuckahoe (McNamara) WMA

the south) onto Rt. 623 toward Marmora. Go 0.2 miles to the traffic light at Rt. 9 and continue straight ahead for 0.1 miles and turn left onto Rt. 631 (Tuckahoe Rd.). Drive about 5 miles to the entrance to McNamara WMA, on the right. [DeLorme 70, N-2]

From the Philadelphia area, you can follow the same directions as just described, or take the Atlantic City Expressway to Exit 17 (Rt. 50). Take Rt. 50 south through Mays Landing for 18 miles to the town of Tuckahoe. Continue about 2 miles on Rt. 50, turn left onto Rt. 631, and drive about 0.3 miles to the entrance to McNamara WMA.

Birding

Drive along the entrance road (where in summer, you will find Pine and Prairie warblers and other common birds of the Pine Barrens) for 0.2 miles to a dirt road on the right; turn onto this road, which leads to the fresh water impoundments. For about a mile, the road passes through pine-oak woodlands where you may find a variety of migrants in spring and fall, and the usual breeding birds in summer. Winter is usually unproductive, although kinglets, Red-breasted Nuthatch, and even Red Crossbill are possibilities.

The road emerges from the woods at a small impoundment on the right that is especially good for herons, waterfowl, and rails. The road continues along the dikes for almost 2 miles, past a large impoundment and then a smaller one, both on the left. On the right are the tidal salt marshes of the Tuckahoe River and Cedar Swamp Creek, which feed into Great Egg Harbor Bay at the east end of the WMA.

Many herons and egrets from the nearby coastal colonies feed in the impoundments from spring through fall, and Least Bittern and Green Heron nest. Migratory waterfowl include all of the dabbling ducks, and some divers, such as scaup, Common Goldeneye, Common and Hooded mergansers, and Ruddy Duck. Only Wood Duck, Blue-winged Teal, and possibly American Black Duck remain to nest. Large flocks of Canada Geese can be found most of the year, and Snow Geese drop in occasionally in the fall. Tundra Swan is a regular migrant, and will remain all winter if the ponds stay open.

Several species of rail nest in the impoundments and in the adjacent salt marsh. Among these, the most unusual is the Black Rail, which has been found nearby in modest numbers during the past few years. (Interestingly, the first nest of Black Rail in New Jersey was found in 1844 at Beesley's Point, site of the power plant visible just a couple of miles east of Tuckahoe). Most of the Black Rails found here recently have been on private property, but some have been heard from the dikes at Tuckahoe. Be aware that the WMA is officially closed at night, so obtain permission at the headquarters before venturing onto the dikes after dark.

Raptors are usually conspicuous at Tuckahoe. In summer, you will find nesting Turkey Vulture, Osprey, and Northern Harrier, while in winter you can expect harrier, Red-tailed and Rough-legged hawks, and possibly Bald and Golden eagles. The impoundments attract many migrant shorebirds, especially in late summer when the water levels are low. You can expect such common species as Black-bellied and Semipalmated plovers, Greater and Lesser yellowlegs, Solitary, Spotted, Semipalmated, Least, and Pectoral sandpipers, Short-billed Dowitcher, Common Snipe, and American Woodcock, but you never know when a rarity might appear.

Shortly after the road leaves the dikes, it intersects with the main road through the WMA. Here you can turn left, and drive through a pine-oak woodland with occasional wet areas, where Acadian Flycatcher and Yellow-throated Warbler nest. After 1.2 miles, turn left onto a road that leads toward Tuckahoe Lake. In about 0.25 miles, you will come to a short road on the right that leads about 100 yards to Tuckahoe Lake. Prothonotary Warbler nests around the lake, and Common Nighthawk has been seen here in summer.

Return to the main road, and turn right. After about 1.6 miles, you will come to a fork, leading, on the right, to a boat landing on the Tuckahoe River; this area should be checked for raptors, especially in winter. Continuing on the main road, you will come to pavement in about 0.4 miles, and then to Rt. 50 after another 0.3 miles. Turn right onto Rt. 50, where you will immediately cross the bridge over the Tuckahoe River.

To reach the Corbin City portion of the McNamara WMA, go north from the bridge for 0.9 miles to Griscom Mill Rd., where there is an old schoolhouse and a sign for the John S. Hembold Education Center. Turn right onto Griscom Mill Rd., which becomes dirt after 0.3 miles. After about 2 miles, you will come to the first of three large impoundments.

For several miles, the road follows the dikes of the impoundments, which are excellent for wintering raptors and for many of the migratory species as well. Then the road passes through some Pine Barrens woodland that has nesting Red-bellied Woodpecker, Brown Creeper, Yellow-throated Vireo, and Hooded Warbler. After having traversed almost 7 miles of dikes and woods, the road rejoins Rt. 50 about 3.6 miles north of Griscom Mill Rd. A small sign marks this north entrance to the WMA, which is just opposite the Holiday Haven Campground. Since the birdlife of the McNamara WMA has not been thoroughly surveyed, further investigation by birders may reveal that this area has more of interest.

Corson's and Townsend's Inlets

From Ocean City south to Cape May, a stretch of salt marsh and tidal bays border the coast, separating mainland New Jersey from the barrier beaches of Cape May County. Four inlets cross the barrier beaches, linking the salt-marsh islands and bays to the Atlantic Ocean. These inlets provide a variety of feeding, breeding, and roosting habitats for many species of birds. A visit at any season can be rewarding, but in summer you will have to contend with thousands of beachgoers at the popular summer resorts along this strip.

At Corson's Inlet, the northernmost of the four inlets, 341 acres of salt marsh and coastal dunes have been preserved as Corson's Inlet State Park. Here you can find a wide variety of loons, grebes, cormorants, and diving ducks from late fall through spring; a good selection of shorebirds in spring and fall; and an abundance of herons, egrets, gulls, and terns from spring through the fall. Townsend's Inlet is the site of an annual fall seabird-migration watch, which has recorded numerous rarities along with staggering numbers of migratory ducks and cormorants.

Directions

Take the Garden State Parkway to Exit 25 (Ocean City and Marmora). From the exit ramp, turn east (left if coming from the north, right if coming from the south) onto Rt. 623 toward Ocean City. Go 2 miles to West Ave. (second light after the bridge), and turn right onto West Ave (Rt. 619 South). Drive 2.1 miles to the traffic light at 55th St. Following Rt. 619, turn right onto 55th St., which soon becomes Ocean Dr., and go 0.9 miles to a parking lot on the left with a sign for Corson's Inlet State Park. [DeLorme 73, B-20]

Birding

The wet, marshy area on the left, just before the parking lot, is a favorite feeding area for herons and egrets from the nearby colonies, and for shore-birds in migration. From the parking lot, walk across the dunes toward the ocean. On the dunes, you may find Horned Lark, Snow Bunting (winter), and several species of sparrow, including the Ipswich race of the Savannah Sparrow (winter).

In and around the inlet, from October through April, you will find a variety of waterbirds, including Red-throated and Common loons, Horned Grebe, Double-crested Cormorant, Brant, Canvasback, Redhead (rare),

Greater and Lesser (uncommon in winter) scaup, Long-tailed Duck, Black, Surf, and White-winged scoters, Common Goldeneye, Bufflehead, and Red-breasted Merganser. Rarely, a Red-necked Grebe or an eider is seen.

Starting in spring, the salt marshes around Corson's Inlet attract many herons, egrets, and Whimbrel (in migration), plus breeding Clapper Rail, Willet, American Oystercatcher, Laughing Gull, Common and Forster's terns, and Salt-marsh Sharp-tailed and Seaside sparrows. On the beaches, there are Black Skimmer, Least Tern, and Piping Plover, three species that have become endangered in New Jersey, primarily because of loss of breeding habitat to beachgoers.

The mudflats around the inlet attract many migrant shorebirds, including Black-bellied and Semipalmated plovers, Willet, Ruddy Turnstone, Red Knot, Sanderling, Semipalmated, Western, and Least sandpipers, Dunlin, and Short-billed Dowitcher. In late summer and fall, large flocks of Forster's and Royal terns gather on the sandbars to roost; at these times, there are frequently a few Caspian Terns among them, and, rarely, a Sandwich Tern.

From the parking lot at the State Park continue south along Ocean Dr. across an island that is part of the State Park. You can pull off and park along the side of the road (carefully—this is a busy road) and scan for birds. Piping Plover nest above the high tide line along this stretch of island. After about a mile, you will come to the tollbridge across Corson's Inlet. Stop just before and just after the bridge to scan the water and the mudflats for birds.

Townsend's Inlet

The next inlet south is Townsend's Inlet, which can be reached by continuing south on Ocean Dr. through Strathmere and Sea Isle City for almost 7 miles. The sandbars that form on either side of this inlet sometimes attract immense concentrations of shorebirds and terns in fall.

The southeast corner of Townsend's Inlet is probably the best spot in New Jersey for observing the fall migration of waterfowl and seabirds. Since 1993, New Jersey Audubon's Cape May Bird Observatory has maintained an annual seawatch from early September into December, recording nearly a million birds in some years. Double-crested Cormorant, Black Scoter and Surf Scoter are the predominant species, accounting for about three-quarters of the total, but Red-throated Loon and Northern Gannet are also recorded in impressive numbers, typically 40 to 50 thousand of each. Red-necked Grebe, Parasitic Jaeger, Little Gull, Common Black-headed Gull, Black-legged Kittiwake, and phalaropes are some of the less-common species seen regularly.

As might be expected, the seawatch has also recorded a good list of rarities, although these are all flybys, of course, and not likely to be relocated.

They included Eared Grebe, Franklin's Gull, Sabine's Gull, possible Ross' Gull, Long-tailed Jaeger, Razorbull, and Black Guillemot.

To reach the seawatch site from the south end of the bridge over Townsend's Inlet, continue about 0.3 miles to 7th Street and turn left. Go 0.4 miles to the end of the road and park at the seawall. If you go during the fall, there will be observers there to assist in identifying the sometimes distant seabirds.

The seawatch can also be reached from the Garden State Parkway, Exit 13. Take Avalon Blvd. east for 3.5 miles to Dune Dr. and turn left. Go 1.2 miles north to 7th Street, turn right, and drive to the end.

🐦

Belleplain State Forest

This somewhat fragmented state forest contains more than 11,000 acres in Cape May and Cumberland counties. It consists of pine-oak woods, mixed deciduous forest, and Atlantic White Cedar swamps, with several lakes and ponds. Birdlife is similar to that of Dividing Creek, but this forest is more accessible. Beginning in the mid-1980s, birders began to explore this area more thoroughly and recognized the tremendous birding potential. Some of the breeding birds to be found here in spring and summer are Bald Eagle, Red-headed Woodpecker, Acadian Flycatcher, Yellow-throated Vireo, Northern Parula, Yellow-throated, Pine, Prairie, Black-and-White, Blue-winged, Prothonotary, Worm-eating, Kentucky, and Hooded warblers, American Redstart, Louisiana Waterthrush, and Scarlet and Summer tanagers. The best birding is to be found along Sunset Rd., Pine Swamp Rd., Savages Bridge Rd., New Bridge Rd., or on the many trails and abandoned roads that can be explored with the help of a map of the forest. There is a campground at Lake Nummy.

Directions

From the coast, take the Garden State Parkway to Exit 25 (Marmora). Go west into Marmora to the traffic light at Rt. 9, continue straight ahead for 0.1 miles and turn left onto Rt. 631 (Tuckahoe Rd.). Drive about 4.3 miles to the traffic light at Rt. 610. Turn left onto Rt. 610 and follow it for about 8.5 miles to Rt. 47, and turn right. Drive 1.9 miles to Washington Rd. (Rt. 557) and turn right.

From the western counties, take Rt. 55 south to its end at Rt. 47 south of Millville. When Rt. 47 and Rt. 347 diverge, take Rt. 347 for about 9 miles

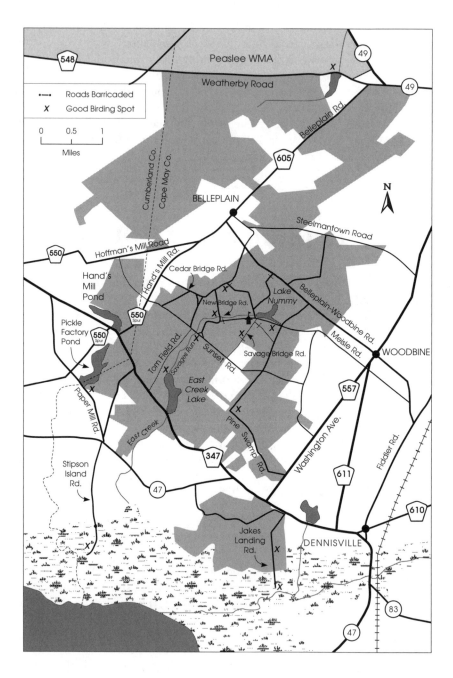

Map 86. Belleplain State Forest

until the two highways rejoin. Continue on Rt. 47 for 0.8 miles to Washington Rd., the first left turn.

Birding

To begin the tour, go one-half mile north on Washington Rd., and turn left onto Pine Swamp Rd. Drive west along Pine Swamp Rd., stopping occasionally to listen in spring for Pine, Prairie, Kentucky, Prothonotary, and Hooded warblers. Prothonotary is an uncommon breeder along this road, but can usually be found in the wet woods. At the junction with Sunset Rd., turn left and drive about 0.7 miles to Savages Bridge Rd., on the right, listening along the way for the ubiquitous Pine and Prairie warblers. Turn right onto Savages Bridge and proceed about one-half mile to the barrier across the road. Park here and walk the closed road for several hundred yards. Summer Tanager is a regular breeder here, along with such common species as Blue-winged Warbler, Eastern Wood-Pewee, Brown Thrasher, Yellow-throated Vireo, Ovenbird, and others.

Return to Sunset Rd., turn right, and continue about 0.6 miles to a right fork at New Bridge Rd., which is split to form a triangle with Sunset. Park here, and walk along Sunset to the bridge over Savages Run. This is an excellent spot for many of the specialties of the Forest. Look and listen for Northern Parula, Prothonotary, Worm-eating, and Hooded warblers, Louisiana Waterthrush, Acadian Flycatcher, Blue-gray Gnatcatcher, White-eyed Vireo, among others. A similar, but somewhat less productive spot is on New Bridge Rd. Drive about 0.4 miles to the bridge over the creek and park. This is especially good for Acadian Flycatcher.

Continue on New Bridge Rd. for about 0.4 miles to Cedar Bridge Rd., and turn right. Go about 0.2 miles to a blocked paved road on the right and park. Explore Cedar Bridge Rd. in both directions for Summer Tanager, Red-headed Woodpecker, Great Crested Flycatcher, Prairie, Pine, and Blue-winged warblers, and watch overhead for Black Vultures, which are common. A Bald Eagle from the nearby nesting site at East Creek Lake might fly over, as well.

To continue this loop tour, take Cedar Bridge Rd. another 0.8 miles to Belleplain-Woodbine Rd., pausing to listen for Orchard Oriole in the residential area. Turn right and go about 1.5 miles to Pine Swamp Rd., and turn right at the sign for Lake Nummy, go 0.6 miles and turn right onto Meisle Rd., following the signs for Lake Nummy and the Forest Headquarters. The White Pines along the entrance road have nesting Yellow-throated and Pine warblers, and a variety of other species can be found around the lake. A map of the State Forest is available at the Headquarters or can be obtained by writing to Belleplain State Forest, Box 450, Woodbine, NJ 08270. Modern restrooms are available at the Headquarters.

Finish the loop by driving east on Meisle Rd. for about 1.4 miles to Washington Ave. (Rt. 557), turn right, and go about 3 miles to Rt. 47. To continue birding at two nearby spots, turn right onto Rt. 47, go 0.7 miles to the traffic light, and turn left, staying on Rt. 47. Continue another 3.1 miles to Stipson Island Rd., and turn left. Drive 1.6 miles to a parking area on the right, where there is a nature trail. The road continues another 0.2 miles to a second parking area at West Creek.

The salt marsh here is part of a 578-acre Dennis Township Wetland Restoration Site, a project of Public Service Electric and Gas, in cooperation with the Nature Conservancy and the State of New Jersey. Most of the area consists of tidal marsh that had been diked for salt hay farming for over a century. By restoring the site to tidal flow, it once again benefits the aquatic life of the Delaware River Estuary.

The short nature trail soon forks, with the left fork leading to a floating platform viewing area. The marshes here, as elsewhere along the bayshore, provide excellent habitat for wintering raptors and waterfowl. Scan for Northern Harrier, Red-tailed Hawk, Rough-legged Hawk (most winters), and Bald Eagle, all of which can be seen with a little patience. In summer, there are nesting Clapper Rails and Seaside Sparrows.

Return to Rt. 47, then turn left and immediately right onto Lehner Rd. Go 200 yards and turn left onto Paper Mill Rd. (Rt. 550 Spur). In about 0.7 miles, you will come to Pickle Factory Pond, on the right, a good spot for Bald Eagle at any season. Prothonotary Warbler nests in the wet woods on the west side of the road, and Pileated Woodpecker, extremely rare in Cape May County, has been seen here.

Another interesting spot at the northern boundary of the Forest is found on Weatherby Rd., just off Rt. 49 (see Map). From the junction of Rt. 49 and Weatherby Rd., go west on Weatherby for about 0.6 miles to a bridge with a small pond on the left. Park on the right here, and look and listen for Eastern Bluebird, Indigo Bunting, Prothonotary Warbler, House and Carolina wrens, swallows over the lake, Eastern Phoebe, Eastern Kingbird, Louisiana Waterthrush, and many others. Cerulean Warblers were found nesting here in the early 1990s, the only breeding site in the southern half of New Jersey, but they have not been found recently.

Explore the rest of the Forest with the help of the map, and you may turn up something new, as well. Jakes Landing Rd., which passes through a section of Belleplain State Forest is nearby, and has interesting birds of its own.

🦆

Jakes Landing Road

Jakes Landing Rd. is the main access road for the Dennis Creek WMA, and is one of the premier places in New Jersey to observe wintering raptors, especially Bald Eagle, Northern Harrier, Rough-legged Hawk, Golden Eagle, and Short-eared Owl. In spring and summer, Yellow-throated Warbler and sometimes Northern Parula nest in the pine woods along the road, and Virginia and Clapper rails, Seaside and Saltmarsh Sharp-tailed sparrows nest in the marsh at the end of the road.

Directions

Follow the directions for Belleplain State Forest to Rt. 47 in Dennisville. Turn right onto Rt. 47 and drive 1.4 miles to Jakes Landing Rd., on the left (the first left turn you encounter after turning onto Rt. 47). [DeLorme 72, D-7]

Birding

Jakes Landing Rd. is only about 1.4 miles long. The first mile passes through a section of Belleplain State Forest, most of which is open deciduous woods, where you will find many of the common upland species of the Delaware Bayshore. The last 0.25 miles of this section has several pine and spruce plantings; the mature pines are where the Yellow-throated Warblers and Northern Parula can be found. Pine Warbler is common here, as well.

Continue to the parking lot at the end of the road. This is where you will hear, and perhaps see, the several species of rails in summer. Seaside Sparrow is abundant, but the Saltmarsh Sharp-tailed is much harder to see. Eastern Meadowlark can usually be heard singing from the salt hay fields on the opposite side of Dennis Creek, and Northern Harrier nest in the marshes. In winter, Northern Harriers and Rough-legged Hawks are always in evidence, and there are usually several Bald Eagles and Golden Eagles in the area. A little time and patience will often be rewarded by views of these magnificent raptors.

Beaver Swamp Wildlife Management Area

The Beaver Swamp WMA is a little-known, but very birdy expanse of swamps, dense deciduous forests, creeks, and small ponds between Swainton

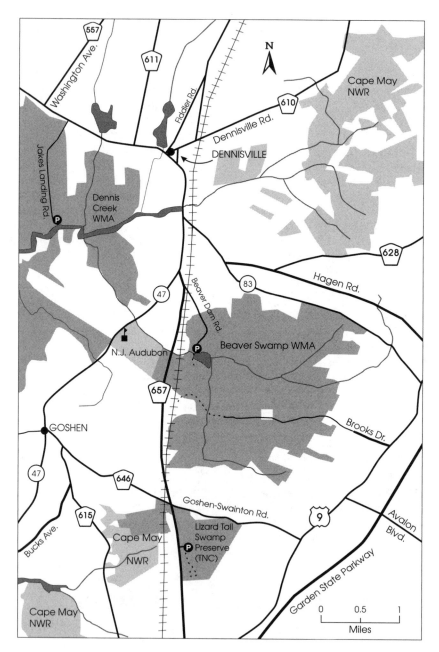

Map 87. Central Cape May County

and South Dennis in Cape May County. Among the more interesting birds that nest on this 2,700-acre tract, also known as Timber-Beaver Swamp, are Acadian Flycatcher, Yellow-throated and Prothonotary warblers, and Summer Tanager.

Directions

From the intersection of Rt. 47 and Rt. 83 in South Dennis, go south on Rt. 47 for 0.8 miles to the traffic light at Rt. 657 (Court House-Dennis Rd.). Turn left onto Rt. 657, go a short 0.2 miles and bear left onto Beaver Dam Rd. Follow Beaver Dam Rd., which soon becomes dirt, for about 0.8 miles to a parking area at the edge of a large marsh. Along the way, you will pass through wet woodlands where Prothonotary Warbler and numerous other species nest. [DeLorme 72, F-10]

Birding

Walk through the gate and continue onto the causeway that divides the marsh and Clint Millpond. Here there are nesting Wood Duck, Blue-winged Teal, Eastern Kingbird, Tree Swallow, and many other species. Forster's Terns from the nearby colonies hunt over the ponds and roost on trees and stumps. Recently, Gull-billed Terns have begun to frequent the ponds, but where they are coming from is uncertain. The road continues into the woods, where Orchard Oriole sings from the tall trees, for a short distance, then ends.

Another point of entry into the WMA is along the abandoned railroad track that forms the western boundary of much of the property. To reach this access, return to Rt. 657 and turn left. Go about 2.3 miles to a railroad crossing, marked with a sign although no longer in use. As you approach the crossing, you will notice signs on the trees on the left placed by The Nature Conservancy, which has purchased the land between Rt. 657 and the tracks that did not belong to the WMA. Park on the side of the very busy road and walk north along the tracks. All of the species noted above can be found here. After about 0.75 miles, you will come to a dirt road leading east into the WMA.

The WMA can also be entered from the east side, but only with a high-clearance vehicle. From the intersection of US 9 and Avalon Blvd. in Swainton, go north on US 9 for 0.9 miles to Brooks Rd., and turn left. Brooks Rd. is paved for the first one-half mile, but then becomes a very rough dirt road for another 0.4 miles, where you reach a gas and power line right-of-way. The dirt road continues another 1.6 miles as a one-lane track through the woods, but you can continue on foot another half mile to the railroad tracks noted above.

The nearby Lizard Tail Swamp Preserve, a 407-acre property of The Nature Conservancy, protects rare plant species, but has many of the same birds as Timber-Beaver Swamp. From the turnoff from Rt. 657 onto Beaver Dam Rd., continue south on Rt. 657 for about 3.2 miles (0.4 miles past Goshen-Swainton Rd.), to the preserve, on the left. Pull in the short driveway and park in the marked spots. A sheltered kiosk has an information board describing the preserve and the one-half mile nature trail through the swamp. The entrance to the trail is on the right, between the gate and the kiosk.

☝

Cape May County Bayshore

The Cape May County Bayshore from Goshen Landing to Fishing Creek includes a mixture of habitats from bayshore to tidal marshes to wet woodlands and even dry deciduous woodlands. Access to the bay at Reeds Beach, Cooks Beach, Kimbles Beach, and Norburys Landing provides birders with a view of the spectacle of shorebird migration in late May and early June and wintering waterfowl during the colder months. The Cape May NWR, headquartered on Kimbles Beach Rd., is assembling a diverse collection of properties throughout the county that will eventually preserve more than 16,000 acres. Likewise, The Nature Conservancy has been active in acquiring land for preservation throughout this part of the county. The following account covers many of these areas.

Directions

To reach the town of Goshen, take the Garden State Parkway to Exit 13 (Swainton, Avalon). Turn right onto Avalon Blvd. and go one-half mile to US 9. Turn left, drive 0.8 miles to Rt. 646, Goshen-Swainton Rd., and turn right. Follow Rt. 646 for about 3.7 miles to the junction with Rt. 47 in Goshen. [DeLorme 72, G-7]

Birding

Proceed directly across Rt. 47 onto Goshen Landing Rd., which runs about 0.75 miles ending in the salt marshes of Dennis Creek WMA. The last few hundred yards can be rough and muddy. The open water on the right just before the end of the road can be good for waterfowl and has had nesting Black-necked Stilt. Several species of rail, including both Yellow and Black rails, have been heard at night at the end of the road. Shorebirds feed along the

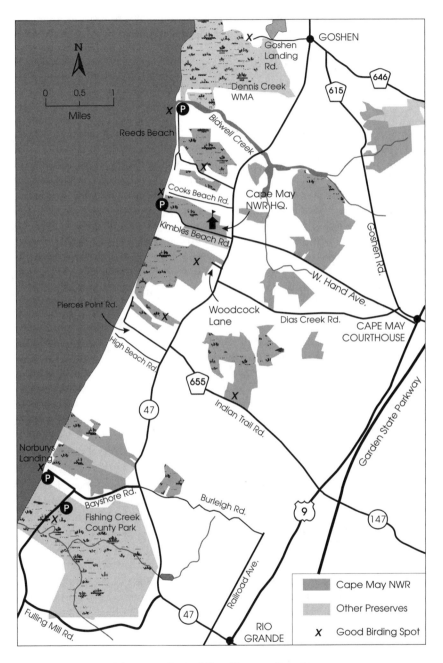

N

0   0.5
Miles

GOSHEN

X Goshen
Landing
Rd.

646

Dennis Creek
WMA

615

X P

Bidwell Creek

Reeds Beach

Cooks Beach Rd.

X

X

P

Cape May
NWR HQ.

Goshen Rd.

Kimbles Beach Rd.

X

W. Hand Ave.

Pierces Point Rd.

Woodcock
Lane

Dias Creek Rd.

CAPE MAY
COURTHOUSE

X

High Beach Rd.

655

47

Indian Trail Rd.

X

Garden State Parkway

Norburys
Landing

X

P

Bayshore Rd.

Burleigh Rd.

9

147

P

X Fishing Creek
County Park

Railroad Ave.

Cape May NWR

Other Preserves

Fulling Mill Rd.

47

RIO
GRANDE

X Good Birding Spot

Map 88. Cape May County Bayshore

banks of Goshen Creek when the mud is exposed, and terns feed along the channel. In winter, scan the marshes for raptors, especially Northern Harrier and the occasional Rough-legged Hawk.

To continue along the coast, return to Rt. 47, turn right, go about 2.6 miles to Reeds Beach Rd., and turn right. In one-half mile, there is a swamp pond on the right that attracts wading birds and waterfowl. In spring it is a favorite roosting and resting place for Green Heron, Black-crowned Night-Heron, and flocks of Glossy Ibis. In May 2001, an adult and an immature White-faced Ibis were regular visitors to the pond. Continue another one-half mile to Reeds Beach, turn right, and drive 0.7 miles to the end of the road, where there is a parking area (parking fee $1). Here, overlooking the Delaware Bayshore at the mouth of Bidwell Creek, is an excellent spot to view the spring gathering of shorebirds. In late May and early June, tens of thousands of Ruddy Turnstones, Red Knots, Sanderlings, and Semipalmated Sandpipers gather to feed on horseshoe crab eggs along the Delaware Bayshore before flying on to their nesting grounds in the Arctic. Although you may see birds as you drive along the road, do not stop, as there is no place to park and the local residents have become understandably impatient with inconsiderate birders.

Another good spot to observe shorebirds is Cooks Beach. Return to Rt. 47 and go right for just 0.25 miles to Cooks Beach Rd. It is 1 mile to the end of the road at the beach. Continue on Rt. 47 another one-half mile and turn right just past the Wawa at the sign for Cape May NWR on Kimbles Beach Rd. The NWR headquarters is 0.3 miles on the right, where there is a signboard and information. All of the land on the north side of the road is part of the NWR, while on the south side, the refuge property is a strip near the road with The Nature Conservancy's 112-acre Hand's Landing Preserve behind it. There are several trails through both properties and a small parking area at the end of the road for scanning the bayshore.

Back at Rt. 47, turn right and go about 0.4 miles to Woodcock Lane, on the right. Turn here and drive a few hundred yards to a parking area and kiosk at the end of the road. A loop trail here with a side trail provides access to a large tract of NWR property that includes fields, woods, salt marsh and beachfront near the outlet of Dias Creek. Breeding birds include Northern Bobwhite, Eastern Bluebird, Indigo Bunting, Field Sparrow, Orchard Oriole, and many others. From late fall into spring, the area is great for migrant and wintering sparrows. A Lark Sparrow wintered at a contiguous part of the refuge accessible from Rt. 47, 1.1 miles south, just past the first house south of Dias Creek.

Two other roads off Rt. 47 that lead to the beach and provide some shorebirding access are Pierces Point Rd. (1.6 miles from Woodcock Lane) and Highs Beach Rd., another 0.2 miles south. A better spot, however, is

Norburys Landing. Continue for 1.8 miles beyond Highs Beach Rd. to the traffic light at Bayshore Rd. (Rt. 603), and turn right. Drive about 1 mile, then bear right onto Millman Blvd. when Bayshore curves left and continue one-half mile to the parking area at the end, where there is a sign about the horseshoe crabs and the shorebird migration. In addition to being a good spot for the spring migration, Norburys is good at other times of the year for migrant shorebirds, waterfowl, and occasionally seabirds when wind conditions are right.

The nearby Sunray Beach Preserve of The Nature Conservancy is accessible at the end of Eldredge Ave., 0.3 miles south of Millman on Bayshore. Just beyond Eldredge, Bayshore Rd. crosses the marshes of Fishing Creek, which is part of a Cape May County Park. Before the *Phragmites* grew too high, this was a good spot for American Coot, Common Moorhen, various ducks, and migrant swallows in spring. Although this large park covers more than 1,000 acres between the Bayshore and Rt. 47, there is limited access at present.

Some other properties of the Cape May NWR that you may want to visit are shown on the map. One of these is on Indian Trail (Rt. 655), a little over 1 mile east of Rt. 47, where you can often hear Kentucky Warbler singing deep in the woods in May (before the traffic gets too heavy). The Nature Conservancy also owns a 10-acre preserve on the south side of the road. There is a trail into the woods by the guard rails on the side of the road about 1.5 miles from Rt. 47. Another large NWR site lies north of W. Hand Ave., about 1 mile east of Rt. 47 (turn at the Wawa just north of Kimbles Beach Rd.). One final area lies east of Goshen-Courthouse Rd. (Rt. 615), about 2 miles south of Goshen. This property is contiguous with The Nature Conservancy's Lizard Tail Swamp Preserve, covered in the Beaver Swamp WMA entry.

↟

Cape May County Park

This attractive little park in southern Cape May County was long known for its small colony of Red-headed Woodpeckers. The woodpeckers have become less reliable in recent years, but the park has a variety of the more common species, including a few like Hairy Woodpecker, White-breasted Nuthatch, and Tufted Titmouse that are hard to find south of the Cape May Canal. Among the nesting species are Eastern Bluebird and Pine Warbler.

Directions

Take the Garden State Parkway south to the traffic light at Mile 11. Turn right and go one block to Rt. 9. The entrance to the park is straight ahead across Rt. 9.

Birding

From the entrance to the park, continue straight ahead alongside the playing fields for about 0.3 miles, until the road bends right at the zoo. Park on the right at the stone wall, where there are some steps up to the group picnic area. When present, the Red-headed Woodpeckers inhabit the open woods around the picnic area and the playgrounds further in. Walk north (away from the zoo) through the woods listening for their characteristic call and watching for the flashes of black and white as they fly from tree to tree.

After about 200 yards, you will come to a dirt road along the northern edge of the park; on the other side of the road is a golf course. The area along this short stretch of road on either side is good for the woodpeckers, Northern Flicker, Eastern Bluebird, Pine Warbler, and Chipping Sparrow. On the north side, the open fairways with scattered trees are especially popular with bluebirds. Scan for them from the edge, however, and do not venture out onto the golf course. Pine Warblers usually arrive at the end of March, and are easy to locate by their distinctive trilled song.

To complete a visit to the park, continue walking along the dirt road for a short distance west, where it turns left. The road then passes through a pine-oak woodland for about 0.2 miles, turns left, then left again to return to the zoo area where the car is parked. Common resident species in the park include Downy Woodpecker, Blue Jay, American Crow, Carolina Chickadee, Tufted Titmouse, White-breasted Nuthatch, Carolina Wren, American Robin, Northern Mockingbird, Northern Cardinal, and Song Sparrow. Other, less common, nesting species include Hairy Woodpecker, House Wren, Blue-gray Gnatcatcher, Gray Catbird, Brown Thrasher, and Eastern Towhee.

There are modern restroom facilities in the large building at the west end of the playing fields.

➤

Stone Harbor

Stone Harbor was famous for its heronry, a 21-acre oasis in a sea of residential development. It was formerly the most accessible heronry in New Jersey and one of the biggest on the Atlantic Coast north of Florida. In the early

1990s, however, a Great Horned Owl took up residence in the heronry, and the other nesting birds abandoned the site and relocated to neighboring locations. Although the owl has long since departed, the herons, egrets, and ibis have never returned in significant numbers. There are still many other birds to be seen at Stone Harbor: the causeway leading from the Garden State Parkway into town is excellent for shorebirds in the fall; and Stone Harbor Point, at the south end of town, is noted for shorebirds, gulls, and terns in fall, and for Short-eared Owls in winter.

Nummy Island, between Stone Harbor and North Wildwood, is the best place of all for terns, skimmers, and shorebirds, especially American Oystercatcher, and Hudsonian and Marbled godwits. Neighboring Ring Island has the largest Laughing Gull colony in New Jersey—upwards of 10,000 pairs.

The Stone Harbor area can provide good birding at any time of the year, but the most productive months are May and August through October. In August, you will have to contend with the swarms of summer beachgoers.

Directions

Take the Garden State Parkway south to the traffic light at Mile 10, the well-marked exit for Stone Harbor. Turn left (east) onto the Stone Harbor Causeway. [DeLorme 72, J-10]

Birding

From the traffic light at the Parkway, go about 2.7 miles to the parking lot for the Wetlands Institute on the right. Along the way, you may see flocks of shorebirds on the mudflats. If you decide to stop, pull well off the road to park and bird, and watch out for the heavy traffic. The mud flats here attract many shorebirds in migration, especially in fall. Common species are Black-bellied and Semipalmated plovers, Greater and Lesser yellowlegs, Willet, Semipalmated, Western (fall), Least, Pectoral, and Stilt (mainly fall) sandpipers, Dunlin, and Short-billed and Long-billed (fall) dowitchers. Along the way you will probably see many Forster's Terns fishing in the nearby channel; Laughing Gulls are everywhere from April to October. The salt marsh on the south side of the road is a favorite area of Red Knot, Whimbrel, and many herons and egrets.

The Wetlands Institute is a private, nonprofit organization, which offers exhibits and information about the ecology of coastal New Jersey. The ponds around the institute have their share of the shorebirds noted earlier, and a pair of Ospreys usually nests in the "backyard."

Continue along the causeway, across the bridge over the intracoastal waterway, for about 0.8 miles to the first traffic light in Stone Harbor. Turn right onto Third Ave. and go about 1 mile to the Stone Harbor Bird Sanctuary,

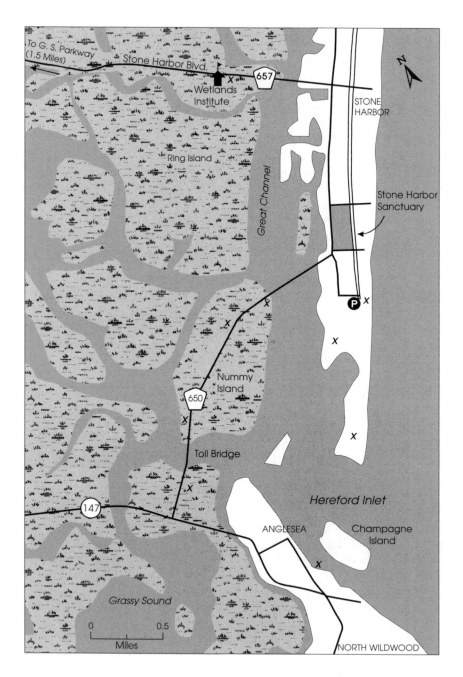

Map 89. Stone Harbor

which is on the left. The parking lot and main viewing area are opposite 114th St., about halfway down the long block containing the sanctuary. Established in 1947, the Stone Harbor Sanctuary is a dense tangle of shrubs and small trees, remnants of the typical vegetation that formerly covered much of New Jersey's barrier beaches. It formerly supported the largest heronry in New Jersey, but few breeding pairs remain.

At the end of the Sanctuary, turn left for one block to Second Ave., and turn right. Continue south on Second Ave. to its end at the parking lot for Stone Harbor Point. If you arrive between Memorial Day and Labor Day, you will need to buy a beach tag. Waves and currents change the point annually, so it is difficult to predict its condition or the birds that might be there. Over the years, however, it has been a good spot in fall for Piping Plover (formerly nested), a variety of other shorebirds, especially American Oystercatcher, Black-bellied Plover, Dunlin, dowitchers, Caspian Tern, and large flocks of Royal Terns, in addition to the local breeders such as Black Skimmer, Least, Common, and Forster's terns.

To reach the birding area, walk south from the parking lot along the dirt road until you come to the water. Turn right and walk along the shore, searching for the many shorebirds, gulls, and terns that frequent the area. Brown Pelicans have been frequent visitors to Hereford Inlet during late summer and early fall in recent years, so your chances of seeing them at those times are good. Depending on the tide, you can cover a large area of mud flats before returning to the parking lot. In late fall and winter, you may see Short-eared Owls hunting over the scrubby dunes at dusk. A large impoundment for dredge spoil was under construction in late 2001, so what this area will look like in the future remains to be seen.

To reach Nummy Island, return north on Second Ave. to 117th St., turn left, and go one block to Third Ave. Turn left onto Third Ave. and follow it south across the bridge for about 0.5 miles to Nummy Island. Stop at the west end of the bridge to scan the water and mudflats for waterfowl and shorebirds. Black-crowned Night-Herons nest in the dense tangle on the right side of the road. The large island off to your right as you cross the bridge is Ring Island, which has the enormous colony of Laughing Gulls. Although there may be birds anywhere along the 1.2-mile stretch of road that traverses the Nummy Island salt marsh, two areas are usually the most productive. The first of these is located about one-half mile beyond the bridge, where there are several ponds on both sides of the road (watch for Boat-tailed Grackles in the shrubby growth along the way).

The ponds on the right (northwest) side of the road are best. In addition to many of the herons and egrets from the neighboring colonies, there is usually a wide variety of shorebirds here. All the regularly occurring shorebirds

Least Tern

SUMONEEN FINNEGAN 2.81

mentioned above can be expected, plus American Oystercatcher and Ruddy Turnstone. Additional possibilities include Lesser Golden-Plover (rare), Hudsonian and Marbled godwits, and Wilson's and Red-necked phalaropes. Among the birds that nest on Nummy Island are Osprey (on an artificial platform), Clapper Rail, Willet, Laughing, Herring, and Great Black-backed gulls, Common Tern, and Saltmarsh Sharp-tailed and Seaside sparrows.

Continue southwest for about 0.4 miles, to just before the road bends left. The ponds on the right frequently have American Oystercatcher and are favored by godwits. A variety of other shorebirds, gulls, and terns can be expected. Just ahead about 0.2 miles is the bridge to North Wildwood Rd. Stop just before the bridge and scope the sandbar on the opposite side of the channel—a favorite roost site for Black Skimmer, American Oystercatcher, shorebirds, gulls, and terns. High tide is the best time to visit Nummy Island, while a low or falling tide is better at Stone Harbor Point. (The tides at Hereford Inlet occur at about the same time as those at Sandy Hook and Cape May Harbor).

Cross the toll bridge, and go about 0.3 miles to North Wildwood Rd. (Rt. 147). To return to the Garden State Parkway northbound, turn right and go about 2.5 miles to the entrance. To go south on the Parkway, you will have to continue another 0.3 miles to Rt. 9, turn left, and go about 2.6 miles south to Rt. 47, then left again and 0.4 miles east to the Parkway entrance.

✝

Ocean Drive
to Wildwood Crest

Ocean Drive along the north side of Cold Spring (Cape May) Harbor passes through salt marshes where migrant and wintering shorebirds gather and where the "salt sparrows" nest and sometimes winter. The jetties at the inlet that protect the entrance to Cape May Harbor are excellent but seldom birded spots for finding such winter specialties as eiders, Harlequin Ducks, and alcids. The property that includes the north jetty, formerly the U.S. Coast Guard Electronics Station, is now part of the Cape May NWR, and plans are to provide access at some time in the future.

The "Coast Guard ponds," along Ocean Drive near the entrance to the former base, provide excellent habitat for both dabbling ducks and shorebirds. Because they are brackish and partially tidal, they are among the last ponds to freeze in winter. Species seen at the jetty on the north side of the

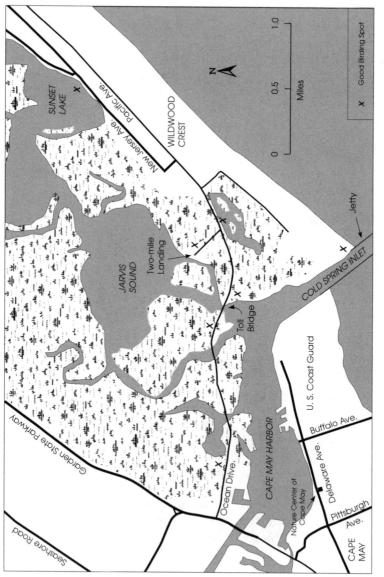

Map 90. Ocean Drive to Wildwood Crest

inlet include Northern Gannet (regular close to shore), Great Cormorant (regular in winter), Common and King eiders, Harlequin Duck, Purple Sandpiper (regular November to May), Little Gull, Black-legged Kittiwake, and Thick-billed Murre.

Directions

Take the Garden State Parkway south to the traffic light at the southern terminus, and continue another 0.3 miles to the next traffic light, just before the bridge across the Cape May Canal. Turn left toward Wildwood Crest, onto Ocean Drive. [DeLorme 73, L-21]

Birding

As you drive east along Ocean Drive toward Wildwood Crest, watch the tidal mud flats along the north side of the road for shorebirds at any season. Just before the toll bridge (1.6 miles), the large fish processing plants attract hordes of gulls, including some of the rarer ones in winter. Access is difficult, however, as birders are not particularly welcome. You can, however, park along the road near the bridge and scan the roofs and shoreline where the birds roost. Just across the toll bridge, on the right, is a marshy area where Seaside Sparrow and Saltmarsh Sharp-tailed Sparrow nest and are joined in fall and spring by Nelson's Sharp-tailed Sparrows. A few of each species sometime try to overwinter.

Continue along Ocean Drive for another mile to the ponds, on the right. The ponds (actually one large pond separated into smaller sections by small marshy islands, are a good spot for shorebirds at any season and ducks in the colder months. They have also attracted a wide variety of less-common species, such as Eurasian Wigeon, American Avocet, Red-necked Phalarope, and Eurasian Green-winged Teal. In winter, you might find Black-bellied and Semipalmated plovers, Greater and Lesser yellowlegs, Western and Least sandpipers, Dunlin, Long-billed Dowitcher, and even a few lingering herons and egrets, along with a good assortment of ducks.

Directly opposite the pond, on the north side of Ocean Drive, is the entrance to Two Mile Landing, which has some restaurants and commercial fishing operations. Drive in the 0.3-miles road and park at the right-hand end near the salt marsh. This is an even better place for all of the "salt sparrows" mentioned above and has "Ipswich" Savannah Sparrows in winter. It also provides good viewing of a large expanse of tidal channels and marsh where many shorebirds gather in migration. Marbled Godwit has been seen here regularly, and has even wintered.

Continue on Ocean Drive another 0.7 miles to the traffic light at Jefferson Ave. and turn left. Take the first right onto New Jersey Ave. and go about

1 mile to Sunset Lake, on the left. The lake is really just a large area of open water in the salt marshes that separate the mainland from the barrier islands. Sunset Lake attracts a good variety of diving birds in fall, winter, and spring, including grebes, loons, and diving ducks.

Return to the traffic light at Jefferson Ave. and turn left, toward the beach. Go 0.25 miles to Atlantic Ave. and turn right. Park where you can find a legal parking spot and cross over to the beach. Pay attention to posted signs, because access may be restricted at certain times. Walk south for about 1 mile to the jetty. Do not venture onto the jetty if conditions are rough, but scan from the shore. Scan the jetty on the south side of the inlet, because birds are sometimes along it, as well.

⌐

Cape May

To the birders of New Jersey and the northeast, Cape May is a mecca. In the fall, we are drawn by the thousands to witness a spectacle that is unsurpassed in eastern North America and has few equals elsewhere in the world—the migration of thousands of hawks, shorebirds, flycatchers, thrushes, vireos, warblers, sparrows, and other songbirds heading south for the winter. Although fall is the best season in Cape May, winter is outstanding, spring is superb, and summer is rich in rarities. Even on a dull day, Cape May is better than most other birding spots in the state.

As of this writing, the Cape May County bird list has surpassed 400, and most of the species on the list have been seen on Cape Island. Cape Island is what birders refer to when they talk about Cape May; it is a triangular wedge of about 6 square miles at the extreme southern tip of the state, separated from the rest of New Jersey by the Intracoastal Waterway canal. Cape Island contains several municipalities, including Cape May city, West Cape May, Cape May Point, and part of Lower Township. There are numerous good birding areas around the Island, and each will be covered separately.

In addition to seeing swarms of hawks, falcons, and songbirds, it is the hope of seeing a rarity that brings many birders to Cape May. The list of rarities that have occurred here is far too long to list here and includes many first records for New Jersey. In 1984 alone, there were sightings of Brown Pelican, Anhinga, White Ibis, Greater White-fronted Goose, Common Eider, King Eider, Swallow-tailed Kite, Mississippi Kite, Swainson's Hawk, Golden Eagle, Sandhill Crane, Marbled Godwit, Baird's Sandpiper, Wilson's Phalarope, Black-headed Gull, Sandwich Tern, Roseate Tern, Arctic Tern, Common Ground-Dove, Western Kingbird, Scissor-tailed Flycatcher, Fork-tailed

Flycatcher, Sedge Wren, Loggerhead Shrike, Orange-crowned Warbler, Townsend's Warbler, Dickcissel, Clay-colored Sparrow, Lark Sparrow, and Brewer's Blackbird.

Other species added to the list since then are Brown Booby, White-tailed Kite, Whiskered Tern, Black-chinned Hummingbird, Rufous Hummingbird, Allen's Hummingbird, Calliope Hummingbird, Bell's Vireo, Cave Swallow, Violet-green Swallow, Brown-chested Martin, Rock Wren, MacGillivray's Warbler, Painted Bunting, and Smith's Longspur.

If you have never been to Cape May before and are visiting in September or early October, I recommend that you start at Higbee Beach at dawn. Later in the day you can explore the other areas. Directions for all locations are given from Cape May Point State Park, the location of Cape Island's most conspicuous landmark—the Cape May Point Lighthouse.

Directions

To reach Cape May Point State Park from anywhere else in New Jersey, take the Garden State Parkway south to its end. Turn right onto Rt. 109, following the signs for the Lewes–Cape May Ferry. Go 0.6 miles and take the jughandle turn for the ferry at the junction with Rt. 9. Follow Rt. 9 (Ferry Rd.) for one-half mile to the traffic light at Seashore Rd. (Rt. 526), and turn left. Take Seashore Rd. (the name changes to Broadway in West Cape May) across the bridge over the canal (from which you can see the lighthouse to the south) for about 2.4 miles to the traffic light at Sunset Blvd. Turn right onto Sunset, and go 1.7 miles to Lighthouse Ave. on the left (along the way, you will pass the South Cape May Meadows, a good birding spot discussed below.) Turn left onto Lighthouse Ave., and drive 0.7 miles to the state park entrance, on the left just before the lighthouse. Drive into the state park, and park in the large paved lot. [DeLorme 73, N-18]

An alternate route, which takes you into picturesque but congested Cape May city, is to continue straight ahead on Rt. 109 at the end of the Parkway. This road becomes Lafayette St. after you cross the bridge over the canal. After about 2 miles, bear right onto Perry St. at the stop sign where Lafayette ends. In about 0.4 miles, you will come to the traffic light at Broadway and Sunset. Continue straight ahead on Sunset for 1.7 miles to Lighthouse Ave.

Birding

Cape May Point State Park

The state park occupies about 300 acres of land at the southern tip of New Jersey. It has been the site of a lighthouse since 1823, when the first one was constructed about 0.3 miles south of the present lighthouse. The rising sea level (which is continuing today) necessitated moving the lighthouse twice,

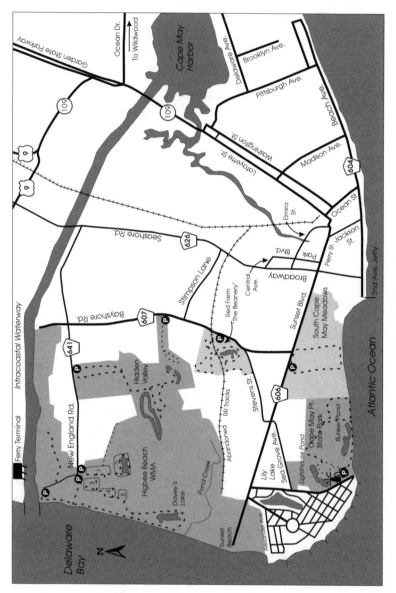

Map 91. Cape May

the last time in 1859 to the present site. The land around the lighthouse served as a coastal defense base and radio relay station until 1963, when it was given to the state of New Jersey. Most of the buildings around the park date from the military period. The headquarters building, which has a nature museum and modern restrooms, is on the west side of the parking lot, not far from the lighthouse.

Cape May Point State Park is the site of a hawk watch, conducted by New Jersey Audubon Society's Cape May Bird Observatory, where comprehensive tallies have been kept every year since 1976. The hawk-watching platform is located on the east side of the parking lot and is usually crowded with people in September and October. It is manned by an official counter every day from late August through November, weather permitting, and is a "must" stop on any visit to Cape May in the fall. In addition to being an excellent spot to observe the migration of raptors, it is also the place to find out what rare birds might be in town and to meet old friends.

Most of the hawks that migrate through Cape May are accipiters and falcons that spend their summers in the forests and tundra of the northeastern United States and Canada. On their fall migration, many species reach the Atlantic Coast, which they then follow southwestward. For the falcons, the coastal route is the principal one, and they are uncommon inland, but for the Sharp-shinned and Cooper's hawks, their abundance along the coast depends very much on the passage of cold fronts with strong northwest winds. When they reach Cape May, many individuals are apparently intimidated by the 14 miles of open water between the Point and Cape Henlopen, Delaware. Instead of crossing, as the falcons and Ospreys do, they turn and head north and then west along the Delaware Bayshore toward Philadelphia.

The hawk flight at Cape May begins in late August, with the appearance of the first Ospreys and a few Bald Eagles; it peaks in late September and early October with the big flights of accipiters and falcons, and dwindles in November, when Red-tailed Hawks and the occasional Golden Eagle and Goshawk pass through. The numbers of hawks in a good season can be staggering; 1981 was the record year, with almost 89,000 hawks passing the Point. Sharp-shinned Hawks dominate the tally every year, with a record 61,167 in 1984, (including 7,000 on October 4). However, Cooper's Hawks, which are scarce at most other hawk watches, can be almost common at Cape May. A record 5,009 were counted in 1995. Clearly, Cape May is the place to learn to distinguish Sharp-shinned from Cooper's.

Even more than the accipiter flight, the migration of falcons at Cape May excites the hawk-watcher. American Kestrel is abundant, although this species has shown a disturbing decline in recent years. Almost 22,000 were recorded in 1981, but in 2000 there were fewer than 7,000, the smallest count ever. The rarer falcons, Merlin and Peregrine, are what birders come to see, however, and Cape May is the place to see them. In late September and early

October, these two are hard to miss, especially on days with easterly or southerly winds. The largest Merlin flight was in 1985, with 2,869, and daily tallies of over 100 are routine. Peregrine Falcons have shown a remarkable resurgence in the past few years, and the seasonal total regularly exceeds 1,000 birds (1,791 in 1997). Daily counts of 25 or more are unremarkable, and the record is 291 on October 7, 1997.

Osprey are also a big attraction at Cape May Point, with as many as 6,734 seen in a season, mainly in September and October. Other regular migrants include Turkey Vulture (all fall), Northern Harrier (September through November), Red-shouldered Hawk (October to November), Broadwinged Hawk (September to October), Red-tailed Hawk (October to November), and Rough-legged Hawk (November). Rarities that show up annually are Mississippi Kite (more often seen in spring), and Swainson's Hawk (maximum of 7 in 1981).

There are many things to see other than raptors at the state park. Walk toward the beach from the hawk-watching platform and you will pass a small pond on the right that has harbored Baird's Sandpiper and Sedge Wren in the fall. A little further along is a much larger pond on the left, known to birders as Bunker Pond. This is a favorite feeding and roosting site for herons and egrets, ducks, gulls, terns, and shorebirds, including Baird's Sandpiper. Least Bittern nests in the reeds around the pond and may be seen flying about, especially in spring.

Continuing on to the beach, you will see the bunker, a large concrete structure that served during World War II as a magazine for four anti-aircraft guns mounted just offshore from it. The bunker is being rapidly undermined by the sea, and is no longer accessible, but check the waters around it for loons, ducks, gulls, and terns. In late fall and winter, you may see Northern Gannet, Common Eider, King Eider, jaegers, or even an alcid, if you are very lucky. A walk along the dunes toward Cape May city should produce Palm Warbler and Savannah Sparrow in October.

Return to the parking lot of the state park. The bushes around the edges of the large open area can be very good for migrant songbirds in the fall. New Jersey's first Chestnut-collared Longspur was found feeding on the grassy area in June 1980, and other ground-feeding birds such as sparrows frequent the edges of the parking lot. Purple Martins nest in the martin houses around the headquarters from late April through the summer. A sight rivaling the big Sharp-shinned flights is the enormous flocks of Tree Swallows, numbering in the tens of thousands, that sometimes gather on the wires around the state park from late August to early October.

A network of nature trails begins on the east side of the parking lot, just north of the hawk-watching platform. To the left of the hawk watch, as you face it from the parking lot, is a picnic pavilion, and to the left of the pavilion is the entrance marker to the trails. A map showing the trails can be obtained at the headquarters. The main trail makes a loop, with one side spur, through the dense shrubs and trees, and provides access to Lighthouse Pond at two points. The trails can be good for migrants in spring and fall. In summer, White-eyed Vireo and Yellow-breasted Chat are common along the trails. Blue-winged Teal and Least Bittern nest around the pond, and a Purple Gallinule spent several weeks here in the summers of 1981, 1982, and 1985. Least Terns hover over the pond searching for minnows from May through August. This is the kind of spot where a rarity might show up, so it is always worth checking.

Lily Lake

Drive out of the park and turn right onto Lighthouse Ave. Drive 0.5 miles, past Seagrove Ave. on the right, and bear left onto Lake Dr. Park immediately on the right, at the sign for the Cape May Bird Observatory Northwood Center. Lily Lake is across the street on your left. The observatory, a unit of NJAS, is located in the white house in the woods on the right, and is a good place to visit to find out what birds are in town. The staff conducts field trips and birding workshops, operates the hawk watch, and runs a small bookstore.

The woods along Lighthouse Ave., and along Seagrove Ave. are excellent for migrant songbirds in spring and fall. You can easily spend an hour or two walking the roads near the observatory on a good flight day in the fall, watching for thrushes, vireos, warblers, and sparrows. A favorite route is a walk around Lily Lake, scanning the bushes for migrant songbirds and the water for migrant ducks. Watch the wires around the north end of the lake for Western Kingbirds in the fall; this seems to be a favorite spot for flycatchers—two Scissor-tailed Flycatchers were here in June 1984.

Lily Lake is a surprisingly good spot for migrant waterfowl and for feeding herons, egrets, Belted Kingfisher, and Spotted and Solitary sandpipers. Redhead and Ring-necked ducks are regular in the fall, and Eurasian Wigeon is seen almost every year. Rarities that have shown up at the lake include White-faced Ibis, Wood Stork, Fulvous Whistling-Duck, Sandhill Crane, Swallow-tailed Kite (seen soaring over the lake in spring on several occasions), and Northern Shrike.

Sunset Beach

From the state park, take Lighthouse Ave. back to Sunset Blvd. and turn left. Go one-half mile to the end of the road and park. Offshore is the wreck of a concrete ship, built during World War I, but decommissioned soon after. It served as a restaurant for a short time, but it has long since deteriorated. From October through May it provides a roosting place for Purple Sandpipers, especially at high tide.

Sunset Beach is a good spot to scan for Red-throated Loon and for passing gulls and terns including Roseate Tern in May. Forster's and Royal terns like to roost on some pilings down the beach to your right, and have occasionally been joined by Sandwich Tern. Jaegers, Black-legged Kittiwakes, even storm-petrels, shearwaters, and alcids have been seen from this spot after strong southeast winds, as well as extreme rarities like Sooty and Bridled terns and Black-capped Petrel during hurricanes. Recently, 125 acres around Sunset Beach, including the site of the former magnesite plant, have been purchased and added to Higbee Beach WMA.

South Cape May Meadows

From the state park, take Lighthouse Ave. back to Sunset Blvd. and turn right. Go about 0.9 miles to a parking area on the right. The South Cape May Meadows is a large, wet pasture, which, along with some adjacent marsh on the east side of the meadows, was acquired by The Nature Conservancy in 1982. Covering a little more than 180 acres, the area is bounded on the south by some low dunes that (usually) protect it from the Atlantic Ocean. The pasture is periodically flooded by sea water, but also has numerous ponds that collect rainwater.

"The Meadows," as it is known to birders, was an outstanding spot for migrant shorebirds; for migrant or summering herons, egrets, and terns; for migrant or wintering gulls; and even for migrant songbirds. Due to the lack of grazing by cattle and inadequate water-level control, the Meadows has been much less productive in the past 15 years. To explore it, walk out the dirt road that bisects the pasture as far as the dunes, scanning the fields and ponds along the way. From the dunes, you can scope the water offshore for loons, grebes, and ducks from fall through spring. To return to your car, you can either retrace your steps, or walk along the beach toward Cape May city for a couple of hundred yards, then bear left along the sand fence to a path that runs along the east side of the meadows back to Sunset Blvd. This path is often the better one in the early morning, because the sun is behind you. When walking through the Meadows, do not stray from the two main paths.

Piping Plover and Least Tern nest on the sandy overwash near the ocean; in recent years, the tern colony has attracted Arctic, Roseate, and Sandwich terns for brief visits. Both White-winged and Whiskered terns appeared here during the 1980s, and Cave and Violet-green swallows have been recorded here during their occasional visits to the area.

Spring shorebird migration brings many plovers and sandpipers to the Meadows, but it is mainly the fall migration (early July through October) that attracts the greatest numbers and variety. Semipalmated Plover, Killdeer, Greater and Lesser yellowlegs, Semipalmated, Least, and Pectoral sandpipers, and Short-billed Dowitcher are the most common species, but virtually all of New Jersey's shorebirds can be found during the course of a season. The meadows is an especially good place to see Stilt Sandpiper and Long-billed Dowitcher. Such rare or uncommon species as American Golden Plover, Upland Sandpiper, Hudsonian Godwit, White-rumped, Baird's, and Buff-breasted sandpipers, and Wilson's Phalarope occur, but no longer every fall. Often they can be viewed at very close range when present. Other rarities that don't show up every year include Black-necked Stilt, American Avocet, Curlew Sandpiper, Ruff, and Red-necked and Red phalaropes.

The Meadows was the best place in New Jersey to see migrant Logger-head Shrike in August (formerly one or two a year), but this species is almost gone as a migrant. A little later in the year you might find a Lark Sparrow or an Orange-crowned Warbler. One of the highlights of the fall season is watching the numerous Merlins and Peregrines chasing shorebirds around the Meadows.

Throughout the year, the Meadows is a gathering place for gulls. In sum-mer, they will be mostly Laughing Gulls; the rest of the year, you'll find Her-ring, Ring-billed, Great Black-backed, and sometimes Bonaparte's gulls. Every year there are rarities, however. Iceland and Glaucous gulls are now regular in winter, while Lesser Black-backed Gulls are becoming more com-monplace. Little and Black-headed gulls are occasionally seen with Bona-parte's in the spring, while Franklin's Gull has occurred at least twice in late summer.

The South Cape May Meadows is worth a stop anytime you are in Cape May, but especially in late summer and fall. Rarities that have appeared here in recent years, in addition to those already mentioned, are Brown Pelican (along the beach), Fulvous Whistling-Duck, Wood Stork, Black Rail, Wil-son's Plover, Fork-tailed Flycatcher, Gray Kingbird, Sedge Wren, and Smith's Longspur.

The Beanery (Rea Farm)

For the past several years, and hopefully into the future, Cape May Bird Ob-servatory (CMBO) has leased birding privileges at the Rea Farm, also known as The Beanery. Stop at CMBO to obtain a birding map and pass, which is free for members of CMBO or New Jersey Audubon, and $15/week for non-members. From the state park, take Lighthouse Ave. back to Sunset Blvd. and turn right. Drive 1 mile to the junction with Bayshore Rd. and turn left (this is just past the parking lot for South Cape May Meadows). Continue 0.4 miles on Bayshore Rd. to a former lima-bean processing plant (the beanery) on the left. Park in the open area and explore the trails, staying off the fields and the areas marked No Trespassing.

As you enter the area, you cross an abandoned railroad bed. The weeds on your left and the wet woods on your right are good for migrants in fall.

The field edge is excellent for Ruby-throated Hummingbird (September), Connecticut Warbler (September to early October), and Orange-crowned Warbler (October). Yellow-headed Blackbird has occurred several times among the Red-wings in the cornfield, and Red-headed Woodpeckers like the dead trees around the edges in the fall. Be alert to the possibilities at this spot; all the regular migrant songbirds can be expected here, and any rarity might occur.

The hedgerow and weeds along the field edge near the railroad tracks are a favorite spot for migrant Mourning, Connecticut, and Orange-crowned warblers, and for sparrows. New Jersey's only MacGillivray's Warbler spent two months in the hedgerow in late 1997. Lincoln's and White-crowned sparrows are regular here, and Clay-colored has been found. Blue Grosbeaks and Indigo Buntings are also attracted to the weed seeds.

The wet woods around the pond on the west side of the property are good for migrants in spring and fall. From the railroad tracks here you can see another pond surrounded by willows between the tracks and the Rea house. There is a trail around the pond, which has had Wood Stork and Ash-throated Flycatcher. New Jersey's only Brown-chested Martin spent most of its ten-day stay flying around the Rea Farm. In addition, the area around The Beanery is the best spot to look for Mississippi Kites in late May and early June. Several immatures (up to about 7) show up in Cape May every spring. The parking area is an excellent spot to sit and scan. Be careful to observe the posted rules for birding the Rea Farm, as these privileges could be withdrawn at any time if abused by birders.

Hidden Valley

From the state park, follow the directions for The Beanery, but continue north along Bayshore Rd. for 1.2 miles past the railroad tracks to the stop sign at New England Rd. Scan the wires around this intersection for Western Kingbird in October and November; the field on the southeast corner of this intersection attracted a Fork-tailed Flycatcher for three days in May 1984. Turn left onto New England Rd. and drive 0.3 miles to the parking lot for the Hidden Valley access for Higbee Beach WMA. Watch for Cattle Egret in the fields along the way; this formerly abundant species has become uncommon in the state.

The 192-acre Hidden Valley Ranch was acquired by The Nature Conservancy in 1986 and transferred to the state Fish and Wildlife Division. Part of the property remains in active use as a riding stable, but most of the property is accessible through a network of trails (see map). The trail from the parking lot makes a loop around an open field that is good for Bobolinks and sparrows in migration and for many songbirds along the edges. It is also a busy spot for migrant raptors in the fall, when a hawk banding operation is set up in the adjacent field.

At the southwest corner of the loop, a side trail branches off and passes by a small pond, which is a good spot for Green Heron and Eastern Phoebe. It then passes along the edge of a horse pasture and turns left to enter the wet woodland. Prothonotary Warbler nests in the woods, which are also good for migrants in spring and fall. Eventually, the trail emerges into a horse pasture. The field edges can be great for sparrows in October and many different migrants, in season. It is also a very good place for raptors, including kites. Mississippi Kite, Swallow-tailed Kite, and New Jersey's only White-tailed Kite have been seen from this field. To return to your car, retrace your route through the woods and complete the loop around the first field.

Higbee Beach

Higbee Beach WMA, which now includes Hidden Valley and the magnesite site, is a 1,003-acre preserve that was acquired by the New Jersey Division of Fish and Wildlife starting in the early 1980s, in recognition of its importance to migratory birds. It is the best place in Cape May for migrant songbirds, and is excellent for raptors as well. The combination of upland deciduous woods, weedy fields, beach, dunes (including the highest in New Jersey), and a well-developed low forest of American Holly, Eastern Red Cedar, Pitch Pine, and Beach Plum behind the dunes, provides a diversity of habitat that attracts and holds the hordes of migrants at Cape May in the fall. From the Hidden Valley parking area described above, continue west on New England Rd. for 0.9 miles to the end at the parking lot. If it is full, a second lot is on the south side, about 200 yards before the end of the road. Don't park on the sides of New England Rd., which is posted, or you will probably get a ticket. You can also take the dirt road on the right at the end of the pavement. This leads to the Cape May Canal, and there is room for parking near the end.

To be at Higbee Beach at dawn on the morning of a major fallout of migrants in late August, September, or October is an experience never to be forgotten. This usually happens only once or twice a year, when the right combination of cold front, clear skies, and northwest winds push a wave of songbirds down from the north. As day is breaking, many of these birds find themselves over the Cape May Peninsula or out over the ocean. Turning toward land and the protection offered by the woods at Higbee Beach, the birds swarm through the trees by the thousands. At such times, one can only stand in awe as the birds zoom by and hope to identify one in ten. As the sun rises higher, the passage slows down and it is easier to identify the many species present.

Even on days when there is only a minor flight of migrants, Higbee Beach can produce exciting birding. Many raptors roost in the trees at night, especially Osprey, Sharp-shinned Hawk, Cooper's Hawk, Peregrine Falcon, and Merlin, and in the morning they sit in the trees or fly about overhead. Northern Flickers are everywhere, flying from tree to tree and screaming in distress when pursued by a Sharpie. In late September and October, every locust tree plays host to Yellow-bellied Sapsuckers.

But it is mainly the songbirds that provide the excitement at Higbee Beach. All the migrant passerines that occur in New Jersey can be expected here in fall. Thirty species of warblers have been tallied in a single day, plus all of the vireos and thrushes and most of the flycatchers. Sparrows arrive a bit later, and any species is likely to occur. Some of the more sought-after migrants that are found at Higbee are Olive-sided Flycatcher (in late August), Yellow-bellied Flycatcher (fairly common), Western Kingbird (rare), Gray-cheeked Thrush (late September to early October), Philadelphia Vireo (fairly common), Orange-crowned Warbler (regular in October), Connecticut Warbler (almost daily in September), Mourning Warbler, Dickcissel, Clay-colored Sparrow (annual), Lark Sparrow (annual), LeConte's Sparrow (rare), and Henslow's Sparrow (very rare). Rarities that have occurred here in recent years are Anhinga, Magnificent Frigatebird, Swallow-tailed Kite, Mississippi Kite, Common Ground-Dove, Ash-throated Flycatcher, Bell's Vireo, Townsend's Warbler, Swainson's Warbler, and Painted Bunting.

Although the Cape May area is known primarily for its fall migration, spring can also produce some excellent flights of migrant passerines. Under the right conditions, Higbee Beach can be alive with the songs and calls of vireos, warblers, tanagers, orioles, and grosbeaks. As in fall, they don't tend to linger, but one can run up a good list in a couple of hours of birding, then head north to Belleplain for the nesting species there.

Higbee Beach is not noted for its diversity of breeding birds, but it does have good populations of Chuck-will's-widow, Carolina Wren, White-eyed Vireo, Yellow-breasted Chat, and Blue Grosbeak. In late fall and winter, there are many American Woodcock and numerous sparrows, plus a few year-round residents, such as Carolina Chickadee, Tufted Titmouse, and Northern Cardinal.

The best birding at Higbee Beach is along the trails and dirt roads that radiate from the parking area. At the entrance to the parking area, a road on the right leads down to the Cape May Canal. This road can be driven, but it is better to walk it, as the birding is excellent. After several hundred yards, the road emerges into some *Phragmites*. Here there is a spoil dike of dredgings from the canal. Climb up on the dike and walk right to where you approach the woods. This spot provides an excellent vantage point for seeing birds moving through the woods, as you are high enough for them to be at eye level.

The best birding at Higbee is usually along the edges of the fields numbered on the map, especially fields 1 and 3. Well-maintained trails provide good access to all these areas, which can be covered in a couple of hours. The central path between fields 1 and 3 is bordered by small trees on both sides and can be especially good for chat and migrants. It leads to the pond in field 2, where you may find a heron or sandpiper. Ospreys like to sit in the trees around the edges of the fields to eat the fish that they catch in Delaware Bay. The trail along the west sides of fields 3, 4, and 5 is also excellent for migrants and eventually leads into some woods at the end of field 5. If you have time, you can follow it to the beach or on to Davey's Lake, a small pond hidden in the dunes, then walk back along the beach to the short trail that leads to the parking lot.

Note: Higbee Beach is a WMA and is used by American Woodcock hunters, primarily in November and December. Although you can bird the area at these times, it is advisable to stay out of the woods and to wear bright clothing, preferably a blaze orange cap or vest. Sundays are best, because there is no hunting.

Cape May City

Cape May city offers birding only along the oceanfront, but the Second Ave. jetty is a good local spot for Purple Sandpiper, Red-throated Loon, Great Cormorant, Northern Gannet, and various other seabirds. To reach the jetty from the state park, take Lighthouse Ave. back to Sunset Blvd. and turn right. Follow Sunset 1.7 miles back to the traffic light at Broadway and turn right. Go 0.4 miles to Beach Ave., turn right, then go 0.2 miles to the end of the road and park on the left.

The jetty is the last jetty in town, and protects the cove that stretches between Cape May city and Cape May Point. From the edge of the jetty, scan the ocean and the cove. In addition to the species mentioned above, Common Eider and King Eider are often seen here from late fall to early spring, usually with a flock of Black Scoters. There are many other jetties northward along Beach Ave., but they seldom have much to offer. Royal Terns are common on the beaches in late summer, and Bonaparte's Gulls are offshore from fall through spring. A large flock of Black Skimmers roosts here in the fall.

☈

Heislerville Wildlife Management Area– Thompsons Beach

The Heislerville WMA, located along the Delaware Bayshore in southeastern Cumberland County, comprises almost 4,000 acres of diked salt-hay marshes, impoundments, tidal marshes, and pine/oak upland. Access to the area is from three roads: Matts Landing, East Point, and Thompsons Beach Roads. East Point Rd. provides the only access to Delaware Bay, while the road at Thompsons Beach now ends at a tidal observation area.

Waterbirds are the main attraction at Heislerville. A variety of herons and egrets can be found here from spring to fall, although there are no known heronries nearby. Migrant waterfowl include a good selection of puddle ducks in the ponds and large concentrations of Snow Geese (offshore). Many species of shorebirds occur in the impoundments at Heislerville and at Thompsons Beach, but the best show is the spectacular concentrations of Ruddy Turnstones, Red Knots, Sanderlings, and Semipalmated Sandpipers that gather along the bayshore in late May. Sometimes numbering in the hundreds of thousands, these flocks are the biggest spring gatherings of shorebirds on the east coast of North America.

Among the rarities that have been reported from the Heislerville area are Brown Pelican, White Ibis, Greater White-fronted Goose, Black-necked Stilt, Curlew Sandpiper, Ruff, and Northern Wheatear, Loggerhead Shrike, and Townsend's Solitaire. Noteworthy nesting birds include Least Bittern, Osprey, Bald Eagle, Yellow-throated, Prothonotary, and Kentucky warblers, Blue Grosbeak, and Orchard Oriole. Sedge Wren and Henslow's Sparrow were formerly common nesters along the Bayshore through the late 1950s and may someday return.

Directions

To reach Thompsons Beach: From the Philadelphia area, take I-76 or 676 south to Rt. 42, the North-South Freeway. Exit at Rt. 55 and go about 41 miles to the end of Rt. 55 at Rt. 47. Continue on Rt. 47 for about 5.7 miles to Rt. 740 (Dorchester-Heislerville Rd.), and turn right. In 0.4 miles, continue straight onto High St., then bear right in 0.2 miles onto Main St. (Rt. 616). Go 2.3 miles to a T intersection at East Point Rd. (Glade Rd.). Turn left, go two hundred yards, and turn right onto Thompsons Beach Rd. Drive 1.2 miles to the end of the road at the parking lot.

From the north, take I-295 to Exit 26 (Rt. 42, the North-South Freeway), follow Rt. 42 for about 1.7 miles and exit onto Rt. 55 South. Proceed as already described.

From the coast, take the Garden State Parkway to Exit 25 (Marmora). Go west into Marmora to the traffic light at Rt. 9, continue straight ahead for 0.1 miles and turn left onto Rt. 631 (Tuckahoe Rd.). Drive about 4.3 miles to the traffic light at Rt. 610. Turn left onto Rt. 610 and follow it for about 8.5 miles to Rt. 47, and turn right. Take Rt. 47 another 8.5 miles to Glade Rd., and turn left. Go 1.6. miles to Thompsons Beach Rd., turn left, and proceed as already described.

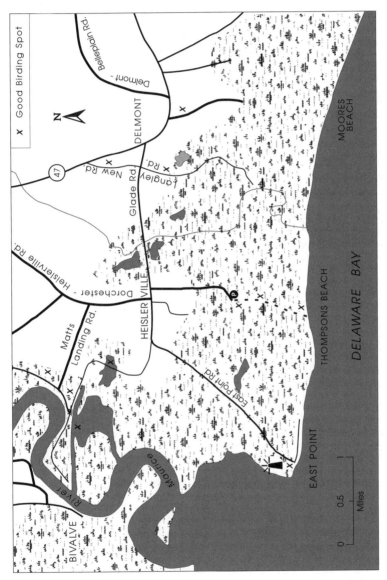

Map 92. Heislerville–Thompsons Beach

Birding

The impoundments at Thompsons Beach are now part of the Maurice Township Wetlands Restoration Project of Public Service Electric & Gas. At the parking lot there is an observation tower that provides a good elevated view of the creek and marshes. The area is at its best during the spring shorebird migration, especially in the last half of May and early June, when the horseshoe crabs are mating and laying eggs. Birds come and go with the changing tide. Best times seem to be about half-way between the low and high tides, which occur about two hours later than at Cape May.

At the appropriate times, tens of thousands of shorebirds gather at the impoundments. The majority by far are Semipalmated Sandpipers, but many other species occur, as well. Regular visitors are Semipalmated and Black-bellied plovers, Greater and Lesser yellowlegs, Dunlin, Stilt, Least, and White-rumped sandpipers, Ruddy Turnstone, Short-billed Dowitcher, Red Knot, and Sanderling.

The remains of the former Thompsons Beach Rd. form a dike that stretches for 0.75 miles from the parking lot to the Delaware Bayshore. You can walk this road, although you may need wading boots at times because of the mud and high water. This puts you out among the masses of shorebirds, which fly away to let you pass, only to return to the road and mudflats as soon as you move by. At the end of the road is yet another spectacle of shorebirds feeding on the eggs of horseshoe crabs. The biggest concentrations of Ruddy Turnstone, Sanderling, and Red Knot prefer to stay on the outer beaches, where the tides are an hour or so earlier.

Nesting birds in the marshes of Thompsons Beach include Osprey (on artificial nest platforms), Clapper Rail, Seaside Sparrow, Saltmarsh Sharp-tailed Sparrow, and Red-winged Blackbird. Rarities seen here include White Ibis, Curlew Sandpiper (up to three in 2001), and Black-necked Stilt.

Upon returning to Glade Rd., go left toward East Point. After one block, you will pass the Dorchester-Heislerville Rd. on the right. Continue straight ahead on what is now called East Point Rd. In about 0.5 miles the road will bend left and a dirt road will continue straight ahead. Don't take the dirt road now, but note it for the return trip. East Point Rd. continues for another 2.4 miles to a quaint little lighthouse on Delaware Bay. Along the way it passes through some woodland and a great deal of salt marsh. The beach at East Point is another good spot for the masses of shorebirds in late spring. Both Loggerhead Shrike (twice) and Townsend's Solitaire (once) have wintered along this road in recent years.

Head back toward Heislerville and turn left on the previously noted dirt road, which leads to a dike along several impoundments. After about 0.6 miles, you will reach a water-control structure separating the impoundment on the right from the tidal salt marsh on the left. This is a good area for

Green Heron

herons and egrets, ducks, and shorebirds. If the water in the impoundment is not too deep, at high tide it is an excellent spot for shorebirds.

Continue along the dike and you will soon come to another impoundment. Forster's Terns hover over the pond in search of fish, and Black-crowned and Yellow-crowned night-herons can sometimes be seen roosting in the trees at the east edge of the pond. To your left is the mouth of the Maurice River. At low tide, a vast expanse of mudflats is exposed and in migration tens of thousands of shorebirds will be feeding on them. Unfortunately, most of them will be too far away to identify, even with a telescope; as the tide rises, they are forced in closer to the dikes, so your chances are improved. (High tide at East Point occurs about one-and-a-half hours later than the published tides for Sandy Hook and Cape May Harbor, and about four hours earlier than high tide at Philadelphia; the tides at Heislerville are a little bit later).

The dike road ends at Matts Landing Rd. Turn right toward Heislerville, and go about 1.5 miles to the junction with Main St. (Rt. 616, Dorchester-Heislerville Rd). Turn left to return to Rt. 47, and go about 1.7 miles to the fork where Rt. 616 bears left and Dorchester-Heislerville Rd. bears right. Just beyond the fork is a bridge over a stream with wet woodlands on either side. There is always at least one pair of Kentucky Warbler nesting here. Continue another 0.3 miles to Rt. 47.

⌖

Peaslee Wildlife Management Area

One of the larger, at more than 18,000 acres, but least birded WMAs, Peaslee is located primarily in eastern Cumberland County, with small sections in Atlantic and Cape May Counties. It has more of a Pine Barrens flavor than does nearby Belleplain. Nevertheless, Peaslee has many of the same birds that draw so many birders to Belleplain, it just requires a little more searching and exploring off the beaten path to find them. The following description is based on material provided by Clay Sutton.

The forested wetlands of the upper Manumuskin River in the northwestern part of Peaslee have Acadian Flycatcher, Yellow-throated Vireo, Prothonotary, Black-and-white, Yellow-throated, and Hooded warblers, American Redstart, Ovenbird, and Louisiana Waterthrush. The same species can be found in the headwaters of Muskee Creek in the southwestern part between Rt. 49 and Rt. 548.

Directions

See Map 84. Follow the directions for Dividing Creek but instead of exiting Rt. 55 at Rt. 47 continue another 3 miles to Exit 24 (Rt. 49, Cumberland Rd.). Go east on Rt. 49 for about 4.8 miles to Hesstown Rd., Rt. 644, and turn left. [DeLorme 69, H-19]

Birding

Unlike Belleplain, there is no traditional route for birding Peaslee. Drive north on Hesstown Rd. (also known as Dorothy Rd. and, farther along as Beaver Rd.) and you will enter the main part of Peaslee after about 1 mile. In about 0.6 miles, there is a dirt road on the left, which can be traveled (with caution). It will lead you deeper into the wilds of Peaslee and eventually come to a junction where you can turn left to head back to Rt. 49 or right to go even deeper into the WMA. To reach another point of entry, continue on Rt. 644 for 3.4 miles from Rt. 49 to an unmarked gravel road on the left (shown as Main Ave. on some maps). This road and many unmarked roads and paths off it provide additional access to the interior of Peaslee.

Wild Turkey and Northern Bobwhite are widespread throughout the WMA, especially near fields. Check any wet woods or stream area for most of the breeding birds noted above. In the more open areas you may encounter Red-headed Woodpecker, Eastern Bluebird, Summer Tanager, Northern and Orchard orioles, plus many typical Pine Barrens species. In winter, the fields and hedgerows are good for sparrows and other passerines.

Returning to Rt. 49 and Hesstown Rd., continue east on Rt. 49 for 1.7 miles to Cumberland Rd. (also known as Estell Manor Rd., Rt. 637). A left turn will take you through more of the WMA, while the road to the right has WMA on its right for 3 miles. Continuing on Rt. 49 from Cumberland Rd. for 3 miles will bring you to Hunters Mill Pond on the left. This pond is formed by a dam on the Tuckahoe River and can sometimes be good for waterfowl when the water level is high.

Just before you come to Hunters Mill Pond there is a dirt road on the right, Hunters Mill Rd. Take this road south for 1.9 miles to Rt. 548, Weatherby Rd. Along the way there are a couple of side roads to be explored. At Weatherby Rd., you can turn left to bird the next 3 miles, which has Peaslee WMA on the left (north) and Belleplain State Forest on the right (south) side.

Union Lake Wildlife Management Area

One of the newest WMAs, this tract contains almost 5,000 acres of pine-oak woodland and deciduous forest, as well as Union Lake, the largest lake in southern New Jersey. It is located on the outskirts of Millville, Cumberland County. The birdlife in this WMA is similar to that in the Edward G. Bevan WMA, just south of Millville (see Dividing Creek chapter). Among the more interesting breeding species is Summer Tanager.

Directions

Take Rt. 55 to Sherman Ave. (Rt. 552), about 4 miles north of downtown Millville. Go west on Sherman for about 1.5 miles to a dirt road on the left and a sign marking the entrance to the WMA. [DeLorme 68, C-9]

Birding

You can follow the dirt road for almost 3 miles through the tract, to the junction with Carmel Rd., just west of Millville. The nesting season offers the best birding along the road, especially in the area where the road crosses Mill Creek, about 1.4 miles from Sherman Ave. Near the south end there is a side road that leads left to a parking area on the lake, where you can scan for waterfowl, loons, cormorants, and possibly a Bald Eagle. Union Lake, 898 acres, was created in 1868 by construction of a dam on the Maurice River. From this point on, the Maurice River flows unimpeded into Delaware Bay.

If the dirt road should be impassable, as it sometimes is, the same point can be reached by returning to Sherman Ave., driving 1.7 miles west to Carmel Rd. (Rt. 608), turning left and going about 3.4 miles to the dirt road and sign for the WMA on the left. Another vantage point for scanning the lake is near the dam at the south end. Continue on Carmel Rd. for 0.7 miles to Rt. 49, go left for 0.25 miles to Sharp St. and turn left. Take Sharp St. 0.7 miles to Sunset Dr. and turn left into Union Lake Park, where you have a good view of the water and surrounding trees.

Another good spot for birding along the river is the Maurice River Causeway. To reach this point, return to Rt. 49 and go east for 1 mile to the intersection with Rt. 47. Turn right and follow Rt. 47 south for about 8 miles to the traffic light at Rt. 670. Turn right and proceed through a second traffic light onto the Maurice River Causeway. About 1 mile from the second light, there is a pulloff on the right, where you can drive down to the Maurice River. This is an excellent spot to scan for raptors in winter; Bald Eagle is a daily occurrence, usually several of them. For a view down the river, take the

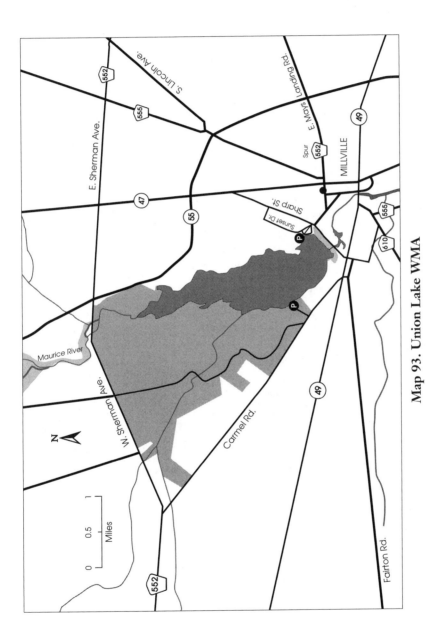

Map 93. Union Lake WMA

short dead-end road opposite the pulloff. From here you have a good view of scenic historic Mauricetown. In late August, thousands of Purple Martins gather on the wires in town in the evening prior to their departure on migration.

✝

Dividing Creek and Vicinity

Bald Eagle, Black and King rails, Acadian Flycatcher, Sedge Wren, Northern Parula, Yellow-throated, Prothonotary, Worm-eating, Kentucky, and Hooded warblers, Summer Tanager, Blue Grosbeak, and Orchard Oriole are just a few of the many species that nest in the vicinity of the village of Dividing Creek in Cumberland County. Except for the wren, all of these species occur annually, and most of them are fairly common. This interesting variety of breeding birds attracts increasing numbers of birders from all parts of New Jersey and neighboring states.

The Cumberland County June Bird Count focuses on the Dividing Creek area and turns up 130–140 species. Although the list includes numerous migrant shorebirds and summering nonbreeders, it reflects the tremendous variety of birdlife to be found here in the early summer. The following list of birding spots concentrates on the more unusual species, but in searching for them, you will encounter a long list of the more common birds of southern New Jersey. Nearby Heislerville WMA and Thompsons Beach, also excellent birding spots from spring through fall, are covered separately.

Although the Dividing Creek area is noted mainly for its breeding birds, it also has a high diversity of wintering species. Large numbers of raptors feed and roost in the woods and marshes along Delaware Bay at this season, including a few Bald and Golden eagles. Nearby Fortescue has long been famous for the spectacular concentrations of Snow Geese that gather offshore in early spring. The PSE&G Wetland Restoration Site project in Commercial Township (Port Norris) has added some important areas for waterfowl and shorebirds.

Directions

From northern New Jersey or the Philadelphia area, take Rt. 55 south from Rt. 42, the North-South Freeway, for 33 miles to Exit 27 (Rt. 47 South). Take Rt. 47 into Millville for about 2.3 miles to the intersection with Rt. 49 (Main St.), then turn right. Go 0.3 miles to Cedar St., the second left after the

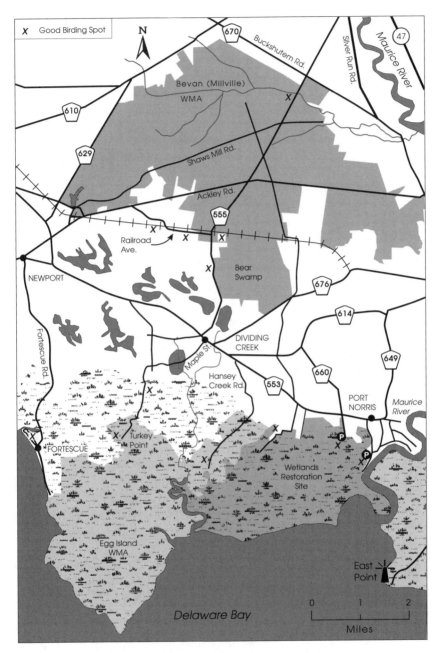

Map 94. Dividing Creek and Vicinity

bridge across the Maurice River, and turn left; this is Rt. 555. After about 0.2 miles, stay on Rt. 555 as it turns left onto Race St. (not well marked). Bear right with Rt. 555 at another poorly marked intersection about 1.2 miles further along. Continue south on Rt. 555 for almost 2 miles until you cross Buckshutem Rd., where you will enter the Edward G. Bevan WMA. About 0.3 miles beyond Buckshutem Rd., park on the right at a swampy area where Buckshutem Creek flows under the road. [DeLorme 68, I-11]

From coastal New Jersey, there are several options. The shortest is to take the Garden State Parkway to Exit 44 (Pomona). Follow Rt. 575 for 8 miles through Pomona to US 40. Take US 40 west for about 7 miles, past Mays Landing, to the junction with Rt. 552, which leads to Millville. Follow Rt. 552 and Spur Rt. 552 (continue straight ahead on the spur when Rt. 552 turns right) for 16 miles to Rt. 47 in Millville. Turn left and go one-half mile to the intersection with Rt. 49 (Main St.); proceed as described above.

Birding

The birding spots around Dividing Creek include several WMAs and much private land that can be birded from public roads. Observe No Trespassing signs and help make birders welcome.

The Edward G. Bevan WMA encompasses more than 12,000 acres of oak-pine forest in southern Cumberland County. Buckshutem Creek, where you have parked, is the main stream that drains the half of the WMA lying west of Rt. 555. The associated Buckshutem Swamp offers much interesting habitat. Prothonotary Warbler and Louisiana Waterthrush often can be heard singing from the spot. A dirt trail on the north side of the stream leads into the woods for one-half mile before turning away from the swamp. Here you might find Hooded Warbler, plus many more common species.

The best way to explore the WMA is with the help of a topographic map (Cedarville and Dividing Creek quadrangles). About 0.7 miles south of the creek, a dirt road (Shaw's Mill Rd.) goes right toward Newport. Two roads that turn right off Shaw's Mill Rd., one after 0.6 miles and another after 1.5 miles, will take you through some of the back woods areas toward the upstream sections of Buckshutem Creek.

Continue south on Rt. 555 toward Dividing Creek. About 3.6 miles south of Buckshutem Creek you will cross some railroad tracks and come to a paved road on the right. Park on the left, opposite the paved road, and walk east over a dirt mound (away from the paved road) along the dirt road that parallels the tracks. The tracks border the northern edge of Bear Swamp and provide some of the most interesting birding in the area. Species that nest here include Yellow-billed Cuckoo, Common Nighthawk, Whip-poor-will, Ruby-throated Hummingbird, Red-bellied Woodpecker, Acadian Flycatcher, Eastern Bluebird, Wood Thrush, Yellow-throated Vireo, Yellow-throated,

Pine, Prairie, Black-and-white, Kentucky, and Hooded warblers, American Redstart, Summer Tanager, Scarlet Tanager, and Chipping Sparrow. Although you can walk the road for almost 2 miles before coming to a sand plant that is private property, the first mile is the most productive.

Return to your car and drive west along the railroad tracks on the paved road toward the sand mine. After about 0.3 miles, there is a dirt road on the left. Park and walk down the dirt road, where, in 1975, the second known nesting of Summer Tanager in New Jersey in this century occurred (the first one being in 1955). Within two years, however, five male Summer Tanagers were found in the immediate vicinity, and from this foothold, the species spread north through most of the pine barrens to Middlesex County, though it is still uncommon.

Return to you car and continue along the paved road past the sand plant, where a large colony of Bank Swallows nest. About 1.3 miles from Rt. 555 the road crosses the railroad tracks. Park on the right and walk west along the railroad tracks for a few hundred yards. This area has nesting Barred Owl and Kentucky and Hooded warblers, plus numerous other species. The paved road continues through some mature deciduous woods to Ackley Rd., where a left turn will lead you toward Newport. Blue Grosbeak nests in the overgrown fields along the road.

Retrace your route back to Rt. 555 at the railroad tracks, and turn right toward Dividing Creek. Drive slowly south for the next few miles, stopping occasionally to listen for singing birds. Acadian Flycatcher and Yellow-throated, Prothonotary, Kentucky, and Hooded warblers are regulars along this stretch of road; Worm-eating Warbler has nested here, and Northern Parula seems to be making a comeback. The *dominica* race of the Yellow-throated Warbler first established itself as a breeding subspecies in New Jersey near Dividing Creek in the 1970s. Since then, it has spread east into Cape May County, north into Atlantic County, and even to Allaire State Park, Monmouth County.

The land along Rt. 555 is private, but the birds can be heard from the wide apron of the road and, usually, coaxed into view by squeaking or "pishing." About 1.5 miles south of the railroad tracks, the woods end and some borrow-pits appear on both sides of the road. Osprey, Belted Kingfisher, and various swallows are often around the ponds, and a loon or two usually lingers late in spring.

After another 0.8 miles, you will come to the junction with Rt. 553 in the town of Dividing Creek. Turn left and go about 200 yards east to Maple St. on the right; the junction is very inconspicuous, so watch carefully for the hidden street sign. Turn right on Maple and drive south toward Turkey Point. After about one-half mile, you will come to a causeway that crosses two tidal pools. Spotted Sandpipers are frequently on the rocks along the causeway. A little farther on are some agricultural fields on the right, where Killdeer and

Black-bellied Plover stop off in migration. About 1.4 miles south of Dividing Creek, Maple St. merges into Turkey Point Rd. Continue straight ahead on Turkey Point Rd., through a deciduous woods where both Chuck-will's-widow and Whip-poor-wills call at night.

After leaving the woods, the road continues another 0.75 miles to a dead-end, where there is an observation tower. Along the way you pass through a mixture of salt marsh, wet meadows, and small stands of trees. Sedge Wren has nested irregularly along this stretch in recent decades and Black Rail is an annual breeder, although virtually impossible to see. A couple of Yellow Rails were calling here in May 1999. From the tower you can scan the vast marshes of Turkey Point, which is not a point in the usual sense of the word (it is, in fact, 2 miles inland from Egg Island Point on Delaware Bay.)

King Rail and Virginia Rail are common nesters in the marshes of Turkey Point, and Short-eared Owl possibly breeds here on occasion. By day, you will see numerous herons and egrets, although they do not nest nearby. Both Northern Harrier and Bald Eagle nest in the area and may be seen hunting over the marshes or soaring above the trees.

Drive back toward Dividing Creek to the junction with Maple St., and turn left, following Turkey Point Rd. The next 0.6 miles is good for Yellow-breasted Chat, Blue Grosbeak, and Orchard Oriole. After about 1.5 miles you will rejoin Rt. 553. To reach Fortescue, which is famous for its Snow Geese in the spring, continue west on Rt. 553 for about 2.6 miles to Newport, then turn left on Fortescue Rd. (Rt. 637). Follow this road for about 3 miles to its end at Delaware Bay in Fortescue, where the Snow Geese gather.

Another good spot for night birds is Hansey Creek Rd. From the junction of Rts. 555 and 553 in Dividing Creek, go east on Rt. 553 for about 0.9 miles to Hansey Creek Rd., the first right turn after crossing the bridge over Dividing Creek. This road runs through woods, fields, and marshes for about 2 miles to its end at the northeast corner of the 2,000-acre Egg Island–Berrytown WMA. Great Horned Owl, American Woodcock, Chuck-will's-widow, and Whip-poor-will call from the wooded areas at night, while King Rail and Virginia Rail are abundant in the marshes.

Commercial Township Wetlands Restoration Sites

The wetlands restoration project covers 4,200 acres of wetland, forested upland and open fields south of Rt. 553 in the town of Port Norris. Several parking areas, boardwalks, and observation platforms provide a good access to the area. From the intersection of Rts. 555 and 553 in Dividing Creek, drive east on Rt. 553 for about 2.5 miles to Berrytown Rd., on the right. Follow Berrytown for 0.7 miles and turn right, birding along some fields and woodlands for another 0.6 miles to a dike. From here a narrow, one-lane road not well suited for low clearance vehicles leads 0.3 miles to the end in the marsh. You may choose to park and walk this last stretch.

Return to the right angle turn on Berrytown Rd. and turn right. Go about 300 yards and turn left, then drive another 0.25 miles to Robbinstown Rd. where there is a ramp for launching car-top boats. Drive north on Robbinstown Rd. for 0.6 miles to Rt. 553 and turn right. Continue 0.8 miles to the intersection with Rt. 660, which is named Strawberry Ave. or Warren Lane on different maps and signposts, but is referred to as Strawberry Ave. in the PSE&G literature. Turn right and drive one-half mile to the parking area, where a short trail leads to a boardwalk and observation platform. This is an excellent spot for observing waterfowl, herons and egrets, terns, Osprey, and many shorebirds.

Return to Rt. 553 (Main St.), go right for one-half mile to Rt. 631, High St., and turn right. Follow Rt. 631, which becomes Shell St., south for about 0.9 miles to the little fishing village of Bivalve and watch for a short street on the right, Germantown Ave., that leads 200 yards to a parking area. From the parking area, there is a boardwalk out into the marsh to another observation platform. Rt. 631, now called Lighthouse Rd., continues another 0.3 miles to another observation platform. A Nature Trail connects the Strawberry Ave., Germantown Ave., and Lighthouse Rd. sites.

To continue on toward Mauricetown, Heislerville, or Cape May, return to Rt. 553 and turn right. Drive 0.3 miles to Rt. 649, North Ave., and turn left. Mauricetown is 4 miles on Rt. 649.

☚

Dix Wildlife Management Area

Located about 4 miles west of the town of Fairton in southwestern Cumberland County, Dix WMA comprises 2,600 acres of agricultural fields, hedgerows, oak/holly woodland, salt marsh, and tidal creeks. In addition, large tracts of adjacent private lands provide even more wildlife habitat, much of which can be viewed from the roads. This area is roughly bounded by the Cohansey River on the north, Delaware Bay on the west, and extensive salt marsh to the south.

The WMA harbors an interesting selection of breeding birds in late spring to early summer, including many Yellow-breasted Chats, Indigo Buntings, Blue Grosbeaks, and Orchard Orioles. In winter, the varied habitat is a haven for sparrows and other songbirds, and has produced rarities such as

Sandhill Crane, Gyrfalcon, Northern Goshawk and Lincoln's Sparrow for the Cumberland County Christmas Bird Count.

Directions

From most of New Jersey, the easiest way to get to Fairton is to take State Rt. 55 south toward Vineland and Millville. Take Exit 29 (County Rt. 552) just north of Millville and go west on Rt. 552 for 6.2 miles to County Rt. 553 and turn left. Go south on Rt. 553 for about 5 miles to its intersection with County Rt. 601 in Fairton. [DeLorme 68, G-1]

From the coast, take State Rt. 49 west to Millville, and continue 8 miles to Rt. 553 at Gouldtown. Rt. 601 is about 3.6 miles south.

Birding

Dix WMA is situated in a remote and little-birded part of the state, and is a good destination for those who like to get away from the crowds. It is a patchwork of different habitats almost completely surrounded by salt marsh. The route suggested by Paul Guris takes you through the different habitat types, is suitable in winter or spring to summer, and should provide a good variety of species in just a few hours of birding.

From the intersection of Rt. 553 and Rt. 601 in Fairton, take Rt. 601 (Back Neck Rd.) west for 0.1 miles and turn right onto Duck Cove Rd. At the end of the road is a good view of the Cohansey River, where Bald Eagle can sometimes be seen perched in the trees nearby. Least Bittern has nested in the reeds along the river.

Return to Back Neck Rd., and go right for 3.7 miles to the entrance to the PSE&G Green Swamp Estuary Enhancement Project (A). The trail here should provide many of the common woodland birds. For another view of the Cohansey River marshes, walk 0.25 miles further on Back Neck Rd. to a boat ramp, where parking is not allowed.

The next stop on this tour of Dix is 0.6 miles beyond the PSE&G site (4.4 miles from Fairton), where a large field on the right has nesting Grasshopper Sparrow, Field Sparrow, and Eastern Meadowlark in season (B). This area is a private hunting preserve, so don't leave the road, but bird from the edge.

Another 0.3 miles on Back Neck Rd. brings you to the intersection with Schoolhouse Rd. (C). Don't turn now, but the corner is good for Eastern Bluebird, and the woods here and on Schoolhouse Rd. are excellent in the nesting season for woodpeckers, Great Crested Flycatcher, Wood Thrush, Ovenbird, and Scarlet Tanager.

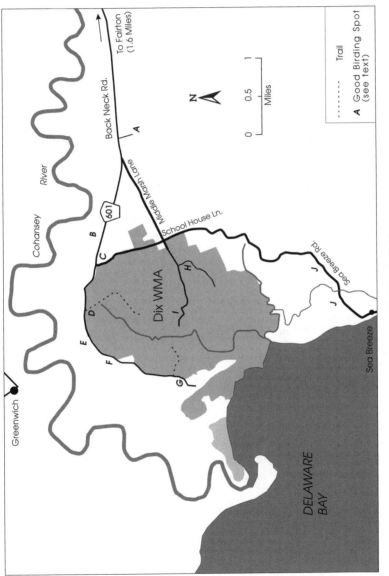

Greenwich

Cohansey River

601

Back Neck Rd.

To Fairton
(1.6 Miles)

Middle Marsh Lane

School House Ln.

A

B

C

D

E

F

G

H

I

J

Dix WMA

Sea Breeze Rd.

Sea Breeze

DELAWARE
BAY

N

0   0.5
Miles

.... Trail

A Good Birding Spot
   (see text)

Map 95. Dix WMA

Continue on Back Neck Rd. for 0.5 miles to a dirt road on the left (D). The New Jersey Division of Fish and Wildlife has planted numerous hedgerows here and elsewhere in the WMA to break up what were formerly large fields. These have grown to form a dense and impenetrable cover which, combined with overgrown wood edges, provides an abundance of habitat for passerines.

If there is no cable across the road, you can drive it (conditions permitting) for almost one-half mile. You'll probably find more birds by walking, however. During the breeding season, check the hedgerows and wood edges for Black-billed and Yellow-billed cuckoos, White-eyed Vireo, Yellow-breasted Chat, Indigo Bunting, and Blue Grosbeak. Willow Flycatcher nests on the right side of the road near the salt marsh, while Ruby-throated Hummingbird and Acadian Flycatcher have nested in the wet woods in back of the first field on the left.

In winter, this area and similar habitat in the WMA can be excellent for sparrows and other songbirds. White-throated Sparrow is the most common species, but Swamp, Song, Savannah, Tree, and Fox sparrows are usually here as well, along with Gray Catbird, Brown Thrasher, Eastern Towhee, and Dark-eyed Junco. The abundance of prey attracts many raptors, especially Cooper's and Sharp-shinned hawks. Red-tailed Hawks and Northern Harriers patrol the open areas.

The pavement continues another 0.3 miles, where there is a large farm field on the right and more good hedgerows on the left (E). You can bird the hedgerow for another 0.3 miles until the road (now dirt) enters a wooded area, where, in the breeding season you can expect the typical woodland species noted above (F).

The dirt road can be driven for another 1.3 miles as it passes through several changes of habitat, including a stand of dead trees where Northern Flicker is usually present. The wet woods along the road have both Barred Owl and Red-Shouldered Hawk in winter, and both may nest here, as well. When the road forks, you have reached private property (G).

Turn around and drive 2.4 miles back to Schoolhouse Rd. and turn right (C). Bird the woods for the next mile to the stop sign at Middle Marsh Lane. At night, this stretch of road is one of the better areas for Whip-poor-will and Chuck-will's-widow.

Turn right at the stop sign and drive 0.3 miles (the pavement ends after about 0.2 miles) to another dirt road on the left (H). Turn here and bird the road for the next 0.7 miles; if you drive, be especially wary of the road conditions in wet weather. Orchard Oriole is common in the breeding season along this stretch, which passes through a variety of good habitat.

Return to the last intersection and turn left. Drive 0.6 miles, past a pond on the right that has had nesting Green Heron, to some pines on the right. The area opens up to a large farm field on the right and a big hedgerow

ahead (I). Don't attempt to drive any further, as the road rapidly deterio-
rates. Park and walk to the hedgerow, which seems to harbor a variety of
birds at any season.

As you walk back toward your car, watch for a narrow path on the right
that runs along the top of an old dike, now covered with trees. After about
200 yards, you will come to an open area of the marsh with tidal creeks and
mudflats visible. This is a good area for waterfowl and shorebirds.

The last stop on this tour is the tiny town of Sea Breeze, which consists
of a small set of vacation cottages. Go back to Schoolhouse Rd. and turn
right. This road meanders through woodlands, farm fields and finally salt
marsh for 3.4 miles until it comes to a dead end in Sea Breeze at Delaware
Bay. Common breeding birds in the salt marsh (J) are Black Duck, Clapper
Rail, Marsh Wren, and Seaside Sparrow. In winter, there are usually many
Northern Harriers and Red-tailed Hawks, and Rough-legged Hawk, Peregrine Falcon, Merlin, and Short-eared Owl have all been seen. Scan the bay
at the end of the road for scoters and other diving ducks.

🦆

Johnson Sod Farm and Vicinity

The productivity of sod farms varies over the years, but at the turn of the century, Johnson Sod Farm is the best spot in the state to find some of the shorebirds attracted to this type of habitat. From August through September, this
farm in northwestern Cumberland County is excellent for Upland Sandpiper,
Buff-breasted Sandpiper, American Golden Plover, the occasional Baird's
Sandpiper, and the omnipresent Killdeer. Adding to the recent interest in this
area has been the continuing presence of a small group of Sandhill Cranes,
including an apparent nesting pair, often seen at nearby Bostwick Lake.

Directions

Take the New Jersey Turnpike to Exit 2 (US 322). At the end of the ramp,
turn right onto US 322 and go east for 3.3 miles through the town of Mullica
Hill, where US 322 joins Rt. 45. When US 322 turns left, continue straight
ahead on Rt. 45 for another one-quarter mile, then turn left onto Rt. 77, the
Bridgeton Pike, toward Bridgeton. After about 12 miles, you will cross
Rt. 611 (Elmer-Shirley Rd.) In one-quarter mile, you will come to the

Cumberland County line and then in another 1.1 miles you will come to Griers Lane (Rt. 688), and the beginning of the sod farm, on the left. [DeLorme 61, K-28]

Birding

You can bird along the east side of Rt. 77, but pull well off this heavily traveled road to scan the fields. Even better, if the birds are accessible, use one of the side roads that lead east away from Rt. 77 along the edges of the sod farm. The first of these is Griers Lane and the second is Hannans Lane, Rt. 690, another 0.6 miles south. The sod farm continues for about another 0.4 miles, just past Friesburg Rd., Rt. 640, on the right. It may take a little exploring to locate the birds on the large expanse of grass, but they tend to stay in loose flocks rather than spread out over the whole area. A spotting scope is useful.

To search for the Sandhill Cranes, take Friesburg Rd. west from Rt. 77. The cranes have been seen in many different spots in an area bounded roughly by Friesburg Rd. on the north, Seeley Rd. on the west, Walters Rd. on the south, and Rt. 77 on the east. One regular spot is the sometimes dry Bostwick Lake, which is off Friesburg Rd. about 1.7 miles west of Rt. 77 (stay right at the fork after 1 mile).

Pelagic Trips

Boat trips out into the Atlantic Ocean offer the only opportunity to see some of the seabirds that rarely or never come close to shore at our latitudes. And, for species that do occur more regularly within sight of land, boat trips offer the best opportunity for observing these birds closely and in large numbers. Pelagic birding is the last frontier for bird explorers in North America, and the information gathered on pelagic trips continually produces surprises. The oceans are large and interconnected and seabirds wander widely. No other type of birding activity can match pelagic trips for the possibility of the sudden appearance of an extreme rarity, nor can any activity match the endless, inescapable hours of boredom that can haunt an unsuccessful trip across an empty sea. The rewards can be spectacular, however, as in October 1984, when a chartered pelagic trip out of Barnegat Light, New Jersey, found a Buller's Shearwater—a species never before recorded in the Atlantic Ocean.

Opportunities to go on organized pelagic trips out of New Jersey are, unfortunately, few. The only regularly scheduled trips are by Focus on Nature Tours, Wilmington, Delaware, and by Alan Brady or Paul Guris from the Delaware Valley Ornithological Club. These are typically run from Brielle, Monmouth County or Cape May. The best way to stay informed about organized pelagic trips is to check the various web sites or call the rare bird alerts (RBAs) regularly; when a trip is planned it will be advertised on the RBAs.

There are other ways to see pelagic birds, however. You can always make a pelagic trip on your own, especially if you are already familiar with some of the species you are likely to see. Innumerable party fishing boats depart regularly during most of the year from ports along the New Jersey coast, such as Atlantic Highlands, Belmar, Point Pleasant, Barnegat Light, Atlantic City, and Cape May. Most of the boats do not go that far offshore, but many of them go 30 to 40 miles out, which is far enough to see some of the pelagic species. A few boats make scheduled trips farther offshore, including some to

DA Sibley 1985

Storm-Petrels

the Hudson Canyon (about 90 miles out) for tuna and tilefish. "The Canyon," as it is known to birders and fishermen alike, is the destination of most of the chartered pelagic trips out of Barnegat Light, because it is the beginning of the deeper water and is the place where the largest numbers of seabirds are found off the New Jersey coast. Many (but not all) of the captains who sail to the Hudson Canyon are willing to take birders along, usually at a substantial discount from the price the fishermen pay; the only requirement is that you stay out of the way. If you are interested in such a trip, watch the Philadelphia, Newark, or New York City newspapers for ads for trips to the Hudson Canyon, then call the captain to see if he will take you along as a nonfishing rider for a reasonable fee ($40–$50 for a 24-hour trip); the worst he can say is no.

If you go on the chartered pelagic trip at the end of May, you can expect to see Cory's Shearwater (a few), Greater Shearwater (many), Sooty Shearwater (many), Wilson's Storm-Petrel (very many), Red-necked Phalarope (usually a few), Pomarine Jaeger, and South Polar Skua (one or two most years). Other species often seen at the season are Northern Fulmar, Manx Shearwater (annual in recent years), Leach's Storm-Petrel, Northern Gannet (stragglers), Red Phalarope, Parasitic Jaeger, Long-tailed Jaeger, and Arctic Tern. A pelagic trip in summer or early fall should produce larger numbers of Cory's Shearwaters and possibly Bridled Tern. All New Jersey records of Audubon's Shearwater are from July and August, and there are a few summer records of White-faced Storm-Petrel and Band-rumped Storm-Petrel, mostly from beyond 100 miles offshore. Sabine's Gull is a possibility in September and October.

From late fall to early spring, different species of seabirds can be expected. Northern Fulmar is a rare, but regular, visitor at this season. Northern Gannet is common, as is Black-legged Kittiwake. The few records of Great Skua for New Jersey have been on pelagic trips from November to March. Winter is also the season to look for alcids, which can be frustratingly difficult to identify because they dive at the approach of a boat, or speed away on whirring wings. Dovekie, Razorbill, and, more recently, Atlantic Puffin are the most frequently encountered species, but Thick-billed Murre is possible. The murre is more apt to be seen along the shore, but even there it is rare.

In addition to the birding opportunities, pelagic trips also offer the chance to see marine mammals. Fin Whale, Pilot Whale, Common Dolphin, and Bottle-nosed Dolphin are the species most frequently encountered off New Jersey, but Minke Whale, Right Whale, and Risso's Dolphin (Grampus) have been seen. There are many other possibilities in North Atlantic waters, especially from late spring to late fall.

Another option for birders who want to see seabirds is to take a pelagic trip from one of the nearby states. There are occasional trips run from Montauk, Long Island, by the Federation of New York State Bird Clubs. These trips, which are irregularly scheduled, are advertised on the New York Rare Bird Alert—(212) 970-3070. Farther afield are the many whale-watching and bird-watching trips run from Cape Cod, Massachusetts, by the Brookline Bird Club, Massachusetts Audubon Society, Manomet Bird Observatory, and other organizations.

Be sure to take along plenty of warm clothing on a pelagic trip, preferably with a waterproof outer layer. The long hours of wind and wet can chill you to the bone. It is always colder that you think it will be, especially in late spring, when the warm temperatures on land can deceive you; the ocean warms up much more slowly than does the land. If you are at all prone to motion sickness, be sure to take something to help ward off seasickness—nothing can be more agonizing than a 24-hour pelagic trip during which you are seasick for 23 hours. In addition to the pills or ear patches used to prevent motion sickness, many birders take along a generous supply of pretzels, crackers, or similar fat-free munchies and keep nibbling on them constantly. Sometimes it even works.

Hawk Watching

Fall hawk watching continues to grow in popularity and has even spread to the American tropics, but some of the best sites in the United States are in or near New Jersey. Cape May is nationally famous for enormous numbers of accipiters and falcons during fall migration, while nearby Hawk Mountain in Pennsylvania is equally famous for its large flights of buteos, numerous eagles, and many other species. Several lesser-known places in northern New Jersey are part of the same migratory flyway as Hawk Mountain; however, these places usually get smaller numbers of birds. A few other hawk-watching sites in neighboring parts of New York and Pennsylvania are also frequented by New Jersey birders. Most of the regularly staffed hawk watches are members of the Hawk Migration Association of North America, which compiles and coordinates data. The association maintains an excellent and informative Web site at http://www.hmana.org.

Except for the coastal locations, all of the hawk-watching sites are associated with mountain ridges. In fall, many species of raptors follow the ridges, which provide updrafts that assist the birds' flight as they work their way south. The best conditions for a big hawk flight usually occur a day or two after the passage of a cold front, followed by strong northwesterly winds. However, good flights are possible whenever there is a northerly wind. Large Broad-winged Hawk movements have been observed on southerly winds, but the bigger buteos and eagles generally appear only when the wind has a northerly component.

The fall migration begins in late August, and the largest numbers of Ospreys, Bald Eagles, Broad-winged Hawks, and American Kestrels occur in September. Late September and early October are the peak times for Merlin and Peregrine Falcon, both of which occur mainly along the coast. October is the prime month for Sharp-shinned and Cooper's hawks, while late October and early November bring most of the bigger raptors, such as Northern Goshawk, Red-shouldered, Red-tailed, and Rough-legged hawks, and Golden

Sharp-shinned Hawk

Eagle, Turkey Vulture, many of which are nonmigratory, and Northern Harrier occur throughout the season. Rarities such as Swainson's Hawk and Gyrfalcon occur annually but unpredictably at one hawk-watching site or another, so there is always the unexpected to anticipate.

Hawk watching is the most sociable of birding activities; hours of staring at the horizon, often with long periods between hawks, are enlivened by discussions of birds, birders, birding locations, field guides, knotty identification problems, and the fortunes or misfortunes of the local pro football teams. Most of the sites mentioned below are staffed on a fairly regular basis (especially on weekends) by dedicated hawk watchers, so there is usually someone to talk to and to help in identifying the hawks. Trying to identify a distant raptor can be a frustrating experience for the beginner, so it helps to go to a site where knowledgeable raptor enthusiasts can provide assistance.

If you are going to one of the mountain ridge sites, be sure to dress warmly—it is always much colder than you think it will be. On the best days in October and November you may be standing outside for hours in 30- or 40-degree temperatures with a 20-mile-per-hour northwest wind. Running around the hawk watch for exercise might warm you up a bit, but the other hawk watchers won't appreciate the distraction. A thermos of hot cocoa or other libation can help sustain a chilly birder on a cold, windy day.

Spring hawk watching is a generally neglected activity, although the Cape May Bird Observatory has run a hawk watch at Sandy Hook since 1979 and several of the ridge sites have been monitored occasionally. In recent years, the Montclair Hawk Watch has been monitored daily in spring. April is the biggest month; Sharp-shinneds and Kestrels predominate along the coast, while Broad-wings are the main species along the ridges.

The twelve sites listed below are separated according to state; the first nine are in New Jersey.

Raccoon Ridge, Warren County (Northwest)

The best of the northern New Jersey hawk-watching sites, this is also the most difficult to reach. Take I-80 west to Exit 12 (Rt. 521, Blairstown). Follow Rt. 521 north for 5 miles to Rt. 94 and turn left. Go about 3.8 miles to Walnut Valley Rd. and turn right (there is a Dairy Queen on the left just before the turn and a sign on the left directing you to turn right for the Yards Creek Pumped Storage Power Plant. Drive 2.6 miles on Walnut Valley Rd. to the entrance to the Yards Creek Power Plant. Stop at the gate and tell the guard that you are going hawk watching.

Note: Access to this site was closed in September 2001. Hopefully, it will reopen in the future.

Access has changed a couple of times in recent years, so the following may not be up-to-date. Continue on the road, staying right at the first fork, left at the second fork and right at the third fork (0.4 miles from the gate), following a road to a former Boy Scout Camp. After 1.1 miles (from the entrance), you will have entered the camp property and will find a parking area on the right; park here. Just ahead on the left, an old road starts up the mountain. Hike up this road for about 0.75 miles (staying right when the road forks just past an old stone building) until it intersects with the Appalachian Trail at the top of the ridge. Turn left onto the Appalachian Trail. The first lookout is a short distance up the trail, but the main lookout is an exposed outcropping of rocks about 0.25 miles southwest along the trail. Although the distance from the parking lot to the main lookout is only about 1 mile, the elevation gain is 700 feet (to 1,560 at the lookout). The strenuous hike takes 25 to 30 minutes.

The view from Raccoon Ridge is breathtaking. Looking down to the northwest, you will see the Delaware River, only a mile away as the Raven flies, but over 1,200 feet below. To the northeast you can see High Point, 30 miles away, and to the west, Camelback Mountain in the Poconos, only 15 miles distant. At Raccoon Ridge, the Kittatinny Mountains have narrowed to a single, steep ridge, so all of the hawks migrating along the chain are concentrated at this point; consequently, the numbers and variety of raptors at Raccoon are always better than at Sunrise Mountain, 22 miles to the northeast. This is the best place in northern New Jersey during the fall migration to see Osprey, Bald Eagle, Northern Goshawk, Golden Eagle, and Common Raven. Raven was formerly one of New Jersey's rarest birds, but is gradually increasing as a breeding bird in the northwest.

Scotts Mountain, Warren County (Northwest)

Follow the directions to Merrill Creek Reservoir Overlook Area Parking Lot. This is the site of the current hawk watch that was formerly run from the communications tower on Fox Farm Rd. All the regular fall migrants are seen here, although not usually in as large numbers as at Raccoon Ridge or Sunrise Mountain. On September 14, 1983, however, the biggest hawk flight recorded in New Jersey in recent years occurred at Scotts Mountain. The tally of 18,500 Broad-winged Hawks, 31 Ospreys, 18 N. Harriers, and 7 Bald Eagles shows that even the lesser-known spots can produce exciting results.

Sunrise Mountain, Sussex County (Northwest)

Follow the directions for Stokes State Forest (see that chapter) to Culvers Gap. Turn right at the sign for Sunrise Mountain onto Rt. 636 (Upper North Shore Rd.), go 0.2 miles, then turn left onto Sunrise Mountain Rd. Drive about 4 miles on this road, then bear right when the road forks at the sign for Sunrise Mountain. This road ends at a parking lot after another 0.75 miles.

Walk up the Appalachian Trail south (to your right as you enter the parking lot) for 200 yards to a covered pavilion on top of Sunrise Mountain. The best viewing is from the open area on the south side of the pavilion. This is the most popular hawk watch in northern New Jersey and is the second best, after Raccoon Ridge. All the usual species are seen here, including Northern Goshawk and Golden Eagle. Winter finches, including Purple Finch, Red and White-winged crossbills, Pine Siskin, and Evening Grosbeak often pass by later in the season. Boreal Chickadee has occurred at the hawk watch several times, and Townsend's Solitaire was seen here twice in the 1980s, including one that stayed a week in November 1980. There are primitive toilets at the parking lot.

Wildcat Ridge, Morris County (Northwest)

This was one of the lesser-known sites for hawk watching, but with the regular monitoring by Bill Gallagher has become increasingly popular and has an excellent raptor flight. The watch was founded in 1997, replacing a former watch conducted from the Rockaway Valley, and is manned in spring and fall. Information is at http://home.netcom.com/~billyg/.

Take I-80 to Exit 37 (Rockaway/Hibernia). Turn left at the traffic light onto Rt. 513 North, drive 6.3 miles north to Upper Hibernia Rd. and turn right. Follow Upper Hibernia Rd. for 2.7 miles (it becomes dirt) to a white gravel parking lot on the right at a brown sign reading Wildcat Ridge WMA, Hawk watch/Overlook Trail Access. Just past the parking area, on the left, are two white gate posts. Walk past the posts and turn right just before the yellow gate onto a trail marked by orange blazes. Take this trail to the hawk-watch site (20- to 25-minute walk).

From the north, take Rt. 23 to the exit for Rt. 513, LaRue Rd. and Green Pond Rd. Cross over Rt. 23, go a short distance, and turn right onto Green Pond Rd. (Rt. 513). Go south for 5.1 miles to Upper Hibernia Rd., and turn left. Follow the directions in the preceding paragraph.

Skyline Drive, Passaic County (Northeast)

This lookout is located on Ramapo Mountain in Ramapo Mountain State Forest. Take the Garden State Parkway to Exit 160 (Fair Lawn). Turn left at the end of the ramp onto Paramus Rd., then go about one-half mile to the exit for Rts. 4 and 208 (Fair Lawn and Hawthorne); this will put you on Rt. 4. After about 0.3 miles, bear right onto Rt. 208 toward Oakland. Follow Rt. 208 for about 11 miles to its end in Oakland, where it becomes West Oakland Ave. Go about one-half mile and turn right onto Skyline Dr., following the signs for Ringwood Manor. Go about 2.4 miles to where a pipeline right-of-way begins on both sides of the road. You can park on the right at the entrance to the pipeline right-of-way or continue a short distance along Sky-line Dr. and park on the side of the road just before a sign that reads "Bor-ough of Ringwood Helping Hands." Parking is difficult, so be careful. Cross to the west side of the road and take the Blue Dot Trail for a few hundred yards to the lookout. All the regular migrants can be seen at this site, espe-cially Broad-winged Hawks.

Montclair, Essex County (Northeast)

Take the Garden State Parkway to Exit 151 (Watchung Ave., Montclair). Drive west on Watchung Ave. or about 2.1 miles to its end at Upper Moun-tain Rd. then turn right. Continue north for about 0.7 miles to Bradford Ave. and turn left. Go about 0.1 miles on Bradford and take the second right turn, Edgecliff Rd. Follow Edgecliff for about 0.3 miles to a parking area on the right. The trail to the hawk lookout is on the south side of the street and leads to a former quarry, which is the hawk watch. Montclair gets most of the regu-lar migrants, but is best known for its Broad-wing flight, the peak year being 1974, with 23,899. Northern Goshawk and Golden Eagle are rare, but Bald Eagle is fairly common in September. This watch has been staffed regularly in fall for about 40 years, daily in recent years by Else Greenstone, who also monitors the flight in spring.

Chimney Rock, Somerset County (Central)

Chimney Rock Hawk Watch is located in Washington Valley Park, Martins-ville, at the southern end of the Watchung Ridges, and gets many of the same birds that pass over Montclair. The hawk-watch platform and parking lot are maintained by the Somerset County Park Commission and the watch is monitored daily in the fall by Chris Aquila and volunteers. Complete information, including several years of data are on the Web page at http://rci.rugters.edu/~magarell/chimney_rock/index.html.

From the north or south, take I-287 to the exit for US 22 East. Go east on US 22 for about 1 mile and exit right onto the jughandle turn at Vosseler Ave. Turn left onto Vosseler, cross over Rt. 22, and proceed uphill for 0.6 miles to unpaved, inconspicuous Miller Lane, on the left. Turn left onto the gravel road and proceed one-half mile to the parking lot. The short trail to the hawk watch begins at the far (west) end of the lot.

Sandy Hook, Monmouth County (North Coast)

Follow the directions in the chapter on Sandy Hook. The official hawk watch is located on an observation platform just north of parking Lot K, but any-where on the peninsula is good, especially along the beach. This is primarily a spring (especially April) hawk-watching site; Sharp-shins and Kestrels make up the bulk of the flight, but Merlin and Peregrine are regular, as are most of the other migrant raptors except eagles. Swallow-tailed Kite occurs once or twice annually, and Mississippi Kite is seen in most years.

Cape May, Cape May County (South Coast)

This is *the* place to see hawks along the coast in the fall. The hawk watch is described in detail in the section on Cape May.

Mount Peter, Orange County, New York

Take the Garden State Parkway and the New York Thruway to Exit 15 (Suffern, Rt. 17). Continue north on Rt. 17 for about 9 miles to Rts. 210 and 17A, then turn left. Go about 8 miles on this road until you reach Greenwood Lake, where Rt. 210 branches to the left. Follow Rt. 17A north for about 2 miles, watching for two large microwave towers. The hawk watch is at the crest of the ridge, where there is a New York State DEC sign and parking lot. The DEC has provided a platform from which the watch is maintained. The birds are much the same as at Montclair.

Bake Oven Knob, Lehigh County, Pennsylvania

Take I-78 west through Allentown to Exit 15 (Rt. 309). Go north on Rt. 309 for about 16 miles to the intersection with State Rd. 4024, Mosserville Rd. (2 miles past the Rt. 143 junction). Turn right onto Rt. 4024, go 2.1 miles, then turn left onto Ulrich Rd. (may be unmarked). When this road bends right after one-half mile, you should continue straight ahead on unpaved Bake Oven Rd. Follow Bake Oven Rd. up a steep hill to a parking lot. Walk north (right) along the Appalachian Trail to the two lookouts, one about one-third of a mile from the parking lot and the second about one-half mile from the lot. The birds here are basically the same ones seen at Hawk Mountain, which is 15 miles southwest along the same ridge, but there are far fewer people. The watch is regularly manned in the fall.

Hawk Mountain, Berks County, Pennsylvania

Take I-78 west to Allentown. Continue on I-78 (US 22) for 18 miles from the intersection with the Northeast Extension of the Pennsylvania Turnpike to Exit 11 (Rt. 143). Go north on Rt. 143 for about 3 miles, turn left toward Eckville at the sign for Hawk Mountain Sanctuary, and drive about 7 miles to the sanctuary. This is the most famous of all the hawk watches and the most heavily visited. The sanctuary is open all year (a small fee is charged on the trail to the lookout) and the watch is manned in spring and fall. The South Lookout is only 200 yards from the entrance, but the North Lookout (the better one) is about 0.7 miles along a rocky, winding trail. The Broad-wing flight in September can be spectacular, while mid-October boasts the greatest variety of species. Falcons are scarce, but excellent numbers of all the other regular migrants are recorded each year, including numerous Bald Eagles, Northern Goshawks, and Golden Eagles. Swainson's Hawk and Gyrfalcon have occurred. Every birdwatcher should make at least one fall pilgrimage to Hawk Mountain. Once you've done so, however, the crowds (almost 50,000 visitors each year) will probably make you want to do your hawk watching elsewhere.

Nature Clubs and Audubon Chapters

The largest and most active natural-history society in the state is the New Jersey Audubon Society, which operates nine nature centers and sponsors many field trips and educational programs. In addition, the centers are good sources of information about other nature activities or clubs in your area. Addresses for the nature centers sanctuaries are:

Cape May Bird Observatory
Center for Research and Education
600 Rt. 47 North
Cape May Court House, NJ 08210
(609) 861-0700

Cape May Bird Observatory
Northwood Center, 707 E. Lake Dr.
Cape May Point, NJ 08212
(609) 884-2736

Lorrimer Nature Center
790 Ewing Ave.
Franklin Lakes, NJ 07417
(201) 891-2185

Nature Center of Cape May
1600 Delaware Ave.
Cape May, NJ 08204
(609) 884-9590

Plainsboro Preserve Nature Center (to open in 2002)
Scotts Corner Rd.
Plainsboro, NJ 08536

Rancocas Nature Center
794 Rancocas Rd.
Mount Holly, NJ 08060
(609) 261-2495

Sandy Hook Bird Observatory
2 Hartshorne Dr.
Fort Hancock, NJ 07732
(732) 872-2500

Scherman-Hoffman Sanctuaries
P.O. Box 693, Hardscrabble Rd.
Bernardsville, NJ 07924
(908) 766-5787

Weis Ecology Center
150 Snake Den Rd.
Ringwood, NJ 07456
(973) 835-2160

There are presently seven chapters of the National Audubon Society active in New Jersey. For the names and addresses of the current membership chairmen and officers, contact the National Audubon Society, 700 Broadway, New York, NY 10003; (212) 979-3000. The chapters and the locus of their activities are:

Atlantic Audubon Society
P.O. Box 63
Absecon, NJ 08201

Bergen County Audubon Society
P.O. Box 235
Paramus, NJ 07653-0235

Highlands Audubon Society

Jersey Shore Audubon Society
P.O. Box 1800
Point Pleasant Beach, NJ 08742

Monmouth County Audubon Society
P.O. Box 542
Red Bank, NJ 07701
(732) USA-BIRD
http://www.monmouthaudubon.org
mcas01@bellatlantic.net

Morris Highlands Audubon Society
c/o J. Knapp
5 Geraldine Ct.
Denville, NJ 07834
(973) 627-1223

Washington Crossing Audubon Society
P.O. Box 112
Pennington, NJ 08537
(609) 730-8200

Some of the other bird and nature clubs around the state are:

Audubon Wildlife Society
P.O. Box 34
Audubon, NJ 08106
http://www.audubonwildlifesociety.org

Burlington County Natural Sciences Club
c/o Dr. Sam Moyer
911 Larkspur Pl. S.
Mt. Laurel NJ 08054
(856) 222-0713

The Fyke Nature Association
P.O. Box 141
Ramsey, NJ 07446
FykeNature@aol.com
http://www.FykeNature.org

Gloucester County Nature Club
c/o EIRC
606 Delsea Dr.
Sewell, NJ 08080

Hunterdon Nature Club
c/o Hunterdon County Park Headquarters
Rt. 31
Lebanon, NJ 08833

Montclair Bird Club
c/o Donna Traylor
34 Gunn Rd.
Branchville, NJ 07826

Sussex County Bird Club
P.O. Box 138
Lafayette, NJ 07848

Trenton Naturalists
c/o Mr. Louis Beck
7 W. Franklin Ave.
Pennington, NJ 08534

For the many New Jersey birders who live near Pennsylvania or in Pennsylvania, there are also multiple clubs to join.

Birding Club of Delaware County
35 Letitia Ln.
Media, PA 19063
(610) 565-2873

Bucks County Audubon Society
6324 Upper York Rd.
New Hope, PA 18938
(215) 297-5880

Delaware Valley Ornithological Club
Academy of Natural Sciences
19th and The Parkway
Philadelphia, PA 19103
http://www.acnatsci.org/dvoc/

Golden Eagle Birding Club
3554 New Hampshire Ave.
Easton, PA 18045

Lehigh Valley Audubon Society
P.O. Box 290
Emmaus, PA 18049
(610) 317-1618

Unami Audubon Society
P.O. Box 75
Harleysville, PA 19438
(610) 326-3874

Valley Forge Audubon Society
P.O. Box 866
Paoli, PA 19301
(610) 544-4217

Wyncote Audubon Society
1212 Edgehill Rd.
Abington, PA 19001
(215) 233-9090

Sea Ducks

DA Sibley 1985

Bibliography

Akers, James F. *All Year Birding in Southern New Jersey*. Pomona, NJ: Stockton State College, 1981.

American Birds. Published bimonthly by the National Audubon Society, 950 Third Avenue, New York, NY, 10022.

Birding. Published bimonthly by the American Birding Association, Box 4335, Austin, TX, 78765.

Boyle, William J., Jr. *New Jersey Field Trip Guide*. Summit, NJ: Summit Nature Club, 1979.

Brady, Alan, W. Ronald Logan, John C. Miller, George B. Reynard, and Robert H. Sehl. *A Field List of the Birds of the Delaware Valley Region*. Philadelphia: Delaware Valley Ornithological Club, 1972.

Bull, John. *Birds of the New York Area*. New York: Harper and Row, 1964.

Cassinia. Published annually by the Delaware Valley Ornithological Club, Academy of Natural Sciences, 19th and the Parkway, Philadelphia, PA, 19103.

Dann, Kevin. *25 Walks in New Jersey*. New Brunswick, NJ: Rutgers University Press, 1982.

Drennan, Susan R. *Where to Find Birds in New York State*. Syracuse, NY: Syracuse University Press, 1982.

Fables, David G., Jr. *Annotated List of New Jersey Birds*. Newark, NJ: Urner Ornithological Club, 1955.

Geffen, Alice. *A Birdwatcher's Guide to the Eastern United States*. Woodbury, NJ: Barrow's Educational Series, 1978.

Halliwell, Tom, Rich Kane, Laurie Larson, and Paul Lehman. *Historical Report of the New Jersey Bird Records Committee: Records of New Jersey Birds*, 26 (1), Spring 2000: 13–44.

Harding, John J., and Justin J. Harding. *Birding the Delaware Valley.* Philadelphia: Temple University Press, 1980.

Heintzelman, Donald S. *Autumn Hawk Flights: The Migrations in Eastern North America.* New Brunswick, NJ: Rutgers University Press, 1975.

———. *A Guide to Eastern Hawk Watching.* University Park, PA: Pennsylvania State University Press, 1976.

Lawrence, Susannah. *The Audubon Society Field Guide to the Natural Places of the Mid-Atlantic States: Coastal.* New York: The Hilltown Press, 1984.

Leck, Charles F. *The Birds of New Jersey: Their Habits and Habitats.* New Brunswick, NJ: Rutgers University Press, 1975.

———. *The Status and Distribution of New Jersey's Birds.* New Brunswick, NJ: Rutgers University Press, 1984.

Perrone, Steve, ed. *Guide to Wildlife Management Areas.* Trenton: Division of Fish and Wildlife, N.J. Dept. of Environmental Protection, Box CN400, Trenton, NJ 08625.

Pettingill, Olin S. *A Guide to Bird Finding: East of the Mississippi.* 2nd ed. New York: Oxford University Press, 1977.

Records of New Jersey Birds. Published quarterly by the New Jersey Audubon Society, 790 Ewing Avenue, Franklin Lakes, NJ, 07417.

Stone, Witmer. *Bird Studies at Old Cape May. 1937.* New York: Dover Publications, 1965.

Sutton, Clay. *Birding Guide to Cumberland County.* Bridgeton, NJ: Cumberland County, NJ, 1993.

Sibley, David A. *The Birds of Cape May.* Cape May Point: New Jersey Audubon's Cape May Bird Observatory, 1997.

Walsh, Joan, Vince Elia, Rich Kane, and Tom Halliwell. *Birds of New Jersey.* Bernardsville, NJ: New Jersey Audubon Society, 1999.

Some Useful Web Sites

Adrian Binn's very helpful site
http://www.delawarevalleybirding.com/

Atlantic County Division of Parks
http://www.aclink.org/parks/homepage.htm

Bergen County Department of Parks
http://www.co.bergen.nj.us/parks/

Camden County Parks
http://www.ccparks.com/

Gloucester County Parks
http://www.co.gloucester.nj.us/parks/parks.htm

Hunterdon County Department of Parks
http://www.co.hunterdon.nj.us/depts/parks/parks.htm

Info on pelagic trips, etc.
http://www.acnatsci.org/dvoc/

Jack Siler's all-inclusive Web site
http://birdingonthe.net/

Mercer County Park Commission
http://www.mercercounty.org/_private/park_commission.htm

Monmouth County Park System
http://www.monmouthcountyparks.com/

Morris County Park Commission
http://parks.morris.nj.us/asp/parks/info.asp

New Jersey Dept. of Environmental Protection
http://www.state.nj.us/dep/index.html

Ocean County Department of Parks
http://www.oceancountygov.com/county/parks/default.htm

Passaic County Parks
http://www.passaiccountynj.org/facilities/facilities.html

Somerset County Park Commission
http://www.park.co.somerset.nj.us/

Union County Parks
http://www.unioncountynj.org/

Annotated List of
New Jersey's Birds

William J. Boyle Jr. and Thomas B. Halliwell

This list provides a capsule summary of when and where you are likely to find the birds that regularly occur in New Jersey. It includes about 370 species that can be expected to occur during a five-year period, with an emphasis on recent trends in the state's birdlife. You can obtain additional information about each species by consulting the index and referring to the individual chapters noted in the list. Most of the species in the list occur every year; a few show up somewhat less often. A number of species are marked with "RL" following the name. These are rare birds that are on the New Jersey Bird Records Committee's Review List. If you observe one of these species, it is important that you take careful notes describing the plumage of the bird, or procure identifiable photos; either, or both, should be submitted to the Committee. At the end of the main list is a compilation of those extreme rarities that are called vagrants in birding jargon—birds that have occurred in New Jersey at least once in the past 25 years, but not frequently enough to warrant inclusion on the main list. If you are so fortunate as to encounter one of these, it is critically important that documentation be submitted to the Records Committee (see address at end of list).

The format of this list is, as in the first edition, a modified version of that used by John and Justin Harding in *Birding the Delaware Valley*. Each entry includes a summary statement of the seasonal pattern of occurrence of each species in New Jersey, its general habitat preference, and its abundance in that habitat. Judgments on the abundance of individual species are somewhat subjective and use descriptive terms such as *common* and *uncommon* that are difficult to quantify. Nevertheless, these terms are widely used, and despite their imprecision, most birders understand what they mean. The number of individuals of a particular species that are present in a given habitat does not necessarily reflect the ease of finding and seeing it, however. Sora is far more common than Great Blue Heron at Troy Meadows, but you can guess which one you're most likely to see. The following terms are used:

Common Always or almost always present, and usually numerous, in its preferred habitat at the appropriate season

Fairly common Usually present, but sometimes only one or a few individuals, in its preferred habitat at the appropriate season

Uncommon Occasionally present in its preferred habitat at the appropriate season, but not to be expected

Rare Of infrequent occurrence (not necessarily annual) or only a few individuals present each year even in preferred habitat

The second part of each entry suggests some of the places that you are most likely to encounter a particular species and an estimate of the likelihood of seeing it at that spot at the stated time. This reflects not only the abundance of the species, but how easy it is to locate or see. Using Sora as an example again, this species is fairly common at Trenton Marsh, but you will be lucky to see one (you have a better chance of hearing it).

We have tried to select sites covering a wide geographical range, while still choosing those where a species is most likely to occur. For the more common species and those that occur in a variety of habitats, the sites suggested represent only a sampling of the places that you can expect to find them. Other places within the species' range that provide similar habitat may be just as likely to produce the bird. So, if you live near Eagle Rock Reservation, don't think you have to go to Princeton or Stokes Forest to see a Wood Thrush. For the less common, rare, or local species, the sites suggested are those that have proven most reliable for birders over the past 10 years or so.

The number of asterisks next to each location corresponds to the probability of your finding the bird at that site and season during a field trip of several hours and reasonable weather conditions. Obviously if you only spend a few minutes at a spot or if it is pouring rain, your chances are greatly diminished. On the other hand, if you spend an entire day, your chances of finding even uncommon and rare species improve greatly. The ratings, which we have borrowed from Jim Lane's series of state *Birder's Guides*, are as follows:

**** *Hard to miss*—your chances are virtually 100 percent.

*** *Should see*—unless the fates conspire against you. This may depend very much on the conditions. If you hit a big wave of migrant warblers at Garret Mountain in May or of migrant sparrows at Island Beach in October, many uncommon or even rare species might be seen. On the other hand, if you bird Cape May in September after several days of southerly winds, even an American Redstart can be hard to find.

** *May see*—these are species that require more effort or more luck at that particular site, but are frequently present at the proper season. This includes birds that are uncommon or for which limited habitat exists at that location; it also includes species that, although common, may be hard to see, such as rails and some sparrows.

* *Lucky to find*—the species has often occurred at that location, but is generally rare or uncommon anywhere in New Jersey. You will probably have to make many trips at the appropriate season before you see the bird.

† *How lucky can you get*—these are rare birds that cannot be expected to show up at that particular site or even in New Jersey every year. The location mentioned is, however, one of the few places where the species has occurred.

For many of the entries, dates of occurrence are stated for the entirety of New Jersey, necessitating a number of cautions. In the first place, the times given are averages; in some years, conditions can skew whole seasons forward or back. Even in a normal season, early-arriving and late-departing individuals are always noted. Also, there is often a difference in migration timing between northern and southern New Jersey (e.g., American Redstarts are regularly seen at Cape May in fall migration, weeks after they have completely abandoned Stokes Forest). Note, too, that summer, as an ornithological season, really just means the breeding season for the particular species mentioned. For neotropical migrants, like most of our warblers, fall migration may be underway for more than a month before the calendar end of summer in late September. Finally, don't expect waterbirds to be present if the water is frozen—even if the annotated list says it should be fairly common in winter.

The names used for each species and the order in which they are listed follow the American Ornithologists' Union *Check-List of North American Birds* (Seventh Edition, 1998). In the list, *Brigantine* refers to Brigantine [Forsythe] NWR, not Brigantine Island; designations such as "State Park" and "WMA" have been omitted from the location names—all names should be understood to refer to the specific locations discussed in the text (e.g., *Lebanon* refers to Lebanon State Forest, not the town of Lebanon).

Annotated List

Red-throated Loon Common migrant and uncommon to fairly common winter resident along the coast; uncommon migrant inland. Typically found October–April, but most common November–December and March–April: ****Avalon, Cape May; ***Barnegat Light, Holgate, Island Beach, North Shore, Sandy Hook; **Merrill Creek, Round Valley.

Pacific Loon (RL) Very rare winter visitor, November–April, at coastal inlets and inland reservoirs. In the past decade seen about every other year. Multiple records at † North Shore (Manasquan), Sandy Hook.

Common Loon Common migrant and fairly common winter resident along the coast; uncommon to fairly common migrant inland. Normally occurs September–May with peak numbers October–November and April–May. Often seen overhead. ***Barnegat Light, Cape May, Holgate, Island Beach, North Shore, Sandy Hook; **Culver's Lake, Merrill Creek, Round Valley, Swartswood Lake.

Pied-billed Grebe Fairly common to common migrant on fresh or brackish water statewide; uncommon in winter; rare summer resident at widely scattered marshes. Maximal numbers occur April and October–November: ***Brigantine, Cape May, Lake Musconetcong, North Shore, Swartswood Lake. Summer: **Assunpink, Cape May, Kearny, Mannington, Pedricktown, Wallkill, Whitesbog.

Horned Grebe Fairly common migrant and winter resident along the coast; uncommon migrant inland. Occurs October–May, but most easily seen November–December and March–April: ****Sandy Hook, Shark River; ***Barnegat Light, Brigantine, Cape May; **Culver's Lake, Liberty, Merrill Creek, Round Valley.

Red-necked Grebe Uncommon to rare migrant and winter resident. Numbers vary widely from year to year. Can occur October–mid-May, but best chance is on inland lakes in April. *Assunpink, Cape May, Culver's Lake, Liberty, Merrill Creek, Round Valley, Sandy Hook, Swartswood Lake.

Eared Grebe (RL) Very rare along the coast. Recorded about every second year, mostly between December and March. †Cape May, Liberty, North Shore, Sandy Hook.

Northern Fulmar Irregularly uncommon to rare far offshore. Most often seen in winter, but records span all months except July and August. *Pelagic trips.

Cory's Shearwater Uncommon to fairly common far offshore late May–October. Seen from land only rarely. **Pelagic trips.

Greater Shearwater Fairly common to common far offshore late May–October; most common late May–June. ***Pelagic trips.

Sooty Shearwater Fairly common to common far offshore, generally in May and June. ***Pelagic trips; *Cape May.

Manx Shearwater Rare to uncommon far offshore spring to fall. Most records are in May–June and October–November. *Pelagic trips.

Audubon's Shearwater Rare to uncommon far offshore July–September. *Pelagic trips.

Wilson's Storm-Petrel Common far offshore; rare from land. Recorded May–November, but numbers diminish by late summer. ****Pelagic trips; *Cape May.

Leach's Storm-Petrel Rare to uncommon far offshore. Mostly seen on late May pelagic trips. *Pelagic trips.

Northern Gannet Common offshore October–April. Inshore, may be present September–May, but most common November–December and March–April. ****Pelagic trips; ***Avalon, Barnegat Light, Cape May, Island Beach, North Shore, Sandy Hook.

American White Pelican Very rare, nearly annual, visitor from the west, especially along the coast in spring or fall. †Brigantine, Cape May.

Brown Pelican Uncommon summer visitor along the southern New Jersey coast in varying numbers. Often present May–October, but most likely June–August. **Barnegat Light, Cape May, Stone Harbor.

Double-crested Cormorant Common migrant along the coast, uncommon to fairly common on inland lakes. Peak flights are April–May and September–October. Rare, but increasing, breeding resident at widely scattered colonies. Summering non-breeders are fairly commonly found on coastal bays and inland lakes. Variously uncommon to fairly common in winter on coastal bays and ponds. ****Avalon, Brigantine, Cape May, Sandy Hook; ***Barnegat Light, North Shore.

Great Cormorant Fairly common winter visitor (November–April) along the coast; rare inland. ****Sandy Hook; ***Barnegat Light, Island Beach, North Shore.

Anhinga (RL) Very rare April–June visitor from the south. Five records in the 1990s, from all regions of the state. Best chance is †Cape May, but beware of soaring cormorants.

American Bittern Uncommon and difficult-to-observe transient in fresh and brackish marshes. Rare in summer and winter. Breeding birds are more often heard than seen. Migration (September–November and March–April): **Brigantine, Cape May, Island Beach, Sandy Hook; *Celery Farm. Summer: *Great Swamp, DeKorte, Troy Meadows, Wallkill, Whitesbog.

Least Bittern Uncommon and secretive summer (May–September) resident of fresh and brackish marshes statewide. Seems to be declining. **Black River, Brigantine, Cape May, Celery Farm, Great Swamp, Kearny, Salem County, Trenton Marsh, Troy Meadows, Wallkill, Whitesbog.

Great Blue Heron Common transient; fairly common winter resident; common, but local breeder. ****Brigantine; *** Cape May, Great Swamp, Stone Harbor, Tuckerton, Wallkill, and many other locations.

Great Egret Common along the coast, primarily April–October, especially from Ocean County south; uncommon at inland lakes and marshes, mainly in late summer. Usually rare in winter. Spring and summer: ****Brigantine, Cape May, Stone Harbor, Tuckerton; ***Mannington Marsh.

Snowy Egret Common along the coast, primarily April–October, especially from Ocean County south. Very rare at inland, northern lakes in late summer. Usually rare in winter. Spring and summer: ****Brigantine, Cape May, DeKorte, Stone Harbor, Tuckerton.

Little Blue Heron Fairly common, April–October, in coastal marshes and heronries, especially from Ocean County south; rare inland in late summer. Only a few in winter. ****Brigantine, Stone Harbor, Tuckerton; ***Cape May.

Tricolored Heron Fairly common, April–October, in coastal marshes and heronries, especially from Ocean County south; quite rare in winter. ***Brigantine, Stone Harbor, Tuckerton.

Cattle Egret Uncommon summer resident in coastal marshes from Brigantine south; also in southern New Jersey farm fields and pastures. The species is most likely seen in April and August–September. Breeding birds have dramatically declined. **Brigantine, Cape May, Salem County.

Green Heron Fairly common migrant and breeding bird throughout the state in freshwater marshes and wooded swamps. Present April–September at ****Assunpink, Great Swamp, Manahawkin, Troy Meadows, Whitesbog, and many others.

Black-crowned Night-Heron Fairly common along the coast, April–October, primarily from Ocean County south; uncommon inland, mainly in late summer; uncommon in winter. ***Brigantine, Cape May, Stone Harbor, Kearny, Tuckerton; **DeKorte, Sandy Hook.

Yellow-crowned Night-Heron Uncommon and local summer resident mainly near the coast, April–October. **Brigantine, Celery Farm, Island Beach, Stone Harbor.

White Ibis (RL) Rare visitor from the south, usually young birds July–September. Nearly annual. Can occur anywhere along the coast or even inland. †Brigantine, Cape May, Tuckerton.

Glossy Ibis Common along the coast from Ocean County south, April–September. Rare inland in April–May and again in late summer. ****Brigantine, Cape May, Stone Harbor, Tuckerton.

White-faced Ibis (RL) Very rare visitor from the west, not seen every year. Has been found by searching flocks of Glossy Ibis between April and August at †Brigantine and †Cape May.

Black Vulture Fairly common, local permanent resident in less developed areas statewide. **Great Swamp, Kittatinny Valley, Bull's Island, Salem County, and many other places.

Turkey Vulture Common permanent resident of farmland and forests throughout the state; uncommon along the coast. Some migration in spring and fall. Easily found soaring almost anywhere and any season, except in the urban areas of the northeast.

Greater White-fronted Goose Rare visitor generally found in large flocks of migrating or wintering Canada Geese. Has been annual in recent years. Many records from †Brigantine and other coastal locations, but has also occurred at several inland goose congregations in recent years.

Snow Goose   Common migrant along the coast, less common inland; fairly common in winter. Highest numbers occur October–November and March–April. ****Brigantine, Fortescue (Dividing Creek); ***Cape May, Salem County.

Ross's Goose (RL)   Rare visitor most often found in large flocks of migrating or, occasionally, wintering Snow Geese. Reports have increased in recent years. †Brigantine, Salem County.

Canada Goose   Common migrant, winter and summer resident. Breeding birds occur throughout the state on any body of water, corporate lawns, parks, cornfields, and marshes. ****Brigantine and virtually anywhere in New Jersey.

Brant   Common migrant and winter visitor in coastal bays and estuaries from Sandy Hook to Cape May. Generally present October–April. ****Barnegat Light, Brigantine, Sandy Hook, Shark River, Tuckerton, and many other locations.

Mute Swan   Fairly common and increasing permanent resident of lakes, corporate ponds, and impoundments throughout. Large flocks winter in coastal bays when interior fresh water freezes. ****Brigantine; ***Cape May, Lake Musconetcong, Shark River, Tuckahoe, and many others.

Tundra Swan   Fairly common transient and uncommon winter resident along the coast, Delaware Bay, and in Pine Barrens cranberry bogs. Birds may be present mid-October–early April, but are most reliably seen November–mid-December and mid-February–March. ***Brigantine, Mannington Marsh, Tuckahoe, Whitesbog.

Wood Duck   Common summer resident of swamps and wet woodlands throughout the state; rare to uncommon in winter. Generally present late March–October. ****Great Swamp; ***Trenton Marsh, Wallkill, Whittingham, and many other locations.

Gadwall   Common migrant and fairly common winter resident on lakes and impoundments statewide; local summer resident in widely scattered marshes. Peak numbers found October–November and March: ****Brigantine, DeKorte, North Shore, ***Cape May. Summer: ****DeKorte, Kearny Marsh.

Eurasian Wigeon   Rare, but annual, visitor found in flocks of American Wigeon. Can occur anywhere, but most often found at *Cape May and *North Shore, September–April.

American Wigeon   Common migrant and fairly common winter resident on fresh to brackish water statewide. Present September–April with maximal counts in October–November and March. ****Brigantine, Cape May, Liberty, Mannington Marsh, Shark River.

American Black Duck   Common migrant and winter resident of coastal bays, estuaries, and marshes; fairly common inland in migration. Uncommon to fairly common summer resident at scattered sites around the state. Most plentiful October–March: ****Brigantine, Liberty, Manahawkin, Sandy Hook, Shark River, Tuckerton. Summer: ***Brigantine, Cumberland Marshes.

Mallard Common at all seasons on virtually any body of fresh or brackish water. ****Brigantine, Liberty, Mannington Marsh, Spruce Run, and many other locations.

Blue-winged Teal Fairly common migrant statewide and uncommon summer resident at scattered fresh and brackish marshes; rare in winter. Peak numbers found September–October and March–April: ***Brigantine, Cape May, Mannington Marsh, Tuckahoe; **Great Swamp, Trenton Marsh. Summer: **Cape May, Dividing Creek, Mannington Marsh.

Northern Shoveler Fairly common migrant and uncommon winter resident of fresh and brackish marshes and impoundments statewide; very rare summer breeder. Maximum counts occur October–November and March–April: ****Brigantine; ***DeKorte, Kearny Marsh, Mannington Marsh, Tuckahoe; **Assunpink, North Shore. Summer: *Brigantine.

Northern Pintail Common migrant and fairly common winter resident of fresh and brackish marshes and impoundments statewide. Seen September–April with maxima in late September–October and late February–March. ****Brigantine, Pedricktown; ***Kearny Marsh, Mannington Marsh, Tuckahoe.

Green-winged Teal Common migrant and uncommon to fairly common winter resident in fresh and brackish marshes throughout the state; rare breeder at few widely scattered locations. Most common October–November and March–April: ****Bivalve, Brigantine, Goshen Landing, Mannington Marsh; ***Kearny Marsh, Pedricktown, Tuckahoe. Summer: *Brigantine, Kearny Marsh, Wallkill, Whitesbog. Individual males of the Eurasian race (Common Teal) are seen annually in the state, occasionally at †Brigantine or †Cape May.

Canvasback Uncommon migrant and winter resident on coastal bays, estuaries, and freshwater ponds as well as inland lakes and reservoirs. Typically found November–March. Has declined markedly in the past two decades. ***North Shore; **Liberty, Merrill Creek, Sandy Hook.

Redhead Uncommon migrant and uncommon to rare winter resident statewide. Usually occurs in small numbers among flocks of Canvasback or scaup. Noted November–March: **Merrill Creek, North Shore.

Ring-necked Duck Common migrant and uncommon to fairly common winter resident on favored freshwater ponds, lakes, and reservoirs statewide. Present October–April with migratory peaks in November and March–early April. ***Assunpink, Culver's Lake, Lake Parsippany, Lake Takanassee, Mannington Marsh, Merrill Creek, Spruce Run, Swartswood Lake.

Tufted Duck (RL) Very rare along the coast late November–March. One or more birds have been reported annually in recent years. Recent records at †North Shore, Sandy Hook.

Greater Scaup Common migrant and winter resident of coastal bays, estuaries, and open ocean from the Hudson River to Cape May and up the Delaware River to Gloucester County; uncommon inland. Usually noted November–March. ****Sandy Hook; ***Barnegat Light, Holgate, Liberty, North Shore, Stone Harbor.

Lesser Scaup Fairly common migrant and winter resident on ponds, lakes, reservoirs, bays, and estuaries statewide; less common on open ocean. Present November–March. ***Culver's Lake, Lake Parsippany, Mannington Marsh, North Shore, Swartswood Lake, and many other spots.

King Eider Rare winter visitor along the coast, usually near jetties. Typically found November–March. Formerly the more "common" of the two eiders, it is now less frequently encountered than the Common Eider. *Barnegat Light, Cape May, Island Beach, North Shore, Wildwood Crest.

Common Eider Rare to uncommon migrant and winter visitor along the coast, usually at jetties. Typically found November–March. *Barnegat Light, Cape May, Island Beach, North Shore, Stone Harbor, Wildwood Crest.

Harlequin Duck Rare winter visitor at jetties along the coast November–March. Quite reliable at Barnegat Light for past decade. ***Barnegat Light; *North Shore, Sandy Hook, Wildwood Crest.

Surf Scoter Common migrant and fairly common winter resident along the coast; rare inland. Generally present October–April, but most common during huge autumn scoter flights in October–November. ****Avalon, Barnegat Light, Island Beach; ***Corson's Inlet, North Shore, Sandy Hook, Stone Harbor.

White-winged Scoter Fairly common migrant and uncommon winter resident along the coast; rare to uncommon inland. Typically noted October–April, but most common October–November. ****Avalon, Barnegat Light, Island Beach; ***North Shore, Sandy Hook, Stone Harbor.

Black Scoter Common migrant and fairly common winter resident along the coast; uncommon migrant inland. Found October–April, but most common October–November. ****Avalon, Barnegat Light, Island Beach; ***Cape May, Corson's Inlet, North Shore, Sandy Hook, Stone Harbor.

Long-tailed Duck Common migrant and winter resident on bays, estuaries, and oceanfront from Sandy Hook to Cape May; uncommon inland in migration. Can be found in coastal New Jersey October–April. ****Avalon, Barnegat Light, Corson's Inlet, Sandy Hook, Stone Harbor; *** North Shore.

Bufflehead Common migrant and winter resident on fresh and salt water. Common migrant on inland lakes and reservoirs as well. Present mid-October–April. ****Barnegat Light, Cape May, Island Beach, Liberty, North Shore, Sandy Hook, Stone Harbor; ***Culver's Lake, Merrill Creek, and many others.

Common Goldeneye Common migrant and winter resident of coastal fresh and salt water; fairly common on inland rivers, lakes and reservoirs. Typically found November–April. ****Barnegat Light, Sandy Hook, Shark River; ***Island Beach, Merrill Creek; **anywhere along the Delaware River.

Barrow's Goldeneye (RL) Very rare along the north coast, on inland reservoirs, and the Delaware River between November and March. Individuals often return for several winters. Recent records at †Sandy Hook, Merrill Creek, Cinnaminson.

Hooded Merganser Common migrant and fairly common winter resident on fresh or brackish water statewide; rare breeding bird of wooded swamps in northern New Jersey. Peak migratory numbers November–December and March: ***Brigantine, Cape May, Merrill Creek, North Shore, Swartswood Lake, Tuckahoe. Summer: *Great Swamp.

Common Merganser Common migrant and winter resident on fresh water; uncommon breeder along the upper Delaware and a few other rivers of northwestern New Jersey. November–December and March are peak gathering times at ****Assunpink, Culver's Lake, Lake Parsippany, Merrill Creek, Swartswood Lake. Summer: **Stokes, Wallkill, Worthington.

Red-breasted Merganser Common migrant and winter resident along the coast from Sandy Hook to Cape May; uncommon migrant inland; extremely rare breeder along the coast. Present November–April: ****Barnegat Light, Cape May, Holgate, Island Beach, North Shore, Sandy Hook.

Ruddy Duck Fairly common migrant and winter resident on lakes, ponds, bays, and estuaries; wintering numbers much reduced in past few decades. Rare breeding bird at a few scattered locations. Peak numbers November and March–April: ***Brigantine, Floodgates, Kearny Marsh, Liberty, North Shore. Summer: *DeKorte, Mannington Marsh.

Osprey Fairly common migrant statewide and fairly common summer resident along the coast. Typically found March–November with migratory peaks in April and September–October: ****Cape May; ***Sandy Hook and inland hawk watches. Summer: ****Brigantine, Salem County, Sandy Hook, Stone Harbor, Tuckerton.

Swallow-tailed Kite (RL) Rare, but annual, spring visitor. Has occurred between April and June in many different locations, but most often at †Cape May and †Sandy Hook.

Mississippi Kite Rare, but annual, spring visitor; much rarer in fall. Usually there are several reports between mid-May and mid-June from *Cape May.

Bald Eagle Uncommon migrant and winter resident; rare breeder. Has increased in past decade. Migrants peak at **hawk watches in September. Winter: ***Dingman's Bridge, Worthington; **Brigantine, Delaware Bayshore. Summer: **Merrill Creek, Round Valley, Salem County.

Northern Harrier Fairly common migrant and winter resident in marshes (especially salt marshes) and farmlands; uncommon and declining breeder in southern salt marshes; rare breeder elsewhere. Most prevalent during fall migration peak October–November: ****Brigantine, Cape May, Dividing Creek, Jakes Landing, Manahawkin, Salem County; **inland hawk watches. Summer: **Dividing Creek, Jake's Landing, Salem County.

Sharp-shinned Hawk Common migrant (especially fall) and uncommon winter resident statewide; rare breeding bird, primarily in northern New Jersey forests. Most plentiful September–October and April–early May. Fall: ****Cape May and all other hawk watches; Spring: ***Sandy Hook. Summer: *High Point, Pequannock Watershed, Stokes.

Cooper's Hawk Common migrant (especially fall) and uncommon winter resident statewide; uncommon but increasing woodland breeding bird statewide. Peak migration October and April–early May. Fall: ****Cape May and all other hawk watches. Spring: ***Sandy Hook. Summer: *Dividing Creek, High Point, Pequannock Watershed, Stokes.

Northern Goshawk Uncommon fall migrant, mainly along the mountain ridges; rare summer and winter resident especially in northwestern New Jersey. Most likely October–November at: **Raccoon Ridge, Sunrise Mountain; *Cape May, and other hawk watches. Summer: †High Point, Pequannock Watershed, Stokes.

Red-shouldered Hawk Uncommon to fairly common fall migrant along the mountain ridges and coast; uncommon spring migrant and winter or summer resident statewide. Breeding numbers continue to decline. Peak migratory numbers October–November at ***Cape May, Raccoon Ridge, Sunrise Mountain; **Montclair, Wildcat Ridge. Summer: *Cumberland County, Great Swamp, Pequannock Watershed, Stokes.

Broad-winged Hawk Common migrant, especially in fall; uncommon summer resident in woodlands statewide. Peak migratory flights mid-September and late April. Fall: ****Merrill Creek, Montclair, Raccoon Ridge, Sunrise Mountain; ***Cape May. Spring and summer: **Cumberland County, High Point, Pequannock Watershed, Pine Barrens, Stokes.

Swainson's Hawk (RL) Very rare visitor from the west; most records are of immature birds at *Cape May, between September and November.

Red-tailed Hawk Common migrant (especially fall), winter and summer resident throughout the state. Peak numbers October–November particularly at migration watches along the mountain ridges. Fall: ****Merrill Creek, Montclair, Raccoon Ridge, Sunrise Mountain, Wildcat Ridge; ***Cape May. Summer: almost any area with woods and open country.

Rough-legged Hawk Uncommon winter resident of marshes and farmland, especially near the coast. Typically noted November–March. Numbers vary from year to year. ***DeKorte, Manahawkin, Wallkill; **Dividing Creek, Jakes Landing.

Golden Eagle Uncommon migrant and winter resident. Most often seen mid-October–mid-November at hawk watches. Winter residents most likely on salt marshes of southern New Jersey or near the Delaware River. Fall: **Raccoon Ridge; *Cape May, Sunrise Mountain. Winter: *Brigantine, Dividing Creek, Jakes Landing, Worthington.

American Kestrel Common migrant (especially fall), particularly along the coast; less common and declining winter resident statewide; uncommon and declining summer resident of much of rural New Jersey away from the coast and Pine Barrens. Peak migratory flights September–mid-October and April. Fall: ****Cape May; ***Raccoon

Ridge, Sunrise Mountain. Spring: ****Sandy Hook. Summer: Salem County, Sussex County, Warren County.

Merlin Fairly common fall migrant along the coast; rare to uncommon winter and spring. Uncommon fall migrant inland. Best time is mid-September–mid-October at ****Cape May; ***Island Beach; **Brigantine, Sandy Hook.

Gyrfalcon (RL) Very rare November–March visitor from the north, usually seen only a few times per decade. Has occurred most frequently along the Kittatinny Ridge and the coast: †Brigantine, Raccoon Ridge, Sandy Hook.

Peregrine Falcon Fairly common fall migrant along the coast; rare spring migrant and winter resident. Rare inland. There is also an introduced, nonmigratory breeding population in certain salt marshes and a few urban areas. Peak migratory flights are mid-September–mid-October at ***Cape May; **Island Beach, Sandy Hook. Introduced birds are usually easily found at ***Brigantine and Thompsons Beach.

Ring-necked Pheasant Introduced species that is an uncommon to fairly common permanent resident of fields, farmlands, and hedgerows over much of New Jersey. Rather rare on the outer coastal plain. Numbers are augmented annually by released stock. Appears to be declining. Most easily found in WMAs. ***Assunpink, Collier's Mills, Liberty.

Ruffed Grouse Uncommon permanent resident of deciduous woodlands throughout the state, most common in the northwest. Often heard drumming in April and May, but most easily seen in June and July when hens have their broods. Has declined in past few decades, especially in southern New Jersey. **High Point, Pequannock Watershed, Point Mountain, Stokes, Wawayanda.

Wild Turkey Successfully reintroduced over much of the state. Common in the northwest; fairly common and increasing in southern New Jersey. Often seen on farm fields at edge of woods. ***Allamuchy, Belleplain, Stokes, Worthington, and many other places.

Northern Bobwhite Uncommon permanent resident of hedgerows and shrubby fields in the southern half of the state. Declining despite annual restocking in many areas. ***Assunpink, Dividing Creek, Glassboro Woods, Higbee Beach.

Yellow Rail (RL) Very rare and difficult-to-detect visitor to New Jersey marshes, most often along the coast. Probably occurs more often than the few-times-per-decade records would indicate. Most are from September–October, although one recent record is of calling birds from †Dividing Creek in April–May.

Black Rail Rare summer resident of southern salt marshes and, even more rarely, inland fresh marshes; difficult to hear, even harder to see. Recent records from †Dividing Creek, Goshen Landing, Jakes Landing, Tuckahoe.

Clapper Rail Fairly common summer resident of salt marshes from Raritan Bay south to Cape May and up to Salem County; rare in winter. ***Brigantine; **Dividing Creek, Jakes Landing, Manahawkin, Stone Harbor, Tuckerton.

King Rail Uncommon to rare summer resident of fresh and brackish marshes along the Delaware Bayshore and in the interior; difficult to observe. **Dividing Creek, Salem County; *Black River, Great Swamp, Makepeace Lake, Pedricktown, Wallkill, Whitesbog. Beware of Clappers in brackish areas.

Virginia Rail Fairly common migrant and summer resident in fresh and brackish marshes; rare in winter. Most easily observed in spring, when they readily respond to tape recordings of their call. ***Dividing Creek, Troy Meadows, Wallkill; **Great Swamp, Princeton, Trenton Marsh.

Sora Uncommon migrant and summer resident of freshwater marshes, mainly in the northern half of the state; very difficult to observe. Summer: **Brigantine, Cape May, Great Swamp, Trenton Marsh, Wallkill. Fall (September): **Cape May, Sandy Hook.

Purple Gallinule (RL) Very rare visitor from the south occurring, on average, every other year. Most often seen in spring or fall and most often near the coast. Recent records from †Brigantine, Cape May, Sandy Hook.

Common Moorhen Uncommon summer resident of freshwater marshes; rare in winter. Typically seen late April–September. ***Brigantine, DeKorte, Kearny Marsh, Mannington Marsh, Trenton Marsh, Wallkill.

American Coot Common migrant on ponds, lakes, reservoirs, bays, and estuaries throughout the state; fairly common winter resident; uncommon and local summer resident of freshwater marshes. Most frequent October–May: ****Brigantine, Cape May, Mannington Marsh, North Shore, Spruce Run, Tuckahoe. Summer: *Kearny Marsh, Mannington Marsh, Wallkill.

Sandhill Crane Rare migrant, winter visitor, and summer resident. Migrants (a few each fall and spring) are most likely along the coast or at southern New Jersey farm fields. In recent years, breeding has occurred in Salem County. Whether this will continue remains to be seen. †Cape May, Salem County.

Black-bellied Plover Common migrant and uncommon to fairly common winter resident, mainly on mudflats along the coast; uncommon inland. Biggest numbers found May and August–November: ****Brigantine, Holgate, Stone Harbor; ***Barnegat Light, Cape May, Island Beach, Liberty, North Shore, Tuckerton.

American Golden Plover Rare spring and uncommon fall migrant at sod farms and coastal mudflats; seen mainly April and mid-August–October. Spring: **Mannington Marsh, Pedricktown; *Brigantine. Fall: **Brigantine, Cape May, Great Meadows, Johnson Sod Farm.

Wilson's Plover (RL) Most records of this very rare southern visitor occur in April–May, and all are along the coast. There are only a few records each decade at places such as †Brigantine, Cape May, Wildwood Crest.

Semipalmated Plover Common migrant at coastal impoundments and tidal mudflats, uncommon on inland shores; rare in winter. Numbers peak May and August–September: ****Brigantine, Cape May, Holgate, Stone Harbor, Tuckerton, and many other places.

444   🦃   Annotated List

Piping Plover Uncommon, and endangered, summer resident of ocean beaches from Sandy Hook to Cape May. Typically present March–September: ***Cape May, Island Beach, Sandy Hook.

Killdeer Common migrant on sod farms, fields, wet meadows, and mudflats; uncommon to fairly common in winter. Common summer resident on fields, gravel areas, and rooftops of schools and shopping centers. Most common late-March–early April and August–October. Fall: ****Cape May; ***Johnson Sod Farm, Spruce Run. Spring and summer: hard to miss in proper habitat in most areas of the state.

American Oystercatcher Fairly common migrant and summer resident of coastal salt marshes and mudflats from Raritan Bay to Cumberland County; uncommon to fairly common in winter, especially south. Most easily found in large assemblages, September–November, at favorite southern coastal haunts: ****Holgate, Stone Harbor, Tuckerton; ***Brigantine, Corson's Inlet, Island Beach.

Black-necked Stilt Rare spring and summer visitor to impoundments, wet meadows, and tidal marshes. *Brigantine, Cape May, Dividing Creek, Goshen Landing.

American Avocet Rare to uncommon migrant at fresh to brackish ponds and impoundments along the coast. Most likely August–September: **Brigantine.

Greater Yellowlegs Common migrant in wet meadows, tidal mudflats, and along the edges of ponds, impoundments, and reservoirs; much less common inland. Rare to uncommon in winter, mainly in southern New Jersey. Major flight periods are April–mid-May and mid-July–October. ****Brigantine, Cape May, DeKorte, Mannington Marsh, Pedricktown, Stone Harbor, Tuckerton.

Lesser Yellowlegs Similar to Greater Yellowlegs, with which it is often found, although somewhat less common in spring and winter.

Solitary Sandpiper Fairly common, but solitary, migrant along freshwater ponds, marshes, streams, and rivers. More likely inland than coastally. Main flight times occur late April–early May and late July–September. ***Black River, Great Swamp, Princeton, Trenton Marsh, Wallkill.

Willet Common and conspicuously vocal summer resident of salt marshes from Raritan Bay to Cape May and up Delaware Bay to Salem County. Present April–October, but most easily found mid-April–mid-August: ****Brigantine, Dividing Creek, Jakes Landing, Manahawkin, Stone Harbor, Tuckerton.

Spotted Sandpiper Common migrant and uncommon to fairly common summer resident of fresh and brackish water. More common as a breeder in northern New Jersey. Present late-April–September, but most likely May and July–August. Usually solitary. ***Assunpink, Brigantine, DeKorte, Spruce Run, Trenton Marsh, Wallkill.

Upland Sandpiper Uncommon late July–early September migrant on fields, meadows, and sod farms; rare and local spring migrant and summer breeder on inaccessible military bases. Numbers of both residents and migrants have declined in recent decades. Fall: ***Johnson Sod Farm, Great Meadows.

Whimbrel Fairly common migrant in coastal salt marshes. Present mid-April–mid-May and July–September; most numerous late-April–mid-May and late July–August. ***Brigantine, Corson's Inlet, Manahawkin, Stone Harbor, Tuckerton.

Hudsonian Godwit Uncommon August–October migrant at coastal ponds, impoundments, and mudflats; very rare inland or in spring. *Brigantine, Cape May, DeKorte, Stone Harbor.

Marbled Godwit Uncommon fall migrant along the coast; rare in winter and spring. Most likely August–November at *Brigantine, Stone Harbor, Wildwood Crest.

Ruddy Turnstone Common migrant and fairly common winter resident on outer beaches, jetties, the Delaware Bayshore, and tidal mudflats. Most common May and August–October: ****Brigantine, Cape May, Stone Harbor, Tuckerton; especially common in late May and early June along the ****Delaware Bayshore (Thompsons Beach and Reeds Beach). Winter: **Barnegat Light, Cape May.

Red Knot Fairly common coastal migrant, especially in late spring; rare winter resident. Most common May and late July–September: ***Brigantine, Stone Harbor, Tuckerton; especially common in late May and early June along the ****Delaware Bayshore (Thompsons Beach and Reeds Beach). Fall migrants may be found at the same oceanside locations, but in far smaller concentrations.

Sanderling Common migrant and fairly common to common winter resident along the outer beaches and on tidal mudflats. Abundant along the ****Delaware Bayshore in late May (Thompsons Beach and Reeds Beach). At other times: ***Barnegat Light, Brigantine, Holgate, Island Beach, Stone Harbor; **North Shore, Sandy Hook.

Semipalmated Sandpiper Common migrant at impoundments and tidal mudflats along the coast; uncommon to fairly common inland. Peak numbers occur May and late July–mid-September: ****Brigantine, Cape May, Stone Harbor, Tuckerton; ***DeKorte, Mannington Marsh, Spruce Run. Abundant along the ****Delaware Bayshore in late May (Thompsons Beach and Reeds Beach).

Western Sandpiper Fairly common to common fall migrant along the coast; rare in winter and spring. Peak numbers occur August–October. ***Brigantine, Cape May, Stone Harbor, Tuckerton; **DeKorte.

Least Sandpiper Common migrant at impoundments, tidal mudflats, reservoirs, and pond shores statewide, though far more common along the coast. Peak numbers found late April–May and late July–September. Occurs at the same places as Semipalmated Sandpiper, plus numerous shores and wet meadows inland.

White-rumped Sandpiper Uncommon to fairly common migrant at reservoirs, impoundments, and tidal mudflats, mostly along the coast. More numerous in fall. Maximal numbers occur May–early June and August–mid-October. **Brigantine, Cape May, Stone Harbor, Thompsons Beach, Tuckerton.

Baird's Sandpiper Rare fall migrant at sod farms, reservoirs, impoundments, and wet meadows, most often near the coast. Most are found mid-August–September.

*Assunpink, Brigantine, Cape May, DeKorte, Great Meadows, Johnson Sod Farm, Spruce Run.

Pectoral Sandpiper Fairly common migrant on grassy mudflats, both inland and along the coast. Major flights are April–early May and late July–October. ****Pedricktown (spring), Brigantine (fall); ***Cape May, Manahawkin, Mannington Marsh, Stone Harbor.

Purple Sandpiper Common winter resident on rocky jetties along the coast, typically present from November–April, with some lingering into May. ***Barnegat Light, Cape May, Island Beach, Manasquan.

Dunlin Common migrant and winter resident on coastal mudflats and impoundments; uncommon inland. Present late September–May: ****Brigantine, Holgate, Stone Harbor, Tuckerton; ***Cape May, Corson's Inlet, DeKorte, Island Beach, Sandy Hook.

Curlew Sandpiper (RL) Rare visitor in May and mid-July–September on coastal mudflats and shallow impoundments. Reports fewer in recent years. *Brigantine, Cape May, Heislerville, †Thompsons Beach.

Stilt Sandpiper Rare spring and fairly common fall migrant at shallow ponds, impoundments, and tidal pools, mainly along the coast. Birds occur May and July–October; most commonly in late July–mid-September: ***Brigantine, Cape May, DeKorte, Stone Harbor, Thompsons Beach, Tuckerton, Tuckahoe.

Buff-breasted Sandpiper Uncommon fall (mid-August–mid-September) migrant on sod farms and grassy mudflats statewide. **Brigantine, Cape May, Great Meadows, Johnson Sod Farm, Spruce Run.

Ruff Rare migrant, more likely in spring, on tidal mudflats and impoundments, mainly near the coast. Usually solitary. Most reports mid-March–mid-May and mid-July–mid-September. *Brigantine, Cape May, DeKorte, Pedricktown, Thompsons Beach.

Short-billed Dowitcher Common migrant, more so in fall, on coastal mudflats and impoundments; rare to uncommon inland. Peak flights mid-April–May and mid-July–September. ****Brigantine, DeKorte, Stone Harbor, Tuckerton; ***Cape May, Mannington Marsh, Pedricktown, Thompsons Beach.

Long-billed Dowitcher Uncommon to fairly common fall migrant at mudflats and impoundments, mainly along the coast; rare in spring and in winter (when more likely than Short-billed). Found August–November, but most likely late September–October. ***Brigantine, Cape May; **DeKorte, Stone Harbor, Thompsons Beach, Tuckahoe.

Common Snipe Fairly common migrant and uncommon winter resident in freshwater marshes, wet meadows, and impoundments; rare summer resident. Mainly found September–early May: ***Mannington Marsh, Pedricktown; **Assunpink, Brigantine, Cape May, Great Swamp, Manahawkin, Thompsons Beach, Trenton Marsh, Tuckahoe, Wallkill.

American Woodcock Fairly common migrant and summer resident in wet woodlands; rare to uncommon in winter. Most easily observed during evening courtship flight in spring. Easiest to see at ***Higbee Beach in late October–mid-November. Otherwise, visit a nesting area for courtship flight in March–April: **Assunpink, Black River, Glassboro Woods, Great Swamp, Rancocas, Trenton Marsh, Troy Meadows, Wallkill, Whittingham.

Wilson's Phalarope Rare to uncommon migrant at fresh or brackish ponds and impoundments, mainly along the coast. Occurs May and mid-July–September: **Brigantine, Cape May, DeKorte.

Red-necked Phalarope Fairly common migrant well offshore; rare migrant at ponds and impoundments along the coast. Most likely May–early June and August–September. **Pelagic trips; *Brigantine, Cape May.

Red Phalarope Fairly common migrant far offshore; rare onshore and inland. Mainly found April–May and September–November: **Pelagic trips; *Avalon, Brigantine, Cape May.

Great Skua (RL) Rare visitor far offshore in winter. *Pelagic trips.

South Polar Skua (RL) Rare visitor far offshore in spring and summer. *Pelagic trips.

Pomarine Jaeger Uncommon to fairly common migrant far offshore; very rare onshore or on inland lakes and reservoirs. Usually seen May and September–early December. ***Pelagic trips.

Parasitic Jaeger Fairly common migrant offshore; rare in spring and uncommon in fall from land. Most are noted May–early June and September–early December: ***Pelagic trips; *Avalon, Barnegat Light, Cape May, Island Beach, North Shore.

Long-tailed Jaeger Rare migrant far offshore, mostly in May and September–October. Very rarely seen from land. *Pelagic trips.

Laughing Gull Common migrant and summer resident along the coast; fairly common inland in the southern counties, although it does not nest there; rare in winter. Generally present March–November. Noisy, conspicuous, and hard to miss anywhere along the coast in summer.

Franklin's Gull (RL) Rare visitor to New Jersey, mostly along the coast. Annual in recent years. Records run from August–April, with most in fall. †Atlantic City, Avalon, Cape May, Florence, South Amboy.

Little Gull Rare migrant, winter resident, and summer visitor, mainly along the coast. Summer birds are usually subadult. Usually found between November and May: *Avalon, Barnegat Light, Cape May, Liberty S.P., North Shore, Sandy Hook, South Amboy.

Black-headed Gull Rare migrant and winter resident at bays, estuaries, and inlets along the coast. Typically found between November and April. *Cape May, Hackensack Meadowlands, Liberty, North Shore, Sandy Hook, South Amboy.

Bonaparte's Gull Common migrant and fairly common winter resident along the coast, usually in small flocks; uncommon migrant on inland lakes and reservoirs. Often present September–May with biggest numbers mid-November–December and April: ****Barnegat Light, Cape May, Island Beach; ***Corson's Inlet, Holgate, Liberty, Sandy Hook, South Amboy, Stone Harbor.

Ring-billed Gull Common migrant and winter resident at shopping centers and fast-food parking lots, garbage dumps, fresh and salt water statewide. Large flocks gather on inland farm fields in April. Some nonbreeders remain through the summer. Hard to miss from August through May.

Herring Gull Common permanent resident, breeding colonially near the shore; abundant in winter at garbage dumps statewide, and on fresh and salt water. Occurs in many of the same places as Ring-billed Gull, but less likely to be found at malls, small ponds, or plowed fields. Hard to miss at any season, especially along the coast.

Thayer's Gull (RL) Very rare winter visitor at garbage dumps and other large gull concentrations. Annual in recent years. *Florence; †Cape May, Sandy Hook, Thompsons Beach.

Iceland Gull Rare to uncommon winter visitor from the far north at garbage dumps statewide, and lakes, estuaries, and beaches along the coast; rare on inland lakes and reservoirs. Usually reported November–April, but most likely December–March. Most sightings are of first-year birds. ***Florence; **Cape May, North Shore, Sandy Hook, and many others.

Lesser Black-backed Gull Uncommon migrant and winter resident at the same gull concentration sites listed above, especially ***Florence. Typically reported September–May, but most often noted in winter. Sightings have exploded in the last two decades.

Glaucous Gull Rare to uncommon winter visitor (mostly first-year birds) from the far north. Look for it at the same times and places as Iceland Gull, which tends to be a bit more common than Glaucous.

Great Black-backed Gull Common permanent resident along the coast, most abundant in winter; uncommon to fairly common, fall–spring, at inland on lakes and reservoirs. Nests in coastal mixed gull and tern colonies. Hard to miss where gulls concentrate, especially along the shore.

Sabine's Gull (RL) Very rare visitor, not seen every year. Records have occurred March–April and August–November. Best chances are †Cape May and †Pelagic trips.

Black-legged Kittiwake Fairly common winter visitor offshore November–March; uncommon from land, especially on southeast winds in November. ***Pelagic trips; *Avalon, Barnegat Light, Island Beach, Manasquan Inlet, Wildwood Crest.

Gull-billed Tern Uncommon and very local summer resident of salt marshes along the southern New Jersey coast. Most easily found May–August at ***Brigantine, where there is a nesting colony, or at Pine Barrens feeding ponds (e.g., **Whitesbog) in August; also at *Cape May, Stone Harbor.

Caspian Tern Uncommon spring and common fall migrant; very rare summer resident of southern New Jersey salt marshes. Found mid-April–mid-May and August–October at coastal and lower Delaware River inlets, flats, and impoundments, and occasionally on inland lakes and reservoirs. Fall: ***Brigantine, Corson's Inlet, Holgate, Salem County, Stone Harbor. Spring: **Mannington Marsh.

Royal Tern Uncommon spring and common fall migrant along the coast; has nested at least once in Cape May county. Most easily seen August–October at coastal inlets: ***Cape May, Corson's Inlet, Stone Harbor; **Barnegat Light, Island Beach. From mid-April–mid-May: try *some coastal locations.

Sandwich Tern Rare visitor from the south, most often seen in Cape May county, July–September, in flocks of Royal Terns; very rare spring visitor in May. *Cape May, Holgate, Stone Harbor, or anywhere Royals gather.

Roseate Tern Rare spring migrant along the coast in May–mid-June. Most likely at *Cape May though other coastal points have recent reports (e.g., †Island Beach, Sandy Hook, Tuckerton).

Common Tern Common migrant and summer resident along the coast, nesting on beaches and in salt marshes. Present late April–October, but best seen May–mid-September. ****Barnegat Light, Cape May, Corson's Inlet, Island Beach, Sandy Hook, Stone Harbor, Tuckerton.

Arctic Tern (RL) Rare migrant far offshore; very rarely seen along the coast, and then usually storm-related. Recent reports from May–September. *Pelagic trips; †Cape May.

Forster's Tern Common migrant and locally common summer resident at coastal and Salem County salt marshes; rare inland in migration and along the coast in winter. Most reliably found April–November at: ****Brigantine, Cape May, Heislerville-Thompsons Beach, Manahawkin, Stone Harbor, Tuckerton.

Least Tern Uncommon to fairly common migrant and summer resident at beaches and inlets along the coast; an endangered breeding species in New Jersey. Easily seen, May–early September, near the noisy nesting colonies. ****Brigantine, Cape May, Corson's Inlet, Sandy Hook, Stone Harbor; ***DeKorte, Island Beach.

Bridled Tern (RL) Very rare tropical visitor far offshore in late summer. Has been seen nearly annually in recent years on August–September *Pelagic trips. The few recorded sightings from land have been associated with hurricanes.

Sooty Tern (RL) Very rare tropical visitor, almost always in the wake of hurricanes. Unfortunately, your best though far from likely chance is not the safest—to scan the ocean during or just after the passage of the hurricane. †Cape May has had the most recent records.

Black Tern Rare spring and uncommon fall migrant at marshes, ponds, impoundments, bays, and inlets, mainly along the coast. Numbers are declining. Most likely July–September: **Brigantine, Cape May, South Amboy. In spring (May): *Cape May, South Amboy.

Black Skimmer Locally fairly common migrant and summer resident along the coast, often associated with colonies of Common Terns; rare in winter. Endangered breeding species in New Jersey. Most are noted late April–October. ****Corson's Inlet, Stone Harbor; ***Barnegat Light, Brigantine, Cape May, Island Beach, Tuckerton.

Dovekie Irregularly uncommon to fairly common winter visitor well offshore (10–30 miles); rare along the coast. Most are seen November–December. **Pelagic trips; †coast and inlets from Shark River to Cape May.

Common Murre (RL) Rare winter visitor well offshore; very rare from land. Seen recently, on average, every other year. *Pelagic trips; †Manasquan Inlet.

Thick-billed Murre (RL) Rare winter visitor offshore and along the coast. Reported most years; in recent years most reports have been in February. *Pelagic trips; *Manasquan Inlet and other inlets and jetties from Shark River to Cape May.

Razorbill Uncommon winter visitor well offshore; rare along the coast, though more likely than other alcids. Found November–March. **Pelagic trips; *Manasquan Inlet and other inlets and jetties from Shark River to Cape May.

Atlantic Puffin (RL) Rare winter visitor far offshore; least likely of the alcids to be seen from land. In recent years seen almost annually on *Pelagic trips between December and May.

Rock Dove Common permanent resident, especially in urban areas. Hard to miss in a day's birding anywhere in New Jersey.

Eurasian Collared Dove (RL) Very rare visitor from the south. Very likely to occur more frequently in the future since the species' range is expanding rapidly. †Cape May is the site of New Jersey's first two records.

White-winged Dove (RL) Very rare visitor from the west, now noted in New Jersey nearly every year. Most records are from April–May and September–November in †southern Cape May County.

Mourning Dove Common resident statewide in fields, farmlands, and suburban areas at all seasons. Hard to miss at parks, reservations, and WMAs anywhere in New Jersey.

Black-billed Cuckoo Uncommon migrant and summer resident in thickets and deciduous woodlands over much of New Jersey; numbers fluctuate widely from one year to the next. Spring (May): **Assunpink, Bull's Island, Garret Mountain, Princeton, Trenton Marsh. Summer: **Black River, High Point, Pequannock Watershed, Stokes, Wawayanda. Fall (August–September): **Cape May, Palmyra, Sandy Hook.

Yellow-billed Cuckoo Fairly common migrant and summer resident in thickets and woodlands statewide; numbers fluctuate widely from year to year. Occurs at the same times and places as Black-billed Cuckoo, but is also a fairly common breeder at **Lebanon and elsewhere in the Pine Barrens, and **Dividing Creek and elsewhere along the Delaware Bayshore.

Barn Owl Uncommon permanent resident of farmlands throughout the state, but almost wholly nocturnal and difficult to see. There is a small movement of migrants through Cape May in the fall, when the bird can be seen flying around the lighthouse at Cape May Point during the night. For several years a pair has inhabited a disused Peregrine Falcon hack-box at **Brigantine, where they can sometimes be seen during the day.

Eastern Screech Owl Fairly common, but highly nocturnal, permanent resident of woodlands over much of the state; more widespread in northern New Jersey. Readily responds to tape recordings of its call, especially August–winter. Most often seen in winter or spring sunning itself in the opening of a tree hole or Wood Duck box.

Great Horned Owl Fairly common permanent resident in woodlands; nocturnal, but often seen flying away when flushed from a roost or nest. Nests in old Red-tailed Hawk nests or those of other species, occasionally in conspicuous sites where they can be observed at leisure during the day, as at *Great Swamp and Salem County in recent years.

Snowy Owl Rare winter visitor from the far north, occurring in widely fluctuating numbers that reflect prey populations in arctic Canada. Most reports are near the coast: *Barnegat Light, Brigantine, Holgate, Island Beach, Liberty, Sandy Hook.

Barred Owl Uncommon permanent resident of wooded swamps in northern and far southern New Jersey, and of deciduous woodlands in the Highlands and Kittatinny Mountains; generally absent from the Pine Barrens and rare in the central part of the state. Nocturnal, but occasionally found at daytime roosts; will readily respond to imitations of call. Most likely at *Great Swamp, Black River, Dividing Creek, High Point, Parvin, Pequannock Watershed, Sparta Mountain, Stokes, Wawayanda.

Long-eared Owl Uncommon migrant and winter resident; rare summer resident. Mainly found in conifers. Wholly nocturnal, this species is seldom seen unless found roosting, often colonially, from November–March. Few areas are reliable year after year; some recent accessible locations are *Allendale, Palmyra, Round Valley, Whittingham.

Short-eared Owl Uncommon migrant and winter resident, mainly in coastal marshes, but occasionally over inland farm fields and marshes; probably extirpated as a breeder in southern New Jersey salt marshes. Try scanning at dusk in winter at: **Jakes Landing, Manahawkin, Wallkill; *Brigantine, Liberty.

Northern Saw-whet Owl Uncommon migrant and winter resident throughout the state; rare breeder in the Pine Barrens and northwestern New Jersey. Numbers fluctuate from year to year. Nocturnal transients moving through Cape May in fall are rarely seen during the day. Best chance is to search for birds roosting in small conifers during winter; recent sites include: **Palmyra; *Allamuchy, Stony Brook-Millstone Reserve.

Common Nighthawk Uncommon spring and common fall migrant throughout the state; uncommon summer resident in the Pine Barrens and scattered, often urban, sites in northern New Jersey. Present May–mid-October; peak migratory flights occur May and late August–early September when flocks may often be seen at dusk anywhere in the state, including: **Brigantine, Cape May, DeKorte, Great Swamp, Princeton, Trenton Marsh, Troy Meadows. In summer (at dusk): Lebanon, Wharton.

Chuck-will's-widow   Local and uncommon summer (late April–September) resident of deciduous and mixed woodlands mostly near the coast from Ocean to Salem Counties. Easily heard at dawn or dusk May–July (but much more difficult to see) at ***Brigantine, Cape May, Dividing Creek, Jakes Landing; **Manahawkin.

Whip-poor-will   Fairly common summer (late April–September) resident of pine and mixed woodlands through the outer coastal plain; rare in the mountains of the northwest. Nocturnal and difficult to glimpse, but easily heard, May–July, at dawn and dusk, at ****Brigantine, Colliers Mills, Dividing Creek, Lebanon, Manahawkin, Wharton.

Chimney Swift   Common summer resident throughout New Jersey, excepting the Pine Barrens. Often near towns and cities. Easily seen overhead in summer and migration in most localities, including: ***Bull's Island, Cape May, Great Swamp, Parvin, Princeton, Stokes.

Ruby-throated Hummingbird   Fairly common migrant and uncommon, but widespread, summer resident over most of the state. Most easily found during May and August–September migration peaks at ***Cape May, Princeton, Stokes; **Allamuchy, Assunpink, Bull's Island, Garret Mountain, Great Swamp, Parvin, and many other sites. In summer, try **Allamuchy, Belleplain, Dividing Creek, High Point, Stokes, Pequannock Watershed, Wawayanda, among others.

Rufous Hummingbird (RL)   Very rare, but now annual, fall visitor. Individuals have appeared at hummingbird feeders in all portions of the state between July and December. A few have been easily identifiable adult males, but most are young birds which are inseparable from Allen's Hummingbird.

Belted Kingfisher   Fairly common migrant and summer resident over much of New Jersey; uncommon winter resident. Always found near water. ***Brigantine, Bull's Island, Cape May, Dividing Creek, Manahawkin.

Red-headed Woodpecker   Rare to uncommon migrant, mainly along the coast in fall; rare winter resident, and rare, and declining, summer resident at a few scattered sites across the state. Does not seem to remain at a breeding site more than a few years. During September–October try: **Cape May, Great Swamp. Birds have bred at *Cape May County Park, Great Swamp, Lebanon, Peaslee, Stokes.

Red-bellied Woodpecker   Fairly common permanent resident of deciduous woodlands throughout the state, but uncommon in the Pine Barrens. ****Allaire, Cape May, Dividing Creek, Great Swamp, Parvin, Stokes, Whittingham, and many others.

Yellow-bellied Sapsucker   Uncommon to fairly common migrant in April and, especially, in late September–November; uncommon in winter; very rare summer resident in the northwest. Spring: **Bull's Island, Princeton, Sandy Hook, Trenton Marsh. Summer: *High Point. Fall: ***Cape May, Island Beach, Sandy Hook; *many inland sites. Winter: **Princeton, Ringwood, Stokes, Worthington.

Downy Woodpecker Common permanent resident of woodlands and suburban areas across the state. Hard to miss in any woods.

Hairy Woodpecker Fairly common permanent resident of woodlands throughout. Numbers seem to have declined in recent years, but still easily found on a day's birding in most localities.

Northern Flicker Common migrant and summer resident in woodlands across New Jersey; fairly common in winter. Should be easily found at most localities in a day's birding.

Pileated Woodpecker Uncommon permanent resident of mature woodlands in the northern part of the state. **Allamuchy, Black River, Jockey Hollow, Kittatinny Valley, Pequannock Watershed, Scherman-Hoffman, Stokes, Wawayanda, Whittingham.

Olive-sided Flycatcher Uncommon migrant in late May–early June and late August–September. Usually perches in the tops of dead trees, often near water. **Allamuchy, Cape May (in fall), Great Swamp, High Point, Princeton, Rifle Camp, Stokes, Trenton Marsh, Whittingham.

Eastern Wood-Pewee Common migrant and summer resident in woodlands throughout mid-May–September. Easily heard and seen in most wooded localities.

Yellow-bellied Flycatcher Uncommon woodland migrant in mid to late May and, especially, August–September. Regular spots for this species include **Allamuchy, Cape May (fall), Garret Mountain, Palmyra, Princeton, Sandy Hook.

Acadian Flycatcher Fairly common summer resident of wet woodlands in southern New Jersey and mostly hemlock woods in the north. Present mid-May–September, though difficult to identify if silent in migration. ***Allamuchy, Belleplain, Cape May (fall), Dividing Creek, Glassboro Woods, High Point, Parvin, Pequannock Watershed, Stokes, Wawayanda, Whittingham.

Alder Flycatcher Uncommon migrant mid-May–early June and August–September; uncommon summer resident, mostly in the northern counties. Nonsinging birds are virtually indistinguishable from Willow Flycatcher. Recent breeding locations include ***Black River; **High Point, Stokes, Wallkill.

Willow Flycatcher Uncommon to common summer resident of shrubby fields, wet thickets, and marsh edges, mid-May–September. Essentially absent from the outer coastal plain (including the Pine Barrens) except for salt marsh edges. Fairly common migrant, but virtually indistinguishable from Alder Flycatcher. Summer: ****Assunpink, Black River, Great Swamp, High Point, Stokes, Troy Meadows; ***Cape May, Manahawkin, Princeton, Salem County, Stony Brook-Millstone Reserve, Wallkill, and many other places.

Least Flycatcher Uncommon summer resident, mainly in the north; fairly common migrant throughout, but especially in fall along the coast. Present in open deciduous woodlands, usually near water; most easily identified by its call during the nesting season. Occurs May–September. Recent breeding sites include **Black River, High Point, Pequannock Watershed, Stokes, Wallkill, Wawayanda, Worthington.

Eastern Phoebe Common migrant throughout the state; fairly common summer resident, especially in the north; rare in winter. Usually found near water, often nesting under bridges, or under eaves or ledges. Late March–early October: ***Allamuchy, Assunpink, Bull's Island, Great Swamp, High Point, Kittatinny Valley, Princeton, Stokes, Wawayanda.

Say's Phoebe (RL) Very rare western visitor seen only a few times per decade. Usually found near the coast in late September or October. Recent records for †Cape May, Goshen, Island Beach.

Ash-throated Flycatcher (RL) Very rare, but annual, late fall visitor along the coast. Most often seen in *Cape May in November.

Great Crested Flycatcher Fairly common to common migrant and summer resident in deciduous woodlands statewide as well as the Pine Barrens. Easily heard and seen at most wooded birding sites from May–September .

Western Kingbird Rare, but regular (about 5 to10 each year), fall migrant, mainly along the coast; only a few winter or spring records. Occurs late-August–early December. **Cape May; *Barnegat Light, Brigantine, Island Beach, Sandy Hook.

Eastern Kingbird Common migrant and common summer resident of farmlands, open woodlands, hedgerows, and marsh edges. Widespread, May–September, including ***Assunpink, Brigantine, Great Swamp, High Point, Parvin, Pedricktown, Princeton, Troy Meadows, Wawayanda. Large flocks gather at ****Cape May in late August–early September.

Gray Kingbird (RL) Very rare visitor from the south in September–October. The three records in the 1990s were from †Brigantine, Cape May, and Sandy Hook.

Scissor-tailed Flycatcher (RL) Rare, nearly annual, visitor from the southwestern United States. Most records are in spring or fall. Best chance is †Cape May in May–June.

Fork-tailed Flycatcher (RL) Very rare visitor from South America. Amazingly, there were nine accepted records from New Jersey in the 1990s! Your best chance, though remote, is May and September–November at †Brigantine or †Cape May.

Loggerhead Shrike (RL) Very rare migrant and winter resident. Has declined dramatically in recent decades. Formerly noted inland in March–mid-April and along the coast in August–September, as well as numerous places in winter. Recent records in spring from †Great Swamp, in fall from †Cape May, and for a few consecutive winters from *Bay Point Road, Cedarville.

Northern Shrike Rare, irruptive winter visitor; prefers shrubby fields and hedgerows. Numbers vary from one or two to a few dozen, typically between November and March. Has occurred in all regions of the state, but most likely in the north. Two places that seem to be especially attractive to shrikes are *Great Swamp and *Flatbrook.

White-eyed Vireo Fairly common summer resident in dense undergrowth, thickets, and shrubby fields over much of the state, although uncommon and local in the northernmost section. Found most easily late April–September at ****Assunpink, Brigantine, Cape May, Dividing Creek, Glassboro Woods, Great Swamp, Parvin, Sandy Hook.

Yellow-throated Vireo Common summer (May–September) resident in northern New Jersey in tall deciduous trees, usually near water; uncommon over the remainder of the state. ****Allaire, Allamuchy, Assunpink, Bull's Island, Great Swamp, High Point, Sparta Mountain, Stokes, Voorhees, Whittingham.

Blue-headed Vireo Fairly common migrant in woodlands throughout the state; uncommon and local summer resident of hemlock forests in the northwest. Migrants noted April–early May and late September–October at ***Allamuchy, Cape May, Garret Mountain, Palmyra, Princeton, Sandy Hook, Trenton Marsh, and many other places. Breeding locations include *High Point, Pequannock Watershed, Sparta Mountain, Stokes, Wawayanda.

Warbling Vireo Fairly common summer (May–September) resident in mature deciduous trees along lakes, rivers, and streams, mainly in the northern and central counties. ***Allamuchy, Assunpink, Bull's Island, D & R Canal, Garret Mountain, Great Swamp, Princeton, Rancocas, Scherman-Hoffman, Troy Meadows, and many other locations.

Philadelphia Vireo Very rare May and uncommon late August–September migrant in second growth deciduous woodlands; found statewide, but most numerous along the coast. ***Cape May, Island Beach, Palmyra, Sandy Hook; **Allamuchy, Kittatinny Valley, Princeton, Trenton Marsh.

Red-eyed Vireo Common migrant and summer resident in woodlands throughout New Jersey. Hard to miss in the breeding season and at migration hotspots.

Blue Jay Common migrant, and summer and winter resident in woodlands and suburbs across the state. Hard to miss in a day's birding at any location in New Jersey that has trees. Large flights of fall migrants pass through ****Cape May in October.

American Crow Common permanent resident in farmland, woodlands, and suburbs. Hard to miss in a day's birding anywhere in New Jersey. Some migration is evident in fall at mountain ridges and along the coast.

Fish Crow Common summer resident in central and southern New Jersey, uncommon, but increasing, north; fairly common migrant and winter resident in the southern half of the state. Most easily found (when calling) along the coast: ****Barnegat Light, Brigantine, Salem County, Stone Harbor, Tuckerton; ***Cape May, Trenton Marsh.

Common Raven Rare, local, but increasing permanent resident in northwestern New Jersey; rare fall migrant along the northwestern ridges; very rare elsewhere. In recent years has nested on the microwave tower at ***High Point. In fall (October–November) try *Raccoon Ridge or *Sunrise Mountain. In winter occasionally found at *Yard's Creek (where it may breed) or *near the Delaware River from the Water Gap north.

Horned Lark Uncommon to fairly common migrant and winter resident on coastal dunes and grassy, plowed, or manured fields statewide; uncommon and local summer resident in the same habitats, especially in southwestern New Jersey. November–March: ***Alpha, Salem County, and similar farmland throughout the state; **Barnegat Light, Cape May, Holgate, Island Beach, Sandy Hook. Breeding: **Alpha, Salem County, Wallkill.

Purple Martin Fairly common to common migrant and summer resident April–September in open, rural, and suburban situations; usually nests in "martin houses" provided by parks and homeowners. Most common in southern New Jersey, quite uncommon in the northeast. ****Brigantine, Cape May; ***Pedricktown and many other places. In the last decade, a major mid-August–early September staging area for thousands of migrants has been located along the Maurice River near ****Mauricetown.

Tree Swallow Common migrant and fairly common summer resident across the state; breeds in wooded swamps, beaver swamps, in nest boxes near water. Present March–October, later in the south. The flocks of thousands that gather in September are a "must see" spectacle at ****Cape May, Corson's Inlet, Island Beach, Mauricetown, Sandy Hook, Stone Harbor, Tuckerton. Common breeder at ****Brigantine, Great Swamp, Princeton; ***Stokes, and many other places.

Northern Rough-winged Swallow Fairly common migrant and summer resident; nests under bridges, around lakes, and along rivers and streams. Typically present April–August. ***Bull's Island, Cape May, Pedricktown, Princeton, Trenton Marsh, Wallkill, and many other places.

Bank Swallow Common migrant and fairly common, but local, summer resident statewide. Most migrants pass mid-April–mid-May and mid-July–August at ***Cape May, Pedricktown, Princeton, Trenton Marsh, and in mixed swallow flocks over numerous lakes and ponds. In summer check for colonies at abandoned sand quarries statewide.

Cliff Swallow Uncommon migrant throughout the state; rare and local (but increasing) summer resident, especially under some bridges over the Delaware River and near farmland in the Kittatinny Valley. Look for it mid-April–mid-May and late August–September among flocks of other swallows at **Cape May, Pedricktown, Trenton Marsh, and many lakes and ponds statewide. The breeding colonies at ****Bull's Island and Lambertville (see Bull's Island) are very accessible.

Cave Swallow (RL) Very rare, but now annual, visitor. Most often noted in †Cape May in November.

Barn Swallow Common migrant and common summer resident in open areas, such as farmland, parks, marshes (fresh or salt), swamps, or ponds. Hard to miss, April–September, almost anywhere in New Jersey in appropriate habitat.

Carolina Chickadee Common permanent resident of woodlands, shrubby fields, and suburbs south and east of a line running roughly from South Amboy to Lambertville (however, Black-capped Chickadee occupies Sandy Hook). Hard to miss in this area.

Black-capped Chickadee Common permanent resident of woodlands and suburbs north and west of the South Amboy to Lambertville line; numbers augmented by winter visitors from the north, especially in flight years, when this species may occur south of its normal range. Almost certain to be seen in most locations.

Tufted Titmouse Common permanent resident in deciduous woodlands, Pine Barrens, and suburbs across the state. Hard to miss anywhere in New Jersey that includes appropriate habitat.

Red-breasted Nuthatch Irregularly uncommon to common migrant and winter resident, usually in coniferous woodlands or at suburban suet feeders. Rare summer resident of coniferous woods (often Norway Spruce plantings) in the northwest and at highly scattered locations around the state. In a big fall flight year birds can occur anywhere August–November, but especially along the coast at, for example: ***Cape May and ***Sandy Hook. Summer: *High Point, Pequannock Watershed, Stokes.

White-breasted Nuthatch Fairly common permanent resident in deciduous and mixed woodlands and suburbs across most of New Jersey. Uncommon along the coast, in the Pine Barrens, and Cape May peninsula; usually seen in a day's birding in appropriate habitat anywhere else in the state.

Brown Creeper Fairly common migrant and uncommon winter resident in woodlands; uncommon summer resident in mature, deciduous woodlands and hardwood swamps, most frequently in the north. Quiet and not easily found, but can often be detected by its high, thin call and song. Migration or winter (October–April): ***Allamuchy, Cape May, Jockey Hollow, Princeton, Sandy Hook, Stokes, and many other places. Breeding birds occur in ***High Point, Pequannock Watershed, Wawayanda, Worthington; **Great Swamp.

Carolina Wren Fairly common permanent resident of thickets, hedgerows, and shrubby deciduous woodlands in the southern two-thirds of the state; uncommon in the northern third, especially following very cold winters. Easy to hear, more difficult to see, at ****Cape May, ***Assunpink, Bull's Island, Dividing Creek, Glassboro Woods, Parvin, Princeton, Rancocas, Sandy Hook, Trenton Marsh.

House Wren Common migrant and common summer resident of woodlands, thickets, shrubby fields, and hedgerows throughout the state. Present mid-April–early October; hard to miss in a day's birding anywhere in New Jersey.

Winter Wren Uncommon migrant (April and October–November) and winter resident in wet woodlands, shrubby fields, and hedgerows throughout the state. Rare and local summer resident, usually at higher elevation in northern New Jersey. In migration: ***Cape May, Palmyra, Sandy Hook; **Garret Mountain, Great Swamp, Princeton, Scherman-Hoffman, Trenton Marsh. Some recent locations for breeding birds are: *High Point, Pequannock Watershed, Point Mountain, Stokes, Wawayanda.

Sedge Wren Rare migrant and winter resident in wet meadows and marshes; endangered summer resident at a few, widely scattered, locations, and these are often not occupied in consecutive years. Best chance is from October–January at Atlantic coast marshes such as *Brigantine, Cape May, and Manahawkin or the many Delaware

Bayshore marshes such as *Dividing Creek, Goshen Landing, and Jakes Landing. Has bred in recent years at †Brigantine and †Warren Green Acres.

Marsh Wren Common, but local, summer resident of cattail, *Spartina*, and *Phragmites* marshes across the state; rare in winter. May–October: ***Allendale, Brigantine, Cape May, DeKorte, Goshen Landing, Great Swamp, Heislerville, Jakes Landing, Kearny Marsh, Trenton Marsh, Troy Meadows.

Golden-crowned Kinglet Common migrant and fairly common winter resident especially in partially or wholly coniferous woodlands or plantings. Rare and local summer resident in Norway Spruce plantings in the northwest. Easily found virtually anywhere in the state during migration peaks, March–mid-April and October–mid-November. Recent breeding areas include *High Point, Pequannock Watershed, Stokes.

Ruby-crowned Kinglet Common migrant and uncommon winter resident in woodlands and thickets. Less partial to conifers than is Golden-crowned Kinglet, and less likely to be found in winter, particularly in the north. Peak migration times are April and October, when it can be found anywhere in the state; it can be especially numerous at coastal hotspots in October.

Blue-gray Gnatcatcher Common migrant statewide; common summer resident in deciduous woodlands over most of New Jersey. Easily found in proper habitat mid-April–mid-September.

Northern Wheatear (RL) Very rare visitor from the far north, usually in September–October. In the past two decades has occurred about every other year, mostly along the coast, but occasionally inland as well. Has occurred several times at †Brigantine and †Cape May.

Eastern Bluebird Common migrant and fairly common summer resident over much of the state; fairly common in winter. ****Colliers Mills, Great Swamp; ***Cape May County Park, Stokes, Stony Brook-Millstone Reserve, Whittingham. Huge migratory flights of hundreds of birds can occur at ****Cape May in mid-October–mid-November.

Veery Common migrant and common summer resident in deciduous woodlands, primarily in northern and central New Jersey. Found May–September at ****Allamuchy, Great Swamp, High Point, Pequannock Watershed, Stokes, Wawayanda; ***Cape May (fall migration), and many other places.

Gray-cheeked Thrush Rare to uncommon migrant in deciduous woodlands. Has declined severely. Peak times are mid-late May and mid-September–mid-October. **Cape May, Garret Mountain, Palmyra, Princeton, Sandy Hook.

Bicknell's Thrush A recent split from Gray-cheeked Thrush; probably, at best, an uncommon migrant through New Jersey with timing similar to Gray-cheeked. Field identification criteria are not fully established for the separation of these two thrushes, so we know next to nothing about their relative abundance.

Swainson's Thrush Uncommon, and declining, migrant in deciduous woodlands. Flight periods are May and September–mid-October. ***Allamuchy, Cape May, Garret Mountain, Great Swamp, Palmyra, Princeton, Sandy Hook, Scherman-Hoffman, Stokes, and many other places.

Hermit Thrush Fairly common migrant and uncommon winter resident in thickets and woodlands; uncommon and local summer resident in the Pine Barrens, and in hemlock glens and on dry ridgetops in the northwest. Migrates earlier in spring (April) and later in fall (October–November) than Swainson's Thrush, but is found in the same places and is more common. Summer: **Sparta Mountain, High Point, Lebanon, Pequannock Watershed, Stokes, Wawayanda, Wharton.

Wood Thrush Common summer (May–early October) resident in deciduous woodlands statewide, easily located by its beautiful song. ****Allaire, Allamuchy, Dividing Creek, Glassboro Woods, Great Swamp, Jockey Hollow, Pequannock Watershed, Princeton, Stokes, and many other places.

American Robin Common migrant and summer resident in open woodlands, edges, and suburbs; fairly common winter resident, more so along the coast and in southern New Jersey. A common and familiar bird, easily found at parks and on corporate and suburban lawns anywhere in the state.

Gray Catbird Common summer resident of dense thickets in deciduous woodlands and suburbs; rare to uncommon in winter, mainly south. From May–October found in appropriate habitat anywhere in the state.

Northern Mockingbird Common permanent resident of shrubby fields, thickets, hedgerows, and suburbs statewide. Hard to miss in appropriate habitat.

Brown Thrasher Fairly common summer resident of shrubby fields, hedgerows, and thickets statewide, but, especially, the thick undergrowth in the Pine Barrens, where it is one of the characteristic birds; rare in winter, mostly south. Typically noted April–October: ****Lebanon, Sandy Hook, Wharton, and many other places.

European Starling Common permanent resident throughout the state in almost every habitat. Unfortunately, hard to miss in a day's birding anywhere in New Jersey.

American Pipit Uncommon to fairly common migrant on farm fields, wet meadows, sod farms, and ocean dunes; rare to uncommon winter resident. Look for it, or listen for its flight call, in April and October–November at **Alpha, Cape May, DeKorte, Holgate, Island Beach, Kittatinny Valley, Pedricktown, Sandy Hook, and on plowed fields throughout the state.

Bohemian Waxwing (RL) Very rare visitor from the west, November–March. The three records from the 1990s were from †Brigantine, Cape May, and Sandy Hook.

Cedar Waxwing Common migrant at woodland edges, hedgerows, holly woods, and orchards; fairly common, but erratic, in winter; fairly common summer resident in woodlands across the state. Summer: ***Cape May, Dividing Creek, Great Swamp, High Point, Lebanon, Pequannock Watershed, Stokes, and many other places. In migration and winter, often unpredictable, but may occur anywhere there are good berry crops. ****Cape May's fall flight (late August–mid-November) is notably heavy.

Blue-winged Warbler Fairly common migrant and summer resident in shrubby fields, woodland edges, and hedgerows. Present May–early September: ****Assunpink, Cape May, Dividing Creek, Great Swamp, Stokes, Stony Brook-Millstone Reserve; ***Glassboro Woods, Lebanon, Parvin, and many other locations.

Golden-winged Warbler Uncommon migrant; uncommon, local, and declining summer resident in shrubby fields in the northwest. Not often seen in migration, but good spots are *Princeton in May and *Cape May in mid-August–mid-September. Recent breeding sites are at: **High Point, Mahlon Dickerson, Pequannock Watershed, Sparta Mountain, Stokes, Wawayanda.

Tennessee Warbler Uncommon to common migrant in tall deciduous trees. Exhibits cyclical increases and declines; recent years have shown declines. Main passage May and late-August–September: **Bull's Island, Cape May (mainly fall), Garret Mountain (mainly spring), High Point, Palmyra, Princeton, Scherman-Hoffman, Stokes, Wawayanda, and many other places.

Orange-crowned Warbler Rare fall migrant in thickets and shrubby fields, especially along the coast; rare in winter and very rare in spring. Occurs from late September, but most reports mid-October–mid-November. **Cape May, Sandy Hook; *Island Beach, and in appropriate habitat elsewhere.

Nashville Warbler Uncommon to fairly common migrant (May and September–early October) in shrubby deciduous woodlands statewide; rare and local summer resident in bogs or in scrubby, open woods in the northwest. Migration: ***Cape May, Garret Mountain, Palmyra, Princeton, Sandy Hook, Trenton Marsh. Summer: Recent nesting records from *High Point, Sparta Mountain, Stokes, Wawayanda.

Northern Parula Common migrant in deciduous woodlands throughout; uncommon, but increasing, summer resident in the northern Delaware Valley and at scattered sites across the state. Migration (May and late August–early October): ****Allaire, Allamuchy, Bull's Island, Cape May, Garret Mountain, Palmyra, Princeton, Sandy Hook, Trenton Marsh, and many other places. Summer: **Bull's Island, Dividing Creek, Wharton, Worthington.

Yellow Warbler Common summer resident in marshes, swamps, and shrubby fields throughout the state; less common in the Pine Barrens. Present May–early September at a multitude of locations including ****Assunpink, Brigantine, Cape May, Great Swamp, Pedricktown, Trenton Marsh, Troy Meadows, and Whittingham.

Chestnut-sided Warbler Fairly common migrant in deciduous woodlands statewide; fairly common summer resident in scrubby second-growth deciduous woodlands in the north. Migration (May and mid-August–September): ***Allaire, Allamuchy, Cape May, Garret Mountain, Palmyra, Princeton, Sandy Hook, Scherman-Hoffman, Trenton Marsh, and many other places. Summer: ****Allamuchy, Black River, Clinton, Pequannock Watershed, Wawayanda; ***High Point, Stokes, Worthington.

Magnolia Warbler Common migrant in woodlands throughout New Jersey; very rare and local summer resident in conifers in the northwest. Migration (May and late August–September): ****Cape May, Garret Mountain, Princeton; ***Palmyra, Sandy Hook, Trenton Marsh, and many other migration hotspots. Summer: Recent breeding reports from *High Point, Stokes, Worthington.

Cape May Warbler Uncommon spring and fairly common fall migrant in deciduous and coniferous woodlands. Exhibits cyclical increases and declines; recent years have shown declines. Spring (May): **Cape May, Garret Mountain, Princeton, Scherman-Hoffman, and other spots for migrants. Fall (September–mid-October): ***Cape May, Sandy Hook.

Black-throated Blue Warbler Fairly common migrant in deciduous woodlands statewide, where it prefers the understory; rare and local summer resident in the northwest in deciduous woods with dense Mountain Laurel understory. Migration (May and late August–early October): ***Cape May, Garret Mountain, Palmyra, Princeton, Sandy Hook, and other spots for migrants. Summer: Recent nesting at **Pequannock Watershed, Stokes; *High Point, Wawayanda, Worthington.

Yellow-rumped Warbler Common migrant in shrubby fields, woodlands, and coastal thickets; fairly common in winter, especially along the coast; very rare summer resident in the northwest. During migration (April and October–November) can be abundant anywhere in New Jersey, especially ****Brigantine, Cape May, Island Beach, and Sandy Hook. In summer try conifer groves in *High Point, Pequannock Watershed, Stokes, Worthington.

Black-throated Gray Warbler (RL) Very rare visitor from the west, averaging about one record every two years. Most records are September–December. Multiple recent records have come from †Cape May and †Island Beach.

Black-throated Green Warbler Common migrant in deciduous and coniferous woodlands statewide; uncommon summer resident of hemlock glens in the northwest and, locally, White Cedar swamps in the Pine Barrens. Migration (May and late August–early October): ***Cape May, Garret Mountain, Palmyra, Princeton, Sandy Hook, and other spots for migrants. Summer: Recent nesting records at ***Pequannock Watershed, Stokes, Wawayanda; **High Point, Lebanon.

Blackburnian Warbler Fairly common migrant in deciduous woodlands throughout; uncommon and local summer resident in hemlock glens in the northwest. Migration (May and late August–September): ***Cape May, Garret Mountain, Palmyra, Princeton, Sandy Hook, and other spots for migrants. Summer: Nests at **High Point, Pequannock Watershed, Stokes, Wawayanda.

Yellow-throated Warbler Uncommon and local summer resident of tall pines along the Delaware Bayshore (*dominica* subspecies) and sycamores along the upper Delaware River (*albilora* subspecies); a few scattered sites away from the Delaware, both north and south. Can be found April–August at ***Belleplain, Bull's Island, Dividing Creek, Jakes Landing.

Pine Warbler Uncommon to fairly common migrant in mixed deciduous-coniferous woodlands; very common summer resident in the Pine Barrens and much of the outer coastal plain, but uncommon in pines northward; very rare in winter. Occurs late March–October: ****Belleplain, Dividing Creek, Glassboro Woods, Lebanon, Wharton, Whitesbog; ***Brigantine, Cape May County Park, Parvin, Tuckahoe; **High Point, Pequannock Watershed, Stokes, Voorhees.

Prairie Warbler Uncommon to fairly common migrant in overgrown fields throughout; fairly common summer resident in overgrown fields (especially those with Red Cedars) in the north and very common summer resident in the Pine Barrens and much of the outer coastal plain. Migration: **at the usual migrant hotspots, late April–mid-May and September. Summer: breeds at ****Glassboro Woods, Lebanon, Wharton, Whitesbog; ***Brigantine, Cape May, Dividing Creek, Tuckahoe; **Stokes, Whittingham, Worthington.

Palm Warbler Fairly common to common migrant in shrubby woodlands, overgrown fields, and ocean dunes; rare in winter along the coast. Spring (April): ***Allendale, Garret Mountain, Great Swamp, Palmyra, Trenton Marsh, Troy Meadows, and many other places. Fall (mid-September–October): ****Cape May; ***Great Swamp, Island Beach, Palmyra, Sandy Hook, and many other places.

Bay-breasted Warbler Uncommon to fairly common migrant in deciduous woodlands throughout. Exhibits cyclical increases and declines; recent years have shown declines. Spring (May): **Garret Mountain, Princeton, and other spring hotspots. Fall (September): ***Cape May, Sandy Hook, and other migrant locations.

Blackpoll Warbler Common migrant in woodlands. Spring (May–early June): ****Garret Mountain, Princeton, and woods across the state. Fall (September–mid-October): ****Cape May, Sandy Hook, and other fall hotspots.

Cerulean Warbler Uncommon summer (May–August) resident of mature deciduous woodlands in the north. ***Allamuchy, Bull's Island, High Point, Jenny Jump, Stokes, Worthington. Hard to find in fall migration (mostly August) at *Cape May, Sandy Hook.

Black-and-white Warbler Common migrant and fairly common summer resident in deciduous and mixed woodlands statewide. Migration (late April–May and mid-August–early October): ****Cape May, Garret Mountain, Princeton, Sandy Hook, and other good places for migrants. Summer: ***Bull's Island, Dividing Creek, Great Swamp, Lebanon, Princeton, Rancocas, Stokes, and many other places.

American Redstart Very common migrant statewide; fairly common summer resident in deciduous woodlands throughout, though more common in the north. Migration (May and mid-August–early October): ****Cape May, Garret Mountain, Princeton, Sandy Hook, and other good places for migrants. Summer: ****Allamuchy, Bull's Island, High Point, Lebanon, Princeton, Stokes, Wawayanda, and many other places.

Prothonotary Warbler Uncommon to fairly common summer resident in the southern part of the state; sporadic at a few scattered locations in central and northern New Jersey. Found May–August at ****Hawkin Road, Parvin; ***Belleplain, Cape May, Dividing Creek, Glassboro Woods, Wharton.

Worm-eating Warbler Uncommon migrant throughout; uncommon summer resident on dry, deciduous slopes in the north; very local summer resident at scattered wet woodland sites on the coastal plain. Migration (May and August–early September): **Cape May, Garret Mountain, Princeton, Sandy Hook, and other migrant spots. Summer: ***High Mountain, Jenny Jump, Point Mountain, Worthington; **Allamuchy, Dividing Creek, Medford, Pequannock Watershed, Scherman-Hoffman, Stokes, Wawayanda.

Swainson's Warbler (RL) Very rare spring visitor from the south, almost always in May. There were four records in the 1990s, three of them from †Cape May.

Ovenbird Common summer resident of woodlands throughout the state; abundant in the northwest. Present late April–early October. Hard to miss its ringing song on a June day's birding in any woodland in New Jersey.

Northern Waterthrush Fairly common migrant in wet woodlands; local, but fairly common, summer resident in the north; very rare breeder in central and southern New Jersey. Migration (May and late July–September): ***Cape May, Garret Mountain, Princeton, Sandy Hook, and other good migrant traps. Summer: ***High Point, Pequannock Watershed, Stokes, Wawayanda.

Louisiana Waterthrush Fairly common summer resident along wooded streams in northern New Jersey; uncommon summer resident of streams in coastal plain swamps. Occurs early April–August: ***Allaire, Allamuchy, Belleplain, Bull's Island, Dividing Creek, High Point, Jockey Hollow, Parvin, Pequannock Watershed, Scherman-Hoffman, Stokes, Wawayanda, and many other places. Nearly all depart New Jersey by the end of August.

Kentucky Warbler Uncommon and local summer resident in the dense undergrowth of deciduous woodlands scattered across the state, though more common in the south. Present May–August: ***Glassboro Woods; **Assunpink, Belleplain, Dividing Creek, Hawkin Road.

Connecticut Warbler Uncommon late August–early October migrant in hedgerows and shrubby woodland edges statewide. **Cape May, Palmyra, Princeton, Sandy Hook.

Mourning Warbler Uncommon migrant in thickets, hedgerows, and shrubby woodland edges. Spring (mid-May–early June): most often detected by its loud song at **Garret Mountain, Princeton, Scherman-Hoffman, and other good habitats. Fall (mid-August–mid-September): probably more common, but quiet at **Cape May, Sandy Hook, and other fall migrant traps, especially near the coast.

Common Yellowthroat Common summer resident in marshes, swamps, brushy fields, and thickets; rare in winter along the coast. Generally found late April–October: ****Assunpink, Brigantine, Cape May, Great Swamp, Kearny Marsh, Princeton, Stokes, Trenton Marsh, Troy Meadows, Whittingham, and dozens of other places.

Hooded Warbler Locally fairly common summer resident of open deciduous woodlands, often with Mountain Laurel understory; not often seen in migration. Can be quite common, May–mid-September, in its preferred habitat, though it is more often heard than seen. ****Allamuchy, Belleplain, Glassboro Woods, Pequannock Watershed; ***Allaire, Assunpink, Dividing Creek, Hawkin Road, High Point, Parvin, Stokes, Wawayanda, Worthington.

Wilson's Warbler Uncommon migrant in thickets, hedgerows, and shrubby woodland edges. Spring (mid–late May): ***Garret Mountain; **Black River, Cape May, Kittatinny Valley, Princeton, Scherman-Hoffman, and many other places. Fall (mid-August–early October): ***Cape May; **Palmyra, Sandy Hook, and numerous other fall migrant locations.

Canada Warbler Fairly common migrant in deciduous woodlands and shrubby woodland edges; fairly common, but local, summer resident in the northwest, frequently in association with Hooded Warbler; very rare summer resident in the Pine Barrens. Look for it, May and mid-August–mid-September, at all the usual spots for migrants, especially ***Cape May, Garret Mountain, Princeton, and Sandy Hook. Summer: ***High Point, Pequannock Watershed, Stokes, Wawayanda.

Yellow-breasted Chat Fairly common summer resident in overgrown fields, thickets, and hedgerows from Salem to Cape May Counties; uncommon and scattered over the rest of the state; rare in winter. Generally present May–September: ****Cape May; ***Dividing Creek, Moores Beach, Salem County, Stony Brook-Millstone Reserve.

Summer Tanager Uncommon and local summer resident in oak-pine woods, mainly in the south; numbers appear to be slowly increasing. Rare spring migrant north of the breeding range. Present May–mid-September: ***Belleplain, Dividing Creek; **Lebanon, Wharton; *Parvin.

Scarlet Tanager Common migrant and summer resident in deciduous and mixed woodlands, though less common in the Pine Barrens. Can be found May–early October in appropriate habitat nearly anywhere in New Jersey.

Western Tanager (RL) Rare visitor from the west. Occurs nearly annually in the state, usually between October and January. Several records from †Cape May.

Eastern Towhee Common summer resident in thickets, shrubby woodland edges, and pine-oak woodlands statewide; uncommon in winter in the south. One of the commonest birds of the Pine Barrens. Present April–October: ****Assunpink, Cape May, Dividing Creek, Glassboro Woods, Great Swamp, High Point, Lebanon, Rancocas, Troy Meadows, Wharton, and many other places.

American Tree Sparrow Fairly common winter resident in fields, thickets, and brushy woodland edges, decreasing in abundance from north to south. Typically found November–March: ***Allamuchy, Assunpink, Cold Brook Preserve, DeKorte, Great Swamp, Stony Brook-Millstone Reserve, Troy Meadows, Warren Green Acres.

Chipping Sparrow Common summer resident of lawns, fields, woodland edges, and even dense coniferous woodlands; rare in winter in the south. Occurs April–October at ****Brigantine, Bull's Island; ***Assunpink, Cape May, Dividing Creek, Princeton, Sandy Hook, Stokes, Wawayanda, and many other places.

Clay-colored Sparrow Rare visitor from the west, mainly along the coast; very rare in winter and spring. Most records (usually more than 10 per year) occur late September–early November. *Cape May, Island Beach, Sandy Hook.

Field Sparrow Fairly common migrant and summer resident in shrubby fields and hedgerows statewide; uncommon in winter. Look for it at any season, but especially April–October at ***Assunpink, Cape May, Cold Brook Preserve, Glassboro Woods, Great Swamp, Mercer County Park, Sandy Hook, Stony Brook-Millstone Reserve, Troy Meadows, Whittingham, and many other places.

Vesper Sparrow Uncommon migrant, especially in fall; rare and local summer resident of farmlands in central and northern New Jersey; rare winter resident in the south. Migration (mostly mid-October–mid-November): *Cape May, Island Beach, Sandy Hook. Summer: **Alpha, Colliers Mills, Wallkill.

Lark Sparrow Rare visitor (several per year) from the west, mostly in fall, and mainly along the coast. Typically occurs mid-August–October, often at *Brigantine, Cape May, Island Beach, Sandy Hook.

Savannah Sparrow Fairly common migrant and winter resident in fields, marshes, and dunes, especially near the coast; rare and very local summer resident of farmlands at widely scattered locations. Migration and winter (September–April): ****Brigantine, Cape May, Cold Brook Preserve, DeKorte, Holgate, Island Beach, Mercer County Park, Sandy Hook, Stone Harbor, Tuckerton. Some current nesting locations are **Alpha, Brightview Farm, Hoffman Park, Salem County, Wallkill. The "Ipswich" subspecies winters in small numbers in dunes along the coast. Try **Barnegat Light, Island Beach, Stone Harbor.

Grasshopper Sparrow Uncommon summer resident in weedy fields and grassy meadows at scattered locations statewide. Some current breeding sites (May–October) are **Alpha, Brightview Farm, Colliers Mills, Hoffman Park, Salem County, Wallkill.

Henslow's Sparrow (RL) Very rare migrant, mostly fall, in weedy fields; endangered and sporadic summer resident in weedy fields in the interior and, formerly, at the edges of salt marshes along the coast. Most years there are no nesting birds. Migration (October): try †Cape May where there have been multiple sightings in the past decade.

LeConte's Sparrow (RL) Very rare visitor from the west, now nearly annual in October–December, or even later. Try †Cape May, , Palmyra, or Sandy Hook, each the site of multiple records.

Nelson's Sharp-tailed Sparrow Uncommon spring and fairly common fall migrant; rare in winter. Much remains to be learned about the occurrence of this recently split species in New Jersey. Apparently best observed in May and, especially, October–November in salt marshes where it mixes with its salt marsh cousin. Also noted inland in smaller numbers, unlike the Saltmarsh Sharp-tailed. Some places where it seems reliable, at least in fall, are ***Bass River, Brigantine, Cape May, Sandy Hook, and Tuckerton. No doubt many other locations will emerge as we learn more.

Saltmarsh Sharp-tailed Sparrow   Fairly common summer (May–October) resident in salt marshes from Raritan Bay to Cumberland County; rare in winter. Most easily seen by walking through marsh grass or "pishing" at ***Brigantine, Conaskonk Point, Manahawkin, Stone Harbor, and Tuckerton, among others.

Seaside Sparrow   Common summer resident of salt marshes from Raritan Bay to Salem County; uncommon winter resident. Generally in the same places as Saltmarsh Sharp-tailed Sparrow, but often perches in small shrubs along the edges of the marsh. ****Jakes Landing; ***Brigantine, Dividing Creek, Manahawkin, Stone Harbor, Tuckerton, and many others.

Fox Sparrow   Fairly common migrant and uncommon winter resident in thickets, shrubby fields, and wet woodlands. Most likely during migration peaks March–early April and late October–November. ***Cape May, Great Swamp, Palmyra, Princeton, Sandy Hook, Scherman-Hoffman, Troy Meadows, Whittingham, and many other places.

Song Sparrow   Common migrant and summer and winter resident in fields, thickets, marshes, swamps, suburbs, and woodland edges across most of New Jersey; not common in the Pine Barrens. Hard to miss in a day's birding in appropriate habitat.

Lincoln's Sparrow   Uncommon migrant in shrubby fields, thickets, and woodland edges. Occurs May and mid-September–October; more common in fall. **Cape May, Cold Brook Preserve, Great Swamp, Island Beach, Mercer County Park, Palmyra, Princeton, Sandy Hook, Thompson Park, Warren Green Acres.

Swamp Sparrow   Common migrant and uncommon winter resident in shrubby fields, marshes, swamps, and wet woodlands; fairly common summer resident in marshes around the state, especially in northern New Jersey and along the Delaware Bayshore. ***Black River, Cape May, DeKorte, Kearny Marsh, Princeton, Salem County, Trenton Marsh, Troy Meadows, Whittingham.

White-throated Sparrow   Common migrant and winter resident of shrubby fields, thickets, woodlands, and suburbs; very rare breeder in the northwest. Can be found October–April almost anywhere in the state. In summer try *High Point or *Pequannock Watershed.

Harris's Sparrow (RL)   Very rare visitor from the west, most often occurring at feeders between October and May. There were four New Jersey records in the 1990s, two in †Cape May.

White-crowned Sparrow   Uncommon migrant and winter resident in shrubby fields, thickets, hedgerows, and coastal dunes. In winter, most numerous in southwest New Jersey; seen over most of the state during May and October migration. **Alpha, Cape May, Cold Brook Preserve, DeKorte, Island Beach, Liberty, Salem County, Sandy Hook.

Dark-eyed Junco   Common migrant and winter resident in shrubby fields, woodlands and suburbs; very rare and local breeder in the northwest. Hard to miss in a day's birding October–April anywhere in New Jersey. In summer, search for it at high elevation at *High Point, Stokes, and Wawayanda. Juncos of western races (RL), particularly "Oregon" Junco, are reported almost every fall–winter, but rarely documented.

Lapland Longspur Irregularly rare to uncommon winter resident on fields (often plowed or manured) and coastal dunes, usually in the company of Horned Larks or Snow Buntings. Most noted November–March: *Alpha, Barnegat Light, Cape May, Holgate, Island Beach, Liberty, Sandy Hook.

Snow Bunting Fairly common winter resident on farm fields and, especially, on beaches and dunes; usually in flocks. Most occur November–March at ***Barnegat Light, Holgate, Island Beach, Sandy Hook; **Alpha, Liberty, Round Valley.

Northern Cardinal Common permanent resident in open woodlands, shrubby fields, thickets, and suburbs. Hard to miss in a day's birding anywhere in New Jersey that includes the appropriate habitat.

Rose-breasted Grosbeak Common migrant in deciduous woodlands; fairly common summer resident in the northern half of the state. Migration (May and late August–early October): ****Cape May, Garret Mountain, Princeton, Sandy Hook, and other good migrant spots. Summer: ***Allamuchy, Bull's Island, High Point, Jockey Hollow, Pequannock Watershed, Stokes, Wawayanda, and many other places.

Black-headed Grosbeak (RL) Very rare winter visitor from the west; usually found at feeders. Has occurred in all parts of the state (six records in the 1990s) between October and March.

Blue Grosbeak Uncommon summer resident of hedgerows, shrubby fields, and farm roads from the vicinity of the Raritan River south; most widespread from Salem to Cape May Counties. Present late April–early October: ***Assunpink, Higbee Beach; **Brightview Farm, Dividing Creek, Moores Beach, Rancocas.

Indigo Bunting Common summer resident in hedgerows, overgrown fields, and woodland edges; uncommon in much of the Pine Barrens. Found May–October: ***Assunpink, Black River, Bull's Island, Cape May, Dividing Creek, Mercer County Park, Rancocas, Stokes, Troy Meadows, Whittingham, and many other places.

Painted Bunting (RL) Very rare visitor from the south; annual in recent years. Records are usually in May or November–March, often at feeders. There are multiple recent records from †Cape May and the †North Shore.

Dickcissel Uncommon migrant along the coast in fall, and rare winter visitor. Very rare and sporadic summer resident in farm fields at scattered sites in central and southern New Jersey; not breeding every year. Listen for the distinctive flight call in fall (September–November) especially at **Cape May and Sandy Hook. Summer: Try *Brightview Farm.

Bobolink Common migrant in fields, marshes, and woodland edges; uncommon summer resident of fields, and farmlands, mainly in the northwest and north-central part of the state. Widespread in May; hard to miss from mid-July–October, especially calling overhead along the coast. Fall: ****Cape May; ***Brigantine, DeKorte, Island

Beach, Sandy Hook, and elsewhere. Spring and early summer: ***Alpha, Brightview Farm, Hoffman Park, Wallkill.

Red-winged Blackbird Common migrant and summer resident in marshes, swamps, wet meadows, and farmlands statewide; uncommon in winter except at huge, localized blackbird roosts. Hard to miss, March–October, in appropriate habitat anywhere in New Jersey.

Eastern Meadowlark Fairly common migrant and fairly common, but declining, summer resident of grassy fields and meadows in rural areas around the state; uncommon in winter, mainly south. Fall (September–October): ****Cape May; **Brigantine, Jakes Landing, Sandy Hook, and many of the breeding locations below; Spring and summer (March–August): ***Alpha, Assunpink, Brightview Farm, Hoffman Park, Salem County, Stony Brook-Millstone Reserve, Wallkill.

Yellow-headed Blackbird Rare visitor (several each year) from the west; usually found in marshes or fields with flocks of other blackbirds. Has occurred in every month, but most often August–March. *Brigantine, Cape May, and Salem County have been the most consistent reporting localities, although one could pop up in any huge blackbird gathering.

Rusty Blackbird Fairly common migrant and uncommon winter resident in wet woodlands and swamps. Peak flights are late October–November and mid-March–April: ***Allaire, Great Swamp, Princeton, Scherman-Hoffman, Troy Meadows, Whittingham.

Brewer's Blackbird (RL) Very rare visitor from the west to farms and pastures in central or southern New Jersey. From the mid-1980s to mid-1990s there were multiple annual reports, but at present there are no records most years. Several records have come from †Cape May and Salem County.

Common Grackle Common migrant and summer resident in farmlands, deciduous woodlands, swamps, and suburbs throughout; uncommon to fairly common in winter, especially south. Often occurs in flocks numbering in the tens of thousands from late fall to early spring. Hard to miss, March–November, in a day's birding anywhere in New Jersey.

Boat-tailed Grackle Locally fairly common, and increasing, permanent resident of coastal salt marshes from Raritan Bay to Cape May and up Delaware Bay to Salem County. Some of the more northern birds may withdraw in winter. ***Barnegat Light, Corson's Inlet, Holgate, Manasquan Inlet, Stone Harbor; **Cape May, Island Beach, Mad Horse Creek (Salem County).

Brown-headed Cowbird Common migrant and uncommon winter resident in pastures, farmland, and suburbs. Common summer resident in open deciduous woodlands and suburbs. From fall to spring often in large flocks with other blackbirds. Hard to miss, March–November, in a day's birding anywhere in New Jersey. From December–February, more common in the southern part of the state.

Orchard Oriole Fairly common summer resident along the wooded edges of fields, farmland, or streams; widely distributed, but scarce in the northeast, the Pine Barrens, and at higher elevations in the northwest. One of the first breeders to leave, it is on territory only May–July: ***Assunpink, Belleplain, Dividing Creek, Garret Mountain, Moores Beach; **Bull's Island, Cape May, Great Swamp, Mercer County Park, Princeton.

Baltimore Oriole Common migrant and summer resident in open deciduous woodlands, woodland edges, and suburbs statewide; rare in winter at feeders. Migration (May and mid-August–September): ****Cape May, Garret Mountain, Palmyra, Princeton, Sandy Hook, and other spots for migrants. Summer: Hard to miss in appropriate habitat statewide.

Pine Grosbeak Irregularly uncommon winter visitor to the northern part of the state. Most recent years have had no reports, but in the 1970s–mid-1980s birds were found in most winters. Prefers coniferous stands, but is also found in deciduous woods and along freshly salted roads.

Purple Finch Uncommon to fairly common migrant and winter resident in orchards, woodland edges, and suburbs; uncommon and local summer resident in mixed woodlands and conifer plantings in the northwest. Migration (April–mid-May and September–November): **Allamuchy, Cape May, Princeton, Sandy Hook, Sunrise Mountain, or other migrant spots. Summer: **Pequannock Watershed, Wawayanda; *High Point, Stokes, Worthington.

House Finch Common permanent resident in shrubby woodland edges, coastal dunes, woodlands, and suburbs; ****Barnegat Light, Cape May, Island Beach, Sandy Hook, Stone Harbor, and at fields and feeders anywhere in New Jersey.

Red Crossbill Irregularly rare to fairly common winter visitor in conifers throughout the state, but absent most years; has nested in the Pine Barrens a few times. More frequent in the north during some flight years, more frequent along the coast in others. Reports in a flight year typically run November–March.

White-winged Crossbill Irregularly rare to uncommon winter visitor in hemlock glens and spruce plantings, mainly in the north; absent most years. In flight years present November–March.

Common Redpoll Irregularly uncommon to common winter visitor at overgrown fields (especially those with birches), hedgerows, and suburban feeders, mainly in the north. Numbers fluctuate widely, and some years none are found. During flight years good spots (November–March) can be *Allamuchy, Allendale, Flatbrook, High Point, Kittatinny Valley, Liberty, Stokes, Worthington.

Pine Siskin Irregularly rare to common migrant statewide; rare to common winter resident in coniferous and swampy (with Sweet Gum) woodlands, and at suburban feeders; has nested a very few times. In flight years often more common along the coast in fall, but more common in the north in winter. In fall during a flight year (October–November) try ***Cape May, Sandy Hook, Island Beach, and other inland and coastal migrant spots. In winter try **High Point, Kittatinny Valley, Pequannock Watershed, Ringwood, Scherman-Hoffman, Stokes, Wawayanda, and conifer plantings and feeders in many places.

American Goldfinch   Common migrant and summer and winter resident in weedy fields and hedgerows; visits feeders in winter. ****Allamuchy, Assunpink, Cape May, DeKorte, Great Swamp, Mercer County Park, Sandy Hook, Troy Meadows, and a multitude of other places.

Evening Grosbeak   Irregularly rare to fairly common migrant and winter visitor; has declined markedly in past two decades; very few birds seen in recent years. In fall, often has been noted at mountain ridgetops or along the coast; in winter found in deciduous woodlands, Pine Barrens, and at feeders. Best chances in fall are *Cape May, Raccoon Ridge, Sunrise Mountain.

House Sparrow   Common permanent resident in cities, suburbs, and farmlands throughout the state. Hard to miss in a day's birding in appropriate habitat anywhere in New Jersey.

Vagrants

The following list is of extreme rarities that have been seen from one to a few times in New Jersey in the past 25 years. All have had at least one record accepted by the New Jersey Bird Records Committee. All are on the Review List and require written, photographic, or other unambiguous documentation for acceptance of any further records. There are a number of other species accepted on the state list which have not been seen in the last 25 years; see Walsh, *et al.*, *Birds of New Jersey* or Halliwell, *et al.*, *The Historical Report of the New Jersey Bird Records Committee* for an enumeration of these. Several additional species have been reported, but not accepted, in New Jersey, due to a lack of conclusive documentation.

Western Grebe	Wood Stork
Yellow-nosed Albatross	Fulvous Whistling-Duck
Black-browed Albatross	Black-bellied Whistling-Duck
Buller's Shearwater	Cinnamon Teal
Fea's Petrel	Garganey
Black-capped Petrel	White-tailed Kite
White-faced Storm-Petrel	Mongolian Plover
White-tailed Tropicbird	Spotted Redshank
Red-billed Tropicbird	Long-billed Curlew
Brown Booby	Bar-tailed Godwit
Frigatebird sp.	Little Stint
Roseate Spoonbill	Red-necked Stint

Ross's Gull

Ivory Gull

Large-billed Tern

White-winged Tern

Whiskered Tern

Brown Noddy

Black Guillemot

Band-tailed Pigeon

Common Ground Dove

Groove-billed Ani

Black-chinned Hummingbird

Calliope Hummingbird

Allen's Hummingbird

Black-backed Woodpecker

"Western" Flycatcher

Bell's Vireo

Brown-chested Martin

Violet-green Swallow

Boreal Chickadee

Rock Wren

Bewick's Wren

Mountain Bluebird

Townsend's Solitaire

Varied Thrush

Sage Thrasher

Townsend's Warbler

MacGillivray's Warbler

Green-tailed Towhee

Spotted Towhee

Black-throated Sparrow

Lark Bunting

Golden-crowned Sparrow

Smith's Longspur

Chestnut-collared Longspur

Western Meadowlark

Hoary Redpoll

Index